THE SOCIAL TEACHING OF THE CHRISTIAN CHURCHES

HARPER TORCHBOOKS / The Cloister Library

Tor Andrae	MOHAMMED: *The Man and His Faith* TB/62
Augustine/Przywara	AN AUGUSTINE SYNTHESIS TB/35
Roland H. Bainton	THE TRAVAIL OF RELIGIOUS LIBERTY TB/30
Karl Barth	DOGMATICS IN OUTLINE TB/56
Karl Barth	THE WORD OF GOD AND THE WORD OF MAN TB/13
Nicolas Berdyaev	THE BEGINNING AND THE END TB/14
Nicolas Berdyaev	THE DESTINY OF MAN TB/61
J. H. Breasted	DEVELOPMENT OF RELIGION AND THOUGHT IN ANCIENT EGYPT TB/57
Martin Buber	ECLIPSE OF GOD: *Studies in the Relation Between Religion and Philosophy* TB/12
Martin Buber	MOSES: *The Revelation and the Covenant* TB/27
Martin Buber	THE PROPHETIC FAITH TB/73
Jacob Burckhardt	THE CIVILIZATION OF THE RENAISSANCE IN ITALY [Illustrated Edition]: *Vol. I*, TB/40; *Vol. II*, TB/41
Edward Conze	BUDDHISM: *Its Essence and Development* TB/58
F. M. Cornford	FROM RELIGION TO PHILOSOPHY: *A Study in the Origins of Western Speculation* TB/20
G. G. Coulton	MEDIEVAL FAITH AND SYMBOLISM [Part I of "Art and the Reformation"] TB/25
G. G. Coulton	THE FATE OF MEDIEVAL ART IN THE RENAISSANCE AND REFORMATION [Part II of "Art and the Reformation"] TB/26
H. G. Creel	CONFUCIUS AND THE CHINESE WAY TB/63
Adolf Deissmann	PAUL: *A Study in Social and Religious History* TB/15
C. H. Dodd	THE AUTHORITY OF THE BIBLE TB/43
Johannes Eckhart	MEISTER ECKHART: A Modern Translation TB/8
Mircea Eliade	COSMOS AND HISTORY: *The Myth of the Eternal Return* TB/50
Morton S. Enslin	CHRISTIAN BEGINNINGS TB/5
Morton S. Enslin	THE LITERATURE OF THE CHRISTIAN MOVEMENT TB/6
Austin Farrer, *ed.*	THE CORE OF THE BIBLE TB/7
G. P. Fedotov	THE RUSSIAN RELIGIOUS MIND: *Kievan Christianity, the 10th to the 13th Centuries* TB/70
Ludwig Feuerbach	THE ESSENCE OF CHRISTIANITY. Intro. by Karl Barth TB/11
Harry E. Fosdick	A GUIDE TO UNDERSTANDING THE BIBLE TB/2
Sigmund Freud	ON CREATIVITY AND THE UNCONSCIOUS: *Papers on the Psychology of Art, Literature, Love, Religion* TB/45
Maurice Friedman	MARTIN BUBER: *The Life of Dialogue* TB/64
O. B. Frothingham	TRANSCENDENTALISM IN NEW ENGLAND: *A History* TB/59
Edward Gibbon	THE END OF THE ROMAN EMPIRE IN THE WEST [J. B. Bury Edition, illus., Chapters 36–43] TB/37
Edward Gibbon	THE TRIUMPH OF CHRISTENDOM IN THE ROMAN EMPIRE [J. B. Bury Edition, illus., Chapters 15–20] TB/46
C. C. Gillispie	GENESIS AND GEOLOGY: *A Study in the Relations of Scientific Thought, Natural Theology, and Social Opinion in Great Britain, 1790–1850* TB/51
Maurice Goguel	JESUS AND THE ORIGINS OF CHRISTIANITY I: *Prolegomena to the Life of Jesus* TB/65
Maurice Goguel	JESUS AND THE ORIGINS OF CHRISTIANITY II: *The Life of Jesus* TB/66
Edgar J. Goodspeed	A LIFE OF JESUS TB/1
H. J. C. Grierson	CROSS-CURRENTS IN 17TH CENTURY ENGLISH LITERATURE: *The World, the Flesh, the Spirit* TB/47
William Haller	THE RISE OF PURITANISM TB/22
Adolf Harnack	WHAT IS CHRISTIANITY? Intro. by Rudolf Bultmann TB/17

Edwin Hatch	THE INFLUENCE OF GREEK IDEAS ON CHRISTIANITY TB/18
Karl Heim	CHRISTIAN FAITH AND NATURAL SCIENCE TB/16
F. H. Heinemann	EXISTENTIALISM AND THE MODERN PREDICAMENT TB/28
S. R. Hopper, *ed.*	SPIRITUAL PROBLEMS IN CONTEMPORARY LITERATURE TB/21
Johan Huizinga	ERASMUS AND THE AGE OF REFORMATION. Illus. TB/19
Aldous Huxley	THE DEVILS OF LOUDUN: *A Study in the Psychology of Power Politics and Mystical Religion in the France of Cardinal Richelieu* TB/60
Flavius Josephus	THE GREAT ROMANO-JEWISH WAR: *A.D. 66–70* TB/74
Immanuel Kant	RELIGION WITHIN THE LIMITS OF REASON ALONE TB/67
Søren Kierkegaard	EDIFYING DISCOURSES: A Selection TB/32
Søren Kierkegaard	THE JOURNALS OF KIERKEGAARD: A Selection TB/52
Søren Kierkegaard	PURITY OF HEART TB/4
Alexandre Koyré	FROM THE CLOSED WORLD TO THE INFINITE UNIVERSE TB/31
Emile Mâle	THE GOTHIC IMAGE: *Religious Art in France of the 13th Century.* Illus. TB/44
T. J. Meek	HEBREW ORIGINS TB/69
H. Richard Niebuhr	CHRIST AND CULTURE TB/3
H. Richard Niebuhr	THE KINGDOM OF GOD IN AMERICA TB/49
H. J. Rose	RELIGION IN GREECE AND ROME TB/55
Josiah Royce	THE RELIGIOUS ASPECT OF PHILOSOPHY: *A Critique of the Bases of Conduct and Faith* TB/29
Auguste Sabatier	OUTLINES OF A PHILOSOPHY OF RELIGION BASED ON PSYCHOLOGY AND HISTORY TB/23
George Santayana	INTERPRETATIONS OF POETRY AND RELIGION TB/9
George Santayana	WINDS OF DOCTRINE *and* PLATONISM AND THE SPIRITUAL LIFE TB/24
F. Schleiermacher	ON RELIGION: *Speeches to Its Cultured Despisers* TB/36
H. O. Taylor	THE EMERGENCE OF CHRISTIAN CULTURE IN THE WEST: *The Classical Heritage of the Middle Ages* TB/48
Paul Tillich	DYNAMICS OF FAITH TB/42
Ernst Troeltsch	THE SOCIAL TEACHING OF THE CHRISTIAN CHURCHES. Intro. by H. Richard Niebuhr *Vol. I,* TB/71; *Vol. II,* TB/72
E. B. Tylor	THE ORIGINS OF CULTURE [Part I of "Primitive Culture"]. Intro. by Paul Radin TB/33
E. B. Tylor	RELIGION IN PRIMITIVE CULTURE [Part II of "Primitive Culture"]. Intro. by Paul Radin TB/34
Evelyn Underhill	THE GOLDEN SEQUENCE: *A Fourfold Study of the Spiritual Life* TB/68
Evelyn Underhill	WORSHIP TB/10
Johannes Weiss	EARLIEST CHRISTIANITY: *A History of the Period* A.D. *30–150*. Intro. by F. C. Grant *Vol. I,* TB/53; *Vol. II,* TB/54
Wilhelm Windelband	A HISTORY OF PHILOSOPHY I: *Greek, Roman, Medieval* TB/38
Wilhelm Windelband	A HISTORY OF PHILOSOPHY II: *Renaissance, Enlightenment, Modern* TB/39

HARPER TORCHBOOKS / The Science Library

Angus d'A. Bellairs	REPTILES: *Life History, Evolution, and Structure.* Illus. TB/520
L. von Bertalanffy	PROBLEMS OF LIFE: *An Evaluation of Modern Biological and Scientific Thought* TB/521
R. B. Braithwaite	SCIENTIFIC EXPLANATION TB/515
Louis de Broglie	PHYSICS AND MICROPHYSICS. Foreword by Albert Einstein TB/514
J. Bronowski	SCIENCE AND HUMAN VALUES TB/505
A. J. Cain	ANIMAL SPECIES AND THEIR EVOLUTION. Illus. TB/519
T. G. Cowling	MOLECULES IN MOTION: *An Introduction to the Kinetic Theory of Gases.* Illus. TB/516
W. C. Dampier, *ed.*	READINGS IN THE LITERATURE OF SCIENCE. Illus. TB/512
H. Davenport	THE HIGHER ARITHMETIC: *An Introduction to the Theory of Numbers* TB/526

(*continued on next page*)

Arthur Eddington	SPACE, TIME AND GRAVITATION: *An Outline of the General Relativity Theory* TB/510
Alexander Findlay	CHEMISTRY IN THE SERVICE OF MAN. Illus. TB/524
D. E. Littlewood	THE SKELETON KEY OF MATHEMATICS TB/525
J. R. Partington	A SHORT HISTORY OF CHEMISTRY. Illus. TB/522
H. T. Pledge	SCIENCE SINCE 1500: *A Short History of Mathematics, Physics, Chemistry, and Biology.* Illus. TB/506
John Read	A DIRECT ENTRY TO ORGANIC CHEMISTRY. Illus. TB/523
George Sarton	ANCIENT SCIENCE AND MODERN CIVILIZATION TB/501
Paul A. Schilpp, *ed.*	ALBERT EINSTEIN: *Philosopher-Scientist: Vol. I,* TB/502; *Vol. II,* TB/503
O. G. Sutton	MATHEMATICS IN ACTION. Foreword by James R. Newman. Illus. TB/518
Stephen Toulmin	THE PHILOSOPHY OF SCIENCE: *An Introduction* TB/513
A. G. Van Melsen	FROM ATOMOS TO ATOM: *The History of the Concept* Atom TB/517
Friedrich Waismann	INTRODUCTION TO MATHEMATICAL THINKING TB/511
W. H. Watson	ON UNDERSTANDING PHYSICS: *An Analysis of the Philosophy of Physics.* Intro. by Ernest Nagel TB/507
G. J. Whitrow	THE STRUCTURE AND EVOLUTION OF THE UNIVERSE: *An Introduction to Cosmology.* Illus. TB/504
A. Wolf	A HISTORY OF SCIENCE, TECHNOLOGY AND PHILOSOPHY IN THE 16TH AND 17TH CENTURIES. Illus. *Vol. I,* TB/508; *Vol. II,* TB/509

HARPER TORCHBOOKS / The Academy Library

James Baird	ISHMAEL: *A Study of the Symbolic Mode in Primitivism* TB/1023
Henri Bergson	TIME AND FREE WILL: *An Essay on the Immediate Data of Consciousness* TB/1021
H. J. Blackham	SIX EXISTENTIALIST THINKERS: *Kierkegaard, Jaspers, Nietzsche, Marcel, Heidegger, Sartre* TB/1002
Walter Bromberg	THE MIND OF MAN: *A History of Psychotherapy and Psychoanalysis* TB/1003
G. G. Coulton	MEDIEVAL VILLAGE, MANOR, AND MONASTERY TB/1020
Editors of *Fortune*	AMERICA IN THE SIXTIES: *The Economy and the Society* TB/1015
G. P. Gooch	ENGLISH DEMOCRATIC IDEAS IN THE SEVENTEENTH CENTURY TB/1006
Francis J. Grund	ARISTOCRACY IN AMERICA: *A Study of Jacksonian Democracy* TB/1001
W. K. C. Guthrie	THE GREEK PHILOSOPHERS: *From Thales to Aristotle* TB/1008
Henry James	THE PRINCESS CASAMASSIMA: A Novel TB/1005
Henry James	RODERICK HUDSON: A Novel. Intro. by Leon Edel TB/1016
Henry James	THE TRAGIC MUSE: A Novel. Intro. by Leon Edel TB/1017
Arnold Kettle	AN INTRODUCTION TO THE ENGLISH NOVEL: *Vol. I, Defoe to George Eliot,* TB/1011; *Vol. II, Henry James to the Present,* TB/1012
L. S. B. Leakey	ADAM'S ANCESTORS: *The Evolution of Man and His Culture.* Illus. TB/1019
Arthur O. Lovejoy	THE GREAT CHAIN OF BEING: *A Study of the History of an Idea* TB/1009
J. P. Mayer	ALEXIS DE TOCQUEVILLE: *A Biographical Study in Political Science* TB/1014
John U. Nef	CULTURAL FOUNDATIONS OF INDUSTRIAL CIVILIZATION TB/1024
Samuel Pepys	THE DIARY OF SAMUEL PEPYS: Selections, ed. by O. F. Morshead; illus. by Ernest H. Shepard TB/1007
Georges Poulet	STUDIES IN HUMAN TIME TB/1004
Priscilla Robertson	REVOLUTIONS OF 1848: *A Social History* TB/1025
Ferdinand Schevill	THE MEDICI. Illus. TB/1010
Bruno Snell	THE DISCOVERY OF THE MIND: *The Greek Origins of European Thought* TB/1018
W. H. Walsh	PHILOSOPHY OF HISTORY: *An Introduction* TB/1020
W. Lloyd Warner	SOCIAL CLASS IN AMERICA: *The Evaluation of Status* TB/1013

The Social Teaching of the Christian Churches

VOLUME II

Ernst Troeltsch

TRANSLATED BY OLIVE WYON

HARPER TORCHBOOKS *THE CLOISTER LIBRARY*
HARPER & BROTHERS · NEW YORK

THE SOCIAL TEACHING OF THE CHRISTIAN CHURCHES

Printed in the United States of America

This translation of *Die Soziallehren der christlichen Kirchen und Gruppen* (German edition, 1911) was first published in 1931 by George Allen & Unwin Ltd., London, and The Macmillan Company, New York, and is reprinted by arrangement.

First HARPER TORCHBOOK edition published 1960

DEDICATED

IN DEEPEST GRATITUDE AND RESPECT

TO

THE EMINENT PHILOSOPHICAL FACULTY

AT GREIFSWALD

AND

TO THE EMINENT LAW FACULTY

AT BRESLAU

CONTENTS OF VOLUME TWO

CHAPTER III

PROTESTANTISM

CONCLUSION

CHAPTER III

PROTESTANTISM

1. THE SOCIOLOGICAL PROBLEM OF PROTESTANTISM

Protestantism: A New Sociological Type

Mediaeval Christianity produced two great classic types of social doctrine: first, the relative type of the idea of Christian Society which is represented by Thomism; and, secondly, the radical idea of Christian Society which was evolved by the sects.

The position of the first type may be stated thus: the Church, which is regarded as a universal institution, endowed with absolute authoritative truth and the sacramental miraculous power of grace and redemption, takes up into its own life the secular institutions, groups, and values which have arisen out of the relative Natural Law, and are adapted to the conditions of the fallen state; the whole of the secular life, therefore, is summed up under the conception of a natural stage in human life, which prepares the way for the higher supernatural stage, for the ethic of grace and miracle, for the spiritual and hierarchical world-organization.

The position of the second type may be thus summarized: the religious community has evolved its social ideal purely from the Gospel and from the Law of Christ; according to this type of thought the Christian character and holiness of this ideal should be proved by the unity reigning within the group and by the practical behaviour of the individual members, and not by objective institutional guarantees. Therefore, either it does not recognize the institutions, groups, and values which exist outside of Christianity at all, or in a quietly tolerant spirit of detachment from the world it avoids them, or under the influence of an "enthusiastic" eschatology it attacks these institutions and replaces them by a purely Christian order of society.

In each instance the nature of the Christian fellowship itself is conceived from a different point of view; in the first instance it is conceived as an institution, not dependent on individualism, possessing a *depositum* of absolute truths and wonderful civilizing sacramental powers; in the second instance it is conceived as a society whose life is constantly renewed by the deliberate allegiance and personal work of its individual members. This is the reason why the champions of the "Church" theory were able to discard the ideal of a strict Christian perfection, or at least to limit it to a particular group, that is, to monasticism; this also explains why the supporters of the "sect" theory upheld the ideal of Christian perfection as binding on all Christians alike.

Further, in both instances the Christian fundamental ideas of sin and grace are interpreted in a different sense. In the case of the Church-type, its doctrine of sin facilitated the acceptance of the existing secular social order, whose merely relative non-Christian character is regarded as the result of sin; this social order, therefore, must be frankly accepted and tolerated. At the same time "grace" is regarded as the miraculous power which purifies these institutions, uses them as the basis of a higher structure, and subordinates them to a universal central authority. This authority is conceived in its essence as a wonderful supreme authority, transcending Nature, even pure and unfallen Nature; as supernature it is superimposed upon Nature in the graded structure of the entelechies of the universe.

In the case of the sect-type, the existing institutions, groups, and values of the secular life are equally explained by the fact of sin; this, however, does not mean that they are inevitable, and must simply be accepted; on the contrary, the supporters of this theory use this fact as an argument for the radical rejection by Christians of the secular life and all its works, and as a challenge to create a social order which is based purely upon the principles of the Gospel. According to this theory, grace means the "calling and election" which separates the Christian from the life of this present world, and inspires the pure gospel ethic with knowledge and power (an ethic which vindicates itself by its subjective influence and not by its institutional system); "grace" also means the hope that the Christian Church will be finally vindicated at the great reversal of all secular values in the Last Judgment. Grace is not a superstructure erected upon the basis of Nature—whether sinful or innocent—which has to be accepted, but it is identified with the complete, pure, ideal nature of the Primitive State. So far as fallen humanity is concerned, grace does not mean the purification of nature and the ascent to supernature, rather it means pure and radical hostility to the whole principle of sin, expressed in a genuine Christian spirit, and in the Christian moral law.

This theory is connected with a whole series of further distinctions, which belong to the subtler realm of religious psychology and to theological thought. Christology, in particular, was obviously connected with the idea of the Church as a "fellowship" which prevailed at that time, in so far as the "Church" regarded Christ as the Founder of the Church and the Founder of the objective treasury of grace and of salvation; whereas the "sect" regarded Him as the Law-giver, the Divine example, the stimulating energy, the presence of the supra-historical Exalted Christ, the source of all immediate influence and activity. All this, however, really belongs to the history of doctrine. For our present subject it is vital to remember that the idea of the Church as an objective institution, and as a voluntary society, contains a fundamental sociological distinction. This distinction leads to a corresponding distinction in the sphere of ethics: on the one hand, the Christian ethic is supplemented by the natural ethic, and is thus enabled to dominate the masses; while on the other, this idea of nature as the "complement" of grace is rejected, and the influence of this group is therefore confined to small circles of passive resisters or revolutionaries. The Church-type accepted a natural ethic whose standards differ greatly from those of Christianity; the sect-type rejected this idea entirely. Those who regarded the Church as an objective institution looked upon "Nature" as something which, though different from grace, was yet capable of being moulded by it; whereas those to whom the Church was a voluntary society regarded "genuine Nature" as something which was identical with grace, while they rejected "fallen Nature" altogether as something which could not possibly be harmonized with grace at all.

This distinction can be traced right back to Primitive Christianity and the Early Church. We see it in embryo in the contrast between the love-communism of the local Church in Jerusalem and the conservative adjustment to the existing social order proclaimed by Paul. The Church only reached her full development, however, when, in the days of Constantine, she became a State Church. Only then was it possible for her to realize her universal and absolute unity and supremacy, which, during the time of the Holy Roman Empire, then enabled her to subdue the State itself to the unity which had been gained with the help of the State; this meant that the Church was also able to assert her authority over the whole of the non-religious civilization as well. Since, however, it was only the Middle Ages which thus created a Christian unity of civilization, so also it was only the Middle Ages which produced definitely and clearly the complementary movement of the sect. At this point the social doctrines of Latin Christianity ceased to develop. Henceforth it became clear that Christian social doctrine could only produce further developments if it were to receive a fresh infusion of new life. Only an inward change, and a further development within Christian thought itself, could pave the way for new ideals in the Christian doctrine of Society.

It is well known that a new development of this kind did take place in the critical period of the later Middle Ages, and that with the rise of Protestantism it succeeded in coming out into the open at the Reformation. At the same time, in various directions, both positively and negatively, the Reformation was restricted by the forces which had already been developed during this crisis. More than two hundred years separated the Reformation from Thomism, which was the classic expression of the mediaeval spirit; meanwhile opposition of various kinds had developed, as well as development of the attempts at adaptation to its ideals. The spirit of opposition to Thomism was expressed, in the main, in three ways: (*a*) in the development of the sect-type, which had an increasing influence; (*b*) in mysticism, which fostered a radical religious individualism, preoccupied with the endeavour to free itself from the shackles of scholasticism and ecclesiasticism; (*c*) in the critical self-destruction of the Thomist system in the late mediaeval theological school of thought, in Nominalism, or rather, to be more exact, in Occamism. Nominalism, in particular, had an important influence on the Reformation. This philosophy severed the connection between Reason and Revelation, destroyed the idea of an ascent from Nature to Supernature and the carefully graded theory of the connatural and supernatural end for which humanity has been created. It intensified psychological self-analysis by its appeal to experience and its emphasis on the doctrine that "the individual is the real"; it also emphasized the positive nature of the Divine Will and altered the theory of the sacraments. According to Nominalism the sacraments do not convey a supernatural life, but they impart the righteousness which belongs to human nature by right, but which had been lost by sin. Otherwise, however, this school of thought still retained the fundamental idea of the universal dominion of the Church—peculiar to Catholicism (in this particular it discarded the elements peculiar to Occam and the Conciliar theologians)—and the idea of the Christian unity of civilization; the moral Law of Nature was still recognized, alongside of the positive Divine order, which was now far more strongly emphasized. By means of treaties between the different States and the Church, the ancient ecclesiastical system was once more secured, both legally and doctrinally, but both in doctrine and in ethics much uncertainty remained, and under the surface a spirit of hostility towards the Church was widespread. The general effect of Nominalism was to dissolve the unity created by Thomism between dogma and philosophy, between a natural and a supernatural ethic, between Natural Law and the positive Divine decrees. This philosophy reflected the prevailing disharmony between the life of the Church and the life of the world; by laying increased emphasis upon the Divine authority, however, it maintained the old ecclesiastical idea of unity; in other directions it provided a safety-valve for reason and the natural powers in the dispositions for grace, in the co-operation of free-will. Luther himself was a product of this school of thought; Thomism was already a matter of ancient history. It was against it that Luther first directed his polemic; yet its way of formulating problems, its dualistic and authoritative habit of mind, its irrationalism towards philosophy, and its psychology of inner experience, also formed the primary positive assumptions of Luther's most fundamental ideas. These ideas, however, are still going through a process of elucidation, and they do not belong to our subject. For us the main point of interest is the result of these ideas, and the new religious idea of the Reformation.[197a] This, then, is our problem: in what did this change of Christian thought consist? What were the new religious ideas, and what were their sociological results?

Although the forces which converged in the Reformation and in Protestantism were very varied, and although they gave rise to a rich development of movements and personalities, all this many-sided development was, in the last resort, based upon Luther's fundamental principles. These principles were the absolute standard, doctrinally, for all these groups, even though later on many of them may have developed along very different lines. The Humanistic groups alone were independent of Luther, and for that reason also they speedily lost their significance, so far as he was concerned, at least for the next few centuries; only on the scientific and scholastic side did they make a contribution to Protestantism, as well as to renewed Catholicism.

Luther and the Protestant Ethic

Thus our fundamental concern is with Luther's religious ideas, and with the sociological results to which they gave rise.

At this point, however, we must emphasize the fact that although Luther's religious ideas were based upon an inward change in the whole situation which covered a century, they were still highly original and personal, and, above all, they arose simply out of the inner development of religious thought itself. Luther's religious

[197a] See p. 821.

ideas were not due to the reflex action of social, or even of economic, changes; they were based essentially and independently upon the religious idea, which alone gave rise to the social, economic, and political consequences. In order to carry out the religious idea in practice, and to make it victorious, in questions of practical organization, social, economic, and political causes did, it is true, play a very important part; but they had nothing whatever to do with the fundamental question of origin. So far as this was concerned the predominant and primary cause was the religious idea, pure and simple. At least, only very indirectly can we here discern certain traces of the influence of social, economic, and political causes. That is to say: the theories proclaimed by the Nominalism of later Scholasticism and the mysticism of the pre-Reformation opposition parties, were doubtless to some extent connected with the social changes which took place during the later Middle Ages. The whole tendency to emphasize the value of personal religious experience which this movement expressed, and the severance of the religious interest from the secular and political interest, was a result of the general situation, of the city-civilization, of the growing independence of national States, and of economic interests. Nevertheless, this influence was only indirect. It only cleared the ground for the new ideas which arose out of the intensely personal struggle and labours of the Monk of Erfurt and Wittenberg, and it penetrated them with the influence of an atmosphere in which a profound religious spirituality was combined with an impulse towards activity and order. That, however, was the atmosphere of the German city-civilization of that period. This phenomenon, as is always the case at the great turning-points of history, was due to a combination of very different causes, originally entirely independent of each other; only a doctrinaire fanaticism would try to reduce these causes to one. In this instance the religious idea was clearly the primary and the dominant impulse. For that very reason it is impossible to connect the Reformation world of thought with any particular social class. These ideas seized the imagination of peasants and democratic artisans, of the lesser nobles who were fighting for their very existence, and of the greater nobles who belonged to the class of great land-owners and princes, of city magistrates, guilds, and the proletariat of the towns. At the outset the Reformation was entirely free from social distinctions. If, however, it is claimed, and in a certain sense rightly, that upon the whole its tendency was bourgeois (especially as compared with the aristocratic Church of the early mediaeval period, and also with the sects, which were steeped in democratic and proletarian ideas), the reason for this can only lie in that indirect connection to which we have just alluded. This, again, was due to the fact (which it is not difficult to understand psychologically) that the growth of intellectual and spiritual individualism among large masses of people is invariably connected with the formation of cities; within the city population, however, the Reformation—which from purely religious reasons was strongly conservative in temper—united with the bourgeois class, while, for the most part, the proletariat adhered to the more radical Protestant sect-type. It was only the later practical turn of events which constrained the Reformation to link its fortunes with those of the civil authorities, who could guarantee the preservation of order, that is, with the territorial princes; but this did not alter its fundamentally bourgeois character. This whole development, however, was a very complicated affair, which cannot now be clearly and directly determined. The actual tendency, which was fostered by the religious emphasis upon the value of the individual, arose out of Luther's own inner struggles.[198] What, then, was his religious position, which forms the basis of the sociological development of Protestantism?

Theology of Luther

It is customary to describe Protestantism as the revival of the Pauline and Augustinian religion of grace, in contrast to the Catholic religion of law. In the main this is true, but it needs a good deal of clear explanation and expansion. For in this renewed emphasis upon the Pauline and Augustinian doctrine of grace, the heart of the matter does not lie so much in the reassertion of "Grace" against "Law", as in the new conception of grace itself. The emphasis upon free grace and the exclusion of free-will was, however, directed immediately only against the dominant doctrine of later scholasticism, which was prevalent in Luther's day and which he outgrew. But this emphasis on "free grace" did not constitute an attack upon Catholicism in general.[199] To Catholicism as a whole Luther's opposition was far more deep-seated. Catholicism, too, was a religion of grace, but its view of grace was that of sacramental grace, of supernature, of a higher, mystical,

[198] See p. 821.

[199] This is strongly emphasized by *Krogh-Tonningh: Der Letzte Scholastiker, 1904*, by whom he means the Thomist and Dutch Carthusian Dionysius. The contrast, however, does not lie in the polemic against Nominalist semi-Pelagianism, but in the idea of grace which is also opposed to St. Thomas and his ideas of predestination.

and miraculous power, imparted by the hierarchy, entrusted to the Church, which has a double effect: the forgiveness of sins and the mystical elevation of humanity.

The idea of law was easily combined with this idea of grace. For, if the ethical character of grace were to be preserved, it had to be prepared for by ethical examination and earnest aspirations after holiness, both of which required a legal standard; for the same reason it had to be proved by good works, which again require a legal standard, and which without harm could be thought into the framework of the conception of Law, although it was still the power of imparted grace, which, at bottom, with the release of the natural energies of man, alone produced good works and merits. Luther's new idea was therefore not merely the general re-emphasis upon grace, which makes a clean sweep of all compromise with legalism, but beyond that, it gave a new meaning to the idea of grace itself.

On the other hand, however, neither Luther nor Protestantism in general ever really removed the idea of Law from its central position. The Law remained as a stimulus to repentance, and as the pre-supposition of faith and the Gospel of grace. The Law remained as the most direct and primal expression of the Divine Will and Being, which only required a joyful and willing obedience in a spirit of love and confidence, but which precisely on that account required that the Law should be fulfilled in a complete and spiritual way. The Law remained as the pre-supposition for the Redemptive Work of Christ, who in His Death annihilated the Law, and only then made men free of the order of grace. Finally, the Law remained, although in a rather anomalous position, as the rule of life in the state of grace, only now severed from the idea of merit and of the achievement of salvation, because the grace on which salvation is founded does not consist in "merits" and "good works", but in a transformed personality, in principle already wholly united with God.

Thus, from this point of view also, it is clear that the new element in Protestant theology was not the overcoming of the conception of Law in itself, but the special content of the conception of grace, which gives to the Law a different meaning and position from that which it has in the Catholic idea of grace. Now the essential element in this new conception of grace is this: that grace is no longer a mystical miraculous substance, to be imparted through the sacraments, but a Divine temper of faith, conviction, spirit, knowledge, and trust which is to be appropriated; in the Gospel and in the Love and Spirit of Christ towards mankind it can be discerned as the loving will of God which brings with it the forgiveness of sins.[200] Religion thus steps out of the material substantial sphere, which was merely accompanied by thought and feeling, and enters into the intellectual, psychological, spiritual sphere. This does not mean that it ceases to be a miracle. But the miracle now consists in the fact that man in his weakness, rebellion, despair, and impurity can grasp such an idea from the Gospel; it is so entirely beyond the reach of his natural powers, and the religious idea of redemption is so far removed from the natural intellectual sphere, that only through the miracle of predestination can it come to pass. It is an inner miracle of faith in the Gospel and in Christ, not an interior-external miracle of the hierarchical-sacramental impartation of grace, which produces the power to do good works and to acquire merit. Moreover, it is not an idea that can be altered and changed at will, but a knowledge which is offered with the absolute certainty of revelation, which starts from the picture of the incarnate, suffering, and risen Son of God, and possesses in the Bible an absolute, wonderful, and authentic representation of this picture of Christ, even though, in detail, the Bible is not free from all kinds of human imperfections. In Protestantism, therefore, the heart of religion consists in the spirit of faith which is thus effected by the "Word", just as for Catholicism it consists in priesthood and sacrament, in obedience and in mysticism. Religion is now a matter of faith and conviction, instead of one which is bound up with a hierarchical-sacramental system. The two Protestant sacraments which are retained are special methods of representing the Gospel; their spiritual influence does not exceed that of the influence of the Word of God in the Scriptures; hence, in the Catholic sense, they are no longer sacraments.[201]

Now, however, this fundamental position contains, directly and indirectly, further implications.

The first result is the reduction of the whole of religion to that which alone can be an object of faith and trust, that is, to that idea of God—evolved from the apostolic picture of Christ—which represents Him as a gracious Will, holy, forgiving sins, and thus leading men upwards into a higher life. All that needs to be added to this idea is that which will bring assurance to the sinner, namely, the knowledge of the Divine Revelation and condescension in the Incarnate Son of God or the Logos. Further, the important element in this view of Christ is not the dim mysterious essence of His being, but the assurance of His Love which is

[200] See p. 823. [201] See p. 824.

conveyed by His self-abasement in the Incarnation, by His sufferings, and by His kindness—whereby sinful man can know for a fact that God forgives sins.

This constitutes an immense simplification in doctrine, and a new method of basing doctrine upon its conscious power to awaken faith and trust. The unlimited authority of the apostolic picture of Christ, which guarantees all this, is taken for granted, as well as the miraculous nature of the Bible. The problem is not, how can this be proved? but, how can one gain this personal assurance? Surely this certainty is only possible through the predestinarian miraculous influence of the God who Himself creates faith. In every impulse towards trust the believer may feel something of the miraculous saving power of God.

The second result of Luther's teaching was that of religious individualism, that inwardness of communion with God which is independent of man or of a priesthood. Thus the whole idea of mediation through a hierarchy, and through sacramental grace, is swept away. This leads to the doctrine of the priesthood of all believers, and to lay religion, to the renewal of the primitive Christian independence and autonomy of the knowledge of God effected by "the Spirit". At this point Luther came into touch with the corresponding tendencies in the sect-movement, which were also derived from the Bible. All that was actually discarded, however, was the idea of sacerdotal mediation; mediation through the Word, that is, through the Bible (and, since this is essentially a witness to Christ, through the Scriptural picture of Christ) is emphasized all the more strongly. Only thus can God be known. Only thus does He reveal Himself as the God of Grace; everywhere else, outside of Christ, He appears as the God of the awful metaphysical riddle and of the terror of the Law. Trust in Christ alone is genuine trust in God. Only through contact with Him does the soul enter into communion with God. Since, then, this picture of Christ is incarnated in the Bible, which is the work of God, the Bible or "the Word" is the only real means by which a personal relationship with God is mediated; this idea totally excludes every kind of "direct" mysticism, which aims at union with God apart from Christ. This Bible, however, with its message of Christ, forms the centre of the Church, which God has founded through Christ as the fellowship of believers which ought to result from the preaching of the Word. For this fellowship He has also established the ministry of the Word, or the preaching of the message of Christ, as the permanent objective foundation and mediation of salvation. All that is indifferent and left to human choice is the method of calling to this ministry of the Word, and the technical-juridical details of organization. All that is needed is regular order and a proper training for one's calling, in order to exclude self-will and mistakes due to lack of knowledge.[202]

The third conclusion to which this fundamental position leads is the principle of a pure spiritual ethic. If the whole value of man consists in a right attitude of faith and trust towards God in the Word, then this general spirit also forms the basis of the standard for the ethical consequences to which it gives rise. Henceforth there is no ecclesiastical, authoritative, moral law; the Church does not shoulder the responsibility of the individual; the only rule for conduct is the impulse of the individual conscience. "Good works" exist no longer; all that matters is the general spirit and attitude of the individual. No longer can one reckon in terms of "merits" or "demerits"; everything hinges on whether the new life is checked and hindered or allowed to develop freely. The system of future rewards and punishments has disappeared, and all that remains is the blessedness of the new creation, out of which all that is good will arise spontaneously. At the same time it was, of course, taken for granted that the standard of this spiritual ethic was still the law of the Decalogue and of the New Testament, since, as before, both agree with the natural moral law and therefore constitute the formula of the natural moral impulse—which merely became a "revealed" formula through those statements of Scripture. Those demands which were stabilized in the Decalogue, and which also formed part of the natural consciousness, only needed to be filled with the religious spirit which issues from faith in order to signify the good as presented by Christianity. It is therefore evident that this equation of the Decalogue and the Natural Law and the Christian Law, which is here taken for granted and continued, means the assimilation of the intra-mundane ethic into the Christian ethic, just as it had been assimilated previously in the whole of the patristic and mediaeval ethic.[203]

[202] On this point cf. *Herrmann: Der Verkehr des Christen mit Gott*[5], *1908*. Here, however, the Lutheran Christology has been greatly modernized, and the significance of the sacraments, in particular that of the Real Presence in the Eucharist, has been very much modified. We only get a true picture when we add to this the Incarnational Christology and the objective sacramental doctrine.

[203] On this point cf. *Gottschick: Ethik, 1906*. Here the motives and the spirit of the Lutheran ethic are excellently explained; one misses here, however, as everywhere else, a detailed treatment of Luther's conception of the content of the Christian moral law, of which more anon.

This spiritual ethic (or ethic of disposition) leads to the acceptance of the world, to the disuse of monastic asceticism, to the new meaning given to the idea of vocation or "the calling". The religious individualism of the religion of faith, which does not mean the acceptance of a certain number of authoritative ecclesiastical dogmas, but simply a spirit of whole-hearted conviction, also affects the ethical temper. Everywhere this ethical temper is a whole, and therefore in principle it is everywhere the same, in spite of various ways of expression. This means that the ideal of perfection is the same for all alike; hence it does away with the naïve position of Catholicism which takes for granted the various degrees, grades, and ranks of perfection. It also discards all the works of supererogation and vicarious oblations which this idea involved. Above all, the Protestant ideal of perfection discards the whole idea of the monastic state as a false ideal of some special higher perfection. But this perfection, which is the same for all, is still not the rigorism of the Christian law, as in the sect; rather it means the spiritual equality, in principle created by the blessedness of forgiveness, from which the "doing" of the "new creature" issues freely.

The religion of faith which denies the sacramental grace of Supernature also tends in the same direction. There is no longer any room for the conception of "Supernature" at all; the whole idea of a graduated system, leading from Nature up to Supernature, from secular morality to that which is spiritual and supernatural, has faded away. Monasticism in any form only appears to be a special condition of moral behaviour, man-made, which flees from the natural conditions given by God; and by creating artificial conditions appears to set itself heavier tasks, although in reality it renders it easier for a Christian to overcome the world. The real problem, however, is to overcome the world wherever we find it, and in the midst of the life of the world to free our hearts from the world and to live in a spirit of detachment. There is no longer any room for self-chosen spheres of action, for forms of fellowship alongside of the life of the world, which claim to rise above it. It is precisely in the spirit of mutual service within the life of the world that Christian love is demonstrated. This also throws a fresh light on the system of vocational organizations, which, on the whole, Protestantism also regards as derived from the Natural Law. This system is no longer regarded as the organization of Natural Law in the lower sphere, above which rises the structure of the Church and of the mystical fellowship of love, but it is the sphere appointed by God for all, which includes the whole of Christian behaviour, in which each man must accept his own calling as the life-task assigned to him by God, and the contribution desired from him for the purpose of forming the Christian unity of love.

The main types of "calling", therefore—such as the calling of a house-father, or of marriage, the calling to be a paternal ruler, or to the exercise of authority in general—are held to have been specially instituted by God Himself. This idea does not contradict the other idea, that is, that these callings are equally derived from Natural Law; it is merely a special Divine confirmation of the most important "callings" appointed by Him.[204] Thus the previous conceptions of *ministerium* and *officium* are replaced by that of *vocatio*; this means that the whole system of callings is not a product of the lower sphere of Nature, a sphere which still has to be transcended, but that, like the natural sphere itself, it is a direct and immediate institution of God.[204a] It proceeds directly from Him, not indirectly from Nature, which is quite distinct from Him. This, however, is a new conception of Nature, as an inward and essential union between God and Nature, in which Nature is regarded as an immediate decree of His essential Will, and not as a lower degree of His self-emptying. To put it briefly: this system of vocational organization is a stable class-system of a patriarchal kind, fixed by Divine appointment in the Old Testament and by the Law of Nature, to which each individual belongs, in permanent categories, usually receiving at birth his assigned calling. Further, we must not forget that this immediate Divine character of Nature is due to a simple, positive decree of the Will of God, which a Christian must accept in a spirit of humble obedience without any attempt at understanding it; there is, however, no real inner essential connection between God and Nature; this is not asserted, nor is it felt to be so. Further, Nature has been so deeply corrupted by the Fall that not merely the present nature of man, but Nature in general, only reveals God in exceptional circumstances; on the whole it reveals far more the wickedness and cunning of the corruption of the Devil, and the misery which is the punishment of sin. Thus this ethic of vocation within the life of the world certainly means an accep-

[204] See p. 824.

[204a] In order to understand the distinction between these two kinds of terminology we need to realize that the word *officium* was the official Latin term for "guild" (*Zunft*), *von Oncken: Geschichte der Naturalökonomie, I, p. 112. Officium* means the natural organization, *vokatio* means at the same time the Divine appointment which it contains; the latter, however, is much more strongly emphasized by S.

tance of the world, but this acceptance is an act of obedience and surrender rather than one of joy in God's world; the idea of joy in the life of this present world because God made it, only appears now and again. At bottom, the acceptance of the world does not cease to be asceticism, that is, denial of the world, only it is a different kind of asceticism from the heroic asceticism of the Church, and it also differs from the legalistic detachment from the world practised by the sects. It is an asceticism which is in the world, yet not of it, which conquers the spirit of the world without fleeing from it; it means the practice of self-denial within one's calling, which is regarded as a service to the whole community; it means the obedience which remains where it is set, and there overcomes the "natural man" and the Devil.[205] As we proceed we shall often have to deal with the tension and difficulty which this acceptance of the world involves, an acceptance which far transcends the Catholic position and which is of great significance for the social philosophy of Protestantism.

Ultimately, of course, more or less consciously, behind all this there are new conceptions of the fundamental ideas of religion: of God, the world, and man. We cannot here pursue this general question any farther[206]; all we can do is to single out certain important points which are relevant to the subject of this book.

In the doctrine of Man the influence of the new ideas appears most clearly in the doctrine of the Primitive State. Here the idea of an ascent from natural to supernatural perfection has disappeared. In its stead we find the theory that the perfection of the Primitive State consisted in a spirit of complete and filial trust in God as an inherent element in the essential nature of man. Sin, therefore, is the destruction of human nature, and redemption is the restoration of human nature to full trust in God within the natural order of life. Here the new conception of the relation between God and man is perfectly clear.

So far as the conception of the world is concerned, the natural consequence is the disappearance of the gradation idea. It disappears not only in ethics, and in the doctrine of redemption, but in the whole conception of the world itself. Matter and Nature do

[205] On this point cf. *Karl Eger: Die Anschauungen Luthers vom Beruf, 1900,* and *Max Weber: Der Geist des Kapitalismus und die protestantische Ethik, Archiv. f. Sozialwiss., XX and XXI.*

[206] On this point cf. the closing chapter in *Harnack's Dogmengeschichte* and *F. Ch. Baur: Der Gegensatz des Kath. u. Prot. nach den Prinzipien und Hauptdogmen², 1836.*

not constitute a stage in the Divine creation of the world which is more remote from the pure world of spirit; Nature is the sphere appointed by the Creator for the realization of ideal values. These values were completely realized in the Primitive State in the perfection of human nature, and they are restored by Redemption. They form an integral part of the life of the world as it now is, and do not transcend it by a higher degree of mystical-sacramental miraculous powers. The miraculous element is present, certainly, but its purpose is simply the healing of the misery of sin and the restoration of Nature, not the achievement of Supernature. This is a different conception of miracle altogether. In the thought of Luther the miraculous element proceeds from the saving will of God which takes away sin, not from Supernature which constitutes the inmost heart of the Divine Being. This means, however, that the idea of evolution has disappeared in its Catholic form of an ascent from Nature to Grace, which Catholicism had combined with the Aristotelian doctrine of the steady process of the development of latent potentialities into actualities, or of the whole process of Nature as a struggle towards perfection. Man does not ascend from the Primitive State to a supernatural perfection which has already been prepared by Nature; the universe and the earth do not evolve from Nature into the realm of Grace; Society is not linked with a natural basis in order that there may be a natural continuity between it and the supernatural fellowship of Grace. In the Protestant theory everything is complete in a moment, and the Aristotelian doctrine of evolution disappears, as well as the Neo-platonic theory of emanations. The Fall does not mean a relapse into Nature, and Redemption is not the ascent from Nature to Grace; rather the idea is that the Fall means the removal of Nature, and Redemption is its restoration. This theory leaves no room for compromise, adaptation, transitional processes, or evolution as in Catholic dogma; all that matters is the Fall of Man and his restoration to God. That is why the Christian ethic is also not connected with and developed out of a natural basis, but is restored by the miracle of Grace, and then merely transferred, in a quite external manner, into the sphere of activity provided by natural conditions which have to be accepted in the spirit of obedience. This point of view shatters the whole fabric of Catholic reconciliation in the realm of metaphysics and of ethics, as well as its doctrine of Society. Out of the ruins there arises a very hard and artificial conception of life—one in which there is no room for relative conceptions nor for any process of evolution. This comes out very clearly in the difficulties and inconsistencies of the Lutheran ethic,[207] which we shall be studying later on.

Last of all, the whole change of view in Protestantism is summed up and expressed in its Idea of God. This is no longer a blend of the natural idea of the infinite absolute Substance which reveals itself in varying degrees, and the personalistic conception of the Divine Law which controls everything in Nature and in the spiritual world and which, by grace, makes it possible to fulfil the highest mystical law of revelation, with corresponding merit and celestial happiness as a result. In his Idea of God Luther discards scientific metaphysics and all attempts to reconcile the finite with the infinite; with resolute anthropomorphism this Idea of God is conceived as the Divine Will. No longer are the ideas of Nature and Supernature placed side by side, but their place is taken by the antitheses of the Law and the Gospel, the moral demand and the loving will which forgives sins, retribution, and grace. The method of harmonizing these elements is found in the Atoning Death of the God-Man. The Atonement, therefore, becomes the central doctrine of Protestantism, and the idea of vicarious achievement, discarded in every other connection, is here developed to its fullest extent.

In such a conception of God the motives and aims of religious fellowship, and the justification of the natural social forms of life, are quite different from those inspired by the Catholic Idea of the Absolute Being, and of the development of the world from Nature up to the miracle of Supernature. As we pursue this inquiry further, it will become quite clear that this changed Idea of God is the final cause of all the other changes which we are now about to consider.

The preceding analysis has noted the essential elements in the religious thought of the Reformation. It is manifest that these ideas are not a mere renewal of Scriptural Christian piety, whether of the Synoptic or of the Pauline and Johannine tradition, but that they represent a transference of mediaeval dogma, the Mediaeval Church, and the mediaeval ethic, to a conception of religion (drawn from Paul) as a matter of inward faith and a new spirit; in short, the Pauline religion of grace and of Christ. This comes out particularly plainly in the new value given to the natural life, which was only brought fully under Christian influence in the Middle Ages. This connection between the natural life and Christianity is retained; it is only justified and made practical for different reasons. Beneath the thought of the Protes-

[207] See p. 825.

tant Reformation there lay the fact of the mediaeval expansion of Christianity. All that took place was that this mediaeval contribution was based afresh on new religious ideas and was reshaped by them.

Sociological Effect of Luther's Thought: the New Conception of the Church

We now come to our second main question: What were the sociological results of this religious transformation of Christianity? The preceding paragraphs have already suggested a simple reply to this question, at least so far as actual essentials are concerned. But as we proceed with the inquiry in detail we shall discover many difficulties which were caused by the complication of these ideas.

In this connection the decisive element is not the peculiar juridical form of the Lutheran conception of the Church (with which the next section will deal), but, primarily, it is the fundamental fact that, from the very outset, this whole intellectual outlook belongs, essentially, to the Church-type. This means that the new conception of the Church fundamentally determines the sociological outlook of all the Protestant groups and gives to them its peculiar difficulties.

In spite of the fact that this school of thought has many affinities with the sect-type, in spite of its individualism, its lay religion, its appeal to the authority of the Bible, its emphasis upon the subjective realization of salvation in personal and inward Christian piety, and on the restriction of the true Church to real Christians, who have been truly "born again"—in spite of all this, in its inmost being it reveals no tendency whatever towards the sect-type; indeed, it regards the Church-type, in the most natural way, as the only Christian type of ecclesiastical organization.

From the very outset this is what Luther intended: (1) the reform of the ecclesiastical organ of grace and of redemption, so that its true basis of grace may be revealed in the Word, in the knowledge of Christ, and in the assurance of the forgiveness of sins which springs from Christ; (2) the reform of the priesthood, in order to restore it to its true office, instituted by Christ Himself, of the proclamation of the Word, or "preaching Christ"; (3) the reform of the sacraments—that is, from rites which impart the "substance of grace", they are to be transformed into rites appointed by Christ as "means of grace" which seal the assurance of the Gospel of the forgiveness of sins.

Luther took for granted that, along with these demands for

reform, all baptized Christians, however immature or nominal they might be, were included in the Church; that Infant Baptism should be retained and universally practised, and that the efficacy of the means of grace is independent of the subjective state both of the celebrant and of the soul which receives these mysteries. Luther had no desire to found a new Church; he simply wished to introduce an *instauratio catholica*, that is, to lead the One Catholic Apostolic Church, founded by Christ and endowed by Him with ministry, Word, and Sacrament, back to its purely spiritual activity of proclaiming the Word which creates faith.

The Word itself, however, its foundation in the Bible, its manifestation in the Sacrament, and its proclamation in the sermon, is to him an objective and precious endowment, intended for the benefit of all the individuals in the world, which the Church (as an institution) appropriates, and which is to be administered in an orderly manner by officials appointed for that purpose. Where officials of this kind do not exist laymen may officiate in their stead. The layman who discharges this duty, however, is thereby entitled to that precise share in the objective treasury of grace. In this respect, in the significance of a *Depositum* which the organ of grace established by Christ appropriates, and in the complete independence of the organ of grace from any standard of subjective realization, Luther's conception of grace is precisely the same as that of Catholicism. The differences lie only in the conception of the content of grace. From that point of view, however, both the nature and the method of influence of the ecclesiastical institution are considerably different.

The hierarchical sacramental Church is replaced by the Church which lays the main emphasis upon the Word of Scripture and its proclamation by the preachers. This Church, however, is also an institution set over its members as their supernatural source, instituted and directed by God Himself. This Church is entirely unaffected by the occurrence or non-occurrence of the subjective effects of conversion in particular individuals: in itself it is holy and Divine, through the converting power inherent in the "Word"; its position as a Divine institution is still supreme, even when very few are actually "converted" souls, while as a united body it extends its influence through all its special developments in the form of a national church, or in other ways. For, where there is the Word and the Sacrament, there is the Church, and the supernatural source of all experiences of salvation; and faith is certain that "the Word of God never returns unto Him void", that is, that finally its indwelling miraculous power will yet overcome all obstacles, and that in the end it must also inwardly convert humanity to Christ. This will certainly never be a comprehensive conversion including the whole of humanity. The Devil and sin are too strong for that, and the confusions of the present Church point to the End of the World, in which the great conflict between Christ and Antichrist will bring the struggle to a conclusion.

This conception of the Church is extremely spiritual and idealistic, making the essence of the Church to consist in the Word, the Sacrament, and the office of the ministry, and restricting it to a purely spiritual sphere of influence. It is, however, always and supremely a "Church" conception. It is the Catholic theory of the Church, only purified and renewed (in the New Testament there is very little support for these ideas at all); it is a transformation of the idea of a merely universal, all-inclusive Church, with an unbroken priesthood, and an absolute possession of truth, into the earlier and more primitive conception of a pure Christocentric religion which exalted the ideas of grace and faith, and whose only objective support is the word of Christ in the Scriptures. The whole of the supernatural element in this Church is focused in the "Word"—this idea gathers up all the objectivity and holiness, the sense that the Church as an institution is independent of the individual and personal point of view, and is, in fact, entirely objective—this idea of the "Word", however, is of the very highest importance for the Protestant conception of the Church. It constitutes the sociological point of contact, freed from the subjective element, secured quite simply, and endowed with a supernatural power of influence, from which, it is held, the Church is to be reconstructed. This conception was the Protestant equivalent for the Catholic episcopate, with its final centralization in the Papacy. In addition, of course, stress is laid upon the fact that the Church does not consist merely in the "Word", but in the interior personal influence of the Word, and thus in the "holy community", the fellowship composed of those who have been truly born again. This reveals Luther's principle of personal piety and of spirituality, and (as will appear later on) it was to this aspect of his teaching that the Anabaptists and the sectarians actually appealed. In Luther's mind, however, this renewed inward fellowship was always only the correlate of the Word of Grace, and the ministry of the Word which has produced this fellowship; this holds good whether the message was given by an ordained minister or by some lay Christian brother. Since, however, in practice it was impossible to distinguish the converted from the unconverted by any external sign, this attempt to limit the meaning of the Church had no practical significance at all. In reality, wherever the Word is preached, there is the Church. Even if there were only one solitary believer in a certain place, there the Church would exist as an institution, for the Church is virtually contained in the Word, as the creator of the fellowship perpetually exercising its miraculous influence, and never in vain. The Church would still exist even if there were nothing left save the Word. From that source it would ever arise anew. It is the duty of all Christians, and especially of Christian rulers (in whom alone, indeed, at first Christendom is rightly represented), to render the Word accessible to every one, to arrange for its regular proclamation, and thus, at least in external matters, to do what is necessary to ensure the establishment of the supremacy of the Word, in order that everywhere the Church may arise out of the Word "in spirit and in truth". The method by which this is to be effected—whether through some future General Council, or, if that is impossible, through the nearest authorities who can be appointed in the district and in the whole country, together with their natural counsellors, the professional theologians—is simply a matter of convenience, a question of linking on to the positive law which is already in existence. In all this, however, as far as possible all violent excitement is to be avoided, and until order has been evolved out of confusion the matter may be handled in very different ways—Luther, indeed, expresses very varying and inconsistent opinions on this point. When he is confronted with the question of a non-Protestant Government he feels it needful to organize a body which shall be entirely independent of the State; when this happens he emphasizes the fact that the secular power must not interfere in spiritual matters.

The result of these ideas is obvious: if universal order is not affected by the Empire or by a Council, and if the expectation of the approaching End of the World which is rife amid all this confusion is also not fulfilled, it then becomes the duty of the laity, and especially of the rulers, to help the Word of God to have free course, as Occam and the Conciliar theologians had already demanded—a demand which was entirely in accord with the whole previous outlook of Christian Society. This does not do away with the idea of the "holy Church throughout the world" which Catholicism preserves; for wherever the Word is present in any Church at all, there is the universal Church, and the particular Church in question is only a section or a corruption of the one universal Church. The "Invisible Church" is not the right term for Luther's conception of the Church, although he himself sometimes uses this confusing expression; what he really meant was that the Church is visible in the Word and the Sacrament, but invisible and incalculable in her purely spiritual influence. His idea might be expressed rather differently, somewhat in this way: the Church of the Word is purely spiritual, effecting the New Birth by means which cannot be defined outwardly, while at the same time she is present in the Word and the Sacrament and endued with the possibility of exercising a universal influence upon the State and upon Society, (which for that very reason means that she requires an external Christian organization of the State) which will make it possible for the Church to reach everyone, while otherwise her own organization is left very free.

Luther and the Reformers, like the Catholic theologians, focus Christian thought in the theory of the conception of the Church. This, however, is no mere relic of mediaeval thought, a barrier which can easily be swept away, but it is part of the very essence of its religious thought, which, in this respect, is entirely in agreement with the mediaeval and primitive conception of the Church, traced back to its very beginnings in St. Paul. Stated quite simply, the one thing we need to realize is this: Luther conceived and understood Christianity essentially as grace, as the basis of the assurance of salvation. A soul with this point of view is predestined to belong to the Church-type. To this type of mind salvation is something finished, certain and sure, a pure gift of God, independent of the ego, of all one's own struggles and subjective efforts, and only has to be appropriated by faith; the soul then absorbs the great principle of an objective Divine creative energy, which effects everything in and through the individual, while it is itself quite independent of the individual.

It is the profound conception of an historical life-substance which first produces all individuals, combined with the religious idea of grace, in accordance with which the possession of faith is a gift, not an achievement. This means, further, that it is only through this most precious gift that the powers of the individual are set free to develop their highest and richest possibilities. Both these phenomena, however—the historic substance and the element of grace which it contains—are conceived as a supernatural institution, strictly distinguished from all that is secular, whose fundamental supernatural elements, the Word and the Sacrament, produce faith, freely and inwardly, without compulsion and apart from external law, through the Divine energy which they contain.[208] In Luther's view a Divine operation of this kind could not be based upon the subjective foundation of individual illumination and mystical knowledge—experiences which often cannot be disentangled from the phantasy of the individual. He felt that the Divine operation must be manifested in something objective, "given", the same for all, something entirely authoritative, miraculous, and definite, standing out in clear relief against all that is merely human. To him this objective element was summed up only in the Divine institution of the Church, and in the Divine Word, through which the Church becomes outwardly visible, and is, indeed, its creative centre. This is the reason why Luther opposed the sectarians with such heat, because they regarded the basis of salvation and the bond of fellowship as consisting in obedience to the Law of God and therefore in subjective attainment. All forms of sociological development which were made concrete in the idea of law were suspect to Luther. In spite of the fact that the Law was part of the Divine revelation, he still insisted that it could not serve as a basis for salvation or for fellowship because law cannot exist without subjective achievement, and therefore it would again lead to placing the main stress upon the subjective achievement of man rather than on the "givenness" of the Grace of God. Likewise he would have nothing to do with mystics, enthusiasts, or fanatics. He held that in their "illuminations" there was nothing objective, no creative element of unmistakably Divine origin, upon which their fellowship was based. Rather, he believed that these "lights" were the creation of their own minds—auto-suggestion, in fact—which they tried to prove, later on, to be of Divine origin, by practical achievements or by the subjective fulfilment of the Law. This is why, in his study of the Bible, Luther discerned solely the Pauline and Johannine type of doctrine; that is, the type in which grace, and its objective assurance in the Body of Christ and in the Person of Christ, is everything. The Christ of the Synoptic Gospels, however, the Christ proclaimed by the Franciscans and the Waldensians, made no appeal to him whatsoever. Neither had Luther any interest in the Law of Christ, so far as this could be regarded as a general rule of life and a basis of Christian fellowship. It never seems to have occurred to him that there might possibly be some other interpretation of Christ and His Law than that proclaimed by legalistic orthodox sectarians. Luther makes Paul his doctrinal standard in everything, and even in Paul he ignores all the "enthusiastic" and mystical

[208] See p. 825.

features, and concentrates on his idea of the Church. To Luther, therefore, Infant Baptism was absolutely essential, as it is to all men of the Church-type. He held that this Sacrament is the outward sign and seal of the objective, universal, world-wide claim of the Church, asserting her will over every individual; it also represents the pure "givenness" of grace, the independence of the Church of all individualistic subjective effort and achievement, and, finally, it stands for the utmost comprehensiveness, implying that the Church is composed of Christians at all stages of experience, from the simplest believer to the greatest saint. Luther regarded Adult Baptism and rebaptism, on the contrary, as a symbol of legalism and of the sectarian spirit, which bases fellowship and salvation upon personal subjective achievement. The doctrinal expression of the idea of Baptism itself was still regarded as a matter of no particular importance, but logically it approximated more and more to the idea of an actual miracle of regeneration, which gives to all who have been baptized—in the possibility of appealing to the fact of their baptism—a *character indelebilis*. Every experience of repentance and conversion, and the entire work of the religious and moral life, means a renewal of baptismal grace, in which grace is fundamentally assured to every member of the Church, just as an entail belongs to all those who have been born into it. As time went on, in the interest of this objective institutional character of the Church, Luther laid more and more emphasis upon the sacraments, in which the Word which creates salvation reveals its objective aspect, and in which the Sacrament of Holy Communion in particular, in the Real Presence of Christ in His Flesh and Blood, reaches the highest point of objectivity. In this emphasis Luther established the distinctive character of Lutheran theology, whereas the Calvinists were content to regard the sacraments simply as tokens which conveyed the certainty of grace and the spiritual character of the Word. Thus Luther restored the practice of confession as a means of conveying the objective assurance of absolution through the ministry of the Word, and also in order to ensure a thorough preparation, through self-examination, for the reception of the Word of God which was contained in the Word of absolution.[209] This whole tendency arose quite logically out of Luther's own personal position, which was determined by his training in scholastic theology, as well as by his original interpretation of the Bible. For lack of more exact knowledge it is impossible to decide, at this distance of time, to what extent his views may also have

[209] Cf. *E. Fischer: Zur Gesch. der evangelischen Beichte, 1903.*

been affected by his personal temperament, as well as by the atmosphere in which he lived, which was steeped in the idea of authority. It is manifest that Luther was strongly inclined towards the side of authority, in spite of all his sense of the need for inner freedom, and it is likewise evident that he was essentially conservatively inclined, in spite of all his fearlessness and recklessness in instances when he was urged forward by his conscience. It seems, however, almost certain, that while these ideas affected the special form in which, later on, he formulated his conception of the Church (and above all, as we shall see, his conception of Natural Law), yet they did not affect the central idea, the conception of the Church itself. This central conception was essentially bound up with his idea of grace and the Word, with his conservative attitude in questions of revelation, especially in cases of supposed "illumination" and "new revelation", and with his aversion to every other rule of life save that of the revelation through grace, which possessed its objective standard in the Word and the Church, upon the basis of which it was then possible to adapt oneself to the life of the world. To erect any other standard seemed to Luther to savour of subjectivism and fanaticism, or of dependence upon "good works", and therefore to betray a legalistic spirit.[210]

Thus we see that the whole of the thought of the Reformation was dominated by the Church-type, which was due in the last resort to the religious originality of the Reformation itself. Luther was only able to exert his enormous influence on world-history as a Reformer of the Church. It was only because he held so firmly to the idea of the supernatural universal character of the Church that he was able to have an influence on institutions of a universal character. Without this conception Luther would have been merely the founder of a new sect, or of a new Religious Order, or even a solitary individual like Sebastian Franck.

Sociological Effects of this Conception of the Church

This predominance of the Church-type, however, meant that all the essential sociological effects also appeared. It led first of all to the demand for the uniformity, unity, and universal dominion of the Church, which, in the impossibility of carrying through a thorough Reformation, either European or German, finally led to the establishment of united Territorial Churches. Secondly, this emphasis on universality led to the extension of the ecclesi-

[210] See p. 827.

astical ethic into the sphere of secular civilization and of the social order, to the acceptance of the general order of life which did not harmonize directly with the Christian moral ideal, but which was inevitable; and, finally, to the perpetuation of the fundamental conception of the *Lex Naturae*, which was the complement of the purely Christian ethic.[211]

That these effects were the natural product of the Church-type is apparent from the fact that Luther himself did not accept these conclusions at all easily; only gradually did they force themselves upon his mind with increasing insistence as inevitable and logical deductions from the idea of the Church. He only developed the idea of universality with difficulty, and almost in spite of himself. This was due to the fact that the idea of the compulsory dominion of a Universal Church was opposed to his spiritual and inward conception of the nature of the Church, and also because his preoccupation with the idea of the priesthood of all believers incidentally brought him very close to the sect-type, with its method of building up a Church fellowship on the basis of voluntary individual membership. Nor did the extension of the ethic of the Church into the social sphere take place without hesitation and misgiving; this was due to the fact that Luther's emphasis upon the Bible led him into deep sympathy with the Gospel ethic of love, which was utterly opposed to the ordinary life of the world, to the secular nature of the struggle for existence, to the lust of power, to law, and to the desire to amass possessions; thus in this direction also he came into touch with the sectarian ethic.

Let us now turn to the first result of Luther's conception of the Church.

(I) Absolute Conception of Truth

With the supernatural idea of the Church—which regards the Church as a Divine foundation, endowed with a truth absolutely authoritative, and secure against all merely human opinion—there was constituted the absolute conception of Truth, which implied unity, unchangeable character, universality, and infallibility of the Church in the heart of the organization upon which it was based.

In Catholicism this idea was achieved through dogma and tradition, through the hierarchy and the sacraments, and from this fundamental impulse it developed into the world-dominating system which was finally forced to inscribe upon its banner its principle of compulsion, in direct opposition to its original principles.

[211] See p. 829.

In Protestantism this central fact was the Word of the Scriptures, and the Sacrament which was the sign and seal of the Gospel, with the natural result of an ordered ministry of the Word, which was, however, dependent upon circumstances for the way in which it was to be exercised. Protestantism, therefore, was faced with a twofold problem: (*a*) to stabilize the definition of the "pure Word", and (*b*) to organize a ministry of the Word, which would proclaim the Faith in its purity. In both directions, however, the new conception of the Church experienced considerable difficulty. The Word which lay at the root of this conception should be, in Luther's great and free way of thinking, the activity of Christ—the Pauline and Johannine conception of Christ contained in the Bible, interpreted in the sense of the Nicene Creed and the Creed of Chalcedon, through the doctrine of the Trinity. But how was this Word to be defined within the Bible? Its free development beyond the Bible, and its basis upon personal experience, opened the door to the most varied interpretations, and to new mystical interpretations which went far beyond the standpoint of the Bible. The only course to pursue was to close the door, to make a very clear distinction between the free proclamation of the Word and its written foundation in the Bible. Then the proclamation of the message was closely connected with its written basis, the Bible as a whole was canonized, in harmony with the dogma of the early Conciliar legislation, while its exposition was regulated by fixed standards, drawn from the Scriptures themselves, that is, from Paulinism. Thus the Protestant dogma of the Bible was created, according to which the Bible is the centre of the Church, the absolutely inspired authority, and the operative power of salvation through the converting power which dwells within it. The Bible proves and manifests its own infallibility by the Holy Spirit who dwells within it; its meaning is sufficiently clear to enable it to overcome all difficulties arising out of varieties of interpretation. This result was inevitable, if the conception of the Church were really to be based upon the Bible, and thus to attain genuine stability. Thus with Luther himself the rudimentary beginnings of a free historical human interpretation of the Bible disappeared, and the process was completed in the subsequent period of orthodoxy. The conception of the Church as the organ of salvation, Divinely instituted, required once for all a truth which should be firmly established, clearly defined, equally binding upon all, and this conception of truth required the absolute authority of the Bible, which would be impossible apart from a kind of literary Incarnation of the Divine. The Protestant extension of the Incarnation in the Bible corresponds to the Catholic extension of the Incarnation in the priesthood. The historic-human Bible criticism, and the establishment of the validity of the Bible upon the personal experience of salvation, was the weak point in the whole idea of the Church.[212]

(II) The Ministry of the Word

The other question, namely, the problem of the organization of a ministry for the proclamation of the Word, was no less difficult. The Word is the support of the Church, and not a hierarchy based on apostolic succession. The essence of the Word, however, consists in its power of forming personal conviction and of producing the New Birth. Thus the real supporters of the Church are Christians who have been born again through the Word, genuinely converted and live Christian people, and the direction of the organization of the Church is in their hands. Thus the Church seems to be constituted by the co-operation and strict Christian piety of its members. This, however, only seemed to be the case. In reality, the situation was quite different. In the confusion of the period of transition, when the adherents of the old religion and the associates of the Augsburg Confession still worshipped together, when the order of the Roman Church had not yet been discarded, and the new order had not yet been established, when men still hoped that a Council or an order on the part of the Empire might find a way out of the impasse, and when these hopes had been shattered, Luther began to believe the End of the World was imminent, and that the only Church organization which mattered was the gathering of the faithful into groups to prepare for the Second Advent. It was then that Luther gave several instructions about the formation of smaller groups of genuine believers, with their own Christian order of life, and a distinct practice of confession and communion, based on the principle of financial self-support and the right to call their own pastors. This happened during the period of ferment, when the attempts at reform were purely local, the time when Luther allowed the congregations to make experiments based on the principle of the priesthood of all believers. By some this period has been described as a complete break with the Catholic idea of the Church; by others, on the contrary, it has often been excused as a temporary deviation towards the sect-type. In reality, both these interpretations are incorrect. This "congregational ideal" does not in any way mean that the idea of the Church as an institution

[212] See p. 830.

has been renounced. For these smaller and purer Christian groups have also been created by the Word, and their view of doctrine is always exercised by means of a wonderful agreement produced by the Word and its miraculous power; the congregation is only the product of the heart of the institution, of the Word, and never the factor which produces the Christian fellowship itself. Moreover, these groups are only regarded as the kernel of Christendom, as a temporary means of education, which by their example and influence are to educate men from whom the Word shall again go forth to mankind in general. Not only, however, is the institutional conception of the Church preserved, but the tendency towards universality, and towards a state of affairs in which, ultimately, a given territory and the religion of that territory would coincide, with some unimportant fluctuations, is also retained. In all this, however, it is assumed that, sooner or later, matters will come to a head, and that the final issue of all these events will be either the End of the World, or, if the world is to continue in existence, a universal reform of the Church. Luther, indeed, only turned to the idea of this group organization after the appeal to the nobility (that is, to the ruling princes) had failed, and the hope of a General Council had been indefinitely postponed. In his mind these groups were to be meetings of the faithful during the dissolution of the Church before the coming of Antichrist; he regards the vital unity of the Church as so essential and natural that he can only account for its breakdown by regarding it as a sign of the beginning of the final throes of a dying era. These groups were to be merely temporary forms of organization; there was to be nothing final about them. It is also obvious that in addition to these groups he was counting on the power of a Christian Government to maintain the Christian order of life, and to defend it against "tumult" and open blasphemy. Indeed, he only recommends this new form of congregational organization in cases where the existing Church-order and the rights of patronage exclude the reform of the whole parish in the Protestant sense. In such a case the Christians who have become genuinely "evangelical" ought to form a group, and if they appoint one of their members as a preacher it should be a priest who has adopted the new views; in this way the continuity of Church-order will be secured. Further, these groups ought to act as far as possible through their natural representatives, the local authorities, in order that all should be done in harmony with the existing order, and in the interests of the Church and not at the caprice of individuals. Public worship should be open to all; it is only the more select body of communicants which is to have a closer form of special organization; Infant Baptism, of course, is to be administered as before, and the children and young people must receive religious instruction. All these experiments, however, are to cease from the moment that it has been decided that a Reformation of the Church at large is out of the question; that is, when action no longer has to be regulated by the points of view prevailing in the various parishes which often were entirely opposed to each other, but when the countries which have accepted the principles of the Reformation proceed to undertake an independent united organization of their ecclesiastical affairs. When that took place it was quite natural that the ruling princes and the civil authorities, as parishioners who are bound to obey the Word of God, and as the appointed representatives of the parishes, should undertake to set the Church in order by means of special "Visitations", and to establish the dominion of the "pure Word", which, at least in its purity, must be set everywhere upon the lampstand, that all may rejoice in its light. This "group ideal", which had only been understood in a very relative sense, disappeared entirely, and the idea of a universal world-wide Church was replaced by the Territorial Church system, without, however, doing away with the idea of the universal Catholic Church, since wherever the ministry of the Word and the administration of the sacraments are practised, even under very different forms, there is the Catholic Church. With his conception of the universal united Church, Luther can only explain the apostasy of the Roman Church by declaring that the Pope is the Antichrist who was prophesied in the Apocalypse; in this way he removes the stumbling-block created by the falling away of so large and permanent a section from the original pure Church of the Word, so long as the ideal is retained of a universal Church, ruled by God Himself, outside which there can be no salvation. That which has already been Divinely foretold can be no argument against the institution of the "pure Church" set up by God Himself.

(III) The Territorial Church System

The Territorial Church system, therefore, finally secures the following elements: the universal character of the Church, its claim to dominate the life of the world, the maintenance of "pure doctrine", and an ordered ministry on orthodox lines. Naturally Luther did not want the ruling princes to control the Church; this development was due rather to a logical development from the situation in the later Middle Ages, and, in any case, it was inevitable once the whole organization had been entrusted to the rulers of the different States. All that Luther desired was to secure the kind offices of the various Governments for the Church, but he also expected that the Word of God within these churches would be left entirely free. This ideal of Luther implied a division of authority within the social order which involved many difficulties from the very outset. In its purely Lutheran sense it was only possible to maintain this ideal in the over-idealistic belief that the Word would spontaneously produce within the Church a harmonious understanding of the truths of Scripture and a clear message; further, so far as events outside the Church were concerned, Luther held that the Word would teach the Government what to do, and that the laity would accept its ruling in free and willing obedience, so far, that is, as the right way had not already been made plain by the Law of Nature. Since church-order is no longer regulated by the legal supremacy of the hierarchy, the whole question is now entrusted to the influence of the Word itself, an influence which can never fail to produce an effect, an influence which is both united and uniting, an influence, which, apart from violent human efforts, will create the unity of the *Corpus Christianum.* When the Word fails to do this the only conclusion that can be drawn is that this failure is due to the power of sin and of the Devil, as so often happens in this wicked world. At this point Luther came very near to the eschatological apocalyptic point of view, in which the one thing that matters is that in the evil of these latter days individuals shall save their souls through faith and patience. This close connection between the renunciation of the uniform Christian order and the eschatological temper, as well as the close connection between plans made with permanent conditions in view and the reform of the whole life of Christendom, reveal more clearly than anything else that in his conception of the Church Luther had not given up the idea of universality, nor the ideal of a spiritual dominion over the whole of life; it would, indeed, have been impossible for him to give up this hope, since it was based upon the assumption that the purified Church also possesses the absolute Truth which alone can bring salvation to mankind. These fluctuations and these early expressions of a "group ideal" do certainly show very plainly the peculiar nature of the Lutheran church conception. Luther evidently believed that it was possible to base the uniform and all-embracing dominion of the Word purely upon inward personal conviction and fellowship, purely upon faith in this Word working through love, while the question of external organization was ignored. In his conception of the "Word" and of "Faith" Luther wished to combine the objective character of an institution with the subjectivism of personal Christian piety, as the fundamental creative forces within the Church. He found it very difficult, however, to combine these two opposite ideas, and it is therefore not surprising that this conception of the Church went far beyond Luther's own ideal, first in one direction and then in another.[213]

Since, however, the universal character of the Church was thus restored, not merely through the power of the Word, but by the maintenance of an external Christendom on political lines, and by the creation of a Territorial Church organization, Luther's conception of the Church was obliged to adopt a further element, which was quite alien to his own thought, but which became logically necessary if the unity and universality of the Church were to be retained, that is, the compulsory supremacy of this uniform ecclesiastical system.

The principle of a pure religion based on faith and personal conviction alone logically implied the voluntary principle of Church membership. And in fact, in his early days as a Reformer, Luther spoke out very strongly in favour of liberty of conscience and freedom to proclaim the Word by purely spiritual means. He had no desire to see the adherents of the "old religion" compelled into any kind of conversion by force from outside; much less did he desire to see this policy applied to those who lived under the new conditions. The Word was to be left free and untrammelled, and to overcome everything by its own spiritual influence. The emphasis, however, was laid upon faith in the miraculous power of the "pure Word", which alone contains converting power. "Set the Word free", he seemed to say, "and the human and priestly illusion will fade away and disappear." Thus Luther was not a champion of religious toleration; the cause for which he fought was the freedom of the Word to exercise its purely spiritual influence without the aid of external compulsion. The religious toleration which was possible from the standpoint of the Lutheran conception of the Church may be thus expressed: it did not consist in a toleration based upon the right of individuals to hold varying convictions, because in religious matters it is impossible to judge objectively, and compulsion in such matters is futile; it was rather the absolute certainty of the sole truth of the Lutheran position, or, rather, of the Divine nature of the Word, and of its capacity to propagate itself on purely spiritual lines. Here also,

[213] See p. 831.

however, the cessation of conflict was only to be a provisional arrangement during the time of ferment and transition; Luther never doubted that the Word would finally triumph, that is, as soon as he realized that these conflicts were not the sign of the approaching End of the World, but the birth-pangs of a new and more settled era. He was, however, obliged to go through the experience, common to every faith of this kind, and one which the Primitive Church had already undergone—namely, that thought and faith alone can never attain an unlimited universal dominion by purely spiritual methods, and that restriction to these methods indeed endangers the stability both of the universality and of the unity of the Church. Thus Luther also was obliged to resort to compulsory methods, which, just as in the case of the Catholic Church, were not exercised by the Church but by the State. The Church was to exercise her functions in freedom and in love, and in the face of opposition she was merely to warn and exhort. But in order to ensure that all citizens should be baptized and come under the control of the Church, the custom was introduced of uniting all civil rights with the exercise of the Christian religion, and in cases of permanent heresy the State intervened with its penalties, since heresy also is a breach in the social order. Both institutions, the unity of the social and civil order and of the ecclesiastical and spiritual order, are, quite naturally, co-terminous, just as they were in the Middle Ages. If, however, this agreement does not evolve quite automatically, it then becomes the duty of the State, at least outwardly, to make any sign of permanent opposition impossible.[214] Further, in view of the illiteracy and immaturity of the masses, it might seem as though it were quite justifiable to compel them to accept truth and salvation; even at the present day the State is still in the compulsory stage, and in countless ways, by the compulsory creation of a certain atmosphere, it forces men for their own good, just as every party, every group, and indeed even artistic and scientific movements only maintain their spiritual unity by compulsory methods of a coarser or more refined kind, whether direct or indirect. In the last resort no sociological cohesion can possibly exist permanently without some method of compulsion This is a fact of life, and all faith in the exclusive power of pure thought is an idealistic illusion; it does not belong to the sphere of reality. Above all, however, an association which is based upon that absolute Truth which alone can "make men wise unto salvation" (which requires, at the very least, that this truth

[214] See p. 833.

should be made accessible to all, and also needs protection against the obstinate undermining of its influence) cannot do without such methods of compulsion. On this question Luther completely revised his earlier idealism, since, in addition to the claim that this truth should be made accessible to all, he also demanded that all heresies which disturbed the order of the Christian commonweal in general should be removed forcibly by the authorities. This demand was aimed primarily at the Anabaptists, with their different ideal of Church and State. Finally, however, and quite logically, purely doctrinal heresies came under the heading of a "disturbance of Christian society", which, in the interest of the *Corpus Christianum*, it was the duty of the State to suppress. In the kind of penalties inflicted, too, the Wittenberger authorities became increasingly severe. Exile was followed by imprisonment for life, and then even by capital punishment—all these penalties were inflicted in the name of the State, after the offenders had been duly warned by Christian exhortation. But even the Catholic Church did not thirst for blood in this harsh manner; it allowed heretics to be punished by the State as obstinate disturbers of the peace and harmony of the Christian Society. Melancthon's attempt to justify these methods shows how much the Reformers felt this was a question of the preservation of Christian social unity; he argued that the punishment of heretics is required by the Natural Law, the fundamental law of a united society, to which the Christian Law is its complement, since the Natural Law itself desires the protection of religion. It is obvious that this position was entirely opposed to Luther's earlier point of view; yet it was not an entire denial of his earlier ideals. It was, indeed, a logical development from the ideal of a united Church, as soon as he realized that the Word could not be established upon a purely spiritual propaganda, and a permanent church-order became desirable. Luther was not driven to adopt this position by the law of the Empire, or by the political situation of the day. This point of view developed spontaneously out of the idea of the Church as the only organ of salvation which is obliged to protect sinners, great and small, from the forces of temptation. It is undeniable that Luther and the jurists of Wittenberg did set up a terribly cruel system of compulsion against "Zwinglians, despisers of the sacraments, fanatics and Anabaptists". They did this not simply under the pressure of the ruling princes, whose own interests were involved in the unity of the Church, and who were also very nervous about the influence of the Anabaptists. No, they adopted this policy deliberately, of their own free will, without, however, giving up the theory that the Church ought to exercise her influence solely on spiritual lines. It was a form of self-deception which is possible to men who believe that they are in possession of absolute Truth, and who are therefore honestly convinced that it is right to claim from the political authorities toleration for the Truth, but no toleration for falsehood. It is not the Church, as such, which punishes the rebels, and gets rid of them by violent methods, but the ideal created by the Church of the universal dominion of the only saving Truth over Society, the absolutist objective conception of truth, and the universal idea of Christian society supported by it.[215]

The Protestant Ethic and Compromise

Parallel with the development of this first logical outcome of the Church-type is the second result, namely, the steady development of an ethic which accepts the life of the world.

At first Luther's ethic had a tendency towards a radical Christianity, which was only concerned with "spiritual" matters and was aloof from and indifferent to the world. It was only gradually that Luther learnt to balance this tendency with the idea of the Christian nature of society required by the ecclesiastical conception, which always seemed very natural to him, and with the natural institutions of the State. Here, too, this development did not take place without many violent contradictions, and, just as the contradictions in the idea of the Church caused the complicated character of the Protestant relation between Church and State, so the contradictions and tensions contained in the Lutheran ethic caused the difficulties in the Protestant social philosophy.[216]

In itself Luther's Christian piety was a return to the purely religious character of the Christian ethic, to which he was led in like manner, even though with varieties of emphasis, by the mystical doctrine of the supreme and unique value of the love of God, by the main Augustinian formula of the Christian ethic of the love of all things in God alone and for the sake of God, and the Gospel message of Jesus of sanctification of the self for the love of God, and of love of the brethren for His sake. As law, the moral law disappears entirely, and he again exalts the free purposive character of ethics, which knows only one absolute aim, that of self-surrender to God in faith. Luther then claims that out of this supreme end (which alone is valid) the whole Christian Ethos with a great variety of motive will evolve quite naturally. The fluctuations in these various motives only show that in

[215] See p. 833.

[216] See p. 836.

Luther's mind the attainment of a fundamental religious position was the one genuine moral imperative, and that, as soon as the central question had been settled, everything else seemed comparatively indifferent and obvious. It is the return to the ethic of the Gospel; the only difference is that its imperative character has been transformed by the apostolic doctrine of grace, which means that the element of demand is only interpreted as a result and a gift of faith, through surrender to the grace which is revealed in and guaranteed by Christ. Faith is the highest and the most real moral demand, and at the same time it is a gift of grace: this is the high paradox and the leading idea of the ethic of Luther. Conduct, however, flows from this naturally. From this point of view Luther rejects all legal moralism to the point of the danger of antinomian consequences. Above all, Luther discards all the reconciliations and transitions of the Catholic ethic, which, by means of its casuistry, had always managed to connect the natural stage of life with the higher stage of asceticism, mysticism, and supernature. Luther defines as the heart and centre of Christian morality solely that pure inwardness of spirit, of trust in God in pain and trial, and that brotherly love which is completely self-sacrificing, which renounces all secular rights, the use of power and of force, and, indeed, of all right over one's own property. From the very beginning this genuinely Christian ethic had been strongly tinged with a kind of mystical spirituality, and to a large extent it remained so, in contrast with the purely practical ethic of the Gospel, which treats moral behaviour as a means of entering into union with God, and estimates it according to its power to effect this union.[217]

Over and over again, in countless passages, Luther has expressed the characteristic principles of this ethic, which consists in aloofness from the world, and in the concentration of attention upon the question of personal salvation and of the unity of the brethren in the love of God. He also makes it quite plain that this ethic of love and salvation is opposed to the ethic which is produced by the struggle for existence, with its concern with questions relating to law, honour, war, the State, and retribution. The Christian is actually only concerned with the life of the world on the side of his physical existence, because his life is temporarily involved in the conditions of earthly existence. To him the real laws of Christian behaviour are those laid down in the Sermon on the Mount: "Resist not evil". . . . "Love your enemies". . . and all that suggests that evil can be overcome by

[217] See p. 836.

love. True Christians have no need of the State, nor do they need the protection of the law for their private property. Natural opportunities for exercising this faith—which for the sake of happiness in God renounces all else and puts itself out freely in love—are to be used when they occur, just as the Gospel suggests; there is no need to create special conditions or to induce an artificial state for extraordinary sacrifices, as in monasticism. But this radical religious ethic, especially in the earlier statements of Luther, is entirely remote from the whole sphere of reason, might, law, force, to which the Christian only submits because it all forms part of this sinful world, and because, as things are in this world, it is impossible to render loving service to one's neighbour without using these secular institutions.[218]

The deduction of ethical behaviour from the religious element is still not very certain; it was, however, evidently intended, for Luther's faith is a "living, busy, and active thing". It is more difficult to determine in what way from the standpoint of this definitely religious general ethic of sentiment the real standard of the content of the Christian life was formed, and especially to estimate its attitude towards the "this-world" (intramundane) values and institutions which are so difficult to adjust to the demands of the radical ethic of love. Theologians usually deal exhaustively with that first general question of the basis of the ethical element in the religious sphere, but they neglect this second problem, because even in the Gospel itself they usually do not feel that there is any difficulty at all in discovering how it is possible to develop a "this-world" morality out of an ethic based on the absolute religious values of love to God and love of the brethren. In reality, however, it is this fundamental problem of Christian ethics which reappears in Luther's teaching. The Catholic compromise of a natural and a supernatural ethic has been destroyed, since to Luther a natural ethic, produced by human strength alone, would have seemed a complete denial of grace, and the limitation of the ethic of grace to the mystical higher life which exists alongside of the natural life would have seemed a misinterpretation and a narrowing of the Christian ethic which ought to influence the whole man. Luther's ideal was the restoration of the purely religious ethic, which, at the same time, should be applied unceasingly to the whole man. Since—whether in the mystical and spiritual sense, or in the spirit of the Sermon on the Mount—Luther emphasizes the real Christian ethic of the love of God and man in its completely radical sense,

[218] See p. 837.

while at the same time he alters the whole idea of Christian piety by transforming the idea of piety as mere membership in a sacramental institution into one of real complete inwardness of spirit; from this point of view also he seems to come very near to the sect-type, and to its radical Christianity of detachment from the world; just as he also emphasizes repeatedly the rarity of true Christians and the smallness of the true Church, which he explains by saying that the last Judgment and the great apostasy are near at hand. In reality, those elements in Luther, which, in the traditional view, are often held to be relics of monasticism, are in the main, though not entirely, due to evangelical radicalism, for the understanding of which it is true that monasticism in certain respects is certainly a help. It is also, for the very same reason, an approximation to the sect-type.[219]

There is here, however, no real fusion whatever with the sect-type. Luther always rejected such ideas very clearly and even passionately. But he never systematically and theoretically formulated the reasons for this refusal. One of the great fundamental self-evident elements of Luther's thought, however, lies behind this refusal, and in order to discover this our first endeavour must be to try to discover the ultimate reason for the form in which he shaped his positive ethic.

The reason which Luther gives most frequently is the definite rejection of legalism. In his mind insistence on the necessity for a radical Christianity expressing itself in life and behaviour meant an emphasis on "works" instead of upon "grace". He held that although the inner spirit of these "works" might be strongly emphasized, the real criterion of the state of the Christian would still be human achievement. Such an idea, however, is opposed to the fundamental idea of grace, which can only be appropriated through faith and trust, by which alone its presence can be recognized, and not by practical results and practical achievements. Although this insistence on freedom and this hostility to all rules and regulations, to all levelling tendencies, and to all compulsion forms part of Luther's character and temperament, it does not become really intelligible until we see that his basic idea is that of grace as the gift of God, which objectively precedes and implies everything else, and that this Divine grace is only obscured by human effort. Thus this stress upon free grace and human impotence leads Luther into an emphasis upon spiritual freedom and abandonment, which merges almost imperceptibly into a kind of Quietism. The active and legal spirit of Calvinism is based

[219] See p. 838.

upon a different idea of grace and of the Church; this helps us to discern the peculiar nature of Lutheran freedom. Essentially it is based upon the fact that the Church possesses the grace of God, which makes everything else superfluous. It is, of course, true that Luther believed that grace ought to bear fruit in a genuine Christian piety expressed in daily life, but he taught that Divine grace is in no way dependent upon this result, and that in general, owing to the sinfulness of mankind, it is only very imperfectly realized.[220]

This now brings us to his second main reason. Original sin is only overcome by faith in the grace of God and in the forgiveness of sins; again and again, however, it attacks the soul which is in a state of grace, but, in spite of this, sin cannot destroy the state of grace if the soul abides steadfast in faith. In Luther's opinion, to make radical Christianity the standard of the Christian state of grace and of the Christian fellowship would be to dream of a perfection which is seldom or never found, even among the finest Christians, and which the majority do not even imagine. If we must talk of Christian perfection at all, it consists in faith and trust, in the acceptance of an individual by God, not in an active fulfilment of the Christian ideal. Upon earth this is impossible, and it will only be realized in the future life. Thus the Lutheran conception of grace and the impossibility of overcoming sin render it impossible to draw any external line of demarcation between perfect and imperfect Christians; and the bond of Christian union does not lie in the realm of practical achievement at all, but in the objective possession of grace guaranteed and preached by the Church. This ideal persists, even when in actual life the Church contains Christians at very different stages of experience, as well as souls which fall grievously into sin. Luther insists that Christianity consists in this objective possession of grace alone, and not in any kind of subjective achievement, although to some extent faith should always issue in works. The extent to which this takes place, however, affects neither the quality of Christian piety nor the fact of personal salvation.[221]

This brings us directly to the third reason. Luther believed that any attempt to estimate the "state of grace" in individuals by the standard of radical Christianity would lead to the making of distinctions and divisions among Christians, to self-made agitations and sects. The result of this would be to break the unity of the Body of Christ, which would result in the pride of the sectarians and the lovelessness of separation. Imperfection and sin

[220] See p. 839.

[221] See p. 840.

within the Church should be overcome rather by mutual instruction and love and wise admonitions. This point of view implies the unity of the *Corpus Christianum*—a unity which ought never to be deliberately broken, but which should be maintained rather by the spirit of love and service. Within this unity of the Body of Christ even coarse and open sinners and non-Christians ought to be tolerated, at least outwardly (for it is never possible to decide quite positively about the real Christianity of any individual), and, further, the primitive masses of the people ought to be kept, at least outwardly, under the control of the Christian way of life, partly as a means of preparatory discipline and education, and partly with the aim of repressing—at least outwardly—external evil behaviour. Grace must not renounce faith in mankind too quickly, but it must gradually permeate a whole people, and for the sake of the religious element in the nation, society must restrain the activities of open sinners.[222]

At this point, however, a whole host of other reasons appear which explain why Luther rejected "sectarian" views. These reasons are not directly connected with the idea of grace. As a matter of course Luther regarded secular institutions and natural possessions as appointed and ordained by God. Nature and the life of the senses, a humanity almost entirely dependent upon mutual help and organization, government and property, law and oath, war and violence—all is willed by God; therefore this social order has its good side; so far as the rest is concerned it is an inevitable state of affairs, and is necessary, owing to the presence of sin, as the arena in which the conflict with evil must be fought. The Christian, therefore, is not set in the midst of a social order controlled solely by the radical Christian ethic of the Sermon on the Mount, nor by the mysticism which preaches self-denial and detachment from the world. As an individual, of course, in questions of personal piety and in the sphere of purely personal relationships, the Christian is bound to try to obey this higher law. But the Christian also belongs to the secular order of Nature and of reason. This natural order has been, in part, directly instituted by God, and in part it is indirectly permitted to exist by Him. It serves the end of material well-being as well as that of repression of evil; the Christian, therefore, ought to submit to it in so far as this does not require him to deny the pure doctrine. This means, however, that for fallen humanity the Christian ethic is a dualism: on the one hand, it is a pure and radical Christian ethic, a personal ethic which is mainly con-

222 See p. 840.

cerned with the preservation of the Christian spirit and temper; on the other hand, it is "natural"—governed by reason—and therefore only relatively Christian, that is, it is an official morality appointed and permitted by God. This view of the natural order means that the Christian may and should use law and compulsion, swear in courts of law, take part in divorce proceedings, strive to acquire wealth, property, whenever such action is required by his official or social position, or by the demands of the State or of the civil order—in fact, whenever it is necessary for any cause whatsoever; the individual, however, the "spiritual" Christian, on the other hand, must ignore everything of that kind; in utter love he must be the servant of all, to the entire exclusion of all personal interests.

In his *Sermon on Good Works*, and also in the treatise addressed *To the Christian Nobility of the German Nation*, in spite of all his mystical spirituality and the radical emphasis upon love in his ethic, Luther had no difficulty in immediately outlining a programme of Christian social reform and of a Christian world order, in a spirit which accepts the life of the world from a very broad point of view. In this programme Luther was thinking mainly of external Christendom, of the Christian as a citizen and a member of the State, of the *Corpus Christianum* or the Christian Society, within which, however, the only real and spiritual Christianity is the Christianity of the individual and of the spirit. To what a limited extent, however, these two aspects coincided is revealed by the fact that during the early years of experiment and reorganization Luther would have liked to see some outward institution representing the true Christians who formed the smaller groups within the Church.[223]

To some extent there is a familiar ring about these ideas of Luther. This is due to their presence in the earlier Christian ethic, and the fact that they are here gathered up into one central thought, which is regarded as self-evident, is not difficult to understand when we remember the analogous patristic and mediaeval developments. This self-evident idea which is here predominant is precisely that conception of the Church which implies that Christian piety and holiness do not consist in the subjective achievement and activity of individuals, but in the objective Divine nature of the wealth of grace which belongs to the institution as such. This idea of the Church also contains these further elements: the universality of the Church, which includes the most varied degrees of the practical realization of the ideal; its system

[223] See p. 840.

of religious instruction which aims at educating all who have been baptized with the aim of full Christian maturity; its acceptance as a logical result of this universality, of secular, political, and social institutions, as institutions which have been founded by natural Divine Reason as they had to be developed within fallen humanity; this is why these institutions should and must represent a relative contrast to the radical ethic of the Sermon on the Mount, with which, however, by means of the Decalogue, a final unity is attained.

Since, however, Luther's arguments are based on fresh assumptions, they naturally carry a different meaning from that of analogous statements by Catholic theologians. The objective holiness which constitutes the status of the Christian, which relieves the individual of the impossible obligation of even attempting the full realization of the Christian ideal, is not the concrete holiness of the institution, of the priesthood, of the sacraments, in which it is possible to participate by entering into the ritual of public worship. In the Lutheran view this objective holiness consists simply in the Word of the forgiveness of sins, which broods above all sin and imperfection as a consoling and joy-bringing energy; the soul can only enter into this state through a full personal faith, born of repentance, which alone makes the Christian community holy and well-pleasing to God, in spite of their sins and their permanent imperfections; it is a purely objective treasure, and as such it is absolute, even though it can only be appropriated in the spirit of entire surrender.

The Word of the forgiveness of sins, however, is the supernatural agent which creates the Church; it is the treasure which has been established by God; it constitutes both her essence and the treasure which she has to administer; it forms the heart of the institution, from which to all who surrender themselves to it in faith, in spite of all unequal achievement, there radiates the glory of an entirely equal reconciling light which makes everyone well-pleasing in the sight of God.

Characteristics peculiar to the Protestant Ethic

In accordance with this point of view, therefore, Luther's conception of the universality of this ecclesiastical ethic is also different. It does not mean an ordered "scale of perfection" with its various degrees of holiness, combined with the permission of a dualistic morality to various groups within the Church. It implies rather that the same ethical claim is made on all the members of the Church, combined with the belief that no one can attain an active perfection. It requires "faith" from everyone, and this ought to be made possible, or at least accessible, to everyone, through baptism and the proclamation of the Gospel in the ministry of the Word. But this demand is combined with a tolerant recognition of the varied effects of faith, due to the feeling that since it is impossible to overcome sin, and since the only thing that really matters is faith in the forgiveness of sins, the various differences in the exercise of faith really do not matter at all in essentials. The Lutheran ecclesiastical ethic does not imply a lowering of the Christian ideal; its real significance consists in this: that the central importance of practical achievement in general is replaced by the supreme decisive power of a personal "heart-faith" in the forgiveness of sins. It is no longer a service based on "good works", rendered in an anxious or scrupulous spirit, nor a sharing out of "merits" among different classes of people; it is not the compensation for the concrete institutional holiness by the strenuous endeavour to produce "good works", nor, on the other hand, is it the quantitative grading of the idea of perfection, nor does it mean that the ideal is maintained in theory while the attempt to realize it in practice is renounced. The meaning of this Lutheran ethic is rather that all kinds of degrees and stages of Christian development are tolerated for their own sake, because ultimately they do not really matter at all, since everything that does matter is focused in the grace of the forgiveness of sins, and in the blessedness of those who have been justified by faith. The universalism of the Church now means a system of religious education, which includes everyone through the preaching of the Word, and a passive quietistic attitude towards the relics of sin, combined with the hope that the power which proceeds from grace will of itself ever afresh in some measure overcome these sinful tendencies, and that the earthly conflict will be followed by a heavenly victory.

The third characteristic of the Lutheran ethic, therefore—the acceptance of the secular institutions of reason—of law, might, compulsion, and property—which is connected with that universality which tolerates the non-realization of the Christian ideal, is also interpreted in a fresh way. It must be admitted, however, that in the main Luther here carries forward the Catholic ecclesiastical idea of a Christian unity of civilization as something which is absolutely natural and obvious.

But this acceptance of the natural order is now no longer interpreted in the mediaeval sense, in which the natural order and all its institutions are placed under the control of the Church, in order to serve the purpose of life in the supernatural order. In the Lutheran ethic these secular institutions become pure forms and presuppositions; in themselves they have no meaning. Luther's view is that these institutions have either been appointed by God directly, or by reason, indirectly—that therefore they are implied in the creative order of reason and the Divine Law; it is, therefore, the duty of a Christian to accept them just as he accepts sun and rain, storm and wind. This situation happens to be that which has been definitely appointed as the one within which Christian love ought to be exercised, and Christians have no right to leave this sphere for self-chosen conditions of life. The right attitude towards them, therefore, is not the acceptance of the natural order as of a lower stage of development, regulated by the higher standpoint of the purpose of the Church and the community, but it is that of obedience to conditions of life willed by God, which provide natural opportunities for exercising the Christian spirit of love. The intramundane political and social ethic has thus been changed from a doctrine of relative ethical values which have to be subordinated to the supreme aim of Supernature, into a doctrine of forms and presuppositions of the Christian way of love appointed by God, which lie ready to hand in the ordered and law-abiding life of the State, with its guild and class organizations. These forms can be understood from the natural law of morals, and their apparent inconsistency with the Christian ideal can be explained by their adaptation to the conditions of fallen humanity; the right attitude towards them, however, is not one of explanation and ethical acceptance, but of religious obedience and humble submission.[224]

(I) Central Position of the Decalogue

This radical Christian ethic of the love of God, and of that love of the brethren which flows from the love of God, was now to constitute the ethic both of a national Church and of an exclusively Christian Society. If this were to be realized, however, the idea that a living faith would spontaneously generate a spiritual and moral order was felt to be inadequate. Luther saw that a definite moral rule of life must be established, a Christian law of ethics, which could be held up to the masses as an ideal, which would also secure the very important factor of the incorporation of secular morality into the whole Christian order. In order to do this Luther naturally turned to the Bible, in which it

[224] See p. 843.

was quite evident that an expression of that fundamental Christian impulse might be found. It is characteristic of Luther that he found the objective revelation of the moral law which manifested this inward impulse not in the Sermon on the Mount, but in the Decalogue, which, again, in his mind, was identified with the natural moral consciousness or the Natural Law, which has been simply confirmed and interpreted by Jesus and the Apostles. It was thus that the Decalogue developed its characteristic absolute meaning within Protestantism, as the complete expression of the *Lex Naturae*, and of the Protestant ethic with which it was identified.[225]

The Decalogue seemed suitable for this purpose, in part because its significance within the whole of the previous tradition had already developed along those lines; in part, too, because it was most useful in the instruction of catechumens, and also because it formed part of revealed religion, and occupied a central position in the Old and in the New Testament; above all, however, probably Luther seized on it instinctively because it provided the opportunity he sought for incorporating "this-world" morality and "this-world" institutions into his whole ethical scheme. The ethic of a universal Church, and the belief that sin could never be overcome, which arose out of the Lutheran emphasis upon the forgiveness of sins, could certainly not find its watchword in the Sermon on the Mount; the Decalogue alone could provide it. The national religious ethic of ancient Israel was better suited to this purpose than the radicalism of the message of Jesus, which was concerned solely with personal religion, and in his later development of ethical theory Luther drew more and more widely upon the moral teaching of the Old Testament and the moral wisdom of the Jews.[226]

The Decalogue thus became the substance of the Christian moral law, and in so doing it also gained a new theological meaning. The mediaeval ideal, which contained, on the one hand, the *Lex Naturae* and its Christian expression in the Decalogue, and, on the other, the higher theological virtues and the Evangelical Counsels, has been abandoned. The Decalogue, combined with the *Lex Naturae*, in its full original sense, is now steeped entirely in Christian thought, and is proclaimed as wholly identical with the fundamental Gospel law of love to God and man. Luther claims that the Decalogue, rightly understood, is the complete Christian ethical ideal. This is why he lays so much emphasis upon the difference between the First and Second Tables of the

[225] See p. 844.

[226] See p. 847.

Law. The First Table, with its commandments which concern man's relationship to God, contains the fundamental demand for reverence, love, and trust, which can only be fulfilled on the basis of a believing assurance. It requires the right religious attitude, the *motus spirituales*, and it constitutes the purely religious demand. This claim, however, leads to the Second Table, with its demand that our attitude towards our neighbour should be one which expresses love, in a state of life which accepts the natural order as something which God has ordained in order to provide a sphere in which love can be exercised. This Second Table includes the doctrine of the "Calling", and of the teaching on adjustment to existing conditions in the State and in Society, and the idea that love is to be exercised not beyond but within the natural order of human life. Obedience to the Second Table of the Decalogue, however, only has a true ethical value when it issues from the spiritual temper of faith, and when it aims at the exercise of a living faith towards one's neighbour, a gathering up of everything in this one real supreme value of life. Hence the Decalogue and the Natural Law, when they are fully understood, constitute the pure Christian and spiritual ideal. Wherever the Decalogue and the Natural Law are interpreted apart from these motives and aims—as, indeed, pagans have done, and as unregenerate reason still does to-day—neither of them has been fully understood. Thus pagans, and those who have taught a remnant of the *Lex Naturae*, were really only acquainted with the Second Table of the Law; they had forgotten the First Table. Their interpretation of the Second Table was well expressed in positive law, especially in Roman Law and in philosophical morality. But, in spite of that, Luther felt that such an interpretation only became useful when it was inspired and vitalized by the right Christian and spiritual temper—that is, with the spirit of the First Table, which in the Primitive State was also the spirit of the *Lex Naturae* in its full sense. Unless this is borne in mind this ethic is simply cold self-righteousness and pagan self-love. Thus the scientific ethic of Protestantism may expound the *Lex Naturae* according to the Decalogue and according to Cicero and Aristotle, but it is only a vital Christian piety which breathes into these forms that inspiring and radiant spirit—maintained in the midst of trial and sorrow and temptation—of gratitude and surrender to God which is based upon the consolations of grace.

Thus, within the Protestant confessions, the development of a right conception of the Decalogue became a task of primary and fundamental importance. The problem was to formulate a theory in which the inner impulse of faith and the positive revelation of the ideal should unite. Theologically, therefore, the chief problem was to make a clear distinction between the First and Second Tables of the Law, and yet to relate them to each other. This involved the necessity for making a clear distinction between the absolute Decalogue and the Law of Nature, (as it was in the Primitive State and has been renewed by Christ) and the relative interpretation of the Decalogue and of the Law of Nature (as it is when the First Table is misinterpreted by the pagan philosophical ethic, by jurisprudence and the natural conscience). In its absolute form in the Primitive State, however, the essence of this moral law simply meant the religious consecration of natural conditions and natural duties, the permeation of nature with a spiritual atmosphere; indeed, the essence of the doctrine of the Primitive State does not consist in the ascent from Nature to Supernature, but in the perfection of man as a human being. Thus, in spite of the fact that many earlier formulas and theories have been retained, the Protestant ethic still forms a new interpretation of the patristic and mediaeval equation of the Decalogue and the Law of Nature—that is, it is a new conception of the Law of Nature itself. This means that the Law of Nature is no longer regarded as the radical expression of the idea of personality, of equality, of community of property, of a life without compulsion or law, but the inspiration of all natural and necessary activity with the spirit of faith, since everything which is required by Nature (which is itself of Divine appointment) can be combined with the spirit of faith, with love to God and man.

Moreover, from a Natural Law of this kind it is manifestly impossible to draw conclusions in favour of equality and communism, not merely because in its present relative form it is modified by the conditions of fallen humanity, but because, in its very essence, it cannot produce such results. The observance of this Natural Law simply means that the activity required by natural circumstances and by Divine appointment is to be impregnated with the religious spirit of trust in God and of surrender to Him, and also that social behaviour is to be the outcome of love, since social usefulness is emphasized for love's sake, and not simply for its utilitarian character.

(II) Dualism of this Ethic

At this point, however, the question arises: which conditions are the product of Nature? So far as the undefined but painless and harmonious conditions in Paradise were concerned, there is very little to say in answer to this question. It is obvious that at that period both elements agreed with each other, and we do not need to pursue this subject any farther. In any case, unbounded love and freedom from compulsion and pain prevailed. But that which it was possible to unite under such circumstances became, in the course of world-history, separated: the relative Natural Law of the state of sin, which expresses itself in the State, law, and dominion, was at variance with the religious ethic of love, which renounces law, self-assertion, and the effort to achieve its own ends. When, however, the Decalogue and the Natural Law had been renewed and interpreted by Christ, the purely religious aim of life and the purely religious fellowship of love emerges as the real Christian ideal, an ideal which concerns the inner life of the individual, along with the secular ethic of professional life, the State, and Society, to which man belongs either officially, or through being incorporated into the order of Society and the State, with its marks of law and compulsion.

This is the difficult aspect of the Lutheran ethic. The patristic and Thomist doctrine had been able to explain its dualistic morality by interpreting the Law of Nature as an institution which served both as the penalty and the remedy for sin; upon this basis of fallen humanity it then constructed the peculiarly Christian order as a higher form of fellowship. When, however, Luther took over this Catholic theory, he felt that it did not really harmonize with his fundamental point of view; for, although he was prepared to admit that the natural order may have lost its spiritual content through the Fall, he felt that actual opposition between the two was impossible. Either there is no room for the transformation of the Natural Law of Paradise into a largely contradictory Natural Law of fallen humanity (and therefore for the essential contrast between the Natural Law of Paradise and the Natural Law of the present day); if so, then the present Natural Law, and the political and social order which corresponds to it, must be present in it or be transferred to it in a form which is really in conformity with Christian thought. Or, the Natural Law of Paradise has actually been transformed into an empirical Natural Law which is strongly opposed to it; if this is so, then its institutions are not simply forms and presuppositions which can be expanded by the Christian spirit and the spiritual love of God. If the latter is the case, this gives rise to a very definite and clear contradiction in thought. Since, then, Luther adopts this latter point of view between his ideal of Natural Law and the Decalogue, or between his fundamental conception of the Christian moral law and his really dualistic instructions to Christians which decree an inward morality for the individual and an external "official" morality, there exists an extremely painful inconsistency. At this point in Luther's doctrine there breaks out once again the tension which is essential in every Christian ethic—the tension between the Christian ethic and the world and Nature which he had removed in his ideal of the Law.

This contradiction which Catholicism had turned into a contrast between two stages—between the lower stage of development of relative Natural Law and the genuinely Christian higher stage of development—has here been transferred to the individual as the contrast between "person" and "office". Since, like the Catholic theologians, Luther maintained the idea of grace and of universality, and could not possibly have adopted the sectarian attitude of world-denial, his ethic was also obliged to incorporate into its theory the contrast between secular morality and the morality of grace. The solution was provided, not as in the mediaeval Church by apportioning responsibility among various classes and groups, for mutual supplementation and vicarious service, but by placing each individual in the midst of a dualistic ethic; this dualism is then explained as due in part to the ordering and arrangement of God, in part to sin, and in part to the actual conditions of physical existence.

As time went on, however, Luther modified this dualism a good deal. Just as in his conception of the Church the earlier subjectivity of his view gave place to the idea of the objectivity of the institution, so also, and in close connection with this change of view, in the sphere of ethics the opposition between a personal and an official ethic, between the Sermon on the Mount and Natural Law, was increasingly modified. More and more he came to regard secular institutions as mere forms of life, which are due less to the relative tendency of sin than to the positive institution and appointment of God, and the general assumptions arising out of Natural Law.[227] Finally, the Protestant ethic finds it once more possible to use the ethics of Aristotle, Cicero, and the Stoics, and the ancient Humanistic ideas of politics, economics, and social doctrine. These ideas provide material which, lacking the religious motive, in themselves do not yet constitute an ethic at all; as the results of Natural Law, however, they only need to be penetrated by the religious principle which was originally contained in the Natural Law, in order to become a Christian ethic. More and more the contrast between a Christianity of

[227] See p. 847.

disposition and the secular official morality disappears; and the sense of tension and contrast gives place to an attempt to construct a synthesis. Existing conditions, which are permanent either because they are founded on reason or appointed by God, become more and more the normal condition, and the Christian ethic becomes, as modern Lutherans say increasingly, "the truth of the natural order", the work of Redemption consists more and more in the "glorification of the natural order created by God, and not in a species of destruction of that which God has created";[228] also, one might add, not merely in a patient endurance of the natural order, but in a humble and obedient acceptance of it. "Nature", that is, the political and social order which has been evolved by the Law of Nature, is conceived as a stable order of Society, existing for one purpose, which is required by reason in the sense of the territorial state; and the religious sentiment regards it less and less as an opposition to the radical ethic of love, but rather as an institution which has been founded and decreed by God, and which therefore has to be obeyed. In place of the earlier and more spiritual point of view, in which Luther formulated the purpose of life from the point of view of the absolute religious end, and of the opposition to the world to which that gave rise, Luther insisted more and more upon the necessity for obedience to positive authority. As faith was replaced by dogma, so, instead of the *justitia spiritualis* of the individual which was opposed to the relative Natural Law of the "official" ethic, he emphasized obedience to the ordinances of God and to the world conditions which He has appointed. The relative order of reason, tainted by sin, becomes the authoritative, entirely positive order of reality, to which, without thinking very much about it, the Christian has to adapt himself. This is how the problem of the inconsistency of the Lutheran ethic has been overcome.[229] The radical ethic of love disappears, and the ethic of obedience towards authority comes into prominence. Increasingly the Lutheran ethic is summed up in the following characteristic features: confidence in God founded on His grace, and love of one's neighbour which is exercised in the social duties of one's

[228] Cf. *Luthardt: Kompendium 10, Thieme IV;* most decisively in *Uhlhorn: Kath. u. Prot., p. 29:* "With that the dualism of the present and the future life, of the natural and the supernatural, of Christian and worldly, of the perfect Christian and the average Christian, has been overcome. Science, trade, and commerce gain once more their free movement. Therefore *Uhlhorn* thinks that Protestantism will be able to solve the social question" for which Catholicism is inwardly incapable and only externally concerned.

[229] See p. 848.

calling, combined with an obedient surrender to the order of Society created by the Law of Nature.

Thus the deep inner tensions of the Christian ethic, which had always appeared whenever a fresh attempt was made to shape the life of the world according to the Christian standard, were also retained in the ethical theory of the Reformation. This ethic also is a compromise, a dualistic morality, above all in the fundamental conception of Luther. Only the inconsistencies are not distributed among various grades, but are interwoven in such a way that they form a dualistic attitude towards life in each individual. The compromise has become a more interior thing, and in the process it has become increasingly modified, since the world is accepted not so much as a sinful institution or as an order which, through sin, has obscured the light of reason, but as a direct and positive appointment by God. The happy and docile humility which accepts the grace of the forgiveness of sins increasingly resembles the humility which accepts the conditions appointed by God; the converse is also true; therefore on both sides the religious attitude becomes similar. The thread of pure idealism, however, constantly reappears. For as soon as the ideal of the Sermon on the Mount reveals the deep cleavage between existing conditions and the genuine Christian ideal, and as soon as the existing social and political order fails to harmonize with the Church and the Word of God, a spirit of violent anger breaks out against the world of sin and of the Devil—the Last Judgment becomes a desirable end of all things, and the Christian life seems essentially to be a life "under the Cross" and the hope of a blessed life beyond death. Joyful acceptance of the world then becomes patient endurance of the world, and Lutheranism, in particular, oscillates between these two extremes.

From another point of view, however, the same problem reappears. If the spiritualizing of the Decalogue is taken seriously, if all that is done in the earthly secular sphere is really regarded purely from the standpoint of the love of God and as an obvious duty, and if it is precisely in the presence of this motive that the Christian nature of morality is seen, then secular institutions sink to the level of merely concrete conditions; they become forms which are in themselves valueless, within which it is the Christian's duty to live as though the world did not exist at all. The reduction of the world to mere form and presupposition is just as much an acceptance of the world on the one hand as it is a depreciation of it on the other. The outlook on the world, however, then becomes

[230] See p. 849.

ascetic, in the sense that men believe that secular institutions and values possess no independent purpose of their own, nor an inner Divine element. They become purely positive institutions and facts, which only proceed from the Will of God, not from inner necessity. They become entirely formal and hollow, and the endurance of them becomes an act of pure obedience and patience. Within this sphere, however, the world is not accepted, but it is regarded as a matter of indifference and overcome. Here, therefore, asceticism, as depreciation of the world, is no longer (as in Catholicism) merely connected with individual achievements, but it permeates the whole fabric of life and its activity, leaving behind nothing save the expectation of the much desired Last Day, which will set the soul free from those conditions of life which have never quite squared with the Christian ideal, most of which are still wholly perverted by sin. The one thing that is forbidden, however, is the effort to free oneself from these conditions, as is done in monasticism. Instead, the spirit of world-renunciation is to be carried into the natural course of daily life within the world itself. This view also contains some expressions of a real love to the world and to Nature (which, indeed, in themselves are good and have only been spoilt by sin), and now and again the whole ethic can even appear as a religious glorification and penetration of Nature. This only means, however, that the deep inner inconsistency, the deep inner tension, which lies in the whole problem, still remains; it shows that the compromise undertaken by Catholicism has only been removed to a different plane; it has sunk deeper into the inward depths of life, but it is still a compromise. It is the compromise (required by practical life, inevitable in the universality of Christian fellowship, made possible by the transferring of holiness from the activity of the individual into the objective ecclesiastical possession of grace) between a purely religious ethic and the claims of the life of the world.

Retrospect and Forecast

If we summarize all these considerations, and look back at the presentation of our subject in the Middle Ages and in the Early Church, we can then say: Protestantism carries forward the acceptance of the life of the world into the ethic of a universal Christian Society, which had been dimly foreshadowed in late antiquity, but which was only really attained in the Middle Ages, and it intensifies this principle to the highest possible degree. Since Protestantism is a renewal of the primitive Christian religious spirit, its greatest difficulty arose, primarily, at this point. In the endeavour to deal with this problem through the formation of small communities within external Christendom, and in the distinction it draws between the personal spiritual ethic and secular official morality, it approaches the sect-type, which also in reality springs out of Protestantism at this point.

Since, however, on the other hand, Protestantism maintains the ideal of a pure institution of grace which comprehends the whole of Society, and the unity of the Christian Society, it rejects the sect-type as the tendency towards legalism and loveless division. This rejection of the sect-type led Protestantism to an ever-increasing recognition of the life of the world and of the morality of the world. Just as in Thomism the contrast between the relative *Lex Naturae* and the ethic of grace gradually disappeared, till it became a lower stage in the ethic of grace, so here the *Lex Naturae* becomes increasingly a mere form, which the Christian spirit inspires with the glow of religious love and energy, making it the presupposition of its activity. In close connection with the development of the Church as the organ of grace into a unity of life dominating the State and Society as a whole, ethics also are developed into a Christian inspiration of life, into the "classes and callings" ordained by God, and therefore holy, which, further, are given with the Natural Law, and to a great extent, in the Old Testament, have been directly appointed or confirmed by God, and have not been rescinded by the New Testament. The idea of Grace as the perfection and superstructure of Nature may be due to Catholic influence, but the permeation of the existing forms of life with the spirit of faith and love is a Protestant conception. While Catholicism distributes the ethical claim among various classes of people, Protestantism demands the same moral standard from all alike. While Catholicism asserts the possibility of attaining absolute holiness, and therefore maintains special groups for the cultivation of the higher Christian piety, Protestantism proclaims the impossibility of overcoming sin for all alike, and gives to all as a common spring of morals the believing disposition, which can be preserved, even despite the outward conditions of life, granted that complete holiness is impossible to attain. Protestantism usually claims that in relation to the problem of "Christianity and Civilization", which Catholicism and the sects in their own way have both solved along the lines of asceticism and legalism (in Catholicism by reorganizing and secularizing the life of the world, in the sects by the rejection of the world and therefore as a definite rigid asceticism, and in both instances as law), it has maintained the inwardness of Christianity freed from all legalism, and that it has thus made it possible for the life of the world to be freely penetrated with the Christian spirit. Compared with the solution provided by Catholicism and the sects this is only, to a very limited extent, a new solution of the problem. The principle of pure spiritual freedom, which Protestantism certainly did restore, is still in its content a principle which is closely connected with the Bible, and in this respect it comes very near to the ethic of the sect-type, with its general rejection of law, might, the State, force, and self-interest; while the extension of this spirit by means of a Church, as the organ of redemption, controlling a united Christian Society, approximates very closely to the ethic of the Catholic Church-type. The Protestant solution of the difficulty in the dualistic ethic of a "personal" and an "official" kind is no solution; it is simply a new formulation of the problem, and even in Protestantism the problem has sometimes been made superficial by reducing it to the legalism of a secular and Christian ethic deduced simply from the authority of the Bible. This development has sometimes taken place not only in Calvinism, but also in Lutheranism; it has only been emphasized more strongly in Calvinism because that denomination generally lays greater stress on the ethical organization of the Church.[230a]

These similarities and differences between Protestantism and mediaeval Catholicism produced, therefore, on both sides similarities and differences in their social philosophy.

Protestant social philosophy carried forward the patristic and Catholic intellectual point of view based on Natural Law with its close relation to the Christian ideal, but it gave to the relationship and the constitution of both a new meaning. Since, however, the tension between both these elements had only changed its position, it also reappears, in an altered form, in the social philosophy of Protestantism. From this point of view also the same process is repeated with reference to the sect-type. The similarity between Protestantism and the sect-type lies in the emphasis upon the Christian demand as a strict and equal demand upon all men, and thus on Christian individualism. Protestantism, however, always deduces this individualism solely from the influence of the Church as the organ of redeeming grace, and in this way it places the individual in connection with the general cultural life by which it is surrounded. Hence, in spite of its individualism, the social teaching of Protestantism is much nearer to Catholic social doctrine than to that of the sect-type.

[230a] See p. 849.

At this point at last we have before us the presuppositions which are necessary for the understanding of Protestant social philosophy. From this point of view we can clearly distinguish the essential difference between it and Catholic social philosophy, as well as its attitude towards Christian radicalism, which, as a complementary movement, was produced just as much by Protestantism as it was by Catholicism.

In the following sections, therefore, I shall present the social philosophy of Lutheranism which has developed, fairly logically, out of these basic ideas. I shall then present a study of the social philosophy of Calvinism, which introduced considerable modifications into the common stock of the intellectual heritage. The first point to be considered in connection with both confessions will be the conception of the Church, and the way in which it secured the universality and dominion of the Church. The next point will be the ecclesiastical ethic, and the way in which secular culture and secular-social values were incorporated into this ecclesiastical ethic. Since in thus gathering the whole of life under the dominion of the idea of the Church there is implied, consciously or unconsciously, the ideal of a sociological fundamental theory which embraces all these formations, we shall deal further with the sociological fundamental theory which was dominant at that time. Only upon this basis will it then be possible to answer the last question about the particular forms adopted by the main social phenomena in the Family, the State, and Society.

Confessional Lutheranism and Calvinism, however, were not the only products of the Lutheran movement. Alongside of these movements which belonged to the Church-type there arose out of them other movements which burst through the Church-type and, more or less logically, developed the sect-type. From this type there extends a whole unbroken chain of complementary movements, extending from the Anabaptists and all "spiritual reformers" to the Independents, Pietists, and the modern sects. These complementary movements, as has been shown several times already, were a logical development of Luther's world of thought, as soon as its presupposition—the idea of the Church—was broken through; Luther himself, in his "group" ideal and in the radical mysticism of his ethical ideas, in spite of the fact that inwardly he was far from the sect-type, came very near to the ideals of these movements; indeed, he only missed them by a hair's breadth. Only in the light of the contrast which these movements present can we fully understand ecclesiastical Protestantism.

Further, since these movements broke away from the main body which supported the Reformation, they have had an amazingly strong reflex action upon orthodox Protestantism. The effect on Lutheranism was manifest: as it watched the development of these sect-movements it realized the danger of subjectivism, and it reacted violently in the direction of objectivity. Calvinism was influenced by these movements in the sense that it accepted to a great extent their ideal of holiness, and in so doing ultimately made a breach in its national and State Church system. Apart from their influence upon the two leading Protestant confessions, these movements are of universal significance in world-history, since in their various ramifications they produced results which led to and fostered religious subjectivism in general, separation between Church and State, the independence of local congregations, and finally of the individual, thus bringing a whole host of religious motives into the subjectivism of the Enlightenment. Thus in the last section we shall still have to deal with the sect-type within the sphere of Protestantism.

2. LUTHERANISM

The Ecclesiastical Organization of Lutheranism

The whole social fabric of Lutheranism—that is, of those ecclesiastical and cultural organizations which were the direct logical result of Lutheran ideas—was erected upon the basis of the thought of Luther's later period, the period, that is, when he had deliberately decided in favour of the Territorial Church system. This Lutheran system, however, did not spread very far beyond its original home; its chief expansion took place in the German territorial States, in Scandinavia, and in the Baltic States. On the Western frontier of Germany it lost large sections to Calvinism. In France, England, Holland, and Scotland it succumbed before more active and progressive ecclesiastical movements of a very different kind. In the South and East its progress was checked by the Counter-Reformation within the Roman Church, which fused Thomism and the Renaissance in a new combination; the result was, that for some time to come, in many respects the Roman Church once more became superior to Lutheranism in the social and cultural sphere.

Lutheranism was based entirely upon the idea of an ecclesiastical civilization, forcibly dominated by religious ideas. This was actually the case, in spite of the fact that in theory the Lutheran system regarded the civil and the spiritual authority as entirely independent of each other, and in spite of the fact that the Catholic supremacy of an international, hierarchical Church, enforced by directly ecclesiastical methods, had been discarded. Thus the conception of a State Church still remains the centre of the social doctrines of Lutheranism, and all social developments which take place outside the religious sphere are estimated from the point of view of the result of their incorporation into the ideal of a social order composed of a unified State penetrated by the Church with the ultimate aims of religion. In Lutheranism this idea was not simply part of its religious and ethical ideal; it was essential to its very existence. Lutheranism realized that it could not stand alone; it was like some frail sapling which needed the robust support of a Christian State or a Christian Society if its pure spirituality were ever to bear good fruit.

The centre of the whole system, therefore, was the specifically Lutheran conception of the Church, and in this matter the theoretical religious and dogmatic view of the Church, from its own standpoint, was of fundamental importance.[231]

This conception contains two main elements which control the Lutheran view as a whole: (1) The idea of the Church has been greatly spiritualized; this was Luther's intention, and in the main the Lutheran theologians maintained this point of view during the classic period of orthodox Lutheranism. (2) This entirely spiritualized Church, which does not desire any human organ of compulsion for the enforcement of the pure doctrine, and which neither is able nor desires to carry out its work of Church discipline by any external method of compulsion which can be legally formulated, is, in spite of that, based entirely and wholly upon the idea of a fixed and rigid system of doctrine to which all consent, which alone has the power, in its purity and exclusiveness, to secure redemption from sin and from hell. This means that, in spite of her spiritual character, and in spite of her renunciation of the methods of law and compulsion as natural rights, the Church is still obliged to submit unconditionally to the external life of the political sphere which she dominates. Inconsistencies of this kind had existed within every previous theory of the Christian Church, but the tension which they caused never became so acute as in Lutheranism, and their mutual hostility has had a paralysing effect upon the whole course of Lutheran development.

The idealistic aspect of this conception of the Church, which introduces an entirely new element into the history of the Christian idea of the Church, thus becomes manifest. The Word of God as

[231] See p. 850.

the herald of the pure doctrine of that grace which forgives sins and renews men's souls brings everything to pass purely in its own strength, by virtue of its inward miraculous power in assurance of faith. The inward witness of experience proves its unique Divine inspiration, which to an increasing extent is expanded until it covers the whole content of Scripture, even including the literal translation of the text and questions of punctuation. The Scriptures, therefore, are the sole absolute authority, the standard by which the Church is guided, in which Christ Himself is at work, and alongside of which there is no need for any human tradition, infallible ministry, priesthood, or hierarchy. The Bible is its own interpreter, since it illuminates obscure passages by the standard of those which are clear, and through the power of the indwelling Holy Spirit it effects an entirely uniform objective creed; these norms, which the Bible itself has created by its own method of interpretation, are fixed in the Creeds.

The Word, or the Christ who is active in and through the Word, completes the work of the sermon and the sacraments; the ordained minister is only the channel of the Word, and through the pure doctrine it is Christ Himself who speaks, preaches, and judges in him. The Word, or Christ in the Word, imparts faith, love, and obedience, by means of which all submit to the truth of the Scriptures, listen willingly to the preachers, who by spiritual gifts and training for their calling have been fitted to proclaim the Word; the faithful also willingly endure the chastisement of the Church. Thus through the Scriptures Christ rules the Church; in Him resides the supreme redeeming power; it is He who operates in the sacraments, who controls the exercise of ecclesiastical jurisdiction, who is the formative, controlling decisive authority in the Church; He achieves purely by His own spiritual influence all that the Papacy, the priesthood, and the hierarchy, Roman law and Roman compulsion, had achieved by external human methods. The government, the supreme court of appeal, and the executive power do not lie within the hands of the faithful as a community of believers, since this community is indeed only a product of the Scriptures and of the "pure doctrine"; neither does this power reside in the clergy, who are only the appointed channels through which the Scriptures operate along their own lines; nor does it reside in the Prince, who is only a servant of the sanctuary, and who only places his services at the disposal of the self-propagation of the Word. No; this authority is centred solely in the Church of the Word itself, built up upon the miracle of Scripture, whose miraculous powers only need to be given a free course in order to allow this Church of the Word and Christ Himself finally to produce all the results required. If from the Catholic point of view the Papacy is the extension of the Incarnation of Christ, the living authority in doctrine and in jurisdiction, in Lutheranism the same thought is represented by the Word, through which, as in a living being capable of action, Christ Himself is directly operative.[232]

In practice, of course, it was impossible to carry out this extremely "spiritual" conception of the Church, with its miraculous faith which staked everything on the power of the Word. In reality, this idea of the uniform influence of the Word, overcoming all difficulties and bringing order out of chaos, stood in dire need of human support. The uniform interpretation of Scripture did not come about naturally; it had to be enforced from above. The institution of ministers in an orderly way did not come about spontaneously, neither through an outpouring of charismatic gifts nor through the voluntary exercise of love and willing submission to a charismatic ministry; a definite church-order had to be created in order to call ministers and to give them official recognition. Excommunication could not be carried out by expecting defaulters to submit to the jurisdiction of the Church of their own free will, but it needed the help of the State and the imposition of civil penalties for spiritual transgressions.

In addition, the whole ecclesiastical organization needed to be regulated on the financial, administrative, and mechanical side, and the purely spiritual form of Church government through the Word made no provision for this side of the life of the Church at all, nor for the fact that the Church was involved in questions of civil rights and the marriage law. Not only did the purely "spiritual" Church of the Word possess no organ by which this business could be transacted; more important still was the fact that it possessed no inward, inevitable Divinely authorized system of regulation. Thus the Church was obliged to hand these matters over to other courts, since it regarded them as purely external and mechanical, of purely human interest, trusting that these courts, led by the Divine Spirit, would settle these questions as wisely as they could from a purely human point of view. Thus it came about that it was only the ruling Prince—the political authority—who, in any case, was occupied with matters of organization and administration through his official position, and who, as the most important member of the Church, as the *membrum praecipuum*, had the duty of rendering this service to the

[232] See p. 851.

Church. To that, of course, there were added arguments based on Natural Law. The Government protects the Natural Law (which is regarded as identical with the Decalogue), and as a Christian Government it has to maintain this Natural Law in its full sense, since it also includes the First Table, which requires the true worship and the pure fear of God. Thus as *custos utriusque tabulae* it is also bound by Natural Law to support public worship, the pure doctrine, and the ecclesiastical jurisdiction.[233]

Thus it came to pass—at first as far as possible in the spirit which Luther intended—that the purely spiritual church-order was supplemented by a purely secular order of law and authority, which, by means of the compulsory secular methods of the *brachium saeculare* is able to exercise that authority which the Church, as a purely spiritual institution of love and freedom, neither can nor desires to procure by coercion. A legal compulsory church-system has been established. But the element of compulsion is not exercised by the Church, but—in accordance with its inferior status—by the State. The fact that all this takes place in the civil sphere, and under the aegis of the secular authority, saves appearances for the Church as a spiritual body which is controlled by love; actually, however, the effect is the same, for in the majority of cases the secular power only acts upon information and suggestions given by the spiritual authority through the pastors.[234] In practice the whole procedure was very cumbrous. Thus, although it meant a departure from the pure Lutheran theory, in order to simplify matters it was ultimately found necessary to create the consistories, which were ecclesiastical organs of government, ordered by the ruling Prince, which, with the co-operation of ministers and lawyers, governed the Church directly and forcibly, and which could directly decree and impose fines, imprisonment, and corporal punishment, who thus in the Church and for the Church introduced a system of government based on penalties and compulsion in order to uphold purity of doctrine and Christian behaviour.[235]

Thus that very element which from the theoretical and religious point of view was regarded merely as a human insignificant side-issue within the fabric of a Church, which was essentially based upon supernatural powers, became in practice, as we can well understand, the main issue.

The ruling Princes created doctrinal uniformity, and imposed

[233] For the theory of the *membrum praecipuum* (*Sohm, pp. 558–573*) is excellent and clear; for the *custodia utriusque tabulae, Sohm, pp. 549–558.*

[234] See p. 851.

[235] See p. 851.

the Symbolical books upon the Protestant (Lutheran) Church by force.

They created State Church councils which undertook the work of administration and of Church courts with the aid of the pastors. They placed questions of Christian faith and morals under secular control, and spiritual procedure and penalties were followed by civil legal consequences. In theory, the Church was ruled by Christ and by the Word; in practice it was governed by the ruling Princes and the pastors. At the outset, however, this whole system of church-order was something quite human, fluctuating and casual. But when its importance for the whole development of the Church became apparent, to some extent at least, even if only indirectly, the system itself came to be regarded as of Divine appointment. It even came to be linked up with the system of doctrine, for as the proclamation of the Word required an organized ministry, and this ministry was appointed by God Himself in Christ, an organized official ministry became necessary from the doctrinal standpoint. For even when a man who has the requisite spiritual gifts makes the decision to enter the ministry on the strength of an inward Divine "call", he cannot obey this call outwardly unless an official ministry instituted by God does exist, a ministry which is carried on in an ordered succession. Thus even in Protestantism there remains a *jus divinum*, even though it be only a poor apology for the real thing: that is, the necessity for an official ministry is recognized, together with the further implication that a man who is called to the ministry should receive his official appointment in an ordered way. This inevitably involves a church-order *jure divino*, so far as the existence of the ministry in general and a regular procedure for induction to office is concerned. The way in which this is to be carried out is merely a matter of convenience. It is *de jure divino* that at least there should be a church law regulating this point at all. The secular law itself, which arises out of the church law, is a purely human institution. The fact is Divine, the method human. Further, the sanctity of the church-order only extends to the appointment to the ministry of the Word, but it does not affect the other technical duties which form part of the system of church administration. Indirectly, however, this element of consecration of the fundamental element in church-order—the office of the ministry—was sufficient to impart the sense of a Divine mission and a Divine authority to those who exercised the right of appointment to the ministry, that is, to the civil authority; inevitably this meant that the rest of the church-order which was administered by the State shone in the reflected glory of this Divine authority, which gave the whole system the stability which it urgently required.

Thus after the tree of the supernatural church-order had been cut down, the stump which was left put forth branches in the shape of a system of church-order which was, at least indirectly, of Divine appointment, and which entrusted the government of the Church, or rather the official representation of the pure truth of Scripture, to the clergy and the ruling Prince.

Thus the aim which was realized in Catholicism through a directly Divine church-order, Lutheranism, in its purely spiritualized form, stripped of every kind of hierarchical or sacerdotal organ, realized through the government and the civil administration, to which, however, precisely for that reason, there accrues a certain semi-divinity.

The distinction between the temporal and the spiritual elements in this system is not a separation, but only a fresh aspect of their relationship; the State now serves the purely spiritual Church in a spirit of love and freedom, and by this service it dominates the Church which has no independent legal organ of its own. Rivalry between Church and State is excluded, theoretically, by the assumption that in both there is at work the truth of Scripture which unites both in the Faith; and practically by the weakness of the Church, which depends entirely upon the State, and also by the fact that the State incorporates religious motives and tasks into the purpose of its own life.[236] I can only mention in passing that it is a well-known fact that this fresh orientation of the relation between Church and State, in its secondary aspect, had already been foreshadowed in the Territorial Church system of the later Middle Ages. We need, therefore, to realize that the Lutheran ecclesiastical system was not simply the acceptance of a tradition which was essentially foreign to its own nature, but that from its own point of view—with its spiritual conception of the Church, and its decided rejection of a church-order based on the Divine right of the congregation to settle its own affairs (like that which Calvinism evolved later on)—it was simply impossible to pursue any other course.

Unifying Influence of the State Church Conception

This complicated State Church social order was, however, in spite of its artificial construction, a social whole. In this connec-

[236] See p. 852.

tion the important point is that this system included the whole sphere of Church and State, that the interests of Church and State had become interwoven with each other, and that both the ecclesiastical and the political authorities had combined to form a harmonious conception of a Christian society.

It is, of course, clear that within this society the true Church —that is, the fellowship of those who have been truly "born again" through the Word—includes only the vitally religious section of the population. This is the *Ecclesia stricte dicta*, to use the term of the theologians. But between it and the *Ecclesia late dicta*, that is, the total number of those in any given region who belong to the Church, upon whom, through the compulsory religion of a State Church, the Church has set her seal in baptism, and who, at least outwardly, must be constrained to listen to the pure Word, to maintain the Christian way of life, and to respect Christian doctrine,[237] there only exists a difference, but no division. This agreement between the Church and the Christian Society is expressed still more clearly in the Lutheran doctrine of classes, which continues the mediaeval organization of the population into *sacerdotes*, *domini saeculares*, and *vulgares*, as the division into a *Status ecclesiasticus politicus* and *oeconomicus*, and defines these three classes explicitly as ranks of the Church, or as hierarchies.[238]

This classification, which was far too rough and ready, even for the simple conditions in Germany at that time, was, however, very important from the practical point of view. For, as in the mediaeval civilization, it means the distinction between a Church in the real sense of the word and one which is not a real Church:[238a] by the real Church is meant only the institution of the proclamation of the "pure Word", visibly expressed in the clergy and the authorities in Church and State; by the Church in the second aspect is meant the Christian Society—in the whole range of the sphere of Church and State, in the totality of their activity and social groups.

This is simply the mediaeval idea of the *Corpus Christianum*, within which, in the modern sense of the word, there is, as yet, no separation between Church and State, between sacred and secular. The civil authority and the ecclesiastical authority are two different aspects of the one undivided Christian Society, for which reason the Government and the State have directly Christian aims, and the Church includes the whole of Society.

All that has been discarded is the Roman system of social

[237] See p. 852. [238] See p. 853. [238a] See above, p. 283.

grades within the range of a small independent State, and the idea of a Universal Church which has the right to intervene forcibly in all matters of human concern. This order of things has been replaced by one in which, within any particular State, there is a voluntary agreement between the Christian government and the Church which consecrates all the work of the world, in which the civil authority serves the Church through its administration, while the Church hallows all "labour in a calling", in the State, in the administration of justice, in Society, and in domestic life, as the service of God and one's neighbour. In theory the purpose of the whole remains religious, only the relationship between the two authorities, whose business it is particularly to realize this purpose, has become a different one, through their mutual co-operation.[239]

Now, however, this conception of the Church and the harmony between the Church, the State, and the social order, which is expressed in the *Corpus Christianum*, combine to form the final assumption upon which the social philosophy of Lutheranism is based: the whole social fabric is enclosed within the framework of the Church, and is related to the religious purpose of Society. The only question is: how and in what sense is this relationship effected? The answer to this question will become plain as we try to realize clearly the leading characteristics of the Lutheran ethic.[239a]

The Lutheran Ethic

The Lutheran ethic is of dual origin. Just as Church and State exist side by side within Society, so here also we have the ethic of love and grace on the one hand and the ethic of law and reason on the other. The fundamental idea of this dualism is due to Luther, and it here only modifies the mediaeval dualism in ethics. Melancthon carried this dualistic tendency a step farther in the dualism of a philosophical and theological morality, and orthodoxy has only broadened both these currents of thought, which have branched off still farther in various directions. In so doing, however, it was only the philosophical side which was scientifically developed; the theological side of the question remained bound up with dogma. It is only in practical life that we see both tendencies combined and mutually influencing one another. This combination is regarded as something quite natural and obvious, which is carried out in practice without further reflection. Ultimately, indeed, this is true of all the previous Christian ethic.

[239] See p. 854.

[239a] See p. 854.

Even the first scientific ethical development on a larger scale which was embodied in Thomism was in reality only systematic in so far as it followed in the steps of Aristotle and made the Christian virtues square with those laid down by Aristotle. Even Thomism did not dream of presenting ethical problems in their widest range and in their ultimate conceptual origins. Thus, since the Christian ethic in general is rather a practically useful Ethos with individual points which have been developed into theories, so also the ethic of Protestantism, and, above all, the ethic of Luther, is not a theory which is in any way comparable with its dogmatic system. Ethical theory only comes into being when—as at one period in late antiquity, and also at the time of the Enlightenment—the natural ethical foundations of life have been destroyed.[239b]

The Christianity of the Middle Ages and of the confessional period had a scientific theory of its own doctrines, and from the estimate of life based upon this metaphysic it drew the main impulse of its ethic. So long as that was dominant, the ethical results followed as a matter of course. All that needed to be worked out in further detail were points like the following: the relation between the moral element or "good works", and grace in general, the relation between Christian morality and secular institutions and the morality which is not based upon the ethical results of grace, or with the traditions of the ancient "philosophical" morality, which regulated the relations between law and freedom, between the Christian morality of life and the impossibility of overcoming sin. Everything else was settled, naturally, by life itself.

Thus the real Lutheran ethic of the sixteenth and seventeenth centuries has to be sought out and reconstructed by the modern scholar, sought, that is, in the sphere of ordinary human life and in fragmentary theoretical statements, and this ethic will be discovered not merely in theological dogmatic statements, but in the theories of jurists and political economists as well.[240]

So far as Lutheranism is concerned this is a comparatively easy matter. The Lutheran ethic consists primarily in the establishment of a religious relation with God, in that love to God which humbly, joyfully, and thankfully surrenders the self to Him

[239b] This is why it is so mistaken to try to save the honour of early Protestantism by attempting to discover in it "theological moral philosophers". The people of that day neither desired nor needed any ethic alongside of dogma; this only became necessary after the upheaval of the Enlightenment.

[240] See p. 855.

in prayer and self-discipline, and the outpouring of this love of God, which cannot give anything to God, upon one's neighbour. It is an inward impulse which uses to its fullest extent the overflowing happiness produced by justification, making it a means of leading one's neighbour to God and of uniting him with oneself in God.

Since however, as a rule, the Lutheran considered that fulfilling your "duty to your neighbour" meant the wise use of all the obvious opportunities, stimuli, and forms of the natural life, with the avoidance of all unbalanced mysticism and all special cliques, this means, then, in the second place, that "loving one's neighbour as oneself" implies that all the duties and tasks which life brings naturally in its train, especially those connected with the family, the State, the labour and vocational organization, are to be filled with this spirit of love, which makes these forms into methods and means of expression of the Christian love of mankind. The mysticism which centres in love to God and man pours itself into the existing forms of human life: into the life of class and guild, into family and domestic life, into the life of the State and the administration of justice. Sublime religious feeling is clothed in the garb of the most ordinary and everyday forms of service within the home and the ordinary duties of citizenship. Down to the present day the ethical teachers of Lutheranism only differ from each other in this—that some would give more scope for the independent development of the specifically religious and mystical ethic, while others would exhaust its significance entirely in loving service to the brethren in an ordered society as "the great workshop of the love of one's neighbour". In the former there is still a trace of the original tension which Luther set between the sacred and the secular, between love and law, while with thinkers of the latter kind there predominates Luther's demand for obedience towards all natural ordinances which the God who is concealed in history had Himself created, and in which therefore He desires to see the believing soul exercising love and happiness in simple obedience.

The ideal of such a way of life is reflected in the conception of the Christian Moral Law, which here appears not so much as the law which effects conversion, but as the interpretation and the description of the impulse towards activity which is set alongside of the bliss of justification by faith, for which therefore the legal form has only an unreal significance. The Lutheran theory of Christian freedom from the Law is still maintained, but in practice this theory changes into a purely Protestant legalism based on the Catechism. This Law is contained in the Decalogue, which in the usual way is regarded as exactly the same as the Natural Moral Law. The Decalogue is thus held to include all the stimuli, opportunities, assumptions, and social forms of Natural Law under the Second Table, and at the same time, in its First Table, it includes the inspiration of the whole with the Christian spirit of faith and love. This distinction between the two Tables of the Law means that the dualistic ethic was still maintained. But since believers are urged constantly not to allow brotherly love to peter out in vague and indefinite sentiment, or in special cliques and sentimental emotionalism, the purely interior, spiritual ethic which utterly renounces all use of law and force, finds, in actual practice, very little scope; as swiftly as possible it is transferred into the ordered sphere where love is expressed in discharging the duties of one's vocation, in civil life, in a healthy division of labour, and in loyal obedience. This is the channel into which, so far as possible, the currents of purely personal and human relations are guided, in the interests of law and order. Further, domestic and civil authority is to some extent hallowed by the fact that it has been appointed by God, and this sense of consecration almost effaces the stain which clings to it as part of the sphere of law and conflict. Thus, alongside of the ethical labour involved in the effort to attain interior union with God, which culminates in communion with Christ in the Sacrament, for which the soul has been prepared by repentance and self-examination, there is only the ethic of the service of the State and of the "calling" which is consecrated by Divine appointment. The fact that this ethic lays a great deal of emphasis upon order, stability, and peace entirely obliterates in theory, and also modifies in practice, the fact of its connection with the severity of the law and the unrest caused by the struggle for existence.[241]

We do not need to deal any farther with the question of this "morality of the disposition" (*Gesinnungsmoral*), which was to breathe its spirit into the secular forms of life. This has been done by the early theologians in their treatises on dogmatics or on practical asceticism. They do not call this Christian ethic an "ethic" at all but *Pietas*, and treat it in this sense in *Scholae pietatis*, or similar practically edifying treatises, which indeed also include the whole thorny apparatus of the dogmatic doctrine of justification by faith. It is only the modern Lutherans who have

[241] Cf. the tractate *De lege in Gerhards Loci comunes (ed. Cotta), V and VI*. Here also there is a detailed explanation of the Decalogue which contains a great deal of ethical material.

transformed this subject into an independent "theological" ethic, into which they have also incorporated the absolutely necessary component parts of the "natural" ethic. Men felt the need, however, for a detailed presentation of the whole subject, giving a minute and exact analysis of all the natural virtues, social duties, opportunities, and obligations which were to be hallowed, Christianized, and filled with the new outlook on life. This alone was the real "ethic", as early Lutheranism saw it. This "ethic", however, was simply the Aristotelian scholastic ethic, revived by the Stoics and by Cicero, and renewed by the Humanists, which in its scholastic form had been re-edited by Melancthon (whose work was destined to influence thought for two hundred years to come), while at the same time it also made use of the Jesuit Neo-Scholasticism which had dealt with the same material in a more detailed way. The stock of ideas which constituted the intellectual capital of the "ethic" of both confessions was exactly the same; that is, if we only use the term "ethic" in its contemporary meaning of the philosophical ethic; this "ethic", in fact, was simply a purified mediaeval Aristotelianism, or the familiar range of ideas connected with Aristotle's interpretation of Natural Law. Since the Natural Law is only Divinely proclaimed and summarized in the Decalogue, this "philosophical ethic" also could be developed upon the basis of the Decalogue without any loss of its purely philosophical and natural character.[241a] This ethic dealt with the conception of the Natural Moral Law, Natural Right, the Aristotelian conception of virtue, the four cardinal virtues—all on thoroughly traditional lines. Its aim was to show how knowledge of this kind was useful in the following ways: (1) it was a preparation for repentance; (2) as *justitia civilis*, i.e. as a loyal external discipline emptied of all spiritual content, it helped to preserve order; (3) it provided the basis of reason for the idea of the existence of God and of the moral government of the world; and (4) finally, when this knowledge was inspired with a spiritual temper, it merged into the unity of the Christian idea of love.

The other aspects of social life which really belong to the sphere of Natural Law—the Family, the State, division of labour, and economics—were only superficially touched by this ethic, and they were really worked out in the special forms of discipline which were constructed upon the basis of the Law of Nature

[241a] Modern writers and critics who do not know the origin or the significance of this group of ideas usually complain about the "still" confused mingling of philosophical and theological ethics.

and of Positive Law—that is, in jurisprudence, the doctrine of the State, and political economy, and in the sections of dogmatics which had borrowed from them. Roman law, in particular, seemed to be a development both of the Decalogue and of the Law of Nature; every time these materials were used, however, their connection with the positive law, in use at the time, also had to be considered.

The resemblance to the Catholic ethic is obvious. In both instances the Ethos of real life is only constructed with the additional aid of the range of ideas centring in Natural Law and of the ethical material of ancient philosophy. An ecclesiastical ethic which also covers the whole field of secular civilization still makes use of this complementary method, upon which the Early Church had already drawn for the same purpose, and which the Mediaeval Church had developed very fully along scholastic lines. In this question of dealing with a secular civilization which the Church had to accept and assimilate, Protestantism continued the fundamental tendencies of the Catholic tradition; just as she had done in the conception of the Church itself. At the same time the difference between Lutheranism and Catholicism in this respect is clear: Protestantism has no hierarchy which can legally and forcibly regulate the harmonious development and relation between the different stages; in the ethical sphere interpenetration has taken the place of an orderly succession of ascending stages. According to the new conceptions of Protestantism the supernatural is now immanent in the natural sphere; this immanence, however, must not be understood in the sense of modern doctrines of Divine Immanence—it does not mean the Immanence of God in the world—but it is the Immanence of the Love of God which overcomes the world, in obedience to secular institutions—indifferent and sinfully corrupt in themselves, but positively appointed by the Will of God—and the Immanence of love in the religious sense, present in all activity which conduces to material welfare and order, an activity which is the natural method appointed by God for the manifestation of love to humanity. The meaning and purpose of it all is not material progress, but the exercise of the obedience of faith (which renounces all caprice and self-will), and of humble and grateful love.

Lutheranism and the Law of Nature

We cannot, however, fully appreciate either the similarity or the difference between Catholicism and Lutheranism in this respect until we have made a special study of one point in which Lutheranism differs from the Catholic and from the Calvinistic ethic alike; (on this point, indeed, the Calvinistic ethic is finally and essentially in agreement with the Catholic ethic). This question is the peculiar Lutheran conception of the Law of Nature, which exists within the rational idea of Natural Law common to both confessions.

In this question Luther struck out on a peculiar line of his own.[242] At first, it is true, he shared the traditional point of view with which we are already familiar, which indeed did not form part of the province of theology, but of reason and practical philosophy; in rejecting Roman theology and the Canon Law Luther did not need to reject the rest of the tradition as well. All he did was to separate the mediation elements from the rest, making a clear distinction between them and the Scriptural ethic of love; he restricted the former elements to the "official" sphere, the ordinary "calling", to law and to the State, requiring that all should adapt themselves to the forms of life thus conditioned which are so harshly opposed to the ethic of love. In so doing, however, Luther had not merely re-ordered the relation of the Natural Law to the Church and the Gospel, but he had reinterpreted the Natural Law itself. From the very outset he explains the Law of Nature in an entirely conservative sense, which emphasizes solely the utilitarian expediency of the concrete order, in which the shaping of Society itself seems to have been produced by Providence in the natural development of history, and all order and welfare depend upon unconditional obedience towards the authorities which have come into being in the course of the historical process. This interpretation glorifies power for its own sake, which in fallen humanity has become the essence of law; it therefore glorifies whatever authority may happen to be dominant at any given time. Even when this power is most scandalously abused its authority still holds good, and every act of resistance to this authority destroys the very conception of the social order based on Natural Law, and thus destroys the foundation of Society in general.[243]

In Luther's innate conservatism, in his pietistic indifference towards external things from the Christian point of view, in his belief in an omnipresent Providence which moves and works behind human thought, in the comparison between social subordination and the religious humility of absolute dependence upon the Grace of God—above all, in his deep sense of the opposi-

[242] See p. 856. [243] See p. 856.

tion between the order of love and the order of law and the universal struggle for existence: in all these ways Luther instinctively regards Natural Law as the establishment of an unrestricted positive authority, effected by God through reason; no amount of experience of a refractory reality can shake him out of the belief that this authority is based upon reason and the Divine Will. This is why he opposes every attempt to reconstruct Society and mould it on rational lines, which is based on the interests and the reason of the isolated individual; this is why he refuses to consider or permit any individual co-operation at all in the endeavour to build up a satisfying "organic" system which will include them all. In his theory, therefore, the idea of a social contract naturally disappears; in it there is no room for the transference of power based on the explicit or implicit consent of those who are governed, nor for any "right of resistance" or revolution which extends farther than frank criticism, nor for any equalitarian conception of social human relationships, nor for any communistic ideal.[244] This was already excluded from the Primitive State; that glorification of power was already present in the nature of pure unclouded Reason; even in Paradise this meant authority and reverence within the family, and submission to circumstances and duties given by God. Sin has merely vastly increased the significance of that power, since the preservation of order is only possible if positive authority is maintained, which, however, has further been linked up with evil and selfishness. But even when this (evil and selfishness) has been admitted, the fact remains that authority must not be resisted. Non-resistance is, therefore, not primarily a demand of the Gospel, but a requirement of Natural Law, since according to this theory no one is fit to judge his own affairs, and every power which permits resistance destroys its own being, as Luther reiterated unceasingly when the peasants made their demands for reform. When, at a later date, a "right of resistance" for the estates of the Empire was asserted, Luther rightly expressed the opinion that this demand did not accord with their conception of authority over the peasants.[244a]

At this point the course of mediaeval thought had displayed a good deal of uncertainty. The problem was this: if the Stoic-Rationalist ideas which had become an integral part both of Imperial and of Canon Law were logically developed, they led to the idea of a social contract, to the doctrine of the right of

[244] *Ehrhardt, pp. 309 and 310.* Unfortunately *E.'s* work is very far from exhaustive.
[244a] Cf. *von Schubert: Beitr. zur ev. Bekenntnis- und Bündnisbildung, 1529–39* (*Z. f. Kirch.-Gesch., XXX, p. 295*).

revolution and of tyrannicide, to the rational development of the State in accordance with the rights of the individual. If, on the other hand, Aristotle was taken as the guide, this led to the doctrine that Society arose organically and inevitably out of Reason; this meant that all that was natural and necessary was ascribed to Providence, in which the only right course was submission to the natural process which was directed by God, in which sinful extremes alone were to be avoided.

If, however, it was felt that this Divine element in authority needed further support, emphasis was then laid on the Divine appointment of authority and on the mythological glorification of power—on the founding of States by means of the Babylonian confusion of tongues, on the Divine nature of the legislation in the Old Testament. When, however, on further reflection, men realized that all the institutions of fallen humanity were only relatively Divine, there arose the ideal of the Primitive State, with its equality, brotherly love, and community of possessions. The mediaeval doctrine of Natural Law moved uncertainly among these ideas, making various efforts to weld them into a coherent system.[245]

Within this confusion Luther had now created a stable order, even though it was very one-sided, and not always logically maintained. He achieved this by doing away with the Stoic and Rationalist elements entirely, regarding the natural development of actual authority as an institution of Providence to be revered unconditionally, teaching that this natural development was authenticated by Divine appointment and confirmation in the Old Testament; thus Luther came to teach a conservative authoritarian conception of the Law of Nature, which deduced from the conception of authority and its utility for human welfare the demand for an unconditional respect for authority as such. The fact that this authority has to use methods of severity and compulsion, law and dominion, is due to fallen humanity, and serves to keep sin in check. This point of view was combined with an attitude of contempt for the masses, amongst whom he thought it rare to find, not merely true Christians, but even wise and reasonable men. In fallen humanity the masses need to be guided and controlled; to Luther, however, it seems probable that he felt

[245] These different elements are well put together in *K. Köhler: Staatslehre der Vorreformatoren* (*Jahrbb. f. deutsche Theol., XIX*): "The inconsistency of the latter (organic Aristotelian) view with the theory of a social contract which finally depends upon the arbitrary will of humanity does not seem to have entered So-and-so's head" (*p. 359*).

this to be essentially the need of humanity as such. For this development of authority is due precisely to reason. Luther, therefore, believes that peace and order, a slow process of organic development from the existing situation, is a better method of inducing prosperity and progress than a violent break with the old order and a fresh beginning. Since within the Christian sphere the Spirit has to work gradually from within outwards, reason ought to work thus within the natural sphere. All along Luther is opposed to revolutionary schemes which are based on an individualistic point of view, and he is in favour of an authority which controls, conditions, and gradually moulds them, even in case of necessity achieving its end by force. In this glorification of authority there were certain resemblances to the doctrine of Machiavelli, which the early Lutherans had already noted.[246] The only difference was this: Luther lays the duty of the preservation of the law of reason upon the ruling powers, and binds this in a Christian society to free obedience to the Gospel. Even at the present time the followers of Darwin, despotic politicians, and masterful men get on better with Lutheran conservatives than with the representatives of Liberal ethical individualism. The main features of the conservative doctrine of the State and of Society have been foreshadowed in Luther's theory, and the "Christian world outlook" of our Conservatives in its most important political and social sections is based upon Luther's positivist and realistic conception of Natural Law.[247]

Under the influence of the negotiations which led to the Schmalkaldic League it is true that Luther broke through this doctrine and asserted the "right of resistance", not merely upon the ground of the Positive Law of the Empire, but also upon the ground of Natural Law. This, however, was clearly due to foreign influence, above all to the influence of Hesse and Strassburg, and a large number of his followers rejected his conclusions, using his very words to support their case. In the struggle between the citizens of Magdeburg and Charles V the theories about the "right of resistance" revived, but they speedily disappeared. In reality, they did not harmonize either with Luther's opinions or with his logic. He manifested his own view of Natural Law in the declaration that the Greeks and the Romans did not know the true Natural Law, but that the Persians, the Tatars, and people of that kind[247a] observed the Natural Law far better.

[246] See p. 857.

[247] See p. 858.

[247a] Cf. *Cardauns, pp. 8–19.* The passage about the Persians in *Ob Kriegsleute, etc., B.A., IV, 1, pp. 398–402.* Unfortunately, *Cardauns'* treatment is not

Although at this point Luther's views had diverged far from Catholic Natural Law, in other important features, such as the mingling of morality and law, in the comparison of Natural Law with Christian morality, and with the emphasis to which that gives rise upon reasonableness and equity, which modifies formal law in favour of ethical judgment, he remained true to it. This modification, of course, does not apply to the law of the State, nor to the laws of punishment; this, however, will have become clear in the preceding pages. Within the law of the State Luther's rigid idea of Original Sin and his demand for severe discipline, his contempt for the masses, and his conception of the civil authority as the representative of Divine punishment and reward, inclined him to extreme severity, and he was urgent in recommending the exercise of penalties like breaking on the wheel, decapitation, and torture.[248]

Within the sphere of civil law, however, Luther desired to see the Natural Law administered with a leniency which takes all the various factors of motive, necessity, and circumstance into account. In his view the guiding principle of the Natural Law is that we should do to everyone as we would like them to do to us. In this respect love is also the meaning of Natural Law, and is thus conformed to Christian morality. This leads him to demand that Positive Law should adjust itself to Natural Law and to the Christian ideal, with which, in the last resort, it is identical.[249] While in all questions of authority and control, of dominion and of subordination, his conception of Natural Law is a naturalistic recognition of the dominant authority and of prevailing distinctions, with an aristocratic emphasis upon the gulf which separates

exhaustive. How fluctuating opinions were is shown by *von Schubert: Beitr. Z. f. K.-G., XXX, pp. 271–316.* The Natural Law of rational defence, the Natural Law of pure authority as it was worked out against the peasants, the Positive Law of the Empire, of an only conditional supremacy of the Emperor, and the Divine law of mere suffering and endurance, are here all mingled; see *Melancthon's* verdict, *p. 313.*

[248] Cf. the basing of the first great and independent working out of the law of punishment upon these Lutheran ideas by *Ben. Carpzov* in *Stintzing: Geschichte der deutschen Rechtswissenschaft, II, 1884, pp. 70–80.* The great part which trial for witchcraft plays in this law of punishment goes back likewise to Luther's faith in demons, for he could only explain to himself the evil of the world and its resistance to the Gospel from the working of the Devil. Luther, however, always fought against the fantastic eccentricities of the faith in witchcraft; *v. Kawerau* in *W.W., Berliner Ausgabe, IV, 1, pp. 44ff.*

[249] On this point *v. Köhler* in the section *Das Verhältnis zum kanonischen Recht, pp. 111–132.* Here the identity with the mediaeval point of view is rightly emphasized. For *epikie* or *aequität, pp. 46 and 98.*

the rulers and the ruled, on the other hand, in all questions of personal behaviour and of merely civil conflict, his conception of Natural Law was one of reasonable equity, which was opposed to a strictly legal formalism; it was, in fact, an attempt to reduce law, as far as possible, to the principles of human consideration for the suffering and the oppressed, and the deliberate ending of conflict. In this respect also the conservative theory of Society follows Luther even at the present day; in all human relationships which do not affect the problem of authority and domination it urges a policy of goodwill and justice, freed from the rigid formalism of law. This theory is averse to surrounding the individual with abstract legal guarantees, because this is the spirit of the individualistic-rational principle in general, but it likes to replace law by Christian consideration on patriarchal lines and personal fair dealing. In the sphere of authority Natural Law is compared with the Christian idea of authority, in the sphere of private property with the Christian idea of love. The harshness of the doctrine of authority is compensated by a Christian softening of the standpoint of law in private relations. This is the early Lutheran doctrine, and to-day it is still the conservative conception of law,[250] and in reality the Christian nature of morality is expressed more clearly in this than in the public law of authority; here also, however, it is a Christian piety strongly tinged with patriarchalism, which distinguishes it very clearly from the virile individualism and the corresponding legal consciousness of Calvinism.

Since, however, Luther's idea of Natural Law is that of the Divine activity expressed in reason, he loves to emphasize God as the Founder of these institutions, and wherever it is possible he tries to find proofs of their direct Divine appointment.

When, however, he takes that line his assertions cease to have any element of Natural Law at all, and the mythical element predominates. Thus he asserts that the Family is an institution of Natural Law, but he also asserts that it was expressly instituted by God. Indirectly the State was instituted at the same time as the Family; but its Divine origin was also often confirmed in the Old Testament. The economic organization and labour were held to be due to the Divine Command at the expulsion of Adam and Eve from the Garden of Eden. In detail, too, he often supports his statement by Old Testament examples; indeed, it often seems as though he had entirely forgotten his former insistence on the freedom of the Christian from the Jewish law, for he uses

[250] See p. 858.

the Old Testament as though it were a legal code. When he is confronted with problems connected with marriage and the question of serfdom he refers to the Mosaic Law, and his fatal appeal to the bigamy of the Old Testament in the case of the Landgrave of Hesse is well known.

In all this, however, Luther still only considered the Mosaic Law to be identical with reason; he regarded it as the Divine confirmation or proclamation of reasonable rules and regulations, but not as the revealed Law of God. This leads, of course, to the production of a curious mingling of arguments drawn from the Bible and from the Law of Nature; this mixture of arguments, however, only proves (and this is of fundamental importance for our inquiry) that the assumption of an inward unity and conformity of Natural Law with the Christian spirit is the underlying idea; upon this alone the relative uniformity of early Lutheran culture is based, and to-day it still forms the basis of the Christian piety of the conservative section of the population, which includes some very un-Christian elements.[251]

While Luther thus often concealed his idea of Natural Law behind positive Scriptural statements, and further, when he was opposed by the jurists who naturally had to preserve the continuity of technical law, with much use of strong language again withdrew to the position which emphasized the contrast between law and Christian freedom, these ideas were trimmed and shaped and moulded into smoothness by Melancthon.[252] He was the Protestant doctor of Natural Law; further, his scheme was adopted by jurisprudence as a whole. Melancthon laid greater emphasis upon the philosophical character of Natural Law, and he strove so hard for reconciliation that the Lutheran tension between the Law and Christianity, between Reason and Revelation, was ultimately merged in the idea of a friendly harmony which has been Divinely ordained. From that time forward faith in this harmony, and the ideal of such an accord between natural assumptions and spiritual inspiration, became a peculiar feature of Lutheranism. In his ethical works and juridical speeches Melancthon expounded the conceptions of Natural Law with which we are familiar, in the classic formulas of Cicero, with some additional material drawn from Aristotle, upon whose *Politics* he also wrote a commentary. He explains the Natural Law according to Cicero in the light of the Decalogue, which he considers identical with it. This identification of the two enables him to introduce the religious elements which the pagans had

[251] See p. 859. [252] See p. 859.

lost. The result of this is a conception of the State and of a legal right to inflict penalties, which is based upon the idea of reason as the support of discipline and of education against sin, as well as of the protection of order and the common weal. This theory also led to a conception of civil law which recognized in Roman Law the positive legal development of the Natural Law, which is identical with the Natural Law of the Decalogue and makes the Roman Law the objective legal standard for the jurists of the future in exactly the same way as the Bible is the objective standard for the theologians.

Melancthon claims that the Decalogue is valid, not as the Jewish Law, but as the product of Natural Law, and, therefore, that the reasonable Roman Law is also the law for Christians, and not, as the Sectarians say, the Mosaic Law. To this written law he also relates the Aristotelian doctrine of the dominion of law in the State. Here also the Gospel is united with reason. At the same time the Natural Law leads to the organization of Society in classes and callings as well as to private property, which was indeed at first held to belong to the relative Natural Law of the fallen State; now, however, it must be urged all the more decidedly that it is a Divine institution.

All this shows that Melancthon was inclined to be more rationalistic than Luther. This accounts for the reappearance of the old rationalistic ideas of the consent of those who are governed to the ruling authority. At the same time, however, Melancthon argues that the State owes its authority to a *Mandatum Dei*, which was already in existence in Paradise when the authority of the family was instituted; at this point, therefore, he enters into entire agreement with the Lutheran authoritative Law of Nature with its emphasis on compulsion and order. Melancthon lays still greater stress upon this idea by making the formal stringency of the existing legal administration far more binding, while he makes far less use of the idea of equity than Luther.

On the other hand, Melancthon asserts the "right of resistance" far more broadly than Luther; this he does, however, only by appealing to the positive Roman Law, in which the Emperor declares that he desires to exercise his power with the consent of his subjects, and by an appeal to the German Law of the Empire, in which the liberty of a privileged class is justified in resisting an Emperor who breaks his contract with his subjects. Finally, against the worst injustices he recognizes the right to resist also as *de jure naturae*, and Luther accepted this reluctantly enough, commending the problem to the jurists and to reason. This, however, had very little effect upon the Lutheran interpretation of Natural Law. On the whole, Luther's influence was the stronger of the two, and both in dogma and also in Natural Law Melancthon's peculiarities disappeared. Although the Humanist admirer of Aristotle preferred the aristocratic city-republics to the absolutism which tended towards "Tyrannis", with the decline of the cities these ideas also naturally disappeared from the political theory of Lutheranism. In reality Luther's conception of authority was more suited to absolutism, and his dislike of the "Sakramentierer"* was equally a dislike of the republics of Upper Germany.[252a]

The whole system of later jurisprudence developed within the framework constructed by Melancthon, the only difference being that in matters affecting the legal administration of the State the conservative authoritative aspect was emphasized still more strongly, although the formulae of a tacit consent of the citizens to the ruling power were still reluctantly retained.[253] It was only in the seventeenth century that an actual constitutional law and a detailed political theory were really formulated; until then the material was divided amongst dogmatics, philosophical ethics, interpretation of the politics of Aristotle, and the exposition of suitable passages in the Roman law, and it reproduced only the familiar ideas, with increasing emphasis on the Divine appointment of the ruling authority, which corresponded to the increasing absolutism; this also took place in the theories of the State evolved by Catholic and Anglican absolutism. The more exclusive constitutional law of the seventeenth century then turned towards the empirical law material. Thus, in principle, the conception of Luther and Melancthon remained, of the reference of the State equally to reason and to Divine appointment; and within the territorial State itself Bodin's new theory of sovereignty was combined with the earlier doctrine of a humble and trustful surrender to the authority appointed by God. This meant that the elements of Natural Law in the theory were thrust more into the background, and were finally reduced to the bare statement of the Divine guidance of reason in the production of political authority. The more the school of Grotius developed a purely rational theory of Natural Law, severed from theology, the more stoutly the Lutherans maintained this theory of Divine appointment; they assert that, although this "Divine appointment" takes

* I.e. those who denied the Real Presence of Christ in the Sacrament of the Lord's Supper.—TRANSLATOR.

[252a] See p. 860.

[253] See p. 860.

place indirectly, it *is* Divine all the same. The result is that they summarize their theory in this statement: the powers that be, just as they are, come from God.

At a later date, Stahl's theory of an irrational Natural Law instead of the rational Natural Law provided the modern Conservative theory with a scientific foundation. The dominant system of Aristotelian-Scholastic metaphysics provided no scientific support for this theory, and indeed within the Lutheran orthodoxy of the day such support was not required. Pufendorf, who in his general outlook was a good Lutheran, and whose view of the positive value of the State and of civilization was merely more hopeful than that of Luther, sought to find a way of making a bridge over the gulf between the individualistic-rationalistic Natural Law of Grotius and the Lutheran realism and positivism of the idea of law and authority. This proved an almost impossible undertaking, however, partly because the Grotius' school of thought outstripped his ideas altogether, and partly because the orthodox pessimism about sin and the later Lutheran doctrine of the Divine institution of the ruling powers were repelled by his theories. Thus Pufendorf made no permanent contribution to the Natural Law of the Church, and in these circles people were satisfied with a highly aphoristic theory and a theological-absolutist practice. When Christian Thomasius went over to the side of Pufendorf, the Danish Court chaplain wrote a pamphlet against him entitled *The Interest of Princes in the True Religion*. In it he exalted the Lutheran Church as the most secure support of the commonwealth, and urged the Royal House to consider that this dogma that all royal power comes directly from God is greatly to their advantage. At the same time he accused Calvinism and Catholicism of encouraging rebellion and "tumult" because they oppose this dogma. This, of course, is no longer genuine Lutheranism at all; it is simply an attempt to bolster up Absolutism with the aid of Lutheran doctrine. It must, however, be admitted that, to a great extent, this doctrine did lay itself open to such a construction.[254]

The "natural" doctrine of Society and of economics developed on similar lines. At first there was no need of any scientific theory at all, since existing conditions were quite obviously the expression of Natural Law and of the guidance of Providence. All that was required was a general theological and ethical point of view, founded on principle, and with that a practical technique of government, which, in connection with the existing situation

[254] See p. 860.

and the positive-legal conditions, made it possible to carry over the still strongly patrimonial administration of the State into a supremacy of the State, bureaucratically rationalized and financially secure.

In so doing this patriarchal economic doctrine made use of the conservative Natural Law and theological ethical theories, exactly as the doctrine of the State had done. Thus the theory was developed in the closest connection with the likewise very aphoristic philosophy of the State and of the interpretation of Aristotle, which, in the old scholastic style, treated the State, Society, and economics solely from the point of view of ethics and theology; the practical instructions also were still full of Biblical and ancient Humanistic quotations, in which they expressed in theory the theological-juridical fundamental outlook. With the presupposition of sinful and corrupt Nature and of the providential reaction of Nature against this corruption, this is a religiously defined, relative physiocracy, a "natural" economic doctrine which is based upon the conditions of fallen humanity; in essentials it is simply the continuation of the scholastic theory, which only revives Aristotle, and which, by means of a certain observation of reality by modern Humanists, has been made more practical. Above all, however, this Lutheran doctrine of Society and of economics was the source from which the Lutheran Natural Law received its bent towards a conservative and authoritarian tendency, in close connection with its whole conception of the nature of authority and of supremacy.[255]

Thus in classical Lutheranism there is a voluntary agreement between the authorities in Church and State, in order that, together, they may realize the religious end of Christian Society. It represents the fusion of the natural, philosophical, and secular ethic with the Biblical, supernatural, and spiritual ethic, blending into a whole way of life, in which the natural forms of life are to be permeated with the religious spirit of love. This constitutes a uniform system of Christian civilization, like that of the Catholicism of the Middle Ages. Similarly, this social system possesses the ideal of a uniform sociological fundamental theory; only, since the basis and meaning of the uniform system of life are now different, the sociological fundamental theory of Lutheranism is also different. This difference is obvious: the fundamental theory of Lutheranism has not been constructed upon the conception of the organism.

[255] See p. 861.

Social Theory of Lutheranism

The social theory of the Middle Ages had expressed its Christian individualism thus: within every section of Society the individual was legally entitled to have his interests considered, in accordance with the standards of the class to which he belonged, while the regulation of the organism in accordance with these requirements was left to the supreme power of the Church. In Lutheranism, however, Christian individualism becomes purely subjective, with no legal claim on Society or on the Church, without any power of external realization, and at bottom both essentially and theoretically it has no sense of the need for fellowship, since it is only out of love that it submits to the life of the community at all.

Thus Lutheran Christian individualism has retired behind the line of battle of all external events and outward activity, into a purely personal spirituality, into the citadel of a freedom which no events of the external order can touch, a position so impregnable that neither joy nor sorrow, the world or Society can capture it. This spirituality is based on nothing save the "Word", which is guaranteed by the Church; it therefore regards the Church simply as the Herald of the Word, endowed with a purely spiritual miraculous converting power; it has no conception of the Church as an ethical organization of Christendom as a whole. Here, within the sanctuary of this spirituality, Lutheran individualism knows no bounds; its only rule is that of faith and sacrament. On this exalted plane the Christian is king and lord over all things; he has an invincible faith in Providence and an unshakable trust in God; and the Christian spirit which he has received moulds his character in an atmosphere of entire spiritual freedom. However, as soon as the Christian believer turns from this spirituality to take his part in real life, he can only express his inner liberty through submission to the existing order, as a method of manifesting Christian love to the brethren, and to Society as a whole, or as something evil which has to be passively endured and accepted; the only exception which is here recognized is when the Christian is commanded to deny his faith—it then becomes his duty to resist. Unlimited in itself, this Christian individualism possesses no organ by which it can either express its own thoughts or secure its own existence, and its influence on the outside world is nil. To the extent, however, in which the Christian spirit does attempt to permeate the natural institutions of ordinary life, it does not appear outwardly as a fellowship of individuals, formed on a religious basis, but as a spirit which seeks to absorb the whole complex of secular institutions and social life into love; this spirit of love leads the Christian to submit unconditionally to the social order which had been established by God and by reason for the good of the whole; and it regards the Family, the State, Society in general, and all labour merely as methods of realizing and exercising the Christian spirit of love and obedience. Thus, when we recall the two elements of the fundamental theory of Catholicism, the organic and the patriarchal elements, we see that here the organic aspect has entirely disappeared.

So far as real life is concerned, therefore, the patriarchal principle alone remains; this, however, is now developed to its fullest extent, undeterred by the necessity for making any compromise with the organic principle, while at the same time, in the demand for the religious spirit of love and obedience, it gains a fuller expression in theory. Thomist Patriarchalism, however, was always more of a passive acceptance of the various differences in rank and power, in authority over others and in wealth—a situation which it regarded as both a penalty and a remedy for sin; the organic principle within Thomism, on the other hand, laid an emphasis upon individualism which maintained the ideal of the freedom, equality, and fellowship of the Primitive State; and, at least to some extent, the system of the Religious Orders actualized this genuinely Christian order.

Lutheran Patriarchalism, however, more and more came to regard the *jus naturale secundarium* as a purely Divine institution, which the forgiven soul, happy and humble in its surrender to God, accepts unquestioningly, and as the wise order of reason, in obedience to which the natural welfare of man also is best secured; to Christian love obedience to this Divine and reasonable order becomes a joyful duty. The same spirit is revealed in the fact that the comparison of existing conditions with a very different ideal Primitive State is emphasized less and less by Lutheran thinkers, while increasing stress is laid on the "patriarchal" virtues, such as care and responsibility for others, trust and reverence, and these are made the sum-total of the whole ethical system, in so far as it refers to external social behaviour. As the relation of God to man is itself a patriarchal one, so also that of men to each other becomes the same. Since this fundamental theory can be realized most fully within the Family, which is necessarily based on authority and reverence, the terminology and the spirit in this fundamental theory are then expanded from the Family until they cover the whole of the rest of life.

The Prince becomes the "Father of his country", and his subjects are the "children of the country"; the lord of the manor is the "Father of the estate" who cares for his children and expects obedience from them, and in virtue of his inheritance as judge represents God to them, while the dependent peasants become the "children of the estate", who serve their lord with respectful and cheerful obedience; the employer becomes the "house-father" who looks after the servants and maintains discipline within the household community, and the servants and wage-labourers become willing and grateful members of the household, who serve God in the person of the master of the house.

Luther expounded this fundamental theory in a most excellent, clear, cordial, and powerful way in his two Catechisms. These two books formed the basis of Lutheran ethics, and by their means, through a process of infinite repetition, this theory of Patriarchalism was hammered into the minds of faithful Lutherans. When the Catechism was expounded the explanation of the Fourth Commandment became the centre of all social ethics, and its teaching again helped to illuminate "*The Home Table*—some texts for divers holy orders and estates, which may serve to admonish them respecting their offices and duties".*

Thus, down to the present day, through the Catechism Lutheran children are taught the main features of a patriarchal agrarian-ethic, in which they learn to "love and trust God above all things", and also that it is their duty "neither to despise nor be angry with their parents and masters, but to hold them in love and esteem". In the Catechism, too, the Lutheran child gives thanks to God that He "has created me and all other creatures, my body and soul, my eyes and ears and all my members, my reason and all my senses; that He has given and still preserves unto me clothes and shoes, house and home, wife and child, fields and cattle, and all my goods; richly and daily He cares for me, providing me with all nourishment for the needs of my body and my life; He protects me against all danger, and keeps and preserves me from all evil; and all out of pure, fatherly, Divine goodness and mercy; with no merit or worthiness of my own; for all that I am bound to thank and praise Him, to serve Him and obey Him".[256] Children of all classes learn this Catechism; in the city and in the country town, in the prince's castle and in the manufacturer's villa, in the farmhouse and the

* This book accompanied the Catechism.

[256] See p. 862.

peasant's cottage, in the tenements and model dwellings of our great manufacturing towns. It is an epitome of the whole of the Lutheran social ethic.

This point of view throws a light upon all the social doctrines in particular: the Family, the State, economics, and Society. The various forms of social life which these doctrines express, which arise out of Natural Law, are merely so many temporary forms of social life. They are meant to serve as the sphere in which the religious spirit of love is to be manifested—that is, they provide scope for the practical exercise of the spirit which springs out of the certainty of a filial relationship with God, which is bestowed by grace. Thus they become sections of a life-curve which is penetrated through and through with the love of God. This is the reason why they are not an end in themselves, and why they may only be accepted in the spirit of obedience and surrender to God. Even as a means for the exercise of love they are not to be used in a humanitarian way; they are only meant to serve as a means of shedding abroad the spirit of love in the way which God has ordained. This fundamental idea, however, did not develop quite smoothly. For the forms of social life which have arisen out of Natural Law are still meant to serve the ends of natural life, and their independent existence becomes increasingly obvious the more one enters into practical life. It then becomes clear that it is impossible to absorb these natural ends purely into the religious purpose of life. Further, the natural aims of life and their social forms of expression in the fallen State have received a character of law and force, of economic self-interest and of conflict, which in their very nature are opposed to the true ethic of love. These considerations, therefore, led to peculiar fluctuations and inconsistencies in the social doctrines of Lutheranism. Catholicism, in its graduated system, had felt the difficulties less acutely; but Lutheranism, with its separation between the sacred and the secular, in a confused kind of way was bound to feel them more intensely. Even during his own lifetime Luther himself expressed them quite strongly. But in the period of Lutheran orthodoxy the doctrine of the Divine character of the natural order, of the duty of adjustment to the existing order, predominated to such an extent that these difficulties were felt no longer. Thus the final result was a terrible spiritual and intellectual sterility, which formed a glaring contrast to the social doctrines of Catholicism and of Calvinism.[257] It was,

[257] On this point *v. Figgis: From Gerson to Grotius, pp. 62–107*, in which Luther and Machiavelli are classed together.

therefore, not surprising that in the eighteenth century, when Lutheranism was faced by the whole new world of Western thought, its social theory broke down completely, although the practical situation remained unchanged.

The Lutheranism of the Enlightenment produced the elementary school, freedom of inquiry and liberty of conscience, the inwardness of ethical autonomy, and depth of feeling in philosophical speculation, but it changed nothing in the social doctrines. In practice even Kant, with his respect for authority, thought in these Lutheran categories. They then became official and secular in character.[257a] At the Prussian-German Restoration in the nineteenth century these theories were revived; they then became a weapon in the hands of a ruling class and produced that blend of masculine hardness and class-conscious ruthlessness which distinguishes modern Lutheranism from the older kind.

The Lutheran Ethic and the Family

In Lutheranism, as in the Catholic tradition, the Family forms the starting-point of all social development. It owes this position to its origin, since it represents the earliest form of social life—it was established in Paradise or in the Primitive State, and was confirmed and re-ordered after the Fall, from which—either directly or indirectly—all other forms of social life proceed. To some extent the State is regarded as having been instituted along with the Family, although, on the other hand, it is also regarded as having been specially founded by God, after the peoples of the earth had been divided into different languages and nations; in all this, however, the State is only conceived as the grouping of various scattered families under one head. The Family is also the starting-point of all economic conditions of management and service, in so far as the most closely knit domestic economy seems to be the ideal, and, actually, economic theory only thinks in terms of the one-family household, and of the household of the State, ruled by the Prince, which is conceived in a similar manner. The Family is the germ and the precursor of the Church, in so far as the religious fellowship within the home forms the real bond of unity within the Family, and Church-life is first established by the house-father through family prayers and instruction in the Catechism. Finally, the Family is the archetype of all social organizations since it presents the original picture of those relations of authority and reverence which arise out of the

[257a] Cf. *Troeltsch: Das Historische in Kants Religionsphilosophie, 1904, pp. 37–42; Kalweit: Kant und die Kirche, 1904.*

natural organization. Thus it is only natural that Lutheran social philosophy should be permeated through and through with the spirit of the Family, understood in a monogamous patriarchal sense.

The Family itself is an expression of the way in which the Law of Nature regulates and solves the sociological problems which arise out of the relation between the sexes. From the point of view of Natural Law its aim is the ordered union of the sexes, the ordered procreation of children, and the household which is formed by the several contributions of the various energies and powers mutually made, is the heart of all economic activity. But relationships of this kind, founded by Natural Law, become for the Christian also directly the form of the primary and most elementary religious exercise of love, since the relations between husband and wife, parents and children, provide the most immediate opportunity for the exercise of love, and in this relationship both a common self-surrender to God and the Divine commandment of love are to be put into practice.

This means, certainly, that the sex ethic of Protestantism was very different from that of Catholicism. Luther's own marriage meant more than a very manifest and concrete attempt to overthrow the ideal of the celibacy of the priesthood; it was also the proclamation of a principle of sex ethics which regarded the sex-life as something normal, and which gave it an ethical character, making it a means of the most vital ethical and religious functions for all believers. Luther did not conceive the purpose of marriage solely from the point of view of the procreation and nurture of children, as so frequently happens when a fundamentally ascetic spirit is softened and adjusted to other ideals, as, for instance, in Puritanism. From his point of view the purpose of marriage consists in an independent value of its own, in the love to be enjoyed by married persons, in which, however, the specifically erotic element and the universal human element, intensified by the common domestic life, are not combined into a firm spiritual, ethical, and religious unity.

Thus the monogamous family solves the sex-problem in general first of all in relation to the outside world. Sexual union before and outside of marriage is to be avoided, and all sexual intercourse is to be carried on within the limits of legitimate marriage. The natural conclusion to be drawn from this is the desirability of earlier marriage. Resolute faith in Providence sweeps away misgivings about the size of population, and all economic difficulties. Luther held that children should be brought into the world without any artificial restrictions whatever; this is a positive duty, and the possibility of being able to support a family is certain because God wills it. In contrast with the Catholic ideal of chastity, celibacy is regarded as only commanded for exceptional temperaments and circumstances—in general, however, it is vigorously rejected. The process of making marriage ethical from within, in the mutual relations between husband and wife, parents and children, is only achieved by the penetration of the whole with the religious spirit of love, which, given the existence of a personal, religiously deepened inclination, will regulate the sex relationships by mutual consideration for one another, which makes the parent-relationship the school of protective and educative willing self-sacrifice, and the relationship of children to their parents one of trustful reverence and a humble spirit of obedience towards all who are set over them. This, of course, naturally implies the indissoluble nature of marriage, but only as an ethical and legal result; the sacramental character of marriage has disappeared. Therefore when separation is desired (and this is only permitted with great caution for any other cause save adultery) the innocent party is allowed to marry again. The fact that within marriage, both morally and legally, an extensive masculine domination of a patriarchal kind is taken for granted is due not merely to economic conditions, or to Catholic tradition; it belongs to the very essence of Lutheranism, which looks upon the physical superiority of man as the expression of a superior relationship willed by God, and a stable order as the chief end of all social organizations. The house-father represents the law, and possesses unlimited power over others; he is the breadwinner, the pastor, and the priest of his household. By submission to her husband the wife atones for Eve's transgression; she ought, however, to be considered on a level of equality with him so far as religion is concerned; to some extent this modifies her subordinate position. The modern individualistic view of marriage is impossible because the economic, legal, and also the ethical presuppositions do not yet exist.

Marriage in the fallen state, however, is still not regarded as an institution which can be entirely justified without any further argument. For Luther sexual desire and the confusing passion which is bound up with it remain a sign of Original Sin; in the Primitive State there was no sensuality, and the fact that sensuality cannot be avoided is to him the clearest proof of the universality of sin. Thus marriage as the organization of sensuality instituted by God and reason is still at bottom only a *frenum et medicina peccati*, a concession to sin, which God winks at, and the sin which marriage inevitably incurs He restricts and heals. If, from that point of view, misgivings should still arise about marriage, Luther then appeals to the fact that it was positively founded and appointed by God, and he defines it simply as a duty in obedience to a Divine command. From that point of view, then, marriage is hallowed and protected against all scruples; indeed, viewed from the Christian standpoint it is the most important and the noblest social service of a Christian. Later Lutheranism, it is true, did not give up the idea that "sexual desire" is the fruit of Original Sin; but its scruples gradually decreased. Here, as in all other questions, it simply emphasized the fact of its Divine appointment, and thus swept away all difficulties, so that Christian marriage in accordance with Natural Law seemed to be a matter of simple obedience to a positive Divine Command, and henceforth, just as in Catholicism, it was idealized as a symbol of the relation between Christ and the Church. Problems relating to marriage, therefore, lie solely within the sphere of marriage legislation, and the right relationship between the religious and the civil authority. Luther desired to hand over marriage legislation to the State, but instead it passed into the hands of the religious and civil authorities in the consistories—a clear sign of the fusion of sacred and secular functions in a Christian society which here prevailed.

Thus in this conception of the Family the various constituent elements were in no way fully combined into a unity. Luther also was quite conscious of the fact that this ideal of the Family was a very high one, far removed from the actuality of life, with its "*wüsten Rotterei und Buberei*" (wild disorder and knavery). Luther explains the fact that the reality approximates so little to this solution of the sociological sex-problem by saying that it is due to the corruption caused by sin, and to the specially evil character of these Last Days. He has no doubt at all that the ideal can be realized. The ideal only breaks down owing to the resistance of the Devil and the lusts of the flesh, and also to greed and luxury, which, also from this point of view, ought to be restricted by law, in order to maintain class barriers and to stabilize the demands of life.[258]

The Lutheran Ethic and the State

The Lutheran conception of the State presents the same characteristics as that of the Family, and the difficulties which it

[258] See p. 864.

presents are regarded from the same point of view.[259] In each case the State has come into existence in very different ways—through creatures as "channels" and instruments of the Divine Reason, and in each case its existence has been confirmed and authorized by the Gospel, above all in the 13th chapter of the Epistle to the Romans. The State is a product of Reason, and is therefore, by its nature, restricted to the aims of mere Reason, the preservation of external discipline and order, and the securing of human well-being. It is the same "police" and utilitarian idea of the State as in Catholicism, only now, in accordance with the circumstances, there is a greater emphasis upon unity of authority. The means which the State has at its disposal for this purpose is authority, which therefore forms its most peculiar attribute, which it always preserves, and which may not be destroyed by any of its subjects. It is, however, the duty of the State to use this authority according to the Divine Law of Nature and for the purpose of reason, and if the powers that be refuse to observe this Law, just as in scholasticism, they are to be regarded as "tyrants", who may be deposed from their office. According to Luther's own logical doctrine, however, the only resistance to these "tyrants" which he will countenance is that of passive resistance, or endurance, or in a case of religious persecution he would recommend those who are oppressed to go into exile. In this sense the State is always justified, both by Natural and by Divine Law, even among Turks and pagans; indeed, in its natural sense, it is even particularly excellent among pagans, and the ancient doctrine of the State and examples drawn from it can still be used to the profit of the State at the present day.

To this extent the State is something really Divine. Now, however, it is its duty to establish order by force and violence as well as by law and justice, and this is completely opposed to the real Christian spirit of love. The Christian ought to love his enemies and to go to law as little as possible; indeed, at first Luther taught that no Christian should go to law at all; later on he conceded the right to go to law as a means of self-protection against "knaves", with whom it is impossible to come to an understanding in a Christian way. In this concession, however, there is no ethical recognition of justice as such, whether in the form of law, or merely as a general sense of justice. Rather it is the duty of the Government to take the initiative in the administration of the law and of the police force, in order to prevent a Christian from being obliged to make too much use of the law for his own

[259] See p. 865.

sake. There is just as little ethical value in patriotic and "Fatherland" sentiments. In cases where the Government is unchristian a Christian must either refrain from resistance or the Government must be changed. The truly Christian ideal is that of a pure fellowship of love, apart from State or Law. This implies that the State—in spite of its Divine character and its basis in Reason—is still only an institution rendered necessary by and against sin, a product of the merely relative Natural Law, reacting against sin under the conditions of the fallen State. Here, then, there reappear all the Augustinian views about the State as the product of sin, which, however, can only be rightly understood if the State is regarded as a product of Reason working with concessions to sinful brutality and evil, and itself set up by Reason against sin.

From this point of view, however, the State again seems to be something unchristian, directly opposed to a genuine Christian ethic, and it would seem to be quite natural and justifiable for Christian men to seek to contract out of the State, not only by refusing to claim the aid of the State in legal matters or to take part in military service, or in swearing an oath, etc., but also by refusing to take part in the official administration of the government, and in the execution of its laws. Faced by such scruples, however (just as in the case of the Family), Luther appeals with great emphasis to the belief that the powers that be are ordained by God, and confirmed in their position by Him. It is a duty of obedience towards God to exercise authority, to obey the Government, and to use authority for the purpose of justice; God Himself bears the responsibility for His institutions, and does not intend them to be interfered with by human sophistry and argument. The practice of government and the administration of justice are offices appointed by Divine command, and Luther describes with great vigour the contrast between the system of law which is carried out from the ruling prince down to the gaoler and the hangman, in which the work of government, administration, and punishment, including hanging, breaking on the wheel, and beheading, is all a service to God, and the non-official purely personal morality, in which, on the other hand, the true service of God consists in loving one's enemies, in sacrifice, renunciation and endurance, in loving care for others, and self-sacrifice.

It is very evident that he delights in the paradox of these two ways of serving God, and he boasts with great satisfaction that no one has yet proved so clearly from the Scriptures the Divine Right of a government, which is independent, dominated by no

Church, and bewildered by no scruples. It is at this point that Luther inserts the most characteristic and remarkable tenet in his whole system of ethics, the distinction between private and public morality, in which, in his own way, he had solved the great problem which had exercised the minds and hearts of the Christian thinkers of an earlier era. In this demand for obedience to a positive command of God all the Augustinian conceptions of the State disappear, and the State is regarded entirely as the Divinely-appointed authority based on reason, whose business it is to execute all the tasks which affect public order and the common weal; by that very fact the State is distinct from the Church, which is dependent solely upon spiritual influence and vital personal fellowship.

From this point of view war also is justified. It may only be waged by the civil authority, for secular purposes, as part of its official duty, when it is necessary to protect the peace and welfare of its citizens against attack. Victory can only be expected if war is waged in self-defence. Further, war must be waged in a spirit of humility, ascribing nothing to one's own efforts, but all to the Grace of God. This excludes, therefore, all ideas of "holy" wars or Crusades; where religious interests are involved only spiritual weapons may be used, and even the war against the Turks may only be waged by the Emperor as one who is called to that duty, and then only in the secular interest of the protection of his people. This position, however, excludes all specific political thought and activity. Even a "secular" war must be waged for a righteous cause, and if a Prince should undertake an unjust oppressive war his subjects are to refuse to support him, accepting with Christian patience the suffering they will have to endure as the penalty for their disobedience. A just war also requires that those who take part in it should have the right moral and Christian spirit; they must prepare themselves by attendance at church, for God will not grant victory to the proud. In all this there is no question of treaties and political combinations. Every country stands alone, and defends itself when it is threatened, trusting in the providence of God. This is an extremely naïve kind of political idea, dependent in particular instances upon politics of the prophetic moralizing kind. Luther is convinced that all wars which are not undertaken in this spirit are permitted to fail, and that Providence uses defeats as a rod of correction and as a religious method of education. Thus the thing Luther admires most in the Romans is that they were obliged to wage war; everyone wished to force himself on them and to gain a knight's renown from them, so that they had to defend themselves; even Hannibal failed because he began the war, "for it is God who does it. He will have peace, and He is against those who begin war and break peace".

It is easy to see what a disastrous effect this kind of outlook would have upon Lutheranism in the political sphere, and although the Lutheran princes, diplomats and jurists, and later on even Luther himself, did not bind themselves to follow this policy, it was still everywhere a dangerous drag on Lutheran politics; it determined the expansion and the fate of Lutheranism, which was unable to extend beyond the land of its birth. What a contrast was presented by Calvinist politics, with their treaties and alliances and their Wars of Religion.[260]

When, however, we inquire into the relation of the State to the Church, and to the life of the Christian community, we see the question from a fresh angle. For if the State is controlled by a Christian government, then it is no longer merely an institution based on Divine and Natural Law through the order of Creation, but it is one of the forms used for the realization of the Christian fellowship of love and redemption. This means that submission to its institutions and associations is a Christian duty of love to the whole of Society, and indeed one of the most necessary and immediate duties, since it is precisely the utilization of the forms of life within the State which helps our fellow-men more than the self-sought holiness of monastic separation from the world. Then it becomes especially the duty of the Government, as a service of love, to undertake the education and preservation of Society, Christian unity of faith, discipline, and order, and also to care for the Word of God, for purity and for the prosperity of the Church. The Government serves the Church freely, from love, creates its church-order and its financial basis, exercises the office of censor and defender of the Faith, and excludes from its sphere all expressions of false doctrine, measures which are not required of a non-Christian government. The Turks may tolerate several religions at the same time, but a Christian government must place itself at the disposal of the loving service of the Truth. Thus it will take upon itself, it is true, all kinds of secular matters, including education and the care of the poor, but it will deal with them all in a Christian spirit, and with consideration for the progress of the Christian life of faith. The religious end of Society, therefore, is exalted above the end of Natural Law, not, however, in the Catholic sense, with its graded organization, regulated in

[260] See p. 865.

case of need by the supreme authority of the Church, but in the sense of an agreement between the activity of the State and the Christian exercise of love.[261] Thus we have again reached an Augustinian idea, the idea of a Theocracy. Only this theocracy is not a Hierocracy, not the supremacy of the international hierarchy, and it is not a relationship which can be legally formulated; but it is the free agreement in love between the purely spiritual Church built upon the Word, and the secular authority, freely serving the Church, receiving voluntary advice from the theologians; both Church and State, however, are controlled and impelled by the Word of God, and by its miraculous and spontaneous power, which achieves its own end.

In this question, too, Luther was fully conscious that in spite of all his concessions to the State as an institution of fallen humanity, he was promulgating a highly idealistic doctrine, far removed from reality. We only have to read Luther's Catechism to see how the Christian ruler will desire nothing save to use his office with all strictness, in might and right, as God's representative to serve the cause of love and faith; and how, on the other hand, Christians ought to lead a humble and peaceful life, in unlimited love and readiness to help others, without legal proceedings or special privileges, without insistence on their formal rights, and with the greatest possible toleration of injustice. It is quite clear that this ideal of the State is super-idealistic, almost utopian, in a Christian sense. On the other hand, we only need to read his angry and vehement complaints of princes and jurists, feudal lords and magistrates, as well as, above all, his complaints of the masses, "so unteachable, so coarse and brutal", to see that Luther was far removed from the opinion that the existing condition of things in the State corresponded to his ideal. However hard he tried, in contradistinction from the Baptists, to make his ideal fit into the conditions of actual life, it was as little at home in this coarse and brutal world as was his spiritual ideal of the Church, which made no provision for its extension.

This was not due, as is often said, to Luther's lack of political ability, a defect which might perhaps have been remedied. It is inherent in the religious idea itself, which cannot be combined with the political spirit. When a fusion of this kind does take place, the religious expression will also be different; Calvinism is a good example of this fact. With the modern Conservatives, who are certainly not without the political spirit, the political element

[261] See p. 865.

(which is founded upon the essence of a policy of force based on might) and the religious element (with its spirituality which finds its chief happiness in waiting on God) diverge so far in opposite directions that there is a complete severance and disharmony.[262]

In the Lutheranism of more recent times the tension between public and private morality disappeared more and more, and there arose that type which is usually described as Lutheran: that is, unconditional obedience towards the central government, and the subordinate officials, both of whom represent God, and only hold their office by virtue of God's permission; the belief that these authorities are based on Natural and Divine Law, which appear more and more as the fundamental laws of a true Christian Society, and which co-operate without difficulty; the duty of the Government to look after all secular and natural affairs, and, so far as it is possible, with its secular means, and in agreement with the ecclesiastical government, also to promote the Christian virtues; the preservation of external peace at any price, and of internal peace by a thorough guardianship over the restricted understanding of its subjects. The sinful origin and the sinful character of law and of force disappeared in the harmony between the Natural and the Divine Law, and this harmony made possible an ideal of Christian Society, which, in itself, was quite possible to realize, although it was constantly being obscured by sin. In this ideal, revelation and natural science and reason unite to form one great ideal of human society.

L. von Seckendorff gave classic expression to this ideal in the dedication of his *Teutschen Fürstenstaat*: "The wisdom by which Kingdoms, Principalities, and lands are happily governed is, according to its origin Divine, in itself glorious and incomparable, and includes in its breadth and universality all that which in other sciences is found only in fragments. Within the sphere of each land it is the absolutely necessary sun, by means of which all is illumined, warmed, and nourished. It may be compared with an inexhaustible ocean into which all other wisdom and art flow, and in a high and secret manner, to the welfare of all, it is again spread abroad and shared throughout the whole land. It is a Paradise which is ever green with all the most beautiful and useful plants of the virtues and good ordinances, of which each in his time and place brings forth pleasant fruits. This wisdom King Solomon besought the only Wise God for his office of government, by which in addition he receiveth the greatest

[262] See p. 867.

treasures and riches of the world also."[263] The pessimism and idealism of original Lutheranism have disappeared, and the doctrine of society bears the traces of a hearty and inwardly strong, but homely and commonplace, paternal government.

The Lutheran Ethic and Economic Questions

Though, from the modern standpoint, the Lutheran doctrine of the State was to a large extent far more reactionary than the Thomist doctrine of the State, its economic ethic,[264] on the other hand, remained considerably closer to the average Catholic theory. It, however, also underwent great changes. These were mainly connected with the repression of monasticism, and of mendicancy, a practice which was closely connected with monasticism, and fostered by the charity of the cloister. Further, celibacy was considerably restricted, industry was urged upon all as a duty, property held in perpetual tenure (mortmain) was secularized, mass-benefices were abolished; above all the control of the Church in the sphere of economics was removed, which had brought questions like the fixing of a just price, and of usury, before the judgment seat of the confessional. All matters of that kind were now handed over to the secular authority entirely, and to Natural Law. The idea of Natural Law itself, however, whose main characteristics had already been regarded as in full harmony with the law of Christianity by the Middle Ages and by the Canon Law, was retained, so far as its positive content was concerned. The only difference was that that which previously had only been recommended to the layman in virtue of Natural Law, was extended to all without exception, without any quarter for beggars or for monasteries. The sphere which the Church had formerly protected was handed over entirely to the secular system of legislation, as something which was connected with the Natural Law in its harmony with the Christian Law.

Thus we cannot be surprised that all the characteristic features of the mediaeval economic ethic reappear in Lutheranism; the only changes are the necessary modifications caused by the social changes of the day.[265]

Labour with its toil and its cares is in itself contrary to nature. The fruitfulness of nature and the minerals in the mountains are

[263] See p. 868.

[264] See p. 869.

[265] Here also Aristotle is the master, see *Schmoller*, 470, also *Melancthon: CR, XVI*, 427. It is "a natural doctrine of economics". "They approach often very close to the physiocratic doctrines although they proceed from quite different presuppositions" (*Schmoller*, 471).

direct gifts of God to be humbly and gratefully received by man; the idea that these good things can only be appropriated if labour and technical skill are expended upon them, seems scarcely to have occurred to Luther. The fact that God has made the acquisition of these good things dependent upon man's toil simply means that God has instituted labour for educative reasons, as a training for humanity which had been corrupted by sin. Like the State, and the institution of marriage, labour is a *remedium peccati*; it belongs only to the relative Natural Law of the fallen State, and serves the ends of punishment and discipline; essentially, therefore, its significance is ascetic.[266] For that very reason, however, it should be urged as a duty upon all who are able to work. Able-bodied beggars, idle monks, and lazy people who live on inherited incomes are an absolute contradiction to this Law of Nature. Private property, which is the product of labour, is also ordained by God; it also, however, owing to the Fall, is only a means of preserving discipline and order.[267] In special circumstances, as, for instance, in time of famine, or for widows who cannot work, righteousness allows man to return to the original love-communism and to allow robbery from the baker, or a "*Notwücherlein*" (compulsory bargain).[268] The standard of private property ought not to exceed the requirements of one's rank, yet pleasure in possessions, even in gold and silver, is allowed within the limits of a grateful frugality without any scrupulous consideration of the measure of one's needs. Since, however, it is of the very essence of labour and of property to procure a man an income suitable to his rank, but not to exceed it, the traditional character of this economic ethic is obvious. The economic order consists essentially in this: to live within one's own class, according to the social standards of that class, and to regard it as a just claim on the Government to be protected by it within this order. It is against all law, both Natural and Divine, to wish to rise in the world, to break through existing institutions on one's own free initiative, to agitate and destroy Society by individual efforts, to improve one's manner of life, or to improve one's social position.[269] Again, the forms of social organization which ought to be maintained, and which, above all, have a right to be protected and morally recognized, are the classes which live most near to the

[266] Cf. specially *Brandenburg, 6*; *Schmoller, 474 and 478*; *Eck, 499*.

[267] Passages from Luther and Melancthon in *Schmoller, 705–708, 597*; *Uhlhorn, 22*.

[268] *Eck: BA., IV, 1, p. 504*; that is quite the Scholastic doctrine, see above, *XXVIII, 63*. It certainly does not quite agree with the rest of the Lutheran doctrine of the Primitive State.

[269] See p. 870.

natural order: the main class of feudal and peasant agriculturists who, in direct contact with nature, produce goods without any intermediaries between the producer and the consumer; the class of officials and soldiers who are needed for the natural task of caring for the common weal, to which belong the vassals who were liable to military service, the class of workmen in the towns who produce goods which cannot be made by the peasantry; day-labourers, servants, and other functionaries, who are to be exhorted to frugality and obedience; finally also the merchant, whose services are indispensable for exchange, who in addition to the net cost may raise the price to one which will secure his existence. The scholastic doctrine of the *pretium justum*, the recommendation of fixed prices for food-stuffs, the scholastic doctrine of the unfruitfulness of money, and the impossibility of selling time, were also combined with this point of view. In all this the continuation of the patristic and mediaeval prohibition of usury is taken for granted; indeed it is demanded with increased urgency in opposition to the evasions introduced by later Scholasticism; only this ought to take place without revolution, since obligations of interest which have already been incurred are to remain as they are until the capital is either commuted or paid back. The system of guarantees and the system of credit are no less hotly attacked as an intrusion into the sphere which belongs to Divine Providence, and as frivolous presumption. These ideas almost entirely represent the consumer's point of view. This is shown by the desire to establish the most direct connection possible between the gifts of nature, labour, and consumption, and the detestation of all complications which cannot be overcome. It is the standpoint of those who desire law and order and the maintenance of peace; all labour organizations and all titles of possession are regarded as means of preserving a social order which is free from competition. This is required by the nature of things, it is, however, also the demand of morality,[270] in which Natural and Divine Law agree; thus if this theory is carried out in practice everyone will gain a living, order and peace will be preserved, love will be exercised, natural distinctions maintained, while dependence on God and on nature will be accepted in the spirit of faith, and the welfare of the whole community will be furthered.

[270] On the "moral" tendency of this conservatism with an agrarian tendency, see *Schmoller, 476*; on the "naturalness" of the retention as far as possible of primitive methods of production and a closely knit domestic economy, see *pp. 479, 564; Oncken, 131.*

The Christian sanction for this natural economic ethic consists in this: obedient service in the callings which have just been specified comes to be considered the first duty of a Christian, and the true and proper sphere for exercising the love of one's neighbour. Since everyone ought to work and live on the proceeds of his labour, together with the members of his household, labour furthers the repose and harmony of the whole, and makes a most important contribution to the welfare both of the individual and of the community. The discharge of one's duty by honest work is the best service a man can render to God, and the love of one's neighbour which is exercised in the duties of one's calling is better than charity, which exalts beggary, makes almsgiving a merit in the sight of God, while it is indifferent about the practical effect of almsgiving, gives too much to one and too little to another, while the whole idea is corrupted by the ideal of a holiness consisting in "good works".[271] This all implies an extraordinary intensification of the idea of the duty of labour, and an impulse to increased output. Further, in spite of all Luther's preference for agricultural work, this is a civic idea and not a feudal one, since the feudal nobility, which, for many reasons, had been greatly strengthened by the Reformation, was still urged to recognize the duty of work, of looking after their own estates, or of princely official service. Both these elements were forced into existence by the course of events, but they were also a requirement of the economic ethic of the Reformation.[272] In all these respects, in spite of the fundamentally mediaeval view of the nature and ideal of economic life which has been retained, the new system itself is something quite different. The universal duty of work, the abolition of mortmain, the substitution for the charity which tried to deal with all social evils by a social policy of the State, and a system of philanthropy of Church and State combined, which would care for those who were really unable to work: these phenomena altered the whole outlook, and certainly later on these were the features to which the modern economic ethic was able to appeal. In itself, however, the spirit of the economic ethic of Lutheranism was thoroughly reactionary: it was a combination of Natural and Divine Law; it urged contentment with the simplest conditions, and a toleration of the existence minimum according to one's class, accompanied at the same time by the readiness, in case of need, to renounce the right of holding property, a right which was only introduced by sin.

[271] On this Christian inspiration, *Schmoller, 488, 707*; *Uhlhorn, 19 ff.*

[272] See p. 870.

But although this theory seems to present a very agreeable picture of the harmony between natural and Christian ethics, even here the element of conflict is present. The constant fight against self-interest, trust in one's own strength, and confidence in one's own achievements, the demand for a surrendered spirit when loss, scarcity, and distress prevail, since these things are divine penalties and means of discipline, the emphasis upon Providence which gives all without strain or affectation, the brotherly love which renounces all claim on possessions—all this goes far beyond the principles of the natural economic ethic, and approaches the evangelical radicalism of the persecuted and passively enduring sect. When it was suggested that if such principles were put into practice all economic life would be destroyed, Luther replied that it is the duty of the Government to prevent this, but that when this does not take place, the result must be endured as the nature of the world and the right of the Christian. Luther waged war not only on the forms of early capitalism and its social results which he could see quite plainly, and possibly even against special degenerations of the new economic organizations, but ultimately he was the champion of the Christian ethic of frugality and love, of faith in and surrender to Providence, against the never entirely restrained egotism and worldly self-confidence which are implied in all desire to possess property at all.[273] He was fighting against the new principle itself. It is only when, in so doing, he comes very close to the sectarian ethic that he again lays stress on the right to possess property and its uses, on the goodness of the Divine gifts, and the Divine authority of the Government—that is, of the whole organized social system. Here again there are the same fluctuating points of view as there were in the questions of marriage and the State. The dualism of Luther's ethical system is everywhere in evidence.[274]

It is only when we realize this that we see why Luther adhered so firmly to the economic ethic of the Middle Ages. It was not prejudice in favour of a prevailing economic theory, which everyone took for granted. Saxony had already developed beyond the economic system based on agriculture; and it is just Luther's passionate polemic, with its detailed enumeration of prevailing customs, which shows that he knew that he was hostile to the spirit of his age and not in agreement with it.[275] Nor was it simply a bias in favour of the Catholic and scholastic tradition,

[273] See p. 870. [274] See p. 871. [275] *Schmoller*, 479.

for whenever this conflicted with his principles he was clear-sighted enough and decidedly hostile; indeed, in this he was not adhering to Catholic theology, but only to its economic ethic and to Natural Law.

Luther believed that it was possible to maintain the content of mediaeval social teaching for reasons which may be analysed thus: just as Luther's peculiar political conception of Natural Law and of force was the conscious, deliberate result of an individualistic, and yet realistic and religiously super-idealistic, point of view, so also his economic ethic of Natural Law and its connection with the Christian ethic was also consciously based on principle. Whereas in politics he consciously broke through the tradition of the patristic Natural Law of political rationalism, here, just as deliberately, he retained it. The reason was this: Luther was convinced in precisely the same way as were the Catholic ethical thinkers, that this mediaeval conception of the economic ethic was the only one which harmonized with the Christian ethic, that it alone could be combined with the Christian ethic of love, trust in God, and renunciation of the world. With the exception of Humanists trained in the economic politics of the towns like Pirckheimer, Peutinger, Machiavelli, and Vives, the majority of Luther's contemporaries, without confessional distinctions, were on his side. The territorial and Imperial legislation also moved along similar lines and fought against the resistance of the towns. We have already seen that a Christian ethic which could accept the life of the world only became possible within the sphere of mediaeval society and the mediaeval system of economics—a system of economics which was based on agriculture and on the growth of the towns with their handicraftsmen. Luther believed that this still held good, and he desired to maintain the basis, upon which alone the realization of the Christian ethic had, until then, seemed possible. The heightened passion with which he asserted the theory, and the intensity of his ethical exhortations, was due to the fact that the new social type of the capitalistic cities and their social results now confronted this idea of a Christian Natural Law. This new type with its consequences of freely mobile individualism, of competition, of the calculating spirit which aims at increasing its possessions, with its complicated and incalculable connections between consumption and production, was in actual fact for the Christian ethic, at any rate for its essential fundamental ideas, a harsh opponent.

Luther saw this very clearly, and it was from this point of view that he formulated his economic and ethical opposition, which, in this respect, entirely agreed with Catholicism.[276]

To this very day the social ideal and the economic ethic of the Lutheran Conservatives still perpetuate this point of view,[277] and in this respect they still have an affinity with the Catholic ethic, which, however, seeks to direct the democratic element (which it certainly recognizes far more clearly) into a new social fabric, and within the borders of a class framework determined by the Church. Luther's ideas were the same as those which are still held to-day by Catholics, Conservatives, and middle-class people in general. Luther fought against monopolies and against joint-stock companies, against the demand for higher wages for day labourers and servants which was the result of the general rise in prices,[278] against the stipulations laid down by the latter,[279] against the individualism which broke through class barriers and sumptuary laws, just as the Conservatives of the present day fight against the Stock Exchange, the greed of the masses, the right of the workmen to form trade unions, and against free competition.

The difference between Luther and the Conservatives of the present day, however, lies in this: Luther had in mind essentially ethical and religious standards alone; class feeling did not enter into the question at all; in place of that he displayed a passionate intensity which made no effort to discover any possible scientific explanation of the type which he hated, nor did he try to understand the general reasons and necessities for the changes which he observed. From his naïve point of view these changes were due to evil—"works of the devil"—or a Divine discipline for the wild and unruly Germans—or they were a foreshadowing of the End of all things.[280] Luther could not imagine that the universal general changes in the world situation might also cause changes in the economic and ethical sphere, and this is why he summoned the world back to the Natural and Divine Law. The new economic order is contrary to humility, to trust in God, to brotherly love, to Nature, and to God. He stated plainly that in his opinion it was now the duty of the Government, in co-operation with the influencing of opinion through church and school, to intervene.

[276] See p. 871.
[277] Cf. *Oncken: I, p. 147,* who refers to *K. L. von Haller* and *Adam Müller.*
[278] Cf. *Schmoller, 513.* [279] Cf. *Schmoller, 515.*
[280] An example of the naïve character of his arguments in *Schmoller, p. 566*: that seven, eight, nine, and ten per cent. are unchristian is proved by the fact "that robbers and usurers who take that rate of interest frequently die a violent death or otherwise perish miserably".

Social Ideal of Luther

The whole social ideal of Luther—the organization and construction of Society in general—is finally explained by political and economic and ethical ideas. As in mediaeval Catholicism, it was the ideal of the social hierarchy, as a "cosmos of callings"; the only difference is that the duty of the "calling" is now extended to all, which involves the direct incorporation of the idea of "the calling" into the very heart of Christian ethics. The "callings" are in part those which proceed from the economic organization of Society, in which a rigid guild organization would be desirable. In part they are vocations to the Church and to the work of education, to which (as is constantly repeated) it is a Christian duty to lead talented children. Then there are the callings of the prince, the noble, the official, the soldier, and, last of all, the surplus of those who cannot find a place within the established organization, but who can still be used to serve in various ways as they are needed.[281] Serfdom, which had not ceased to exist, and which was extended at the close of the sixteenth century, from this point of view was regarded in precisely the same way as slavery was regarded in the Early Church, as a class, that is, in which men may enjoy the inner liberty of Redemption, but in which they have no right to seek external legal freedom.[282] In Lutheranism there was no idea at all of any new anti-slavery movements, and even down to the present day neither agrarian nor industrial serfdom raises any kind of misgiving in its mind. The reason for all this is perfectly clear. The social hierarchy does away with competition, so far as that is possible in the fallen state, and in so doing it harmonizes both with the ideal of love, and with the ideal of Natural Law which aims at law and order. It is in this sense that Stahl has made a new defence of the class theory as part of the theory of Christian Natural Law.[283] A blind faith in Providence assures the community that a principle of this kind would meet all the needs of the whole population. This system can only be disturbed by unusual accidents and Divine chastisements; when this happens those whose lives have been thrown out of gear by these events are commended to the care of Christian philanthropy, and to the care of the civil authority, firmly believing that these methods will suffice to heal all social evils.[284] At bottom, no one doubts that the Government can achieve all this, provided that it obeys con-

[281] See p. 871. [282] See p. 871. [283] See p. 872.
[284] Cf. *von Seckendorff: Fürstenstaat, p. 193.*

scientiously both the Law of Nature and the Law of God: that is, the characteristic difference between this point of view and that of the present day. The reason for this lies partly in the fact that in reality conditions were—in a quite remarkable way—much simpler than they are now; partly, owing to the lack of all statistical information, there was a total absence of scientific knowledge of the complicated character of the social situation, which was conditioned by and dependent on so many different factors; the right of location did not yet exist, and the problem of population had only just begun to appear as a subject for discussion. Hence a naïve conception of that kind was possible. The later theological ethic therefore, on the side of its social theories, was simply concerned with the vocational system as a whole; in particular it dealt only with the question of the family and the household, which, it felt, ought to constitute the chief sphere for the development of the ethical virtues of Christianity. The regulation of the whole is left to the Government, which, strongly supported by Lutheranism, takes supreme control. It is then the duty of the Government to see to it that in harmony with Christian and Natural Law the different classes are maintained in their suitable way of living, that social evils are remedied, and that whatever progress is necessary, is achieved. These matters come under the province of political economy and police administration; thus the Lutheran theory merges into mercantilism, since, where the good of the community is concerned, the Government is permitted to do that which is forbidden to the individual, that is, to gain an increase of property and profit, to initiate new industrial enterprises, monopolies and royalties, immunities, and alterations in the social structure and its compulsory character. In connection with this subject Seckendorff has given a classic description of the Christian "police".[285]

Social Policy, Social Reform, and Philanthropy

When we gather up all these various particulars and summarize them it then becomes possible to answer the question: to what extent did Lutheranism attempt to mould Society according to Christian ideals, or to introduce a scheme of social reform? The answer is simpler than we would expect when we consider that Lutheranism has been interwoven with an amazingly varied social history. Lutheranism has been mainly interwoven with a social process which extends from the advanced stage of the

[285] See p. 872.

German civilization of the sixteenth century, through the desolation of the Thirty Years War, the formation of the German States, and finally, through the politics of the Enlightenment and the Restoration periods, down to the great social problems of the present day. The simplicity of the answer is due to the fact that down to the present time the Lutheran position is based essentially upon the religious theory of the purely spiritual nature and "inwardness" of the Church, while all external secular matters are handed over to reason, to the ruling Princes, to the civil authority. At the beginning, certainly, there was combined with that the assumption that Natural and Divine Law, both issuing from the same source, will always naturally supplement each other, and that a Christian government will always desire and be able to govern and to mould secular affairs in harmony with Natural and Divine Law, in the spirit of the religious and ethical ideal.

The idea of moulding Society according to Christian ideals certainly existed; but it was left entirely to the Government, to be carried out in accordance with natural reason, which harmonized with the Gospel and was adapted to the fallen state. When, however, the modern conception of Natural Law arose which differed from the Christian Natural Law of the fallen state and of its comparative harmony with reason, then certainly a new situation had been created. Lutheran thinkers found a solution by accepting the new Natural Law just as they had accepted the old, seconding the reforming activity of the State with a partially secularized religious enthusiasm: when, moreover, the political and social development, which had also been emancipated from this idea, passed into the modern conditions of the pure struggle for power and of competition, then the social theory of Lutheranism was in a position of great embarrassment; henceforth it could only preach its doctrine, with scarcely a hope of realizing it, since, unlike Catholicism and Calvinism, Lutheranism possessed no organ by which it could put its theories into practice apart from the State, and the modern State, for its part, no longer feels itself—as in early Lutheranism—to be the secular aspect of the organism of Christian Society. This was the beginning of the social impotence of Lutheranism, in so far as it has not adopted Calvinistic and modern ideas. In its actual primitive sense it only finds support among the Conservatives; and it therefore combines its dogmatic renewal with the political and social views of the Conservatives. Its hopes of a social transformation in accordance with Natural and Divine Law are pinned no longer to the Christian State, but to the Christian Party. As we can understand very well, this brings Conservative Lutheranism into touch with the other Christian Party—against which it had once fought so ardently—that of Catholicism, in a community of "Christian world-outlook", and of opposition to the modern militaristic and bureaucratic sovereign State, with its indifference towards the Church and religion in general.

At first, however, Luther did not exhort the Church to this passive attitude in social questions. At the moment when the seething ferment of German life came into touch with the reform of religion, and when it seemed as though this combination were about to lead to the goal of a Christian commonwealth, renewed in its political, social, and Church-life, Luther, in his appeal *To the Christian Nobility of the German Nation*, outlined a programme of ecclesiastical and socio-political reform for the whole Empire, in which he had interwoven all the suggestions which had come from the opposition and the reform parties with his new ecclesiastical ideal of a Church based upon the priesthood of all believers. In this treatise, however, Luther was carried farther than he intended by the impetus of the whole movement; and even here his theory was foreshadowed, to this extent, that he does not suggest that the spiritual authority should bring about the reforms and thus impose on the nation a new Christian law, but that the princely rulers alone are to bring about the reforms outside the Church, in the strength of reason and love for the pure Gospel.

"Reasonable Regents alongside of Holy Scripture"—these are the separate powers, which, however, each within its own sphere, work together for the reform "of the Body of Christ". But an enthusiastic optimism still conceived both tasks as essentially united and destined to achieve a common victory.[286] After these preparations had been made a General Council would then finally take in hand the reform of Christendom as a whole. Nothing came of this idea of a collective reform, so in the times of ferment the Reformation movement turned to the particular local and communal authorities, which each in its own way undertook the work of "social betterment", and during this experimental period they were supported by Luther's "group-ideal". The municipalities and the magistrates, who already possessed considerable ecclesiastical rights, and a tradition of a

[286] Cf. *Brandenburg*, *pp. 9ff.*; for the origin of thoughts of reform in one who, until then, had been exclusively occupied with theology see *W. Köhler: L.'s Schrift an den Adel im Spiegel der Kultur- und Zeitgeschichte, 1895*.

kind of ethical "police" supervision, now issued new regulations, which made arrangements for the system of public worship, administration of the Poor Law, and the organization of the police force in the new Protestant sense. The Wittenberg Ordinance of January 1522, and the Leisnig Ordinance of 1523, were endeavours (which have often been imitated) to institute a Christian social order which was to use the money formerly locked up in endowments and benefices for the benefit of church and school, for poor relief in general, and also in time of famine, and which desired to leave the administration of these funds in the hands of elected stewards of Church revenues. These "ordinances" were based on similar police organizations in the towns, which had previously exercised similar powers, but they were coloured by the evangelical Protestant Church spirit, and this ecclesiastical flavour certainly entitled them to be described as Christian Socialism on local and communal lines. These "ordinances" were, however, Utopian and visionary, and they were never carried out in practice.[287] Indeed, under the influence of the disillusionment of the Peasants' War, and with the possibility which had now arisen of instituting a new order on territorial and not on local lines, Luther turned away from the dubious "group-ideal" altogether, and henceforth, in accordance with his essential main idea, he handed over all political and social matters, as external secular affairs, entirely to the Government, to reason, and to the jurists, that triad which he praised as much as he scolded it! With his eyes open Luther now maintained that the Church ought to dominate solely the purely spiritual spheres of edification and instruction. Under the influence of the Gospel, he argued, a Christian Government should then be able to settle all social questions which appeared on the horizon of that day on its own authority. These social questions were mainly concerned with the problem of the support of those who, for some reason or another, were unable to earn their living within the social hierarchy, conceived as a system of "callings".

[287] Cf. *Uhlhorn, III, 33–51; Barge: Karlstadt, I, 352, 382–386;* above all, *L. Feuchtwanger: Geschichte der sozialen Politik und des Armenwesens im Zeitalter der Reformation, Berliner Diss., 1908,* and its continuation in the *Jahrbuch für Gesetzgebung, Verwaltung, und Volkswirtschaft, 1909, XXXIII.* In essentials I follow *Feuchtwanger,* who very considerably supplements and corrects the work of *Barge*; cf. the analyses of the *Wittenberger "Beutelordnung"*, of the "*Ordnung der Stadt Wittenberg*", and of the *Leipziger "Kastenordnung"*, *Diss., pp. 9–16.* Cf. also *K. Müller: Luther und Karlstadt, 1907* (*Appendix*), and *Barge: Die älteste evangelische Armenordnung, Hist. Vierteljahrsschrift, XI, 1908, pp. 193–225,* and *Theolog. Jahresbericht, XXVIII, p. 530.*

This might have been the end of all direct ecclesiastical social activity, and the beginning of a policy of purely secular social welfare and care of the poor. The territorial Princes, however, whose authority was still far from being centralized, and the communes (free cities) which were burdened with heavy tasks, undertook this vocation very imperfectly. Luther's helpers therefore intervened, above all Bugenhagen, who was a good organizer, and they took over the task of the care of the sick and the poor, which lay so near to the heart of the Church. This service was undertaken, however, no longer in the Utopian, Christian-Socialist spirit of the "Ordinances" of Wittenberg and Leisnig, but—and in this matter it was essentially the towns which were concerned—in a very matter-of-fact combination of communal-police activity and the ecclesiastical activity of pastoral work and of charity. In accordance with municipal organizations for the care of the poor in the towns, and under the stimulus of the reform of the Poor Law by Ludovico Vives, which started in Belgium, the means were created out of endowments, the poor were controlled by the co-operation of the spiritual and the secular authorities, vagabondage was restricted, hospitals were created, and a fixed system of book-keeping was introduced in which particular care was taken to avoid the confusion caused by mixing up these accounts with those which belonged to the administration of the Church and to education. In the end, however, these new "ordinances" for administering the funds from the "common chest" were not carried out permanently. This was partially due to the fact that the problems connected with the Poor Law had been underestimated, and partially also to their failure to centralize the endowment monies which they did control; another cause was the lack of voluntary officials who could serve in turn upon the board of administration; above all, however, the new religion itself was too much engrossed with the personal interior life, too much imbued with the idea that everyone ought to work, and too much alienated from the old ideal of charity, to succeed in creating the necessary new methods. Thus the Lutheran "Chests" (*Kasten* or funds) merely became meagre funds in support of the poor alongside of other similar institutions.[288]

Thus, in this form also, ecclesiastical Socialism came to nothing, and the task of caring for the common weal was entrusted to the various governments, which were becoming more and more

[288] Cf. *Uhlhorn, III, 102–140,* and *Feuchtwanger: Geschichte der sozialen Politik und des Armenwesens im Zeitalter der Reformation, Berliner Diss., 1908.*

centralized, and were increasingly taking control of all the interests within their sphere; these governments, however, felt that the ecclesiastical arrangements for poor relief relieved them of responsibility, and they therefore did nothing on their side. But, still, the permanent principle had been finally formulated: that all secular and political affairs, and therefore also the question of social welfare, belong to the province of the Government, while the Church is concerned solely with the salvation of the soul and the interior life of personal piety.

Thus the Lutheran social programme merged into the social politics of patriarchal mercantilism. Then, when the State accepted the modern movement of thought, and moved away from a patriarchal Absolutism to an Absolutism of the Enlightenment, the whole system of Christian social effort slipped into the modern policy of social welfare, and Lutheranism lost all inner connection with, and all influence upon, the Government, which was certainly far from being a "Christian" government.

The more, however, that the social policy became purely secular, and the more clear it became that a purely class and vocational system does not enable everyone to gain their livelihood, but that it was always surrounded by a multitude of people who had become *déclassés*, and of people in distress, and especially when the more restless social movement of modern life brought bewilderment and confusion into many lives, Lutheranism was obliged to give up its attitude of simple trust in Providence and in the vocational system; and the Christian desires to express love which it did possess were again exercised in the form of voluntary philanthropy, in institutions, fellowships, clubs, and charities. Under the influence of Pietism, Lutheranism returned to the religious-social policy of charity, without the glorification of mendicancy, and at first without permitting this practice of charity to have any connection with the Church; in every other respect, however, this meant the resumption of the charity of Catholicism and of the Early Christian Church.[289] This has been the position ever since, and, under English influences, during the nineteenth century, as the "Innere Mission" (Home Mission) movement, this Christian social service has developed and flourished in a quite remarkable way. Orthodox ecclesiastical Lutheranism has only taken part in this movement in a rather hesitating way, but it has to-day finally become fairly sympathetic to it as a whole. Strict Lutheranism, which was renewed at the time of the Restoration and which has since then been dominant,

[289] See p. 873.

refused to entertain any further ideas of social reform. It has maintained the position which Stahl represented, i.e. that the social order should be entrusted to a Christian Government, whose duty it should be to ensure the maintenance of the class organization of callings with the restriction of the modern life movement. Wichern's attempt to go beyond the mere exercise of charity and to introduce a Christian social reform from the side of the Church, and in the grand manner to combine organically an ecclesiastical religious philanthropy with the social policy of the State, broke down because Lutheranism was unprepared, inwardly, for action of this kind, and also because his ideas were captured by the Conservative reactionary party.[290] The transformation of the programme of Wichern by Stöcker only led to the demand for a greater independence and power for the Church, and thus to an imitation of modern Catholic social reform; otherwise, so far as the general social ideal was concerned, it was obliged to connect itself with Conservative and middle-class principles in the true Lutheran sense; its rejection by the Conservatives finally drove it back into very small groups.[291]

Thus, down to the present time, the Lutheran Church has never advanced farther than the renewed ideal of charity; it has never made any effort to initiate a real social transformation at all. Most Lutherans simply repeat the old doctrine of the inwardness of the Church and of the duty of leaving all external matters of legislation and social welfare to the State.[292] Others, like the Christian Socialists of the Naumann school, discard the principles of Lutheranism altogether, and feel forced to return to the general political, economic, and social foundations of present-day Society.[293] Others, like those who represent the point of view of the Evangelical Social Congress, fully aware that the situation has entirely changed, discuss from differing points of view the possibility of striking out along new paths.[294]

Wherever the earlier Lutheranism is still a real force—among the Conservatives, that is to say—all social reform consists in breaking up the rationalistic, individualistic nature of modern Society, and in the revival of a society organized on aristocratic lines, bound together by class bonds, i.e. in the struggle against the Liberal world-outlook, and against the creations of Liberalism in the political, economic, and social sphere; alongside of this, then, the "Innere Mission" (Home Mission) may indeed exercise its charitable activity among the poor and the sick, but it must

[290] See p. 873. [291] See p. 874. [292] See p. 874.
[293] See p. 875. [294] See p. 875.

guard against any possibility of shattering the idea of authority.[295] Within these limits the "Innere Mission" has certainly achieved splendid things, although the Christian-social element certainly predominates less within it than the propaganda and the evangelistic element.[295a]

The Lutheran Ethic and the General Situation

This completes the analysis of Lutheranism. Now, however, we have to answer the final question: to what extent are these social doctrines the reflection of existing political and social conditions? So far as the actual ideal is concerned which floated before the minds of Lutheran thinkers, we must give a directly negative reply to this question. The social doctrines of Lutheranism are, like the whole of Lutheran piety, a genuine branch of the whole Christian religion and ethic of love, which either rejects or is indifferent to the world, with its law, property, might, and force, and of that monotheism which proclaims that the religious aims of the personality united to God are the only true and lasting values of life, and from that derives the idea of the union of mankind in love, through the common exercise of these values. To a far greater extent than Catholicism, certainly, Protestantism has accepted the life of the world, and it is therefore similarly determined by the spirit of general social development, which forced itself upon the attention of the Church and found itself in a situation in which this was possible without any particular difficulty. In so doing, however, Protestantism has carefully preserved the dualism of the Christian ideal which arises out of this conception, and which, in contrast with Catholicism, it has both deepened and intensified. Since Protestantism supported the mediaeval ideal of a social hierarchy and the anti-capitalistic spirit, expressed in agrarian and middle-class ways of living, along with a patriarchalism based on authority and reverence, as the right way of reconciling both sides, it drew its conclusions from the ethical and religious ideal, and not from the circumstances which happened to prevail at the time. If we reflect upon Luther's idealistic plans, and remember his bitter complaints of the non-Christian character even of the new Protestant evangelical world, we receive far more the impression of a Christian Utopia than of the justification and glorification of existing conditions, and not without reason. One of the finest and most original Lutheran

[295] See p. 875.

[295a] Cf. *Schäfer: Leitfaden der inneren Mission*³, *1893*, and *Uhlhorn: Liebestätigkeit*.

thinkers, J. V. Andreä, has described Luther's social ideal (in imitation of Sir Thomas More and Campanella) in a Utopia, called *Christianopolis*.[296]

Whenever the social doctrines of Lutheranism are treated solely as the religious sanction of the existing situation, as often happens in orthodox Lutheranism, this always means that Lutheran thought has been weakened and despiritualized; the main impulse of the real Lutheran ethic in its mystics and spiritual thinkers, in its ethical reformers, and finally in the Pietists, has always reacted against this tendency with great vigour. By the very vigour of its protest, however, this opposition often lost its connection with the real leading ideas of Lutheranism, and landed in the other extreme of asceticism. The same applies to the exaltation of Luther's doctrine of the "calling", which is a favourite idea of writers of modern books on the subject, which they try to interpret as a certain religious consecration and sanction of modern civilization. It is not due to thoughtlessness, therefore, when the idea is suggested that modern civilization means essentially an anti-Catholic freedom from sacerdotalism and from monasticism, and that otherwise it is a conservative middle-class restriction or weakening of the modern life-movement.[297]

The religious and ethical ideas of Lutheranism are not a glorification and intensification of definite class and power interests by means of a world outlook based upon those interests. This might perhaps apply to the peculiarly irrational idea of Natural Law which enabled Lutheranism to accept the existing conditions of authority, regarding the Law of Nature as though these conditions of authority, together with sin and inequality, were all part of the unchanging Divine Order, to which the soul (which remains inwardly free) gives itself up to labour and to endure. The reason for this lay, at least originally, and in Luther himself, not in any kind of class interest, but in the authoritative conservative temperament of Luther himself, and in his peculiarly penetrating conception of the nature of authority and power, as well as the essential inequality of the fundamental elements in all human social groupings. In this he is only perpetrating the

[296] Cf. *Joh. Val. Andreae: Reipublicae Christianopolitanae descriptio, Strassburg, 1619.* The spirit of the whole is decided Lutheran. The communism is taken over from the Utopias of the Humanists (private property and the aristocratic constitution are carefully maintained), but the whole is balanced by the principles of Lutheranism; cf. also *E. Ehrhardt: Un Roman Social Protestant au 17ème siècle, Paris, Fischbacher, 1908.*

[297] See p. 876.

patriarchal side of the scholastic Natural Law,[298] while he discards the individualistic rationalistic elements. This, however, is the reason why Luther also called these elements directly unchristian and the product of sin, and he only recognized them as a Divine institution within the sphere of sinful reason, under the impression of their unalterable nature and their absolute necessity. He was only able to combine this idea of Natural Law with his own general Christian idea by inculcating the spirit of humility, trust in God, readiness to suffer, and the fact that man, owing to the taint of Original Sin, deserves to be punished. When, later on, this idea of Natural Law was used simply to justify existing conditions, and the chief heirs of the Lutheran spirit at the present day, the Conservatives, developed this Natural Law into an aristocratic naturalism which is related to Darwin's doctrine of selection and to Nietzsche's ethic of the Super-Man, these are certainly applications of the idea in the interest of political and social domination, in which they display their flagrant opposition to the real Christian ideas and their "class" spirit. Further, this inconsistency is not usually apparent to most people, since they conclude that the non-Christian character of those principles is due to the situation created by sin, and therefore they do not merely retain them in spite of their unchristian character, but they are convinced that they ought to use them, as results of inequality and means of repression willed by God against the individualistic atomistic evil.[299] This theory also undoubtedly contains right views about the "nature" of man, and it contains no less incontrovertible ethical values in the ideas of obedience and of authority, just as in patriarchalism itself.[299a] Thus here also the ultimate cause is the old ideological basis, which only nowadays is so visibly useful to "the sectional interests" and is now associated with them to make some thoroughly impure combinations.

It is more difficult to answer the opposite question: What influence has Lutheranism had upon social history? Here, from the very outset, we must distinguish between the effects of its spiritual individualism, which manifest themselves plainly in the spiritual and ethical development of German culture right down to Kant and Goethe, and which has left traces of its influence in the idea and development of family life, and in the realm of political, social, and economic institutions.[300] It is essentially the latter with which we are here concerned.

[298] Cf. above, *pp. 285–288.*

[299] Cf. the numerous illustrations from modern Conservative literature in *Stillich, pp. 30–50.*

[299a] See p. 876.

[300] See p. 876.

The gist of the matter is this: in itself the late mediaeval tendency in the development of the State and the general social classification was not altered by Lutheranism. The only changes were the disappearance of the priesthood, which was replaced by the Protestant ministry, as well as the abolition of the supreme control by the Church, and the establishment of the system of purely State control which took its place; the process of secularization and the abolition of monasticism were also changes which cut deeply into the social fabric, but they did not initiate new social developments. The social fabric was more profoundly affected by the rise of a Humanistic educated class, which was encouraged by the didactic character of the new religion, and its close connection with education; yet this was rather an effect of Humanism combined with the Reform Movement than an effect produced by the religious spirit itself.[301]

Its political influence was more central. This does not mean that Lutheranism developed a new idea of the State, or even created a new State; but, by its renunciation of ecclesiastical independence, by its deification of the Government and its loyal passivity, it provided a most favourable setting for the development of the territorial State, which was then engaged in the process of self-development. It smoothed the way for territorial absolutism; to the feudal lords of the manor it made easier the development of the manorial estate with its privileges and the growth of a new kind of serfdom,[302] and it fostered the patriarchal attitude and the corporate class spirit.

In relation with foreign countries, however, the same Lutheran spirit hindered the action and expansion of the various States, and finally caused terrible defeats. Its only service to the actual modern State has been to encourage the spirit of absolutism; once that was supreme, however, it became strong enough to strike out on a modern line of its own, and it has thus gone far beyond the Lutheran principles of peace, protection, and punishment based on Natural Law as well as the duty of the Government to promote Christian charity.

The influence of Lutheranism in the economic sphere has been equally indirect. Here its essential spirit is that of traditionalism and agrarian middle-class production, which, by means of corporate solidarity, excludes competition, as far as possible

[301] Cf. *Wittich: Deutsche und Französische Kultur im Elsass, 1900*, a work which goes far beyond its explicit subject.

[302] On this point, see detailed illustrations in *Drews: Der Einfluss der Gesellschaftlichen Zustände.*

combining simplicity in one's requirements with simplicity of the conditions of production and consumption. Since it also abolished mendicancy, urged the masses to work, and by its individualism stimulated individuals, even on the non-religious side, and created a certain elasticity of mind by its system of education (which at first certainly only affected the middle classes), it has, in spite of everything, helped to develop economic life in a more vital way. Here, however, also the chief element in the whole process was the making of the secular authority independent, which, entrusted with social welfare and exalted to supreme power, introduced Western methods of production, and in so doing it profited by the fact that the Lutheran sections of the population were more inclined to work hard than the rest. Otherwise it was not for nothing that mercantilistic rulers introduced Calvinist or Pietist settlers wherever they wished to raise the level of trade or manufactures. The modern economic situation—even in the modest range which it had attained in Germany until the nineteenth century—has been created by the State, and is not due to the influence of Lutheranism.[303] Lutheranism opposed the modern development of the State only one degree less ardently than Catholicism.

Finally, so far as its main social tendencies are concerned, and its theoretical conception of Society, Lutheranism has always represented the principle of patriarchalism and conservatism. This was caused in part by the fact that the fundamental religious temper of trust in God and distrust of human effort and industry, the relation of the sense of sin with suffering and endurance, in itself tended to foster a conservative spirit, and in part by the fact that the bases of the earlier social constitution, with its class organization and the greater simplicity of the relation to the Divine gifts of Nature, are firmly retained by Lutheranism as the presupposition of its ethical ideals. Thus Lutheranism is inclined to endure existing conditions humbly and patiently, even when they are bad, and to glorify them when they agree with those earlier ideals. If, speaking generally, the Protestant countries are the most progressive at the present time, we must not forget, on the other hand, that during the period when the Protestant churches were being formed the mother-lands of modern civilization—Italy, France, and Spain—were Catholic, and that their exhaustion has no connection with their Catholicism—that, thus, on the other hand, the Protestant countries too, and especially the Lutheran, cannot in any case ascribe their present position

[303] See p. 877.

primarily to their religious bases, however important these may be in particular.[304]

The passivity of Lutheranism involved the habit of falling back upon whatever power happens to be dominant at the time. When it was suggested that this attitude left Christians at the mercy of every rogue and brutal tyrant, Luther replied that the Government ought to see that this did not happen, and that if it failed to prevent it, then certainly the Christian must simply suffer for it. Thus everywhere Lutheranism came under the influence of the dominant authority. The yielding spirit of its wholly interior spirituality adapted itself to the dominant authority of the day. This meant, however, that the form Lutheranism took was controlled by the various forms of government with which it was connected. It had no theoretical tendency towards monarchism or absolutism at all[305]; this theory was only an invention of the modern Conservatives. It was only because absolutism and the system of manorial estates arose in Central and North Germany that it there developed the loyal spirit which characterizes *Ostelbiertum*.* In the Imperial towns it glorified aristocratic-republican rule. In Württemberg, where there was no corresponding nobility, although it held the ruling prince in all honour, it did not hinder bourgeois and peasant democratic ideas, but even fused itself with them. In the military national State of Sweden it justified the aggressive policy of Gustavus Adolfus, and in the class struggles in the Austrian territories it justified the rise of the Lutheran nobility[306]; in Denmark and Norway a very firmly established peasant democracy is to-day united most closely

[304] Cf. on the whole subject, *Troeltsch: Die Bedeutung des Protestantismus für die Entstehung der modernen Welt, 1906* (see also *Hist. Zeitschrift, 1905*). *Haendtke* shows the severance of general civilization from the specific Lutheran presuppositions while retaining their formulas.

[305] Cf. *Brandenburg, p. 18.* Luther replied to the question why God has created authorities of so many different kinds by saying: "Is God obliged to give chapter and verse to such useless fools why He wants to have it thus?" Also radical monarchical Divine Right as is taught by *Horn* in his *Politicorum pars architectonica de civitate Traj. a. Rh., 1664* (analysed by *von Gierke: Althusius,*[2] *p. 70 f.*) is not genuinely Lutheran, but it has grown up out of opposition to the Calvinistic doctrine of contract and is filled with the ideas of princely absolutism.

* Translator.—I.e. the Nationalist spirit, which is the distinctive feature of the landed aristocracy in the agricultural districts east of the Elbe.

[306] Thus, for example, *Bernhard von Weimar* was able to justify from the religious point of view his brigandage as "a royal calling" (*Haendtke, p. 19*). Gustavus Adolfus was politically an admirer of the quite un-Lutheran *Hugo Grotius*, whose chief work he always carried about with him; *H. G.: Recht des Krieges und Friedens, Phil. Bibl. 15, p. 8.*

with a sturdy Lutheranism, which is certainly tinged with Pietism; and in America the most orthodox Lutheranism one can imagine flourishes under the wing of democracy.

We must, however, admit that by its very nature Lutheranism adapts itself most easily to political conditions of a monarchical and aristocratic kind, and to an economic social situation which is predominantly agrarian and middle class. Hence it has found its strongest form of expression in the politics and world-outlook of the Prussian and German Conservatives, through whom to-day Lutheranism still helps to determine the destinies of the German people.

Social and Political Significance of Lutheranism

In the aggressive position which, after the eighteenth century had culminated in the French Revolution, the older spiritual forces again adopted towards the modern world, and in which they, with the union of ideological and practical politico-social powers, advanced victoriously against the new world, the restoration of Prussian-German Lutheranism was one of the most important events in social history.[307] It united with the reactionary movement the monarchical ideas of agrarian patriarchalism, of the militaristic love of power; it gave an ideal to the political Restoration and its ethical support. For this reason, then, it in its turn was supported by the social and political forces of reaction, by all the means of power at their disposal. Finally, Lutheranism of this type hallowed the realistic sense of power, and the ethical virtues of obedience, reverence, and respect for authority, which are indispensable to Prussian militarism. Thus Christianity and a Conservative political attitude became identified with each other, as well as piety and love of power, purity of doctrine, and the glorification of war and the aristocratic standpoint. Thus all attempts at Church reform were suppressed along with the world of Liberal thought; the representatives of modern social and spiritual tendencies were forced into an attitude of strong hostility to the Church, and all whose sympathies were Christian and religious were enlisted on the Conservative side. As an essential element in the forces of the Restoration, Lutheranism played an important part in the political and military development of German Prussia which arose out of the forces of the Restoration; and it was thus in violent opposition to all those other elements which worked together to produce a new Germany, the democratic-union elements and modern social and economic move-

[307] See p. 878.

ments. Along with the international Catholic Restoration policy which was akin to it, and yet so very different from it, and with which it is in contact, sometimes friendly, sometimes hostile—Lutheranism occupies the key position of the most difficult and pregnant problems affecting the life of Germany, and does its part towards widening the gulf between the forces which support the patriarchalism of the Restoration and those which support the cause of democracy and progress, a gulf in which all moderate attempts at reconciliation are drowned; the longing to bridge over this gulf in Germany with a Christian-Social programme was an idealistic and praiseworthy but fleeting and swiftly refuted dream.

For the great majority of orthodox Christians in Germany the traditions and the spiritual constitution of Lutheranism made any such reconciliation impossible; and on the other hand, the unrestrained hatred towards the Church which characterized all progressive and democratic elements belonging to that group of movements also made any kind of union impossible. Thus Lutheranism naturally does little towards building up a new social structure. In the main its efforts are confined to the philanthropic activity of the Home Mission Movement; otherwise its tendency is to alleviate but not to re-create. Wherever the Christian-Social ethic and social policy strikes out in another direction we may be sure that other influences are at work than those of genuine Lutheranism. As a rule these influences are due to Calvinism, and thus we come to the second great confessional structure of Protestantism: Calvinism.

3. CALVINISM

Calvinism and Lutheranism contrasted

After a period of initial success Lutheranism ceased to advance. This must be attributed, in the main, to its stress on personal piety, its acceptance of the existing situation, its acquiescence in the objectivity of the means of grace, as well as to its lack of capacity for ecclesiastical organization, and its non-political outlook. It was the destiny of Calvinism to extend the Reformation of the Church throughout Western Europe, and thence out into the New World, and, actually, Calvinism is the chief force in the Protestant world to-day.

The primary reason for this wide-spread extension of Calvinism was the fact that it gained a footing among the Western nations at a time when they were passing through a great process of political development. There is, however, a deeper reason, and one which lies within the essence of Calvinism itself, which explains why it almost or entirely crowded out the rudimentary beginnings of Lutheranism and of the Anabaptist movement, which were also present in those lands. This deeper reason lies in the active character of Calvinism, in its power for forming Churches, in its international contacts, and its conscious impulse towards expansion, and, most of all, in its capacity to penetrate the political and economic movements of Western nations with its religious ideal, a capacity which Lutheranism lacked from the very beginning.[308]

Thus the social doctrines of Calvinism and its conception of the Church also differed considerably from those of Lutheranism. In course of time this difference became more and more pronounced, with the result that at the present day Calvinism feels itself to be the only Christian ecclesiastical body which is in agreement with the modern democratic and capitalistic development, and, moreover, the only one which is suited to it.[309] In spite of the fact that originally it was very closely connected with Lutheranism, Calvinism—while retaining its orthodoxy—has gradually become the very opposite of Lutheranism, with its State Church character, its institutionalism, and its conservatism.

From the political and social point of view the significance of Lutheranism for the modern history of civilization lies in its connection with the reactionary parties; from the religious and scientific standpoint its significance lies in the development of a philosophical theology, which is blended with a religious mysticism and "inward" spirituality, but which, from the ethical point of view, is quite remote from the problems of modern political and social life.

Calvinism, on the other hand (in more recent times under the influence of Pietism and Methodism to which it is closely akin), has, upon the whole, maintained its unphilosophical theology, or at least after the disturbances of the Enlightenment it rediscovered it. In its close connection with English and American racial peculiarities and institutions, however, it has merged with and to some extent produced that political and social way of life which may be described as "Americanism". It is obvious that to-day this "Americanism" has an independent existence, which is almost entirely divorced from a religious basis

308 See p. 879.

309 See p. 879.

of any kind.[310] Calvinism has, however, also had a reflex influence upon the Continent of Europe. It has influenced Lutheranism not only in the conception and constitution of the Church, in the life of Christian social activity and fellowship initiated by the Church, in Home Missions, in Pietism, but, as a universal spiritual force, the type of humanity which it produces affects the whole of European civilization; for the most part, however, this civilization is entirely unconscious of its original connection with Calvinism. During this process of development, Calvinism came into touch with the sects, which, as will become evident later on, tended to approach Calvinism along their own line. Together with the sects, and in co-operation with political and social conditions, Calvinism has produced that particular type of humanity which has just been described. This will become fully evident when we have studied the question of the sect-type within the sphere of Protestantism. Yet it is important to call attention to this fact here, in order that we may take into account that particular point in Calvinism at which, in its main ideas, it came into closer or more permanent touch with the sect-type than was the case with Luther (of course, I am alluding only to his earlier period).

Calvinism has developed into a very widespread movement, which has expanded far beyond its beginnings at Geneva. In order to understand Calvinism, therefore, our primary task is to distinguish the primitive Calvinism of Geneva from its later forms of development. At the outset, however, we must ask the following questions. To what extent are these later developments the logical outcome of primitive Calvinism? How far do they transcend it? and what were the causes which led to this development?

In such great questions, which are connected with the whole history of civilization, from the very outset it is clear that developments of that kind were not influenced merely by the logical dialectic and impelling energy of the religious idea, but also by the particular historical situation at any given time. On the other hand, Calvinism is such a magnificent austere intellectual system that we are bound to try to discover the inner intellectual connection which either persists through all these changes or is restored by them.[311]

[310] On this point cf. *Rauschenbusch: Christianity and the Social Crisis, New York, 1908.* Hundeshagen describes the astonishment of an American student who thought that in Germany Christianity was a science, while in America it was a practical matter.

[311] See p. 879.

Primitive Calvinism

Thus our first task is to analyse the distinctive religious content of primitive Calvinism, upon which was logically constructed the edifice of its conception of the Church, its ethic, and its social ideals. Only when that has been accomplished can we inquire into the later development of Calvinism, and the changes which have taken place in later Calvinism, in the political, economic, social, and ecclesiastico-political sphere.

Primitive Calvinism is the daughter of Lutheranism. Originally it had no other desire than to be purely Lutheran, both from the theological and the religious point of view, part of a great united Protestant body, able to absorb all fanatical movements into its own life. In its second phase, under the influence of Bucer, it assimilated the element of truth contained in the Anabaptist movement, i.e. the practical social development of the congregation, and in so doing it also came into contact with the Reformation in Switzerland. Early Calvinism secured the Lutheran doctrine of the sacraments against Zwingli by making certain concessions, and yet it preserved their original meaning intact. Finally, in union with the Upper Germans, it completed the strict purification of public worship from all Catholic ceremonies, at which point it came into agreement with Zwingli; all it aimed at, however, in this connection, was to carry out more logically Luther's principle of obedience to the Word of God. While Calvin was insisting on the strictest purity and unity of doctrine in Geneva itself, he still believed that by making certain concessions on questions which were not vital to the main principle he would be able to unite the various countries and Churches in one great united Protestant body. It was only the resistance of German Lutheranism, and the independence of Anglicanism, which forced Calvinism to become an independent Protestant Church.[312]

Thus, the central element in Calvin's theology and piety was of Lutheran origin. Calvin always laid great stress upon his agreement with Luther, and upon his personal relations with him. He considered Luther the Reformer *par excellence*, but he was not greatly attracted by Zwingli, and he treated him with reserve. Calvin owed his conversion essentially to Lutheran influences, and he also made use of Lutheran literature. So far as the other influences in his life are concerned—the Humanistic theology of the Reform, the Swiss purification of the Church,

[312] See p. 880.

and the ecclesiastical-social reform and union policy of Strassburg—he himself ascribed all that was really essential to Luther. His Lutheranism was certainly of the Upper German, and particularly of the Strassburg, kind, coloured by Bucer's union tendencies, the conditions in the city itself, the competition of the Anabaptists, and the influence of the neighbouring inhabitants of Zürich, but it was Lutheranism none the less.

The fundamental doctrines of Luther were therefore also the fundamental doctrines of Calvin. Calvin held firmly the Lutheran doctrines of justification and sanctification; indeed, of all the Reformers, he actually expressed them in their purest systematic form. Over against the absolute corruption caused by sin and the helplessness of the natural man, he proclaims the certainty of the forgiveness of sins and of the Divine Mercy freely given by God in Christ, and the transformation of the soul into joyful communion with God, with moral power and strength to undertake active labour in the service of God. Further, just as with Luther, this doctrine of justification and sanctification is firmly embodied in the framework of the idea of the Church. It is only completed through the agency of the Church as an organ of salvation, endowed with the objective means of grace in the Word and the sacraments; everywhere the Church only produces subjective and personal religious life by means of the Scriptures, and of the Christ revealed in Scriptures.

The main features of the Calvinistic religious system may then be summed up as follows: a strict insistence upon the Church as the organ which mediates salvation; a very strong and definite emphasis upon the sacraments as objective Divine means of grace; the fact of the vital connection between Calvinism and the Primitive Church (contrasted with the apostasy of the Papacy); the logical establishment of the Church upon the Bible, as the supernatural element which creates faith, and also proves its supernatural origin by creating fellowship; the catholicity of the Church wherever the Word and the sacraments have been preserved, even under the veil of error and false ceremonies; a universal and uniform dominion of the truth of the Church within the sphere which it can win and control; the theocratic union of Church and State, and the compulsory enforcement of the "pure doctrine", at least externally; the closest union between Church and State, while allowing each to retain its fundamentally distinct character; the acceptance of secular culture and the penetration of the system of "callings" belonging to the realm of Natural Law, with the Christian spirit; the identification of the Decalogue with the Law of Nature and the approximation of positive law to both; and, last of all, its conception of the Church itself.

All these ideas Calvin adopted as finished products, and his system was therefore free from the fluctuations amidst which Luther first of all worked out these conceptions, and he shaped them with the doctrinaire logic which is peculiar to men of a second generation, due to their sense of possessing a secure inheritance.[313]

Distinctive Features of Primitive Calvinism

Thus all the distinctive features of Calvinism have only been evolved out of the main stock of the ideal which it holds in common with Lutheranism. That, however, does not imply that these features are unimportant; on the contrary, they are original, and of the highest significance. These peculiarly Calvinistic elements turned the religious thought of Protestantism into a new channel, and it is not difficult to understand why this new tendency was finally rejected by Lutheranism, whose outlook was so entirely different. The essential differences lie within the sphere of the Idea of God, of the fundamental, religious, and ethical attitude which that involves, and finally in the sphere of the peculiar conception of social duty which this implies.

(I) Doctrine of Predestination

The first distinctive feature of Calvinism, and the most important one, is the idea of predestination, the famous central doctrine of Calvinism. It is the expression—gradually formulated and finally strongly emphasized—of Calvin's peculiar idea of God. In this matter also Calvin is the disciple of Luther, and the doctrine of predestination is primarily only the logical and systematic emphasis upon the main aspect of Lutheran doctrine, which is also a central point in Pauline doctrine, and which, in his strict obedience to the Bible, he regarded as a directly obligatory article of faith. It constitutes that particular element in Lutheran doctrine by which the purity of the Reformed Faith was protected against any admixture with the alloy of human ideas and opinions. Faith is not a human faculty at all, it is a perception given by God as an absolute miracle; at the same time the human element in the shape of all human "merit" and all "natural" human activity is excluded, while the emphasis on "grace" in a religion based on faith is fully preserved.

Thus, at first sight, Calvin's doctrine of predestination seems

[313] See p. 881.

to owe its significance only to the inferior acuteness of a disciple who has systematized his master's teaching and has thus manifested the driving force of the motive behind the whole system. But Calvin was more than a disciple or a mere imitator of Luther.

Behind his doctrine of predestination there lay also that idea of God which was the peculiar element in his own personal piety. In the idea of predestination Calvin is not merely trying to discover and formulate the absolute miracle of salvation, its supernatural character, and the fact that it is a pure gift of free grace (its "givenness"); he is also trying to express the character of God as absolute sovereign will.

Calvin's idea of grace is that of pure unmerited grace, and is not in any way concerned with any thought of justice which the creature, in its misery, might desire to claim from the Lord of the World. It is the Nature of God to give salvation to some without any merit on their part, purely out of His own freewill and choice, and to prepare destruction for others on account of their sinfulness. No one has any right either to boast or to complain. Just as no one can choose whether he will be a human being or an animal, so no one has any right to claim to belong to the "elect" rather than to the "damned". God's majestic sovereign will is the supreme cause, the supreme standard. The reasons and norms which do exist gain their significance only from God; there are none which can be applied to Him, or to which He must bow. In entire and arbitrary freedom He lays down the law for Himself; and this law is the law of His own glory which is served both by the gratitude of the undeserved bliss of the elect and by the misery of the merited despair of the damned. This means that no longer, as in Lutheranism, is the idea of Love at the centre of the conception of God, but the idea of Majesty, in which the impartation and influence of the Love of God is only regarded as a method of revealing the Majesty of God. According to this conception God did not create the world out of a sense of need for the responsive love of His creatures; His world-plan has not been disturbed by the freewill of the creature, and salvation does not consist in the restoration of universal beatitude to all creatures through the miracle of redemption. Rather it is the inscrutable Will of God which is the basis of the world, and the cause of its whole course. God ordained the sin of Adam, and he makes use both of sinners and of those who are justified in His world-economy; the elect are a symbol of His mercy, which bestows all that is good merely through the exercise of His Will, and the damned serve as a symbol of His wrath against all that is unhallowed and evil. To Calvin the chief point is not the self-centred personal salvation of the creature, and the universality of the Divine Will of Love, but it is the Glory of God, which is equally exalted in the holy activity of the elect and in the futile rage of the reprobate. In His Gospel God offers His grace to all, but in the same Gospel He proclaims the duality of His counsel of election and of reprobation, to which reason must submit without making any attempts to harmonize these two aspects of the truth.

Luther also had thus distinguished between the hidden and the revealed God, but in the end Luther held to the revealed God of the New Testament, and gave up speculation. Calvin retained it, and in so doing he transformed the whole idea of God.[314]

This new conception of God contains a wealth of implications. From the outset it frees Calvinism from all the problems of the Theodicy which weigh so heavily upon Lutheranism, and which, while holding fast to the universality of the will of grace, lead again and again to the problem of the righteousness of God, and make salvation dependent upon the receptive will of the creature. Within this conception there is room for different purposes of God to exist alongside of each other; He reveals Himself in the *Gratia universalis*, in all the gifts of reason, and in the beauty of the world, in the elect and in the non-elect, and in all these gifts He does not need to limit His purpose solely to redemption; He reveals Himself in pains and penalties, which are not merely means of education, purification, and expansion, but which are decreed by His Sovereign Will in order to represent His wrath, to steel the courage of His saints, and to prove the nothingness of the material world; He reveals Himself most intimately, though not exclusively, in the bliss of those who are justified, who may have unlimited confidence in God, who, however, must also serve Him without reserve.

Although in his correspondence Calvin expounds with ardour the ways of Divine Providence, this does not mean that he is trying to "justify the ways of God to men"; his aim is simply to prove how God is guiding, testing, and saving the Church; to heroism of this kind suffering, in itself, is no problem at all.[315] This idea of God is not drawn from the Old Testament, except, perhaps, indirectly through Paul. It is the unique product of Calvin's own mind, to which, certainly, certain elements in the thought of the Old Testament were congenial.

A further result of this conception of God is the practical and

[314] See p. 883.

[315] See p. 883.

ethical intention which it gives to the idea of justification; for justification does not mean a quietistic repose in thankful happiness, but a method of activity and a spur to action. The Will, with which the soul has to do, is active; it is not simply the Mercy which forgives sins. God creates, and grants in election, the assurance of the forgiveness of sins, in order that the soul which has been set free from guilt may serve Him as an instrument of His Will. Through justification the elect are made members of the Body of Christ, penetrated with the active spirit of Christ; they become Christ's warriors and champions, subjects in His Kingdom. The proof of justification does not consist in inwardness and depth of feeling, but in energy and the logical result of action. In Lutheranism the real proof and verification of justification is that happiness which the world cannot give, which reaches its highest point in close connection with the Christ who substantially unites Himself in the Eucharist with the believer in the *Unio mystica*, in a mystical union with God.

In Calvinism, with its emphasis upon the transcendence of God, such a proof could not be imagined; union with God can only be understood in the sense of surrender to the electing and renewing will of God, and as an activity of the ever active ("*actuosen*") God in the believer, which indeed in the Eucharist results in an actual union with the exalted Christ, but only in spirit, since communion with Christ is not one of substance at all, but it means being absorbed into the active and effectual spirit of Christ. "*Finitum non est capax infiniti*" is the principle of Calvinism, and that gives both to the idea of justification and to that of faith a different psychological meaning: instead of the characteristic of happiness in the grace of God which forgives sins, we find the certainty of belonging to the elect, and a spirit of active energy.[316]

It is impossible to describe here in further detail the way in which these views changed the whole colour of the body of theology which Calvinism held in common with Lutheranism.[317] It is, however, significant that from this time forward the whole body of doctrine, the "pure doctrine" itself, in spite of its orthodoxy, gained a quite different position in the whole intellectual system. To the Lutheran, salvation and blessedness become objective in the "pure doctrine" (which alone can produce these effects), which is also the heart of the ecclesiastical institution,

[316] This characteristic, above all, has been very well developed by *Schneckenburger* and continued by *Max Weber: Archiv. XXI, pp. 21–25.*

[317] This has been done in a masterly way, although perhaps almost too completely, by *Schneckenburger*.

and the one objective element in Christianity. To the Calvinist, in addition to the "pure doctrine", there is the moral law, as the expression of grace and discipline, as the expression of the active Divine Will. To the Calvinist the creative centre of the Church is the "pure doctrine", combined with a Divinely revealed discipline. In Calvin's mind God cannot reveal Himself solely in purity of doctrine; He must also manifest His active and creative nature as an energy of will. Purity of doctrine, therefore, is not, as in Lutheranism, the exclusive concern of the Church, since, to the Lutheran, purity of doctrine guarantees purity of faith, and with this all else comes naturally. The "pure doctrine" is not an end in itself, but, just as faith is the presupposition of right action, so also pure doctrine is only a presupposition and a means to some further end. That means certainly that, as well as the systematic statement of aim which characterises Calvinism, there is also a theoretical development in doctrine which extends beyond the requirements of Lutheranism; but the doctrine which is developed, in spite of all its system and its comprehensiveness, still remains a means to an end, the presupposition of that which is really valuable—of Christian conduct. This explains why Calvinism, with its severe logic and its acceptance of the culture of Western Europe, maintains a far higher intellectual standard than Lutheranism, and yet lays far less emphasis on doctrine and on system. To Calvin, God is irrational in the sense that He is not to be measured by the standards of human reason and logic. God, he teaches, gave us reason to aid us in our work in the world, and for the glory of God. Thus the keenest and the most cultivated intellect, and the clearest formulation of doctrine, are only of use as tools for purposes which are above the grasp of the intellect and as a preparation for action.[318]

Finally, we must note yet another ultimate effect of this idea of God which has had a considerable influence upon practical ethics: the altered conception of the Bible, the source of, and the authority for, the "pure doctrine". The sovereign Will of God made known in election, and in the preparation of a community of the elect, does not manifest itself merely in the spirit of love and in the atoning sacrifice of the love of Christ, which, as the very heart of the Bible, is seized and isolated by the faith which experiences its power in such a way that the rest of the Bible seems comparatively insignificant, or at least it merely serves the purpose of pointing forward to Christ. Rather the revelation of

[318] See p. 883.

the sovereign predestination of God is, as a whole, a positive revelation of will, a law of faith and of morals. Since the predominant idea in the Calvinistic conception of God is not love, but majesty, holiness, sovereign power, and grace, so also the Bible is regarded less as a means of attaining the assurance of the love of God which forgives sins than a manifestation which should create a community in which the glory of God will be realized, which will also result in the overthrow of evil men and of reprobates. To Protestants of the second generation it seemed quite natural to give the Bible an abstract independent position; this was a logical effect of Luther's attitude to the Bible, in which it constituted the final court of appeal. In Calvinism, therefore, the Bible, regarded as that which had been founded by the anti-rational positive Will of God, then became, further, a law, whose aim and nature were of equal value in every part, in which both the Old Testament and the New Testament bear the common official character of revelation, and in which the only distinction between them lies in the fact that certain Old Testament elements have been explicitly discarded by the New Testament. In Calvinism, therefore, the Old Testament attains a higher and more independent position.

Since the Calvinistic Idea of God is in many ways similar to the Idea of Jahweh whose Being is Will, the necessities of practical life led to an increasing use of the Old Testament, as we shall see directly. This development, however, meant that the Calvinistic Theocracy became a Divine covenant with the Church upon the basis of revelation, in which the State is to serve the Church after the manner of the Kings of Israel, and in which public life is controlled by the pastors after the manner of the Prophets. Thus we may sum up the Gospel of Calvin in the following terms: a new Israel has been born, a new holy city has been founded, established upon the Divine Law, which has been deepened by the spirit of the New Testament, directed by the Will and the Grace of God which deals out punishments and rewards, elected to be the organ for the glorification of Christ, the God-man, in whom the hidden electing will has become flesh, with power to create the community of the Church.

Here, as at several other points, there emerges a certain resemblance to the Baptists, which will occupy our attention a good deal from time to time. The Calvinistic doctrines of predestination and salvation are, of course, poles apart from the Baptist doctrine of freedom, but the idea of the Bible which produces the idea of predestination comes very near to the Baptist conception of the Bible. The Baptists held the same view of the Bible as the moral law, and they also considered the constitution of the Primitive Church to be the ideal Church constitution. The basis of Calvin's argument is certainly very different from that of the Baptists. He does not share their desire to found a new and entirely different religious community instead of the Church. His one desire was to effect a radical reform of the Church in harmony with the teaching of the Scriptures, and for this he found Scriptural authority in a conception of God which was directed at the same time towards the creation of a Church which is Scriptural, pure, and holy. In so doing, however, he went beyond the idea of the Church as the organ of salvation, based purely upon itself, and came into contact with the leading ideas of the Baptist movement. He came very near to their Scriptural purism. The Lutherans were only interested in the Bible to the extent in which it was concerned with the Church as the organ of grace, the forgiveness of sins, and the work of Christ upon which all this is based, and in this respect certainly they often used the Bible as a law which regulates doctrine. Beyond that point, however, they felt no need to make it into a law. Calvinism, however, did feel this need. It extended the authority of the Bible over a wider field, and in the process it transformed the whole conception of the Bible into an infallible authority for all the problems and needs of the Church. Lutheranism controlled the doctrine which it had evolved out of inward experience by the Bible; Calvinism sought to renew the whole of Christianity, in doctrine and the Church, in ethics and in dogma, solely through the Bible. Its greater reforming radicalism was due to this fact, and to the active character of its religion, which was based upon the doctrine of election.[319]

(II) Individualism

Thus as Calvinism has developed the Lutheran doctrine of predestination, and of the idea of God, in a fresh light, the same development also took place in its second distinctive characteristic—that of religious individualism. Luther was always ultimately concerned with the individual's assurance of salvation, and his happiness, flowing from the forgiveness of sins; everything else, however, is merely the overflow which radiates from union with God, it is only a natural result, not an essential end.

Calvin's view is different. He also emphasizes the need for inwardness and the purely personal individual character of all

[319] See p. 884.

piety. He also rejects a faith that is based merely on dogma and authority, and discards all ideas of sacramentarian magic; he also teaches that the new life must spring from faith. But since to him the central point of religion is not the blessedness of the creature, but the Glory of God, so also the glorification of God in action is the real test of individual personal reality in religion. In Calvin's view the individual is not satisfied with mere repose in his own happiness, or perhaps with giving himself to others in loving personal service; further, he is not satisfied with an attitude of mere passive endurance and toleration of the world in which he lives, without entering fully into its life. He feels that, on the contrary, the whole meaning of life consists precisely in entering into these circumstances, and, while inwardly rising above them, in shaping them into an expression of the Divine Will. In conflict and in labour the individual takes up the task of the sanctification of the world, always with the certainty, however, that he will not lose himself in the life of the world; for indeed in everything the individual is only working out the meaning of election, which indeed consists in being strengthened to perform actions of this kind.

Within Lutheranism a position of this kind would be untenable, for Lutheranism believes that it is possible to fall away from the state of grace. This is the point at which there is the greatest divergence of opinion between the two aspects of religious individualism, which characterize the Protestant religion of faith and sentiment. Lutheranism does not think out the doctrine of predestination to its logical conclusion, i.e. the impossibility of losing the state of grace. The reason for this lies in the fact that from the very outset the one aim of Lutheranism is to secure the monergism of grace in all that is good, while it teaches that evil is due to the human will alone. Thus the supreme concern of the Lutheran is the preservation of faith and of the state of grace, a constantly renewed effort to maintain intact the purity and stability of a faith which is independent of "works" or "merit". Hence all the emphasis is placed upon the cultivation of the emotional life of the individual, on the maintenance of the sense of an unmerited happiness, and the Christian ethic is regarded merely as the preservation of the state of grace, which can be lost either by falling into grave sin, or by relying upon one's own strength.

Calvinism, however, does not believe that the individual can ever lose the state of grace, and therefore it has no trace of this fear of losing grace. Hence it does not need to lower the tone of the religious life to the level of self-preservation in the state of grace, and it feels that a constant preoccupation with personal moods and feelings is entirely unnecessary. The Calvinist knows that his calling and election are sure, and that therefore he is free to give all his attention to the effort to mould the world and society according to the Will of God. He does not need to cling to God lest he should lose Him; on the contrary, he knows that he himself is absolutely dependent upon God's sustaining grace. His duty, therefore, is not to preserve the "new creation" in its intimacy with God, but to reveal it.

Thus from all sides the individualism of the "Reformed"* Church was impelled towards activity; the individual was drawn irresistibly into a whole-hearted absorption in the tasks of service to the world and to society, to a life of unceasing, penetrating, and formative labour. This does not mean merely that Calvinistic individualism in its austerity and reserve is more firmly established upon a basis of religious metaphysics; still more important is the fact that it does not suffer from constant breakdowns and reactions like those which characterize the Lutheran way of life, and rivet the attention of Lutheranism again and again simply to the fact of the forgiveness of sins. Calvinism organizes the work of preservation logically and systematically, straightforwardly and with a clear aim in view. Above all, however, this specifically Calvinistic individualism possesses this peculiar characteristic that in its refusal to expand on the emotional side, and in its habit of placing confidence in God in the foreground and all human relations in the background, in going out of itself it always directs its attention towards concrete aims and purposes. Calvin's correspondence reveals an amazing objectivity and personal reserve, combined with an unceasing gathering together of all for the purposes of the Christian community. As an "elect" person the individual has no value of his own, but as an instrument, to be used for the tasks of the Kingdom of God, his value is immense.

This individualism differs not only from Catholic and Lutheran individualism, but also from the optimistic, rationalistic individualism of the Enlightenment. Founded upon a crushing sense of sin, and a pessimistic condemnation of the world, without colour or emotional satisfaction, it is an individualism based upon the certainty of election, the sense of responsibility and of the obligation to render personal service under the Lordship of

* The term "Reformed" is used throughout this book in the technical sense of "Calvinistic.—Translator's Note.

Christ. It finds its expression in the thoughtful and self-conscious type of Calvinistic piety, in the systematic spirit of self-control, and in its independence of all that is "creaturely". The value of the individual depends wholly upon the merciful grace of election, and it may give honour to none save God alone. This leads to the result that against a background of the severest self-condemnation there stands out in clear relief in Calvinism the sense of being a spiritual aristocracy; this produces a detached and aloof manner of handling all that is secular and creaturely, solely with reference to their secular purposes, which extends into all merely secular and natural personal relationships.

Calvin's successors, however—both in the sphere of theology and of practical pastoral work—were soon faced with this question, which became more and more insistent as time went on: How is it possible to be certain that one is of the number of the elect? From the time of Beza the current reply was that the fact of election was proved by good works, which are outward signs of the inward state of grace. This idea, which was developed more and more explicitly as time went on, drove the individual (who, in Lutheranism could rely on the objective means of grace) to the practice of self-examination and to systematic concentration on his own independent achievement. This tended to make the individual increasingly egocentric, and it also produced a strained intensity in the pursuit of the utmost possible perfection. Under certain circumstances this spirit approaches legalism and perfectionism; ultimately, although the effect of election is most strictly bound up with the Church, the Scriptures, and the Sacraments, it makes the individual independent of the Church, and assurance, like election, becomes entirely a matter for the individual to ascertain. Without intending to do so, however, this individualism had developed an individualistic independence of the Church, which bore some resemblance to the individualism of the sect-type. The severe self-control, based on the standard of the Bible, which is characteristic of Calvinism, is also akin to the sect-type, in spite of the fact that the whole idea is steeped in the ideas of the Church and of grace; this self-control is attained again and again by ascribing all individual personality and its achievements to the working out of predestination.[320]

(III) The "Holy Community"

The third distinctive characteristic of Calvinism—the central significance of the idea of a society, and the task of the restoration

[320] See p. 884.

of a holy community, of a Christocracy in which God is glorified in all its activity, both sacred and secular—seems to be opposed to this kind of individualism. This idea of a "holy community", however, has not been evolved out of the conception of the Church and of grace, like the Lutheran ecclesiastical idea; on the contrary, it springs out of the same principle which appears to give independence to the individual, namely, out of the ethical duty of the preservation and making effective of election, and out of the abstract exaltation of the Scriptures.

To Calvin the Church is not merely an organ of salvation which provides the objective means of grace, from which everything else should develop as a logical result, and from the standpoint of which the ungodliness of the world must be supported in patience and humility. The organ of salvation ought rather at the same time to provide the means of sanctification; it ought to prove itself effective in the Christianizing of the community, by placing the whole range of life under the control of Christian regulations and Christian purposes. At the same time it ought to develop the necessary organs by means of which the community can be moulded by the Divine Spirit and the Divine Word, in every aspect of life: in Church and State, in the family and in society, in economic life, and in all personal relationships, both public and private.

This theory represents the final development of ideas, which Luther had suggested during the years of ferment and of local reforms, but which he was obliged to drop for lack of real Christians to carry them out. Calvin's aim, however, was somewhat different from that of Luther; it was also more practicable. In this question Luther, with his emphasis upon freedom and personality, was mainly concerned with the logical results of the principle of the priesthood of all believers—i.e. with the autonomous administration and self-government of the community; the community could, of course, at the same time evolve the means of self-control and discipline, but all was to be done in complete freedom. But, just because his main concern was the universal priesthood of believers, he drew back from realizing his principle through the revolutionary democratic movement, and contented himself merely with ensuring the proclamation of pure doctrine by dependence upon the territorial Princes. Calvin, however, was not concerned with the priesthood of believers, but with making the control and the purity of the Church effective.[321] He was so

[321] Cf. *Rieker, pp. 139 ff.* (he is very good on this point); also *Köstlin: Stud. und Krit., 1868, p. 483.*

deeply convinced that this was necessary that he did not doubt that, just as in the case of doctrine, the Scriptures would provide him with the necessary support and counsel. Thus, in precisely the same way that Luther deduced his doctrine from the Bible, Calvin also evolved his theory of the constitution and Christian organization of the Church from the Scriptures. In his view the Holy Scriptures contained, in addition to the doctrines of justification and predestination, the constitution of the Church in the famous four orders: pastors, teachers or theoretical theologians, deacons or those who relieved the wants of the poor, and the board of discipline, which was to be composed of ministers, and elected representatives of the local congregations or elders. The fact that Calvin made the ethical interest of sanctification and the exhortations of Scripture the starting-point for his theory instead of the requirements of the priesthood of believers, secured his religious system against all democratic and revolutionary excesses, and against the perils of religious subjectivity. The participation of the congregation which was possible within these limits, in the choice of a pastor proposed to them by the ecclesiastical collegium, in the choice of deacons, elders, and administrators of discipline, made room within the ecclesiastical system itself for those ideas of the universal priesthood, and of personal religion, which could then be allowed to continue without harm, and without any danger of being diverted into secular and democratic channels. In Luther's theory ethics and Church organization were not based upon Scriptural doctrine, but everything was left to free development; further, Luther could not admit that the ethical end was more important than the happiness of justification; these two facts made it impossible for him to find a way out of the difficulty along Calvin's lines. Luther was obliged to give up his idea of the Church which he had evolved solely from the standpoint of the priesthood of all believers, and revert to the objective institution of the ministry of the Word, which was merely menaced, and not furthered, by handing over questions of organization and discipline to the local congregations. Calvin, however, saw no difficulty in this question at all. From his point of view the task of the Church and the constitution of the Church supplemented each other admirably, since the same Word which bore witness to the faith as doctrine effected agreement to the moral and constitutional ordinances, and thus from the outset the universal priesthood was placed under effective control without being abolished.[322]

[322] This is told in detail by *Hundeshagen* and *Choisy*.

Calvinism and the Anabaptist Movement

At this point, however, the resemblance between Calvinism and the sect-type becomes very evident. It is here no longer merely an instinctive resemblance which occurs more or less through the influence of the Bible, and which also appeared in Luther's suggestions for a congregational ideal comprising smaller groups of earnest Christians. Rather there is here, through the Strassburg Reformers and through Bucer, a special connection with the Anabaptists. Since the Strassburg Reformers, by instituting the right of excommunication, and by undertaking the supervision of morals, admitted that the Baptists possessed one element of truth in which they were apparently justified, and as they tried to take the wind out of the sails of the Baptists by instituting an austere organization of the Church for the purpose of sanctification, Calvin then convinced himself that these claims were both Christian and Scriptural. In addition, they fitted in quite well with his whole conception of the Christian Faith and of predestination, which was directed entirely towards activity.[323]

Thus in Calvinism there appear a number of important characteristics which are common both to the Calvinistic and to the Baptist ideal of the Church as a society. Pre-eminent among these characteristics are the right of excommunication, and the conception of the Lord's Supper as the fellowship of genuine and believing Christians, from whom unbelievers are to be kept separate. No one is admitted to Communion without being subjected to a thorough process of strict examination and discipline. Thus the Lord's Supper becomes more than the objective assurance of salvation through the forgiveness of sins; it becomes also the occasion for the official inspection and purification of the congregation. This latter element constitutes a complete departure from the Lutheran point of view.

The celebration of the Communion becomes the central point of the life of the congregation. The purity of the body of communicants remains a subject of the most earnest care, and leads to scruples and fear of the Sacrament; in the end it often even led to the formation of separatist movements. While Lutheranism handed over to the secular authority the right of excommunication and the control of morals, the Calvinist community exercised that authority itself, only at a later date restricting itself to spiritual penalties alone.

[323] See p. 885.

The Lutheran preparation for the Communion was personal auricular confession and absolution; the Communion itself was the fulfilment of the blessedness of forgiveness with the Real Presence of the Body and Blood of Christ, which can be enjoyed in isolation apart from a general celebration in church. The Calvinist preparation, on the contrary, took the form of searching inquiry through pastoral visitation, and a careful purging of the roll of communicants, and the Lord's Supper was regarded as having no meaning excepting as an act of the whole congregation. The same thing applies to Baptism. It also is an act of the whole congregation, and signifies the consecration of the child to the Church; in the Dutch and Rhenish churches full church-membership was only permitted after the candidate had passed through a thorough course of instruction as a catechumen. Baptism is regarded as the recognition of the presumed state of election, and is a sign of the candidate's obligations towards the congregation, but it is not a vehicle of grace. Hence there arose, now and again, misgivings about the rite of Baptism, and especially about the baptismal formula, in so far as it attributes a Christian character to the child instead of the mere obligation to become a Christian. It is evident that this point of view of baptism is nearer to the teaching of the Baptists than to that of Lutherans and Catholics.[324]

Again, in the process of sanctification, both of individuals and of the Church as a whole, the Divine Law was regarded both as a method of control and as the rule of life. In Lutheranism the moral law of Scripture was regarded as having been instituted solely in order to produce conviction of sin, to be applied to the souls of those who are "justified" only in so far as the "old man" has not yet been subdued, while the moral achievement itself issues from faith alone, apart from the law; and the Decalogue, interpreted in the spirit of Christ, is used only as a Christian exhortation in popular religious instruction. In Calvinism, however, the Law was regarded rather as a positive Christian moral law, as the standard of personal and congregational discipline, as the rule of life required for that sanctification which flows from the grace of election, and of its realization through the activity of the Holy Ghost.

In Calvinism severe Scriptural legalism in morality prevailed, just as in the Baptist community; this legalism was expressed in self-examination, in Church discipline, and in self-conquest for the sake of sanctification. The Baptist idea of the content of the

[324] See p. 886.

Law was, however, very different from that of Calvinism; this will soon become evident.[325]

Combined with this legalism is the further idea of a continuous progress in sanctification, which in genuine Calvinism, it is true, does not lead to actual perfection, but to a comparative and partial kind of perfection. The Lutheran idea of perfection meant no more than the qualitative perfection of the "justified"; it did not think of sanctification as a gradual growth in actual holiness. The Calvinistic idea was that of a relative "Perfectionism", and only among the Baptists do we find something similar; for this idea has no connection with the Catholic doctrine of an intermittent process of sanctification, which is continually being affected both by mortal sin and by the sacramental inflow of grace. It is an active ideal of holiness, resulting from the fundamental Calvinistic idea of activity, and of the Scriptural doctrine of victory over sin, which belongs inevitably to the ideal of the Holy Community.[326]

Finally, however, the analogy is most complete in the Christology of Calvinism. It is true that it maintains the primitive doctrine of the Two Natures, and the Pauline-Scholastic doctrine of Substitution and Satisfaction, as strictly and firmly as the Lutherans and the Catholics. But Calvinistic theology does not believe that the primary significance of Christianity consists simply in this: that in the Atoning Death of Christ the wrath of God is extinguished, and the bliss of justification is secured, and that this, believingly accepted, in itself actually constitutes the whole status of the Christian, which, mediated solely through the Word and the Church, will spontaneously create all the desired spiritual results amid the continual resistance of the flesh and of sin. In Calvinism, however, as among the Baptists, Christ is rather the Lawgiver, the Example, and, above all, the Lord and Head of the Church, which undertakes to follow Him, and which through the Holy Spirit is drawn by Him into His dynamic power. In Calvinistic theology, within the doctrine of the Two Natures, a relative independence is assigned to the Human Christ, through which He gains salvation through obedience. Since, then, the power of this work of Christ is imparted to believers in Christ by the Holy Spirit, Christ is thus an Example of unfailing

[325] See p. 886.

[326] On this progress in sanctification and relative Perfectionism, see *Schneckenburger, I, 45, 78ff., and 166ff.* It is the preparatory stage for Methodism, as *Schneckenburger* likes to point out; see also *Heppe: Geschichte des Pietismus und der Mystik in der reformierten Kirche, 1879, pp. 49, 126, 415,* who shows the transition to Puritanism and Pietism. *Wernle: Der Christ und die Sünde bei Paulus* is also useful; this book deals with the Scriptural basis of Perfectionism.

faithfulness and holiness, the Law-giver of the Christian rule of sanctification, the guarantee before God for those who follow Him, and who receive into their souls the activity of His Will. Whereas from the Lutheran point of view, through the union of the Divine and Human Natures in Christ in the Word and the Sacrament, He is the visible embodiment of the forgiveness of sins, and along with forgiveness He gives Himself and all His benefits to faith, from the Calvinistic point of view Christ is the Lord and Head of the Church, who has bound Himself to her through His Act of Redemption, and He Himself is incomplete until the Church is perfected in holiness, in a bliss which will be consummated in the life beyond the grave.

From the Lutheran standpoint the *Unio Mystica* with Christ is a substantial indwelling, with a fullness of blessing which constitutes the happiness of faith; from the Calvinistic point of view it is the relation of the members to the Head, who rules and instructs them, and brings them to fruition through the gradual sanctifying power of the Holy Spirit which awakens faith.

Thus, both in the formulation of the doctrine of the Two Natures and in that of the Atonement, the Calvinistic point of view reveals an extensive approximation to the Baptist idea of Christ as Lawgiver, Example, and Head of the Church, who will only attain His maturity in the future Kingdom of God. There is, of course, no trace of the Baptist tendency to reject the doctrine of the Atonement, but, all the same, the Atonement is regarded more as a means of creating the Church than as the decisive act (complete within itself) which turns away the Divine Wrath and fills the ecclesiastical treasury with Grace.[327]

Only when this doctrinal standpoint had been attained did it become possible for the Christian Church to accept the Calvinistic idea of a Covenant. The Church is based upon a Covenant between God in Christ and the body of believers, in which God undertakes to fulfil His Promise of Grace and the Church undertakes to yield obedience to Him. This idea is thoroughly non-Lutheran, and bears a close resemblance to the separatist ideas which led earnest Christians of a certain narrow type to form sectarian groups of their own. Thus in each parish there was actually a double roll of Church membership: on the one side there were the true, genuine, faithful, and active Christians, and on the other those who were merely nominal and worldly. Thus the effect of Calvinism was the separation of the pure body of communicants

[327] See p. 886.

from the impure; in fact it produced the distinction between an open and a closed community, which reminds us of the separation between the world and the "saints" set up by the sect. The true covenant-members are distinguished from the Church which includes the reprobate.[328]

This line of development shows that instinctively Calvinism has logically developed the ideas implicit in the Anabaptist ideal of a holy community, which it accepts and acknowledges as Scriptural, and in so doing it has developed the analogies with this ideal in various directions. These analogies, however, were strictly limited by the ecclesiastical spirit of a Christian national and State Church, which admits the necessity for various stages of human experience, and by the idea of pure grace which excludes every kind of human initiative.

First of all, the Christian moral law and the holiness of the Church are conceived in such a way that precisely those demands of the Baptists which were most striking to the outside observer—abstention from official position, from positions of authority, from law, oath, war, and also their communism—were unhesitatingly rejected, and it was asserted that within the sphere of relative Natural Law which is adapted to fallen humanity, from the Christian point of view, all these things are permitted and commanded. Although, under the influence of Pietism, the later Calvinism now and again had misgivings even about these very questions, yet Calvin himself, and the whole of orthodox Calvinism, joyfully accepted the world, and placed these very things at the disposal of the "holy community". If, then, we attempt to draw comparisons between Calvinism and the sect-type at all, the resemblances will be found to be more in the direction of the aggressive reforming sects, with their "Holy Wars", than in that of the sects which practise non-resistance and endure persecution. In reality, however, to a far greater extent, the underlying current of thought in Calvinism was influenced by the general stream of ecclesiastical thought; we shall see later on how this ecclesiastical outlook was balanced by the demand for a specifically Christian holiness.

Secondly, the whole legal spirit, the appeal to personal resolution, the thought of Christ as the great Exemplar, and of the Law of Christ, the idea of a Covenant and of a fellowship of believers in Christ, is not conceived indeterminately as subordination, confession of faith, and personal fellowship as in the Anabaptist movement, which always fought hard against the doctrine of

[328] See p. 886.

Predestination, but as the effect of election produced by God through the Spirit.

The impression that Calvinism fosters an atomistic individualism, in which the community merely consists of the sum of the individuals composing it, is only a superficial idea, which fastens on the external process through which this society is built up. In reality it is truer to say that all proceeds from the effectual grace of election, and that all the rest—*Unio cum Christo*, the Covenant of the Church with God, the deliberate emphasis on good works, the law, and fidelity to law, self-examination and ethical improvement—is effected by Christ, the God-Man who by means of His Divine Nature effects all this through His human Nature and the Holy Spirit. Obedience and the imitation of Christ, the covenant relationship and Christocracy—in reality, all that means *insitio in Corpus Christi*: this activity has only been awakened by the fact of election. Nothing is left to individual initiative save the recognition that these achievements are signs and tokens of the presence of the Spirit; human initiative itself, however, is the work of the Spirit, and the very fact of its presence shows that it is due to the operation of Christ.[329] Under these circumstances, even the separation between the children of this world and the saints is conceived differently from the idea of the Anabaptists. Since in dealing with one's fellow-men, at least, it is impossible to distinguish outwardly the elect from the reprobate, everyone is to be considered and exhorted as belonging to the elect, while on the other hand the reprobates, at least outwardly, are to be disciplined by the Church, to prevent them from becoming a stumbling-block, and in order that, outwardly at least, they may give glory to God. Both groups are to be included in an ecclesiastical civil commonwealth, and are to be kept in the fear of God by the State and by the Church. The Final Judgment alone will effect the separation between them. In the visible Church men are not to make any difference between the invisible community of the elect, which it contains, and the reprobate. Therefore, until Calvinism came under the influence of Pietism, it did not attempt to separate the wheat from the tares.[330]

Above all, however, Calvinism differed fundamentally from the Anabaptist movement in its ideal of the Law of Christ, which —so far as its content is concerned—governs the holy community.

[329] On this point see especially *Schneckenburger* in the chapter on the *Unio mystica, I, 219*. Since the Church, the Word, and the means of grace belong to the methods of working out predestination, along this line also the ecclesiastical idea itself is included.

[330] See p. 887.

In this matter, as we have seen already, not only did Calvinism not shrink from taking part in the institutions of relative Natural Law belonging to fallen human nature, but it felt no need at all to adjust its ethical ideal to the law of Christ in the New Testament, or the Sermon on the Mount. At this point Calvin diverged from the sect-ideal far more widely than Luther, in the sense of a practical understanding of life. While, on the one hand, Calvin went farther than Luther by adopting and establishing the ideal of the Holy Community, and the disciplinary organizations which maintain it, on the other hand, at the very point where Luther followed the sect-ideal by his recognition of the ethic of the Sermon on the Mount as the really inward and personal ethic of Christianity, Calvin felt no sympathy for it at all, nor had he any sense of its connection with the rest of the Bible. Since in Calvin's conception of God the idea of free omnipotence and sovereign glory transcended the idea of love, so also, from the outset, in his conception of the Christian moral law, the thought of the glory of God outweighed the thought of the claims of a brotherly love which would overcome all conflict and all law through communion with God. In contrast with Lutheranism nothing stands out so characteristically in Calvin's ethic as the absence of any sense of the need to justify and balance the radical ethic of love of the Sermon on the Mount over against the claims of the social ethic of the practical life of politics and of Society. Throughout Calvin's correspondence, in which he gives his judgment on a countless number of ethical cases, there is not even a suspicion of that individualistic morality with its hostility to the world, and its opposition to an official morality which it is forced to accept. Wholly instinctively, and with piercing insight, Calvin singles out of the Christian morality of love the religious element of activity for the glory of God, and of sanctification for God and for His Purpose, which has always distinguished Calvinism from any mere sentimentality and humanitarianism. Without hesitation he regards everything as commanded and permitted which can serve the glory of God—and by that he means that the Church is to be set up, maintained, and kept pure as a community of saints closely connected with the State and with Society. When it is claimed that the Christian ought to renounce authority and law, wealth and possessions, rewards and worldly honours, Calvin takes care to explain that this renunciation only applies within certain limits—that is, that a renunciation of this kind must be solely designed to serve the spirit of holiness and brotherly love, but that it must not be permitted in any way to endanger the glory of God Himself. Where this is concerned, all those methods are not merely permitted, they are commanded; of course it is understood that they are to be exercised within the limits of sincerity, personal gentleness, and disinterested enthusiasm for the cause, without any hatred or injury to individuals. Without further argument he interprets the Sermon on the Mount in this sense; above all he bases his argument repeatedly upon the Old Testament (which cannot fail to harmonize with the Sermon on the Mount, since the Bible is a unity), upon the reforms and the policy of the kings who "feared the Lord", on the Decalogue, on the later ethic of Judaism, on David and the Psalms.

The result of all that is undertaken must always be committed into God's keeping, but the believer is entitled to use every legitimate method, and he may connect it directly with the religious end in view, without appealing to the support of an alien official morality. This idea of an official morality has only been retained in so far as Calvin gives a prominent place to all those who, by virtue of their calling and their official position, are called to use law and authority, to an active participation in political and military affairs. In such cases, however, a direct religious value is assigned to their activity, without any sense of conflict, or need for the reconciliation of opposing ideas. Calvin himself writes and acts like a most practised and accomplished politician, and like a military strategist who has weighed all the risks. In all this, certainly, all that is left to the masses is obedience to their leaders, without any scruples about their Christian right to use force and violence for the glory of God.

Further, Calvin was not opposed to private property nor to the endeavour to acquire wealth, provided that all is done honestly, moderately, and united with a generous charitable activity. It all serves the good of the community (of the Church), of the State, and thus the glory of God; it is only a question of defining its limits; in itself it is no problem at all. Only upon this assumption can we understand Calvin's strong attraction to the Old Testament. Only when the New Testament ethic is thus fused with that of the Old Testament, as Calvin has done, only when the Love of God is conceived as the Will which elects certain souls, and when love to God is regarded essentially as the sanctification of the life of the individual and of Society for the sake of God, does such an interpretation of the New Testament become possible.

Calvin adopted this position entirely instinctively. He had no quarrel with the Lutheran ethic; he was simply acting on his conviction that such a position was only the logical result of his genuine Reformation exaltation of the Bible, in the belief that an ethic of this kind also harmonized with the genuine Reformation predestinarian conception of God. As in increasing measure Luther had already appealed to the Old Testament in order to justify his intramundane ethic of vocation ("the calling"), so Calvin also adopted this position. Here also he believed that he was only developing common principles of the Reformation more strictly and practically. We must remember, too, that Calvin had never passed through the school of monasticism.

Thus he found it possible to make an ethic of sanctification the underlying basis of Church discipline and of the development of the State, which in its severity might be compared with that of the Baptists, without making the radical ethic of love of the Sermon on the Mount into a universal law, since this would be impossible for Society as a whole. This is the actual source of the alleged "Old Testament" character of Calvinism. It is the same instinct which, at an earlier historical stage, had impelled the type of the aggressive reforming sect towards the Old Testament, its "holy wars" and its covenants. This phenomenon is not a revival of Jewish legalism, but of the Old Testament concern with the practical life of the nation. Nor has this ideal of the holy community anything to do with reactions towards Catholicism. It is the sect-ideal, united, however, with the idea of the Church as an institution, brought within the bounds of practical possibility by an extensive application of Old Testament principles; in all other respects it is a most active and vital form of Protestantism. Compared with Luther's teaching about the duty of love and patience and the endurance of suffering, it is certainly a more practical and opportunist point of view. But since everywhere its aim is simply to work for the glory of God and of the Church, with an entire renunciation of all self-interest, it is not a depreciation of Christian morality to the average level; rather it is an emphasis upon that other element in the Christian ethic which is bound up with it, of that fearless heroism which will dare and achieve anything for the glory of God.[331]

Again, if men hold the view that the glory of God is furthered by the institution of a holy community, and not merely by the preservation of personal religion, then this superior heroism will no longer be merely passive but active and organizing, and it must seize the means that it needs in order to achieve its purpose. This, however, is precisely the nature of the Calvinistic ethic, which, while it has exercised the severest self-repression, has

[331] See p. 887.

indeed achieved great things, even when it made use of secular institutions for the Kingdom of God. In Calvin's view the glory of God is not advanced by the repeated surrender of the sinner to the forgiving love of God, but in the evolution of the holy community, by means of self-surrender to God and to His commands.[332]

It is thus quite easy to understand the emphasis which Calvinism lays on fellowship, in the inclusive sense of a State Church association for Christian sanctification, in accordance with the example, law, and lordship of Christ. This is an interesting phenomenon, taken in conjunction with its peculiarly accentuated stress on independence and individualism.

The sectarian ideals which had been absorbed from the New Testament and from the Anabaptist criticism of the Reformation were thus fused with the idea of the Church as an organ of grace, and merged in the idea of predestination, which by its active character intensified the sectarian ideal, and yet kept the balance by its emphasis on the ideal of the Church. This fact, however, explains why, throughout Calvinism, we see a twofold tendency, which aims at the active formation of a society, and also at personal achievement, cômbined with a methodical, rational method and a completeness of action, all of which are directed towards the goal of the happiness of the future life. This leads Calvinism everywhere to an organized and aggressive effort to form associations, to a systematic endeavour to mould the life of Society as a whole, to a kind of "Christian Socialism". This "Christian Socialism" certainly is not primarily concerned (like its modern counterpart) with the material, economic preliminary conditions of higher intellectual culture, neither has it, of course, anything at all to do with the modern class problems which have been created by Capitalism and Industrialism; but it lays down the principle that the Church ought to be interested in all sides of life, and it neither isolates the religious element over against the other elements, like Lutheranism, nor does it permit this sense of collective responsibility to express itself merely in particular institutions and occasional intervention in affairs, as in Catholicism.[333]

The Ethic of Calvinism

This brings us to the fourth point: the peculiar ethic of Calvinism. At first Calvin simply continued Luther's point of view—that is, he evolved ethical principles from the spirit of faith; the only

[332] See p. 887.

[333] See p. 890.

difference he made was that he applied this principle more systematically and more clearly. In so doing, however, the whole idea of ethics was altered; instead of being merely the result of justification by faith it became the end. This transformation, of course, was one which could take place very easily on the assumption of the doctrine of predestination, without any reaction in the direction of a system of "good works" and merit. Further, the standard of Christian ethical behaviour has become more definite in outline, for from the very outset the Holy Spirit provides a clear and definite standard in the moral law of Scripture: the Decalogue, interpreted in the sense of the whole range of Scriptural ideas, and identified with the natural moral law. At this point, indeed, Lutheranism also had not been able to limit its ethical theory to one of obedience to spontaneous impulse in behaviour; it did admit that the Decalogue was the expression of the Divine Will with regard to moral impulse. Calvinism also adopted all the following ideas from Lutheranism: Luther's theory of the Decalogue, of the two Tables of the Law, of the identity between the Divine and Natural Law, and the Christian interpretation of the Decalogue as a law of spirit and of freedom, which depends upon the power of the Holy Spirit in order to realize it in life. Calvin, however, gave the Decalogue a firmer position in the system, since to him the *usus legis* was not a problem bristling with difficulties, but a coherent fundamental theory. Why should the Holy Spirit dispense with that clarity in ethics which He reveals in doctrine? The Bible itself lays stress on ethics as well as on doctrine. In the mind of Calvin this does not signify a reaction towards heteronomy or legalism, since in this law it is only the content of faith in its ethical aspect which is manifested, and since the value of the moral achievement does not consist in particular actions, but in the spirit generated by faith in the whole personality, in the total change of heart effected by conversion.[334] By means of the Decalogue the Holy Spirit solely enlightens the elect about those regulating principles of action which lead to the realization of the Kingdom of Christ, which cannot be left to the mercy of mere instinctive, unenlightened natural feeling. In this respect also Calvin is only the systematic thinker and practical organizer; at this point, however, he leaves the idealistic freedom of Luther behind and moves towards the average constraint of the human sense of the need for authority.

[334] Cf. *Lobstein, pp. 58–60*; the Decalogue as little heteronomous as the natural moral law, both means of the moralizing and Christianizing of Society.

The following features also are peculiar to the Calvinistic ethic: the doctrine of final perseverance, or the impossibility of losing the state of grace, which creates a uniform permanent state of moral achievement and assurance, in place of the Lutheran idea of the possibility of falling away from grace and the renewal of justification; then there is the doctrine of a progressive sanctification, which teaches that the germ of the grace of election becomes increasingly conscious, and that it develops more and more into a mature Christian experience; this is an absolute contrast to the Lutheran suspicion of the whole idea of progress, and to its connection with preparation for Heaven. It is these distinctive features in the thought of Calvinism which have produced those systematic, rational, inclusive, and progressive elements which characterize its personal and its social ethic, creating an ethical ideal which is not merely an ideal for the achievement of individual Christian character, but one which covers the whole life of the world with an all-embracing religious purpose. The natural result of all this is seen in the more closely knit, comprehensive, and penetrating energy of the Calvinistic social doctrines. By treating moral progress and achievement as practical proofs of the state of grace the Calvinist ethic was extraordinarily intensified and also externalized, yet at the same time it also became more accessible to the average attainment of mankind.[335]

Yet all these peculiar aspects of the Calvinist ethic, with their influence on character, in spite of their effectiveness, were still rather external. Far more important is their unique content: the ascetic outlook which was produced by the direction of purpose towards the future life, and by the austere separation between God and the creature; this asceticism also included the most positive kind of work within this world itself. This is one of the most creative elements of the Calvinistic ethic, since it has determined the whole way of life which is peculiar to the nations who have been bred in the atmosphere of Calvinism.[336] As has been already shown, in itself asceticism only becomes connected with Christianity through the pessimistic doctrine of Original Sin, which depreciates the value of the life of the world in comparison with the world of redemption and of salvation, and which at the

[335] Cf. *Lobstein, pp. 75–78*: no conversion conflict as in Lutheranism, but development within and through the community for the community. Otherwise, see above, all *Schneckenburger*, whose analysis of this ethic is particularly masterly, whereas the dogmatic analysis tends to modernize too much.
[336] See p. 890.

same time desires to control the life of the flesh and of the senses by means of a rational system of discipline. The Gospel outlook transcended the things of time and sense, and expected the coming of the Kingdom of God upon earth; it did not renounce the world, nor did it develop a systematic discipline of the life of the senses. Asceticism only found its way into Christianity when the idea arose that the world was permanently lost and steeped in Original Sin, and when the Kingdom of God came to be viewed as something belonging to the future life.

From the very beginning asceticism had a dual significance: on the one hand it was a metaphysical condemnation of the world, and on the other it was a rational discipline of the senses. It was possible for both these elements to unite; it was also possible for them to exist separately. It was quite possible for ascetic world-denial to develop into Antinomianism, and ascetic discipline was quite capable of developing into a severe austere eudaemonistic legalism, with its eye fixed on future rewards. Both kinds of asceticism were practised within Catholicism. Catholicism, above all, felt the difficulty of making room for ascetic morality alongside of the unavoidable necessities of life in the world. It found the solution of the problem in its dualistic theory of morality, and in the full meaning of the word it placed asceticism alongside of and above the life of the world, which only recognizes ascetic obligations now and again, and within practicable limits. Catholic asceticism was, and still is, a form of life which existed alongside of and above the average conditions of life in the world, cultivated particularly in monasteries and confraternities and among the clergy.

Protestantism, however, discarded that dualism, and laid upon all alike the duty of permeating the life of the world with the spirit of world-renunciation and victory over the world. Its ideal was one of spiritual detachment from the things of this world, combined with victory over the world, while remaining within it. Thus it intensified the moral demand by making it apply to all alike, and it intensified the pessimistic doctrine of Original Sin in its desire to make the idea of conversion and of redemption dominant over the whole of existence. Thus to a certain extent Protestantism maintained asceticism, but only in the form of an asceticism within the life of the world. Within this sphere of general agreement, however, Lutheranism and Calvinism developed along very different lines. They divided between them the two fundamentally different aspects of asceticism which have already been mentioned: the spirit of metaphysical depreciation of this sinful world, and the systematic discipline of the senses. Lutheranism depreciated this world, mourning over it as a "vale of tears", but so far as everything else was concerned the Lutheran, happy in the assurance of justification, and nourished by the Presence of Christ in the sacraments, let things remain as they were, quite happy and confident, accepting the world as he found it, exhibiting Christian love in faithfulness to the duties of his calling, leaving results to God, and incidentally thankfully rejoicing in the Divine glory of creation which breaks through the shadows cast by this sinful world. In this attitude there are traces of the mystical Neo-Platonic depreciation of the senses and of the finite, which had already played a prominent part in Catholicism, and incidentally there appeared also, in connection with the freedom of the Spirit from the world—in sharp contrast with the legalism of the "Reformed" churches—the antinomian result. Here also Lutheranism, which is happy in the midst of wretchedness, is entirely illogical; it takes impressions just as they come, both the misery and vexation of the world, and also thankful enjoyment of the gifts of God; neither the one nor the other really matter, since through justification by faith the world has been overcome.

The Calvinist's attitude towards the world is quite different. He finds it impossible to deny the world in theory and enjoy it in practice. This lack of system is contrary to his reflective and logical mind. He cannot leave the world alone in all its horror and comfort himself with the thought of a "finished salvation". That kind of Quietism is totally opposed to his impulse towards activity, and the idea of a "finished salvation" is opposed to his orientation towards the aim of a salvation which is yet to be attained. With his deep sense of the gulf which separates the omnipotence of God from the nothingness of the creature any attempt to find satisfaction in creatures, even of a passing kind, would mean a deification of the creature. The creature in itself is only a means; it is never a Divinely complete end in itself. Moreover, to the Calvinist the sinful creaturely world is an abomination which he must oppose with all his might, and which he feels he must overcome. Thus he knows he must go to work thoughtfully, systematically, and progressively to overcome the tendency to deify the creature, and all the sin which clings to the senses and to self-love. In view, however, of his Protestant estimate of the secular life, and of his ideal of a Holy Community summed up in the form of a State Church, he can only overcome the world by at the same time recognizing the value of its life.

Calvinism, therefore, creates an intramundane asceticism which logically and comprehensively recognizes all secular means, but which reduces them to means only, without any value in themselves, in order that by the use of all the means available the Holy Community may be created. The method by which all that is secular is reduced to the level of a mere means is a rigorous discipline of the instinctive life, a destruction of all merely instinctive feeling, and the limitation of the sense-life to that which is necessary and useful, the practice of self-discipline and self-control in order to lead a holy life in obedience to the Law of God.

These are the ideas which lie behind that combination of practical sense and cool utilitarianism with an other-worldly aim, of systematic conscious effort united with an utter absence of interest in the results of effort, which is a distinctive characteristic of Calvinism, and in which all the qualities which have already been described are merged.

This peculiar combination of ideas produces a keen interest in politics, but not for the sake of the State; it produces active industry within the economic sphere, but not for the sake of wealth; it produces an eager social organization, but its aim is not material happiness; it produces unceasing labour, ever disciplining the senses, but none of this effort is for the sake of the object of all this industry. The one main controlling idea and purpose of this ethic is to glorify God, to produce the Holy Community, to attain that salvation which in election is held up as the aim; to this one idea all the other formal peculiarities of Calvinism are subordinate.

Only when we see Calvinism from this angle can we grasp the full significance of Calvinistic legalism, and its resemblance to Catholic disciplinary asceticism which has often been remarked, even to the point of a righteousness consisting in "works" and the desire for reward. In pure Calvinism, however, all these weaknesses are obviated by the ideas of grace and predestination, which, on the other hand, fostered this tendency to legalism by its teaching about good works as the signs of election.

It is well known that Calvin's judgment in these questions was comparatively free from prejudice , and that he knew how to appraise the values of civilization in the *Gratia universalis*, which also lays hold on the reprobate making them capable of higher achievements, and thus also revealing the beauty of the world. This *Gratia universalis*, however, which softens the ascetic tendency, is still only a foreign body in the system, introduced under the pressure of practical life and under the influence of ancient classical culture. When the problem is viewed in the light of Christianity—and that is the decisive point—there Calvin also ceased to assign any positive value to creaturely achievement and earthly glory; all are regarded simply as a means for establishing the dominion of Christ. The *Gratia universalis*, regarded in the light of a civilization which is not controlled by the dominion of Christ, is valid only for the reprobate and the unconverted. The elect and the converted, on the contrary, use their possessions solely for the purposes of religion. Calvin permits joy, it is true, but only in a very restricted way, as a necessary and useful relaxation.[337]

Moreover, as will easily be understood, later Calvinism intensified and systematized Calvin's rigorism to a pitch of Puritanical legalism and purely utilitarian restraint, which stands out in sharp contrast from Lutheranism, which in this respect is most illogical. It would be wrong to try to find in this development a trace of the influence, whether past or present, of Catholicism, which, indeed, scarcely bears any trace at all of this kind of asceticism within the ordinary life of the world. It is the very essence of the genuine Calvinistic spirit, and it has bred that sober, utilitarian, energetic, and methodical purposive humanism which labours on earth for a heavenly reward, which in its secular form is only too well known to us to-day. Calvin's own attitude, and the spiritual counsel he gives in his letters, provide the most magnificent example of an ascetic and utilitarian ethic of this kind. In his case, however, this way of life was still penetrated by a genuine religious dignity and majesty, with a sense of responsibility and of a wide range of thought, with the consciousness of the greatness of the ultimate End. Thus his ethical system and his methodical habit of mind never became petty; on the contrary, it was characterized by the highest sense of duty towards an objective task in life, which does not consider the feelings and inclinations of the individual, but which concentrates entirely upon work for God. In the greatness of genuine Calvinism there is always an undertone of this kind. But in periods of peace and relaxation, under the influence of the human tendency to sink to the average level, and in connection with the bourgeois life of business, this spirit becomes rather self-righteous and Pharisaical, very full of the consciousness of belonging to the number of the elect and expecting the heavenly reward. These sentiments found apparent support in the Old Testament, and, not without reason,

[337] See p. 892.

the Puritans have been often regarded as Jewish Christians. While the passivity and happy surrender of Lutheranism, combined with its emotional warmth and naïveté, with its tendency to give rein to natural impulses, has left its mark, in the form both of a dependent spirit and of geniality, upon large sections of German civilization right down to the present day, the school of Calvin, on the other hand, has bred in the Calvinistic nations a habit of personal reserve, positive restraint, aggressive initiative, and a reasoned logic of the aim of action.[338]

Since, however the sphere of one's calling provided both scope and a method of discipline for this intramundane asceticism, the idea of the "calling" itself here gained a new and specially emphasized significance, which distinguished it not only from the Catholic, but also from the Lutheran conception. This conception provides the transition to modern vocational humanism. The Early Church, in its defensive attitude towards the world, tolerated the natural organization of labour and the various degrees of Society, regarding them as matters of indifference so far as the question of salvation was concerned; it had only excluded certain callings from those in which Christians might take part, on account of their incompatibility with the Christian Faith.[339] The mediaeval period brought the natural lower grade of secular work and the natural social organization into an inner connection with the spiritual sphere of the Church, but it still regarded it all as a providential classification on the basis of Natural Law, upon which real religious achievements still had to be built up, but which was not binding for the heroes of the religious life, the vicarious representatives and authors of the essential Christian spirit.[340] At this point it was Protestantism alone which drew Nature and Grace together, since in its view the redeeming Will of Grace both gave each man his secular task in the World and made it the normal sphere, necessary for everyone, for the exercise of the spirit inspired by Divine Grace.

From the economic and social point of view the consequences of this conception of the "calling" were extraordinary. It raised the ordinary work of one's profession (within one's vocation) and the ardour with which secular work was prosecuted to the level of a religious duty in itself; from a mere method of providing for material needs it became an end in itself, providing scope for the exercise of faith within the labour of the "calling". That gave rise to that ideal of work for work's sake which forms the intellectual and moral assumption which lies behind the modern

[338] See p. 893. [339] Cf. above, *pp. 118–127*. [340] Cf. above, *pp. 293–296*.

bourgeois way of life.[341] Within Lutheranism, however, the consequences of this conception only had a limited influence. It is only in Calvinism that their full and strictly logical effect appears. Luther's view of vocation agreed with that of Paul, the Early Church, and the Middle Ages. To him the "calling" was simply the sphere of activity in which one was set, and in which it was a duty to remain. He could see no meaning or Divine sanction in the idea of a holiness which was higher than the ordinary ethic of a Christian vocation. Although at the same time Luther pointed out that it is precisely through the ordered work of one's calling, and the intricate network of mutual service that the preservation of the whole community is effected, and with that peace, order, and prosperity, he attributes it all to the wise ordering and the kindly guidance of Providence, and not to deliberate human initiative. The vocational system was not consciously designed and developed for the purposes of the holy community and of Christian Society, but it was accepted as a Divine arrangement. The individual, moreover, regarded his work, not as a suitable way of contributing to the uplift of Society as a whole, but as his appointed destiny, which he received from the hands of God. That is why it was possible for the Lutheran to regard the work of his vocation in an entirely traditional and reactionary way—as the duty of remaining within the traditional way of earning a living which belongs to one's position in Society. This point of view coincides with the traditional Catholic view. Christian morality was exercised *in vocatione* but not *per vocationem.*[342] It is just at this point, however, that the difference between Lutheranism and Calvinism is most manifest. Calvinism aimed consciously and systematically at the creation of a Holy Community.[343] It co-ordinated the activity of the individual and of the community into a conscious and systematic form. And since the Church as a whole could not be fully constituted without the help of the political and economic service of the secular community, it was urged that all callings ought to be ordered, purified, and enkindled as means for attaining the ends of the Holy Community. Thus the ideal was now no longer one of surrender to a static vocational system, directed by Providence,

[341] On this point cf. especially *Max Weber,* who also analyses in detail the linguistic origin of the Protestant conception of the "calling" from 1 Cor. vii. 20, in connection with Eccles. xi. 20–21.

[342] On this point cf. *Weber: Archiv. XXI, 16–17; Lobstein, 143 ff.*

[343] Here I would mention once more *Eger's* excellent book, *Luthers Lehre vom Beruf*; see also above, *pp. 561–564.*

but the free use of vocational work as the method of realizing the purpose of the Holy Community. The varied secular callings do not simply constitute the existing framework within which brotherly love is exercised and faith is preserved, but they are means to be handled with freedom, through whose thoughtful and wise use love alone becomes possible and faith a real thing. From this there results a freer conception of the system of callings, a far-reaching consideration for that which is practically possible and suitable, a deliberate increasing of the intensity of labour. To what extent this rationality and mobility of the conception of vocation was carried through in detail, in the presence of the opposing conception of life with its "guild" and "police" spirit, is quite another question. The instances of ecclesiastical social politics in Geneva which will be cited farther on, however, display considerable freedom of movement.

There is also another element which ought to be taken into account, the significance of which will also only become fully evident at a later stage. It is this: one of the special tasks of the Holy Community was that of ascetic self-discipline in work, an ascetic abstention from all worldly distractions in order to attend to the duties of one's calling, the renunciation of the utilization of the profit gained by one's labour for personal enjoyment; this kind of asceticism produced, as an important by-product, that ideal of hard work, of the prosecution of work for its own sake, as a duty in itself, which is anything but a natural attitude of mind, and which can only be understood in the light of a religious energy which can thoroughly transform the natural instinctive life. Once this psychological state of mind has been created, it can then, through a process of metamorphosis of purpose, be detached from its original meaning and placed at the disposal of other ideas; in various ways this process often takes place at the present day. It is, however, precisely at this point that we can observe the difference between nations which have been educated on Catholic, Lutheran, or Calvinist lines.

To people who have been educated on Calvinistic principles the lazy habit of living on an inherited income seems a downright sin; to follow a calling which has no definite end and which yields no material profit seems a foolish waste of time and energy, and failure to make full use of chances of gaining material profit seems like indifference towards God. From the Calvinistic point of view laziness is the most dangerous vice; it is hurtful to the soul from the standpoint of ascetic discipline, and harmful to the community from the standpoint of social utilitarianism. In this matter, however, Calvin himself did not perceive the full logical result of his idea. His strongly aristocratic outlook, and his connection with the French nobles, gave him a more broad-minded and understanding conception of the services rendered by various callings.

Huguenot Calvinism, within which the aristocratic element predominated, was at first quite different in character; it only became bourgeois after it had been disarmed and fettered; in any case it was this development which made it more difficult for the nobles to join the movement. The permanent remnant of the Huguenot movement, and the Huguenot emigrants, certainly display quite plainly that interest in trade and commerce which is characteristic of a bourgeois society. In the last resort, however, a bourgeois development of this kind was bound to take place as a result of Calvin's social ethic as well as of his ascetic rigorism. It reached its full development in the bourgeois atmosphere of the Calvinism of the Lower Rhine and of the Netherlands. That was the kind of society which provided a congenial soil for this religious ethic, just as the dualistic ethic of Catholicism suited the graduated social system of mediaeval society. Just as the agrarian-feudal and mediaeval city conception of life formed the basis of mediaeval Christian civilization, and made the latter possible, and was in return strengthened and permeated by it, so the nascent bourgeois world was inwardly related to the ethic of Calvinism, and in return it was religiously strengthened and moulded by it into a spiritual and ethical force which was independent of all mere fluctuations in sentiment and opinion.[344]

Up to this point we have been dealing solely with the question of the supernatural, spiritual ethic, which is produced by the grace of election. This ethic, however, needed support in the natural or universal ethic of civilization, such as the ethic of the Catholic Church had already long possessed; all that Lutheranism had done was to regulate afresh the relation between the two. This function was exercised by the conceptions (with which we have already dealt several times) of the moral Natural Law and of the Law of Nature. It is precisely at this point, however, that there emerges an important peculiarity of Calvinism. In the actual wording of this theory Calvin certainly does not seem to be using any different formulas from those employed by Luther and Melancthon about the absolute Natural Law of the Primitive State, and the relative Natural Law of the present day, adapted to the conditions of fallen humanity.[345] Calvin speaks just as they did

[344] See p. 894.

[345] See p. 895.

about the identity of the Natural Law with the Decalogue, in which, not only the Decalogue, but the whole Old Testament Law and the history of Israel appear as illustrations of the Natural Law;[346] of the application of the Christian spirit to the social institutions of the Natural Law, and of the corresponding division of the Decalogue into two Tables, one of which concerns spiritual and religious matters, and the other, the concerns of secular morality;[347] the argument that Positive Law is an application of Natural Law, conditioned and altered by time and circumstances, according to which the positive element in the Law of Moses (Mosaic Code) and in Roman Law, and also in the present law of the State, in civil and in criminal law, is to be understood as the evolution of the Law of Nature, conditioned by time and place.[348] Up to this point Calvin's ideas seem to coincide exactly with the Lutheran conception. Further, Calvin agrees with Luther in a very strict demand for respect for authority, even in cases where those who wield authority are not particularly estimable. The same applies to Calvin's exhortations to frugality, modesty, and adaptation to existing circumstances and situations. Calvin's position seems to have been directly nearer to Luther's positively authoritative conception of the Law of Nature than to the rationalistic conception of Melancthon; Luther's ideas were certainly in closer agreement with his personal instincts than Melancthon's.[349] In spite of that, however, it is precisely at this point that we can discern a great difference between Calvin's position as a whole and that of Luther and Lutheranism.

This distinction appears first of all in two apparently external points. The first point is that Calvin emphasized the difference between absolute and relative Natural Law far less than Luther. He continually describes the Decalogue and the Natural Law as the eternal unchangeable rules of the Divine moral law; the modification of the law by the fact of sin is only alluded to incidentally, it is never dealt with in principle. The State in particular, in the chief passages in which Calvin refers to it, is never regarded as a mere antidote to the fallen State and a penalty for evil, but it is always chiefly regarded as a good and holy institution, appointed by God Himself. Nor is there ever any suggestion that the original communism of love had been modified and transformed into the institution of private property; private property likewise seems to be a directly Divine institution.[350] Far less emphasis is laid, therefore, upon the contrast between the Primi-

[346] See p. 896. [347] See p. 896. [348] See p. 896.
[349] See p. 897. [350] See p. 898.

tive State and the fallen State [probably this was due to the influence of the doctrine of Predestination]—rather, from the outset political and economic institutions are regarded as Divine institutions for the purpose of preserving social peace and harmony. The Augustinian influences which had coloured the Lutheran ethic of the State and of economics, which indeed even in Luther belonged rather to his earlier period, have practically disappeared entirely; in Calvin's mind the problem is simply this: how can these Divine institutions most usefully be moulded to serve the ends of a Christian society?

It is the same thing with the second point: Calvin's conception of the relation between the First and Second Tables of the Decalogue. It is well known that Calvin makes the First Table include four instead of three commandments, by reckoning the command against image-worship as a commandment in itself; to make things right he runs the Ninth and Tenth Commandments into one. This is a feature of every Calvinist catechism. The deeper significance of this change, however, lies in the fact that now the general meaning of the First Table is not the demand for a spiritual union with God, detached from and superior to the world, out of whose interior depths alone goodness streams forth, but it is that of a commandment which inculcates purity of worship apart from pictures, magic, or ritual ceremonies, and lays great stress on strict Sabbath observance. This entirely changes the meaning of the First Table; it places purism of temper and of worship on exactly the same plane as that of unconditional obedience. Hence the Lutheran tension between the absolute religious morality of love of the First Table, and the social demands on justice, compulsion, and force of the Second Table, disappears altogether.

So far as Calvin, like Luther, describes spirituality as that spirit which alone produces obedience to the Second Table of the Law, inspiring it with the Christian spirit, he considers that this spirituality consists in the radical severity and emotional moderation of motive which springs from the "vision of the true God, reverenced and recognized", and not in the pure, loving disposition which is opposed to the whole order of law.[351] Thus, in connection with the "Two Tables", we see the same process at work as there was in the question of the distinction between a "private" and a "public" ethic; while in Luther the differences had already receded behind the formal character of a demand, in Calvin they had altogether disappeared.

[351] See p. 898.

There is, however, more in this than a mere wholesale adoption of Luther's later teaching which obliterated these distinctions. A completely different spirit now prevails. Calvin scarcely ever presents the products of relative Natural Law in the Family, in the State, in Society, and in the sphere of economics as concessions to the fact of sin, which must simply be tolerated; almost always he alludes to them as useful institutions for attacking evil, for the furtherance of good, and for the realization of the glory of God. From Calvin's point of view the objections of the Anabaptists, which Luther partially accepted, in the distinction which he drew between private and public morality, and to which he only added the reservation that the Gospel must not be turned into a Law, seemed to be simply unpractical and fantastic nonsense. Calvin's one reply is to set against the views of the Anabaptists the statement that the Divine Law cannot be divided, that whether it be expressed in the Old Testament or in the New it is all one. He adds that in his opinion their demands are against common sense, since if they were realized they would do away with the Law of Nature as well. Calvin regards the absolute Law of Nature so little as the real standard, and takes for granted that the relative Natural Law is a Divine institution, that he lays all the emphasis on that which is practical, possible, and suitable. The result of this attitude, however, is that the institution of the State and of Law both can and must be adapted to the two following ends: (1) the religious purpose of the maintenance of true religion; and (2) the social and utilitarian end of the promotion of peace, order, and prosperity. These two points are all that really matter; both, however, are primarily the concern of the Government. Calvin entirely excludes any idea of forming Society rationally on the basis of the individuals which compose it, or from the point of view of the "man in the street".[352] But, even so, the intellectual atmosphere in which Calvin's ideas of the State, of Law, and of Economics are bathed is impregnated with a spirit of logical purpose and rationality, which seems to have no connection with the Lutheran attitude of pessimism[353] and mere toleration of all these things. Further, however, Calvin is very cautious and non-committal in his expression of opinion about the positive forms of the State, since in them he perceives the idea of the State conceived in terms of Natural Law, shaped by Positive Law in

[352] *Inst., IV, 20, 31*: "Quibus nullum aliud quam parendi et patiendi datum est mandatum; de privatis hominibus semper loquor." *IV, 20, 8:* "Et sane valde otiosum esset, quis potissimus sit politiae in eo quo vivunt loco futurus status, a privatis hominibus disputari"!

[353] See p. 898.

accordance with the historical situation, with national characteristics, and with political necessity. These forms of the State, however, correspond mostly nearly to the Law of Nature in which it is possible to control and direct the governing authority in the right path, as, for instance, monarchies with various social ranks and legally empowered counsellors, aristocracies in which a mutual influence is exerted upon the rulers, and, above all, republics with a graded system of authority. This is the famous theory of the "right of resistance" and of reform which belongs to the *magistrats inférieurs*, who, if the supreme authority fails in its duty, hold a Divine Commission, which entitles them to intervene for the good of Society and the truth of religion. The private individual alone is forbidden to interfere in public affairs; his only duty is to suffer and obey. The official courts, however, are authorized to make criticisms and to suggest reforms; they can thus work towards the goal of a society framed and ordered according to reason and to Nature. These views, however, breathe into the whole a spirit which desires to see Society shaped and moulded for a definite purpose, and a spirit which can criticise law and authority according to the eternal standards of Divine and Natural Law. Thus that claim which Luther only reluctantly admitted later on as part of the positive German law of the Empire, and which he always limited to the defence of religion against foreign aggression, seemed to Calvin to belong from the very beginning to the requirements of Natural Law, embracing the whole rational ethical formation of the State, because it is this which best develops a system of Positive Law, which provides the necessary subordinate powers for the control and reprimand of the supreme authority.[354] Although this theory still gives no place in the political scheme to the private individual, the wall of partition which prevents him from co-operating in the attempt to introduce an ideal order of the State has worn very thin, and will fall the moment that all the official courts cease to function. In reality Calvin's idea of Natural Law is nearer to the Catholic idea of Natural Law than it is to the Lutheran conception from which it started. In particular it has no trace of that specifically Lutheran anti-rationalism, that glorification of authority for its own sake, as the form which the structure of Society has developed under the influence of sin, which it is possible for God-fearing princes to use, with the blessing of God, for the good of the Church, but which, as a rule, is only to be patiently endured, with all the suffering this involves, as the very opposite of love. As we shall

[354] See p. 899.

see later on, circumstances intensified this distinction, and it assumed a fundamental significance for the whole history of the development of Calvinism.

Social Theory of Calvinism

Finally, however, an Ethos of this kind means—and here we come to the fifth point—the unified society, the *Corpus Christianum*, which is built up by the joint influence—different yet not divided —of the sacred and the secular authority. As in Catholicism and in Lutheranism, so also here, the dominant idea is that of a Christian civilization, of a Christian society, of a compulsory unity of Faith.[355] In Lutheranism this idea is conceived as the voluntary charitable service of the authority instituted by Natural Law, directed towards the ends of justice, natural peace and order, placed at the disposal of the purely spiritual organ of salvation, which must be endowed by the State with its legislative organs, and supported by it in its spiritual activity.

In Calvinism this idea of the *Corpus Christianum* is regarded as the union of the Government which discerns its duties—both from the point of view of Christian and of Natural Law—in reason and in the Bible, and the active independent Church, which administers its own law of Divine justice for the Christianizing of Society, and also works with the State in the spirit of a common obedience to the Word of God. It is a uniform system of life and of Society as a whole, inspired by one common ideal in things secular and sacred, which therefore possesses a comprehensive sociological fundamental theory, developed by the very same methods used by Catholicism and Lutheranism to achieve the same end.[356]

Under the influence of the whole intellectual system of religious thought Calvinism produces, as has already been noted above, a quite different idea of personality from that of Lutheranism. The Calvinist, alone with God and his own soul, feels within himself the "grace of election"; he uses it, and the effect on his own mind is very different from that which fills the soul of a devout Lutheran —whose main sentiment is one of loving self-surrender to God and a loving self-giving to his neighbour—; the Calvinist is filled with a deep consciousness of his own value as a person, with the high sense of a Divine mission to the world, of being mercifully privileged among thousands, and in possession of an immeasurable responsibility. This idea of personality, however, which arises out of the idea of predestination must not be confused

[355] See p. 899. [356] See p. 899.

with modern individualistic and democratic ideas. Predestination means that the minority, consisting of the best and the holiest souls, is called to bear rule over the majority of mankind, who are sinners. It includes the idea that the existing conditions of life and authority—so far as they do not go against the Word of God—are Divine ordinances, to which man must humbly and willingly submit. Within these limits, however, Calvinism gives a value to the personality of the elect soul which is thoroughly in harmony with the idea of Kant, while in this respect Luther tends to remain within the range of ideas controlled by mysticism.

Along with this strong emphasis upon personality, however, the idea of fellowship is also defined in a peculiar way, a phenomenon which is most characteristic of Calvinism and which has already been noted. Fellowship does not arise, as in the Lutheran idea, merely directly out of the conditions of physical life, out of the existing institutions of the *Lex Naturae*, out of the invisible effects of the visible doctrine and use of the sacraments; it arises far more out of the predestinating Will of God itself. Fellowship is not a method of working out the happiness of justification, in which, however, the freed soul, certain of its God, never spends itself wholly, but it is the purpose of justification and of sanctification, into which all the energy of religious renewal ought to flow. In spite of the isolation of the particular elect soul in the process of the working out of election, the same fact of predestination places the soul once more, in principle, in the fellowship which uplifts, supports, tests, and educates its members.[357]

This fellowship, like that of Israel, is always defined as a national community. God makes His Covenant with each nation and requires loyalty in return for loyalty; he educates the nation by punishments and visitations, and gives His Word in order that man should know His Will. Particular nations and churches, however, are closely united among themselves, and have a very strong mutual influence upon each other; all are for each and each for all. The idea of international religious unity belongs to the fundamental essence of Calvinism. A union of Christian nations, in which each nation, in its own sphere of influence, realizes the ideal of the Theocratic State; that is the Will of God, if its Scriptural significance is rightly understood.[358]

[357] See p. 900.

[358] On all these points see *Choisy* and *Kuyper*. The international character of Calvinism was illustrated recently at the Geneva Jubilee, and is also displayed in the active translation activity, by which everything of importance which appears is translated into English for the benefit of the English-speaking peoples. Kuyper's book itself is a monument of this international spirit.

Thus this fundamental theory possesses neither the somewhat vegetative character of the idea of the "organism", (since it is directed towards the conscious and clearly determined aim of the individual), nor does it possess the Quietistic features of a pure Patriarchalism; rather, it combines a strong sense of authority with the idea of the equal dominion of the law over all. Nor is it the conception of Society from the standpoint of the free and voluntary association, for it is produced by the guiding power of Providence in the natural sphere, and by the power of predestination in the supernatural sphere. The creative Divine Will binds together and unites all in one positive aim, to which all are committed, and from which all trace of arbitrary individual choice has been removed. On the other hand, this idea of fellowship is not conceived as the direction and unification of Society by means of a tangible supernatural priestly government, since it arises solely out of the common possession of the Spirit, and out of that harmony with Divine and Natural Law which this effects. Difficulties and complications are solved by the Bible, coupled with the deliberate decision of conscience in the sight of God. This fellowship is a common union in an objective Divine relation of interest and purpose; to this end the particular individual must dedicate his highest and freest personal energies, in which, however, all are most closely united to each other through something which transcends all individualism.

Thus this conception of fellowship is an entirely new form of the Christian sociological idea, in spite of the fact that its forms of expression remind us in innumerable instances of the conceptions of Lutheranism, Catholicism, and the Primitive Church. Down to the present day the peculiar nature of this structure stamps the life of the Calvinistic peoples with a unique emphasis on the cultivation of independent personality, which leads to a power of initiative and a sense of responsibility for action, combined also with a very strong sense of unity for common, positive ends and values, which are invulnerable on account of their religious character. This explains the fact that all the Calvinistic peoples are characterized by individualism and by democracy, combined with a strong bias towards authority and a sense of the unchangeable nature of law. It is this combination which makes a conservative democracy possible, whereas in Lutheran and Catholic countries, as a matter of course, democracy is forced into an aggressive and revolutionary attitude.[359]

[359] *Kuyper's* whole book is steeped in these descriptions of the fundamental theory contrasted with that of the European democracy of France. Hence he draws the conclusion that the two distinct forms of democracy of America and

Closely united with this new form of sociological fundamental theory is the balance between the ideas of equality and of inequality which is peculiar to Calvinism, and the aspirations which it evokes, both in democratic and radical, as well as in aristocratic and conservative, movements. This question has always constituted one of the main problems connected with the Christian conception of Society; it was always further complicated by the fact that the Stoic doctrine, fused with the Christian social doctrines from time immemorial, had always maintained that in the Primitive State all men were equal, on the basis of the equal possession of reason and the power of exercising it, and from that hypothesis often enough equalitarian inferences for the present day had been deduced. Similar ideas have also appeared within the Christian doctrine of Society itself, especially among the sects, and their influence has confused the issue, down to the present day. In the midst of these complications Calvinism adopted a decided position, based on the statement that equality and inequality are nothing in themselves, and that their only value consists in the varying relations of men to one another. In the presence of God all men are equal, for in His sight all men are sinners, and all are equally bound to obey Him. On the other hand, in relation to each other they are unequal, for the Divine Ruler of the world has ordained that some should serve, and some should rule, as part of the essence of human life, and not as a result of the Fall. The essence of the Divine Nature is not reason, and that righteousness which satisfies all the demands of reason, from which one can postulate the equality of all men. It is rather that of the sovereign Will of the Ruler who elects one, and rejects another, according to His eternal and inscrutable purpose, which may not be measured by any order of reason which can be applied to all alike.

Thus the whole social ideal of Calvinism is controlled by the sense that human beings are unequal by Divine appointment, and that the only equality which exists is that of incapacity to do any good in one's own strength, and the obligation to render unconditional obedience to the Divine Will. The result is that the main features of this social ideal are essentially conservative and authoritative. The irrationality of God, of the order of the world, and of election is most strongly emphasized, existing institutions and governments are fully recognized.[360]

of France are the two great world Powers of the future, whereas in his opinion Germany seems foredoomed to weakness owing to its belief in pantheism.

[360] See p. 901.

On the other hand, however, equality before God is not conceived as a mere consolation, a higher point of view which lifts the individual spiritually above the misery of earth, but otherwise leaves everything just as it was before. On the contrary, this idea of equality, combined with the living spirit of Church fellowship and of Calvinistic individualism, had a strong practical influence upon actual conditions of life. The moral tribunal has no respect of persons; its judgment applies even to those in the highest position of all; it reminds all continually of their equality before God, and of their obligations to the Holy Community. The ministers avoided with scrupulous care any display of their position of authority, and in their weekly meetings they appointed a different chairman each time; discussions with the laity about the truths of Scripture were instituted, in order to abolish the distinction between the clergy and the laity. The greatest possible emphasis was laid upon the idea that true Christian dignity regards questions of rank and position as matters of entire indifference, while on the other hand, every position of privilege is regarded as an obligation to the whole community. From the purely logical point of view there undoubtedly exists an unsolved contradiction in this emphasis first on one element and then on the other. Yet the main sociological problem of the relation of the individual to the community, as soon as it becomes a conscious problem in the stages of a higher intellectual development, always remains antinomian. Calvinism has balanced the two aspects of this antinomy in a very important and powerful manner. In so doing, along with the organic and patriarchal fundamental theory of the mediaeval idea of Society, Calvinism has become the second great Christian definite social ideal of European Society, which in its turn has also experienced a similar deep and broad process of expansion. All other social theories were, and are, too Utopian and too idealistic to be able to master the harsh phenomenon of the struggle for existence, and the complications introduced by self-interest. Indeed, the great importance of the Calvinistic social theory does not consist merely in the fact that it is one great type of Christian social doctrine; its significance is due to the fact that it is one of the great types of sociological thought in general. In inner significance and historical power the types of the French optimistic equalitarian democracy, of State Socialism, of proletarian Communist Socialism, and of the mere theory of power, are, in comparison with Calvinism, far behind.[361]

[361] See p. 902.

In spite of its patriarchal spirit of authority, by means of this balance between fellowship and individualism, authority and freedom, compulsion and initiative, sobriety and enthusiasm, aristocracy and democracy, Calvinism still had a positive influence upon social ideals, not only within the sphere of the Church, but within the whole sphere of Christian Society in general. To the individual it gave the possibility of an extensive co-operation, and a claim upon the whole, as far as this was possible within existing limits. On the other hand, those who possessed social privileges were laid under such heavy obligations to the community, and their position of privilege was held to involve such self-sacrifice for the good of the whole, which subordinates should meet with reverence and trust, that all inequalities were swallowed up in a system in which the powers of all were engaged in a mutual effort for the good of the whole community. Calvinism was then, and still is to-day, a united body, with a common feeling and a sense of mutual responsibility among the Church members which, by means of labour and criticism in common, continually subordinates the common life afresh to ethical standards, and moulds it in harmony with ethical principles. Here then—for the first time in the history of the Christian ethic—there came into existence a Christian Church whose social influence, as far as it was possible at that period, was completely comprehensive. As we have already seen, Calvinism was "Christian Socialism" in the sense that it moulded in a corporate way the whole of life in the State and in Society, in the Family, and in the economic sphere, in public and in private, in accordance with Christian standards. It took care that every individual member should receive his appointed share of the natural and spiritual possessions of the community, while at the same time it sought to make the whole of Society, down to the smallest detail, a real expression of the royal dominion of Christ.

From the preceding pages we see clearly why it was that only now did it become possible to make an experiment in social transformation in harmony with Christian ideals which was initiated by the Church-type, founded on real principles, and thorough in its effects and scope. Until that time, in the attempt to realize the ideals of Primitive Christianity in a thoroughly Christian organization of Society, the sect alone had led the way. But as a sect it was immediately placed beyond the legal pale of general civil society. Calvinism had, however, incorporated into its idea of the Church so much of the sect-ideal that it was obliged to make the bold attempt (1) of constituting its national church as a church of professing believers, and (2) of constituting its unity of Church and State as a Christian society in the strict sense of the personal Christian faith and character of each individual member. On the other hand, however, Calvinism did so far remain a "Church" that it never questioned the ideal of a unity which included Society and the State, natural life and worship, and the separation of a holy separate community from the ordinary life of humanity always remained a crime. In order, however, to be able to attain both these ideals, in the last resort it found it necessary to modify and transform the real ideals of the Gospel in order to make them agree with its attachment to the popular morality of the Old Testament. It was by the adaptation of those Gospel ideals to the Old Testament and to the natural ethic that Calvinism so far adjusted itself to the practical conditions of life that it became possible to carry them out in practice. Even so, the demands that were left were highly pitched enough. In the severe earnestness of the religious excitement of the time, and under the pressure of great conflict for a hundred years, Calvinism actually succeeded in carrying out its ideal.

At the same time, as we have already indicated, this "Christian Socialism" was quite different from its modern counterpart of any kind. It retained the institution of the sanitary police (which was part of the life of a mediaeval town), and the system of regulations and supervision created by the Guild-spirit, though without their monopolistic rigidity. But whereas in these previous developments a Christian Socialism had already been formed, which had, however, remained under the control of the secular and civil authorities, the Church co-operating with the Government now took these matters systematically in hand. This ecclesiastical Socialism gave way certainly to the pressure of modern political and social developments. When, however, the technical and social effects of these developments revealed their dubious tendency, once again it was Calvinism which came forward with a new "Christian Socialism", adjusted to modern conditions, yet still bearing traces of the Puritan spirit.[362]

Thus here also, in the last resort, the peculiar essence of Calvinism consists in the combination of the main ideas of Church and Sect in the sense of a fellowship, based upon religion, which, in spite of all that, is still new and original. It is this also which determines the form of its sociological fundamental theory. From this point of view we can understand how Calvinism is able to combine the most alert and active individualism with a

[362] See p. 903.

solidarity which admits all social differences and relates them to each other, its intensification of the sense of personality and at the same time its inclusion (in the scheme of things) of the collective activity of politics and economics, its emphasis upon the equality of all men in the sight of God, and of the inequality of earthly vocations which involves the need for mutual service, its revolutionary habit of measuring all Society by an ideal standard, and its conservative sense for the need of law and order, for authority for actual historical situations.

So much for the religious and ethical special characteristics of Primitive Calvinism; it is actually a new spirit. Upon the whole, everywhere it maintained this spirit, all through that century of vast conflicts, by which, above all, it saved Protestantism from the policy of the Counter-Reformation. Yet in it all there is nothing, consciously and theoretically, that goes beyond the general intellectual level of the sixteenth century, beyond the ancient Catholic, Lutheran, Baptist, or Humanist ideas which prevailed at that time. All that its contemporaries perceived as its distinctive feature was its anti-Catholic radicalism. Lutherans in particular were only conscious of differences in doctrine and in worship. Calvin tried to treat these differences as though they were merely external and terminological, and he strove to maintain the unity of Protestantism as a whole. It was the Lutherans alone who broke the unity, separating from Calvinism as though it were a heresy worse than that of Nestorius or Muhammad. The thinkers of that period concentrated their attention almost entirely upon dogma, and they scarcely perceived that the real heart of the difference lay in the sphere of ethics and of social doctrine. In actual fact this difference only expressed itself tangibly in the peculiar energy which Calvinism displayed in international diplomacy and the organization of churches; everywhere it was busily at work, using every apparently open door in order to gain an entrance to foreign Courts, or to penetrate into the life of foreign peoples. Calvin's corespondence reveals a theological diplomacy and a strategy which embraced the Continent. Where substantial success had been gained, Calvin required a complete break with the rites and ceremonies of the Established Church, and a public confession of faith, which was just as important as an entirely new structure and the organization of a community free from "devilish errors". In this policy Calvin parted company entirely with Lutheranism, which was everywhere ready to make concessions to the ancient Church, wherever the pure preaching of justification by faith was permitted, committing all the rest to the miraculous power of the Holy Spirit. This energy, therefore, is the direct secret of the success with which Calvin outdistanced both Lutheranism and the Anabaptist movement. The programme of the new Church, which spread from Geneva outwards, and stamped a new character upon the nations which accepted it, may be summarized thus: a radical break with tradition; a new Church organization on the principles of Calvinistic church-order, and the international relationship of the new churches which support each other in things material and spiritual.

In all this there is no appreciable advance towards modern civilization. When, however, a *rapprochement* of this kind continually pushes its way to the front as an actual fact, and when, finally, it appears that it has been caused by the development of Calvinism—even though in a very one-sided direction—without any departure from Calvinistic principle, it is evident that this *rapprochement* cannot have arisen out of the religious and ethical fundamental ideas themselves, but that it must be due to an adjustment of these ideas to actual conditions, which at first, scarcely visible, still contained within itself the possibility of future transformations. At the same time, from the very outset this adaptation must have been based inwardly upon the spirit of Calvinism. This particular religious and ethical feature must have been already present in germ in an indissoluble inward connection with the existing political and social conditions of civilization, whose results then came to light in the development of Calvinism, and made possible to it a capacity of adaptation to the modern bourgeois-capitalistic civilization which was lacking in Catholicism and in Lutheranism, or at any rate which did not appear to this extent. Only thus can we understand the comparatively direct development of Calvinism, which led, however, to a result so different from primitive Calvinism.

Primitive Calvinism and Geneva

In reality this is what took place. Since from the very beginning the Genevan situation helped to determine Calvin's political, social, and economic ideal, it led to that adaptation to conditions which only revealed its full significance at a much later period. Therefore we must now inquire to what extent Calvinism itself was influenced by the general cultural situation in Geneva.[363]

The first effect of the Genevan situation can be stated very

[363] The same formulation of the problem in *Marcks' Coligny, I, 1, p. 286.* Here I am only trying to go somewhat further than Marcks.

simply: here alone there were actual conditions within which it was possible to realize Calvin's ideal of a holy community.[364] The ideal which was occupying Calvin's mind was also influencing wide circles of the Reformation movement in Germany.[365] It was only in the States ruled by sovereign princes that there was no prospect of realizing this ideal, since it threatened their royal power. In the great and independent city-republics it came into conflict just as sharply with the traditional power of the great families, which was again becoming dominant after the shattering events of the Reformation. Even in Zürich, Zwingli was obliged to hand over his ideal to the secular authority in the State. In Strassburg, Lutheranism and the oligarchy destroyed the modest attempts begun by Bucer. Geneva's neighbour, the powerful State of Berne, did not merely provide the clearest example of this kind of the exploitation of the Reformation in the interests of the oligarchy—it was also particularly hostile to Calvin; all along it made life difficult for him, and it opposed the introduction of the independent Calvinist Church into the State, fearing that its own Church government might be endangered by this bad example. The fate, however, with which Berne threatened its neighbours hung over all the small dependent communities in Germany which desired to organize "Puritan Lay Christianity" in an independent congregational church. The danger of infection with these ideas was resolutely combated by the territorial lords or the neighbouring princes; finally, those who upheld these ideals saw no other course to pursue than to drift into the Baptist movement.[366]

In Geneva alone, on the contrary—which had won its political freedom and its constitution in the struggle against its bishop and against Savoy, and whose freedom was indissolubly bound up with the maintenance of the Reformation—where a young Government, without[367] traditions, was facing a very complicated

[364] Cf. also *von Bezold: K. d. G., II, V, 1, p. 81*; also *Marcks' Coligny*.

[365] On this point see *Barge: Karlstadt*. This must make us cautious about accepting the view that Calvinism represents the specifically French and Latin aspect of the Reformation; see also *Hundeshagen, I, p. 293*; *Rieker, p. 59*; and *Marcks' Coligny, I, 1, p. 287*; the right restrictions of this statement in *Marcks, pp. 289 and 296*. On Zwingli's reform in this respect, see *Kreuzer: Zwinglis Lehre von der Obrigkeit, 1909* (*Kirchenrechtl. Abdh. hg. v. Stutz, Nr. 57*).

[366] Cf. *Rothenburg's History of the Reformation* in *Barge, II, 295–363*; secessions to the Anabaptists, *II, 452 ff.*

[367] Cf. the Jubilee inscription composed by *Beza* in 1584, in which "the Restoration of the religion and the ancient liberties of Geneva" are summarized; see *Choisy: L'état chrétien, p. 233*.

political situation, was it possible to establish a community of that kind, which by the very fact of its own stability also gave coherence, support, and strength to the State, through the genius of its leader also providing a firm support for the political leaders. Even in Geneva, however, the old families inclined towards a State Church on the Bernese pattern, and Calvin only overcame their opposition after heated struggles; in the end, however, he was successful. He was then able to establish a Church which obeyed the magistrates in all external questions, and exercised an independent system of discipline; its stability was secured by the permanent presidency of Calvin himself; the Church was the backbone of the young and immature State. Only thus was Calvin able to create a holy community which directed its own affairs in freedom according to the Word of God, protected by its pastors as its tribunes, and kept pure through the exercise of discipline, in agreement with the authorities. The general significance of this phenomenon consists precisely in this: we have here the union of a national Church and a voluntary Church, of the Church as the organ of salvation and the sect-ideal, a moulding of the common life on Christian-Socialistic lines which is impossible without the organized rule of Christian thought over Society; that, however, means (since in the end these ideals can only be represented purely and with full knowledge by the ministers) that Society cannot be influenced in this way unless the Church is supreme over Society. Every effort may be made to remove all traces of a hierarchy; the greatest possible emphasis may be laid upon the independence of the secular authority within its own sphere; the free co-operation of each individual may be enlisted to the fullest extent; all this was done in Geneva: still, it is perfectly plain that unless the Church is supreme—unless she controls the State and social life in general—the whole thing is impossible. This is why this first thorough and extensive social evolution of Christianity was also the most theocratic. In his teaching on the independence and secular character of the State Calvin used exactly the same language as Luther; since, however, at the same time he created a strong independent Church (based on the assumption of the *Corpus Christianum* common to all three confessions) through which he desired to effect a Christian and ethical transformation of the whole of Society and civilization, in practice he made the State subordinate to the Church.

But although the actual situation in Geneva thus made it possible to establish Calvinist Christianity, yet on the other hand, in its strong admission of the independence and validity of all secular institutions based on reason, this close relationship between Society and the Church also had a strong reflex influence upon the ethic and the social ideals of the Church of Calvin.

Democratic Tendency of Primitive Calvinism

The first sign of this influence can be traced in a certain democratic constitutional tendency which the Genevan experiment produced. It is, of course, possible to point out that Calvin's personal point of view was as undemocratic and authoritarian as possible; that, further, in spite of the fact that the whole community shared in the life of the Church, Calvin's Church Constitution, with its basis in the Divine Church order and with its special connection with the aristocratic constitution of the city, was still in no sense a congregational democracy,[368] and, finally, that the Genevan Constitution itself, under the influence of Calvin, and in line with the spirit of the period, developed more in the direction of an oligarchy than of a democracy.[369] That is all quite true. Nevertheless, in the last resort, the final effect of this interpenetration of a city-republic with a national Church was a strong impulse in the direction of democracy, towards the principle of the sovereignty of the people. The reason for that is that the whole aim of the Government was to secure the reasonable welfare of the individual which is required by the Law of Nature, and in this sense the State was to be conformable to reason.

A far greater influence in the direction of democracy was, however, exercised by the fact that the final and decisive method of influencing the political authority in this sense was the appeal to public opinion, and to the electors, through the sermon. In all cases of difficulty the *Cri au Peuple* was the *ultima ratio* of Calvin and of his successors. Calvin worked against the dominant families, and influenced the elections, by stirring up the masses by his preaching, and by the use of denunciation and the censure of ungodly or unreasonable laws. The famous section in Calvin's *Institutes* in praise of the republican constitution, the ardour of subjects for its preservation, and the duty of the authorities to respect it, appears first in those editions which were published after 1543, as a later interpolation in the text, which had otherwise remained unaltered since 1536.[370] During the first century of Calvinism, then, this right to the *Cri au Peuple* was also a con-

[368] See p. 904.

[369] The increasing oligarchy in Geneva in *Marcks' Coligny, I, 1, p. 299,* which emphasizes Calvin's share in this development; see, further, *Choisy: L'état chrétien, p. 148.*

[370] See p. 905.

tinual subject of controversy between the magistrates and the ministers, as can be seen from the records of both bodies. Throughout this controversy the ministers always insisted on their conscientious view, which they emphasized very strongly, namely, that they had no right to be "dumb dogs", but that they were the tribunes of the people. By their outspoken criticisms they repeatedly intimidated the Council, which repeatedly requested that difficulties of this kind might be discussed in private before they were ventilated from the pulpit. It was only towards the end of the century that the Council succeeded in limiting the freedom of the ministers.[371] In actual fact, however, the policy of the Consistory really amounted to an appeal to the people as the actual sovereign authority. This becomes still more evident when we remember that in all these matters the main questions were concerned with the interest of the people, with righteous legislation, with the administration of relief funds, with situations of economic and political distress, with bad customs and the like. In spite of the respect for authority inculcated by Calvinism, and the duty of obedience which was laid upon the private citizen, this was its real motto: By the people and for the people.

It is, therefore, not at all strange that Calvin's most loyal disciple and follower, Beza, in face of the Massacre of St. Bartholomew, and the irremediable godlessness of the French Government, finally altogether discarded the theory of the duty of subjects to be obedient, and that for such cases of need he frankly proclaimed the sovereignty of the people as the ultimate court of appeal. That is the meaning of his little tractate *de jure magistratuum*, the authorship of which has only recently been attributed to him with certainty. His view of the question was still no rationalistic artificial law of the State, with State treaties and the like, but only the fundamental simple idea, that Divine and Natural Law make the people the ultimate source of law when all other appeals break down; also that violent revolution is permitted, if no other means are left; that the authorities are bound by the positive laws which in any way contain the Natural Law, and that if these are lacking they are still bound to observe the Natural Law, which is tacitly assumed, and, in a case of tyrannical injury, it is permissible to warn the authorities by the courts which are called to that duty, and if their own conscience does not function they may be compelled to obey the law. This implies the sovereignty of the people, the right of revolution, and the binding nature of a constitution. All this, however, is

[371] See p. 905.

imbedded in a mass of qualifying statements and modifications, which combine with this democratic individualistic spirit both the early Christian doctrine of authority and submission to authority, and the doctrine of Divine Right and the Divine appointment of the traditional authority. Beza points out that all these rights and duties do not directly concern the private individual, but only those whose legal standing in some way involves them in these questions: e.g. professional groups, lower magistrates, elective bodies, which have been appointed and commissioned to represent the interests of the people. Further, the point at issue is not an abstract question of moulding Society according to reason, but one of either improving or replacing a bad Government, whereupon then the old historic, and therefore Divine, rights again come into force; finally, all this is only permitted against a Government which has really deteriorated into tyranny, that is, against an executive power which permanently disregards Natural and Divine Law, and which in principle disobeys both the First and Second Tables of the Decalogue. Beza's theory is still a compromise between the doctrines of the Divine nature of authority which supports, and carries forward, the process of history under the guidance of God, and of the Christian duty of passive obedience enjoined by the Bible, with Calvinistic individualism and its rational ideal of Society, which is practically realized in the execution of one's real duty for the glory of God, and whose inner meaning is summed up in the phrase, "We must obey God rather than man". Even with Calvin it had been a compromise. Beza simply emphasized the individualistic, rational, and democratic element still more strongly. Beza himself suggests what it was which made this development of the theory possible by his appeal to the welfare of the people as the aim of the State, and by his claim for the right of appeal to the people against the Government, which logically involved the right of actual armed resistance as well. The rational idea of Natural Law in Calvinism, which was included in the Calvinistic ethic and combined with Christian individualism, here reveals its significance and its logical results.[372]

Beza and the "Monarchomachi"

Beza used to expound these theories to an international body of students, but the Council decreed that his book must be published anonymously. It had, however, a positive and personal connection with a whole series of similar famous publications

[372] See p. 906.

by theologians, jurists, and politicians. Hotmann read the manuscript, and it seems probable that both men planned the *Franco-Gallia* and Beza's treatise at the same time. These two men, together with Henri Estienne and Gentillet, discussed the theory and the literary plan of campaign.[373] This is the literature of the so-called Calvinistic *Monarchomachi* or "opponents of monarchy", to which belong also the founder of the independent Calvinistic ethic, Lambert Danäus, and men like Duplessis-Mornay, the author of the *Vindicae contra tyrannos*, an energetic supporter of the Centre Party in Calvinistic theology, diplomacy, and Church organization. It was at Beza's suggestion, too, that the first report of the Massacre of St. Bartholomew was reissued, under the title of *De furoribus Gallicis*, although its actual author was the pastor Ricant; the orthodox theologian Jurieu also defended these theological, ethical, and political theories.

In the whole of this literature, the ideas which Beza had developed, which represented the doctrine of the school of Geneva, reappear, with various adjustments and expansions, undoubtedly practically determined by the irreconcilable opposition to the French Crown, and by the fact of the Huguenot and Netherlands Revolt; but these ideas were still only a conceptually theoretical deduction from Calvinistic fundamental principles, and they were therefore characteristic in their range of ideas and possibilities. In all the literature of this kind the sovereignty of the people, the social contract, the right of revolution, the legal obligations of rulers, stand out very clearly; just as clearly, however, there appear also the genuinely Calvinistic limitations of all radical statements about Natural Law by the idea of historic, and therefore of Divine, right, and by the assumption that in principle humanity is unequal.

The idea of a social contract, in particular, which is here introduced, is very far removed from its later purely rationalistic realization, which it experienced in the classical modern Natural Law of the Enlightenment, set free from theology. At no point does it deal with the question of the formation of Society itself on the basis of a social contract. Society rather is regarded in the light of the Aristotelian-organic theory; it is the formation of Society through Nature and reason with the common subordination of the differently placed members through the law which expresses reason. It is always first of all a question of the contract of sovereignty, which, it is assumed, is contained by Natural Law in every kind of sovereignty, and which has no

[373] *Cartier, pp. 204 ff.*

need at all of any positive legal formulation, although such a formulation is mostly, in point of fact, present, and only needs to be brought forward again out of the old popular and class laws.

At the same time this social contract according to Natural Law is interpreted essentially in the light of the Old Testament Scriptures, in which it is regarded as a covenant between God on the one hand and the ruler and people on the other; it is thus something quite different from the primitive social contract of classical Natural Law. The ideas of Natural Law and of a covenant are applied in a thoroughly theological manner, since they represent an original archetypal ingredient contained in the Bible and in every governmental relationship, whose aim is not so much that of making possible a rational construction of the State as that of the exercise of a moral and religious control of the dominant historic powers. Nowhere is there any question of a radical new structure of the State which would be indifferent towards the Divine right of that which had grown up through history. Therefore no kind of definite State organization is deduced from this, but, as in the case of Calvinism, it is left to the play of circumstances. The Calvinistic idea of the mutual obligations of the people and the ruling power, and of the significance of the elective corporations of the subordinate authorities, were only further developed, certainly in a sense which corresponds more to the Thomist and Humanist conception of Natural Law than to the strongly Lutheran authoritarianism of Calvin.[374]

John Knox

John Knox and the Scottish School went farther than Beza and the Huguenots in their departure from the original Calvinist political programme, but even they did not accept the purely rationalistic modern ideas of Natural Law. In his pre-Calvinist period John Knox had been influenced by John Major, who—although he remained a Catholic—advocated the Catholic doctrine (with which we are already familiar) of the sovereignty of the people with a strong democratic emphasis. This teaching seems to have left a deep and enduring impression upon Knox. It seems probable that this accounts for his harsh remarks about the murder of tyrants during this period. While he was in Geneva, Knox, under Calvin's influence, accepted and assimilated the Genevan principles without any reservations. He then instructed the

[374] See p. 908.

Scottish and English nobles in their duty towards the cause of reform. He told them that, as *magistrats inférieurs* they were both entitled, and indeed bound, to support the cause of religious reformation, and to aid the Government in this question; so far as resistance was concerned, he added, they were only justified in that attitude for the sake of the Gospel and of evangelical reform; he deprecated the use of violence, however, and in all secular matters he enjoined strict obedience. When, however, Knox found that this policy rendered it impossible to attain the necessary means of power, and when he saw the danger that both in England and in Scotland the Queens would marry foreign Catholic sovereigns, which would lead to a systematic and entire suppression of the Gospel, he was forced into a position of resolute opposition to the hereditary monarchy, whose right of inheritance could lead to such madness, and which ensured no kind of protection at all against godless and unjust tyrants. He then demanded that monarchs should be chosen and controlled in exactly the same way as judges, and declared that the *magistrats inférieurs* possessed both the right and the duty of leading armed resistance against the "Tyrant", up to the point of capital punishment. Finally, indeed, he summoned private persons, through voluntary associations and on their own initiative, into the work of religious reformation and the formation of churches, implying also that if necessary they ought to take an aggressive share in the exercise of political power.

Doctrine of Popular Sovereignty

This is the doctrine of the sovereignty of the people, based on reason and on Scripture, the theory of the right and duty of violent resistance to godless rulers, even to the point of capital punishment if necessary, for the doctrine of the Covenant, and of the right to urge the people to revolt, and to fight for the sake of the Gospel. This doctrine was advocated by many supporters of the Calvinist ethic; in Scotland it was upheld mainly by Buchanan, who at the same time reveals a very strong Humanist tendency. It was the doctrine of the Scottish and English Presbyterians under the Stuarts, the doctrine of the Generals in Cromwell's Army, who, in the prevailing confusion, regarded themselves as the only legitimate authority which was left. This is the doctrine which cost Charles I his head. But, for all that, its spirit is not republican, nor in harmony with the Natural Law of reason; nor is it Scriptural and conservative, and in harmony with the conception of Natural Law. The aim of this doctrine is only to control the Government in power in accordance with the principles of the rights of the people and the good of the Christian Church; so far as possible it is legitimist, and it is loyal to the most legitimist powers which still remain, after the actual legitimate authority has broken down. It is not concerned with building up the State rationally from the standpoint of the rights of the individual; it only desires to control the powers that be according to the principles of the natural constitution of every State—that is, according to the Bible and the Natural moral Law.

In this sense both the English and the Scottish Presbyterians were Legitimists. Cromwell himself was no theoretical republican, but a man who believed in legitimate authority, who allowed his hand to be forced by events, till they drove him into the situation in which his political genius for government could develop, and then he had to obey his own laws.

The meaning of the whole theory has always been that which Knox expressed in his famous interview with Mary Stuart. She accused him of striving for power, of being an enemy of royalty and an instigator of rebellion. Knox replied: "God forbid that I should grasp at the exercise of power or set subjects free to do exactly as they like. My one aim is that Prince and people alike should obey God."[375]

Althusius (1557–1638)

The first step towards a rational construction of the State, and of the whole of Society, from the point of view of popular sovereignty, was taken by Althusius, who appealed to the example of the Netherlands, just as the opponents of monarchy had evolved their theory after their hopes in the French Monarchy had been shattered. Althusius was a strict Calvinist; he began his career as a master at the Calvinist Academy at Herborn; he then became Chief Magistrate of the Imperial city of Emden, on the frontier of the new Dutch republic; later he was called to Franeker, and then to Leyden, as a recognized leader in the Calvinistic doctrine of the State. Quite deliberately Althusius wished to make politics independent of ethics, theology, philosophy, and jurisprudence; he desired to gather up the scattered materials which were then in existence in order to construct a new and independent discipline, utilizing the Natural Law and the Decalogue merely as bases upon which the actual political theory could then be built up. At the same time he held firmly

[375] See p. 909.

to the idea of a Christian society, and to the idea of close agreement between Church and State; to this extent, therefore, he was still in line with the general thought of Calvinism. The net result of his teaching, however, was to dissolve the compromise which until then had existed between the historic idea of Divine Right and the rights of individuals. This was due to the following reasons: Althusius based his doctrine upon the theory of the original freedom and equality of mankind in the state of Nature, which in its turn produced Society in all its forms as a vast series of associations, rising with increasing degrees of complexity, through the corporation, the parish, the province, to a climax in the State. This theory was based on the idea of a social contract, whether explicit or implicit, and this distinguished it from the territorial sovereignty which alone had been taken into consideration up to that time; sovereignty is vested in the whole body of the people; both the "ephors" and the "chief magistrate" (or the magistrates and the King) only possess their authority as the delegates of the people. The main trend of his thought was influenced by the Humanistic ideas of Stoicism, by the theory of pure Natural Law. In this theory Althusius has discarded the view, current for so long, that the State must be ruled by its supreme ruler in harmony with the principles of Divine and Natural Law, through intermediate courts which take into account the rights of the people and the interests of religion; rather he constructs his theory of Society from the point of view of the freedom and equality of individuals, together with those limitations required by the conditions which govern an ordered Society designed to serve the end of the Christian meaning of life.[376]

GROTIUS

Hugo Grotius, however—the thinker through whom the Law of Nature and the contract theory first gained their importance in world history—explicitly severed the connection between these theories and Calvinism, strove to replace the Calvinist State Church system by a policy of toleration based on rationalistic and political motives, explicitly rejected the anti-monarchic doctrine as the starting-point of his political theory, and on the theological side became an adherent of that Humanistic Rationalism which from the days of Erasmus had never entirely lost its influence, and which reappeared in the Arminian theology. Starting from the idea of the equality and freedom of the Primi-

[376] See p. 910.

tive State, he taught that the State was founded in contract, whose purpose was the purely rational aim of the common good; into this theory he incorporates a theory of international law (in *The Law of War and Peace*), which totally excludes all thought of Wars of Religion at all. In spite of the fact that Grotius himself was a devout Christian, these theories were formulated from an entirely secular point of view. The further history of this doctrine, therefore, does not belong to the history of Calvinism, but to that of the rational idea of Natural Law, whose democratic or anti-democratic development, from this time forward, had only a very loose connection with Christian thought. Grotius's point of view was aristocratic, not democratic. In his case, however, that had nothing to do with religious motives; it was due to purely rational and political considerations; it is well known that Grotius, as a supporter of John of Olden-Barneveldt, was on the side of the merchant aristocracy. The contrast between Calvin's phrase, "*Stat* (in the Being of God) *pro ratione voluntas*", and the doctrine of Grotius, that the Law of Reason would still be valid even if—*per impossibile*—there were no God, throws a lurid light upon the great gulf which separates these two worlds. In taking this stand, Grotius's position, like that of Leibniz, was closer to the Catholic theory of Natural Law than to the Calvinist, or even to the Lutheran theories. In reality this is a new world. When Society is constructed on a rational basis, and individualism is based upon the equality and freedom of the reason of individuals, then the spirit of Calvinism has disappeared, and we are faced with the fact that the rationalistic ideas of Stoicism have been set free from their fusion with Christian thought, and that this has given rise to a specifically modern individualistic habit of mind. In granting the religious conscience exemption from the duties of the contract with the State, so far as these were retained, as in the Anglo-Saxon world, it preserved some traces of Calvinism, although Spinoza also made a similar exception on purely philosophic grounds. But in the Natural Law of French Democracy, and, above all, in Rousseau's theory, every trace of the Calvinist spirit has disappeared.[377]

Locke

John Locke, the second great founder of the modern theory of Natural Law, can only be connected with Calvinism and its conception of the Christian Natural Law with certain reservations. Locke had been educated, it is true, in a Calvinist atmo-

[377] See p. 910.

sphere by his father, who was a Puritan soldier. His whole nature had a tendency towards a Calvinistic sobriety, industry, and utilitarian objectivity, and the whole temper of his mind was always characterized by a piety which was as fine and clear as it was warm and earnest. Early in life, however, he had formulated an essentially independent conception of Puritanism, and his later theories of the Church and of toleration belong to the sect-type and not to Calvinism. On the other hand, equally early in life, he conceived theology in a latitudinarian sense, and later on, under the influence of the Arminians and the Socinians, he developed these ideas in his own peculiar, very able, and original way, which was, however, entirely non-Calvinistic. The latter then combined with the former, so that his advocacy of freedom of worship also meant freedom for philosophical and theological interests, and security for freedom of thought outside the churches. Moreover, his liberal constitutional theory of the State is obviously connected with the theory of the Christian Natural Law of the Calvinistic, scholastic kind. He acknowledged his indebtedness to Hooker, whose *Ecclesiastical Polity*, in its first part, is an epitome of rational Christian Natural Law; in the second part, however, in honour of Elizabethan Anglicanism, it is twisted into a theory of the monarchy as the expression of the will of the people, supported by the obedience of the Church; this is a great contrast to the majority of the Anglican exponents of political science, whose views found their clearest expression in the absolutism of Filmer's *Patriarcha*, which was similar to the Lutheran doctrine of authority. But although Locke's theory of Natural Law bears a great deal of resemblance to the Calvinistic theory, particularly in the following points: in the theory of the *mutua obligatio*, in the idea that the contract of sovereignty is tacitly contained in all State organizations, in the theory of the purely earthly and utilitarian character of the State, and of the right of the people to control and depose their rulers, his theory of Natural Law is fundamentally differently conceived. He blends the various ingredients which composed the previous theories of Natural Law in an entirely fresh way; he starts neither from Stoic rationalism nor from Scriptural revelation, but from a utilitarian empiricism, from which, however, he often reverts towards the older ideas. His Natural Law results psychologically from the idea of the equality and freedom of all mankind in the Primitive State; in his conception the state of Nature was one in which peace and reason prevailed; men possessed equal natural rights to life, liberty, and property, and, in order to maintain these rights, the individuals, by means of a social contract, formed a body politic. This body had the power to protect these natural rights of man; and out of this social contract there arose the forms of government which individuals found necessary for their welfare. This Natural Law is under Divine guidance, it is true, and is Divinely reiterated in the Decalogue, and is thus in agreement with Revelation; but that which it produces is solely for the good of individuals, and not for the glory of God.

The ecclesiastical communities stand completely alongside of the State, and are free associations which in all political and moral questions must adjust themselves to the order of the State; they are free only in worship and theology. Locke feared nothing so much as priestly domination, whether it be Catholic, Anglican, or Presbyterian in form. When friction arises (and this can never be entirely avoided) between Church and State in ethical questions, Locke certainly recommends passive obedience, quite in the manner of Calvin; in the case of permanent injustice on the part of the ruler of a State he would permit revolt, and the resistance of those who are most justified to do so, to the extent, finally, of revolution, since—and to him this is part of the moral order—we must obey God rather than man.

Further, Locke regarded the ruling authorities which have emerged from the process of history as—indirectly—appointed by God, and he was a firm supporter of the positive law of that period, which to him in England seemed to be a particularly happy incorporation of Constitutional Natural Law, and which also implicitly contains this Natural Law as its own presupposition, and its own standard. But these loud echoes of the Calvinistic Christian Natural Law do not drown the underlying tones, which are quite different: the complete removal of the idea of the glory of God as the religious end of the State, the idea of the sole sovereignty of God, of the theoretical inequality of individuals, and their obedient adjustment to things as they are. Here in Locke's theory the dominating idea is rather one of the most versatile individualistic rationalism, purely utilitarian and secular in character, which can be abstracted as it stands from the religious setting of Locke's theory; at a later date this often actually took place. This rationalism rests upon such an independent basis, both in philosophy and in public law, and corresponds so closely to the secular idea of progress, and to the political necessities of the day, that its inclusion in the religious framework no longer had much inward significance. It stands alongside this framework, not within it, just as the religious associations exist alongside of the State. That, however, is the spirit of the Enlightenment and not the spirit of Calvinism.

Thus in the Revolution of 1688 the establishment of the constitutional Kingdom of William III expressed far less of the Calvinistic idea of the *mutua obligatio* than the execution of Charles I had been an expression of the Calvinistic doctrine that the *magistrats inférieurs* have the right to mete out punishment to a tyrant. Still, there were plenty of people ready to justify the second Revolution on religious grounds of that kind. But the Revolution itself was essentially far more secular than the revolt against Charles I.[375]

HOBBES

The third main founder of the modern conception of Natural Law, Thomas Hobbes, was much farther from Calvinism than Hugo Grotius and Locke. It is true that he also used the conceptual material of the Christian Natural Law, and even maintained that in an ideal instance Divine and Natural Law and Order might actually coincide, not in fancy, but in fact. Only, Hobbes did not merely conceive the Natural Law of Society in an anti-idealistic manner, as based on pure egoism alone, but, above all, he regarded the essence of the social process which arises out of this egoism as the establishment of an authority which, according to its conception, must be directly sovereign, and therefore must include power over religion and the Church. It is the induction of a purely absolutist theory from rationalistic premises, which in many respects reminds us of some of the Lutheran propositions.

PUFENDORF

Thus Pufendorf, who was a Lutheran, combined in a peculiar way the doctrine of Grotius with that of Hobbes, and also held that the authority of the Church is delegated to the Government. In a doctrine of this kind there is no trace of the spirit of Calvinism. Lutherans and Anglicans alone understood how to gather grapes

[378] Cf. the *Letters on Toleration of 1685*, and the *Two Treatises of Government of 1690;* also *Lezius: Der Toleranzbegriff*, etc., and the very instructive work of *Bastide*, which describes the whole period, *J. L.: Ses Théories politiques et leur influence en Angleterre, 1906*; the views which are here expressed on matters and theories ecclesiastical are, however, often very misleading, see especially chapters v and vi.—There is an analysis of *Hooker* in *Lang: Ref. u. Naturrecht, pp. 28–33,* his originality, however, is here highly overestimated.

from the thorns of Hobbism; but it was the Enlightenment which reaped the chief harvest.[379]

It would, therefore, be an error to attribute modern French democracy, or even American democracy, directly to the influence of Calvinism. Not even its theories of Natural Law were essentially Calvinistic in origin. Rather, in their essence, they arose out of purely economic movements, and their theories grew up out of the common central stock on which both Christian and Humanist Natural Law was nourished, the culture of the Ancient World. So much, however, *is* true: to a remarkable extent Calvinism, more than Catholicism, and far more than Lutheranism, had prepared the way for the gradual emancipation of those theories from their connection with Christian thought, even though the Baptist movement was more radically effective in this direction, as we shall see when we come to the English Revolution. It would be truer to say that both these movements (the Calvinistic and Baptist movements) have prepared the way for modern democracy, and given it a spiritual backbone, rather than that they actually created it. Even this preparatory process developed against the actual intention of Calvinism. But even though this needs to be strongly emphasized, on the other hand it is evident that Calvinism, by means of the constitutional and critical Natural Law principle which it adopted in the Genevan situation, certainly had a facility for adapting itself to democracy, and that, finally, in its religious ideas, not only was there no hindrance at all, but they helped to create an affinity with it. However little the American lack of respect for authority accords with Calvin's spirit, and, moreover, however alien to it Rousseau's social and political rationalism may be, Calvinism can still combine with both inwardly, if the sovereignty of the religious sphere of life is preserved.

Thus Calvinism has become that form of Christianity which has an inward affinity with the modern democratic movement, and can enter into contact with it without injuring its religious ideas. At the same time, by the very fact of its fundamentally religious and metaphysical individualism, by its retention of the idea of the essential inequality in human life, and by its conservative feeling for law and order, it has escaped the most

[379] Cf. *Lezius* and above, *537*; for the whole subject, see my article *Moralisten, Englische* in *PRE*[3], and my article *Das Stoisch-christliche Naturrecht und das moderne profane Naturrecht* in *HZ*, *1911*, also in *Verhandlungen des ersten deutschen Soziologentages*, *1911*, in which the instructive speeches made in the discussions are also to be found.

dangerous results of democracy: mere majority rule and abstract equality. To what extent it may have itself contributed to this process of democratization it is very difficult to say in particular; some developments which have strengthened it in this direction will be dealt with later on. It cannot, however, be denied that to-day Calvinism is inwardly united with democracy, and that its characteristic world outlook is based upon it. At the same time it has also everywhere come to terms with the sects, which, from the outset established more upon a democratic and individualistic basis, to-day, along with Calvinism, represent the idea of an essential inward connection between democracy and Christianity. This last point will be treated more fully in the last section. In all that, however, Calvinism still remains the supreme spiritual force.[380]

Economic Ethic of Calvinism

The second important point is the economic ethic of Calvinism. Its beginnings were insignificant, but it developed into a factor of the greatest historical importance, both in the development of the modern economic spirit and in that of Calvinism itself.[381]

From the outset, in its main features the economic ethic of Calvinism was also related to the corresponding aspects of Lutheranism. The Calvinistic ethic shared the Lutheran view about work, to which it assigned a high value, regarding it as the practical exercise of a calling appointed by God, and therefore as Divine worship; it also regarded it as a method of self-discipline and of diverting evil desires. Both Calvin and Luther advocated labour as a universal duty, and abolished monasticism and mendicancy. The Calvinistic economic ethic also agreed with the Lutheran ethic in its "anti-Mammon" spirit, its urgent desire for modesty and moderation, its observance of distinctions in rank, its campaign against luxury, which in this respect was prosecuted with unexampled severity by laws against luxury, and which was supported ecclesiastically by the moral tribunal. Calvin also believed that poverty fostered the Christian virtues more effectively than wealth, and he launched out into violent denunciations of the great commercial cities like Venice and Antwerp.[382] In spite of all this, however, Calvin influenced the

[380] This is all brilliantly worked out in the manifesto by *Kuyper*, which is often quoted. The restraining elements due to the religious tradition which English Liberalism contained stand out very clearly in *Held: Zwei Bücher*, etc.—For its influence upon Anglicanism, and its analogy with the sects, which to-day seek refuge within its camp, cf. *Kuyper, pp. 8–10*; *Karl Hartmann* is here also very instructive, see especially *pp. 27–30 and 32*. [381] See p. 911. [382] See p. 911.

"Reformed" economic ethic from the very beginning in such a way that, as in the political sphere, it developed an utterly different spirit from that which animated the Lutheran ethic, both in its primitive and in its present form. This took place, however, without any special and conscious intention on Calvin's part. To a very large extent indeed, the direction in which this ethic evolved was determined by the conditions which governed the practical situation in Geneva.

This was the decisive turning-point: Calvin was convinced that this "anti-Mammon" Christian spirit could express itself and maintain its existence within the sphere of a society which was based essentially upon a money economy, upon trade and industry. Unlike Lutheranism in similar circumstances, Calvin did not hark back to the agrarian patriarchal form of life as the ideal with its closely knit self-contained family life, based as far as possible on primitive methods of production, but he recognized industrial production based on a money economy as the natural foundation and form of professional work alongside of agrarian labour. Calvin himself had a great deal to do with questions of industrial production, and he quite approved of the fact that greater profits were made in trade than in agriculture, since they were simply the reward of carefulness and industry. It is, of course, true that he urged the abolition of certain kinds of business which were questionable from the Christian point of view, such as the manufacture of playing-cards, but in general he was in favour of movement and progress. It was at Calvin's instigation that, with the aid of a State loan, the manufacture of cloth and velvet was introduced into Geneva as a home industry, in order to give work to the poor and unemployed. Later on, when this industry had to be given up on account of the competition of Lyons, the manufacture of watches was introduced with the same aim. He had no desire merely to uphold existing customs and methods of gaining a livelihood. He never denied the necessity for the mobility of an economic system based on industry and trade. All this, however, was due to the Genevan situation and the Genevan atmosphere, which even affected his correspondence; his letters, indeed, deal constantly with the interests of finance, trade, and industry (from the point of view of the manual labourer).[383]

[383] Cf. the following quotation from the letter, *De Usuris, CR XXXVIII, p. 247*: "Quid si igitur ex negociatione plus lucri percipi possit quam ex fundi cujusvis proventu?—Unde vero mercatoris lucrum? Ex ipsius, inquies, diligentia et industria."

As a jurist and a townsman, from the beginning he may have felt differently about these things than Luther who was a monk, but from the sources it is plain that, in any case, in Geneva he could not think or feel otherwise, if he were to have a practical influence, and that he accepted this necessity without scruple or difficulty.[384] The reason why Calvin was able to accept this situation as he did was probably due to the peculiar character of his practical active ethic, which embraced the whole sphere of public life, and which set in the forefront those elements of behaviour which were practically possible to achieve, while the radical commandments about love and suffering were relegated to the background. If Luther had lived in Geneva under the same conditions we can hardly imagine that he would have thought and felt otherwise than in Wittenberg. If Geneva had been a specially large and active commercial town[385] it is of course probable that even Calvin would have felt it much more difficult to submit to the claims of Capitalism. In Geneva, however, which was surrounded by hostile and rival neighbours, and whose territory was very small, the conditions were narrow and provincial. But it was precisely in this form that Calvin found Capitalism acceptable, as a calling which suited the existing conditions in the city, and which was capable of being combined with loyalty, seriousness, honesty, thrift, and consideration for one's neighbour. It was just because the economic conditions at Geneva were so bourgeois, and on such a small scale, that Capitalism was able to steal into the Calvinistic ethic, while it was rejected by the Catholic and the Lutheran ethic.

That is officially expressed, properly speaking, in the important fact that Calvin and the Calvinistic ethic rejected the canonical veto on usury and the scholastic theory of money, and on the contrary supported a doctrine of money, credit, and usury which were nearer to the modern economic idea, with limitations, certainly, with which we shall have to deal presently. In this Calvin abandoned the purely consumer's standpoint of the previous Christian ethic, and recognized the productive power of money and of credit. Calvin's co-operation with the economic administration of the State, and his conception of the importance of a social life which was well ordered from the economic point of view, for the holy community, show that he felt an inner connection between economic progress and moral elevation. Calvin's successors at Geneva went forward in the path which he had traced. Beza and the *Vénérable Compagnie* devoted much detailed

[384] See p. 912.

[385] On this point cf. *Holl: Calvinreden, pp. 61 ff.*

care and thought to questions of economic prosperity and efficiency. They also watched to see that wealth was rightly distributed, and that proper relief was given to the poor, and work to the unemployed. In questions of this kind the Government of the State continually turned to them for their opinions and advice. They took an interest in taxation and in State loans, and in the rate of interest, which was always fixed with their approval. They gave their judgment in favour of the erection of a State Bank, both in order to bring to the State the gain of exchange of business and to create cheap credit for the trades which were needing assistance.[386]

Calvinism and Capitalism

Thus this economic practice of Geneva became the starting-point from which Capitalism was incorporated into the Calvinistic ethic all over the world, though with caution and under certain limitations. Conditions among the French Huguenots, in the Netherlands, and in England, each with their own characteristics, also helped to adjust modern business life to the religious point of view. One very important aspect of the situation is the fact that the Calvinists in France and England, and at the outset also in the Netherlands, and, above all, during their period of exile on the Lower Rhine, as minorities were forced out of public life and official positions in the State; they were thus obliged, in the main, to go into business life. Apart from this, however, the Calvinists displayed a strong tendency in this direction, even in circumstances which were not particularly favourable to business life; their industrious habits, their detachment from the world, and their rational and utilitarian spirit certainly strengthened this tendency.[387]

The economic situation in Geneva, however, contained the germ of logical developments which went beyond the intention of Calvin and the Genevese. Once Capitalism had been accepted, even with many precautions, given the right *milieu*, everywhere it led to results which increased its power; while the specifically Calvinistic habits of piety and industry justified its existence and helped to increase its strength, which gave it in the Calvinistic communities a special character and a peculiar intensity.[388] The exhortation to continual industry in labour, combined with the limitation of consumption and of luxury, produced a tendency to pile up capital, which for its part—in the necessity of its

[386] Numerous examples in *Choisy: L'état chrétien*; banks established, *pp. 36 ff.* and *187 ff.*

[387] See p. 912.

[388] See p. 915.

further utilization in work and not in enjoyment—necessitated an ever-increasing turnover. The duty of labour, coupled with the ban on luxury, worked out "economically as the impulse to save", and the impulse to save had the effect of building up capital. To what extent these developments took place everywhere is a separate question. Upon the whole, however, this result belonged to the very nature of the case, and it is the general opinion that this is what actually took place among the most important Calvinistic peoples.[389]

This, however, is not the main point at issue. The contribution of Calvinism to the formation of the Capitalist system itself is not the most important aspect of the question. This only becomes clear when, with Weber and Sombart, we inquire into the ethical "spirit" and the world outlook, or the "economic temper" which gave the system its firm hold over the minds of men, and which, in spite of its opposition to natural human instincts, has been able to strike root in human minds as a firm conviction. Economic traditionalism, interrupted by unscrupulous individuals who are simply out for gain, is much more in line with ordinary human instincts than the concrete and abstract dominion of labour and profit, as ends in themselves, the continual increase of work produced by every fresh profit from labour.[389a] It is here that we perceive the importance (together with the related, yet different, effects of Judaism) which the peculiar Calvinistic type of the inward ethical attitude has gained towards the performance of labour in business life, and its religious estimate of the earning of money. The Protestant ethic of the "calling", with its Calvinistic assimilation of the Capitalist system, with its severity and its control of the labour rendered as a sign of the assurance of election, made service in one's "calling", the systematic exercise of one's energies, into a service both necessary in itself and appointed by God, in which profit is regarded as the sign of the Divine approval.[390] This conception of the "calling" and of labour, with its taboo on idleness of every kind, with its utilization of every chance of gain, and its confidence in the blessing of God, now, however, to a great extent approached the commercial professions and the business of making money. It laid the foundation of a world of specialized labour, which taught men to work for work's sake, and in so doing it produced our present-day bourgeois way of life, the fundamental psychological principles which gave it birth, which, however, it was

[389] Cf. *Weber: Antikritisches, XXX, 191 ff.; Schlusswort, XXXI, 594 ff.*

[389a] See p. 916.

[390] See p. 916.

not bound to perpetuate once this way of life had become the constitution of the modern world.

Thus there arose a current—definite, particularly powerful, and influential—of the bourgeois capitalistic spirit, which was pre-eminently typical of the bourgeois way of life in general. This was the predominance of labour and of the "calling", of industry for its own sake, a process of objectifying work and the results of work, which was only possible where work was exalted by means of an ascetic vocational ethic of that kind, into the sphere of that which is *necessary in itself* by means of the underlying religious conception. Calvinism, which in its early days included a good many groups of the aristocracy, was at first indifferent to social questions, but in the course of the political development in various countries it became bourgeois; this social transformation, however, was entirely in line with certain elements in its spirit.[391]

It is obvious that such a conception of Capitalism would easily glide into a purely secular conception, once the religious motives had weakened and the religious atmosphere had begun to evaporate. From the time of Adam Smith, indeed, the classical economic theory has constructed the foundations of economics in precisely the opposite sense, in pure hedonism. Here, however, the opposition to the religious ethic was not due to its Utilitarianism. In secular matters, and especially in economics, Utilitarianism was already the exclusive economic principle.

In this respect English economic science only continued the fundamental religious convictions. The modern and anti-Calvinist elements only appear in radical individualism, in the introduction of the idea of equality, and in the abolition of respect for authority, class privilege, and the welfare of the whole. Just as in the case of the formation of the political theories, therefore, the groups of theorists divide into two sections: those who are rather conservative and those who are radically individualistic. Adam Smith himself, like Locke, was still torn in both directions. It was only the arrival of Bentham and his school which finally broke the thread which united the new economic ethic with the old.[391a]

[391] On this point, and on the relation between mediaeval Capitalism and the Catholic ethic, as also on the other kinds of Capitalism which are neither ascetic nor bourgeois in tendency, see *Weber, XXX, pp. 193–197.*

[391a] Cf. *Held, pp. 144–342*; *p. 249* on Bentham: "However little the doctrine was new in itself, its one-sided application in England by Bentham was something new: it signified Rationalism pure and simple, and a complete break with the Puritan traditions of the English democracy." Here also it is of French origin as *Held* emphasizes. For the conservative ethical elements in Smith, see *Held, pp. 154–175.*

The Manchester School, with its doctrinaire optimism, the brutal glorification of competition as the survival of the fittest in the struggle for existence, and finally the thoughtlessness with which to-day capitalistic civilization accepts as its destiny its feverish labour, its crises, its specialization, and its vocational humanism—all this means a completely altered world. All this, however, belongs to the history of economics, and not to that of Calvinism. In connection with the sects there will be a good deal more to say on this subject later on.

The significant point which is important even to-day for our subject is this: that in these Christian circles, and in them alone, was it possible to combine modern economic activity with Christian thought, and, indeed, that down to the present day it is possible to do this with a clear conscience. In this connection we only need to recall the circumlocutions with which Catholicism tries to make this modern form of economic life tolerable, and how, at bottom, it continually attempts to restrain it, or the revulsion with which early Lutheranism and contemporary German Conservatism officially regard Capitalism. Seen in this light, the significance of this new Calvinistic form of Christianity for the whole modern development, and especially for the position of Protestantism within it, becomes plain. It is the only form of Christian social doctrine which accepts the basis of the modern economic situation without reserve. The reason for this does not lie in any supposed "greater insight" into the essence of the economic processes, but in the fact that here the super-idealistic and Pietistic hindrances in the fundamental ethical idea have fallen away, which would have otherwise hindered or restrained this development; because, on the contrary, the Calvinistic ethic contains energies which directly further this economic development.[392]

Whether a Christian ethic of this kind, contrasted with that of Catholicism and of Lutheranism, is entirely an advantage, whether it is not tinged rather strongly with the spirit of "business" and the avidity of a materialistic outlook on life, is another question. The main point is that it is peculiar to the leading modern nations, or at least to majority groups amongst them, and that it here effects an adjustment to the modern economic world which has not been achieved by the Christian piety of other nations.

The Christian element in this Calvinistic justification of Capitalism would, however, be greatly misunderstood if one did not

[392] See p. 917.

at the same time remember the limits with which the real Christian idea of love here also surrounds the ethic of industry, and which have continued to exert a beneficent influence right down to the present day, wherever, in all capitalistic labour, the main Calvinistic ideas have remained vitally alive. Labour is asceticism, an asceticism which is absolutely necessary. Profit is the sign of the blessing of God on the faithful exercise of one's calling. But labour and profit were never intended for purely personal interest. The capitalist is always a steward of the gifts of God, whose duty it is to increase his capital and utilize it for the good of Society as a whole, retaining for himself only that amount which is necessary to provide for his own needs. All surplus wealth should be used for works of public utility, and especially for purposes of ecclesiastical philanthropy. Thus the Genevese assessed themselves to the furthest possible limit for special cases of need, and gave regularly in support of the local poor as well as for the numerous refugees. The charitable activity of the Church which was exercised by the board of deacons was part of the requirement of the Church-order instituted by God, was organized with great energy, and, with the aid of voluntary gifts which were often amazingly large, it was able to cope with the demands made upon it. This is the origin of the practice known among us through the example of American millionaires —in which even men who have become quite indifferent to religion will give a large portion of their profits for public purposes. The actual theory and practice of money and interest has also been determined by this spirit of philanthropy.

Only "productive credit" for business purposes is allowed, not "usury credit", which is simply used for living on interest. From poor men, or people who have been otherwise harassed by misfortune, no interest is to be taken; loans also were not to be refused for lack of securities. Arrangements of that kind are only to be carried out with reference to the good of the community as a whole. The debtor ought to gain just as much from the money as the creditor. The law of cheapness ought to prevail everywhere, in accordance with the principle of the Gospel and of the Natural Law, that "whatsoever ye would that they should do unto you, do ye also unto them". Finally, the rate of interest ought not to exceed a maximum, which is to be legally fixed according to the needs of the situation. This was the theory. In Geneva practical life was regulated in accordance with these principles. The fight against usury and the exploitation of the poor fill the protocols of the Council and of the Consistory, and these Christian-Social elements of Calvinistic doctrine have also left their mark upon ethics. Thus we can understand how it is that within Calvinism, in the face of the modern development of Capitalism, there has always been, and still is, a tendency to merge into a form of Christian Socialism. We have already seen that a Socialism of this kind was contained, from the very outset, in the Genevan ideal of the Holy Community. It was continued in the "communities under the Cross", where the religious idea developed freely. How far it helped to determine the State legislation of Calvinistic countries has still to be discovered.

The great English system of legislation which deals with the poor, with workmen and with wages—in the guild-professional sense and, above all, with respect to education for work—bore traces of its spirit. In opposition to the "Manchester" conception of the State and of economics, Carlyle deliberately asserted the old Puritan ideas. The Christian Socialism of the English people at the present day is essentially of Calvinistic origin, and the activity of the American churches is often of a Christian Socialist kind directed against the abuses of Capitalism. In Switzerland, in the Netherlands, in England, and in America there are to-day Socialist clergy, whereas within the sphere of Lutheranism such a phenomenon is regarded as an offence against the sacred foundation of the Divine order, as taking part in purely secular matters, as a reprehensible revolutionary spirit, and a human intervention in the order of Providence; among us social heresies are more dangerous and more objectionable than doctrinal heresies. The meaning of that is, however, that Calvinism is in closer agreement with modern tendencies of social life than Lutheranism, or than Catholicism, which, at least in the Latin lands of its origin, likewise holds these heresies at arm's length. This also is the basis of that intense self-consciousness of Calvinism, the sense that it is the only form of Christianity adapted to modern life, because, on the one hand, it is able to justify modern forms of economic production before the tribunal of conscience, and because, on the other hand, by means of Christian Socialism, it strives to rectify the abuses of the system when they occur. It is very conscious of representing "modern Christianity"—not because it is in touch with modern theological thought (for its theological tendency inclines to conservatism, and it is only its overwhelmingly practical character which leads to dogmatism being relegated to a secondary position), but because it is in harmony with the political and economic way of life, and understands how to further and yet to define its problems, whereas it considers that Lutheranism is philosophically diseased, unpractical, and remote from the problems of ordinary life.[393]

Calvinism and International Policy

Of less importance for later times, but all the more important during the first century of its existence, was a third tendency, by which Calvinism was influenced by the Genevan situation, and then by later political and ecclesiastical developments. This was the tendency to form a religious system of politics and of international mutual support—that is, the policy of armed intervention. Since the independence of Geneva was intrinsically bound up with the fortunes of the Reformation, it could only be permanently maintained by federation with the Protestant Powers, the Reformed Cantons, and with their German co-religionists, for its independence was menaced perpetually by France, Savoy, and Berne.[394] Further, Calvin was often only able to maintain his position in Geneva itself with the support of the foreign churches, whose opinion and agreement he often solicited, and which aided him in difficult and complicated situations.

To that we must add the missionary impulse, and the urge towards universalism which has already been described, which certainly at first based its confidence solely upon the Word and the power of Truth. In practice, however, it soon found that diplomatic and secular methods were absolutely necessary; moreover, in the school of Genevan politics these measures had forced themselves upon the attention of the leaders as necessary for the primary aim of self-preservation. In foreign policy also these methods became necessary, and had to be recommended to other churches. The diplomatic correspondence of Calvin, the activity of Beza as a political agent, the Huguenot, Netherland, and Palatinate negotiations, are all well-known expressions of this necessity. In theory this practical necessity was reflected in the doctrine of the union of all Protestant churches and their duty of mutual support, which of course implies the same obligations for the States and commonwealths which were united with them.[395] Certainly at first the only immediate result was the necessity for financial, personal, and theological support, and for diplomatic assistance.[396] But immediately the further question

[393] See p. 918. [394] See p. 919.

[395] Cf. *Briefe, 131*; which deals with the question of international mutual support; similarly *I, 137*. On Calvin's international spirit, see *Rieker, p. 184*.

[396] Calvin's letters give very many illustrations of this point; it is his ideal to strengthen a position of power through diplomacy, but apart from bloodshed, as he says with reference to *Condé: Briefe, II, 334*.

arose: to what extent may and should this help take a military form? I.e. how far are Wars of Religion both permitted and enjoined as the ultimate method of decision? The important decision in favour of Wars of Religion—so fundamentally different from the Lutheran position—was not in harmony with Calvin's mind and spirit. His views on war in general were exactly the same as those of Luther.[397] War, he held, is a matter which concerns the State, which is permitted to use it for the secular purposes of defence, provided that it is waged with no confidence in the arm of the flesh and with trust in God, in all humility and Christian austerity of morals. The interests of religion, on the other hand, must be promoted without the power of the sword, purely in dependence upon Providence, through suffering and endurance; they are not to be mingled with secular methods of exercising power. The constant recourse to diplomacy, however, was already, in effect, a use of secular methods, and it was in the very nature of the case that on occasion this diplomacy had to take the ultimate step of armed intervention. Just as Calvin's teaching on the duty of subjects to obey the Government was broken down by his other tenet: that the lower magistrates were entitled, on occasion, to exercise the "right of resistance", and take up the reins of government, so also his teaching about peaceful intervention became ultimately, on occasion, one which admitted the right of armed intervention. Of course, a legal reason had always to be found for this step, just as for the "right of resistance". This was discovered as soon as the ruling power had become a "tyrant", and the lower magistrates had taken his place; they were then also empowered to form alliances with foreign Powers. Thus the doctrine of the expansion and maintenance of the dominion of Christ by purely spiritual means became merged with the recognition of the right of armed intervention and of Wars of Religion, so long as, in so doing, the legal order was preserved.[398] This led to the right and the duty of military support in general; thus that which had been forced upon Calvinism in actual case of need was then justified in theory. In accordance with this Beza thoroughly investigated the whole subject of "Wars of Religion" and of armed intervention, as well as of the "right of resistance", and he based his affirmative reply upon the Bible, upon History, and upon Dogma. From that time forward both questions were closely connected in the literature of the earlier opponents of monarchy.[399]

It is well known that this view attained immense practical

[397] See p. 919. [398] See p. 920. [399] See p. 920.

importance, and that the example of Calvinism finally also affected the Lutherans in the Thirty Years War, who, on the occasion of the War of Schmalkalden, had indeed already discussed the same problem. When the period of the Wars of Religion was over, in which Cromwell had given a last example of Protestant policy, this doctrine then became meaningless, but as a relic of those times there has still remained, right down to the present day, a strong sense of the close connection of all Calvinists with each other, an international Calvinism, with which the very individualistic Lutheranism of the present day, in spite of its Lutheran Conferences, cannot in any way compare.

International Calvinism, after it had given up the theory which justified "Wars of Religion", and the gradual severance of its connection with the State—while it became more and more democratic and capitalistic—went over to the pacifist position in this problem of war, which is so difficult for the Christian ethic. A war, like the Boer War, for example, may possibly be justified for reasons of national self-preservation, but Christian nations in general ought not to bring other nations to such a pass that they feel obliged to wage a war of that kind.

The humanitarian and ethical movement against war, which aims at substituting a system of covenants and courts of arbitration in place of war, is pre-eminently at home among Calvinists and the sects; they take the whole question very seriously, and struggle hard against the Imperialistic tendencies, which are indeed closely connected with the process of economic development of the nations to which they belong.[400]

Social Philosophy of Calvinism

Summing up the results of these inquiries, we then begin to understand the social doctrines which are peculiar to Calvinism, and their development beyond their early position, which at the beginning seemed so much like that of Luther. These social doctrines are a product of the particular religious and ethical peculiarities of Calvinism, which revealed a marked individuality in the doctrine of Predestination, in the voluntary principle, in the tendency towards organization, in activity, and in the idea of a "holy community", and also in its ethic, which aimed at achieving that which was possible and practical. On the other hand, however, they are a product of the republican tendency in politics, the capitalist tendency in economics, the diplomatic and militarist tendencies in international affairs; all these ten-

[400] See p. 921.

dencies at first radiated from Geneva in a very limited way; then, however, they united with similar elements within the Calvinistic religion and ethic, and in this union they became stronger and stronger; until in connection with the political, social, and ecclesiastical history of particular countries, they received that particular character of the religious morality of the middle classes (or bourgeois world) which is so different from the early Calvinism of Geneva and of France. The results of this development were gathered up by the natural-philosophical and theological ethic, which, quite unlike Lutheranism, was highly developed in Calvinism, and which made steady progress from Calvin to Jurieu and Lampe.[401] The social doctrines of Calvinism have already been described sufficiently fully in the preceding pages. The fundamental sociological theory of Calvinism, its doctrine of the State and of economics, have emerged clearly from this analysis, and there is no need to sum them up again. The only point in which a summary of this kind would be useful is the conception of the Church. In Calvinism the Church is both national and free, a holy community, and an objective institution, a voluntary and a compulsory organization, since it is based upon the assumption that all the elect, if they are sufficiently well taught, will open their minds to the Truth, while it is required that all the non-elect must be suppressed, to the glory of God and for the protection of the elect, and must be prevented from expressing both their unbelief and their non-morality in public. Thus this is the union of the sect and the Church ideal, minus a Royal Head of the Church and patronage. The Church consists of the whole body of the elect, but that does not mean that its main idea is democratic, for the congregation is only allowed to give its silent consent to the decisions of the Church leaders, and the right to protest is only permitted in extreme cases. The Church government is in the hands of the official office-bearers, who are placed in office according to the Divine Church-order: i.e. the ministers; the courts of discipline, the teachers and deacons, who are systematically appointed apart from the tumult of the popular vote, and who do not represent the Church but the Word of God. The classical constitution and the system of synods made this Genevan idea suited to the conditions among great nations, but it did not alter its spirit.

In questions of faith and morals the Bible constitutes the final court of appeal. Throughout it is assumed that its meaning is

[401] See p. 921.

plain and clear; when uncertainty arises the meaning may be settled by reference to some of the most highly respected congregations, whose opinion would give added weight to any decision. This Church showed its independent position in the following ways: by its independent exercise of moral judgment; by a widespread system of supervision and denunciation of individuals; by its authority to exclude members from the sacraments, which meant a civil boycott as well; and by its respect for, and its occasional influence upon, the municipal legislation. In addition, however, the Genevan Church also counted upon the voluntary support and co-operation of the civil authorities, who also took the Bible as their standard. In practice, however, there was continual friction between the Church and the civil authority on the question of excommunication. Thus in spite of the supposed unity of the *Corpus Christianum* Calvinism found it impossible to avoid friction with the State. There was conflict everywhere, not only in Geneva. In England and in the Netherlands this friction led to serious conflict and vast catastrophes, the effects of which we still have to consider.[402]

The Calvinist doctrine of Society has already been described sufficiently in the preceding pages. In Geneva it bore a quite overwhelmingly bourgeois-industrial and financial character. We have yet to discover how it worked out in the rural regions influenced by Calvinism, where the peasants were under the control of the landed nobility. In any case, the general idea of Society was overwhelmingly bourgeois, and became so more and more. Calvinism was even accused of hatred of the aristocracy. This is enough to account for the class and guild organizations of the day, although unlike Lutheranism the question of stability is practically ignored; indeed, the frequent changes of work, and the vicissitudes of fortune in the refugee communities in general, made stability impossible. Characteristically there is no trace of the crude Lutheran doctrine of the three classes.

Wherever class distinctions do appear, as in the legislation against luxury, we see that the social organization was varied; social distinctions, however, depend entirely upon a man's possessions. Possibly certain plutocratic characteristics which are still visible in the life of Holland and America may be connected with this fact. Above all, however, the idea of equality in the sight of God is emphasized far more strongly here than in Lutheranism, and in Church-life, especially in the exercise of

[402] See p. 921.

discipline, it was carried out far more explicitly. In Geneva violent conflicts raged round this question. We all remember how John Knox explained to Mary Stuart how all men, even kings, are equal before the Law of God. The Board of Discipline did not hesitate to deal with the Huguenot nobility. In spite of the retention of external differences, and of the strict loyalty which this involved, this idea of the equality of all men in the sight of God undoubtedly caused a ferment of democratic ideas. Kuyper has rightly pointed this out in his manifesto of modern Calvinism; this tendency was, however, modified by the characteristically patriarchal elements within Calvinism. From the very beginning it was a social ideal which combined democratic and aristocratic elements, which also exercised a restraining influence upon each other. This social ideal attained an exalted spirit of independence from earthly authority, by the way it subordinated all classes of Society to the sovereignty of God; at the same time, however, it gained unity and stability through the conception of law, and through the definition of its sole aim as the glory of God. This fact explains the passionate and often successful attacks made by united Calvinistic minorities upon a whole nation, such as those which appear again and again in French, Dutch, and English history.[403]

So far as the ethic of sex and of the Family is concerned, Calvinism has the same principles as Lutheranism. Possibly, however, we may say that the personality of woman is granted a higher degree of independence, and that the purpose of marriage is conceived in a more rational way; the scholastic dualistic idea of its relative value, and its necessity for the restraint of concupiscence, has given place to the rational idea that the Family is a means of building up Society. Here also we have a glimpse of the difference between Lutheran and Calvinistic asceticism. Under the influence of its doctrine of Original Sin Lutheranism abandons concupiscence entirely to sin, but permits the element of sinful impulse to exist within the restrictions of marriage, whereas Calvinism lays less emphasis on that element, urging rather that marriage should be strictly regulated by the rational view of its service to the common good, while the natural instincts and passions are to be controlled by objective considerations and the attempt to direct them into other channels. This is merely a difference of emphasis, but it is important, and it throws light on the inmost distinctions[404] between the two systems.

403 See p. 922.

404 See p. 922.

Influence of later Calvinism

In the main, in this section we have been concerned almost exclusively with primitive Calvinism, and only some of the characteristics which have affected its modern development have been mentioned. This, however, does not provide an adequate explanation of Calvinism as it is to-day, nor of those great developments of the seventeenth century, which produced movements which have profoundly affected the life of the present day. Two important phenomena, both of which were the direct product of Calvinism, have not yet been mentioned: the rise of the Free Churches, and the rise of Puritanism within the Church, or Pietism.

(I) Rise of the Free Churches

Through the development of the Free Churches, Calvinism forged a bond of union with democracy, which was totally different from the ethic of the State which has already been described. This earlier ethic of the State was only concerned with establishing a constitution or a system of control over against a State which was doing injury either to the glory of God or to the welfare of nations; otherwise its ideas were as conservative and legitimist as possible. The essential meaning of the Free Church system, on the contrary, is the destruction of the mediaeval and early Protestant idea of a social order welded together by one uniform State Church, and of one infallible authority with a uniform control of the whole of civilization. From the very outset, therefore, its attitude towards the fundamental social ideas of the previous era was revolutionary. As a system, therefore, it represented a subjective and relative form of religion, which indeed only meant the renunciation of that earthly authority which possesses and promotes the extension of absolute Truth; for this very reason, however, it felt obliged to permit the different religious communions to exist alongside of one another, since they appear to have some right to exist until the final separation at the Return of Christ. This meant that the question of Church membership now became a matter of individual choice, and that, at least outwardly, the form of Church-order becomes that of a voluntary association, even although theologically the community which thus comes into being may still continue to be considered as an objective, ecclesiastical institution. Thus the conception of the Church was moving towards individualistic democratic ideas, and it is obvious that an ecclesiastical ideal of this kind would have a close affinity with political democracy; on the other hand, also, a democracy which regards the State as a unity of individuals can more easily co-operate with a Church-conception of this kind than with the idea of a State Church, which at bottom in some way always dominates the State with its absolutist ideas. In course of time, therefore, the Free Church system, or the separation of Church and State, became the religious and political principle of democracy, while, on the other hand, the Free Churches produced democratic impulses. It is clear that this represents a new development of Calvinism, and one which goes far beyond all its previous experience; above all, the Free Churches approximate more and more to the sect-type, even when the idea of the Church is preserved, with all its dogmatic and ethical consequences.

Finally, whereas the result of the development of the Free Churches was a somewhat formal analogy with the sect-type, the second development forms a very obvious analogy with the sect-type, both in form and content. Pietism has no direct concern with Church constitutions and democratic tendencies or results; its one desire is to create a "pure" Church. Pietism intensified the fundamental asceticism of Calvinism, and in so doing it broke with the world and with secular culture, having no use for anything which goes beyond all that is directly utilitarian and necessary. This certainly was a reactionary tendency, compared with the much freer and finer attitude of Calvin himself, and also the earlier Calvinistic idea of civilization, which was distinguished precisely by its urbane refinement and humanistic culture; naturally this idea did not cease to exist, but it was forced into the background by the more active and more Puritanical form of Calvinism. Pietism, therefore, developed some affinities with the Ethos of the sect, although the very distinct differences between it and the genuine Baptist Ethos still remained, although they had been distinctly modified.

Both these movements, however—the Free Church system and Pietistic Puritanism—were not by any means identical with each other. The Free Church movement can be understood in the sense of a dogmatic and ethical Calvinism of the most correct kind, and can, if it will, decidedly assert or increase the freer attitude towards the world. Pietism, on the other hand, does not need to urge the necessity to break up the uniformity of the State Church system, since it hopes, either, that it will succeed in bringing the whole of Society under the yoke of Church discipline and of the Puritan ideal, or that it will be able to form smaller groups within the Church, which would virtually create a distinction between a religious community in the wider, more pedagogic, and relative sense, and one which would be conceived in the narrower, more Perfectionist, and absolute sense. At times, however, both tendencies merge into one another. The *motif* of the Free Church, in addition to its emphatic rejection of compulsion in religious matters, can be also that of the "holy community", and the Pietist system of creating small groups within the Church can also lead to the development of a Free Church; instances of this kind actually happened, especially in the early days.

The question now arises, To what extent are both these developments to be attributed to the logical development of Calvinism, and to what extent has this result been affected by external influences of a foreign kind? Both these changes took place preeminently in the great conflicts in England, and in the Netherlands, between the State and the supremacy of the Church, between the ideal of holiness and that of the Renaissance and of national customs. Was this the logical result of Calvinism, or was this situation created by influences of a special character?

First of all, we may say that both these developments, in spite of great changes, can still be explained in the light of the Genevan basis; it must be admitted, of course, that they were not the direct result of the Genevan situation; on the contrary, they arose out of a quite different setting. They took place in fact in conditions in which the situation was no longer controlled by the life of a small State, but by the problems which arise where masses of people are concerned, which increasingly necessitated strong compulsion in religious matters. Geneva was a small State, and this made it possible for this comparatively limited number of people to be permeated with the ideals of Christian holiness. For a long time also its civil government was weak, and therefore it submitted to the control of the Church. In both respects this situation was unique, and unattainable under other conditions. In other places too, however, where Calvinism was organized on similar lines, it was always at first the religion of an aggressive minority. Within a smaller setting it was possible to set up the ideal of the "holy community" as a national Church, and a Christian civilization which covered the whole of Society, while the opposition of this minority to the civil authority meant in practice that the problem of a State Church did not exist. But as soon as it became a question of influencing the life of actual sovereign States with the Calvinistic ideal of the State and of

Society, or as soon as the Calvinistic churches were placed within a general system of secular mass civilization, the problem then arose: How was the civil authority to adjust itself to the predominating ecclesiastical and theological interests? This led to the further question: How could a "holy community" composed of sterling Christians, whose faith was a matter of profound personal conviction, and whose lives were controlled by an exalted and austere ideal, be at the same time a Church which would provide a spiritual home for the masses of the population? The pressure exercised by Calvinism provoked the resistance of the political authority which demanded "Erastianism", i.e. the control of the Church by the State, and the resistance of the civil authorities which had no desire to adapt themselves to the hard and one-sided rigorism which Calvinism required from its adherents.

The fact of this resistance, however, produced a great change in Calvinism itself, by forcing it into a new position. Calvinism had to face this question: Is this ideal of a "holy community", and of making God's glory dominant in the whole life of the world, actually practicable? Long before, the Anabaptists had denied this possibility, but Calvin had asserted that it was possible (in resolute confidence that the non-elect were in the minority, and that, at least outwardly, they could and must be made to submit to the Christian Church). And now the question had reappeared. And with this, too, it became quite evident that the Calvinist ideal possessed a certain affinity with the Baptist ideal, although at first no one had been aware of the fact. Like the Baptists the Calvinists now began to question the validity of the whole State Church system, and to replace it by a voluntary Church which the State cannot touch. Like the Baptists the Calvinists undertook to separate themselves from the world by a Puritanical strictness of life. It was only an approximation to the Baptist ideal, however; there was no real unity between the two. Even as a Free Church Calvinism still remained as far as possible a national Church, nor, in practice, has Puritanism ever disputed on principle the existence of secular offices, power, war, law, and the oath. There is, however, a certain resemblance between the Calvinistic Free Church and the Baptist ideal, and it is clear how deeply this is due to the problem raised by Calvinism in general of the really active "holy community" which represents the sovereignty of God.[405]

Further, it is clear that, in any case, Puritanism and Pietism

[405] See p. 922.

were able to proceed more directly out of the fundamental ideas of the Calvinistic Church than the Free Church movement, although the latter is the more enduring and important principle in world-history. The Free Church movement has been described as a "subsidiary ecclesiastical ideal" of Calvinism, produced when the "primary" ideal proves insufficient or unsuccessful. On the other hand, however, some thinkers look upon it as an aspect of the Calvinistic idea of the Church connected with Natural Law, which only thus finds its logical expression. Modern Calvinists like Kuyper do not hesitate to ascribe the existence of the Free Churches directly to the influence of Calvin's most essential ideas; his idea of a State Church, with its compulsory Christian civilization, they regard as a mediaeval idea, involving mediaeval limitations, which it is easy to discard. Others trace its origin to influences derived from the Baptist idea of the Church, in which, indeed, adult Baptism is only a symptom, but not the heart of the matter. The question of the origin of this development is thus a very real problem.[406]

When we remember that in primitive Calvinism there was not the slightest tendency towards the formation of these "Free Church" ideals, but that, on the contrary, it considered it the greatest crime to tolerate the existence of several churches alongside of each other, and a withdrawal of the State from the sphere of its Christian duty; when too we realize that primitive Calvinism believed that the absolute and unbroken nature of the idea of truth requires both the unity of civilization and the sole dominion of the Truth, coupled with intolerance towards untruth; when, further, we consider that the Calvinistic idea of the Church from the very outset was certainly not democratic, but that it carefully avoided the logical consequence of democratic ideas, and that, although the doctrine of Predestination did permit an immense individualism of personality, it permitted no "enthusiastic" emphasis on "direct" religious experience, with very great variety of expression, but, rather, that by connecting it with the means of grace in the Church, the Word, and the Sacrament it extended its solemn sense of awe to all these means of grace: we then feel that it is impossible to come to such conclusions.

To that we must add these further considerations: whenever, in any particular instance, Calvinism was forced to take its place alongside of other denominations, it always regarded this situation as something which was only compulsory and temporary, and

[406] See p. 924.

that where, in the beginning, it was forced into the position of a Free Church, or a secret society, it regarded this explicitly as a serious lack, that in England and North America, under Presbyterian influence, as soon as it had the power to choose, it gave up its principles of toleration and returned to the principle of Theocracy; that at the Synod of Charenton it directly and solemnly condemned Independency and Congregationalism in the French Church. The early Puritan communities in England also, which at first had been Separatist, under more favourable circumstances became the great Presbyterian party, which desired to replace the Anglican State Church by a Presbyterian State Church. Even the communities on the Lower Rhine regarded their Free Church form of existence as merely provisional, and aspired to become a State Church, after the pattern of that which the Calvinists had attained in Holland. Even the idea of a Church covenant is not Calvinistic in origin, for the Scottish Covenants were not Church institutions but associations for the protection of the Church.[407]

The Brownists

In reality, the historical starting-point of the Free Churches, as a normal principle, does not lie in those Free Churches which were the fruit of necessity, but in Congregationalism. The origin of Congregationalism was similar to that of Puritanism, but it was not identical with it. Robert Browne, the Father of Congregationalism, was at first a member of the strict Puritan body; then, however, he developed Separatist principles which were expressed in the idea of complete separation between Church and State, in basing the life of the Church solely upon the inward power of the Spirit, in a Scriptural austerity of worship, in the demand for "converted" preachers, in the ideal of the purity of the body of communicants, in the principle of self-government in individual churches, and finally in the idea of a covenant and the voluntary character of the Church.

In this ideal the only Puritan and Calvinist feature is the emphasis upon the holy community. All the other characteristics are Baptist, and in part akin to those of the spiritual reformers; the idea of the Church Covenant especially is decidedly Baptist. It does not affect the argument that Browne himself, his spirit broken by suffering, made his peace with the Established Church, with mental reservations; further, his mental reservations were of a "spiritual" nature, for Browne believed that the spirit was

[407] See p. 924.

all that mattered, and that externals were insignificant. The retention of Infant Baptism also, and the recognition of the validity of Anglican Baptism, certainly shows that these "Holiness" groups were not concerned with the question of Adult Baptism at all. They were based upon a covenant with God and with each other, and their constitution was simply that of purer and more closely knit groups within the universal Church; they did not intend to be new forms of Church organization. This comes out clearly in the controversy with the General Baptists, who, in common with Robinson's Leyden Church, had arisen out of a Brownist community at Gainsborough, but who, under the influence of the Dutch Mennonites, had adopted the principle of Adult Baptism. In doctrine, too, the Brownists remained completely orthodox in a Calvinistic sense.[408]

The Barrowists

Henry Barrowe, the second "Father" of Congregationalism, held opinions which were very similar to those of Robert Browne. Barrowe was a gentleman and a layman who had been converted to Puritanism; in his opinion a Separatist position was the only logical inference to be drawn from Puritanism and the ideal of a holy community. For this reason he opposed the Puritans of the Cartwright school (whom he stigmatized as "illogical") just as bitterly as the High Church Party, which on its side thought it was entitled to reproach Puritanism with the very existence of the Brownists and the Barrowists, which, it was careful to point out, had really been caused by the behaviour of the Puritans. Along with many of his followers Barrowe died the death of a martyr, a sacrifice to the cruel spirit of Elizabethan conformity, which saw in these Separatist movements the principles of anarchy at work, threatening the very existence of Church and State, and of Society as a whole.

Barrowe evolved his ideal from the Bible and the Calvinistic idea of holiness; to some extent also he was indirectly influenced by Brownism, and actually to a far greater extent by the Baptist movement, though this he himself would not admit. Also, just as in the case of Browne, he had been deeply influenced by books dealing with interior religion, although he did not go so far as to set the Inner Word above the Bible, as it was alleged was done by some of those who laid most emphasis upon the "religion of the Spirit". His recognition of the function of lay preachers and of spiritual gifts, which may have been deduced directly from

[408] See p. 925.

the Bible, points in the same direction. His ideal of the Church may be summarized thus: it is a "pure" Church, separate from the State; each congregation is completely independent, constituted upon the basis of a Church covenant; the sacraments are merely the sign and seal of this covenant; its officials—pastors, elders, deacons—are called independently, in a purely democratic way, yet without equality; it exercises Church discipline and excommunication independently, supports itself and its officials by the voluntary gifts of the faithful, and in all particulars it upholds the ideal of early Christian love and holiness among all its members. Synods of the whole Church will only act in an advisory capacity; the individual congregation is to be entirely independent; the Holy Spirit will preserve the spirit of unity. In doctrine his point of view is strictly Calvinistic and Predestinarian. The only ecclesiastical function left to the State is the expulsion of those who profess false doctrines; the building up of the Church is to be left to its own efforts and to the Spirit, in harmony with the principles of Scriptural Church-order. Marriages and funerals are civil functions. The authority of the State is to be treated with conservative respect, yet at the same time excommunication can be exercised even against princes without injury to their high civil position. Infant Baptism is retained, and the baptism of false churches is also recognized, since election and the influence of the Word are not bound by the limits of the purely visible Church.

In spite of certain resemblances with the Baptist ideal of the Church as a voluntary association and with the Baptist ideal of holiness, there is in this last point a relic of the Calvinistic national Church ideal, in the light of which these "purely independent communities" appear merely as particular Perfectionist groups. Thus in spite of much controversy the thread which connects this movement with Puritanism has not been entirely severed.[409]

At this point two lines of possible development lay before Congregationalism: on the one hand, a merely subjective development in the direction of freedom of conscience, and the formation of more spiritual exclusive groups, without any definite ecclesiastical constitutional ideals, or, on the other, the organization of independent individual congregations into a Church, based on a covenant, in which each congregation is based upon the voluntary principle. The English Independency of Cromwell's Army developed in the first direction. The Congregationalism

[409] See p. 926.

which has maintained its existence down to the present day followed the second line of development. But, whichever line it took, Congregationalism stood midway between the Calvinistic church-type and the sect-type; to some extent this was involved in the fact that Calvinism itself had many affinities with the sect-type; in reality, however, Congregationalism only arose under Anabaptist influence; above all, as we shall see later, it was influenced by a type of spirituality which differed greatly from Anabaptist ideals. The close connection between this movement and the sect-type appears not only in the fact that the General Baptists went over to the Anabaptists, but also in the fact of the development of the Particular Baptists, which followed an entirely independent course. These Particular Baptists likewise had split off from originally Independent communities, and adopted Adult Baptism as a result of the Free Church principle; otherwise, however, they remained strict Calvinists, and had no further connection with the Baptists. Frequently bodies of Congregationalists went over to the Baptists *en bloc*; indeed, there were some congregations which were composed of both elements. There were also Baptist congregations which organized themselves on the basis of a Church covenant, an explicit agreement of the Church members with each other and with God, which each member had to sign and solemnly swear to observe. That is an entirely Baptist idea. On the other hand, however, Congregationalism was closely akin to the Calvinistic church-type. It is shown in the different ways in which this fundamental Church covenant is expressed; sometimes it is only implicit, and sometimes it is explicit. When it is only implicit it is supposed to be contained in the covenant of Infant Baptism and in the existence of the Calvinistic national Church; it then only means the idea of a Church which is under strict obligations to be a "holy community", and leaves to it its significance as a method of popular education. When it is explicit it means the constitution of a separate body upon a basis of voluntary membership and strict consistency, which does away with the idea of a national Church. Thus we can understand why it was that many people went over from Congregationalism to Pietism and Presbyterianism and vice versa, while others found it possible to hold these views and yet to remain in the Established Church.

In all this, however, the fundamental element is still non-ecclesiastical and akin to the sect-type; only it has not severed its connection with Calvinist theology, and it does not, therefore, need to be constituted by a baptismal rite of its own. This explains, above all, the inconsistencies in the Congregationalist Church-life of New England.[410]

"Pilgrim" Communities

Let us now follow first of all the line of development which led to the so-called Congregationalist Church principle. To it belonged the Refugee or "Pilgrim" communities, which arose out of the early beginnings (which have just been described), and which emigrated first to Holland, and then to New England, in order to preserve their nationality, and in the interest of their mission to found a "purely democratic church".

The English Government modified their persecuting laws to this extent that they allowed the Separatists to emigrate—with this proviso, however, that if they returned they would forfeit all their property and be executed. While Browne had founded a congregation in Middelburg, which soon went to pieces, Barrowe's followers then formed a similar Church in Amsterdam. Under these circumstances the social position of this Church was a difficult one. Farmers and scholars alike had to become manual labourers, or to go into business. Meanwhile the anarchy prophesied by Whitgift soon began to rear its head in the congregation. The main democratic element, the majority principle, lay-preaching or "prophesying", brought all kinds of strife, hair-splitting arguments, and rivalries in its train. There was a great deal of argument about the constitution: should it be aristocratic and Presbyterian, or ought it to be more democratic? The statement that the Church is governed not by man but by the Spirit of Christ is only another illustration of the influence of a pre-eminently "spiritual" type of thought upon the whole; in practice, however, this idea had no influence at all. Robinson led a section of the congregation away from all this confusion to Leyden; he solved the problem by making a distinction between the Church government exercised by the elders, and the authority of the Church exercised by the congregation, which really amounted to this: that less important matters were settled by the elders, and important questions by the majority of the Church members. At the same time Robinson approved of the idea of a "Church fellowship", an advisory council representing the congregations which in themselves were independent.

Pilgrim Fathers

The Pilgrim Fathers then carried these principles with them to New England. There they succeeded in infusing their spirit

[410] See p. 927.

into the numerous groups of Presbyterian settlers which arrived later on. Not yet did that mean, however, freedom to organize churches of all kinds. In New England, Calvinistic Congregationalists alone were recognized, and even the most important political rights were bound up with Church membership. The actual communicant body consisted only of those who were considered "genuinely converted", and who had signed the Church Covenant. The children, however, were all baptized, and were regarded as an outer circle within the Church, which, without belonging to the central group of communicants, was still regarded as Christian; these "adherents" also had to pay Church taxes. They were only required to sign what their enemies called a "half-way covenant", however, which laid on them merely the obligation to act in a generally Christian way. Thus, in the colonies of New England, Congregationalism became the State religion, and the local churches were brought into closer relation with each other. This formed the starting-point of American Congregationalism, which under the influence of the Methodist Revival lost one section of its members to the Presbyterians and another section to the Unitarians, but which still forms a large and influential community, whose constitutional principles have come to be shared by a whole series of other denominations, like the Baptists, the Seventh Day Adventists, and the Unitarians.[411]

Independency

The other process of development which has already been mentioned, the Independency of the Cromwellian period, is an entirely different phenomenon. It did not unite with the English Congregationalists, who likewise had their origin in Leyden, and who started with the Church of Jacobs, composed of Congregationalists who had returned to London, who later on, together with the Presbyterians and the Baptists, combined to form English Dissent.

In Parliament, in the Westminster Assembly, and among the clergy, this form of English Congregationalism was only represented by a very small minority, and it was here prepared to allow the continuance of the Established Church, merely stipulating that the individual congregation should be independent, have the right to excommunicate when required, and to elect its own officers; it was prepared to admit a certain amount of State control. The real support of the movement, however, came,

[411] See p. 927.

not from these "Dissenting Brethren", but from Cromwell's Army. It is, however, quite evident that this movement was neither Brownism nor Barrowism, and that, owing to the course of political history, it was also a good deal influenced from abroad. Rather, in relation to the Established Church, it was a confused and theoretical impulse towards inward illumination and experience, coupled with the demand for the right of lay-preaching, which was exercised both by officers and by soldiers, a demand for converted pastors, and for freedom to constitute churches around a preacher who has been freely called by the Church. It was a much more idealistic "spiritual" movement than either Brownism or Barrowism; in many ways it resembled Luther's earlier teaching, and also Schwenckfeld's smaller groups, which were formed on the model of the Early Church.

These Independents claimed toleration towards themselves, out of respect for tender consciences and for the witness of the Spirit within individual souls, but they were then obliged to grant it also to the "other sects", on account of which the Independents seemed to the Presbyterians like "Anabaptists and Antinomians"; they soon found, however, that unlimited toleration itself produced difficulties. The Independents even accepted pastors appointed by the Parliamentary Commission, provided that they were "genuinely converted". On the question of lay-preaching they went farther than Browne, claiming it as a right, and in this they verged on fanaticism. At the same time the whole ecclesiastical situation and the theory of the Church were still most obscure.

In so far as Cromwell allowed himself to be influenced by Harrison, the real patron of the sects in the Army and later of the Fifth Monarchy Men, it is possible that he was actually influenced by Baptist ideas. He always adhered, however, to the idea of a union of toleration for all Protestants, and of Christian unity and government of the nation without discarding the technical organization of the Established Church. It was only when the majority in the Barebones Parliament abolished the system of tithes, which would have meant that parishes and universities would have lost their means of support, and would have been obliged to resort to the voluntary principle, that an attempt was made to reorganize on a new basis. This attempt it was, however, which caused Cromwell to dissolve this Assembly, which was a convention of notables rather than a Parliament. His own Church policy then took the line of appointing a Parliamentary Commission of Inquiry, composed as far as possible of excellent people of different groups and tendencies, including Presbyterians and Anglicans; these men were called the "Tryers". Catholics alone were excluded on political grounds, and later, after an attempt at rebellion, the Anglicans were also excluded. Alongside of them, of course, the Separatist groups of the Baptists, Congregationalists, and the Quakers were tolerated. Thus in reality Independency was the religion of the State, since nearly all the official positions were occupied by its followers, for the most part earnest men of a Pietistic kind. The desire and choice of individual congregations could thus be taken into consideration. The whole procedure, and the toleration which was combined with it, was characterized by a strong emphasis upon "spiritual religion"; as we shall see later on, Cromwell's chaplains were enlightened men of this type. Nevertheless, Cromwell's leading ideas were Calvinistic. He also desired to see a Christian State. He only extended the borders of Christian experience: the conviction of sin, assurance, and a theology of grace; these are the marks of Christian experience. He also exercised moral supervision over the people; only this was done not through ecclesiastical courts of discipline, but through the State General Majors.

Cromwell

Cromwell was also a firm believer in a theocracy. He classed his own proceedings, and those of the Army, with the measures taken by the *magistrats inférieurs* when the legitimate government had failed. He regarded his own position as sanctified by Providence and the course of history, and therefore as his by Divine Right. His religious convictions remain Calvinistic and Predestinarian. Thus in principle both Cromwell and the Independency of his Army were quite different from the Baptist movement, in spite of various resemblances between the two.

His teaching about the *Salus publica* and the sovereignty of the people is the Calvinistic doctrine of the duty of the nation to establish a government according to the Will of God, and he discerns the Will of God in the course of events. In questions concerning property, law, and government he is therefore conservative in principle; more and more clearly his own position is differentiated from that of the democratic, communistic, and Chiliast radicals. From the very outset his Independency had differed from theirs; it had far less affinity with the Baptist movement than had Brownism, but, unlike the latter, it had a greater tendency towards "inwardness"; the latter tendency, however, was modified by the Calvinistic idea of the State as an institution which exists to serve and glorify God.

From this standpoint, as Lord Protector, Cromwell also accepted the universal Calvinistic policy of the union and protection of Protestants. This was a Protestant international policy, the last great expression of a denominational Protestant world policy, after the manner of Bucer, Zwingli, Calvin, and the Landgrave of Hesse. All the same, the Independency of Cromwell was only an interim phase. The final revolution of 1688 fell back upon ideas which were vital before Cromwell, and Independency dispersed its remaining faithful adherents among the various Dissenting bodies: the Quakers, the Baptists, the Congregationalists, and the Presbyterians.[412]

At first Congregationalism and Independency were phenomena whose range was limited, and moreover Independency was not permanent. But the influence of both was great. The first result, which was of universal importance in world history, was the transition from the independent theory to the Locke doctrine of the State, which developed into a theory which favoured freedom to form churches, and to the separation between Church and State which was closely connected with political Liberalism. We have already had a hint of this in the preceding pages, and it now becomes plain in its historical setting. From the time of Locke onwards this theory has been extended and developed as a philosophy of the State right down to the present day. It has become the ecclesiastical policy of Liberalism and of democracy.

The second still more important result is this: that in the constitution of the United States of North America, and in the constitutions of the North American individual States, the ordering of the ecclesiastical situation was practically shaped along these lines, partly as a result of the actual existence of several churches alongside of each other in the various States, partly, however, also as the expression of the Congregationalist Calvinist idea of the majesty of the Church, and of a freedom of conscience which cannot be touched by the State. Although, in a general way, it was held that the State was Christian in character, yet so far as the churches were concerned it ought to have no authority over them, nor be under any obligations towards them, but it ought to leave the religious conscience alone; this is in sharp contrast with the attempted separation between Church and the State which has been taking place in Latin lands since the French Revolution; in reality this movement is the struggle

[412] See p. 928.

of a free-thinking society against the power of the churches, and, above all, against the Roman Catholic Church. The ecclesiastical policy of the present day is being determined more and more by those theories, and by this example of America.[413]

Calvinism and the Free Church Principle

After this detailed examination into the question, it is impossible to attribute these results directly to Calvinism itself; they may rather be described as due to the influence of a modified Calvinism affected by Baptist and "spiritual" influences. It is, however, always a fact that even the genuinely Calvinistic Churches, in face of the mingling of peoples and religions, and of the increasing tendency to secularize the State, have followed this example.[414] This fact is, however, of decisive importance for the modern forms of Calvinism. Nearly everywhere Calvinistic Free Churches have grown up alongside of National Churches. In Geneva itself separation prevails to-day. The manifesto of Kuyper, often mentioned, which the University of Princeton has almost made official, teaches the Free Church system directly as a fundamental Calvinistic theory. Everywhere then, connected with that is the tendency towards the liberal or democratic constitutions which make possible to every ecclesiastical party, and to every church, freedom of movement, and an honourable place in public opinion.

In its passage through the Free Church phase the main block of Calvinism became Liberal in politics, and it participates so closely in the tendency of the sects towards an individualistic and purely utilitarian conception of the State that to-day, in this respect, there is scarcely any difference between it and them. Above, in another connection, the tendency of Calvinism to form constitutional theories of the State has already been pointed out. Free Church Calvinism, however, went farther than that, and became receptive towards the idea of democracy itself. It was only in this amalgamation of the Free Church system with democracy that it received its present-day relation to political individualism. Thus at the present day Calvinism (including the sect-movement) is diametrically opposed to the Lutheran State Church system, and it proudly claims to be the only form of Christianity which appeals to the modern mind. It has not, of course, produced democracy, but in its Free Church form it has encouraged it. Wherever natural conditions favoured democracy—as, for instance, in the colonies of New England—Calvinism gave

[413] See p. 930.

[414] See p. 931.

it a decided impetus, adjusted its life in accordance with democratic principles, and inspired it with its own spirit of the independence of the individual of all earthly authority.[414a]

Free Church Principle and Religious Toleration

Religious toleration was one logical result of the rise of Congregationalism and of the Free Church movement. Some time elapsed, however, before this principle was fully accepted. The main obstacles to be overcome were (1) the Calvinistic idea that each religious body was the sole possessor of the Truth, and (2) the theory of the Christian nature of the State. Final acceptance of the principle was also delayed until pure Calvinism had adopted the principle of toleration.

The ideal of the early Congregationalists was expressed in the following terms: freedom to form independent churches; the abolition of State compulsion in religious matters; and the exclusion of all heretical forms of religion from the State. The Congregationalist Puritans of New England perpetuated these principles; they compelled no one to join the Church; but they declined to tolerate the existence of any other church, and they gave important civic rights to the members of the Church. Here, then, we see the purely negative theory at work, which forbids compulsion in religious matters, while at the same time no room is left at all for the positive existence of different religious communions alongside of one another. It was not until the eighteenth century that positive toleration was introduced, and then that was mainly due to a slackening of religious interest and to the growth of various secular trade interests. In England the Long Parliament only granted toleration to the various groups within Calvinistic Protestantism; in order to secure the Christian nature of the State it maintained the Elizabethan legislation which made attendance at public worship compulsory; the only difference was that individuals were now at liberty to choose the religious group with which they desired to worship. As occasion offered, Brownists and Independents then claimed that religious freedom should be granted also to Baptists, Socinians, Arminians, and even to Jews and Muhammadans. They based this demand on "spiritual" grounds, urging that the external form of worship was a matter of comparative indifference compared with the importance of the inward revelation. Milton was the most "advanced" representative of this group; he, however, modified his Puritan and

[414a] See p. 931.

"spiritual" ideas with a strong dash of the intellectual spirit of the Renaissance. Cromwell declared that freedom of conscience was a natural right of humanity; finally, however, on political grounds he was obliged to deny this right to Catholics, Anglicans, and radical Baptists; he had a firm belief also in the Christian nature of the State, and in a State Church system of at least a formal and administrative kind. It was only the Baptists, the Quakers, and Roger Williams, who maintained that from the spiritual point of view all religious denominations ought to receive equal recognition, and that the State, which is based upon the Law of Nature, and only administers the Second Table of the Decalogue, ought to be neutral towards the religious aims of Society; in the same way the State is here conceived in a purely utilitarian sense. Williams threw in his lot with the Baptists, but they very soon turned him out, and he then gave himself up to an undenominational kind of "spiritual religion". As the founder of Rhode Island he persuaded the new colony to found its constitution upon the basis of complete religious toleration; Williams also held the view that the nature of the State was Christian.

As an actual principle religious toleration was not accepted until Locke had formulated his theory of Church and State. In the constitution of the American States it then became a matter of practical politics, in which, out of respect for the majesty of conscience, the human rights of liberty of worship, and of the freedom of the individual conscience, were made the constitutional basis of the individual States; otherwise, however, in America the general Christian character of the State has been preserved quite naturally in various institutions, and above all in the national spirit, down to the present day.

Jellinek has shown us that this formulation of the right to worship according to one's conscience, as a human right which ought to be guaranteed constitutionally, forced its way into juridical formulation, together with the "rights of humanity" already proclaimed by the Natural Law of the Enlightenment, and that this formulation was then carried over into the constitutions of Europe. The idea of the "calling" is another illustration of the same process—which shows plainly that many an independent idea which to-day has no religious basis at all grew originally out of the soil of religion. This fact, and above all the proclamation of liberty of worship as an inalienable human right, can only be attributed to Puritanism in so far as this term includes Quakers and Baptists, above all as we take into account the softening influence of "inward religion" with its tendency to assign a very relative importance to external dogmatic forms. The only real source of toleration is that individualistic form of spirituality which considers that all external religious forms are merely relative; the only Calvinistic element in this point of view is the feeling that the State has no right to interfere with religion.

Further, we ought not to forget that in addition to these religious forces there were many other external reasons, especially "enlightened" rationalistic ideas, which helped to shape these constitutional principles. The principle of religious toleration only penetrated into actual Calvinism with the growth of the Pietistic Separatist churches, coupled with the growth of many forms of religious belief and worship within one nation. At the present time it interprets the early Calvinistic idea of the sovereignty of religion and of the Church in the sense of freedom from the State, and therefore as the principle of liberty of worship. At the same time its main trend is evangelical and orthodox.

So far as genuine Calvinism is concerned toleration is still a purely political question, which aims at making the Church independent of the State; it does not deal with questions within the Church itself. Genuine Calvinism regards the existence of several churches alongside of one another as a provisional arrangement which constitutes a problem incapable of being solved by human minds. Only at the Last Day will this problem be solved in the interest of the pure Truth. The process of sifting truth from error will be carried out by the Judgment of God, not by the effort of man, nor by the decision of the State. These arguments are still based upon the assumption that the State, and Society in general—with their moral foundation of Natural Law and the conscience of rulers—are Christian in character. In this respect as well, however, Neo-Calvinism considers that it is the supporter of modern progress; above all, it differs from primitive Calvinism in the development of the Free Church system and in religious toleration.[415]

Neo-Calvinism

In so doing, however, Neo-Calvinism has adjusted the relative Natural Law of the fallen State, which, originally, was strongly conservative, even though in comparison with Lutheranism it was far more rationalistic, to the modern classical rationalistic Natural Law of Liberalism. This latter conception is, of course,

[415] See p. 933.

not a product of Calvinism. On its theoretical side it was created by Humanistically inclined jurists, who drew their inspiration from a Stoicism which was freed from Christian influences, and from the Roman Law, and also by modern psychological philosophers, with their habit of deducing everything from experience.[416] Since, however, this conception has also been strongly influenced by the Calvinistic and Scholastic conception of the Christian Law of Nature, which some of it has actually assimilated, it is not difficult to understand how it was that Calvinism of the Free Church type, which was democratic and Liberal in its practical political experience, adopted these ideas. The union of Church and State in primitive Calvinism was based upon the duty of the Christian government towards God, and also upon the conviction that the institutions of relative Natural Law are entirely unable to satisfy the needs of human society without the help of the Church as the organ of the Grace of God. When, however, Church and State were separated and the secular institutions were set upon their own feet, i.e. upon the basis of Natural Law alone, it was then inevitable that this basis of Natural Law should throw off the shackles of the ancient, merely relative, Christian Natural Law, and with that the need of being completed by the Church. More and more the idea gained ground of an autonomous rational Natural Law, which conceived and taught men to realize the purely utilitarian ends of the secular institutions by the light of pure reason alone, without the co-operation of the authority of revelation. Or, to express the same thing in theological terms: the Law of Nature expressed in the Second Table of the Decalogue can be realized without also realizing the First Table, which, in the fallen State, no longer belongs to the Law of Nature. This was the kind of argument which had already been employed by Milton, Roger Williams, and Bayle. Thus men felt they could quietly accept the modern secular Natural Law, and indeed all the more, since increasingly, in true English style, it was constructed on essentially empirical and utilitarian lines. But, as in the case of the Calvinists of New England in the eighteenth century, men also found it possible to adapt themselves to the French conception of Natural Law, with its rationalistic and idealistic temper, which was based on the theory of the autonomy and equality of the individual reason. Thus we can understand how it is that Neo-Calvinism has been profoundly influenced by the conception of the Law of Nature, whilst historically and theologically it justified this point of view by stressing

[416] See p. 936.

Calvin's tendencies in the direction of a rationalistic Natural Law, which have already been described in the foregoing pages. The theocratic spirit has entirely disappeared.[416a]

Neo-Calvinism extends the principle of the formation of all fellowship by means of association to every relationship in life, and everywhere it manifests a tendency to form societies for ecclesiastical and religious ends, as well as for civic and cultural purposes. Instead of the endowments, institutions, and corporations of hereditary entailed property belonging to class and guild associations, there arises the principle of the free formation of "societies", since, indeed, at bottom both the Church and the State are themselves "societies". Upon the basis of the uniformity between the laws of Scripture and of Nature, Neo-Calvinism lays stress upon the co-operation of Christianity and Humanity in a sense quite foreign to the older Calvinism. From that standpoint it then proceeds to develop a pacifist international spirit and pacifist propaganda, champions the rights of humanity, encourages the anti-slavery movement, and allies itself with philanthropic and humanitarian movements. The Feminist movement also found some support here, long before other denominations dared to broach the subject. The earnest Christian sections of American and English Protestantism—which, in England, under the influence of the Evangelicals, includes also a large part of the State Church—represent the humane, freedom-loving, and cosmopolitan ethic of Liberalism.[417]

Thus even Cromwell believed that it was possible to combine the *salus publica* of the Natural Law with the Christian idea of salvation, and with this idea of the Christian State he combined a relatively modern and liberal and utilitarian system of politics. In this respect, however, the most interesting example is that of Gladstone, the great modern representative of Christian politics. He was an Anglican, it is true, but he inclined more and more towards Nonconformity. Politically and ethically, his ideals were those of the Nonconformists. Thus for ethical reasons he supported Liberalism, extended the franchise, and declared his conviction that in the settlement of problems of foreign policy the method of arbitration was both possible and desirable. His policy was decidedly Christian, and in the secular sphere he was just as decided that the basis was that of Natural Law. If we compare with that the idea of a Christian State represented by Julius Stahl and Bismarck, the great difference between the continental Lutheran and the Anglo-Saxon world of thought, determined

[416a] See p. 937.

[417] See p. 937.

or influenced by Calvinism, stands out in clear relief. That, however, these differences are not due to the Anglo-Saxon temperament is shown by the fact that the Dutch ex-Minister Kuyper represents a similar Liberal-Natural-Law conception of secular affairs. In all these questions Neo-Calvinism has drifted far away from Calvin—a fact which Kuyper tried in vain to conceal. In the handling of secular questions it has formally come very close to modern Liberalism and Utilitarianism, and the latter finds in it (in Neo-Calvinism) one of the great moral forces which it lacks upon the Continent. At the same time it still keeps a sufficiently clear distinction, which is usually quite explicit, between itself and the abstract French doctrine of democracy and of equalitarian Natural Law.[418]

In surveying this development as a whole it becomes evident that, in the development of Calvinism as a Free Church system, an element was released which, from the very beginning, had been implicit in the idea of the "holy community", which, however, was there combined with the idea of the unity of Christian Society, and with the principle of its sole guarantee in a compulsory religious unity. The separation between these two ideas only took place under the pressure of the English Revolution, and with the help of "spiritual" and Baptist influences. The result was that that social ideal of absolute conformity was set aside, and the secular social doctrines were committed to a conception of Natural Law which was entirely utilitarian, while the Christian standards were maintained, directly, solely in the churches, and only because these ideals were realized, to some extent, within the churches did they spread farther, and penetrate Society as a spiritual and social force. To-day faith believes that finally these two currents will coalesce, since the God who is the source of the Natural Law, is the Same who creates the Church. Thus these nations which have been deeply influenced by Calvinism, in spite of the loss of outer conformity, do believe in an inner permanent conformity. Everything depends on how long both these spheres of life will be immune from the specifically modern type of criticism, and how long they can still consider that the practical demands of life are easily met by "common sense". At present these nations only know the modern world essentially as a political, social-economic, and technical development, and they have been enabled to adjust their religion to this way of life.[419] In this respect, however, great changes have taken place since Darwin, Herbert Spencer, Bentham, John Stuart

[418] See p. 938.

[419] See p. 940.

Mill, and Ruskin, and increasingly such changes will continue to take place.

Influence of Later Calvinism: (II) Puritanism and Pietism

This integral element of Calvinism, however, which centres round the idea of the holy community, found other avenues of expression than those of Congregationalism and the Free Churches, which were soon drawn into close connection with Unitarianism, the Enlightenment, and with intellectual development in general; modern Congregationalism in particular likes to emphasize the connection between its belief in liberty of conscience and the scientific love of truth.[420] This "holy community" idea might also develop within the Church merely as the intensification of the idea of sanctification and asceticism, and this is what actually happened in the development of Puritanism and Pietism. From the very outset this possibility of development belonged to the very nature of Calvinism. Is it not customary to call Bucer, who had such a decided influence over Calvin, "the Pietist among the Reformers"? And Calvin himself is often described as a "Rigorist". Here also, however, this tendency needed to be released and developed in one particular direction by definite circumstances. It emerged first of all within the setting of a wide general national life, which became to Calvinism the menace of secularization, a difficulty which could no longer be solved by Calvin's ideals administered in the Genevan style by the exercise of discipline. This danger did not arise in Geneva itself, where the Huguenots were entirely absorbed in the great political struggle, nor in Scotland, where religion was organized entirely on the principles of Geneva. Puritanism, however, had a very decided development in "Merrie England", with its dominant State Church—in the Netherlands, which never became completely Calvinist, and where the powers of the court of discipline in particular were much restricted—in the West German provinces, which were influenced by the Netherlands, and in America, which had been awakened by Methodism; through these channels Puritanism also penetrated into the life of the French and the Swiss churches in the nineteenth century. In Germany also, which likewise was menaced by the danger of secularization, and above all where Lutheranism was struggling for its life against a rigid and lifeless orthodoxy, it gave rise to a similar reform movement, to some extent stimu-

[420] See p. 940.

lated by the example of Calvinistic Pietism; from that time forward the separation between Lutheranism and Calvinism has been lessened. At the present day the whole of the Church life of the Continent is deeply influenced by the spirit of Anglo-Saxon Methodist Pietism.

Puritanism in England

English Calvinism was founded in the reign of Edward VI; it first appeared in Cambridge, where Bucer had worked,[421] and in London, where the foreign churches, which were under the leadership of John à Lasko, set an example from the very beginning [422] of spirituality and strictness of life. During the reign of Elizabeth, under the influence of the exiles who were then returning from the Continent, English Calvinism drew much closer to the Genevan ideal, and it was also in close contact with Scottish Calvinism. It then gradually divided into three main currents, Presbyterianism, Congregationalism, and Puritanism, which often merged into one another.

Presbyterianism was very clearly defined by Cartwright. Aided by Scotland during the period of the Long Parliament, it hoped to become the State religion of England. This is genuine Calvinism, spread throughout a great nation by a system of synods; it needs no further description here. It seems probable that in the main Cromwell himself belonged to the Puritan movement[423], from which he was only diverted for a time by his respect for the actual providential guidance of the nation through events and by his expectant confidence in the new revelations. A man like Baxter is a good representative of Puritan thought and achievement at its best. Down to the present day, too, the whole of English Pietism and Continental Pietism is still fed and nourished by the devotional books of Bunyan, the Baptist tinker.

The movement began by attacking the Catholic elements in the Anglican Church, coupled with the demand for the institution of a court of Church discipline, and for the formation of "pure" bodies of communicants. Under the Stuarts, however, it then became a real religious awakening, a demand for a second Reformation, in which reform in doctrine should be followed by reform in life, and which desired to realize personal spirituality and holiness as the true essence of Christianity.

[421] See *Harvey: Butzer in England, 1906* (Dissertation of Marburg), with interesting information about Bucer's socio-political proposals from *De regno Christi, pp. 77–85*; here already the conflict had begun against enclosures, monopolies, and miscarriage of justice.

[422] See p. 940.

[423] See p. 941.

The following elements were characteristic of this Puritan movement: "prophesyings" or discussions in church between the minister and the congregation about the sermon and passages of Scripture; family worship, which included catechetical instruction, conducted by the father of the family, care in the religious instruction of the young in matters which "pertain unto salvation", since it is essential that each individual should know for himself all the conditions of salvation, as ignorance leads to Hell, as Bunyan teaches very vividly in the *Pilgrim's Progress*; extempore prayer instead of a formal liturgy; severe self-discipline, systematically aiming at holiness—which explains the number of autobiographies, spiritual diaries and journals, and the stress laid on the duty of meditation; avoidance of all profane pleasures, and a strict voluntary separation between the Puritans and the unconverted "children of this world", or of the state of Nature; the demand for ascetic practices, and, above all, for the most strenuous industry as the best method of spiritual and corporal discipline; a system of casuistry and of careful self-examination and consultation, combined with a very thorough exercise of the cure of souls; its popular character, the provision of elementary education, and the effort to raise the general level of social life among "the people"; extreme simplicity of life in matters of comfort and of dress, which, however, did not prevent a certain dignity and sterling excellence of deportment; practical capacity, reliability, and honesty in every walk in life, which is displayed in a very considerable amount of activity in practical affairs—in politics, in social questions, and in commerce; and, finally, the spirit of unity, which, by laying emphasis solely upon practical experience, and the need to be "living epistles, known and read of all men", abolished the barriers between the Protestant denominations, and united all "believers" in the "saintliness" of Pietism.

In all this the Puritans were consciously opposed to the Renaissance spirit, and the literature of the Elizabethan and Stuart periods. They were also entirely opposed to the policy and economic standards of feudal times, which were expressed in the enclosures and in great monopolies. Shakespeare's hatred of these Pietists with their hostility to sensuous pleasures, and Butler's scorn for their theological narrowness and pedantry, are well known.

The following Puritan characteristics bring out the difference between this movement and that of primitive Calvinism: a far more intense individualism, which, in spite of all the means of grace, sets God and the soul over against each other in solitary immediacy; a detailed estimate of and examination into good works as "signs" of election, which introduces a legalism, self-righteousness, and a systematic asceticism to an extent which was unknown in genuine Calvinism; the spirit of solitary individual self-control and ascetic discipline, which does not exclude pleasure in the gifts and revelation of God in Nature, but which still distinguishes the elect, who use the "speech of Canaan" and whose manner of life is strict, from the children of "the world" and the "children of wrath". In all this the influence of new motives is undeniable. These new motives may be thus briefly summarized: the individualizing effects of the dogma of predestination, the collapse of strict ecclesiasticism through a period of ecclesiastical strife, and the division of Society into the strict and the lax. Naturally that produced a very different situation from that which had obtained in Calvin's strictly uniform Christian State.

On the other hand, this kind of Puritanism differs from Lutheran Pietism in its still unshaken loyalty to the Church, in its lack of emphasis upon a passionate "conviction of sin" and of a sudden emotional "assurance" of grace, and in the systematic logical result of progressive sanctification. Since in Lutheranism justification by faith is regarded as the key which suddenly unlocks the door of the heavenly treasury, and the happiness to which this gives rise is regarded as the only clear proof that the soul is in a state of grace, the central body of Lutheran Pietism naturally concentrated on "conviction of sin" and the "sense of assurance". In Calvinism, however, grace is something which existed before the world was, and slowly and gradually evolves in election. Thus in Puritanism conversion was regarded as the effect of predestination which had gradually evolved, and it believed in the careful control and cultivation of this process, and not in "feelings", which a mere temporal faith can have also. Thus it was easier to combine loyalty to the Church with this conception, since it is precisely the means of grace which mediate this progress, and from the very outset the fact that they are "spiritually" conceived does not hinder the inwardness of faith. In order to compensate for the aridity and austerity of the asceticism of sanctification mysticism is called in to help. Since, however, it was here combined with the Calvinistic idea of the *insertio in Christum non otiosum*, this kind of mysticism had a more practical and active tendency than that of Lutheranism. Chiliastic ideas appeared now and again, but on the whole they were comparatively rare, and it is not certain to what extent they may possibly have been introduced by Anabaptists and fanatics.

Thus this Calvinistic Puritan Pietism was somewhat different from Continental Pietism. It was the moral school of the English middle classes, and after the fluctuations of the great period of the Enlightenment in England it reappeared as early as the eighteenth century—this time, however, in the shape of Methodism, which was indeed in the line of the old Puritan tradition, though it also contained some essentially new elements. There will be more to say about this later on, when Methodism is described, since it finally joined the ranks of the Separatists. The Evangelical spirit which it produced, which repeatedly led the attack on the Enlightenment, in spite of various deviations, reveals even to-day the power of the Puritan Calvinistic Spirit, and has also extended its influence to non-Calvinistic Church-groups.[424]

At the outset the social structure of Puritanism included people from all ranks of Society. To the extent, however, in which it became a "Holiness" movement it became the religion of the middle classes, and since its revival through Methodism in England and America this has become more and more its settled character. The lay element became predominant, and theology and clericalism were regarded as secondary; finally, after the Revolution the court and the aristocracy broke with it altogether. Its way of life did not commend itself to the higher officials and the nobility, and it could only be forced upon the naturalism of the rural population (which was so difficult to break) with great limitations. When this whole movement was classed as "Dissent", alongside of the Established Church and the official world, the groups which composed it were forced from the very beginning into the world of commerce. This bourgeois spirit of the middle classes was carried over to New England at the very beginning by the Pilgrim Fathers, and in spite of the extremely primitive economic conditions of existence which prevailed there at first they developed the bourgeois and capitalist character which forms the predominant element in the American people, and which finally triumphed over the aristocratic and slave-holding colonies of the Southern States.

This is the group which supports Liberalism in politics, and which, from the economic point of view, out of the fundamental conditions of Calvinism which in general were already favourable, developed, with peculiar energy and with a sober realism, the spirit which gave to the bourgeois capitalism of these peoples the

[424] See p. 941.

ideal foundations for its extensive development and success among the masses of the people.[425]

"Precisianism" in the Netherlands

Calvinism in the Netherlands developed along similar lines, but its results were different. With the continuance of the Baptist groups, and of the mystical movements with their emphasis upon "spiritual religion", as well as with the formation of a strong Puritan Pietist group within the Calvinistic State Church, the same elements were present which in England led to the explosion of the great Revolution. All that was lacking was the opposition of a persecuting Catholicizing State Church, and an inner political crisis in the system of government. Here, however, from the very outset the bourgeois republic had a tendency to adopt the secular ideals of Calvinism, and here also the ecclesiastical ideals of Calvinism were finally realized in a comparatively satisfactory manner. Thus the Puritan development in the Netherlands was confined to a strongly ascetic and rigorist movement of those who were nicknamed the "Precisians" or the "Stalwarts". This movement was composed of people who were opposed to the Humanistic culture of the Renaissance, and to its accompanying phenomena of a fabulous economic development, which surpassed that of all the other nations of Europe at that time, and they formed themselves into small groups within the National State Church. A tendency in this direction had already existed within Dutch Calvinism from the time when the first national synod had met outside the Dutch boundaries at Emden in 1571, and had there first felt its solidarity as a national body, and had tried to formulate an ecclesiastical system for the whole nation. While in Holland itself it was impossible to make any attempts at Church organization owing to the Spanish tyranny, and then to the ecclesiastical chaos which was only regulated with difficulty by the local authorities, the exiled Calvinists tried to organize their Church system on the Huguenot pattern. This ecclesiastical system, which made a clear distinction between the wider circle of the baptized and the narrower circle of those who had been explicitly received into the Church through Confirmation, and which also had a strict system of moral discipline, showed its evident connection with small and strict refugee churches. After the Union of Utrecht (1579) the exiles gradually began to return to Holland; they then proceeded to make treaties with the various State authorities of particular

[425] See p. 942.

provinces, by which they created Calvinistic State churches, which, however, alongside of themselves tolerated the existence of minorities which held other opinions; these churches also had to submit to a considerable amount of State supervision, particularly with reference to the exercise of ecclesiastical discipline. Everywhere, too, they were hostile to the earlier and more liberal Reform movement in the Netherlands, and also to the great cities, which were mainly concerned with commerce, and therefore in their own interest were in favour of a policy of religious toleration. Even as early as the Synod of Emden (1571) the hostility between the *Preciesen* (i.e. the rabid Calvinists) and the *Rekkelijken* (i.e. the party of compromise) was quite evident.

After the State churches had been formed the opposition became more intense. The conflict raged round the questions of a strict Calvinistic constitution, a strict creed, the ethical ideal of Rigorism. "Precisians" and "Libertines" now faced each other in hostile camps. In this situation the primary concern of the strict Calvinists was the exclusion of the Arminians, whose outlook was predominantly humanist and deeply influenced by Erasmus, and who also stood out for the ecclesiastical dignity of the State, and for the independence and variety of conditions within each individual State; the strict Calvinists also opposed all the groups which supported the Arminians. Their endeavours were crowned with success by the treaty between the Stadtholder (who in the person of the Prince of Orange was likewise concerned for the attainment of national unity) and the strict Calvinist party at the Synod of Dort in 1618. This Synod laid down a host of regulations, which, with the aid of the Government, they hoped would help to make the Netherlands strictly Calvinist. It was, however, realized that this goal could not be attained by external means alone, and indeed, within a short time, Arminianism and Erastianism had to be tolerated once more, in accordance with the position adopted by the different States in particular. The strict Calvinists now realized that they could best attain their end by personal dealing in spiritual matters; if this were unsuccessful, then the "Libertines" might have to be excommunicated by the Church courts. Taffin and Udemann led the way, but in the main the authorities borrowed their methods of dealing with these difficulties from English Puritanism. Wilhelm Teellinck, the father of Pietism in the Netherlands, began his career under the influence of impressions of English Puritanism which he had gained during a journey in England. The other leaders, and Voet in particular, made great use of English literature, and many English books were translated into Dutch. One of the leading founders of Pietism in the Netherlands, Amesius, was an English refugee, and Lodensteyn also wished to prepare himself for his practical activity by a journey to England.

Here also, therefore, the transition from Calvinism to a Pietism which was more individualistic, based on the "conventicle" pattern, pastoral, and strongly mystical, was almost unnoticeable. But as time went on, and its latent tendencies began to develop, it became very plain that a great gulf separated this kind of Pietism, which was entirely orthodox in theology, and also loyal to the National Church, from the primitive Calvinism of a united national community sanctified by the sovereignty of Christ. A widespread system of conventicles arose with a wealth of ascetic literature; the watchword of the pastors of this school of thought was the *theologia regenitorum*; the laity was permitted to take part in public worship in the conventicles, in which women also were permitted to teach. The children of grace and of election separated themselves from the children of the world; they observed the Sabbath very strictly; they practised casuistry and self-examination and systematic asceticism, in which they were not afraid of taking hints from the Jesuits and from the Catholics in general. Home and Foreign Missions were carried on; and great stress was laid on conversion and the visible signs of conversion. Here too, as in England, the doctrine of good works as the signs and tokens of the fact of election was accepted, with which was combined a similar strict systematic legalism and exercise of self-discipline. Here also the individualistic spirit was revealed in diaries, autobiographies, narratives of edifying death-beds, as well as in the practice of family worship and in the cure of souls. The Pietists found it almost impossible to bring the secularized National Church to this austere way of life, and here too they took refuge in the ideas of eschatology and Chiliasm. Especially they balanced the prevailing hard, sober, and dry spirit of legalism and of discipline with a spirit of mystical devotion akin to the early mysticism of the Netherlands, the mysticism of St. Bernard, and the mystical interpretation of the Song of Songs; in other words, this led to the incursion of an emotional and contemplative individualism which was entirely remote from the spirit of Calvin. Here early national traditions again broke through. Voet explicitly described his teacher Teellinck as a "Calvinistic Thomas à Kempis".

The only difference between this renewed asceticism and the

older kind was this: the Dutch Pietists explicitly claimed that all secular callings ought to be penetrated by this spirit, and they violently opposed every endeavour to exempt secular life from this demand. It was explicitly an asceticism within the ordinary life of the world. Thus the Pietists did not desire Separatism, but the sanctification both of the nation and of the Church. Unbelievers were to be excluded, and believers were to rule; it ought not to be the other way round. In the true spirit of Calvinism the Pietist leaders kept their gaze fixed on life as a whole, and they continually made fresh attempts to gain the aid of the authorities in their endeavours after holiness. Their main efforts were engaged in the struggle against patronage, against luxury, against modern philosophy, and against the principle of toleration; they were, however, not very successful among the upper classes. However, the period of suffering caused by the wars of Louis XIV became a period of great popular success, which also led to a modification of the legal severity into a more evangelical, less Old Testament spirit. The programme of the sanctification of the whole Church, and of the masses, on these lines naturally could not be actually realized. Thus, in the end, Separatist phenomena appeared; and, on the other hand, radical individual mystics severed their connection with ecclesiastical orthodoxy. Mystical inwardness and the sectarian spirit, which had never died out in the Netherlands, carried many religious people away from the Church, as we shall see later on. A strong section of Pietist Christians, however, remained within the State churches all through the whole period of the Enlightenment, and through the confusion of the Napoleonic period.

When the Netherlands became a unified State and a Kingdom, and the Calvinistic State Church also had to be reorganized, then these Pietists broke off as the "separated Reformed Church", that is, as an orthodox and Pietistic Free Church. This Church still plays an important part in the life of the Netherlands, and, under its leader Kuyper (who has often been mentioned in this book), through a common policy with the Catholics, it has won for the time being an absolutely dominant position. In his historical, theoretical, and political writings Kuyper has made an intelligent and even brilliant study of this type of Neo-Calvinism, which is certainly better represented among Anglo-Saxons than on the Continent. Still in many respects this Netherlands Free Church may be compared with English Dissent.[426]

The social composition of this Pietist Calvinism of the Nether-

[426] See p. 943.

lands, which in the seventeenth century generally coincided with strict Calvinism, and by this means dominated the main body of the nation, cannot be ascertained from the material which is at present available. It is well known that the rich merchant class, above all that of Amsterdam, was Arminian in temper, and that the politicians valued toleration as the salvation of the Netherlands; it was certainly to the advantage of the exiled English and French Calvinists, the Mennonites and the sects, as also of the Spanish and Portuguese Jews, that is, of groups which both politically and economically formed an integral part of the Calvinist Republic. It is also well known that the town population was far larger than the agricultural population, and that the peasantry had already begun to turn towards a capitalistic technical method of pursuing agriculture, and were thus not so very remote from bourgeois Calvinism; in spite of that the Pietists fought hard against rural fairs, and we may conclude that among the peasants there was a good deal of resistance to their Rigorism. We may therefore assume that here also this strict Calvinism was mainly bourgeois and middle class. Here, however, it had no occasion to stand out in such pronounced opposition to the aristocratic way of life as English Puritanism and its successors, Dissent and the Evangelical Party. At this point it felt itself in harmony with the spirit of the Republic and of the bourgeois social order; it is impossible to isolate and distinguish any particular social doctrines as peculiar to the Calvinistic Pietism of the Netherlands.[427]

Pietism in the Churches of the Lower Rhine and of Switzerland

The Pietism in the Reformed Churches of the Lower Rhine, which at first was closely connected with the Calvinism of the Netherlands, and which also after the formation of the Netherlands State Churches was permanently influenced by it, does not need to be described in detail. Here the same features recur. In these Churches, however, Pietism was maintained more continuously, since in these lands Calvinism never became a State Church, but always—first of all "under the Cross", then tolerated and supported by Brandenburg, finally taken into the Rhenish-Westphalian Church—it had to prove its right to exist by an intensified practical holiness, and it never had any connection with National or State Churches. In this region, therefore, Pietism has always remained particularly strong, and is so at the present

[427] See p. 945.

time, providing a favourable atmosphere for a very flourishing sectarian movement. This Pietist movement had no visible effect on politics; as a minority religion it was shut out from all wider political influence, although even at the present day it is not regarded with favour by the Prussian authorities. Its economic results are well known. They have not been confined within the limits of a Pietist middle class, but they include the great and rich merchants and manufacturers; this is quite intelligible, since there is here no privileged class of landowners, nor any social group which would be out of harmony with vital Pietist principles.[428]

There is just as little need to describe the Calvinistic Pietism of Switzerland. It owed its origin to the influence of German Pietism; from the outset, therefore, it cannot be interpreted from the point of view of Calvinism. The religious awakenings of the nineteenth century in French Switzerland were also due to foreign influence. The Calvinistic setting has, however, had a strong influence upon this Pietism, and has stamped upon it the characteristics of ecclesiastical Puritanism. Politically the Swiss Pietists belong to aristocratic conservative circles; they really form a republican aristocracy. Its economic and social effects which attract most attention are the industrialism of French Switzerland, the wealth of Basle, and its great services to the common weal.[429]

In North America, moreover, it is impossible to isolate Calvinistic, Puritan, and sectarian influences. Each particular question would need to be studied in much closer detail. In this connection we can only emphasize the fact, which is generally recognized, that everywhere the Puritanism of the leading English section in American life is regarded, even down to the present day, as an essential element of American political and social life, although, so far as I can ascertain, no one has ever yet thrown a clear light upon the precise connection between the two facts.[430]

[428] See *Göbel: Gesch. des christlichen Lebens*. A great part of the more important passages have already been utilized above; here it is mainly clear how Calvinism and Pietism merge into one another. On this point cf. *Ritschl: Gesch. des Pietismus, I; Simons: Synodalbuch und die Kirchen unter dem Kreuz*. The Pietism of the Wuppertal, with its results in economic and ethical life, must be regarded as well known.

[429] See *Ritschl, I*; the rest is based upon general impressions; in any case Basle is a model of social ethics of a Pietist-Calvinistic kind.

[430] See p. 945.

Neo-Calvinism and the Rise of Ascetic Protestantism

If we look back, from the point at which we have now arrived, at this subject as a whole, the difference between primitive and modern Calvinism becomes quite plain. Neo-Calvinism, with its Free Church system, and its accompanying phenomena of democracy and liberalism, as well as with the Pietistic Rigorism of a strong self-controlled individualism, very utilitarian in secular affairs, has moved very far away from the early aristocratic Calvinism of the period of its foundation at Geneva, when it was still close to Lutheranism. For that very reason, however, it has become a great new social and ethical principle within Christendom.

The Christian ethic here bears a quite different complexion from its aspect in other confessions, particularly in Lutheranism. In Lutheranism it was precisely the inwardness of the Christian morality of love which demanded detachment from the external affairs of the order of law and of the State; further, it encouraged the exclusion of competition and of the struggle for existence in the professional guild organization, and from that point of view recommended the individual to withdraw into inward happiness, and in external matters to submit humbly to the existing aristocratic organizations of life. Neo-Calvinism, on the other hand, requires the Christian-Liberal organization of the State and of Society, independence and freedom for the individual, equality of opportunity as well as in the eyes of the law, the organization of international peace, and the conquest of the struggle for existence by means of self-discipline and active social help through associated effort. Only thus does it believe that the Christian ideals of freedom and brotherly love can be realized, and thus it appeals to the Bible as the great social text-book of humanity. The patriarchal conservative elements of the Christian ethic have receded, and the aspects of social reform and love of liberty have come to the front.[431]

Within Lutheranism and Calvinism, therefore, the Christian ethic has developed in diametrically opposite directions. In German Prussia, Lutheranism has become the support of the conservative, aristocratic, legal positivist, and compulsory orthodoxy order of life, and develops in its genuine adherents the Christian virtues of an inwardness which is detached from the world, along with those of submission, patience, reverence, kindly care

[431] See p. 945.

for others, and conservative endurance. Calvinism, on the contrary, has become a Christian intensification of the ideas of democracy and liberalism, and it produces the virtues of independence, love of liberty, love of humanity, and of Christian social reform.

Both the chief elements of the earliest Christian ethic have been divided between the two confessions, and in the process each has been extraordinarily invigorated. Catholicism, on the other hand, has remained until the present day a combination of both these elements, and, as occasion arises, it emphasized sometimes the democratic aspect of Natural Law, and sometimes its aristocratic and patriarchal aspect, quite sure that it can prevent any conflict between these tendencies by means of its central ecclesiastical board of control, which is daily gaining more authority. Calvinism, however, in its fundamental tendency towards as much of a national Church as possible, and in its emphasis upon the inequality of mankind in all relationships which are not directly religious, still remains inwardly aloof from the purely voluntary Church-system, and from the equalitarian communistic ideas of the strict sect, in spite of all the close connection between the two. The individualism which is based upon predestination is, and remains, different from the individualism which is supported by the rationalistic Baptist doctrine of freedom.

Now, however, the last point is certainly not settled by merely emphasizing the difference between Calvinism and the sects, since it is precisely this difference which has become so much less important in recent times. Calvinism has formally drawn nearer to the sects. On the other hand, after the Baptists had reorganized themselves into the Mennonite sect, all the other sects which appeared later on were already more or less under the influence of Calvinism. The Free Church principle and Pietism have, moreover, permitted both the main groups to come still closer to one another.

Only now is it possible to discern the position which Calvinism occupies in the world at the present day, and its social significance for civilization. Calvinism and the sect-group composed of the Baptists, Methodists, and Salvationists to-day constitute a religious unity which also represents a great sociological collective type of Christian thought. It is supported mainly by the Anglo-Saxon nations, but it is not confined to them, but is present in all Calvinist countries. It has also had a very great influence upon the religious and ethical thought and practice of contemporary Lutheranism, especially with the aid of Pietism, which arose from the same source, even although it is characteristically different.[432]

This fusion is based, on the one hand, on the fact that the sect-idea which influenced Calvinism a good deal from the outset became increasingly powerful as time went on, and finally prevailed. The whole of this previous study proves the truth of this statement. The sect-idea was only checked by the fact that Calvinism positively accepted the world, and by its conception of itself as an objective ecclesiastical institution, in spite of all its Free Church tendencies.

The theological idea of predestination which originally distinguished Calvinism so clearly from the Baptist movement has to a great extent receded, without the necessary disappearance of the practical and ethical results which were derived from it. The idea of sanctification which was bound up with that dogma lived on independently, and led to the Free Church ideal with a strict system of ethics. At this point, however, the development of the sect came into touch with Calvinism; this was due to the fact that as the sects extended and settled down under tolerant State conditions they became large national churches, and they then either gave up or largely modified their attitude of separation as "holy communities", and their opposition to "the world" with its political and economic conditions. The modern sects in particular, have been influenced by Calvinism from the very beginning, and they are very different from the Waldensians and the Baptists. Both groups agree in their emphasis upon the voluntary principle, and upon a systematic ascetic strictness in their way of life. Thus together they have developed into a force which in contradistinction to the softer, more easygoing, and less principled Lutheranism has been called "ascetic Protestantism". It might also be called the "individualistic Protestantism of active-holiness", if this description were not too cumbrous. From the point of view of historical influence this "ascetic Protestantism" is to-day the chief force in Protestantism, since it extends its influence far beyond the genuinely Pietistic and ascetic circles of "earnest" Christians. Along with mediaeval Catholicism it constitutes the second great main type of Christian social doctrine,

[432] This is a leading idea of *Max Weber*; and also of *Kuyper*; also see *Knodt, 45–46*, and *Holl* in the *Calvinreden, p. 26. Held* has noticed this also. *P. 303:* "The working classes had long ago turned away from the aristocratic State Church, and their religious needs were met especially by the sects, in which the democratic spirit of Puritanism lived on in a modified form." Finally, I would refer the reader once more to *Weber's* views on this question.

while the more subtle but weaker ideas of social doctrine in mysticism, in spiritual idealism, in Lutheranism, and in philosophical Neo-Protestantism are far behind it in historical influence.

While Catholicism had both the necessary complexity and authority to embrace and to direct the whole of life, ascetic Protestantism has the necessary hardness and flexibility, the religious energy, and the matter-of-fact sobriety, the power to adapt itself to the ethical ideas of the average man combined with doctrinal simplicity, which likewise enable it, in its own way, to dominate the whole of life; and just as Catholicism was connected with the general conditions of mediaeval life, so ascetic Protestantism is connected with modern developments in the political, economic, social, and technical spheres.

In order to understand this fully, however, it will be necessary also to study the development of the sect-type within Protestantism. In so doing we shall discover that mysticism and spiritual idealism contain influences which have a vital effect upon the social doctrines of all confessions. We shall note in particular the significance of the transformation of the sect-type into great mass communities, the development of their freedom within the sphere of the tolerant modern State, and the adaptation of the sects to the bourgeois social order. Since, however, in all this there takes place that adjustment with Neo-Calvinism to which allusion has already been made, the social doctrines of Neo-Calvinism can only be presented in a conclusive manner in conjunction with the social doctrines of the sects.

4. THE SECT-TYPE AND MYSTICISM WITHIN PROTESTANTISM

Introduction

Lutheranism and Calvinism do not represent the whole of Protestantism. In these two great confessions the Reformers were able to work out their basic idea of the Church as an institution. It was thus that they maintained their connection with the fundamental idea of the Early Church, and, above all, with mediaeval Catholicism and its theory of a universal Church of the people, dominating the whole of civilization. Other movements, however, of a sectarian and mystical type, constantly emerged alongside of this mediaeval unity of Catholic civilization, and their ideas had a most decided influence upon the thought of Catholicism. The same phenomena appeared both within and alongside of Protestantism. Thus, in addition to the institutional idea of the

Church, Protestantism also developed the characteristic ideas of the sects and of mysticism. Since these ideas originated in the New Testament,[433] the emphasis laid on the New Testament by Protestantism naturally gave a great impetus to these tendencies. In Protestantism, however, the need to work out its own idea of the Church as an institution, and its relation to an absolute, objective, supreme truth of revelation, was felt to be a matter of paramount concern; the sectarian and mystical movements were therefore thrust aside and forced to adopt an independent position. However, in spite of ecclesiastical antagonism, both these movements still remained in closest touch with the Protestant Churches, and from the middle of the seventeenth century these ideals had an increasing influence upon them. Reference has already been made to the adjustment which took place between these ideals and those of Calvinism. The reason for this is clear. From the very beginning, indeed, the Protestant Reform movement had been permeated by both these tendencies, and its opposition to Catholicism was due, to a great extent, to the co-operation of both these factors.

It was through mysticism that Luther first gained that personal certainty of salvation in which he found that the ennobling and overcoming power of grace was imparted, not through mechanical sacraments which could not deliver from conviction of sin, but through an inner spiritual experience. The strictness and purity of Luther's Scriptural attitude towards ethics made him place the personal ethic of the Sermon on the Mount, and the doctrine of the priesthood of all believers, in the forefront of his ethical teaching. This meant that he had discarded the mediaeval doctrine of the compromise between Nature and Supernature. He strove to find a new interpretation for the forms and values of the natural life: thus, in his earlier period, Luther's outlook was often very similar to that of the sect-type.

Protestantism, however, did not attain its full independence, combined with an ever-increasing hostility towards the sectarian and mystical tendencies, until the following points had become clear: first of all, men had to learn to base their hope of salvation firmly and exclusively upon the objective assurance of the forgiveness of sins through the Death of Christ; this led to concentration of emphasis upon the inward appropriation of the forgiveness of sins, directly offered from without; everything else followed logically from this central fact of experience; on this objective foundation the Protestant Church was firmly established, with

[433] See p. 946.

power to mediate the certainty of redemption through the Word and the Sacrament; the final stage of this process was reached when the spiritual ethic of the Sermon on the Mount spread from the Church outwards into the established forms of professional and social life.[434]

This separation between Church and Sect, however, did not prevent the sectarian and mystical movements from feeling themselves, to some extent at least, at home within Protestantism. In point of fact, within Protestantism these sectarian and mystical ideas have undergone a peculiar process of development, very different from that of the older forms; they differ completely from the development of the same ideas within the sphere of post-Tridentine Catholicism.

At the close of the section on the Middle Ages the main characteristics of the sect-type were indicated.[435] Here, therefore, it is only necessary to bring out the connection between the Protestant sects, or the Anabaptist movement, and the mediaeval sects; we also need to make clear the particular form which they now developed within Protestantism.

The question of mysticism, however, needs different treatment. It was, of course, mentioned incidentally in connection with the later Middle Ages,[436] but its religious nature has not yet been analysed, nor the religious-sociological character with which it is connected. At that stage it was not necessary to go into the question fully, for although even then mysticism was an important factor for theology, for the philosophy of religion, for the history of civilization and for psychology, the religious and sociological peculiarities and results had scarcely begun to appear.

Mysticism meant the rise of a lay religion within the Church, and it greatly encouraged the individualistic tendency of the bourgeois world. But at that time it had no influence upon the life of the religious community, nor had it yet any critical significance in connection with the idea of the Church, or with doctrine. Mysticism was still either under the protection of the Church, or it was connected with the Religious Orders. It never stood alone. Protestant mysticism, on the contrary, learnt to regard itself as the outcome of the idea of the priesthood of all believers, and of the personal religion of conviction, and thus it was able to make an independent stand.

In studying this question our primary aim will be to make clear the sociological results of these phenomena. As we proceed it will become clear that they introduce into the history

[434] See p. 947. [435] See above, *pp. 328–343*. [436] See above, *pp. 376–377*.

of Christianity a principle which has to-day assumed a position of paramount importance.

I. The Baptist Movement and the Protestant Sects

The first question with which we have to deal is that of the Protestant sect, or the Anabaptist movement. At an earlier stage in this work we have shown that the sect-idea was deeply rooted in the thought and creative activity of the great Reformers. Luther made a distinction between the ethic of the Sermon on the Mount, or the ethic of the individual, and the secular or official ethic, or the ethic of the relative Natural Law of the fallen State. He defined the former as the genuine Christian ethic. In so doing, however, he was really only making concessions to the needs of the national Church, necessities which God allowed to exist, but which were actually due to the Fall.[437] Traces of the earlier idea remained, however; it was never entirely hidden, but was only obscured by the hollowness of orthodoxy. This is revealed by the fact that at the outset of his career Luther had reckoned on the influence of smaller groups of earnest Christians to leaven and influence the general compulsory religion of the Territorial Church. It was only the danger of subjectivism which caused these plans to be set aside, and in the uniform Territorial Church of the Visitations they were allowed to disappear.[438]

The opposition within Protestantism has never ceased to appeal to these statements which belong to Luther's earlier days; they are echoed again and again, from the days of the early Baptists down to the time of the English Independents and the German Pietists.[439]

The sect-type has influenced Calvinism still more strongly, though from a different point of view. Calvin adopted the sect-ideal—the idea of the "holy community"—and also the sectarian methods by which this ideal could be realized, such as excommunication and Church discipline, and he applied this ideal to a whole territorial and national Church, instead of to small groups of genuine Christians within the Church. The non-elect and the unbelievers were to be disciplined for the glory of God with the same means which were to be used to develop and establish in the elect a spirit of genuine spiritual piety. Thus in Calvinism the sect-ideal of the holy community became the general ideal of

[437] Cf. *Harnack: Dogmengeschichte, III⁴, p. 904*: "That which was divided between the cloister and the world in Catholicism the Reformers desired to unite in common labour." This, however, is simply "intramundane asceticism".

[438] See p. 947.

[439] See p. 947.

national life and of civilization; at a later stage the inner tension which this produced shattered the solidarity of Calvinism.

It is not difficult to understand why the Protestant sect-type[440] extended its influence far beyond the measure permitted by the ecclesiastical Reformation itself. An entirely natural factor in this development was the influence of the Bible, including that of the Sermon on the Mount, which could only be adapted with difficulty to the compromise which the Reformers had achieved. Again and again it was the direct influence of the Sermon on the Mount which impelled people to form strict Christian communities, whose members wished to live according to this standard; they then found it impossible to remain under the wing of a national Church, and of a general civilized society. This phenomenon is all the more intelligible because both in thought, and possibly also in organization, the religious life of that day was already permeated with these ideas, due very largely to Waldensian or Bohemian influences. Thus the groups which held these views saw in the Reformation simply the development of their own programme, and in its victories the possibility of developing a free, anti-hierarchical, and entirely lay religious movement.

General Characteristics of the Baptist Movement

In fact, under the stimulus of the Reformation, on every hand there sprang into existence an enormous number of small groups of earnest Christians, living apart from "the world", claiming complete civil and religious freedom, whose main ideal was the formation of religious communities composed of truly "converted" persons, on a basis of voluntary membership. Their outward symbol of membership was Adult Baptism, which implied the voluntary principle. They rejected Infant Baptism, with its implications of an all-inclusive, non-ethical basis of Church membership. Another characteristic external sign was the demand for Church discipline, and authority to excommunicate, which was closely related to the demand for "a pure Church". They did not accept the ecclesiastical doctrine of the Sacrament. To them the Lord's Supper was mainly a festival of Christian fellowship, and an expression of personal faith in Christ. Thus they were classed with the "*Sakramentierier*".* Their real strength, however, lay in the

[440] See p. 949.

* Luther's epithet for those who denied the Real Presence of Christ in the Sacrament of the Lord's Supper. He applied it particularly to men like Zwingli, Karlstadt, Oecolampadius, Schwenkfeld, and others.—Translator's Note.

emphasis which they gave to their desire to be a "holy community", "holy" in the sense of the Sermon on the Mount, and implying a voluntary community composed of mature Christians. In practice this "holiness" was expressed in the following ways: in detachment from the State, from all official positions, from law, force, and the oath, and from war, violence, and capital punishment; the quiet endurance of suffering and injustice as their share in the Cross of Christ, the intimate social relationship of the members with each other through care for the poor and the provision of relief funds, so that within these groups no one was allowed to beg or to starve; strict control over the Church members through the exercise of excommunication and congregational discipline. Their form of worship was a simple service, purely Scriptural in character, conducted by elected preachers and pastors who had been ordained by the laying-on of hands, and prayer by the synods representing the local groups.[441] They also accepted the moral Law of Nature, but they opposed the relative conception accepted by the Church, the compromise of Natural Law with Original Sin. Like their mediaeval predecessors, they interpreted the Law of Nature as the absolute Natural Law of the Primitive State; from this interpretation they sometimes deduced conclusions which were as revolutionary as those proclaimed by the followers of Wyclif and Huss. In general, however, they held that it was impossible to carry out the Natural Law, and the Law of Christ with which they identified it, in the world, because the world is of the devil, and is the scene of suffering and endurance until the Advent of Christ, from which the faithful are to prepare themselves by separation from it. Thus this movement displays the main characteristics of the sect-type, with which our previous study of the question has already made us familiar.

Origin of the Baptist Movement

Thus we can understand why some thinkers have even suggested that perhaps these Baptist sects were merely a sign of the reappearance of the mediaeval, Waldensian sect, made possible by the Reformation. To that we must reply: (1) that we have no conclusive proof of the continued existence of any sect of this kind as a uniform international organization, and (2) that there is no evidence that the Baptist leaders came from these sectarian circles. They were all the product of the religious movements of the time; some were originally Lutheran, others Zwinglian or Humanist, while some came from the ranks of the laity whose

[441] See p. 951.

main interest was in the Bible. But in addition to the positive characteristics which have just been indicated—the priesthood of all believers, the central position of the Bible, and their emphasis on personal religion—these movements also contained some negative features—a spirit of criticism, of disappointment with the Reformation, as well as a more thorough emphasis upon its main ideas. This comes out in their emphasis upon Adult Baptism (or rebaptism) as the motto of the new movement; it comes out still more clearly in the struggle against the moral sterility of the great Churches of the Reformation, with their emphasis on compulsion in religious matters, and in the bitter scorn which the Baptist leaders pour upon the friendship of the Reformation leaders with the world, and with royalty. These facts are familiar, though their deeper significance is less generally recognized.

The situation thus created was only the outward expression of the inward difficulty of the Reformation Churches. They had an extremely high, almost Utopian ethical ideal. They had renounced the Catholic system of stages, and had given up the hierarchical authoritative direction of souls, but their great desire was to penetrate the whole mass of the population equally with the miracle of the strict Christian ethic of love, and thus to make the life of the world the direct organ of the love which religion inspires. Lutheranism hoped to achieve this object entirely idealistically, purely through confidence in the miraculous power of the Word; Calvinism, more practically, hoped to attain the same end by means of an apparatus of control, based upon Scripture, and founded by God. It is not surprising that this extreme idealism was grievously disappointed, and that this practical reform did not succeed. In contrast with Catholicism the ideal was universalized, deepened, and intensified, and Catholic methods of compulsion were renounced. Thus, within the sphere of Lutheranism in particular, a process of practical demoralization set in, which was freely admitted by Luther and his companions; down to the present day Catholic controversialists make great capital out of this fact.[442] Above all, it furnished the Baptist opposition parties with plenty of material for criticism. Even in Geneva Calvinism was unable to hold out for more than half a century at its highest level. The deterioration of the Calvinist ideal is clearly visible in that Puritanism which sank to the level of a self-righteous piety, regarding material prosperity as the Divine reward of orthodoxy.

The more that practical and ethical achievement fell away from the ideal, however, the more the churches, in true ecclesiastical

[442] See p. 952.

fashion, concentrated upon the objective possession of salvation, upon the Divine endowment which is entirely independent of a righteousness achieved by good works. In Protestantism this Divine endowment meant Scriptural doctrine, and the predominant position of the pure message in the ministry of the Word. Thus the Protestant Churches fell a prey to an orthodoxy, which, with its limitation to "the Word", "pure doctrine", and the confession of faith, was much narrower and severer than Catholic orthodoxy, which, indeed, finds salvation, not only in correct dogmas, but in worship and in mystical devotion, that is, in non-dogmatic imaginative elements. This emphasis on orthodoxy also led to a closer relationship with the civil authority, which alone could secure, at least outwardly, the supremacy of the true faith. This relation between the Protestant Church and the civil authority naturally resulted in the whittling down of the subtle Lutheran distinction between the real Christian ethic of love and the secular ethic of Natural Law, till it was almost entirely obliterated; this, of course, meant that morality itself became secularized.[443] The problem of the relation of the Christian ethic to war, authority, force, and law was soon no longer felt. On the contrary, men boasted that it was one of the advantages of the pure Reformed doctrine that it provided scope and a Divine sanction for all these things, which would not be countenanced by monks or fanatics, with the natural assent of all the opponents of Christ.

It was at this point that the Anabaptist movement arose. It attacked the new theological dogmatism, the compulsory State Church, and the tendency to secularization.[444] As a movement it throve on opposition; it laid particular emphasis upon certain elements which had originally formed part of the spiritual ideal of the Reformers, which, however, under the stress of circumstances, had become merged in the idea of a national Church which compromises with secular civilization. The Anabaptists deliberately opposed the results of this compromise, and in so doing they also opposed the whole idea of the Church, and of an ecclesiastical civilization. This violent opposition, however, proves that in reality it had been caused by the Reformation itself. This is also proved by its apocalyptic-eschatological temper, an element which we do not find in the earlier evangelical sects. On

[443] The well-known books of *Tholuck* and *Hundeshagen* speak very plainly on this point.

[444] This point is brought out very plainly and vividly by the testimonies which have been collected by *Sebastian Franck*, *Schwenkfeld*, and *Gottfried Arnold*.

this point the Anabaptist movement was in agreement with Luther, who felt that he could only interpret such a collapse of the whole ecclesiastical tradition from the point of view of the approaching End of the World, and the coming Antichrist, who had been proclaimed by prophecy.

To the Baptists, with their principle of small voluntary communities, separate from the world, this attitude seemed quite natural, for it was only possible to combine the idea of the world-wide dominion of Christ with the break-up of Christendom into small groups of this kind which separate themselves from the degenerate Church of the people, on the assumption that the great falling away of the masses, and the gathering up of Christendom into a small group of believers, prophesied in the Apocalypse, had already begun. It was only after these eschatological hopes had been raised that certain individual groups proceeded to try to erect the Heavenly Jerusalem by force. Further, in the excitement caused by this expectation, they opened the door to mystical and "enthusiastic" influences, which later on were forbidden by the pure Baptists of the Mennonite persuasion; these influences, however, were also connected with the excitement created by the Reformation, and in many ways they united with the various mystical movements which branched off from it. All this was alien to the true Waldensian movement, which proves that in the Baptist movement we are dealing with a by-product of the Reformation, which is closely connected with the Scriptural purism and moral earnestness of the Reformation, but whose deep inward opposition to the ecclesiastical idea of the Reformers is also quite evident.

It is, however, probable, and even possible, that the wide expansion of the Baptist movement was greatly assisted by some lingering traces of the influence of the Waldensians and of other sects; it is even possible that this fact alone provides the final explanation of the growth of this movement. It is quite possible also that here and there individual leaders may have been influenced by traditions of this kind, in ways which we cannot now trace.[445] The Reformation, however, and the opposition which it aroused, certainly provoked the rise of this movement, and helped to shape its course. At bottom, therefore, the whole movement belonged to the Reformation. It was caused by the Reformation; it appealed to its principles and ideals, and it remained in closest touch with it; Catholicism, on the contrary, rejected this Anabaptist tendency entirely.

[445] See p. 953.

Catholic and Protestant Attitude towards the Sects

Thus the history of the Christian Church presents us with this strange spectacle, in which the very varied sect-movement, which had formed the complement of Catholicism, was almost entirely vanquished in the Catholic sphere, and then went over as a whole into the Protestant camp. Tridentine Catholicism excluded the unlimited possibilities of development which mediaeval Catholicism had contained; it became such a rigid centralized organization that sect and fellowship movements could no longer exist within its sphere. The motive which led to the formation of sects naturally did not disappear suddenly from within Catholicism. But they were diverted into the formation of new Orders and ecclesiastical confraternities. Thus Tridentine Catholicism of the Counter-Reformation experienced a new and brilliant period, during which many new Orders were founded; since then, however, the sect-impulse within the Catholic Church has died out. The Bible was placed under the strict control of the Church, and every kind of "fellowship" group was obliged to submit to the ecclesiastical authority.[446] This has been the official Catholic position ever since. The only development has been in the direction of increased rigidity.

The Protestant Church, however, with its strong emphasis upon the Bible, its lack of hierarchical centralization, and the possibility which it contains of continually offering fresh interpretations of the Scriptures, from that time forward provided a fruitful soil for the sect-movement. It is true that at first the Protestant Church persecuted and suppressed this movement as cruelly and violently as the Catholic Church had done; but the Protestant movement was unable to eradicate the principle completely, because it contained within itself the elements of this principle. Hence new sects arose continually out of the ashes of the persecuted movements. It is the combination of all these factors which explains the peculiarly complicated position of the sect-movement in relation to Lutheranism and Calvinism.

In its austere ideal of detachment from the world, and its emphasis upon good works, the sect-type is more adapted to Catholicism; for monasticism bears a certain resemblance to it, and the monastic life itself, to some extent at least, acknowledges the sect-ideal. On the other hand, the sect-type, in its insistence

[446] Cf. *Gothein: Staat und Gesellschaft des Zeitalters der Gegenreformation, pp. 139–145, 161–176.*

on the necessity for judging everything by the standard of the Bible, on personal "assurance", and on ecclesiastical liberty, is really more at home within Protestantism. Finally, also the sect-type completely accepted the Protestant doctrine of grace and the idea of the "calling".

At bottom, however, this complicated relationship is not difficult to understand. Both in Catholicism and in Protestantism the sect-idea arose out of fundamental primitive Christianity, but in each case its form of expression was entirely different. Catholicism controlled this tendency by allowing it to express itself in the formation of new Religious Orders and confraternities, and, in the end, it stamped out every trace of an independent sect-movement. The Protestant attempt to destroy the sect-movement was, however, unsuccessful. At first it merely tolerated its existence outside the Protestant Churches, in the form of Dissent. Finally, however, in the form of Pietism, it incorporated the sect-movement into its own life.

Catholicism was more pliable and ready to compromise. Just as in its graded ethical system it accepted secular civilization, and at that particular point in history in the Tridentine Reform absorbed the Renaissance most thoroughly, so also in an equally adaptable manner it assimilated the sect-idea through its new Orders and Confraternities. On the other hand, however, so far as it could, it annihilated every sectarian or cultural movement which attempted to maintain an independent existence.

Protestantism was simpler, narrower, and more Scriptural, and therefore it rejected both non-ecclesiastical culture and the sect-movement. But its unchangeable principle of personal conviction and "assurance", and its emphasis upon Scriptural purity, led it in the end to tolerate the sect-movement as an independent phenomenon. The relationship between the two, however, was so close and intimate that official Protestantism was deeply affected by the influence of the sect-ideal; this, again, led to a wealth of development, compared with which the elastic Catholic synthesis seems hard and narrow.

In the last resort, however, the sect is a phenomenon which differs equally from the ecclesiastical spirit of Protestantism and of Catholicism. It is an independent branch of Christian thought; it is the complement of the Church-type, and it is based upon certain elements in the New Testament ideal. The great national churches represented both the idea of grace, and that of a common spirit which produces individual souls, and thus they also assimilated into their own life the presuppositions of civilization in general. For them the main question was this: how could they gain an influence over the masses? Salvation and grace are as independent of the measure of subjective realization of strict ethical standards as they are pliable in adjusting themselves to the institutions of Natural Law, institutions which have become necessary through sin, which have a healing and disciplinary effect, but they certainly cannot really be called Christian. This adaptation to the institutions based on Natural Law turns the Christian ethic into a compromise which, in one way or another, accepts the world.[447] Thus, from the point of view of their influence upon world history, the great national churches formed the main expression of Christian thought; they are great historic powers, under whose influence the Christian ethic has been carried forward and developed. They were the first great result of the world mission of the Primitive Church. Once they were firmly established, however, they provided both the material and the occasion for the play of forces, through which there was introduced the critical and hostile element of an individualistic form of Christian piety, severely ethical in the Primitive Christian sense, which did not believe in a mass religion at all. This criticism, however, contained a fundamental element of the genuine ethic of Primitive Christianity. Under its influence there arose small groups of earnest souls who judged the life of the world by the high ethical standard of the Gospel. Their sociological expression naturally took the form of a society of persons united by a deep common personal conviction, who were entirely opposed to the ecclesiastical system, with its inclusive character, and its claim to be the sole depository of grace. This development took place within all the Christian churches, because in them all, along with the Bible, and the endowment of grace, the germ of the sect-type was latent. This seed of the sect-type developed along different lines within the different churches, but the end attained was the same. Within Catholicism its main form of expression was detachment from the world, realized in practice on the higher moral level of monasticism; within Protestantism it expressed itself in an individualistic and subjective method of interpreting the Scriptures, and in its emphasis upon the attainment of salvation without priesthood or hierarchy. There is no doubt that Protestantism has proved the more fruitful soil for the growth of the sect-idea. The whole course of Protestant development has been accompanied by and carried through with the aid of a powerful sect-movement. The extraordinary sociological consequences of this development

[447] See p. 953.

of the sect-type within Protestantism have already been shown by its influence upon Calvinism, and in this chapter this will become still more evident.

Space forbids me to give a detailed presentation of the sect-movement at this point; all I can do is to mention the salient features, and to outline the general course of the movement, in the same way as this subject was handled in connection with the Middle Ages.

Anabaptists at Zürich, and First Extension of the Movement

The Anabaptist movement broke out in 1525, in Zürich, in radical Reform circles, to whom Zwingli's application of the principles of Scripture seemed inadequate. The following were its main characteristics: emphasis on Believers' Baptism, a voluntary church, the precepts of the Sermon on the Mount, the rejection of the oath, of war, law, and authority, and, finally, the most far-reaching mutual material help, and the equality of all Church members, the election of elders and preachers by the local congregations, and, to a large extent, the unpaid character of the pastoral office; these principles were in close agreement with the democratic tendencies of the masses. In the main, the whole movement sprang from the lower classes; primarily it was recruited from the ranks of the manual labourers, miners, and similar groups. Its leaders were mostly trained pastors, whose main concern at first was with the literal application of the Word to existing conditions, and with questions of Church discipline. As time went on, however, they learned how to appeal to the democratic instincts of the masses.

The first demands of the peasants were moderate enough, and (probably quite rightly) they have been connected with their doctrines, in so far as they referred to the restoration of the law of Christ and of the apostolic Church. The later radicalism of the Peasants' Revolt, however, was connected with the Hussite and Taborite ideas of the absolute law of God and of Nature, and not with the ideas of the persecuted Baptists.[448] The moderate Baptists, however, who suffered patiently for their convictions, constituted

[448] On this point look up the article entitled *Bauernkrieg* by *Sommerlad* in *Schiele's Lexikon*. He rightly emphasizes the Natural Law in its absolute Taborite significance and connects the radical demands with Hussitism. The moderate early demands of the Twelve Articles are connected by *Berens: The Digger Movement* with the Anabaptist movement; *Stolze: Zur Vorgeschichte des Bauernkrieges, 1908*, calls the Baptist Hubmeier one of the authors.

the main body of the movement. Rioting and violence had no place in their programme. It was only the Moravian groups, under the leadership of Hut, which practised communism, refused to recognize any "man-made law", and abandoned themselves to a Chiliasm of the Joachimite type.

From Zürich the movement spread with great swiftness and intensity: everywhere it attracted to itself all who were dissatisfied with the Reformation, as well as a remnant formed of members of the earlier mediaeval evangelical groups. The whole of Central Europe was soon covered with a network of Anabaptist communities, loosely connected with each other, who all practised a strictly Scriptural form of worship. The chief centres were in Augsburg, Moravia, and Strassburg, and, later on, in Friesland and the Netherlands.

The whole movement was an early premature triumph of the sectarian principles of the Free Churches.

This whole principle, however—apart from the Anabaptists' objection to all forms of official connection with government and the administration of justice—was so harshly opposed to the still dominant mediaeval idea of a social order expressed in a State Church that Catholics and Protestants alike could see in it nothing less than the destruction of the very basis of Society itself. Hence the response of the official Churches to the movement was a horrible and sanguinary persecution. First of all, the leaders of the movement were taken and put to death. Some were burned alive; some were slain by the sword; others were drowned. Then came the turn of the masses, who were decimated with savage cruelty.[449]

Before 1526, while the ecclesiastical conditions in some places were still most unsettled, individual Baptist groups began to organize their own religious system on an independent basis; with all the unlimited possibilities of ecclesiastical organization which seemed to be opening out in many directions, it looked as though there were a sphere and a future for the Anabaptist movement. For that very reason, however, the ecclesiastical authorities brought this provisional period to an end as quickly as possible; they resolutely manufactured an ecclesiastical unity from above, since it did not arise spontaneously from below, through the power of the Spirit. Only where a positive organization of this

[449] Cf. the negotiations of Philip of Hess about the policy to be adopted with regard to the Anabaptists in *Hochhuth: Z. f. hist. Theol.* Only the Landgrave is in favour of a relatively humane policy, but he cannot carry it through against the men of order who want to "preserve the State and Society".

kind was still impossible, as, for instance, in the Netherlands before 1572, did the Baptist movement prolong its existence. Here it finally attained a permanent, though limited, possibility of life. Everywhere else persecution was dominant. This terrible pressure of persecution then drove the Baptist communities into an excited Revivalism and Chiliasm, and thus some fanatics in the Netherlands (just as the Taborites had done at an earlier date), came to the conclusion that the Last Days were at hand, and that they were justified in attempting to set up the Heavenly Jerusalem by force. They based their argument upon the example of the Old Testament and the Apocalypse. This led to the horrors of Münster, which was a disaster for the whole movement, and only made their persecutors feel still more sure that their oppressive attitude was justifiable and right.

The Mennonites

Out of the confusion which ensued, Menno Simons gathered the Anabaptists into a peaceful evangelical community; he excluded the Taborite-Joachimite type of fanatic, and gave the leading position in the movement to the Zürich section, which had been in the majority from the outset; at the same time he appealed to the example of the mediaeval evangelical sects. The following were to be the general lines of organization: each group was to be controlled by the spirit of the Sermon on the Mount, with power to excommunicate and discipline its members; Church members were all to be considered equal; the leaders in the community were to be openly elected to office, otherwise remaining in civil life. The taking of oaths, participation in war and in the administration of justice, were still forbidden. Great stress was laid on separation from all non-Baptist Christians; this went so far as to demand that a marriage should be dissolved in which the husband or the wife had been either excommunicated or convicted of unbelief.

Conditions in the Netherlands, where each individual State organized its Church system independently, and on different lines, gave the Mennonite Baptists the right to a bare existence, although they had no civil rights, and had to endure much oppressive treatment from orthodox Calvinism. Finally, under the influence of the surrounding Calvinism, to an even greater extent they have adopted the Protestant ethic of the "calling", and from this standpoint they have learned, not merely to tolerate the State, law and public life, but they themselves have become part of its life. In time of war they made their contribution to the State through the taxes, and in return they were granted full civil rights. They became bourgeois, prosperous, and wealthy. When, after 1650, the radical element reappeared, they rightly condemned these Baptists for compromising with the world.[450]

Even then, however, the Baptist movement was unable to create a uniform organization. It split up into various Free Church groups, large and small. The Baptists of Friesland and Waterland were inclined to assert the independence of the individual congregation; they also laid a good deal of emphasis upon individual freedom in general. This attitude was opposed to the spirit of those groups which were administratively centralized, and which exercised a strict Church discipline. From this centre the spirit of independence spread through the whole Baptist movement, till at last it either did away altogether with the system of Church government by a supreme Board of Elders, or, at least, it limited their powers to such an extent that, in the end, they became merely nominal.[451]

English Baptists, and the Rise of the General Baptists

The next important development of the Baptist movement took place in England. It had been introduced into that country about the year 1530 by the masses of Dutch emigrants who joined forces with the aftermath of the Lollard movement. At first they were of the Chiliastic Hofmann type, but later on they became Mennonites. Here also they were cruelly persecuted as "Separatists" and enemies of the social order. In spite of all these difficulties, however, they maintained their existence until the period of the English Revolution, when we shall hear more about them.

On the other hand, from England there went forth influences which helped to draw Pietistic Calvinism into closer contact with the Baptist movement. We have seen already that the same phenomenon occurred in connection with Congregationalism, but in this instance the contact was far closer. About 1602 a certain John Smyth founded a Congregational church at Gainsborough; it was from this congregation that there arose the great Church of the General Baptists, which to-day has spread into

[450] See p. 953.

[451] *Ten Cate, Gemeente of oudsten souverein? Doopgezinde Bijdragen, 46, 1906, pp. 141–151:* "Bij een karakteristiek van de innerlijke ontwikkeling der gemeenten van hun ortstaan c. 1650, mag deze trek van overgang der suvereiniteit uit de handen der oudsten in die der gemeente niet worden vergeten: De oudsten verloren hunne macht en te gemeende ontwikkelde zich tot een geheel democratische independente instelling" (*p. 51*).

many parts of the world. At first the basis was Puritan and Calvinistic; but while Browne and Robinson developed their Congregationalism on very similar lines to the Independency of the Baptists, without accepting the specific Baptist doctrines, Smyth, who took his congregation to Amsterdam, and settled there as a Refugee Church, was drawn farther and farther into the Baptist way of thinking. Finally he acknowledged Believers' Baptism as the logical result of Separatism and the "holy community". He baptized himself, and then the members of his church, and thus re-established the church as a Baptist congregation. Then he openly declared his connection with the Baptists and the Mennonites, and joined that body. One section of his congregation, in spite of a fraternal relationship with the Mennonites, did not agree to the fusion of the two elements and, under the guidance of Helwys and Murton, its members returned to England in 1611. It was there that their church became the mother of the great Church of the General Baptists. The main features of this Church are these: it rejects the doctrine of predestination, demands separation between Church and State, establishes Church fellowship upon a voluntary basis, ethical and spiritual fitness, and upon baptism by immersion; it renounces the dogmatic errors of the early Baptists, permits its members to swear in a court of law, to take part in war, and to take official positions under the State for the purposes of citizenship; it rejects communism, and desires to be a corporation which includes all classes without any social distinctions whatsoever.[452] Otherwise this Church maintained its connection with the Baptists of the Reformation period, although, on account of their historic origin and their permanent environment, they became strongly impregnated with the spirit of Calvinism. Throughout the confused period of the English Revolution they maintained a precarious existence; since then, in England, America, and on the Continent, they have developed into a large body.[453] In reality all that they have retained of the original Baptist spirit is the Free Church principle of membership on a voluntary basis, and the requirements of moral discipline; otherwise, however, they have gone far beyond Menno Simons, and have accepted the general Pro-

[452] *Newman, p. 392.* For "spiritualist" features in Smyth's original programme, and which the original Congregationalists with whom he was closely connected decidedly rejected, see *Barclay, 106–109*; such features are always more likely to occur among the Baptists than among people who wield dogmatic authority. Yet he desired to be connected with the external Word as the means of the Spirit, the affirmation of the moral law of the Bible, and strict order in the Church.

[453] See p. 953.

testant ethic of "the calling", together with the recognition of the State, of law, and of economic life. They have thus severed their exclusive connection with the lower classes and have gained adherents from the most varied ranks of Society. To-day it is more accurate to speak of Baptist "Free Churches" than of Baptist "sects". The persecuted Baptist movement with its patience and hope, in ways which had already been prepared by Menno Simons, thus made its peace with the world, very much along the same lines as the Protestant churches of other confessions had done. The only original elements which remained were: the voluntary principle of Church membership, a strict morality, and a very thorough individualism, which—like the individualism of the Congregationalists and Independents (which had been produced by Calvinism) with which it was closely related in religion, and also in positive historical ways—affected the whole of the political and social life of America, as well as that of the English middle classes, and united itself also with other impulses which were moving in this direction.

The radical Baptist element, however, had not died out. It renewed its vigour at the time of the English Revolution. In an earlier section of this book we have seen how Congregationalists imitated the Baptists in their Church constitution, and how the Cromwellian Puritans and Independents, with their enthusiasm for lay-preaching and their aloofness from Church organization, also represented Baptist principles; all these factors then united, to the advantage of the Baptists and the Quakers among others. The chief characteristics of these Independents, however, were a greater emphasis upon the more spiritual and Pietist elements on the one hand, and, on the other hand, upon the Calvinist, Puritan, and theocratic elements. The peculiar feature of this Cromwellian Independency consisted precisely in that union of the toleration of a free Protestant Church organization, with a strict surveillance of Christian morals, combined with the right to carry on a Holy War for the cause of God, and with the inauguration of a Christian-civic commonwealth. Its connection with the Baptist movement lay rather in the Baptist ideals which were generally accepted by Calvinism, and in the explicit freedom of Church organization than in the characteristic Baptist radicalism of a new building up of the Kingdom of God upon the ruins of secular and civil organization. The radical Baptist spirit, however, was very much alive in Harrison and his followers, and it was increased by the newly revived Chiliasm.

In the army, Harrison's regiment formed the real focus for the sectarians, while Cromwell's regiments were the seat of Puritanism. In the Barebones Parliament, moreover, Harrison and his followers wanted to set aside all law and all courts of law, in order to prepare a people, freed from all secular ties, for the Advent of Christ; indeed, many of them attacked the idea of private property, and they wished to break up the Church organization altogether by abolishing its financial foundation—the tithing system; all earthly authority was to be destroyed in order to make room for the Heavenly King and the coming Kingdom of God. It is difficult to judge to what extent these ideas were accepted by the nation and by the army, and how far they are a real link with the original Baptist and Sectarian radicalism. At any rate, we know that the literature of the early Baptists was widely read. In his *Holy War* no less a person than Bunyan had before his eyes the ideal of Münster, while his *Pilgrim's Progress* is connected with the story of Tobias in the *Wanderings of Hendrik Niclaes*.

In the Barebones Parliament both groups came into conflict, and the dissolution of the Parliament of "saints" was the expression of the painful separation of Cromwell from his old companions. This radical sectarianism finally made it impossible for the work of Parliament to continue, although otherwise it had rendered signal public service by earnest political work. It split into two groups: a moderate majority for Cromwell, and a fanatically advanced minority for Harrison; it therefore resigned its commission into Cromwell's hands. From that time forward the radical "saints" were the opponents of Cromwell; they threw in their lot with the popular democratic movements, which, in this general breakdown of previous conditions, now came to the fore. This turn of events, however, threw the republic between the Scylla of dictatorial authority and the Charybdis of doctrinaire fanaticism. Men of energy and political responsibility like General Monk did not hesitate about their course of action; they decided to join the moderate party, under Cromwell, and, as usually happens, the masses followed suit. This ended the last great period of Baptist revolt, which, however, had only been able to reach this point in the wake of the Independent movement, which was more Puritan than Baptist in its outlook. This advanced sectarianism was the last politically important wave of Chiliasm, the last return of the spirit of the Hussites and of the Peasants' Wars, the last attempt by Christian social reformers to prepare the way for the Kingdom of God in the world by means of the sword.[454]

[454] See p. 953.

Radical Baptists and the English Revolution: the "Levellers"

In the last years of the Civil War, and above all after Cromwell's "apostasy", certain groups emerged which bore Baptist characteristics with the addition of some peculiarities of their own. In the unsettled state of affairs, and in the widespread attitude of "spiritual" indifference to forms of worship and to organization, there were now no longer any groups with particular forms of worship; these groups had all become politico-social parties; they, however, display all the more plainly the politico-social conclusions drawn from the religious idea as such. The largest and most important group was that of the "Levellers". These men had strong political interests, and set themselves in opposition to the leaders of the army, but they also based their claims on religious grounds. They represent that current of thought which believes in the radical Law of Nature, of God, and of Christ, which will allow no compromise with the institutions corrupted by sin, but which desires to realize the Christian social and political ideal throughout Society, from top to bottom. Their leader, John Lilburn, came from Puritan circles; he had been a victim of the Star Chamber and an exile in Holland, and later an officer in the Parliamentarian army. He then fell out with the Parliament, inflamed the army by his agitation, and induced the soldiers to assent to the famous proposals to the Commons and to Parliament which are known as the *Agreements of the People*. The leading feature of this movement was the demand for complete separation between Church and State, deduced logically from the standpoint of a "Spiritual" Christianity, and the division of the Church into free, self-supporting congregations; it also included the ideal of a radical democracy, based on the facts of Christian equality and the freedom of the redeemed. The demand was not for equality in possessions, but for full equality before the law, and for a real share of the whole people, so far as it is really Christian and religious, in the work of government; it was also felt that the system of law needed to be simplified, and the practice of capital punishment restricted. In this sense Jesus was the first "Leveller". Forced back by the opposition of the generals, and finally by the Protectorate of Cromwell, they became a passionately hostile opposition partly, which did not hesitate to encourage conspiracies and attempts at assassination, and even union with the Royalists, until finally they were forcibly suppressed. John

Lilburn himself ultimately found a refuge in the quiet haven of Quakerism.[455]

THE "DIGGERS"

The Socialists and Communists of the Revolution were much less influential. While the "Levellers" based their arguments for political freedom on religious premises, in the common interest of the radical middle class and of the workers, these socialist groups represented the interests of the rural proletariat, which also hoped to gain its rights and a reward for its sacrifices in the Civil War by means of the Kingdom of the "Saints". The movement did not spread beyond the agricultural workers, for, at that period, there was scarcely an industrial proletariat worth the name. They called themselves the "Diggers"; they formed a small group organized on communistic lines, and held that it was their Christian duty to place common land and crown property under spade and ploughshare.

Their spokesman was Gerard Winstanley, from whom there has come down a pamphlet dedicated to Cromwell, and entitled *The Law of Freedom*, which contains a programme of Christian Social Reform. Many of his other writings have also been preserved. Originally Winstanley had been a purely "spiritual" man on the lines of Hans Denk, Sebastian Franck, and the Familists. But this Christian-Social ideal, which he upheld as the logical result of this spirituality of the Inner Light and of the Indwelling Eternal Christ, which is in harmony with the creative Divine Reason, is the ancient sect-ideal of the Absolute Natural Law, as it was before the Fall, the ideal of freedom, equality, and brotherhood, which only recognized the use of law, force, and dominion in so far as those things are permitted by the full consent of all the individual members of Society, and as they freely serve the common good. All historic law which goes beyond that, all that the Church and the monarchical and aristocratic principle exalt as the relative Natural Law, which has been instituted by the Fall, is a product of the flesh, of selfishness and externalism; it has only been glossed over with complicated arguments, by the false theology of priests and professors in the interests of a particular class. Christ, the Inner Light, Reason, the absolute Natural Law: it all means the same thing. The victory of Christ, now, in England, means that a new era has begun; and this message ought to be carried over to the Continent as well.

This Christian Natural Law is to be carried through, first of all,

[455] See p. 955.

by the cession of the common land, and of the estates which have no masters, to be worked by the poor and needy as a communistic experiment. The family and the private household are to be retained. The whole scheme is to be realized without the use of force.

The "older brethren", as they called the landowners and capitalists, are to remain in possession of their property and income; only the land which has become free shall be entrusted to the "younger brethren", i.e. to those who have no capital. The Spirit must then carry through the new order Himself. Winstanley conceived this new order as an absolutely democratic society, to be ruled by elected officials changing every year, from which he excluded money, hire, and the exploitation of labour. The example of the law of Israel, spiritually interpreted, was in his mind throughout. Finally, he placed this choice before Cromwell: either to set up the new order and thus to remain a true Christian, or merely to continue the old order under a new name, and in so doing to betray the indwelling Christ.

Winstanley's ideas form an anticipation of theories on the subject of property, similar to those propounded by Locke at a later period, and they foreshadow a reform of the land laws like that of Henry George to-day. At first, however, these ideas had no effect at all, since the next development was in the exactly opposite direction, and brought about the break-up of property held in common, and the dispossession of the free peasants in favour of the Enclosures.

Shortly after Winstanley's death, there appeared in London in the year 1659 two pamphlets by a Dutchman, Peter Cornelius Plockboy, who belonged to the moderate Baptist movement. Stimulated by the Moravian Baptists, and perhaps also by the Labadists, he drew up a programme for a co-operative society on Christian principles, organized in the grand style; in this he hoped to force the bourgeois element to imitate him. We do not know whether these ideas bore any practical fruit or not. Winstanley's ideas, however, influenced the Quaker Bellers; he in turn influenced Richard Owen; thus there is a direct connection between Winstanley and modern Socialism. He himself, however, disillusioned in the same way as Lilburn, finally found a home among the Quakers, together with many of his followers.[456]

The Millenarians

The closest connection with the radical Baptist movement was maintained by the Millenarians. This party taught that the four

[456] See p. 956.

world-empires of the Book of Daniel, familiar to students of the ecclesiastical philosophy of history, covered the whole intervening period, down to the Protectorate of Cromwell; when it broke down they expected the Fifth World Empire of the full dominion of Christ. They looked for the Advent of Christ, and for the setting up of the true Kingdom of the "Saints", without priest or sacrament, law or oath, king or government, for the kingdom of the complete Christian anarchy of love. Some waited for this future in quiet patience, and endured the world; others, like the Taborites and Münsterites, became violent revolutionaries.

The genuine religious fanatics belonged to this section. Their spirit dominated the Left Wing of the Barebones Parliament, and made it impossible for Cromwell to govern through it. They were a real danger to the Protectorate. A smaller group composed of quieter people, split off from the main body of the party. This section was led by a certain John Pordage, who adopted mystical and ascetic ideas. In his teaching, the "Kingdom of the Saints" was spiritualized into a Philadelphian society, very much on the lines of the later Quakers and the Labadists. Many, however, maintained an attitude of bitter hostility to Cromwell.

The radical Baptists were closely connected with the Millenarians. They were strongly represented in the Irish Army, and they greatly desired to choose an Anabaptist general to lead them; in the end Monk cleared them all out of the Army. At the Restoration, these Chiliasts were the only people who could not accept the new order, or who went over to the Pietistic groups. They made an attempt at resistance which was defeated with bloodshed. Their leader, Harrison, died in the conviction that he would soon come again at the right Hand of Christ, at the setting up of His Kingdom. From that time forward the revolutionary Baptist movement was over.[457]

The other religious groups which arose during the Revolution belonged to the mystical spiritual movement, and will be mentioned later in that connection. The Quaker sect, however, in which all these religious tendencies finally merged, was a curious blend of sectarianism and spiritual religion. For that reason it also will be described later.

In this section I only wish to emphasize the sectarian element which played a very distinct part in the Great Rebellion, in the same way as in the previous chapter I was obliged to lay stress on the Scottish and Huguenot element within Calvinism. All that went beyond the sectarian element which I have just described

[457] For the Fifth Monarchy men, see *Gooch*, *260–267*, *324* and *Glass*.

belonged to the sphere where fanaticism was rife. These movements were characterized by mystical ideas and experiences, a great belief in "spiritual religion", and, above all, by that "advanced" interpretation of the Law of Nature which belongs to the aggressive Chiliasm of the Anabaptist movement. This last element in the extremely complicated movement belongs to the subject of our present inquiry. It was not the dominant factor, but it left abiding traces of its influence. Here, as always, the first result of idealistic radicalism was merely to prepare the way for reaction. Nevertheless the movement had a permanent influence. Indirectly, through its connection with Puritan Independency, and directly, through these radical groups, it was the influence of the Baptist movement which helped to loosen the connection between Church and State, which made the formation of Free Churches possible, and which helped to Christianize the ethical and social interests of the English people apart from dogmatic compulsion.

All this took place in an atmosphere of Utopian fanaticism, but in the next generation it became a moderate political and economic programme. It was the last time that a political and social revolution was carried through in the name of Christ, but it was to these Christian ideas that it owed a great part of its power, and only through them has it been introduced, in its secularized form, into the modern world. Here we see very clearly the significance of the Christian outlook on life, expressed in the terms of the sect-type, not merely in the history of the Church and of religion, but also in the sphere of political and social questions.[458]

Pietism

The sectarian energies which were released in the English Revolution were connected with the Pietist and Puritan form of English Calvinism. As we have already seen, this element was also one of the factors in Continental Calvinism. Although this movement had a quieter and less eventful history than its English counterpart, it too had its Left Wing, which developed here and there into sects of the extremist type; the whole movement also spread into Lutheranism. At this point it is customary to gather up all these phenomena under the term "Pietism".

Generally speaking, Pietism simply represents the sect-ideal within the churches, restricted and controlled by the fundamental thought of the Church. It reappears continually throughout the history of the Church. Its characteristics do not vary: always

[458] See p. 956.

there is the same insistence on the New Testament law of morals and on the idea of the Kingdom of God, and the same opposition to all externalism in the ecclesiastical sacramental system. In this sense, like the sect-ideal itself, Pietism belongs to all the churches. At that time (i.e. the seventeenth century), for similar reasons, Catholicism also had its own Pietist movement in the shape of Jansenism. But Catholicism can only tolerate that kind of movement if it is properly controlled by the Church as an Order or a Confraternity, so Jansenism was completely crushed. The corresponding movements within Calvinism we know already as Puritanism and "Precisianism".

Pietism, however, did not remain within the churches; everywhere it took the further step which led to separation and to the formation of sects. In the Netherlands this sectarian development began with Labadism; in England its new phase of development was ushered in by Methodism. The same phenomena also appeared within Lutheranism; and they came into touch with Calvinistic movements of the same kind; this intercourse has gradually become more intimate and vital, and is still a real force at the present day. In this later English and Continental Pietism, however, the whole movement does not come to a head in a process which influences the history of the world—the destruction of an old system of government and the erection of a new system—as was the case in the English Revolution. In that particular instance the religious movement was set, by the course of events, at the very heart of the political and social conflict; that explains the overwhelming force of an upheaval in which a Christian nation actually beheaded a king.

Continental Pietism was not connected with any great events of this time. That is why it remains, especially in Germany, more of a party matter—almost a hole-and-corner affair—which is limited to theological and ecclesiastical circles, and becomes, in the main, tame and colourless. It is true that it displays a great deal of genuine, warm, and self-sacrificing piety, but it also displays that pettiness of religious groups which compensates for their detachment from the world by a still more thorough spiritual pride; affecting to despise worldly influence, they strive to attain it by personal scheming and intrigue, and they give vent to their passions in all kinds of religious bickerings, thus revealing exactly the same characteristics as the darker side of the Baptist movement.

In Germany, when the country had recovered from the Thirty Years War, there arose a reaction against the popular religion of the Territorial Churches, which had become formal in their officialism and rigid in their orthodoxy, while morally they were far too indifferent. The leader of this movement was Spener, who, in addition to his emphasis upon Luther's earlier idea of forming small groups of "earnest Christians" within the Church at large, had also been deeply influenced by the Pietism of England and Holland.

One of his main innovations was the introduction of the conventicle system which he had seen at work in England and in Holland. By this method he hoped to achieve that spiritual and ethical reform of the Church which was needed as the complement of the reform in doctrine which had already been carried out so thoroughly. It was his intention, however, to keep this movement entirely within the life of the Church. But its "Perfectionist" aim of separating "converted" Christians, that is, of mature and conscious Christians, from the rest, in order to form them into smaller groups of real Christians, its stress on the need for "converted" preachers, its emphasis upon lay religion and upon the pure apostolic primitive Church, revealed a spirit which was still inwardly hostile to the spirit of ecclesiasticism. Spener also held that the greatest impulse towards reform lay in the idea of the coming Kingdom of God, and the approaching world transformation.

The ethical point of view which was developed from this belief, of an asceticism active within the sphere of one's calling, but detaching itself from the world, and a rational methodical discipline of self-consecration in preparation for the future life, stood in direct opposition to the Lutheran ethic of moral neutrality, tolerance, and the free outworking of the Spirit. In spite of the fact that it accepted the doctrines of the Church, the Sacrament, and the Territorial Church system, the affinity between Pietism and the spirit of the sects is evident. Its opponents certainly emphasized this fact often enough, for they constantly compared Pietism with the Anabaptist movement, with the followers of Valentine Weigel, the Rosicrucians, and the Quakers. The driving force in this movement was clearly akin to those sects. The opponents of Pietism, however, would not see, or at least they would not admit, that their own Church system really contained certain affinities with the sects. Pietism was based, and rightly so, upon the Bible, and upon Luther's earlier ideals, and it was forced into existence by the formalism of the State Church system. Its attitude towards the world and towards civilization was still only the logical inference from Luther's doctrine of Original Sin and conversion, which prevailed as soon as the Lutheran doctrine of Baptism, and its freer but ill-defined attitude towards the world, was less emphasized. Also its imitation of the Calvinistic conventicle, and the connection with Calvinistic asceticism and moral discipline, was no mere casual, foreign influence of Calvinism, but an appropriation of the means, already closely related, which had been evolved for similar reasons, and which were to lift the German movement out of its distress.

In addition, all the other logically connected phenomena of this sectarian ascetic spirit were also introduced: the emphasis upon the co-operation of the laity; the independent study of the Bible without ecclesiastical control of exegesis; depreciation of the State Church and of the "*subsidia*" *religionis*; the demand for the right to excommunicate and to exercise Church discipline as an activity of the Church, and not merely as a function of the police; the impulse towards personal and experimental religion; the reduction of all secular culture to the elements which were practically useful, and the entire rejection of philosophy and theology; the evangelizing and educating of baptized but not really "converted" children; the introduction of confirmation in place of adult baptism; the new Pietistic Church order of joint ministry, which assumed that the Church began with the gathering together of individuals in groups, but which at the same time maintained the silent transference of authority over these groups to the Government; under these circumstances, for the time being, practical results were impossible. In Germany there were no large Separatist movements, owing to the fact that, unlike the law of England and the Netherlands, the law of the Empire did not permit them.

Pietism remained within the Church; indeed, at the time of the Enlightenment it bound itself very closely with the relics of the old dogmatic ecclesiastical system, and from its reawakening at the beginning of the nineteenth century there arose the great renewal of orthodoxy in this century, through which, however, the Church life of the present day has been impregnated with a mass of Pietist explosive material.

To sum up: Pietism represents the sect-ideal within the Church; the mystical elements with which it was mingled will be dealt with in a later section of this book. The influence of the Church-type upon the sect-ideal is everywhere quite evident; this appears not only in questions of doctrine and organization, but, above all, in its attitude towards social questions. Like Puritanism and the later Baptist movement, Pietism had no trace of the tendency of the sect towards political and social radicalism. It did not need to *become* bourgeois like the early Baptist movement; from the very beginning it *was* bourgeois and loyal. In the spirit of Lutheranism it accepted the existing social order of the State; the idea of Christianizing the social order did not occur to it. On the contrary, Pietism liked to be connected with the ruling class and with the aristocracy; it aimed solely at Christianizing the hearts of men. It carried on Home Mission work, and healed social ills by a new kind of charity, which depended on free group initiative; nowhere did it touch the fundamental facts of existing conditions.

The resemblance between Pietism and the suffering and persecuted Baptist movement is slight. Pietism expressed asceticism and renunciation of the world in the form of the acceptance of existing conditions of labour, rather in the sense in which Puritanism and the later developments of the Mennonite movement had expressed it. In this respect Pietism comes into touch with the commercial ethic of the Calvinistic churches. Pietism teaches that secular business and interests have no intrinsic value of their own; the Christian man takes part in them as the "Lord's steward", simply for the purposes of civil life, and of the "Kingdom of God". Pietism does not seek to reform the world; it simply gathers "earnest Christians" together into a party within the Church, and seeks to convert the heathen; this all shows how indifferent it is to questions of social reform. Its task is simply to seek the conversion of individuals, and to gather "converted" souls into groups for fellowship and edification. Its interest in the release of the third estate, that is, of the laity, is concerned purely with the religious and ecclesiastical sphere, and consists in giving the right to possess an independent personal piety, and the right to form conventicles.

It is precisely at this point that a characteristic distinction appears between German Lutheran and Calvinistic Pietism. When Calvinism, which aimed from the very beginning at the creation of a "holy community", came under the influence of Pietism, it found its supporters mainly in the lower and middle classes, whereas in German Pietism, on the contrary, the lower middle classes preferred to become Separatists, and Pietism within the Church simply concerned theologians and the aristocracy. The Lutheran Church system is, indeed, not inwardly at home in Pietism and its ethic, even though the Lutheran doctrines of sin and conversion come very close to its spirit.

Pietism, of course, has produced some notable effects upon the development of civilization: under its influence life became more personal and inward, social distinctions faded into insignificance, and social existence became more humane. On the other hand, these very influences often became perverted, owing to the Pietists' tendency to be on good terms with the aristocracy, and to form cliques and parties. Pietism is, in fact, a revivalist form of Christianity, fitted to meet the needs of small groups, which seeks and finds its support in the Territorial Church, while it leaves the world and secular civilization severely alone. When it does influence civilization at all, particularly on the political and social side, it does so reluctantly and almost involuntarily. Here, once more, we see the standpoint of the persecuted sect, which here comes to terms with the existing organization in Church and State. This is why Pietism was comparatively popular with the authorities when they had learned—with great difficulty—that it was impossible to maintain the old purity of a State religion. Pietism supplies the State with loyal servants, who practise submission as part of the asceticism of their calling; it does not seek to alter existing conditions; the only obligation it lays on the Government is that of patriarchal kindness and care for the common weal, and it obliterates class distinctions only within the limits of religious intercourse; indeed, this also did not take place to any appreciable extent.[459]

The Moravians

The fact that in Pietism the sect-ideal is so closely connected with the Church explains why the few important Separatist movements which took place were not voluntary, but were the result of actual compulsion. This is true of the only larger Separatist movement, the Herrnhut Community. Like the Quakers, this body was not a simple expression of the sect-idea, even though it was connected with the Church. From the very beginning it contained various elements. On the one hand, it consisted of the Lutheran inwardness of Count Zinzendorf, a man of great personal charm and attractiveness, who, in an age of sentimentality, seemed like some gallant Crusader of olden days. His aim was to unite the true lovers of Christ in small groups, rather after the earlier ideal of Luther and Spener's system of "conventicles". He never dreamed of the impossibility of uniting these supra-ecclesiastical Philadelphian groups with Lutheranism. On the other hand, the Herrnhut Community contained the sectarian impulse of the Moravian Brethren, who, having incidentally settled upon the Count's estate, became to him a "chariot and

[459] See p. 956.

warhorse" for gaining the victory; in the process, however, his conventicle idea developed into that of a sect, organized on an exclusive basis, founded upon the voluntary principle, and upon maturity in Christian experience, exercising powers of discipline and excommunication—a body in which laymen exercised a spiritual ministry. Out of the tension and conflict between these two tendencies, and in consequence of the rejection of the Count's "conventicle" idea by the official Lutheran Church, there arose, finally, a new Church, which gradually settled down into an established existence, with inherited traditions, rather like that of the Society of Friends. It had no objection to Infant Baptism, but its chief aim was to attain the highest possible degree of inward piety and Christ-mysticism, by means of worship, organization, and education. Nevertheless, it still retained important characteristics of the sect-ideal. The body of communicants was to be as pure as possible; and discipline was directed to this end. The small size of the community, its system of mutual control, its independence of the State, its legal character as an "association" (*Verein*), its business undertakings which arose in order to secure its existence, its urgent desire to win souls freely to Christ through missions to the heathen, above all the endeavour after an active purity of the Christian ethic which was to distinguish its members from the "children of this world": all this gave to the Church of the Brethren—partly with and partly against its will—a certain likeness to the sects, which it was in the habit of ascribing to the influence of the Bohemian Brethren, and of the Waldensians, and through them to the Early Church. Traces of an attitude to the Sermon on the Mount similar to that which characterized the Baptists are also apparent. Finally, their ethic (even though it was imparted and established by the Count in the spirit of a happy and childlike Lutheran piety) was comparatively tolerant towards the world, and quite unsystematic; on the other hand, however, through its desire to present an active Christian piety very different from the life of the world, and through Calvinistic accessions to the community, it was, in many respects, related to Puritanism. In any case, the Moravians felt a closer affinity with Calvinism than with Lutheranism. The economic results, too, which were produced by these circumstances soon appeared in the shape of an excellent and increasingly successful business life, characterized by integrity and frugality. This tendency was strengthened by the fact that at first the community was gathered from the shifting element in the population, and that it became limited essentially to active members who were engaged in trade, and also by the fact of the necessity of meeting their own expenses, particularly those connected with their mission work, which meant that they were, and are, forced to depend on the business enterprise of the whole community.[460]

The Methodists

Of much greater importance was the founding of Methodism, which was one of the most important events in the later history of Christianity, and of modern spiritual development. It marked the renewal of orthodox Christianity in a quite individualistic accentuated form; it anticipated the continental revival movement of the nineteenth century, and was one of the means by which the English world was rendered proof against the spirit of the French Revolution; it presented a radical opposition to the whole spirit of modern science and civilization. Methodism, like the Moravian Church—by which, indeed, it had been stimulated, and for which, like the latter, it had been prepared by a Pietist conventicle-movement—was an attempt to leaven the life of the National Church with the influence of smaller groups of genuine and vital Christians. Externally, it was only forced to take up an independent position because the pulpits of the National Church were closed to it. Inwardly, however, this separation was inevitable. For this body, like the Moravian Church, belonged essentially to the sect-type and not to the church-type, in spite of its earnest desire to remain inside the Established Church. Indeed, its own nature forced it to adopt a far more independent attitude than the Moravian Church had felt necessary from its own point of view. For the primary aim of Methodism was not to gather devout lovers of Christ into small fellowship groups, but to awaken the masses, which, under the influence of an "enlightened" Church and the pressure of industrial capitalism, had become indifferent, dull, and coarse. The movement was already faced by the conditions produced by the wide development of modern science, and by the social situation, which, on the Continent, were only developed in the nineteenth century. The Methodist Revival laid renewed and extreme emphasis upon the doctrine of Original Sin, and it taught that the way to salvation consisted in a direct sense of "assurance", based on justification through the Blood of Christ. Its leaders proclaimed that salvation from hell, death, and damnation could not be attained by an inert confidence in baptismal grace, nor by a certain measure of decent

[460] See p. 959.

and correct behaviour, but by a radical change, the conscious passing from the state of condemnation to that of forgiveness and peace, together with the genuine ethical energies released by this experience.

The results of this Revival, however, which the Methodist missionaries carried on amidst dangers and toils like those of the first apostles, and which, with the aid of great open-air services, they finally carried right into the life of the lower and middle classes, had to be secured and gathered up into a coherent whole. In order to achieve this end, however, organization was needed; Wesley, who was an indefatigable and indomitable missionary like Paul, and a dominating, powerful organizer like Ignatius Loyola, was a master in this art. As this process of organization went on, the main characteristics of the sect-type, which were already present in embryo, began to emerge in the stress laid on adult conversion and on ethical Perfectionism. To the emotional elements of the direct "sealing of the Spirit" and of "assurance of salvation", in which Methodism comes very near to the spirit of the Lutherans and the Moravians, there was added a spirit of composure and self-control in which Wesley remained true to Puritan Calvinism.

The aim of Methodism was to win men and women to Christ, who would then be genuine Christians, full of "joy and peace in believing", and who, as far as they could, were aspiring to perfection; the means was the gathering of such Christians into an organized society. At first, during the original period, the Society consisted of adult members who came in from the outside; the question of Infant Baptism did not need to be raised, since all the members belonged to the Established Church which dispensed the Sacrament of Infant Baptism throughout the land. A probation period of six months preceded the final reception into the Society. The members received their Society ticket, which had to be renewed every quarter, and within the Society they were divided up into classes of about ten persons, who gathered themselves together weekly under a lay leader for mutual fellowship, guidance, and Bible study; the renewed grant of the Society ticket, and the final reception of candidates, were dependent upon the leader's report. The groups, again, were gathered together into districts which were visited systematically by an ordained pastor; the latter had at the same time the duty of carrying on evangelistic meetings for outsiders. The districts, again, were placed under the supreme guidance of the General Conference of the famous Hundred, which was constituted at first merely by the arbitrary choice of

Wesley, then according to seniority and then by the addition of elected ministers, and finally also of elected laymen.

We cannot enlarge any further upon the development of this system of Church government, whose main features have remained unaltered to the present day. Its general character is clear. It is something between an Order, established upon a foundation of unconditional obedience and minute mutual control, like the Jesuit Order (with which Methodism was compared in its early days), and a society of earnest Christians, proving the reality of their faith by their lives, founded upon entirely voluntary membership in which the members have a permanent share, as in the Baptist organizations.

The two sociological forms of the sect-type, the Religious Order and the voluntary association, are here combined; at the same time they are made elastic for the reception of increasing numbers, without, however, allowing the opposition to the popular piety of the church-type to disappear. Infant Baptism is, in reality, replaced by the experience of the New Birth, which is connected with conversion, and its recognition by admission to the Society. Nothing was altered in Church dogma, its supernatural character was only intensified, and its general meaning was summed up in conversion and its presuppositions, and in sanctification with its heavenly results. The continuance of the Church was taken for granted, but in spite of that its spirit was denied. This necessarily led to external separation, in England itself last of all.

When this separation and independence had been achieved, Methodism passed through the same experience which had befallen the Baptists, the Moravians, and the Quakers. An inherited position was developed in which the children of members naturally belonged to the community; this fact, coupled with the reception of increasing numbers of people, who to-day (counting all the different branches of Methodism) number about 30 millions, with the increase of the clerical element, which was unavoidable under these circumstances, and with the introduction of scientific theology and general culture, with the many influences which modified the original attitude of opposition to the world and to civilization, finally led Methodism to become less and less of a sect and more and more of a Church, or, rather, a number of churches. All that remained of the original sect-spirit was a certain sensitiveness about questions of organization, which is peculiar to all societies organized on a voluntary basis—a rivalry between laymen and ordained pastors, by which (in the various denominations) laymen attained an increasing but varying share in the general administration. It was this which led to most of the separations and reunions which have taken place. Further, just as in the case of the Baptists, the original restriction to certain classes of Society disappeared. To begin with, Methodism gained its victories in the middle and lower classes, among the miners and in the industrial towns. To the middle and lower classes it brought a new sense of the sacredness of personality; it appealed to the popular imagination, and awakened a devotion which found expression in a most self-sacrificing charity. From the aristocratic classes and the rural population, as well as from the educated professional classes, it remained, on the whole, remote. It had brought the impulse of personality and individuality into the life of the masses, who were being brutalized by the industrial system, and with its charity it helped them in their distress. Otherwise, however, its ethic served to maintain the existing order in Church and State; it balanced the emotional character of its type of conversion by emphasis upon sanctification, which was to be attained by a severe and rigorous course of self-discipline, and a far-reaching practice of asceticism in work. Its attitude towards the social problem was displayed in its zeal for franchise reform, for the liberation of the slaves, for philanthropic activity, as well as in its strict Sabbatarianism, its opposition to modern culture, science, and art. In modern Methodism this opposition to culture has been modified, but it has not been removed.[461]

The Labadists

In the Netherlands also, which were influenced by a certain type of Puritanism, the sect-movement was present, although it did not spread very widely because Rigorism had already been allowed a fairly free course in the State churches. There a man like Lodensteyn pushed the idea of the purity of Church membership to such an extreme that the Sacrament of the Lord's Supper could no longer be observed. Others so changed the baptismal formula that they did not describe the children as "Christians", but merely as "destined for faith"—both strong proofs of sectarian inferences drawn from Puritanism. Labadie alone tried to form a sect, and in so doing he influenced others in the Separatist direction. This sect was like a monastic order; but since his leading idea was not merely the idea of sanctification, but was chiefly mystical in character, we will describe this in detail later on. Further, this movement declined and disappeared during the first generation after it had been founded. In the Netherlands and the

[461] See p. 960.

Church of the Lower Rhine, however, it became the rallying-point for a marked development of the sectarian spirit.[462]

Modern Sects

Almost all the sects which have been mentioned are still in existence. Many new ones of a similar type have been added—the Salvation Army, the Adventists, the Irvingites, the Darbyists, the Württemburg Temple, and others. Everywhere their activity arouses the continental Territorial Churches, and actually within them the so-called "Fellowship Movement" constantly produces fresh analogies to the origin of those sects. From the point of view of social doctrine they all bear the same characteristics: a society founded on a voluntary basis apart from the State, Perfectionism, asceticism expressed in hard work, a conservative-middle-class outlook, even where their political attitude is theoretically one of bourgeois Liberalism. These newer sects represent the natural development of the persecuted Pietist element (within the Church) during a period when the sect is no longer persecuted, and when the absolute necessity of civil and social order for the immensely complicated economic organism has become clear and obvious. With the rise of Capitalism the early ideals of the persecuted Waldensians and Baptists became impracticable. Henceforth the only course to pursue was: either to oppose Capitalism altogether and to propose something entirely new, or, however hostile certain groups might be to the world and to civilization in general, to adjust themselves to the existing order of Society, merely modifying or getting rid of the unchristian phenomena which accompany it.[463]

It is this sense of contrast which has reawakened in the modern world the old ideas of world-renewal which characterized the aggressive sects. These ideas have again come into prominence through the Bible, particularly in the Sermon on the Mount, and the idea of the Kingdom of God. There has been no recurrence of Hussite Wars, it is true, nor of armies of "saints"; and at the present day the aim of Christian Socialism is no longer primarily to attempt a direct transformation of world conditions

[462] On this point, see *Göbel, II, Ritschl, I,* and *Heppe.*

[463] For modern history of the sects, see "*Kirchen und Sekten der Gegenwart*", published by *Kalbe*², *1907*; further, the collection entitled *Kerke en Secte, Baarn, Hollandia Druckerij.* For the so-called "*Gemeinschaftsbewegung*", see the article by *Benser* in *Schiele's Lexikon.* For the connection with the general life of the people, see *Tischhauser: Gesch. d. ev. Kirche in der ersten Hälfte des 19. Jahrh., 1900.* These are things which the modern educated German knows nothing about, but which play an important part in real life.

by means of an organized society inspired by a common religious aim, and strengthened by united worship. To-day men know or feel instinctively far too clearly how complicated are the problems of our common life and our common civilization involved in these great questions, to attempt anything of this kind. With the rise of the great sovereign States which dominate the life of the citizens down to the smallest detail, and with the revelation of the nature of the Capitalist system, the ideal has naturally changed its emphasis.

The ideal of the Christian Revolution has become at once more spiritual and more complicated. Society in general is now summoned to a change of heart and disposition under the influence of the Gospel, which, with the co-operation of all social-technical experts, shall then, and not till then, create a change in the general situation which shall harmonize with the ideas of Christian personality and of the Kingdom of God. To-day a genuine Christian love and sense of the value of personality seems to demand expression along the following lines: a break-away in principle from the individualistic social order which has grown up during the last two centuries; the equal surrender, not merely of individuals, but of all, for the common good; the creation of just and suitable means for a sufficient material existence for all, as a basis for the development of spiritual values.

Thus, in its origin, with Owen and St. Simon, Socialism contained within itself transformed Christian impulses of this kind. By his reference to the Quaker, Bellers, Owen restored the direct contact with the sect-ideal. In Germany this point of view was represented by Weitling. Since, however, Socialism has finally given up all connection with religion, and since the Marxist development of the "class-war" idea and its acceptance of the Gospel of Naturalism, there have been no further developments in this direction.

Christian Socialism

Its place, however, has been taken by Christian Socialism which claims to present the demand of the Gospel for brotherhood, and the coming of the Kingdom of God in its undimmed clarity and uncompromising character, after its eyes had been opened by Social Democracy to these inferences drawn from the Gospel. Christian Socialism rejects the glorification of the prevailing bourgeois order as one which represents a relative Natural Law which owes its necessity to the fact of sin, and its character of a Divine appointment to the Divine permission. Taught by the modern science of the State and of Society, and by the experiences of everyday life, Christian Socialism sees clearly one thing which Calvinism (which was moving steadily in the direction of Christian Socialism) did not see: that the possibility of a spiritual and ethical development depends entirely upon the substructure of a healthy collective social constitution, and that spiritual factors are very closely connected with physical and economic factors. Christian Socialism has learned from experience that the previous exclusive emphasis upon "the ideological" aspect of the problem takes us nowhere. It is this which constitutes its new element. Christian Socialism, therefore, also rejects the Pietistic attitude of withdrawal from "the world" into a sphere of "spiritual life" and evangelistic effort, because it implies an attitude of despair towards the world, and an attempt to quiet the Christian conscience by winning a few souls, many of whom are not of the best. In the view of Christian Socialism, to identify the Kingdom of God with the Church, or to relegate it to the future life, seems to be a position which corresponds neither with the Bible nor with the demands of reality, both of which require a sphere on earth in which it should be possible to rise above the mere struggle for actual existence, and beyond the Gospel of Competition and the survival of the fittest.

In this attitude, however, we perceive once more the familiar characteristics of the primitive Christian tendency, the characteristics of the aggressive sect which believes in an actual transformation of conditions in this world. The Kingdom of God and reason, the Kingdom of God realized *on earth*, the invincible faith in the victory of goodness and in the possibility of overcoming every human institution which is based upon the mere struggle for existence, the Christian Revolution: this is the primitive, splendid ideal of the sect. It is only the Chiliast ideal translated into human and intelligible terms. It is the ideal of a Christianity without compromise, formulated in harmony with modern social views, an ideal which could not be conceived within primitive Christianity with its faith in the miraculous Second Coming of Christ. From the Patristic period the old Christian theories of the nature of Society have been handed down through the centuries (with changes which have been already described), and these same theories still hold good in all communions, and until the present day are continually being repeated, with a naïve ignorance of the world situation, in spite of the wholly altered practical position in Christian ethics. Thus Christian Socialism alone has broken through these theories, and forced men to think out afresh the social ethic of Christianity and its relation to the actual changes in the social order. It has laid bare the worm-eaten condition of the previous conventional Christian ethic, which, at its best, offered something for the ethics of the family and the individual, but which, on the other hand, had no message for social ethics save that of acceptance of all existing institutions and conditions, much to the satisfaction of all in authority. Christian Socialism has regained for the Christian ethic its Utopian and revolutionary character; once more it has brought upon its heralds the reproach of Christ, which officials of Church and State are always ready to hurl at all who indulge in humanitarian sentiment or in idealistic dreams, at all who "wantonly deny the impossibility of overcoming sin", and the absolute necessity of their methods of suppressing it.

The fundamental distinctions within the movement, which expresses itself very differently among Catholics, Calvinists, Lutherans, and Free Protestants, and which, above all, has greatly agitated the Lutheran Church, cannot be described here. This point alone must be emphasized: with this movement all the interior problems of the Christian ethic and of that Stoic idealism which is so closely connected with it, have been reawakened. Once again we are faced with the question: how far is it at all possible for the faculty of thought and of the Ethos, of faith and of the world outlook, to oppose the natural processes of social development, and to overcome and shape them, both from within and from without? Is it possible that ideal laws of the Ethos and of the Divine "nature of Humanity" can overcome, or at least affect, the ordinary natural laws of social development? Can it be, after all, that that which is humanly possible forms the limit of that which is ideally necessary? Is there, in fact, any real hope of a Christianity for the majority of mankind?

Tolstoi

It is a remarkable fact that while Western Christendom was thinking in this way about a real Christian renewal of Society within the modern State, the old radical sect-ideal found a prophet in Russia, who, on the contrary, wished to break with the State entirely, and with the whole technical and legal system of civilization, in order to found a new humanity. It is the radical early Christian ideal, shorn of its apocalyptic element, which also refuses the aid of modern technical Rationalism.

If in spirit men will only break with the present world-order, then out of the spirit of love itself a new world will arise—a world

[464] See p. 962.

without State, law, or compulsion, without mechanization or the desire for material pleasure. Tolstoi can only be completely understood from the point of view of the Russian world, and perhaps also from the point of view of the development of the Russian sect-system. His significance, however, is this: for the West he proclaims the old radical sect-ideal of a realization of the Sermon on the Mount, in the artistic form in which it is alone possible to attract the attention of modern cultivated people to such questions. Tolstoi's message is based essentially upon the Sermon on the Mount; it is, however, characteristically free from all traces of that tension which the expectation of the imminence of the Coming of Christ produced in the Primitive Church; it steers clear also of all the dangers involved in an ecclesiastical ethic of compromise, or of a fusion with the busy activity of the Western world. The fact that Tolstoi founds his whole message upon a conception of God which is strongly coloured by Western pantheism, and which dims the clear spiritual motives of the Sermon on the Mount with a kind of modern ennui, need not detain us here. Tolstoi's understanding of the Gospel may be limited, but the fact remains that his message—like that of the radical sect and of Christian Socialism—is still a reminder of the essential fundamental features of the Gospel, which had been obscured by the doctrine of the relative Natural Law of fallen humanity, and which the classical Natural Law of Liberalism as well as the most modern kind of Socialism had forgotten, and it had therefore obliterated all traces of their connection with the source from which they sprang.[465]

At this point we must leave these questions. They belong to the realm of systematic ethics, not to the history of ethics and of social doctrine.

II. Mysticism and Spiritual Idealism

We must now direct our attention afresh to the second current which flows alongside the main stream of ecclesiastical Protestantism—to "spiritual religion" and mysticism. We have already noticed it frequently in its connection with the sect-movement; in the usual treatment of these questions this second element is unhesitatingly classed with the sect-movement.

"Baptists and spiritual reformers" ("Täufer und Spiritualisten") has become a stock phrase, as if in essentials both were the same. This is, however, an entirely erroneous idea. For these two movements are like separate streams, which only mingle their waters

[465] See p. 962.

now and again, but which historically vary greatly both in their sources and in their development.

The subject with which we are now concerned is Christian Mysticism and its significance within the sphere of Protestantism. This Protestant mysticism also carries forward pre-Reformation ideas and tendencies, like the sect, but it is far more closely connected with Luther's original main ideas, and is therefore still more strongly rooted within Protestantism.[466]

It is, however, a very difficult matter to distinguish clearly between this type of mysticism and the sect-movement; this difficulty is increased by the fact that the old heresiological tradition ignored these differences entirely, and under its influence modern research has only learnt very gradually to distinguish between them. The difference becomes most evident when we consider the sociological consequences to which these movements gave rise; this indeed is the standpoint from which the difference between the Church and the sect is most easily discerned.[467] If, however, we are to gain a right understanding of the sociological consequences of mysticism, our first task must be to understand the nature of the religious source whence these consequences proceed. In the first place, therefore, we must make a general analysis of the religious nature of mysticism. It is only at this point in our inquiry that the time has come to deal with this question, although mysticism itself goes back to the very earliest days of Christianity; the intellectual content which underlies Protestant mysticism in particular was formed partly by the mysticism of St. Bernard and Richard of St. Victor, and partly also by the deep, rich, and splendid German mysticism of the later Middle Ages.

Mysticism: A Direct Religious Experience

In the widest sense of the word, mysticism is simply the insistence upon a direct inward and present religious experience. It takes for granted the objective forms of religious life in worship, ritual, myth, and dogma; and it is either a reaction against these objective practices, which it tries to draw back into the living process, or it is the supplementing of traditional forms of worship by means of a personal and living stimulus. Mysticism is thus

[466] See p. 962.

[467] For the difference between both the remarks concerned in *Hegler*, see information in *Harnack's Dogmengeschichte, ThLZ., 1898, Nr. 9*, and *Luthardt: Gesch. d. christl. Ethik II, 249 f.*; also *Sippell: Chr. W., 1911, pp. 955–957*, gives important information in line with my definition of the conception of the sect.

always something secondary, something which has been deliberately thought out, although this emotional condition which has been deliberately produced is characteristically connected with an immediacy of feeling which is the entire opposite of the former process. Thus it always contains a paradoxical element, a certain hostility to popular religion and its average forms of expression, an artificiality which, however, is again extinguished by its own thirst for direct communion with God. Hence the primitive religious fact itself in which experience and the expression of the experience are simply identical, is never mystical.[468] The vitality of the religious sense, however, when it is faced with objectified religion, easily and often develops mystical characteristics. It expresses itself in ecstasy and frenzy, in visions and hallucinations, in subjective religious experience and "inwardness", in concentration upon the purely interior and emotional side of religious experience. Certainly these visions are rarely creative in the sense of imparting fresh knowledge; they are almost always expansions and interpretations of the common faith, as was the case with the spiritual gifts of the early Christians, and with the innumerable visions and prophecies of mediaeval recluses and saints, an experience which has been repeated all through the centuries, down to the present day.

Alongside of, or within, the recognized forms of worship, mysticism creates special and more intimate mysteries, in which salvation is appropriated in a peculiarly inward manner; in these mysteries the ancient cults of sacred meals, "feeding upon the god", of sacrifice, of a new birth from the divinity into an immediate eating and drinking of the life of the divinity, become intensified and inward to the point of a real new birth and deification. Mysticism creates prophecies and ecstasies as well as fantastic allegories and a "spiritual" interpretation of the objective side of religion. This mystical sense, however, can also create a passionate realism of communion with the gods, which makes the ancient cults or the accepted rites the means of immediate substantial union. The Hellenistic mysteries united the most coarse and material conceptions with "spiritual" theories which reduced them all to a symbol, which still, however, had a wonderful effect. According to Paul, the Christian Supper of the Lord was itself a mystical creation; and when the Eucharist became an objective ecclesiastical rite, Eucharistic mysticism transformed it, for the second time, into a mystical experience.

Above all, eroticism here plays a leading part, since either the

[468] See my articles upon *Revelation, Faith, Faith and History*, in *Schiele's Lexikon*.

sexual stimulation is also used to stimulate religious enthusiasm, or the latter strengthens and expresses itself in sexual stimulation. The imagery of Love and the "Wine-shops" of Sufi poetry, and certain Christian interpretations of the Song of Songs, harp upon the same string in the spiritual life.

On the other hand, this immediacy of feeling likes to escape from the finite world of sense through a spirituality which either treats it with indifference and ignores it, or removes it to a distance by means of ascetic mortifications. Mysticism is thus open to the incursions of a spiritual Pantheism and of a radical Dualism of flesh and spirit, of time and of eternity; and, in connection with it, to the suggestions of an asceticism which crushes all that is finite, or of a Libertinism which treats everything as equally indifferent.

Mysticism in the New Testament

Thus, in all religious systems in these varied forms mysticism is a universal phenomenon. It reached a particularly high stage of development in India, Persia, Greece, Asia Minor, and Syria. It was only natural that it should appear within the primitive Christian movement, where it developed partly from within, out of its own life, and in part was introduced from without and eagerly accepted.[469] It is to this mysticism that the so-called "Enthusiasm" of the Primitive Christian Church, a large part of the "spiritual gifts", the "speaking with tongues", the power of exorcism, the whole of its spiritual activity, belongs; this phenomenon recurs again and again, in the Christian sect-movement, down to the present day, bringing home with great power the redemptive energy of the Gospel to the individual soul. Paul, in particular, on his mystical side represents this type of Christianity which existed along with his Church convictions in a permanent state of tension, though he himself was not aware of a conflict between the two tendencies. Paul took over the Christ-cult of the Primitive Church as a form of religion which had already been objectified in worship, tradition, and organization. But he inspired it with a deep and passionate mysticism, which also utilized the ancient terminology of the pagan mysteries. It is in this alone that his religious originality consists, contrasted with the view of the Primitive Church; and it was only thus that his anti-Jewish universalism became practically effective. Thus the

[469] For the subject in general, see *Edv. Lehmann: Mystik in Heidentum und Christentum, 1901; A. Merx: Ideen und Grundlinien einer allgemeinen Gesch. der Mystik, 1903;* above all, *Erwin Rohdes' Psyche,* also *James: Varieties of Religious Experience.*

Lord's Supper, the centre of the new cult, became to him a mystical, substantial union, and Baptism became an actual dying and rising again with Christ. To him Christ became an actual sphere of life of a supersensual kind, in which the believer lives, feels, and thinks, and becomes a new spiritual personality, "a new creature". Thus all that was merely ceremonial and traditional was relegated to the sphere of "the flesh" and "the world", and the "Christ according to the flesh" fades out of sight. So the history of Israel was allegorized and spiritualized, in order that it could be directly applied to the Christian believer, and the Christian community became the spiritual Body of Christ. Ecstasies and visions were not wanting, spiritual gifts were exalted and cultivated, and incorporated into a new spiritual life.

Here, in this primitive Christian pneumatic enthusiasm, and in the Pauline Christ-mysticism, lie the inexhaustible sources of Christian mysticism. In the Fourth Gospel this mysticism has already become calm and controlled, and adjusted to the historical and objective side of religion. Here, in particular, however, it has also produced or discovered its really characteristic formulas —flesh and spirit, darkness and light, allegory and "the letter".

Other early Christian writings contain similar elements. Through the New Testament, spiritual enthusiasm and Pauline mysticism became a permanent source of power, stimulating the corresponding sense of need and vivifying its formulas. This mysticism has expressed itself in a very vital way at all periods of Church history, and particularly at all periods of criticism of tradition, of religious decline, and of new religious developments.

The germ of the idea of the Church as an institution was already latent within Primitive Christianity, for it was given naturally with the conception of grace, of a finished salvation, and of the salvation of the world. Primitive Christianity also contains the germ of the sect-idea, which reveres the Sermon on the Mount as the moral law of its Master and continues His expectation of the coming of the Kingdom of God upon earth, and gathers the pure and holy into the fellowship of the Church which waits for Christ's return. Primitive Christianity also contains the germs of a mysticism for which this fleeting world is but a symbol, all that belongs to the sense-life and to the earthly sphere a mere limitation; for which every form of worship is only a means of substantial union, and all faith simply a direct translation from the visible to the invisible, into the very life of God and Christ.[470]

[470] See p. 963.

Mysticism and the Philosophy of Religion

Now, however, we must seek to distinguish mysticism in the narrower, technical concentrated sense in which it is used in the philosophy of religion from this wider mysticism with its immense variety. The phenomena which have just been described proceed directly from the emotional sphere, and for that reason they are comparatively instinctive and spontaneous, and can be combined with every kind of objective religion, and with the customary forms of worship, myth, and doctrine. They contain no kind of doctrine and theory about themselves; at the most all they possess is a primitive technique of religious self-cultivation and the production of a certain temper. Their varied forms of expression—enthusiasm, orgiasm, contemplation and Gnosticism, allegorical and spiritualizing tendencies, the renewal or the bringing forth of forms of worship—are quite different from each other, and they develop very different results which often cancel each other out. Hence they do not essentially affect the existing sociological connection with religion, for they simply mean an intensification of its powers, or a particular emphasis upon some of its elements, or perhaps they add new forms of worship; but concrete religion they do not deny.

The whole question can, however, sometimes assume a far more unified aspect, and then a considerable sociological element is introduced into the situation. The active energies in mysticism of this kind can become independent in principle, contrasted with concrete religion; they then break away from it and set up a theory of their own which takes the place of the concrete religion and of its *mythos* or doctrine; this may take place either by means of open denial, or through an allegorical change in interpretation. When this takes place, however, mysticism realizes that it is an independent religious principle; it sees itself as the real universal heart of all religion, of which the various myth-forms are merely the outer garment. It regards itself as the means of restoring an immediate union with God; it feels independent of all institutional religion, and possesses an entire inward certainty, which makes it indifferent towards every kind of religious fellowship. This is its fundamental attitude; it does not vary whether the mystic adheres externally to the religious community or not. Henceforward union with God, deification, self-annihilation, become the real and the only subject of religion.

This theme is then presented as the abstract content of mystical experience, and is made the general universal essence of all inward and genuine religious processes. A union with God of this kind, however, further requires a general cosmic theory in which is established both the possibility and the manner of realizing this process of salvation. It also requires a technique of causation and completion of the mystical experience deduced from this theory.

A theory of this kind must be able to show how it came to pass that, in God, a separation between God and finite spirits could take place, and how this separation can be overcome by the very fact that the finite spirits have their being within God. It shows how all that is finite proceeds from God and returns unto God, for the sense of identity persisting through the separation becomes the very means by which the sense of separation is removed. This theory defines the degrees by which the creature falls away from and then rises up again into God; finally, it shows clearly that reflection upon and understanding of this process explains the religious experience to itself, and thus it attains an understanding of its own particular central content. The purely intellectual process of this association of ideas, so it is said, is, where it is really genuine and independent thought, the religious experience itself, and through this intellectual process the religious experience again interprets and clarifies its own ideas. From this there arise also the degrees of this experience, which are simply the stages of this intellectual process translated into terms of spiritual experience, to the point of the conscious attainment of the full sense of identity.

This type of mysticism becomes an independent religious philosophy, which recognizes that the religious process is the same universal expression and consciousness of the metaphysical connection between absolute and finite being, and which discovers everywhere, beneath all the concrete forms of religion, the same religious germ, which, however, only reaches complete and pure maturity under its fostering care. Thus mysticism becomes independent of concrete popular religion, timeless and non-historical, at most concealed under historical symbols, the only valid interpretation of the religious process, under whatever form it may be clothed. It becomes anti-personal and ascetic, since it allows personality to be absorbed in God, because it regards the senses and finite existence as the wall of separation between God Transcendent and God Immanent. This type of mysticism gives rise to that form of Pantheism which, however, in the philosophical sense is no Pantheism, because in it the separation of the finite ego from God is as important as its reunion with God. This therefore tends to develop into the crudest Dualism or into a gradual descending system of Emanations. It becomes a peculiar kind of intellectualism, an intellectualism which looks down with contempt upon the sense-bound standards of the intellect, and which replaces the common, carnal, and unhallowed ways of thought by a religious logic which is intelligible only to the religious mind. It can, however, also become pure voluntaryism, as soon as the dangers of thought for religious inwardness are felt, and the main stress is laid upon union of the will with God, or upon the decline of the will to live. Thus Brahmanistic speculative mysticism and Buddhistic voluntary mysticism, the Dominican mysticism of knowledge and the Franciscan mysticism of the will and of love, are all able to exist side by side.

This technical mysticism in the narrower sense, with its own philosophy of religion, has also appeared in various religious spheres with a remarkable similarity of form: in Indian Brahmanism and its repercussion in Buddhism, in the Sufism of the Parsees and of Persian Muslims, in the Neo-Platonism of the Greeks, in the varied syncretism of late antiquity which is known as Gnosticism. In the guise of Platonism, Neo-Platonism, and Gnosticism it presented itself to the Early Church, which seized it eagerly as a scientific foundation for its own religious doctrine, in the same way as it took Stoicism into account for its moral and social teaching, as a scientifically worked out analogy for its system of ethics. The stages of this development within Christianity are clearly defined. Jesus is not a mystic. He lives simply with His gaze fixed on God, urges practical sanctification of life, and proclaims the imminent realization of the ideal.

Paul and the "spiritual" men turn inward, spiritualize, and revive the Christ-cult and the Christian tradition which had grown up in the Early Church apart from philosophy and speculation, and with a free use of the mystical language of the ancient mysteries. The Gnostics, and the philosophers and theologians of the Early Church, open their minds to the mystical philosophy of religion, emphasizing more or less the concrete dependence upon Christian history, and affirming in varying tones of emphasis the practical and ethical idea of personality.

Mysticism in the narrower and the technical sense of the word, the mysticism which is concerned with the philosophy of religion, therefore, also developed an immense importance within Christianity. It helped the scientific theology of the early Christians to bring their faith in the Divine incarnation, in the hero of the cultus, in Christ, into line with the scientific formulas of the doctrine of the Trinity, which was conceived at first in harmony with the theory of emanations, and then as the consubstantiality of the Son with the Father (ὁμοούσιον). It helped early theology to define the possession of salvation as something to be attained through union with God in the Christian cultus, and to give a religious and philosophical meaning to its sacraments. It was also of value for the apologetic of the early Christians, since mysticism represented the natural universal religious consciousness which comes to completion in the Incarnation of the Logos and in the sacraments of the Church.

In connection with our present subject, however, all this is only relevant in so far as the relative acceptance of mysticism at that time formed the starting-point of and the justification for an ever fuller penetration of mysticism into Christianity itself. For us rather the significant effects of mysticism only emerge clearly where the sense of need for the inwardness and quickening of the religious process appropriated the technical methods of the soul's ascent to God, worked out by mysticism. This ascent was described as a process by which the soul rose from meditation and self-denial through ripening knowledge and union, to the heights of ecstasy, and thus was able to attain and experience Christian union with God and with Christ. Here Dionysius the Areopagite forms not the only but the noblest bridge of union with the Neo-Platonism which had most thoroughly formulated this doctrine. The Alexandrian theologians and Augustine had also already made their contribution. The decisive point, however, was not reached until mediaeval piety accepted the traditional Christian system, with its foreign elements inherited from antiquity (so remote from the Germanic temperament) of cultus, doctrine, and hierarchy; this it did by way of mysticism, which breathed into it an atmosphere of warm, personal piety. Thus St. Bernard and the Victorines freed the Christian faith from dogmatic rigidity and infused into it new warmth and vigour. Thus also the mystics of the Reformation period describe the gradual ascent of the soul from purgation, through illumination, right up to the heights of blissful union with God.

Further, we must also note the doctrine of mystical union with God or of the Indwelling of Christ as the very heart and basis of all practical religious achievement, and the radiating centre of religious ethics. Along these lines Christian mystics have sought and found a substantial union with Christ, in which the Christian experience became the principle of all religious activity and power, and, on the other hand, practical power to overcome the world became the test of the reality of union with Christ. In this way the gulf between past and present, between doctrine and practice, was overcome, and faith became the principle of direct practical achievement. Thus the Christocentric piety of the Middle Ages restored to believers direct access to Christ; the rock of Byzantine dogma had been struck, and out of it there flowed rivers of living water.

Luther also, sometimes revealed traces of this spirit, and it was through these ideas that Karlstadt, Schwenkfeld, and Osiander developed a mere faith in the doctrine of justification into the power of a life which expressed itself outwardly in direct and practical ways. This, too, was the tendency of the Christology of all the "spiritual reformers" of that day; it enabled them to interpret the Jesus of History and the mystically discerned Christ of Experience by the more general principle of the Logos incarnate in Christ, through whom they were brought into contact with the eternal living fullness of God.

The Divine Seed

This latter element, above all, needs to be taken into account as a means of establishing the mystical impulse towards an interior life, and of breathing fresh life and energy into objective religion upon a general theoretical scientific foundation. This basis is held to be that universal cosmic process, which is also the ultimate underlying truth in the Christian experience of salvation, of the descent of the Absolute into the finite world of sense, in which, however, God remains the Ground of the Soul, the Seed and the Spark even of the Creature, which in selfishness and sin asserts its right to an isolated independent existence. This is the great doctrine of the Divine Seed, of the Divine Spark which lies hidden in every mind and soul, stifled by sin and by the finite, yet capable of being quickened into vitality by the touch of the Divine Spirit working on and in our souls. This "seed" is the source of all religious longing for and awareness of God. Simply quickened by the historic revelation, this "seed" is developed into a complete power of overcoming the world and of return to God by the purely inward movement of the Spirit which is kindled and strengthened within the soul. Here all the emphasis falls upon the present, immediate, interior religious movement of feeling and of thought, in contrast to all external authority, all literalism in faith, to all theories which would make salvation dependent upon historical facts and upon the individual's knowledge and acceptance of these facts. Here the saving energy of

God joins forces with the movement of transient religious emotion, and faith is certain that it is able to distinguish the motion of the Divine Spirit from all merely human opinion and desire, by the practice of self-examination and the cultivation of a selfless spirit. All that is ecclesiastical, historic, dogmatic, objective, and authoritative is changed into a mere means of stimulation, into that which arouses that personal experience which alone is valuable, and on which alone the hope of salvation is founded. This is a theology of the subjective consciousness of salvation, and no longer one which confines itself to the objective facts of redemption. The Spirit, or the present living consciousness of salvation, and the facts of history and of the cultus, have been placed in a new relation. All that concerns the Church, doctrine, and dogma seems to be simply a precipitation of a personal religious life of that kind, and can only be understood in its true sense by the gracious inward influence of the Spirit, the movement of God within the soul. The spirit of God can only recognize His own Presence in the Scriptures and in the Church, and only thus can strength and nourishment be drawn from them; left to themselves both the Bible and the Church are merely a dead letter or an empty ceremonial. This is mystical "spiritual religion" in the service of a direct and personal religious life, preserving that which is alone worthy, a life in the spirit which rises above and conquers the world.

German mysticism evolved this theory as the foundation of practical reform, in connection with the emancipation of late mediaeval lay-Christianity from its ancient setting; at the same time, with varying consistency, it remained in touch with the objective institution of the Church, and, so far as lay in its power, it preserved the main Christian tendency by its emphasis upon personality. According to this theory, the finite spirit achieves actual reality in the world process; in its selfish resistance towards the Spirit of God it commits real sin, and through the working of the Divine Spirit which lays hold of it in Christianity it is raised to the true centre of personality and united with God. It is true that the ultimate end of union with God in contemplation, or in the surrender of the will to the Divine Love, still somehow always involves a certain loss of selfhood in God. In this respect Dante himself found it difficult to preserve the distinction. There can, however, be no doubt that mysticism intends to maintain the elevation, salvation, and deification of the true and genuine centre of personality. The whole mystical idea itself is indeed at the service of a personal living piety, of an "interior life" which has a direct experience of salvation. This fact, together with the relation between the inner working of the Spirit and the stimulation, heightened power, and intensification which come from history (which was somehow always maintained), distinguishes this Christian mysticism from its ancient foundation of Neo-Platonism, quite apart from the fact that the Trinitarian-Christological doctrine was retained and interpreted in this sense.[471]

The mysticism of the period of the Reformation arose out of this old mystical tradition, and its foundation in the New Testament, which constantly inspired it with fresh life. It is a matter of common knowledge that Luther himself was greatly influenced by it. Calvin, however, came far less under its influence. His doctrine of the Eucharist, too, does not agree with it, but rather with anti-Catholicism, and with the tendency to place a great gulf between the Creator and the creature. Calvinism is related to the sect-type, but not to mysticism. In spite of that, however, mysticism penetrated into it through all the avenues which were then possible, just as it penetrated into the Catholicism of the Counter-Reformation and into Lutheran Pietism. While in connection with Catholicism its strength lay in its desire to represent itself as the complement of the exaggerated emphasis upon the purely objective aspect of religion, and in its power to unite itself with the Catholic doctrine of justification in the shape of an inward substantial transformation of the believer;[472] on the other hand mysticism had a great attraction for Protestantism in its fundamental emphasis upon personal assurance of salvation, and, particularly in Lutheranism, in the doctrine of the present happiness of those whom Christ has set free.

The spiritualized conception of the Church in Protestantism, and the unsettlement which prevailed while the new Church organizations were being formed, provided this movement with scope for independent development. When this section was excluded from the churches and needed some other support and fellowship it found a very uncertain support and refuge in the excited "Enthusiasm" of the Anabaptists and in their ascetic system of morality. Some mystics remained entirely solitary, and entrusted their knowledge only to the printed page.[472a] Under these circumstances there arose a Protestant mysticism which, unlike Catholic mysticism, was not a compensation for ecclesiastical formalism, but which was a conscious, active, and independent principle of religious knowledge, inward experience, and morality. Only upon the basis of Protestant individualism

[471] See p. 963. [472] See p. 964. [472a] Cf. p. 739.

and Paulinism did specifically Christian mysticism attain an independent development, with new creative power, which exercised an ever deeper influence upon ecclesiastical Protestantism, and yet always remained inwardly separate from it. Anticipating the results of the modern, speculative, and autonomous philosophy of religion, it pointed forward to the development of modern Protestantism, and, in connection with Pietism, it destroyed ecclesiasticism, making the ecclesiastical exclusiveness and institutionalism of Protestantism increasingly uncertain.

"Spiritual Reformers"

This form of mysticism certainly found its highest and noblest expression only in the most outstanding thinkers and the most "interior souls" among the Protestant "Spiritual Reformers", in men like Sebastian Franck, Valentine Weigel, Dirck Coornheert, and John Saltmarsh. Detached elements of this process of thought, however, often appear among them all in an obscure connection with ecclesiastical statements, as, for instance, in Karlstadt, Schwenkfeld, and others. Conclusions of this kind were not uncommon in the "Enthusiasm" which played such a prominent part in the early Anabaptist movement, in the beginnings of Quakerism and in Methodism. Individuals also came to the same conclusions, even though mere "Enthusiasm" which depends upon sudden, extraordinary, and unregulated manifestations of God in itself certainly has no connection with the mystic's repose in the eternal unchanging Divine Spark within the human soul. Since, however, in all this the "enthusiastic" temperament still presses forward through religious excitement into the direct presence of the Spirit or of God, it has a strong tendency towards mysticism, which was often fully developed by "enthusiastic" and highly educated Baptists. The English Puritans passed from Pietism and Enthusiasm into mysticism and "spiritual religion"—at least in part—and when they did so it was with great vigour. Continental Pietists also came under the same influence; in both instances the older "spiritual" literature was producing a belated effect. As we have already noticed, the Congregationalists and Independents were "Spiritualists" without realizing it. The Quakers, in particular, developed their classic theory of the Inner Light out of an "enthusiastic" movement, and thus found rest of spirit and light in perplexity. It was, however, only when "Enthusiasm" and the urge towards "inwardness" achieved results of this kind that mysticism became real spirituality; at the same time, in its anti-hierarchical tendency to further the idea of the priesthood of all believers, this spirituality reveals its Protestant character.[473]

Thus we see clearly the difference between this "spiritual" tendency and the sect-ideal and the Baptist movement. For the Baptists the decisive element is the Law of Christ, the Sermon on the Mount, and the absolute Law of Nature which agrees with it. The "spiritual reformers", on the other hand, know nothing but the Spirit, its freedom and its inward impulse. They are "Antinomians" and obey the light of conscience which has been unveiled by the Indwelling Christ. The Anabaptists laid passionate stress on Adult Baptism as the external sign of the covenant with God. To the "spiritual reformers" Baptism was a matter of supreme indifference. They recognized solely the "Baptism of the Spirit", and they taught that only those who were spiritually gifted were able to recognize those who belong to the true, pure, Spiritual Church, or fellowship of the Spirit of Christ. The Anabaptists had external organizations and ceremonies: the Lord's Supper, the feet-washing, a constitution. The "spiritual reformers" would admit nothing but the worship of God in spirit and in truth; they recognized no external united Christian body, and, at bottom, they had no use for sacraments. The Anabaptists obeyed the external Word as their literal rule of life and their external authority. The "spiritual reformers" depended upon the Inward Word, the Logos, the Divine Seed, or the Divine Spark, through whose impulses alone they were able to understand the external Word, which they (who also held firmly to the doctrine of inspiration) interpreted in an allegorical manner. The Anabaptists organized congregations, and appointed their members to different offices; they used ordination and carried on mission work. The "spiritual reformers" dwelt within the Invisible Church, in which the Spirit does all, and in which it is not necessary to know each other according to the flesh. The Anabaptists formed a community ruled by Christ and composed of genuine saints. The "spiritual reformers" did not recognize a visible Church at all, but they looked for the Third Age in which all men will

[473] On this point cf. the very valuable writings of *H. Heppe: Geschichte der pietistischen Mystik in der katholischen Kirche, 1875, Geschichte des Pietismus und der Mystik in der reformierten Kirche namentlich der Niederlande, 1879.* The latter book maintains its very considerable value alongside of *Ritschl's Geschichte des Pietismus.*—There is a one-sided ascription of mysticism to Catholicism in *Herrmann: Verkehr des Christen mit Gott, pp. 16–21* (English translation, *Communion with God, pp. 19 ff.*). In the school of Ritschl both mysticism and the sect-type are referred back to Catholicism, in order that they may be excluded the more surely from Protestantism.

be illuminated and led by the Spirit Himself; for them Christ ruled only by the Spirit, which is identical with direct religious experience. The Anabaptists also took the Apocalypse literally, and calculated the Advent of Christ and the coming of the Millennium. The "spiritual reformers" spiritualized even the Millennium, transforming it into an inward return of Christ to hearts which at last are open to the Divine Love. The Anabaptists laid great stress on the teaching of the Synoptic Gospels, on the Jesus of History, and on His proclamation of the coming Kingdom of God. The "spiritual reformers" appealed to Paul and to John: they did not know Christ after the flesh, and through the Spirit they were ever pressing on into an ever new and deeper knowledge of God, which to them was alone the true work of God. These differences are fundamental; their ultimate causes lie in the Bible itself.

The distinctive sociological peculiarities of this kind of "spiritual religion" are also manifest. Mysticism is a radical individualism, very different from that of the sect. While the sect separates individuals from the world by its conscious hostility to "worldliness" and by its ethical severity, binding them together in a voluntary fellowship, established upon mutual control and penitential discipline, laying upon individuals the obligation to follow the example and submit to the authority of Christ, increasing individualism by placing it within the mutual influence of group-fellowship and worship,—mysticism lays no stress at all upon the relation between individuals, but only upon the relations between the soul and God. It regards the historical, authoritative, and ritual elements in religion merely as methods of quickening the religious sense with which, in case of need, it can dispense altogether. "Spiritual religion", in particular, in its intense emphasis upon "first-hand experience", actually tends to sweep away the historical element altogether, and in so doing it eliminates the only centre around which a Christian cult can be formed. Thus this kind of religion becomes non-historical, formless, and purely individualistic, although certainly in very varying degrees of consistency. So long as it remains consciously Christian, the Bible and the historic Figure of Christ still play an important part; this aspect, however, is never stressed sufficiently strongly to produce a firmly established community, with a common centre of worship, history, and authority. Whatever organized forms it does adopt are loose and provisional, mere concessions to human frailty, without any sense of inward necessity and Divine inspiration. Its individualism, therefore, differs entirely from that of the sect. The sect characteristics—personal confession of faith in Christ, and the ever-renewed creation of fresh forms of fellowship through the mutual influence of individuals upon each other—are absent. Instead there is simply a parallelism of spontaneous religious personalities, whose only bond of union is their common Divine origin, their common spirit of love, and their union in God, which is the free and invisible work of the Divine Spirit. In itself, this kind of spirituality feels no need for sacraments or dogmas, for a ministry or for organization. Its spirit of fellowship, like the religious illumination itself, is solely the work of the Spirit, which is the same in each soul, and can be recognized alike by each soul, from which also in each separate instance there arises the interior union of souls and the active expression of Christian love. The individualism of the Anabaptist movement has been transcended, since this "spiritual religion" dispenses with all mediate and organized forms of worship and fellowship, placing faith and feeling in an entirely independent position. On the other hand, this kind of individualism is much weaker than that of the Anabaptist movement—(with its emphasis upon continual activity and the active holiness of its members who are united in a vital fellowship)—since its main tendency is towards quietude and abandonment, in which love is exercised only in individual instances. Individualism can, indeed, mean very different things, and have a very different effect, according to its basis and its setting, as we have already seen in the difference between mediaeval individualism with its emphasis upon differentiation and gradation, and Protestant individualism with its stress on the equal autonomy and equal obligation of all towards the community.

So far it might seem as though this kind of "spiritual religion" had no positive sociological character at all, or as though it only achieved fellowship incidentally through lack of clarity. This, however, is not the case. First of all, as we have already seen, "spiritual religion" presupposes both the unity of the "Divine Ground" which is the source of all personal religion, and the unity of aim which binds all souls together in one. Only it does not strive to create fellowship and unity by its own human activity—by founding organizations and societies—but it leaves this work to the Divine action through the Spirit. Further, this "spiritual religion" is still Christian. This does not mean simply that the Spirit is fully incarnate and visible in Christ, thus gathering believers into an historic and definite unity, but also that the ethical element of Will in the Christian and prophetical idea of

God, urges it towards active charity and self-giving to the brethren.

Sociological Theory of "Spiritual Religion": The "Invisible Church"

Hence at this point there arises the idea of fellowship peculiar to this kind of "spiritual religion": the idea of the Invisible Church, of the purely spiritual fellowship, known to God alone, about which man does not need to concern himself at all, but which invisibly rules all believers, without external signs or other human means. The conception of a purely spiritual fellowship, which is carried forward independently by the power of the Spirit, is the background of this sentiment, and in this the individual is therefore relieved of all obligation to organize and evangelize, and from all connection with ecclesiastical and sectarian organization. There is no need to make any efforts to prove and maintain the historical basis of faith; it appears spontaneously wherever the Spirit beholds Himself. Since in reality all Christianity is identical with the stirring of the divine "Seed" in the soul, Christ also is omnipresent, not merely in His historical form, but also in every true believer. Non-Christian religious souls can thus also be revelations of the Christ. Once again, however, this means that all forms of religion, viewed from the Christian standpoint, are regarded as identical with Christianity. The best method, therefore, of making this fellowship an active and practical force is the practice of toleration, coupled with faith in the power of God to make this fellowship effective by the might of His Spirit. Thus the "spiritual" man everywhere seeks to reach others at the deepest levels of the soul, wherever these are at all accessible. He exercises Christian charity, however, not in founding institutions or societies, but in practical life, wherever the claims of love present themselves in the guise of homely duty. Thus in this Christian "spiritual religion" there is an element of fellowship which is closely related to Luther's earlier ideas; the only difference is that Luther required the "spiritual life" to be kept in close relation with the Word, the Sacrament, and the ministry, whereas the "spiritual reformers" proclaimed the need for the free and untrammelled movement of the Spirit, an increase of knowledge and of freedom in opposition to "the letter" of Scripture.

But the sociological element in mysticism goes still farther. Even the mystic is human, and he feels the need for the give-and-take of intimate fellowship with other souls. In the mystic, too, this is no mere human weakness but a Christian duty, inculcated plainly by the example of the pure love of the Primitive Church as a command of the Spirit of God. Where, however, mystics do form groups they do not intend them to take the place of the great Invisible Church (as a sect would tend to do), or to interfere with God's own work of spreading the influence of the Spirit; the aim of these groups is purely personal; they are intimate circles for edification. This kind of fellowship expressed itself in various ways, as for instance in Philadelphianism; and in the formation of groups round spiritual directors and deeply experienced leaders. There was nothing rigid about these groups; they formed and re-formed naturally and easily, according to the situation in any given place. At other times this spirit expressed itself in organizations which were formed on the family pattern; these groups were formed by religious people who lived a community life which was similar to that of the cloister; they were controlled by ideas which were in entire agreement with the mystical ideas contained in monasticism. They had no intention, however, of claiming to be "the true Church" or "the Christian community"; they were merely personal and casual in character, groups within the Invisible Church which the Spirit calls into being, through which, in some incalculable manner, He influences the whole.[474] Only in an intimate group of this kind can worship be offered in purity and truth, arising out of a spiritual fellowship in which love has been truly kindled on the altar of intimate friendship and union in God. In this method of worship there are no magical "means of grace" and no ritual ordinances; all the stress is laid upon the mutual fellowship of hearts—"representative action" as Schleiermacher very unecclesiastically describes the cultus. Within such groups the Lord's Supper and the Agapé can be renewed and spiritualized in their true mystical meaning, in a way which is impossible to the Church of the masses, or in the quarrelsome exercise of discipline among the sects. As the polemical writers of that day used to say, "spiritual religion" is super-ecclesiastical, "syncretistic", "indifferent", or "fanatical". In reality this movement reabsorbs rigid historical dogma into the living movement and development of the Spirit; in the psychological processes themselves it seeks the essence of revelation and a present redemption.

Effects of "Spiritual Religion" on Dogma

Since all mysticism first arises in opposition to objective dogmas and forms of worship, it assumes in a very aristocratic way that

[474] See p. 964.

the concrete forms of worship will continue to be the religion of the masses. It is its mission, however, to call the true children of God out of that external worship in order to lift them up into the Kingdom of God which is purely within us. From every side it sees souls growing into this Kingdom. From this point of view these more intimate groups are merely personal and changing forms of fellowship, which express in a particular circle, with enhanced vitality, the universal unity of the Spirit. That is why so many mystics remain within the Church, which they do not wish to replace by any other new organization; they look upon their own circles as special groups which can quite well exist within the Church itself. Several, of course, do reject the Church altogether and live an isolated existence, but they comfort themselves with the thought of a better future, of a "third revelation" when all shall be taught of God, and when an "unsectarian Christianity of love" will unite all Christians in one fellowship of love. Mystics are far less inclined to separate from the Church than are the sectarians.

Naturally this whole way of thinking reacts upon the world of doctrinal conceptions. As the main doctrines of the Church—of Christ, the Trinity, the Work of Redemption through the Atonement, and the sacraments which appropriate this redemption—are closely connected with the ecclesiastical idea and with the worship of the Church, the mystical movement stands out in opposition to the current ecclesiastical doctrine of Redemption and of the Sacrament. It recognizes no "finished salvation" with which the Church is endowed as an organ of grace, but only, primarily, the facts of revelation and redemption in the present religious experience of each soul. Thus it feels no need of the doctrine of the Atonement, and it sees in it only the logical, ethical, and metaphysical inconsistencies which cause its disintegration. "Spiritual religion" of this kind does not admit the possibility of appropriating the benefits of redemption through worship, the sacraments, or through Church organization. It rejects the whole idea of an objective deposit of salvation upon which the Church can draw in order to impart its benefits to those who need them; its main emphasis is upon the example of Christ as the source of His continuing spiritual influence. Primarily it does not know the "Christ after the flesh" at all, and it has no interest in the doctrine of the Incarnation; it sees the Divinity of Christ solely in the Spirit of Christ of which the Jesus of History is merely the concrete symbol. Therefore it either deifies Christ entirely, even in His human nature, or it loosens the connection between the Divine and human elements in Christ. Thence there arise now and again attacks upon the doctrine of the Trinity, which come very near to placing Christ within a Neo-Platonic Emanationism.[475] This type of religion does not strive after a mass Christianity, for which, naturally, the forgiveness of sins stands in the foreground, as a release from the unattainable degree of sanctification without giving up the comfort of salvation; in it the forgiveness of sins recedes into the background, and it is replaced by a direct experience of God and actual victory over sin through the deification of the soul.[476]

In all these aspects, however, "spiritual religion" is also opposed to the sect, which presupposes the God-Man as the ruler and founder of the religious community, and the work of salvation as the complement of the efforts of a life of sanctification which is still always imperfect. Nor has it any use for the ideas of the sect with its literal historic Christ, and its retention of the Synoptic message of the Kingdom of God. Only where the sect merges into mysticism do we find it exercising this kind of doctrinal criticism, as, for instance, among some Baptist and Quaker theologians. On some other points, however, mysticism approaches the sect point of view in doctrinal matters, but, characteristically, for very different reasons. This applies, above all, to its repudiation of the doctrine of predestination. The coupling together of the doctrine of original sin and reprobation, with the doctrine of election, seemed to these "spiritual reformers" to imperil moral seriousness, and also to destroy the very foundation of mysticism: that inward Divine Seed which in some mysterious way is present and active within every soul. These "spiritual reformers" were also akin to the sect-type in their insistence on the necessity for focusing faith in a simple, experimental, and tangible unity of thought, as originally Luther also had desired to do, a desire which reappears indeed in every fresh impulse towards inward and direct religious experience. It was, therefore, not merely the moralistic Anabaptist movement which strove against the ecclesiastical and orthodox tendency to develop this practical and simple heart of religion into a doctrinal system;[477] the Protestant mystics of that period also threw all their influence into that effort.

[475] This has given rise to the suggestion that various "spiritual reformers" ought to be numbered among the Anti-Trinitarians, a group which in the average history of doctrine is still continually presented to us, whose members, however, belong to quite different connections, and which can only be gathered together in this group from the external, heresiological point of view.

[476] See p. 965.

[477] See p. 965.

Through this criticism of doctrine, and through the appeal to a permanent unchanging "Divine Ground" within the soul, which is only quickened into life when it meets with the Bible and the message of Christ, mysticism establishes another still closer relationship, namely, the relationship with rationalism. We need, however, merely to glance at the Humanistic theology, at Socirianism and Deism, in order to notice the important distinction which, for all that, still exists between mysticism and rationalism. Several Humanistic ideas have crept in, as is quite clear in the case of Sebastian Franck, Castellio, and Coornheert. But in principle a great distinction remains. Mystical "enthusiasm" with its constant "illuminations", and divine "openings" and "communications", spiritual idealism with its asceticism, its rejection of the "letter" and of the external knowledge of the senses, is still at heart hostile to the spirit of scientific rationalism. Scientific rationalism is more at home in the rational apologetic and scholasticism of the churches, and genuine rationalists, like the Socinians, preferred to remain within the churches, because purely critical scientific theology has no fellowship principle of its own. Where they were forced into a separatist attitude they certainly did create their own communities, which, however, were more like schools than religious fellowships of like-minded people bound together in love. Nevertheless, this kind of spirituality has many points of contact with the general intellectualist spirit of rationalism; and when its mystical glow fades it easily slips into it, as was the case with Spinoza, Edelmann, and a section of the Deists.

Mysticism which draws its nourishment from the immediate perception of the Presence of God, is a process which is repeated everywhere and always in the same manner, and thus it comes into touch with the autonomy and universal validity of scientific thought. Both assimilate each other. Further, to the extent in which mysticism of the Neo-Platonic type bases its experience on a universal cosmic foundation, regarding it as the actualization of the Divine Spark contained in every soul, mystical religion in general becomes a process which completes itself in attaining to the knowledge of God through the intellect, and the redemption of the spirit through that knowledge. It thus leads to a Universalism which recognizes in all the concrete positive religions that fundamental process which arises from the essential relationship between God and the finite. In spite of its reverence for the Bible it still reduces the sense of difference between Christianity and the other religions, and recognizes the Indwelling Christ also in the non-Christian faiths. It places the universal religious consciousness which is interpreted as an inward necessity, over against an active and personal faith, which has an objective historic basis. In so doing, however, it leaves the realm of positive theology and enters that of the universal philosophy of religion. With the disappearance or decrease of the gulf between the Christian and the non-Christian world this school of thought approaches the system of comparative religion and criticism, for which Erasmus had already prepared the way. It turns its attention, first of all towards those elements in traditional theology and worship which constitute the greatest stumbling-block to the mystic—against the practice of isolating the Christian facts of salvation and making them static, which is so uncongenial to the mystical thirst for direct experience. The historic time-element and the magical sense-element are willingly handed over to a more or less penetrating criticism, and, in place of these elements, stress is laid upon the timeless and universal element which Christianity contains. Thus the full significance of this kind of spirituality does not emerge until it appears in mystics like Franck, Coornheert, and Castellio, who, together with their mysticism, had also imbibed the spirit of Humanistic culture and criticism.

Finally, this movement exhibited a spirit of tolerance which went far beyond the Anabaptist demands for toleration. In the view of the "spiritual reformers" toleration did not consist in merely refraining from forcible compulsion in religious matters, coupled with the conviction that one's own section of the Church contains the whole and the sole Truth; it was a spirit of religious toleration which granted to each individual the actual right to his own convictions; its outlook is relative, since in all that is relative the Absolute is present. It was that relative conception of Truth which was current neither in the churches nor in the sects, and which alone completely eradicates the urgent desire for the sole dominion of an absolute conception of Truth. Luther's strongly mystical statements about toleration sank into oblivion because instinctively he would not and could not give up the absolute conception of truth and Revelation. On the other hand, the toleration preached by "spiritual reformers" did gain ground, because it everywhere recognized Truth and Revelation in every relative approach to the one Truth, which, ultimately, could only be experienced in the present. Only among the "spiritual reformers" was there liberty of conscience within the religious community, whereas the sects and the Free Churches recognized liberty of conscience only from the standpoint of the State, and alongside of the ecclesiastical organizations. But in this respect also this "spiritual" movement differs from strict rationalism, which, with its absolute demand for the truth of its ideas, tends rather towards intolerance, like the churches, and is only ready to tolerate the opinions of others out of contempt and opportunism. Real toleration was and is found only among those rationalists who have steeped themselves at the same time in mystical and "spiritual" ideas.[478]

These conclusions, however, only represent the final development of these ideas. Few of the "spiritual reformers" in early Protestantism went as far as this. Their chief aim was simply to breathe new life into the Christian movement, and to make it active and effective; most of them therefore did not go beyond a Christ-mysticism of the type of St. Bernard. Schwenkfeld is the leader, or at least the type, of most of them. The doctrine of Original Sin, too, which increased the gulf of separation between the Christian and the non-Christian world, was indeed forced into the background by the idea of the "flesh", and of that selfishness which revealed itself in external matters; but the underlying dualism was still rarely completely dissolved. These reflections are only modern deductions from these ideas, which were certainly latent within these doctrines, but which did not reveal their significance until they were developed to their full logical extent.

The early "spiritual reformers", even the most radical, were still very sure of their essentially Christian faith, and they particularly liked to appeal to similar "spiritual" expressions of Luther's early period, when Luther, too, had expected everything from the Spirit who is contained in the Word. Everything centres in confidence in the Spirit, who, wherever He may be, is always the Spirit of Christ, and who Himself will make humanity Christian. Ecclesiastical differences are softened or even removed; but Christianity itself was not drawn into this relative outlook; these results of a relative point of view were still only latent. The outward Church has been dissolved, but the inward Church and the support which it provides still exists. The main interest of these thinkers is not intellectual but emotional. They hold that the religious spirit is not produced by criticism of doctrine and of the Bible, but by the opposite method. The starting-point of all criticism is the need for direct experience, the ethical seriousness and the sociological standpoint of the mystic or the "spiritual" man. Doctrines, so far as they are opposed to this, or which have

[478] See p. 965.

become unnecessary for the emotions, certainly come under its criticism, which is further strengthened by Humanistic and other forms of criticism. The main interest, however, is religious, and the whole relative element is felt to be a possible point of view within the Christian position. This main religious and Christian tendency could not be destroyed until it came under the influence of modern natural science, and of the new philosophical systems which were erected upon this foundation. Only since then has this type of spirituality been fused with a really rational "universal Theism".[479]

The Ethic of "Spiritual Religion"

The ethic of this "spiritual religion" also is peculiar. It is an ethic which aims at holiness and at perfection, and it reproaches the churches particularly for their ethical laxity and their effortless acceptance of the objective aspect of Christianity in their faith in the vicarious removal of the curse of sin by the Death of Christ. At this point "spiritual religion" seems to come very close to the sect, and often enough it has been fused with it. It has points of contact also with the Catholic ethic, which therefore it often praises more highly than the Protestant ethic. This "spiritual" ethic of sanctification, however, is quite differently interpreted from that of the sect. Its ideal is the untrammelled freedom of the Spirit; not control, community discipline, and the strictness of the law of the Sermon on the Mount. It was just at this point, too, that this school of thought came into contact with Luther, and it was fond of appealing to his earlier expressions of opinion. In the moral sphere, also, the freedom of the Spirit is paramount. Here again there is nothing literal and nothing external. Within this movement there was a strong sense, it is true, of deep opposition to the world, a hatred of the carnal and selfish worldly temper; in this respect it was much closer to the ascetic ideal than were the churches. As a movement, however, it lacked that other element of asceticism, the legalistic spirit and the practice of regular discipline. It recognized a method of degrees in the life of communion with God, and of self-discipline for the aim of "deification", but it felt no need of a moral purification with a supernatural end in view, or of a gradual process of sanctification which proves the existence of a "state of grace". This form of spirituality is as remote from the sober and legal spirit of Calvinism and of Puritanism as it is from that of the Anabaptists and the Mennon-

[479] See p. 966.

ites. When it did take root in Puritanism (as in Dell and Francis Rous) it appealed to Luther and to Catholic literature. Further, there is at this point a distinct difference between Calvinistic and Lutheran mysticism. Tersteegen considered Count Zinzendorf superficial; the latter represented more logically the ethic of this mystical spirituality. The goal of this movement is an immanent, free happiness, which does good quite spontaneously, and which is as little bound to the conventions of men as it is to the moral law of the Bible. Nor has the idea of the natural moral law any special significance for this school of thought. Its followers prefer to speak of the Inner Light, of the Illuminated Reason, of conscience as identical with the revelation of Christ which awakens it to life. The primary aim of this ethic of freedom is the enjoyment and practical proof of personal salvation. The outpouring of the Divine Love upon the brethren is only something additional, though it is strongly and particularly emphasized. Religion is placed above ethics. It is perfectly natural, therefore, that problems of secular morality, of the State, of Society, and of economics are regarded as unimportant; in fact they are actually treated with entire indifference. Wherever people attempted to solve these problems in smaller groups they either formed societies on the model of the family or the cloister, or they assimilated certain features of the sect; every ethical experiment, indeed, brought the "spiritual reformers" into closer relation with the sect-type, with which they were already on the verge of fusion at many points. In actual practice both of these religious types were constantly merging into each other. The sect aspired to the inwardness of mysticism; mysticism strove to actualize the sacred fellowship of the sect. "Enthusiasm"— the result of great excitement and of the oppressive hostility of the churches—also played its part in drawing both these groups closer together. But inconsistencies and tensions, due to this partial fusion of the two types, still remained.[480]

This general description must now be supplemented by concrete examples. In so doing we are as little concerned with a new presentation of the subject-matter as we were in dealing with the sect; our one aim is to shed light upon the sociological significance and social influence of particular groups, in which their opposition to the group-fellowship and the social ethic of the Church becomes plain.

[480] See p. 967.

Thomas Münzer

Thomas Münzer is the first instance of this pronounced opposition to the Protestant church-type. At first he shared Luther's views, but from the outset he was influenced by the mystical writings recommended by Luther, and he was also conversant with Joachimite literature. Further, while he was pastor in Zwickau, he came under the influence of the conventicles which existed in that town, and he imbibed their idea of a fresh outpouring of "spiritual gifts" before the swiftly approaching End of the World. His theology consisted of the mystical doctrine of passive deification, and the doctrine of the Holy Spirit, revealing His presence independently within the soul, merely stimulated and authenticated by the Word; this view he combined with the Zwickau fanaticism. From the outset also he united with this doctrine the ideal of establishing an exclusive community of mystical adepts and of the elect; this ideal was broadened until it included ideas of communistic social reform. It seems probable that this later development was due to the influence of Hussite and Taborite ideas, because when Münzer was driven out of Zwickau he went to Bohemia, where he hoped to realize his ideals. This hope, however, was doomed to disappointment. From that time he developed still more strongly the idea that, since in these latter days the authorities had failed, it had now become the imperative duty of the laity to use violence in order to realize the ideal of the perfect spiritual community. From the same standpoint also he deduced the rejection of Infant Baptism, on the ground that external sacramental ordinances belong to "the flesh". Münzer did not belong to the Anabaptists. It is true that the Zürich Anabaptist movement which had just come into existence welcomed him, but its members warned him against the use of violence, and they blamed him for laying so little emphasis upon Believers' Baptism.

Münzer represents a reawakening of mystical ideas combined with fanatical Hussite and Taborite revolutionary ideas. This combination, however, was merely accidental; it did not represent a real fusion of these various elements. It can only be explained by the character and destiny of this restless man, who was always eager for peculiar and spectacular activities. In the end the waves of the Peasants' War engulfed him. The so-called "Zwickau Fanatics" are also connected with Münzer, through his residence in Zwickau. These men, however, are of no special importance for our inquiry, save that of being representatives of "spiritual enthusiasm", and the "spiritual" criticism of the sacraments, in the sense of an excited religion of the common people which was nourished by fragments of mysticism.[481]

Karlstadt

The mysticism of Karlstadt was far more important and influential. It led to a passionate disagreement with Luther, who clipped the wings of his former colleague first of all by exile, and then by internment in a place where he was kept under observation, until at last Karlstadt fled to Switzerland, and thus gained his freedom. Karlstadt also could not accept the doctrine that salvation consists in the mere acceptance of the forgiveness of sins by the soul which has trembled before the awful majesty of the Law on the bare authority of the Word, and its proclamation by the ministers of Christ. He also, after the manner of the mystics, conceived salvation to be a gradual process leading upwards from self-emptying to complete conformity with the Will of God. In his view this sanctification was to be realized not merely on the bare authority of the Word of Scripture, but rather by the free inward movement of the Spirit which is merely aroused and controlled by the Scriptures. Moreover, he felt that the genuine character of the purely inward process ought to be recognized by its practical results, by the ethic of love and self-sacrifice made possible through spiritual conformity with the Will of God. This led him—in line with the true mystical tradition—to exalt the "spirit" above the "letter"; to a "spiritual" criticism of the sacraments; to the idea of a lay-religion of spiritually enlightened souls, who are to be shepherded by particularly gifted spiritual men, recognized and approved as such by the whole "illuminated" group; to the free formation of congregations exercising their individual choice of such a "spiritual" man as their pastor; and to a strong emphasis upon the practical results of conformity to the Mind and Will of God; through these ideas he came into contact with the social reform movements of his own day. In this instance, as a result of his contact with these ideas of social reform, mysticism seemed to be approaching the ideal of the sect. In reality Karlstadt's main concern, however, was not with the ethic of the Sermon on the Mount, but with the spirituality of self-negation, not with Adult Baptism as the sign of mature Church-membership, but with a "spiritual" explanation of the sacraments;

[481] Cf. the article on *Münzer* by *Kolde: PRE.*[3], *Gottfried Arnold, II, 14–17*, with the characteristic expression of opinion: "Even although at the beginning he may without doubt at times have received grace from God, yet Nature retained the upper hand" (*K. Müller: KG., II, 310–326*).

not with the formation of a "holy community", but with the gathering together of individuals who are freely moved by the Spirit, for whom all visible fellowship is a merely external matter. Although he withdrew from co-operation with Münzer, yet, later on, he did not join the Anabaptists.

Karlstadt laid down his spiritual offices and dignities at a time when everyone was still making ecclesiastical experiments, for he wished to form a community at Orlamünde which in itself would not have been wholly against Luther's earlier principles. Luther, however, was alienated from Karlstadt on the following points: Karlstadt replaced the doctrine of justification by faith by the doctrine of the degrees of salvation; he set the freedom of the Spirit in contrast to the Word; he linked the demand for practical proof of the reality of the inner life with the demand for social reform, and, above all, he assailed the rights of the patron.

Luther's passionate hatred regarded Karlstadt simply as another comrade of Münzer, and a muddle-headed fool. So he drove him into misery and want, from which the Swiss churches, with their more lenient views of mysticism, rescued him. The conflict was, however, not a personal one; it was purely objective. It meant that an essentially individualistic, irreconcilable form of mysticism (which, moreover, had incidentally come into touch with the democratic reform tendencies of the small Communes), stood out in opposition to Luther's idea of a mediated salvation, bound up with an objective authority, which, for that reason, was capable of leading to an ecclesiastical organization. Otherwise, however, Karlstadt tried to unite the "Word" and the "Spirit" just as Luther had tried to do in his early days; Zwingli also had made the same experiment. This is why the problem was never really solved. The only result of the controversy was that Luther coined some decisive polemical formulas which came into permanent use.[482]

Schwenkfeld

The doctrine of Schwenkfeld, and his organization of conventicles, marks a distinct step forward. Schwenkfeld was a most delightful man, and one of Luther's noblest followers and most spiritual colleagues in the cause of reform; his "spiritual religion" always remained moderately ecclesiastical. He had been influenced by the teaching of Luther's early period, and also by German mysticism, particularly by Tauler. Later he came into touch with Karlstadt, and with the Basel and Zürich Reformers who

[482] See p. 968.

were very sympathetic towards mystical ideas. The impulse to his particular form of mysticism arose out of his evangelistic work in Silesia, where he discovered the hopelessness of a people's church which was simply a mass of baptized individuals; his desire was to combine Luther's "spiritual" idea of an inner circle with the Scriptural primitive conception of a society for worship endowed with spiritual gifts. In order to achieve this end the merely objective "Word" was insufficient; what was needed was the quickening Spirit, as distinct from the "Word", whose presence can be felt, and its reality proved by its fruits. Accordingly Schwenkfeld's idea was that of the present inner activity of the converting and renewing Spirit of God, and the absolute necessity of practical religious and ethical fruits to prove the reality of this activity. In order to protect the inner movement of the Spirit from dissolving into a purely psychological process, like Luther he laid the most vigorous emphasis upon predestination and the self-witness of the Spirit as true in the elect. He admitted that the inward activity of the Spirit is mediated through the objective authority of the Word and of preaching to the extent that he regarded the Word or the Bible only as a vessel which contained a deposit of inner spiritual experience, and he admitted its importance in kindling a similar inward spiritual movement, like that out of which it had itself arisen. The Bible was also useful as a standard by which the inner working of the Spirit could be tested. He also accepted the doctrine of the Atonement through the Death of Christ, but in this he laid all the emphasis upon the appropriation and imitation of this "dying of Jesus" through the absolutely real indwelling of the Exalted Christ within the elect.

To Schwenkfeld salvation did not consist in faith in the validity of the Gospel proclaimed by the Church, nor in the salvation which the Church holds in trust for humanity, but in a personal direct Christ-mysticism of dying and rising again with Christ. This belief led him to emphasize very strongly the great difference between the "letter", the "flesh", and the "creature", and the directly Divine element in life, the Spirit, the inward result of "election". Above all, he deduced from all this the idea of the Divine Christ whose Nature must not be stained with any "creaturely" element at all, for even His human Body from the very beginning of creation was a spiritual and supernatural Body. This remarkable dogma formulated by Schwenkfeld, which is connected with speculations of the ancient patristic mystical type, and which also gives form and substance to the mystical idea of the process of salvation, was, in reality, only an attempt to express his desire to empty the idea of Christ of all historical content while retaining the Christological dogma.

One result of this doctrine was to empty of meaning the external sacraments. At the most they might possibly be regarded as outward tokens of the spiritual fullness which was already present. Therefore, in spite of the fact that Schwenkfeld rejected Infant Baptism, and that he happened to be on friendly terms with the Anabaptists, inwardly he held himself aloof from their movement. The only baptism which he could admit was the Baptism of the Spirit; the only law, that which works through the Spirit, the only religious community, that which Christ Himself has brought into being, conventicles endowed with spiritual gifts and ruled by the Spirit, which, while they may continually change their form, are the leaven and the salt working within the visible churches. In Schwenkfeld's theory these conventicles were to be smaller groups of genuine communicants, which were to be kept as pure as possible by means of discipline. The Primitive Apostolic Church has passed away; it soon became formal, and from the time of Constantine it became purely secular. The visible Church, which has been in existence since that time, and which at the present day is divided into four sections: Baptist, Lutheran, Zwinglian, and Anabaptist, may continue to exist as an auxiliary institution for the protection and furtherance of the true Church, the spiritual community of those who have been truly "born of the Spirit". Connection with the State is an evil; force in religious matters is wholly unchristian. The conventicles are persecuted because they oppose the spirit of the world. Only an apostle obviously raised up by God, or the Return of Christ, will make it a final organization, or lead it to victory. Here again we see how the Chiliast idea always springs up afresh when there is a clash between universal hope and actual failure. This conception of the Church was certainly sharply opposed to the idea of a Church composed of those "born again through baptism" proclaimed by the Lutheran preachers, who were only thinking of a church in terms of a mass movement. This is why it aroused in Luther such intense anger that he soon made it totally impossible for "Stenkfeld" to live in any Lutheran country. Schwenkfeld was to share the fate of Karlstadt.[483] In a wandering life of self-imposed exile from his homeland of Silesia, protected mainly by aristocratic members of his own class of society, Schwenkfeld created conventicles which consisted of believers united by ties of personal fellowship who shared in the life of the churches but abstained

[483] See p. 968.

from the use of the sacraments, waiting for the settlement of this vexed question by the Protestant leaders.

In many respects Schwenkfeld reminds us of Zinzendorf; but Schwenkfeld was much nearer to true mysticism than Zinzendorf. Schwenkfeld's ideal was that of smaller groups within the churches who are to be guided and built up in the faith by a truly "converted" preacher, who, naturally, will be really effective; this pastor may, of course, be a layman. Like the Moravians and the Methodists at a later date, his followers were forced by persecution to form independent communities of their own. Only a few groups survived these persecutions, and in Silesia, towards the end of the sixteenth century, they united with the Baptists. After 1720 the few who remained fled from oppression to England, Holland, and America.

Schwenkfeld's ideal may be broadly described as a union of the sectarian principle with mysticism; it was, however, influenced less by the sectarian and mystical tradition than by Lutheran, Scriptural, and Patristic ideas. It is non-ecclesiastical, with a supra-confessional outlook, but it also recognizes and uses the churches as the outward means of preparation for making the world Christian. The real rebirth of the Church is still to come, and pure conventicles are only a preparation for that consummation. But this rebirth will be a work of Divine miraculous power and the outpouring of the Spirit before the End.

The influence of these ideas was great and widespread. Nearly all the "spiritual reformers" show traces of its influence, and the English Congregationalists in particular can possibly only be explained from this point of view, even though their outlook was also strongly coloured by Calvinism.

Weigel

Valentine Weigel, a disciple of Schwenkfeld, at a later date carried the mystical element a step farther, at least in one of its aspects. Weigel despised the mere externals of religion to such an extent that all his life he passed for an orthodox Lutheran pastor. It was only after his death that his writings made known to a horrified world his view that salvation was bound up entirely with purely inward, directly personal movements of the Spirit. He developed the purely philosophical foundations of mysticism in a very logical way, the idealistic conception of the idea of God in humanity. His ideas, therefore, are more significant for philosophy than for Church History.[483a]

[483a] See p. 970.

Although the mysticism of Schwenkfeld remained within the borders of the Church, making a distinct effort to establish a relationship with the specific organized Christian communities, it went far beyond these limits in the most important and independent representatives of this school of thought. It became an entirely individualistic principle, akin to the critical Rationalism of the Humanists. Its spokesmen were distinctly hostile to the Reformation, which was beginning to settle down as an objective ecclesiastical organization. This is why the Reform movement regarded this type of religion as its most dangerous enemy, and pursued it with such deadly hatred and persecution. The chief leaders in this movement are Sebastian Franck, Sebastian Castellio, and Dirck Coornheert, alongside of Erasmus and the Reformers (*Reformatoren*).

Sebastian Franck

The most original member of this group was Luther's contemporary, Sebastian Franck. Greatly distressed by the sterility of the new teaching, by the impossibility of making men good simply through the proclamation of the Word, and by the inconsistency of a concrete ecclesiastical holiness which gave up all idea of subjective results, he resigned his post as a Lutheran pastor, and lived as a literary prophet of the sole redeeming power of the Spirit and of the Inward Word, supporting himself at the same time, like Paul, by the work of his hands. To him the central point of the whole of Christianity came to be summed up in the inward power of the Spirit, expressed in the terms of mediaeval mysticism, ascending through the different degrees from self-renunciation and detachment to the heights of ecstasy and deification. This power of the Spirit must then issue in the practical ethic of self-conquest and brotherly love; beyond that the State and Society must be left as they are, since God permits them to exist. In Franck's experience there are few genuine Christians with a personal experience, and most of these are scattered about all over the world without any cohesion or connection with each other, united only in the Spirit, and mutually recognizing each other through the voice of the Spirit. A Church does exist of those who have been led by the spirit in a marvellous manner into communion with God. This Church, however, is present to faith alone; it has no external form of worship, no external bond, no outward means of grace and no mere authority of the "letter". This Invisible Church is created by God alone. The very spirit which brings it forth, however, is a spiritual movement arising from the centre of the soul, from the immanence of God in the creature, from the Divine Seed and Spark in man; everywhere it is the same, since it arises out of the subconscious sphere, and harmonizes with the Spirit of Christ. This is the Logos or the Indwelling Christ, whose spirit is poured out upon all flesh, and it identifies all genuine piety with the Christian faith, which is visibly represented by the Incarnation of the Logos. The only advantage of the Christian revelation is that it is able to offer this universal, unchangeable substance of truth in a complete manner, since through the Scriptural tradition it is summed up in Jesus, who was filled with the Spirit, and in the Biblical writers, and it is from this source that the Spirit within us is quickened into life. This, however, only takes place where the inner spiritual Spark goes out in search and longing to meet the incarnation of the Spirit in the Scriptures. The Spirit alone can interpret the Bible, which represents in an allegorical manner the eternal inward truths of spiritual experience in the form of the historic myths of the Fall and Redemption; otherwise the Bible in its literal form is something completely human and historical which can only be quickened into life by the Spirit. This point of view leads Franck to a Theism which is expressed in the terms of the universal history of religion; it recognizes only an eternal and unchanging substance of truth, along with an allegorical interpretation of Scripture which is ever on the watch for the transformation of general conceptions into historic myths. This, again, leads to a universal philosophy of history, which interprets the whole of history in terms of an ever-recurring conflict between a faith which is directed towards invisible, spiritual, and disinterested aims, and an unbelief which is bound up with visible, external, and selfish aims. Franck is, therefore, completely indifferent to churches, parties, or sects. In his view a new Reformation is unnecessary, since every reformation only produces a new Church. Of course, if a spiritual prophet were to arise, obviously sent by God, he might possibly be the leader of a new movement. But so long as such a leader does not appear all that can be done is to maintain an unsectarian, independent, purely personal, and individualistic type of Christianity, of sanctification and brotherly love, with no outward ceremonial and no external authority. Franck believes that the ultimate stage in the history of Christianity will be reached when churches and sects disappear, and the Invisible Church, the "community of the Spirit", will alone remain in every land, to serve as the spiritual "salt of the earth". This last idea is evidently a modified adaptation of Schwenkfeld's idea of a coming Reformation through an "apostolic man", possessing Divine credentials; it also means that in the coming outpouring of the Spirit the Church will play no part; the whole expectation is "purely spiritual" in character. In this doctrine Franck comes very near to the old mystical doctrine of the *evangelium aeternum* or the Third Era. From the point of view of his contemporaries these views made him an impossible person. Everywhere he was an outcast; finally he disappeared, leaving no trace. Through his writings, however, he continued to exercise a living influence in Holland and in England.[484]

Castellio

Just as Franck was the critic of Lutheranism, so Castellio was the critic of Calvinism. As an outstanding Christian-Humanist and Principal of the *Collège* he seemed destined to become the Melancthon of Geneva. But a difference of opinion in Biblical criticism separated him from Calvin, who was the dominating theological authority of that period. From that time forward the great task of Castellio's life was the protection of personal freedom of conviction as the palladium of a genuine Christian Reformation. As the friend of Occhino and David Joris, and as an admirer of the *Theologia Germanica*, Castellio based his convictions upon the spiritual and mystical doctrine of the power of the Holy Spirit, through which alone the Bible can be rightly understood, and its vital power experienced, apart from all human effort. He also shared the views of those who taught the doctrine of the degrees of the interior life, from detachment and death to self, up to the sphere in which the Spirit of Christ is in full control. He rejected the doctrine of imputed righteousness, and taught that forgiveness of sins springs out of the Heart of God, who reveals Himself through the Spirit, and who can only be conceived as angry and unreconciled by defiant and unilluminated souls. At the same time his mysticism was strongly tinged with moral and active ideas, and verged on an ethical Rationalism. Castellio was, however, never an Erasmian; his whole outlook was that of a "spiritual reformer". His view of the Bible (which in his immense industry he translated into Latin and French) coincided with that of Sebastian Franck. Although he believed in the inspiration of the Bible, his philological and critical attitude towards the Bible was both inwardly free and amazingly bold. This was due to his theory that the Spirit alone can interpret the Scriptures, for He alone can recognize His Presence in the inner inspiration of the

[484] See p. 970.

writers of the actual text. Above all, after the burning of Servetus, Castellio fought for the principle of the relative character of all the outward forms of the Spirit, which, however, does not in itself destroy the identity of the Spirit. He became one of the great early champions of religious toleration based on spiritual and mystical ideas. He supported his point of view by appealing to the teaching of Luther's earlier period, and to Sebastian Franck, to the theory of the separation between the temporal and the spiritual authority; in his view the spiritual authority may use no other weapons than those of the Word and the Spirit, in entire dependence upon their final and purely spiritual victory. This is not the toleration of scepticism or of opportunism, but the tolerant spirit of mysticism, which regards every kind of dogmatic formulation as merely approximate knowledge. Through these views he hoped to overcome the horrible physical cruelty and the moral unfruitfulness and dogmatic externalism of the Reformation.

We cannot now discover on what grounds he believed it would be possible, under these circumstances, to maintain a popular and national Church, whose existence he accepted without hesitation. Apparently he believed in the invincibility of the Spirit, in the possibility of a dogmatic simplification which would unite all Christians, and he regarded excommunication or exclusion from the community (which he also desired in the interest of ethics) as a measure which need rarely be used. In any case he did not accept present conditions in the resigned spirit of Schwenkfeld, nor did he share his eschatological expectations. Living in the little town of Basel he may have felt that such an ethical simplification and spiritualization of the whole Church would be possible; influenced as he was by Humanism, too, his ethic was more suited to practical life than that of Schwenkfeld or Franck. His enemies at Geneva, however, saw clearly how dangerous these "relative" ideas would be to the idea of a Church of the people with the infallible authority which such a Church would need. They denounced his idea of the victory of the Spirit and of the Word as "fantastic", pointing out that we must not reckon on miracles taking place, for "we do not relieve the starving by looking for the intervention of angels, but we make suitable provision for them ourselves".

Castellio, meanwhile, had taken refuge in Basel; his opponents tried to make his life there impossible, but they were unsuccessful. After his death both his published and his unpublished writings were used afresh in the struggles of the Remonstrants, and, like the writings of Franck in the Netherlands, they exercised an influence which they were unable to exert during the lifetime of their author.[485]

COORNHEERT

The important Dutch Humanist and politician, Coornheert, represented a point of view similar to that of Castellio. He wished to translate all Castellio's writings, and he actually translated a certain number of them. At the time when he lived and worked, ecclesiastical conditions in the Netherlands were still unsettled. This was the period when the Baptist communities, which have already been mentioned, were being reorganized. Coornheert urged on his contemporaries the need for a Christianity of the "Inner Word", which would reveal its reality in practical life. Entirely rejecting the idea of forming any kind of new Church, Coornheert wished to do away with all denominations and parties within the Church, and to retain no doctrinal basis beyond that of the Bible and the Apostles' Creed. At the same time he did not accept the literalist attitude of the Baptists towards the Scriptures; his one desire was to make way for the free inward dominion of the Spirit, who alone can open men's minds to understand the Scriptures, and who witnesses to His presence within the hearts of men by the fruits of tranquillity, self-sacrifice, and brotherly love. He urged that the presence of the Spirit and of the Indwelling Christ ought to be manifest in everyday practical life, and that it should be actually realized in its utmost perfection. The Spirit Himself can convey the forgiveness of sins, and there is no need to refer to the supposed connection between the forgiveness of sins and the historic fact of the Atoning Death of Christ. This Indwelling Christ reaches out far beyond the actual borders of Christendom, since, apart from the Scriptures, the Logos has brought new light and life to many souls in the non-Christian world.

In all these ideas Coornheert's mysticism, like that of Castellio, has strongly marked rationalistic and practical features; he has no desire to probe into the deeper mysteries of the Trinity or of Christology; he wishes only to see them made effective. Although he approved of the simplification of the Gospel proposed by Erasmus, he differed from him in his definitely Protestant doctrine of Grace, in his mystical strain, and in his entire repudiation of the visible Church. Otherwise, however, like Erasmus and Castellio, he made the Christian ethic harmonize with that of the Stoics, and in so doing he modified their "spiritual" Dualism.

[485] See p. 971.

Under these circumstances his attitude towards the ecclesiastical organizations of his own day, and to the whole idea of a community bound together by a common form of worship, is particularly characteristic. Like Franck he rejects the whole idea of a reformation and of the establishment of a purified Church, since he believes that the visible Church is inherently wrong. At the same time he holds that it is quite possible to take part outwardly in the old forms of worship, since a bad form of worship does not make a man bad, nor a purified form make a man good. It is possible to take part in everything and yet to remain inwardly independent and remote from it all. It is, however, also possible to take the other line, and to live in a spirit of pure inward holiness and brotherly love, apart from sacraments and external worship. Like Schwenkfeld and Franck he will only admit the possibility that a new Church might arise if a prophet were to appear endowed by God with supernatural powers.[486] He does not believe that he himself is called to be that prophet any more than any of the Reformers. Nor does he recognize this man of God in the visionaries of his day, like David Joris and Heinrich Niklaes. In case Christians may still think they need some form of fellowship, however, he outlines a programme of fellowship which is certainly most peculiar. Faith is to be based simply upon the Bible and the Apostles' Creed, and it should be urged, above all, to prove its truth in practical life. These groups, formed on a free and voluntary basis, are to receive as members those who accept this very simple form of faith, and who avoid the grosser forms of sin. For the sake of the weaker brethren it is permissible to make a rule that obstinate and hardened sinners, and all who oppose the Glory of God, should be avoided; this, however, should be done without splitting hairs over trifles, and without censoriousness. For the sake of the weaker brethren, the sacraments of Baptism and the Lord's Supper may be observed as outward signs of the New Birth, but all in complete freedom. There is no authoritative teaching ministry, but only exhortation from the Scriptures for edification. These congregations should be quite free, and no one should be compelled to join them.

This whole scheme seems to be a modified and rationalized form of Schwenkfeld's ideal; indeed, in many particulars it resembles it very closely. It is, indeed, a highly Utopian Church-programme; if it had ever been put into practice it would have led to interminable "splits" in the different congregations.

[486] See *Hegler, pp. 256 ff.* As already in Franck this idea also reappears in Coornheert, especially against the Anabaptists.

Indeed, it could only have been carried out in the spirit of Castellio, and of Luther in his early days, through confidence in the spontaneous power of the Holy Spirit to unite men's hearts in love. Thus it is not surprising that its practical influence was slight, and that it did not arrest the development of ecclesiastical organization in the Netherlands.[487]

The Collegiants

The later influence of Coornheert can only be clearly discerned in the movement known as the Collegiants, or the Rynsburgers. Their position was peculiar; they represent a kind of half-way house between a Free Church (or sect) organization, and a purely individualistic mystical fellowship of kindred souls. Outwardly they were obliged to belong to the Baptist denomination, although they had no desire to encourage the establishment of a Baptist Church; when a number of Remonstrants joined the movement it became strongly tinged with rationalism. Pre-eminently, however, the movement bore the impress of the idealism and mysticism of Coornheert.

The Nineteen Articles of Galenus Abrahams and Spruyt (about 1650) declare that the Apostolic Church, with its obviously miraculous gifts, had long been extinct. They can discover no command in the Bible to attempt to erect it once more "solely by means of the Scriptures which are all that is left", and they find no encouragement in the new churches, since they are all (including the Mennonites) divided by constant controversy. A prophet who can be compared with the apostolic teachers, and whose mission is attested by signs and wonders, has not appeared; thus there is no possibility of restoring the Church at the present time. Therefore they declare that their Society is a purely human institution, instituted without Divine commandment or Divine authority. They base their whole confidence on the hope "that the Great Father of the Family will still be pleased with it, and that, in so far as their efforts are made in good faith, He will regard it graciously out of the depths of His Infinite Mercy". They believe, therefore, that in the churches of their own day the office of the ministry, the various forms of service, the ritual, the work of teaching, and the sacraments of Baptism and the Lord's Supper "do not possess the same value as in the Early Church". The most that can be said for them is that "they are permissible if they are exercised without any claim to authority, in all lowliness, with patience and endeavours to rectify them, without any

[487] See p. 972.

attempt to bind men's consciences very closely to this doctrine and to the observance of the same". Provided due care is exercised, "Believers' Baptism and the Lord's Supper may still be observed with profit". The real truth, however, lies in a "pure inwardness" of spirit and in the Invisible Church. A more detailed declaration of 1659 says that "at the present time, when the visible Church is decaying, among many nations, there are believers, who turn away with their whole heart from all discord and from all sectarianism; who in the midst of divisions possess an undivided heart, built up as a united body upon the one and only foundation, even upon Christ Himself, completely one in the ground and the power of God". As in Coornheert himself, these sentiments are a clear echo of the ideas of Schwenkfeld, although they have been somewhat altered. The only elements which are missing are Schwenkfeld's pronounced supernaturalism, substantial mysticism, and his eschatology.[487a]

Mystical Ideas and the Baptists

It is also well known that a section of the Baptists adopted mystical ideas, and on that account both groups have often been identified with each other. These ideas, however, were only held by individual Baptist theologians and their followers. In itself the Baptist Movement was non-theological and needed nothing beyond the Bible. When, however, the more reflective minds within this movement studied the theological ideas which the Bible contains, there was certainly aroused in them a sense of need for a firmer basis and for clearer conclusions which opened the door to a more spiritual religion, as soon as men wished to escape from the crude literal meaning or the inconsistencies of the Bible. Then, too, the fanaticism which arose in times of persecution, when men tried to justify their "new revelations" by proclaiming that the new situation was the beginning of the End of the World, by the very fact that in making these statements it had advanced beyond the literalist interpretation of Scripture, had formed a bridge which led to a more "spiritual religion". In themselves, however, fanatical Anabaptists and spiritual mystics still differed greatly from one another. On the other hand, mystical thinkers who wished for religious fellowship could not find it in the churches, so they sought for it in the ethical lay-religion of the Baptists. Franck, for example, made this experiment at one stage of his career.

[487a] See p. 972.

Hans Denk

This was also true of one of the most human and attractive personalities of the age of the Reformation, Hans Denk. He was a disciple of Tauler, of the *Theologia Germanica* and of Humanism; yet, as principal of a school at Nürnberg, having come under the influence of Karlstadt, Münzer, and Staupitz, he could no longer agree with the Lutheran ecclesiastical doctrine, which he reproached for its ethical sterility, and its rigid depreciation of the individual in comparison with the reconciling grace which belongs to the Church.*

Henceforward Denk led the life of a fugitive and a wanderer, which seemed the appointed destiny of souls of this type. For a time he was in communion with the Baptists; in the end, however, he left them also, commending himself wholly to the redeeming power of the Inward Word, and of the Eternal Christ, who everywhere inwardly creates His Church, among circumcised and uncircumcised, Catholics, Zwinglians, and Lutherans, if only one will allow oneself to be led by the Spirit into quietness of spirit and brotherly love. In his view, Christ and the Bible are the Spirit-filled means by which the inner "Seed" or "Spark" is quickened into life. God carries out His work of redemption through the kindling of this "Spark", which is everywhere latent in every soul, and has to be fostered by the surrendered will; Christ can only be described as "Redeemer" in so far as he sets these inward processes in motion. But in order that Christ may do this, the Spirit must already be in man. It is only because the Divine Spirit in man meets the Divine Spirit in the Bible that redemption becomes a fact which triumphs over externalism, the flesh, selfishness, and worldliness, leading to the love of God and the brethren as the sign and seal of every genuine experience of salvation.

It was because he held these views so strongly that Denk opposed the externalism which clung to the contradictory "letter" of Scripture, the substitutionary theory of the Atonement, the exclusive limitation of salvation to the historic Christ, the division of men into the two groups of the elect and the damned, as a denial of the Divine source of souls, the current exaggerations of the doctrine of sin, the division of man's final destiny into heaven and hell, ecclesiastical Christology and the ecclesiastical ethic which compromises with the world. He admitted the necessity for the State, but he counselled Christians against accepting

* That is, "grace" as a doctrine was exalted almost at the expense of the individual.—Translator's Note.

official positions under the State. Hätzer, Bünderlin, and Entfelder held similar views. They were disciples of Denk, and, together with him, they influenced Sebastian Franck. Theobald Thamer's position was peculiar; he interpreted the Spirit in terms of the natural conscience or the natural moral law, a remarkable anticipation of the transformation of Christian thought into moralistic Deism which took place two centuries later.[488]

Mystical Natural Philosophers

The mystical natural philosophers of that period, Ludovico Vives, Campanus and Servetus, Agrippa of Nettesheim and Paracelsus, enter far more deeply into the Neo-Platonic and natural philosophical argument for the Spirit, and of the struggle between the flesh and the spirit. From the religious point of view, they all represent an inwardness of temper which is indifferent to the churches, and a mystical love which overcomes selfishness; most of them also remained within the Catholic Church, but their main influence was exercised among Protestant mystics. Servetus, in particular, in his revival of the Gnostic elements in the Bible and their connection with Neo-Platonic speculations, was one of the most interesting and brilliant thinkers of the day. To some extent Sebastian Franck also had been influenced by all these thinkers.

Böhme, Gichtel, and Others

The theosophy of Jacob Böhme, too, was founded on impressions received from Paracelsus, Schwenkfeld, and Weigel; from the religious point of view it was essentially mystical and combined with an orthodox reverence for the sacraments of the Church. Gichtel, Poiret, van Helmont, and Fludd (both father and son) also belonged to the same school of thought. When all heretics were banished from Germany and Switzerland, they took refuge in the Netherlands and in England, where the spiritual piety of the period of the Revolution was, to a large extent, nourished on their writings. Böhme's works were printed in Holland and then translated into English; thus his influence was exercised in these countries just as Franck's influence had spread to Holland and to England.

Kepler

Among great natural scientists, Kepler had leanings in this direction; it is, indeed, otherwise a well-known fact that he had

[488] See p. 973.

a close affinity with Neo-Platonism, which in principle is the underlying philosophy of all mysticism. He compared his new doctrine of Nature with the Bible in the limitation of revelation to the religious "intentions" of the Spirit, and through the Spirit's "accommodation" through the "letter" of Scripture to the popular way of thinking and speaking; he also had to wage a furious conflict with the theologians, and he only saved his mother's life (she was accused of witchcraft) by a heated literary controversial campaign.

Comenius

Another of the important reformers and prophets of the future who belonged to this group was Amos Comenius, the last Bishop of the Bohemian Church of the Brethren, who, after terrible sufferings, like so many others, found a refuge in Amsterdam. In natural matters, like the Pietists and Quakers at a later date, he was the champion of an empirical-sensationalist-utilitarian conception, which also formed the point of departure for educational reform. On the other hand, from the religious point of view, he held Chiliast views, and was a Platonist and a mystic. He looked forward to the spiritual unity of mankind, and hoped for the time when all religious denominations would disappear. Like Sebastian Franck, he belonged to the number of those who are secretly pledged to a better future; only to-day can his hopes be completely understood.

David Joris

The Jorists and the Familists belonged originally to the entirely different realm of frenzied and fanatical mysticism. The idea of the approaching End of the World, which was closely connected with the collapse of the previous Church—an idea often expressed by Luther—and the examples of the "enthusiasm" of the Early Church and of the Apocalypse, were closely akin to that kind of fanaticism, especially to that of the Anabaptists, with their exclusive emphasis upon Scripture. This expectation was intensified by the terrible nervousness produced by the horribly cruel persecution to which these people were exposed. Both these groups represented the development of a more settled mystical and "spiritual" movement which had emerged out of this undisciplined fanaticism; thus they became significant forces in

[489] See p. 973.

the formation of the great mystical movement which issued later on in the English Revolution and in Pietism.

The Jorists arose with David Joris, a Dutch contemporary of Luther, who took part first of all in the Reform movement and then in the Anabaptist movement. He sought to unite the two wings of the Anabaptist movement—the radical violent wing and the passive section—in the one supreme principle of mysticism. He taught a mystical ethic consisting of serenity and brotherly love; but within his teaching there were some traces of Libertinism and Antinomianism, deduced from the principle of the freedom and perfection of the Spirit. The peculiarity of this movement, however, lay in the fact that he made this mysticism the basis of a community which, without worship or sacraments, was attached to his own person, since in wonderful visions he described himself as the herald of the Spirit of Christ, or as "the third David" at the dawn of this new era in world-history, of the Third Dispensation, the era of the Spirit. At the same time he gathered round his own person a group of individuals, based on the family principle, for which in fantastic "revelations" and "messages" he demanded recognition from the authorities in Church and State. He claimed for himself that miraculous vocation which Schwenkfeld, Coornheert, and the Collegiants had just as emphatically disclaimed. He united the sense of this vocation with his doctrine of the three eras of world-history, and of a special indwelling and unveiling of the hitherto imperfectly revealed Spirit of Christ, gathering all this up in his own person. This is why Coornheert, who otherwise agreed with his mystical principles, attacked him so vehemently. Joris was willing to conform outwardly to any form of religious worship; meanwhile he lived in Basel as a respected citizen, secretly controlling a large and widespread movement with many branches, which likewise only grew in secret. Long afterwards radical Pietists were accused of being "poisoned by Joris", for his writings were still being reprinted at the close of the sixteenth century. The indignant citizens of Basel, who had only seen in him a noble foreign gentleman of exemplary piety, were only able to exercise the law against heretics on his corpse. The modern sect of the Nazarenes is an interesting example of a similar movement; their prophet, Wirtz, claimed a similar position for himself and the movement was also propagated in secret; in other ways it was in line with the primitive mystical tradition, and circulated its literature.[490]

[490] See p. 973.

Hendrik Niclaes and the Familists

At the same time there arose alongside of the Jorist movement an important counterpart, the "House of Love" or the "Familia caritatis". This movement was founded by a merchant named Hendrik Niclaes. Niclaes had left the Roman Catholic Church, and, without joining any of the Reform parties, he had swung over into a visionary "Enthusiasm", combined with the familiar ideas of German mysticism, of "deification" and of "tranquillity", of the "Divine Spark" of Light and Love; he also taught an ethic of religious perfection with its victory over "the flesh" and "the letter". He found his sphere of influence, however, first of all in Protestant circles, since he represented himself as the Prophet of the Last Days on the strength of his visionary vocation and of his "deification"; proclaiming the well-known three eras of the religious history of the world, he took upon himself the rôle of the prophet of the last era. In this last era the inwardness of the Spirit is dominant, as it was formerly in the Primitive State; pure ascetic holiness and love prevail, and that complete freedom from law, history and the "letter", which is the ultimate sign of a full-grown fanaticism. It is, however, significant that this "prophet" did not merely bind the members of his community together in a personal way round himself, but that he created a hierarchical and communist organization. In creating this Society Niclaes had a twofold aim: (1) after the example of the Anabaptists, he sought to create the pure community of the New Jerusalem; while (2) after the example of Catholicism, this Society ought to represent a holy priesthood; the second aim, however, could only be realized through an inner "election". Coornheert also opposed this group, since it renewed the idea of the hierarchy, and because its fanaticism spoiled the disciplined simplicity of the Spirit's ministry made known to us in the Scriptures. But these ideas spread far and wide, especially in England, where Bunyan transformed the allegorical mystical journey of the Prophet into his *Pilgrim's Progress* and where almost all fanatical phenomena could be traced back to the Familists. The so-called "Ranters", in particular, a very eccentric "spiritual" group, were supposed to derive their ideas from them. At the English Revolution the movement disappeared. The Catholic-Apostolic Church of Edward Irving is a modern movement which bears a certain resemblance to the Familists. Alongside of these two groups there were still several smaller "prophetic" communities of a similar kind, but of less historical significance, consisting in part of the dissatisfied members of both groups.[491]

Labadie

While these movements, which have just been described, arose at the time when the ecclesiastical situation in Holland was still unsettled, the Labadists represent a domestic community founded on monastic and communistic lines, in opposition to the Calvinistic State Church system of the Netherlands. Jean de la Badie was originally a Catholic priest, and had been in close touch with the Jesuits. He fell under the spell of Quietism, and of the doctrine of the "Inner Word"; he adopted Augustinian views on grace, free-will, and predestination. Finding that he had more in common with the Reformed Church he went over to Calvinism; he was soon driven out of France, however, and then found an enthusiastic welcome among the Dutch Pietists. He became pastor of a French-speaking congregation at Middelburg; here, however, he began to reorganize his congregation on the basis of the "Inner Word", the "ladder of contemplation", and of strict asceticism, striving to form a new community of the "Heavenly Jerusalem". In consequence his old friends deserted him. Uniting the mystical principle with that of monasticism and of the Chiliastic Anabaptists, he then created his communistic house-community, which was doomed to an unrestful wandering life until it finally disappeared; but during its short existence it had succeeded in scattering seeds of mystical thought in all directions. This movement thus belongs to the history both of the sect-type and of mysticism—a double aspect which we have been forced to admit several times; this, however, does not do away with the fact that both types are distinct.[492]

Mysticism in the Netherlands in the Seventeenth Century

In addition to these movements, about the middle of the seventeenth century a fresh tide of mystical life swept through the Netherlands, similar to the movement which was spreading at the same time through England. This awakening was in line with the Dutch religious tradition; early mystical influences from the fifteenth century continued to affect the religious life of the country, for in the pre-Reformation period Holland had served both as a centre and a place of refuge for every imaginable kind of mystical movement. As we have already seen, the Pietistic

[491] See p. 974. [492] See p. 974.

Puritanism which came into the Netherlands from England led to a form of mysticism which regarded the ecclesiastical doctrine of salvation, public worship, and the story of Redemption as matters of absolute indifference. The younger Teellinck, Lodensteyn, and Brakel in the seventeenth century, and Schortinghuys in the eighteenth century, pressed this theory to its extremist limit, and very nearly succeeded in entirely destroying the connection between the "inner life" and the salvation offered by the Church.[493] Others, like the followers of Jakob Verschoor or Pontiaan van Hattem, tended towards Pantheism. The whole atmosphere provided the background for the ethic both of Spinoza and of Geulinex.[494] The Collegiants awakened out of their quiet life, and, in the person of Galenus, they carried their spirit of Independency, and of "prophesying", and their doctrine of the Inner Light, into the Baptist movement, with reforming power; this activity aroused deep and passionate controversy down to the eighteenth century. New prophets of "enthusiasm" and of holiness arose, urged forward by the passionate tension caused by the great new Dutch struggle for existence against Louis XIV.

Lutheran mystics and the followers of Böhme, as well as the heralds of French Quietism, spread their message far and wide. Quaker missionaries also awakened in the Netherlands the idea that the real Reformation of Christendom was only now beginning, since the Reform of Luther and Calvin had merely resulted in a fresh form of Catholicism, which had left Christendom inwardly unchanged. Thus, in the second half of the seventeenth century, mysticism in the Netherlands developed into a widespread movement, touching large masses of the population. It affected all classes of Society, even though the various groups differed greatly from one another. The Pietism which was simply the complement of the Church, remained quite distinct from the non-ecclesiastical "religion of the Spirit", although in the end the Pietist mystics were only separated from it by their desire to remain loyal to the Church.

In practice this "spiritual religion" usually gained a footing in the following manner: first of all it penetrated into the Baptist movement, which for some time past had already made its peace with the State; once that had been achieved, and in spite of very strong opposition from the Baptist sect itself, it proceeded to use the Baptist movement as a kind of springboard from which it plunged into a purely non-ecclesiastical mysticism; then it

[493] Cf. *Heppe, pp. 169–204, 375–489.*

[494] See p. 975.

revived the old passion for social reform which marked the earlier stages of the Baptist movement. This process of development, therefore, accounts for the fact that from the very outset this movement also revealed a practical, fanatically reforming tendency, a characteristic which it did not possess in the time of Sebastian Franck and Coornheert. However greatly these groups differed from each other, in this respect they were all one: they all repudiated the sacramentalism of the Church and the literalism of the sect, popular Christianity and external authority, and all the previous history of the Church from Constantine down to Luther and Calvin. Everywhere this movement exhibited the traits of an extreme form of the "religion of the Spirit", with its radical individualism, its criticism of all literalism, authority, and doctrine, with its impulse towards "direct" subjective experience, and its exclusive dependence on the "inward Christ", apart from external Christianity with its historical miracles.

Its forms of fellowship were certainly most varied and curious. Some of its adherents, as we have already said, for a time utilized the Baptist movement, upon which they exercised an inwardly disintegrating effect. Others maintained purely individualistic groups of the "prophetic" order, or exclusive fellowship groups meeting in private houses like the Labadists. Others again sought to found new associations, or even denied all need for social organization at all, looking for the entirely free activity of the Spirit in a new era with a purely spiritual Church.

Their ethic also was equally varied, though everywhere it reflected the main characteristic mystical asceticism, with its desire to conquer the "flesh" and the "world". In individual cases, however, we find a purely passive Quietism, the purely spiritual, super-sensible freedom of those who have been "born of the Spirit", combined with an entire independence of all the conventions of bourgeois morality, even in sex questions. This movement also revealed that asceticism of labour and the "calling" which is characteristic of Puritan Pietism; all this was combined with a more or less detached attitude towards State institutions, and the customs of Society, with fantastic expectations of world peace, and the renunciation of all use of the law, of authority and force, in every sense of the word; above all, it was combined with that indifference to all morality in general which belongs to this type of extreme spirituality, and finally with an inner impulse to the most self-sacrificing labours of charity. In this ethical system, of course, the following ideals are taken for granted: toleration and freedom of conscience; exclusion of the

State from all religious matters; the ideal of a State built up as far as possible upon love, peace, and the common good, combined with an active opposition to the existing order of the State, with its tyranny, its use of force, and its "carnal" selfishness. In spite of this attitude towards the State, however, the leaders of this movement stated explicitly that all reform must come from within, through the power of the Spirit, quite naturally, without revolution and without external violence. Therefore, greatly to the annoyance of the presbyteries and the ministers, the civil government in general left these people alone, so long as they did not become a practical danger to its institutions and to generally accepted customs. Like all exaggerated idealism, this movement gradually faded away and died out. Its emphasis upon the "Holy Spirit of Christ", which, indeed, it interpreted in the sense of conscience, reason, and Natural Law, finally (as usually happens) changed into rationalistic and philosophical reason.[495]

Mysticism in England in the Seventeenth Century

The spirit of mysticism had a still more important development in the conditions created by the English Revolution.

The English, whose practical sobriety and common sense we are accustomed to consider a racial trait, had their great mystical period. It is true that the mysticism which waits and suffers in silence, looking for deliverance only to the power of the Indwelling Christ, plays a smaller part than the more aggressive and practical forms of Christian morality, expressed first of all in the political religion of the Presbyterians, and then in the ideals of the radical Baptists. But alongside of and beneath all this more aggressive movement there flowed a strong current of "spiritual religion" which bore to the masses of the people the ideas of complete separation between Church and State; of a radical lay-Christianity; of freedom to preach and prophesy; of an ethical renewal, springing out of all this, and characterized by readiness for self-sacrifice and brotherly love; of a pure doctrine free from all academic scholasticism, freely springing up from within. It was the impact of these ideas which first inclined the masses of the people to turn partly to Independency and partly to the Baptist movement. Both these tendencies were full of elements which provided a favourable soil for mystical ideas. On the other hand, however, mysticism also led easily to the conclusion that a Free Church movement was needed, in which the sacraments should be dis-

[495] See p. 975.

pensed only to those who were worthy of them, just as those movements were accustomed to proclaim. From this point of view also it was not difficult to persuade Puritan Pietism to give up its ecclesiastical way of thinking. Where mysticism steered clear of all these fusions, or freed itself from them, there it created groups which concentrated on "inward religion" like the "Seekers" or "Waiters", and the Quakers, or orgiastic-libertine groups like the Ranters. Thus it came to pass that at this time mysticism became a power in the general life of the English people in a way that it had never before attained, and which it never reached again.

The sources of this movement lay deep in the history before the period of the Commonwealth. Pietism had already opened its gates to mysticism through Hall, Francis Rous, and James Janeaway. Even under the Stuarts there had already been radical mystics, of whom John Everard, whom a Dutch writer regards as the precursor of Quakerism, is an outstanding example. Everard was a preacher and writer who lived at the beginning of the seventeenth century; he translated Poimandres, Dionysius the Areopagite, the writings of Tauler, the *Theologia Germanica*, the *Widerruf* of Hans Denk, and other mystical works into English, while he himself, in his *Treasury of Revelation*, expounded the most advanced ideas of the "Inward Word" and of redemption through interior union with God. In support of his views he quoted from Plato, Plotinus, Proclus, Origen, Augustine, Bernard, and St. Francis of Assisi. During a life of continual conflict with the authorities in Church and State, in which he suffered greatly, Everard gained a large band of adherents, with whom the Familists and other branches of mysticism seem to have been fused.

Further, there were the groups composed of the disciples of Jakob Böhme, whose works reached England by way of the Netherlands, and were translated into English at this time. This movement had a strong influence on George Fox at the beginning of his ministry, until he turned away from it because the followers of Böhme retained the sacraments.

Neither must we forget the great school of the Cambridge Platonists, the real philosophical Enlightenment of the England of that day, which illuminated the darkness of ecclesiastical Aristotelianism, and proclaimed a mystical ethic of a Neo-Platonic kind. The rationalistic technical philosophy of progress of the court-official Bacon, which belongs to the same period, had no practical significance.

The movement did not culminate, however, in this scientific intellectual mysticism which was based upon stable, eternal spiritual principles. There arose alongside of it, nourished by Baptist literature and Dutch influences, and intensified by the terrible confusion of the period, the "Enthusiastic" mysticism of visionaries, ecstatics, and "prophets". This form of spirituality had a strong tinge of Chiliasm, while doctrinally it was entirely at the mercy of all kinds of sudden and changing ideas and whims; still, it contributed something to the spiritual life of the day by awakening the desire for first-hand religious experience, and by the endeavour to prove the reality of its religious experience in ethical and ascetic practice. Then, in a thousand different ways, this "visionary" movement merged into genuine mysticism.

This wave of mystical experience was not confined to small groups, but it permeated the religious life of the time. Even statesmen and generals acted according to "lights" and "revelations", and listened respectfully to the "prophets" who arose at this time, believing that they might possibly have a real "word" from God. Cromwell, for instance, believed that further intercourse with George Fox would lead him into agreement with his views; Fox, however, rightly maintained that Cromwell was mistaken.

Another element of the seething religious life of that period was the rise of the anarchic movement of Independency. Originally it was a purely Calvinist tendency which merely claimed the independence of congregations consisting of genuine Christians, but it subsequently developed the desire for liberty into licence. The Independents demanded and exercised entire freedom to preach, both for men and women; they claimed to have received "direct illumination" from God and the "witness of the Spirit", and they developed the inferences drawn from the principle of a regenerate community into a theory of advanced individualism. Alongside of the General Baptists, whose outlook had been strongly influenced by the Mennonites, the rest of the Baptists displayed their old tendency towards "Enthusiasm" and mysticism.

Out of all these groups and influences there arose the "spirit-mongers", as they were called by the bitter polemic of the Puritans. Thus we are able to understand how it was that both the great preachers at Cromwell's Headquarters, John Dell and John Saltmarsh, were enlightened mystics.

John Dell taught that the true Church ought to be founded solely upon the Word and its inherent miraculous power, because the Word is the spontaneous source of the congregational life which clusters round it: the one essential is to permit it to follow its free course, unhindered, as Luther had taught in his earlier days. When men raised this question: How then are believers to know which is the true teaching, and how are they to recognize the genuine Heralds of the Word? he replied that true believers were endowed with the faculty of recognizing one another. In Dell's teaching certainly "the Word" is always the "Inward Word", which is immanent both in the Scriptures and in the heart of the believer, which, like the Logos, is timeless and broods over both.

John Saltmarsh preached the old mystical doctrine of the three dispensations: from Adam to Christ, from Christ to the age of the Spirit, and from this third era, which has now begun, to the Celestial Jerusalem. In this Third Dispensation there is no longer any need for the "letter" of Scripture nor for the law, neither for an ordained minority nor for an external Church at all; everything is summed up in the Indwelling Christ, who reveals Himself in love.

We have already met these ideas in Sebastian Franck, Coornheert, and the Collegiants; there is also much in them which reminds us of Schwenkfeld. As in the mysticism of the Netherlands, there were many different exponents of this "spiritual" movement, and yet all had something in common. Some of them formed new communities of their own for worship; under the régime of freedom others accepted appointments within the Church, while others again strenuously opposed all official ecclesiasticism, and every organized form of worship. Some accepted the system of tithes and the official ecclesiasticism which was built upon it; others rejected both.

This movement affected all classes of Society. Everywhere it was characterized by that asceticism which extreme fanatics easily transformed into the "liberty of the flesh". All these groups found the question of war, and of an authority which is based upon external compulsion, the most difficult problem of all. Some held that a "holy war" was justified in "the Last Days"; others repudiated this idea. Some wished to recognize the State and the law under Christian auspices only; others were willing to accept existing institutions for the sake of order.

The whole movement represents an enormous variety of ideas and opinions. Yet underlying it there was an immense Utopian idealism, which confidently hoped that the "Age of the Spirit" would make it possible to establish a social order free from all compromise with the world, which would be "Christian" in the true sense of the word.[496]

These "spiritual" hopes met the same fate as the dream of world-renewal cherished by the radical Baptists: they were shattered by the hard facts of political and social life. These struggles resulted in the Protectorate on the one hand, followed by the Restoration and finally by Whig Liberalism, and on the other by the revulsion from all Christian super-idealism, the secularization of the "Spirit" into Reason, with which Deism initiated the great period of the criticism of the history and philosophy of religion of the new era. All that remained of the mystical upheaval was "the Children of the Light" or the "Society of Friends", as the Quakers called themselves. In the final form of their doctrine they are the direct descendants of the spirituality of the Reformation period, heralds of the Inner Light, of an individual rebirth through the Eternal Christ, in whose message the Spirit in the regenerate soul and in the Bible is one; heralds of the presence of the Divine Light, that Light which lightens every man coming into the world, and which is only released from the prison house of the flesh when it comes into contact with the Bible. It would, however, create a false impression, if we were to interpret them from this point of view alone. In reality the Society of Friends represents the union of this mystical doctrine with the Baptist ideal of the pure and holy voluntary community, based on genuine conversion and freedom from State control.

The Society of Friends

The Quakers overcame the natural anti-social, or rather individualistic, tendency of mysticism by adopting the Mennonite constitution, and, above all, that of the Collegiants. Like them they have an inner and an outer circle, elders and overseers for poor relief, meetings and love-feasts, free lay-preaching—(to the lay-preaching they add the Meeting for silent worship, where the members wait on God together for light)—community discipline and excommunication. The sign of admission into membership, however, is not Adult Baptism; the candidate for admission simply has to satisfy the Society that he is "converted" or "born again"; the candidate's outward behaviour is also taken into account, and this matter is left in the hands of the overseers. The free community of the Spirit must act on the assumption that the Spirit bears witness to Himself in the election of elders and in the acceptance of candidates.

[496] See p. 976.

So far this Quaker constitution is very similar to Luther's original "spiritual" ideal of a congregation. The problems which arise out of this ideal, in connection with the reception of new members and the election of elders and overseers, are solved by committing all to the guidance of the Spirit. But they had to discover through experience that this Society, formed by the Spirit in freedom, became, through the sheer force of the habit of community-life, an inherited membership handed down from one generation to another, a "birthright" membership, instead of the free adherence of all who are truly converted to the Society of Friends.

It was not only their constitution, however, which linked the Quakers with the Baptist movement. In ethics also, like the Baptists, they avoided Antinomianism, took the Sermon on the Mount as their ethical ideal, and required their members to renounce all worldly honours and official position; further, they were to take no part in war, nor in the administration of the law; in all exercise of authority over others, on the positive side, the members of the Society were urged to practise a most generous love of the brethren, and charity towards the poor.

At this stage of its development—as has been often pointed out—the Society of Friends represents the final expression in its purest form of the Anabaptist Movement. Later, however, like the Mennonites, to whom they were closely akin, they became distinctly bourgeois. They found it impossible to continue to live in their original detachment from the world; more and more they combined the Calvinistic ethic of the "calling" with their ascetic way of life. Then God "blessed their business" with those economic results which this ascetic Protestant idea of the "calling" usually brings with it. Thus a religious body which sprang into existence out of an entirely unworldly spiritual movement, developed into a community with an entirely different ideal; in its ultimate form it exhibited the following characteristic traits: a high sense of the duty of labour; the limitation of the kind of work which may be undertaken to useful and practical undertakings in trade, industry, manual labour, and agriculture; strict personal economy and a minimum amount of luxury, with a maximum amount of effort for the welfare of the community; supervision by the Society of the business honesty and solvency of its members, of family life, of the education of the children; in short, it is the same ideal as that of Geneva in the days of early Calvinism, the only difference being that this community is founded upon a voluntary basis. The Quakers, therefore, became bourgeois precisely because they had accepted the Puritan ascetic idea of "the calling"; this only harmonizes with Bernstein's theory that asceticism is a "bourgeois" virtue, that is, that it produces the bourgeois attitude towards life.

It is, however, particularly significant that, in the person of Penn, the greatest of the Quakers, who expressed their ideals in their purest form, the Society of Friends had the opportunity of forming a State and a society upon the virgin soil of America, with the aid of this most severe, and in many respects most logical, conception of a true Christian ethic. The Quaker State of Pennsylvania was the "Holy Experiment", the creation of a real Christian State upon the joint basis of the freedom of the Spirit and a strict ethic. It was a State without compulsory religious organizations, and with complete separation between Church and State. In actual practice, of course, it was affected by the fact that the Quakers were in the majority, and their Christian spirit influenced the State; this situation was maintained by the general confidence felt in the Quakers, whose representatives were continually re-elected to public office. In this colony, where civilization was only in its initial stages, the circumstances were favourable: the only possible conflicts that could arise were those between the colonists and the Indians, or with neighbouring colonies. Simple, quiet, God-fearing farmers, who lived in a small circle where everyone knew the affairs of everyone else, freed from all the hindrances of a crowded population, were able to simplify their lives and order their affairs in peace. They were able to establish relations with the Indians by peaceful methods, and within the State, at least in the beginning, most personal difficulties were settled by friendly arbitration, apart from law or compulsion. When this method did not succeed, no objection was raised against formal proceedings in a court of law, nor even against capital punishment. The exercise of force towards impenitent disturbers of the peace was regarded as being in a different category from that of war; it was, indeed, considered to be the duty of a Christian Government to deal with such matters. Finally, after an existence of seventy years, this Christian State went to pieces over the problems of war and of religious toleration. This is how it happened: the colony was forced by the Mother Country to take part in the war between England and France. The Quakers then refused to take part in the administration of the colony, in order to avoid giving their consent to the imposition of war taxes. The result of this was that the other religious denominations in the State, which had always been tolerated by the

Quakers but not converted to their views, gained the upper hand. With their loss of influence in the administration of the Colony, the Quakers also lost their spiritual influence. When the great War of Independence broke out, the Quakers had to submit to the tragic fate of being mere passive spectators of a struggle which was being waged, to a very large extent, for their own ideals. From that moment they came to the conclusion that public life was not for the Christian at all, and they gave up the "Holy Experiment" for ever. Another section of the Society, however, among whom was Franklin, gave up the early Christian idea of non-resistance, and threw itself all the more ardently into the democratic movement, as a directly Christian duty. But the main body, which was increasingly forced into a minority existence, withdrew into the life of the religious Society itself, closed its ranks, and developed a magnificent philanthropic activity. In spite of that, however, the process of secularization was not arrested. The glory of this later period was the successful campaign for the liberation of the slaves and for the humane education of the negroes; while the Quakers were dominant they had already shown the way by personal example, and so far as they were concerned they had freed all their slaves.

European Quakerism developed along similar lines, and it arrived at the same result, the only difference being that it reached its term far more swiftly than in America, since the détour of the "Holy Experiment" was absent. European Quakers excel in the economic virtues, in honesty, and in Christian philanthropy; lacking the propagandist spirit, however, they do not increase in numbers; this also is very significant for the understanding of the religious life from the sociological point of view: the spirit of toleration and "inwardness" which is produced by opposition to compulsory Christianity is not favourable for the maintenance of an organic body.

Within their own society the Quakers were content to solve the problems of Christian social life upon the basis of private property, honest hard work, and the care of the poor. Beyond their own circle they worked through philanthropic and humanitarian movements. It is particularly interesting that one of their number, John Bellers (d. 1725), recognized the inadequacy of these bourgeois ideas, and proposed, first of all to the Friends, and then to Parliament, a Socialistic scheme of productive co-operative societies founded on Christian, as well as economic, social, and political ideas. At the same time, however, he took into account the whole general situation—with its bourgeoisie and its capitalism

—as well as the habits of the Friends. For all that, he went right to the root of the problem of poverty and riches, since, in addition to a better organization of labour, he also proposed a more just and equal division of the fruit of toil for the sake of the Gospel. Thus in the nineteenth century Richard Owen appealed to Bellers' ideas, and found some of his best helpers among the Quakers.[497]

With Quakerism the wave of mysticism in England was spent. Even the Society of Friends itself increasingly lost its spiritual vitality. From that time forward either the modern bourgeois spirit of "enlightenment", which took place in connection with the rise of the middle classes, or an ecclesiasticism, which, in its better section, was inclined towards Pietism, has been the prevailing feature in the situation; both these elements are characterized by that utilitarian spirit which Calvinism so often evinces towards secular questions, and which only too often also affects the spiritual life.

Methodism and Pietism

The second great period of religious awakening, therefore, the Methodist Revival, was not based upon mysticism at all. Certainly it felt a very urgent and deep desire for a direct personal experience; but it satisfied that desire by indulging in "Enthusiasm" and emotional revivalism. We have already seen how widely this differs from "spirituality" and mysticism, and how very differently it works out in the organization of a religious community. The overwhelming effect of the Methodist Revival upon the masses, an effect which was constantly renewed and apostolic in its power and fervour, was based explicitly upon this emotional revivalism; it was along this path that Methodism was able to reach individuals and classes of Society whom it would have been impossible to reach in any other way. This form of "Enthusiasm" certainly contained within itself the danger of an anarchical individualism; but, as we have seen, Methodism met this danger by a still more careful and effective system of organization, through which the individual was definitely linked up with the whole. Methodism is as masterly in the art of organization as it is in the art of revivalism.

On its ethical side, the emphasis upon liberty and joy represented the "enthusiastic" aspect of the movement, and might very easily have led to Antinomianism. Here, however, the full logical result of the mystical idea was forestalled by the introduc-

[497] See p. 978.

tion of Calvinist austerity, which was the method which preserved and made known the state of grace; this point, too, has already been mentioned. The only really important result of the exclusive emphasis upon "spirituality" was an extreme simplification of the practical and dogmatic content of Christian thought. After the initial success of the Methodist Revival, however, it passed through the experience which, at an earlier period, had often befallen the Religious Orders, when a period of ardour and growth would be followed by one of complacency and stagnation, and a fresh reform movement would be required. Thus, in order to avoid the danger of lapsing into secularism and indifference, or even into a formal Church life, Methodism in all its branches has constantly felt the need for fresh revivals, sweeping the whole movement with the wind of the Spirit.[498]

Continental Pietism has been considerably influenced by mystical ideas. Pietism has often been described as a phenomenon composed of many heterogeneous elements; this is due to the fact [which applies equally to Quakerism and to various groups within the Baptist movement] of the prevalence of these very ideas. German Calvinist Pietism, which was largely influenced by the Netherlands and the mystical elements in English Pietism, has already been mentioned. To that we can only add, at this point, a brief allusion to the deeply spiritual poet, Tersteegen. Like Sebastian Franck and Coornheert, Tersteegen was entirely aloof from the organized Church life of his own day; he acted, however, as the chosen leader of a group of mystical souls which resembled the fellowship of an earlier period known as the "Friends of God". Lavater and Jung Stilling must also be noted; as mystics of the Reformed Church it is true, of course, that both of them, under the influence of modern ideas of Immanence and of Humanitarianism, did not lay a great deal of stress upon the opposition that exists between the world and holiness, between the flesh and the spirit. Their faith centred in a Christ-mysticism, which was authenticated by experiences of "answered prayer"; it developed a piety which was full of light and independent of all confessions, and it evolved a purely individualistic form of group-fellowship. On the whole, however, the mysticism of the

[498] For this Enthusiasm, see *Lecky, II, 582–589*, and also *James: Varieties of Religious Experience, London, 1902*. The illustrative material for this study in the psychology of religion is drawn almost entirely from this sphere.—For the mystical element in Methodism, which was mediated through Moravian influences, see *Schneckenburger: Kleinere Kirchenparteien, pp. 150 ff.*; what *Loofs* says against this point of view in *PRE., XII, 774 and 779*, does not seem to me to alter it.

Calvinistic churches, after its first attempt to reform the whole Church on sectarian and ascetic lines, to a great extent retired into a mysticism which was indifferent to organized Church life altogether, and cultivated a strict holiness of life which bore many traces of the influence of Quietism.

Lutheran Pietism was already far more predisposed to experience a similar development, owing to the fact of Luther's high estimate of mediaeval mysticism, and to the orthodox doctrine of the *Unio Mystica*. At an early date the Christ-mysticism of St. Bernard penetrated into and revitalized its dogmatic Christology. The early Lutheran ascetic writers and hymnologists, who laid great stress on the need for "inwardness" and fervour within the Protestant churches, were particularly open to influences of this kind. In this connection Arndt ought to be mentioned particularly. Arndt did not belong to the rigorous "conventicle" type of piety, and his tendency was wholly in the direction of mysticism and spirituality; at the same time he was always careful to maintain his connection with Lutheran theology, and he laid great emphasis upon the power of "the Word". As a friend of Valentine Weigel, and an admirer of Paracelsus, with a thorough knowledge of devotional mystical literature, he instinctively made a compromise between the Lutheranism of the ministry and the Word, and the religion of direct inner illumination, between the dogma of justification and the doctrine of deification, between the radical doctrine of Original Sin and panentheistic ideas of Immanence—a compromise which is full of inconsistencies and contradictions, but which still possesses a strong spiritual vitality and influence. Arndt's ideas met with a good deal of opposition, but the current of thought which he had set in motion continued to develop, and Pietism in particular was greatly influenced by it. This tendency was intensified by influences from England, the Netherlands, and from Jakob Böhme, in addition to those which emanated from the older literature of mysticism. On the whole, however, this school of thought did not advance beyond this position: it held the doctrine of the "degrees of orison", or the "ladder of contemplation" which led to union with God; it adapted the Christ-mysticism of St. Bernard (rather sentimentally) in accordance with the tastes of the day, and it fostered a mystical hope of the Kingdom of God, which, however, did not expect the ministry, the Word, and the Sacrament to be entirely discarded until the spiritual Advent of Christ. Ecstasies and visions, miracles and prophets also formed part of the phenomena of the movement. Spener himself, whose scrupulous mind had little in common with mysticism, certainly loved the mediaeval mystical literature, and would often describe the Church as the "hidden Seed of the beloved souls in every Church" : a favourite phrase in English mysticism. With Spener and his disciples the emphasis upon inward experience and its practical results in daily life was certainly almost as important as the doctrine of justification by faith which constituted the Church's treasure-house of grace; from that standpoint it was easy to pass on into mysticism, especially when ascetic holiness was no longer conceived in the Calvinistic sense, but was based upon "spiritual" and Quietistic ideas. Spener's chief opponent, Dilfeld, was, however, only able to accuse him of "a subtile enthusiasm".

Franke

Franke, who had adapted Pietism to the purposes of theological education, and thus to that extent directly assumed the existence of the Church, still furthered the "enthusiastic" side in many respects by insisting on the doctrine of conviction of sin, and of an explicit experience of conversion, with a definite date—a point of view which it is difficult to combine with a belief in Infant Baptism. This emphasis on the need for a direct "consciousness" of the "state of grace" had a certain mystical tendency. Thus Franke used to quote Tauler with great approval as an illustration of a *praxis interioris Christianismi*, and he also translated a treatise by St. Catherine of Genoa. This is why Löscher was able to accuse Pietists of that type of great offences against Church life: "An indifferentism which had the appearance of religion, lack of appreciation of the means of grace, and particularly of the preaching of the Word; a tendency towards mysticism, Enthusiasm, and Chiliasm; a habit of talking about the "image of God", in Nature, and in Man; a confusing of Nature with Grace; talk about "begodded" (deified) men; faith interpreted as experience and spiritual feeling; the harbouring and defending of fanatics."

At this point the way for a transition to real mysticism had been opened up, but, on the whole, this did not often happen, for German Pietism is essentially definitely ecclesiastical, and "Enthusiasm" and Christ-mysticism of the St. Bernard type, which belongs to the non-intellectual realm of fantasy, did not appeal to it.

Arnold and Dippel

Apart from all kinds of narrow-minded groups and dishonest hypocrites, the only names we need to consider are those of

Gottfried Arnold and Dippel, both of whom, it is true, were men of outstanding importance. They were thoroughly individualistic mystics, who refused to join any organized Christian body at all. Their particular theories may be summarized thus: they believed that Christian fellowship only existed in its purity in the Primitive Church, before the time of Constantine; that the significance of Christ and of Redemption consists in quickening the Divine "seed" which is latent within the soul of every human being; they emphasized the fact that religious men within the non-Christian faiths possess a similar faculty in the "Divine Ground of the soul"; from the spiritual nature and spiritual unity of mankind they deduced the doctrine of ascetic holiness, and an attitude of indifference towards the existing social order which is based upon Nature; they taught that the "Inward Word" is the same as the natural moral law of love of humanity, and they looked for the coming of the Kingdom of God, in which there would be no ministry nor compulsory religion, nor a State Church.

In the last resort these are the characteristic features of a Spirituality which is based upon a substructure of Neo-Platonism, combined with the Spirit of Christ, and through Him with the history of Christianity. From that position the interesting and sarcastic Edelmann passed over to a Monism which openly declared that historical Christianity was a sham and a delusion—a point of view which must have given infinite pleasure to Arthur Drews and his friends.

Thomasius

Christian Thomasius also belonged to the friends of the mystical "Indifferentists" more than to those of real Pietism with whom he was at first connected. Upon that "Indifferentism" he built up his system of church-order, and sought to unite Christians in self-denial and in love, apart from the organization of any religious society, which, under present conditions certainly, always has to reckon everywhere with the positive order of the State Church. His anti-ascetic temper, however, separated him from the mystics, and thus he arrived at a Christian position which otherwise resembled that of the "Enlightenment".[499]

The Moravian Church

The mystical element within genuine Pietism reached its zenith in the Moravian Church. The Count himself was its most outstanding representative—indeed, it was Zinzendorf who expressed

[499] See p. 979.

this type of piety in a form which was intimate and spiritual, but also in extremely bad taste; the language and the hymns used by the earlier members of the Church of the Brethren usually drive the modern reader to distraction. Zinzendorf no longer regarded Pietism as an attempt to reform the Church; to him it was a voluntary association of individuals who are united with the Saviour who is spiritually present and who can be found in the Word, just as he regarded the Early Church as due solely to the personal influence of Jesus and as a personal union of believers. He transformed Spener's conventicle ideal into a form of free Christian social life, through which he and the brethren, in this community, guided by Providence, have been granted a special relationship with the Person of the Saviour.

It is evident that here we are not dealing with a spirituality which regards Christianity as an all-pervading spirit, which is merely present in Christ in a special way, but with a Christian mysticism which retains the doctrines of the Church, while, like St. Paul and later St. Bernard, it entwines the objective fact of Redemption with the sense of direct inward experience and feeling. In this respect Zinzendorf was in thorough agreement with the Jansenists. The only difference was, as Ritschl, with his usual acuteness, rightly divined, that this Pietist Christ-mysticism, and especially that of the Zinzendorf variety, always regarded this direct experience as an entirely personal and private relation with the living Saviour, whereas the older Christ-mysticism satisfied the desire for a personal relationship in a much more general manner. Pietism thus looks back over the whole history of the development of Christian individualism, and already it has a tinge of modern sentimental aesthetic individualism. In other directions, however, the relation between Moravian mysticism and ecclesiasticism is most obscure. Zinzendorf always considered himself in agreement with Lutheran theology. In reality, however, he only agreed with certain sections of Lutheran doctrine. With the ecclesiastical and sociological side of Lutheranism he certainly did not agree. As we have already seen, with the help of the Moravians, he was obliged to form a sectarian organization. This sectarian idea, however, was again and again contradicted by the Count's peculiarly personal motive which was contained in his strongly "spiritualized" Christ-mysticism. Behind the strong emphasis upon a direct experience of the Living Christ, and the extremely personal nature of the soul's relation with the Saviour, there lay concealed a certain indifference towards the historical aspect of Christianity, and a certain warm affection for individual religious peculiarities in their relative values. The disintegrating results of this type of mysticism began to appear in the so-called "sifting period" in Herrenhag, when Jesus was styled the "chief elder" in the Moravian Church; they appeared also in the stress which was laid on the "general spirit" of the Bible instead of on literal interpretation; and in the emphasis upon a "general" interest which extended far beyond the existing denominations, in the depreciation of the importance of religious denominations, which was expressed in the idea that they existed merely as different methods of educating souls for the true love of Christ. Above all, however, the exclusive emphasis upon personal piety—which the Moravians displayed in their practice of mutual confession, in their habit of including reports on the inner life of individuals, in their practice of reading aloud these confessions for purposes of personal edification—had a great influence, far beyond the borders of the Moravian Church itself. In this sense Schleiermacher and Novalis always remained true to the ideals of Herrnhut; they merely developed explicitly the ideas which were implicit within them. In Fries also the clothing of the universal religious idea with an individualizing and relativizing symbolism was probably mainly due to the influence of the Moravian Church.[500]

Pietism at the present Day

This whole world of ideas has endured down to the present day. It appears under various forms in the whole Pietist movement with its various branches, and also in the foundation of fresh mystical or even directly "spiritual" groups. There has never been a time when the old mystical treatises have not been read and studied, and people are still reading and expounding them to-day. These movements are undercurrents of religious life which mostly pass unnoticed; socially, too, they chiefly affect the lower classes. To-day, to a great extent, they have joined forces with spiritism and theosophy; the only new movement in the grand manner is Swedenborgianism; Swedenborg was really a modern Paracelsus, translated into terms of modern natural science; with his mysticism he combined occultism.[501] But these ideas, however, did not affect a large number of people: in America the movement is still in existence; William James had leanings in that direction.

[500] See p. 981.

[501] See also on this point *Kalbe: Kirchen und Sekten der Gegenwart*; also *W. Bruhn: Theosophie und Theologie, 1907*.

Place of Mysticism within the Philosophy of Religion

There is, however, another fact to be considered which is more important for spiritual life in general. This is the presentation of the ultimate spiritual meaning of mysticism and its place in the philosophy of religion; this has become a matter of vital importance to all the religious people of the present day who are either outside the churches altogether, or who at least do not belong specifically to a Church or to a Pietist group. The problem may be stated thus: when modern thought came under the influence of the conception of universal world laws, and of a universal world unity, which meant that morality, religion, and art also had to be regarded as universal fundamental laws for the spiritual development of mankind, the only hope of bridging the gulf between this type of thought and religion in general and Christianity in particular, lay in "idealistic" mysticism. Everywhere already mysticism essentially represents the same phenomenon: a religious experience based on direct and vital contact with God, which, in its ethical and religious content, was obviously related to Christian thought; further, in the historical elements of Christianity, mysticism was able to discern an historical incorporation and symbolizing of its own ideas in a specially living and primitive form, in so far as it remained linked with the historical element at all. All that was necessary was to connect this mysticism with the general psychological or epistemological ideas of modern philosophy; this yielded the common fundamental conception from which it was possible to open up a way to the particular within the concrete religions, after the naïve age-long dominion of the positive and particular, that is, of supernaturally established Christianity, had been shattered. The whole of modern philosophy tends in this direction.

This, however, meant that the whole historical concrete element in religion became a problem, and it opened up the possibility for the most radical solutions. Since, at the same time, the historical element in religion was incorporated in a general historical point of view, and was thus open to criticism, very often the need for release from historical uncertainty led to the demand for the pure immediacy, present character, and inwardness of the *evangelium aeternum*, to the expectation of the Third Dispensation in which each individual, out of the depths of his own life, independently and personally, and yet essentially in agreement with others, gains his own knowledge of God. The ideas which Sebastian

Franck had expressed with such depth and clarity had again become operative.

Mysticism of this kind lies at the heart of the philosophy of religion taught by Leibniz, however deeply orthodox this reconciler of philosophy and religion appeared. Spinoza had already taken this path. In a theistic and personal sense Herder and Goethe took this line; Goethe had imbibed these ideas from Church History through Gottfried Arnold. Lessing, too, saved religion from mere intellectualism and criticism by appealing to the emotional piety of the Moravians. Kant, who regarded religion simply as spirit and thought, also treated the story of Redemption from this point of view, although in other ways he was purely ethical and theistic and not at all mystically minded; his spiritualization of doctrines into symbols of eternal truths and ever-recurring present processes is entirely in accord with this kind of spirituality. There is no need to prove this in the case of Fichte, Schelling, and Hegel; the two last have drawn explicitly upon the old mystical religious literature; and the belated Gnosticism of Schelling is a "spiritual" theory borrowed from Böhme. Above all, however, in Hamann, Friedrich Heinrich Jacobi, and Lavater, it is obvious that their infinitely stimulating ideas spring either from Christian mysticism or directly from general "spiritual religion" itself. If they figure as the Theistic and Dualistic opponents of the Monism of the period, the opposition is still only relative, and within the common whole.

As the Monism of those thinkers was impregnated with the irrational character of the individual, and was crowned with an idea of God filled with an ethical content, so the Dualism of these was no mere Dualism of Natural Law and Christian miracle, but, rather, of externally mechanical Nature and fullness of the Spirit, in short of lower and higher nature. In them spirit becomes genius, and the physical is treated as an external intellectualism which is calculable and tangible. In them faith is treated as a feeling which the Presence of God effects in the soul, in which He alone and all His works can be experienced. It is obvious that here the old "spiritual" ideas are only being continued, or renewed, in a fresh form. The religious-philosophical element of Neo-Platonism, which Christian mysticism had assimilated, became ever more evident and independent, combined with the aesthetic colour of Platonism, which Christianity had set aside entirely, and which modern aesthetic culture has renewed in such a differentiated manner.[502]

[502] See p. 981.

The Romantic Movement

In this movement of thought Romanticism was the most important phenomenon; its religious element was represented by Schleiermacher and Novalis, and it influenced the whole group in varying degrees of truth and depth. Everyone who has read Schleiermacher's *Discourses* knows that there is clearly proclaimed in them the "spiritual" idea of a direct revelation of religious feeling, and a mutual understanding of all Spirit-filled men and of all revelations, and that the sociological conclusions are also drawn quite definitely from these ideas: a system of loosely connected groups, varying from time to time, gathered round particularly strong leaders and prophets, serves to unite the faithful in ever new groupings for mutual fellowship, in order to awaken the spiritual consciousness which all possess; the "spirit" is not tied to the historic Christian community, but, reaching out beyond its borders, it can allow religious feeling, which is in itself everywhere the same, to form ever new concrete groups. The prophets and seers, Christ Himself included, are merely those who arouse and enkindle that spark of direct religious life which is the possession of every human being.

It is undeniable that this conception has some connection with Herrnhut, even though the general outlook is determined by the main features of the modern view of the world, and the whole tendency towards inwardness and immediacy is intimately connected with the personality of Schleiermacher. However, whether this is simply an analogy or one which is based on history, the whole idea is very closely related to Protestant mysticism. In Novalis, Moravian Christ-mysticism was also placed within this setting; later on, Schleiermacher developed this idea still farther; here, too, it is, however, a genuine Christ-mysticism, i.e. the view which regards the whole of life as full of a power which is only concretely incarnate in Christ; the Lord's Supper means that the believer is fed with the materialized and concrete Divine Spirit, who indwells the universe; the whole rite is a symbol of the unity between the Spirit and Nature, between the prophet and the community.

This religious Romanticism possessed two most important new features: (1) On the one hand, under the influence of modern conceptions of law and world unity, the dualistic opposition between the flesh and the spirit disappears, and with that the asceticism which was so characteristic of the older Protestant mysticism. Whereas the latter had scarcely reconciled its ascetic

Dualism with the idea of Divine Immanence by means of the Neo-Platonic theory of Emanations, and further, within this framework, had made room for the freedom of the creature, the new Protestant mysticism tended absolutely and directly towards Immanence and Determinism. Where this was not the case, freedom is still only the principle of an ascending and victorious evolution, not that of an ascetic and dualistic opposition between the redeemed soul and the flesh which is tainted with sin. Hence the mystical religious philosophy of the present day has a strong affinity with the Pantheistic idea of Immanence, and the ancient idea of the opposition between the flesh and the Spirit is transformed into the idea of progress through the stages of an evolutionary process. (2) The second important change is the coalescence of the fully developed religious "inwardness" and individuality with the aestheticism of individuality, with the differentiation of the altogether individual artistic feeling. This far transcends the aestheticism of Platonism which still always clings to the universal, of which we hear echoes from time to time in the Christian mysticism of the Ancient World, and which reappeared at the Renaissance. Under the influence of Christian thought and of modern life, this is an extremely differentiated aesthetic of entirely individualistic feeling. With that it is only too easy to combine that whole aesthetic relativism which regards everything as right in its own place, and as contributing to the harmony of the whole. Although Schleiermacher, Novalis, Fichte, Schelling, and Hegel all strenuously opposed this tendency, it has continued to grow and increase down to the present day, combined with the growth of an aesthetic world-outlook, and under the impression of the extreme variety in history. This double combination, however, signifies a most important complement to pure Christian "inwardness". Whereas the older mysticism had absorbed the Neo-Platonic doctrine of deification, and natural philosophy, the newer mysticism now drew into itself the modern conception of humanity and aesthetic individualism. This meant that it was now able to play its part in the practical tasks of modern life.[503]

This religious romanticism, together with the aesthetic differentiation and the mysticism which is connected with the philosophical idea of Immanence, is the source of that which the modern German Protestant of the educated classes can really assimilate—his understanding of religion in general. This is the secret religion of the educated classes. Mystical and spiritual litera-

[503] Cf. also the article by *Koch: Zur Beurteilung der modernen Persönlichkeitskultur*, and the reply by *J. Müller: Chr. W., 1908.*

ture, therefore, celebrates to-day its resurrection. Lutheranism, in particular, provides a very fertile soil for these ideas, since from the outset Lutheranism had certain affinities with this type of spirituality in its most genuine form. This kind of spirituality meets with far less understanding in Anglo-Saxon countries and among Calvinistic peoples; to them it appears unpractical, anti-social, non-ecclesiastical, and unethical. Yet from the literature of the Emerson group, and in the works of Carlyle—(Carlyle's spirit was, it is true, actively ethical and not aesthetic)—even there (among the Anglo-Saxon peoples) this line of thought had been pursued for a long time: History is a symbol; thought wells forth eternally, only reaching special intensity in the heroes of mankind. Finally the aesthetic spiritual temper entered into English life through Ruskin and his school; this has rightly been described as the end of Puritanism.

The sociological consequences of this fundamental position soon became evident. The religious community—both the Church and the conventicle—had lost all significance. Public worship had become entirely unnecessary, and without any meaning for religion. The historical element had simply become a symbol, a means of stimulus, while some went farther and regarded it with great suspicion. The historical element had almost entirely lost any connection with public worship; instead it had become a theme for scientific treatment, a subject for the free play of the imagination, or a means of stimulating certain moods according to one's own private fancies. Literature, poetry, and the old Philadelphianism, the formation of small groups governed by personal impressions, took the place of the old fellowship in worship, just as Schleiermacher describes in his *Discourses*, only usually with much less earnestness.

In the meantime also the Naturalistic Monism of modern nature philosophers, and Brahmanic and Buddhist ideas, added their quota to this confused mingling of ideas; moreover, all relation to Christian history, and indeed to Christian Personalism in general, was thrown into great confusion, or even into a complete break with the past and passionate opposition to it. But even where this complete severance from the spirit of Christianity had not taken place, or had not done so consciously, in these romantic ideas the tendency was to identify Christianity with an entirely personally differentiated and entirely inward spiritual religion.[504]

[504] See p. 983.

Mysticism and Modern Theology

The intellectual formulas of the newer scientific theology, in so far as they are in touch with the modern mind, and at the same time are seeking religious warmth and vitality, since Schleiermacher, Hegel, and de Wette, have also been moving in this direction. Certainly the need is here more clearly felt of doing justice to history and to revelation, but only on the fundamental assumption that salvation is not a static quality, belonging to institutional religion, but an experience of the union of the soul with God which is new every time it takes place. Therefore the meaning of history for faith has also become the central problem in modern theology. It is more closely related to Meister Eckhart and Sebastian Franck than it is to Luther and Calvin, and all that it values in Luther for the present day is his early period with its "spiritual" teaching. This all means the revival of the earlier mysticism. Its best ideas have either been foreshadowed in it or developed from it. It merely transplants them into the historico-critical method of thought which has arisen meanwhile, and into the modern knowledge of the world.

This is the theology of subjective experience in contrast to the theology of objective revelation; the sole value it assigns to Jesus is that of serving as the original stimulator of the religious consciousness. This, however, means that so far as the sociological situation is concerned it renews the experience of the earlier mysticism. It creates no community, since it possesses neither the sense of solidarity nor the faith in authority which this requires, nor the no less necessary fanaticism and desire for uniformity. It lives in and on communities which have been brought into existence by other ruder energies; it tries to transform these groups from confessional unities into mere organizations for administration, offering a home to very varying minds and energies. It is opposed to the ecclesiastical spirit by its tolerance, its subjectivism and symbolism, its emphasis upon the ethical and religious inwardness of temper, its lack of stable norms and authorities. Therefore it is obliged to utilize the forms of reorganization which the more robust period of the State Church compulsion had created and which would have never arisen without violence.

Sometimes, however, it goes farther still and envisages a new situation altogether, in which it will no longer be necessary to connect religion with the decaying churches. Richard Rothe and Hegel did not prophesy in vain that the Church would become merged in the State, that is, the complete autonomy of the religious "mind" directly united with the collective reason and its social organization. In an extremely instructive and deeply thoughtful summary of Church History[504a] Rothe has laid bare the ultimate tendencies and the most difficult problems connected with this form of spirituality, while at the same time he argues that this type of spirituality itself is the logical result of the evolution of Christianity.

Sociological Results of Modern Spiritual Idealism

All these considerations, however, help us to understand the sociological reaction which followed this Romanticism—the return to the earlier ecclesiasticism. Even in Novalis this was not an impulse arising out of Romanticism itself; on the contrary, it was an attempt to guard against the relativity and radical individualism which resulted from this type of thought. As Novalis steeped himself, in his romantic way, in the study of history he realized the utter poverty of modern Society and of its prevailing religion in sociological content and the power of producing fellowship. From this point of view, and not without good reason, the mediaeval period seemed to him richer and more natural. At the same time St. Simon also expressed similar views; in his desire to discover a new form of social order, which he felt to be an urgent necessity, he turned to religious thought, and held romantic views of Christianity. French Catholic Romanticism also developed along similar lines. The romantic outlook on history and the need for satisfaction through symbolism and imagination was only one method of this counter-movement. The true spirit of Romanticism did not move in this direction at all. The new ecclesiasticism, therefore, freed itself as soon as possible from these unsuitable methods, and sought to replace them with others, which were contained in Pietism or in pure orthodoxy. To-day, in actual fact, within both the Catholic and Protestant Churches, the dominating tendency is the very opposite of Romanticism; it is the tendency towards institutionalism, authority, and uniformity. Nothing is left of Romanticism save its phraseology, which some theologians like to use who wish to be clever and to be considered "modern".

Such a reaction, however, in some form or other, was necessitated by the real nature of Christianity itself, which is never merely individualistic mysticism, but is always at the same time an ethical driving-power, a recognition of the fact that fellowship

[504a] See p. 984.

is required by the Divine Will, and which, in the form of religion, can only be nourished by a living form of worship. In some sense or another, however, this form of worship must be the worship of Jesus as the Revelation of God. Thus even Schleiermacher discarded his youthful ideals of an individualistic "spiritual religion", and returned to the idea of the Church, centring in the worship of Christ, as the original source from which religious energy ever flows forth anew.

In Schleiermacher's opinion this worship ought to be exercised within the territorial churches (so long as they exist) in great congregational freedom and with a large measure of elasticity for individuals. The whole unified body of the Territorial State Church ought to be penetrated with a Christian spirit working out personally through the individual groups for worship. It is the ideal of a synthesis consisting of the collective spirit of a Church and an individualistic mysticism, of a popular National Church and a Congregationalist Independency; of the worship of Christ and the shaping of life by the Spirit of Christianity—an ideal which requires both from the congregations and from the ecclesiastical authorities the greatest wisdom and broadmindedness, circumspection and willingness to renounce one's personal views; for that very reason this ideal was only realized in a kind of caricature, that is, as the orthodoxy of the Territorial Church combined with the compulsory toleration of liberal theologians. The educated laity, therefore, so far as it is attached to Christianity at all, has in reality a religion without a Church or forms of worship, a Christianity of "the Spirit" and of disposition, a religion of humanitarian activity, and an entirely individual interpretation of the intellectual aspect of religion.[505]

The position of Christianity in the modern educated classes is determined by all these factors. Another point which we must not overlook is the fact that certain religious types tend to belong to certain social strata of Society; this fact has practical significance and gives to those types their permanent support. Certain sections of Society desire the sect, its stimulus, and its satisfying sociological organization which gives the individual a share in co-operative activity. Others again desire the Church because they believe that it provides those sociological and religious features of support and authority which form the most favourable equalizing and reconciling element for the control of the masses. In general, however, the modern educated classes understand nothing but mysticism. This is due to the reflex action of the atomistic indi-

505 See p. 985.

vidualism of modern civilization in general, of an individualism which in non-religious spheres of life is already losing its hold, and is beginning to develop into its exact opposite. In its depreciation of fellowship, public worship, history, and social ethics this type of "spiritual religion", in spite of all its depth and spirituality, is still a weakened form of religious life, which must be maintained in its concrete fullness of life by churches and sects, if an entirely individualistic mysticism is to spiritualize it at all. Thus we are forced to this conclusion: this conception of Christianity, which alone meets the needs of the educated classes, assumes the continuance of other and more concrete living forms of Christianity as well; it can never appeal to all. Rather, we may even express the sure conviction that Lessing's prophecy of the *Evangelium aeternum*, and of the knowledge of God as the original and equal possession of every individual, will never be fulfilled. What the actual course of development will be, however, and what significance this modern type of "spiritual religion" will have for the future, no one can foretell. To-day the problem of the organization of religious groups is more obscure than ever. The growth of sects and of mystical movements, combined with the problematic character of the relation between Church and State, has produced a situation analogous to that which existed at the beginning of the period of the Reformation.[506]

This completes our survey of the phenomena of the sect-type and of idealistic mysticism. Although both these movements differ essentially from ecclesiastical Protestantism, yet both belong to Protestantism, since they reveal the ever-renewed aspirations of the sect and of mysticism which arise out of the Bible, and which accompany every form of church-type, in their specific and definite Protestant form, the sect in its final acceptance of the Protestant idea of the "calling", and mysticism in its fusion with Protestant autonomous individualism. Thus we see that their ideals were already latent within the Protestant churches themselves; the idea of the sect on the whole belongs to Calvinism, while mysticism is more at home within Lutheranism. Through Pietism, which stands midway between Protestant ecclesiasticism and sectarian or mystical piety, these tendencies have constantly

[506] Cf. my work entitled *Die Kirche im Leben der Gegenwart* in the collection which has already been mentioned called *Weltanschauung*, etc., and the article *Gewissensfreiheit Ch. W., 1911*; also my lecture *Die Bedeutung der Geschichtlichkeit Jesu für den Glauben, 1910*; *Eucken* expresses the same views, *a.a.O.s., 136.* Cf. also *Harnack's Dogmengeschichte, 4. Aufl. III, pp. 902–908.*

formed the complement of the Church. The early exclusion of the sectarian and mystical groups (which were connected with the democratic tendencies of the period) from the main current of the Reformation did a great deal of harm at that time to the popular influence of Protestantism, throwing it more than ever upon the ruling powers for support; this fact again immensely increased its natural tendency towards the church-type. But the ideas which had been banished reappeared; they then produced the Pietist movement, which has had a deep influence upon the churches until the present day, the independent sect-movement, and the idea of Christian Social reform, as well as that type of "spiritual religion" which is either free from the Church or indifferent to it.[507]

Social Philosophy of Mysticism and "Spiritual Religion"

Finally, all that we now have to do is to formulate the social doctrines of these groups and their sociological significance. All that is required, therefore, is a brief summary of the various observations which have already been made, and a definition of the relation of these social doctrines to those of Catholicism, Lutheranism, and the primitive Calvinism of Geneva.

Spiritual idealism and mysticism—to begin with the subject which we have just been studying—has no impulse towards organization at all. Only in so far as these groups retain their hold on ethical Christian Theism (and among the Quietistic and Pantheistic groups only under the pressure of the ineradicable natural urge towards fellowship) do these movements produce any form of independent social organization as the outcome of their religious ideas. As a rule people of this type care solely for the individual and his eternal welfare, while they believe at the same time in the universal fellowship of the spirit in love. Under certain circumstances they emphasize this idea of universal spiritual fellowship, but the idea of the Church and of religious organization is alien to their thought. Within that "communion of the spirit", however, they only form narrower groups of a brotherhood [Philadelphian] kind, or of select circles of spiritual leaders and experts. The sense of need for public worship and an historical basis, in which churches and sects find the rallying-point of their organization, is not evident; it either disappears out of

[507] Cf. also *Göbel, I, p. 145*. This is also the right element in *Barge's Gesamtanschauung vom Verlauf der Reformation*, which manifests very little understanding of the Church-type, but is accurate in its main characteristics.

sight altogether, or it is changed into a strong emphasis upon a personal direct relation with God and Christ, or into spiritual exaltation. It is, of course, true to say that these tendencies have a sociological fundamental theory, a union of the hearts of all in one common aim, and a complete toleration of all other souls on an equal basis, because, as Lagarde says, "upon the ascent towards God the various lines do not cut across each other but converge and meet". People of this type, however, do not carry this fundamental theory systematically and actively into Society.

This fundamental theory is of value only for those who are seeking and experiencing God, and for those who are illuminated by Him, and its power can only be extended as the Spirit is shed abroad in the hearts of men. Here nothing can be planned and organized. The question is only how far this spirit will work of itself, and in this respect individuals differ according to temperament. Resignation, a sense of superiority, pessimism, Quietism, and optimistic expectations all have their place within this movement. The result is, naturally, that there is a complete indifference, or impotence towards all social problems which lie outside the directly religious sphere. Fundamentally, this school of thought has no idea at all of the way in which to deal with questions of the State or of economics; it only knows that everything ought to be altered and begun entirely afresh. When? And how? It is, indeed, hard to say. As we can understand, it is only within the sphere of the sex ethic and of the family that this type of thought displays features which are peculiar to itself, since these matters are very closely connected with an entirely personal intimate valuation of life. In this respect it is very independent and unconventional. Its aim is to spiritualize these most important processes, which have such a strong influence on the emotional life; it wishes to effect the fusion of the erotic with the ethical and religious element. This is the reason for those phenomena known as Antinomianism and Libertinism, of which, both rightly and wrongly, these circles have constantly been accused. To-day it is just these circles which deal most finely with the problem of sex ethics. The spirit of restraint and the possibility of penetrating erotic relationships with religious feeling, or also, on the contrary, ascetic misgivings about the erotic competition of feeling, are here emphasized, and from this standpoint they develop marriage ideals which are in strong opposition to the conventional legal "property-regarding" viewpoint of marriage, which is legitimate from the standpoint of the Church. The very fluctuating details connected with this point of view could only be described within the framework of a monograph, but they would present many features of great interest. In any case, the connection between erotic and religious feeling which in this interior subjectivity makes possible a mutual penetration of both, and which does away with the coarse ecclesiastical doctrine of concupiscence as the result of the Fall, is important. When, however, great idealistic mystical thinkers of recent times, like Schleiermacher and Richard Rothe, deal with ethics in connection with the practical tasks of civilization, their ideas proceed obviously and avowedly from the modern world of thought. The difficulty, then, is how to fuse this world of thought with Christian spirituality and its supernatural character. Rothe, in particular, is a very characteristic example of the difficulty of this task.[508]

Turning to the question of the sect, we find that it falls into the same divisions which characterized it in the Middle Ages: the aggressive, world-reforming type, and the type which endures persecution and contempt with patience and is indifferent to the world.

Social Doctrines of the Aggressive Sects

The aggressive type with its apocalyptic violence burnt itself out in the seventeenth century, but through the Great Rebellion in England it has certainly exerted an immense influence on world history. The only relic of it which now remains is that Christian Socialism which, logically or otherwise, and by very varied methods, attempts to bring in a new order of Society which shall be in harmony both with the Will of God and with reason.

In Catholicism, which in any case only takes up this problem in inter-confessional groups, the sect-type has been almost entirely obliterated. There, ultimately, the idea is simply to introduce a new class into the social organism which is directed by the Church, whose inner harmony will thus be restored by the grace and power given to the Church and to its controlling authority; naturally that does not exclude a very energetic and successful activity along certain lines, all the more since it has the immense influence of the Church behind it.

Within Calvinism, Christian Socialism finds its main expression in the formation of associations, in the endeavour to influence public opinion, and in the establishment of co-operative societies. Within Lutheranism, where it had no point of contact within the churches at all, it has had the greatest development in theory. There also, however, it falls into two sections: first there is the

[508] See p. 986.

school of thought which merely tries to influence the general ethical temper and to bring the spirit of reconciliation into the class war, and there is another, which believes that a socialistic renewal of the whole constitution of Society is a Christian duty; and which believes that this movement should be incorporated into the steady upward march of progress which is willed by God. Of course it is only natural that particular social and ethical problems should pale in importance before these general problems, which are of fundamental significance. Either they break up into an infinite number of questions of detail, or they disappear altogether in the very vague and general sketch of a future social order. Their special features, which, in part, are very instructive, could only be made clear in a special monograph.[508a]

In our present inquiry all that matters is that we should gain a thorough insight into the association of ideas. This study, however, throws much light on the whole problem of the relation of Christianity to the idea of social reform, and forms a definite conclusion to the observations on this subject, which have already been stated.

In this respect the Gospel was completely ideological and indifferent towards the world, whose transformation it only expected from the great miracle of the coming Kingdom of God; in great things as in small it left everything entirely to God; the only thing which was taken into account was the view that the poor and the suffering were in a more advantageous position than others, since they feel more warmly and humbly towards God; beyond that it regarded every act of love which the opportunity required as the exercise of the right attitude towards God. The Ancient Church absorbed the world into its own life, making a few absolutely necessary changes while it preserved a spirit of interior detachment from it, and in order to overcome material distress it began the work of philanthropy.

The mediaeval period produced a relative harmony between the actual situation and the Christian ideal; but it only developed the dominion of the Church over this life-harmony of Nature and Supernature, and dealt with social wrongs no longer through the Church and the congregation, but through institutional monastic charity, which was made possible by the endowment system.

Lutheranism left all secular questions to a government which was guided by the Gospel, leaving it to struggle with the existing difficulties as best it could, certain that the Gospel possesses the

[508a] On this point see the various works of *Ragaz* and *Rauschenbusch*, which have already been mentioned above.

power to inspire and establish the order of Nature through love.

Calvinism, which had adopted the sect-ideal of the Holy Community, and had come to terms with the State Church spirit, for the first time, alongside of the sects, set a Christian social ideal in the forefront of its life; it did this, however, in a thoroughly conservative sense; it held that the existing civil order of the State should be maintained, on the assumption that this social order, guided by relative Natural Law, along with good-will and the necessary earnestness in the pursuit of holiness, could be made the foundation of a truly Christian social order.

The idea of a radical social reform, which regards the existing order of Society and property as radically incapable of developing Christian personality and Christian love in any comprehensive way, was held only by the sects, and by them only in the measure in which they passed from patient endurance of persecution, under the influence of the eschatological idea of the Kingdom of God and in the expectation of its speedy realization, into the attitude of a thoroughgoing reform according to the ideal of the Kingdom of God and of primitive Reason. Further, the more the idea of the Natural Law of the Stoics agreed with these hopes, the more this reform became democratic and communistic. These were the sole supporters of a Christian social ethic which was radical, allowed no compromise, and did not accept the existing social order.

Then Christian Socialism arose, with its penetrating criticism of the existing social order. It threw out a clear challenge, claiming that the urgency of the situation demanded either a radical change in the fundamental social outlook, or the destruction of the present economic system in order to make room for a new social order, which would be in harmony with the ideals which also dominate the Socialistic Reform parties, groups which have sprung into existence under the pressure of the economic situation. These demands show, however, that Christian Socialism again is fired with the old spirit of the aggressive sect; like it, it interprets the movements of the day as a challenge to change the whole principle of the existing order, a change which can be effected by God alone; it renews the hope of realizing the Kingdom of God upon earth, and revives the sense of the intimate connection between mind and body; and its ideals bear a close resemblance to the ancient Stoic-Christian conceptions of absolute Natural Law. Modern ideas of Immanence, and of the importance of secular civilization, have also had some influence upon it. It regards itself as the product of intellectual, cultural, and technical development. For Christian Socialism, therefore, the day of ascetic "Enthusiasm" and Dualism is past. No longer, like the early sects, does it supplement the social message of the Gospel by ideas drawn from the Old Testament and the Apocalypse, but it utilizes the conclusions of modern social science, and the technological conception of progress. It therefore renounces the apocalyptic revolutionary idea of violence, and looks for a revolution only from within. In so doing, however, it severs itself from the Church of the present day not so much from the actual institution as from its inner spirit. On the whole, the Church requires the masses to acquiesce in existing social conditions because they have been appointed by God; moreover, since it is essentially on the side of law and order, its only idea of social reform is charitable activity and a Christian control of the civil order. Socialistic churches are nonsense. The task of the Church is something different from radical-ethical endeavour and the re-ordering of life. But a Christian Socialism which is separate from the Church in spirit can appeal to the Gospel. The Christian piety of the churches is inwardly very different in its outlook from that of a free community, earnestly endeavouring to bring in the Kingdom of God. At the same time, of course, there are numerous points of contact between the two schools of thought. The heart of the problem, however, lies in the contrast between an ecclesiastical institution realistically focused towards mankind and a free voluntary community unconditionally striving after the ideal.

The Non-Aggressive Sect and Neo-Calvinism

The passive persecuted sect is represented by the Mennonites, the Baptists, the Quakers, the groups which came into being through Pietism, and the modern sects. It also has assumed a different character from that of its mediaeval and early Protestant ancestors, like the Waldensians, the Bohemian Brethren, and the early Protestant Baptists. They have given up their previous attitude of passive resistance, and have accepted the State, Society, and the economic order. Based on the Protestant ethic of the "calling", they have all developed into groups which, in the sociological sense, must be described as "bourgeois", and which therefore accept existing conditions. Their only contribution to social reform lies in the sphere of Home Missions through evangelistic work and social service, coupled with an influence on Society through Christian public opinion and the Press. This middle-class development, and the adoption of the ethic of the "calling", is a natural result of the change in its own position, due to a more settled existence, increase in numbers, and the inheritance of stable conditions, as well as to an inevitably intimate connection with the immensely powerful organism of modern political and economic life, which can no longer, as in the anarchy and simplicity of mediaeval life, leave untouched islands to exist in its current. Another important factor in their development has been their Calvinistic environment. Both in their own sociological process of evolution and in their social ethic they have grown into a very close relationship with Calvinism, or, rather, with Neo-Calvinism. On the other hand, Neo-Calvinism itself has entirely severed its connection with the State, and on the ethical side it has been fused with these sects to such an extent that it is practically impossible to distinguish them from each other. The main question, however, in which these sects still differ from the churches is that of freedom from the State, and the demand for the ecclesiastical neutrality of the State; but since the churches are now being separated from the State in any case, this question is naturally less urgent than formerly.

It is not difficult to see why these sects have followed this line of development. The passive persecuted sect is only possible as an interim organization, while it awaits the Divine Revelation of the Kingdom. If, however, these bodies give up this "waiting" attitude, and accept the existing world-order as something permanent, they then adopt a relative standard, and make their own compromise with the world. Of necessity, therefore, they then develop in the direction either of the churches or of the radical sects, or they die out. Thus they have become ecclesiastical and bourgeois, just as Calvinism, on the contrary, has become Free Church and legalistic. From the point of view of religious sociology they have become churches, founded, like the true churches, upon the doctrine of sin and grace; the only difference is that, either in theory or in practice, their ideal of Church membership is stricter than that of the churches.

As churches, therefore, which by the very fact of their separation proclaim their independence, their freedom from the State, and the sovereign power of religion over against a secular civilization, and as highly individualistic organizations based on personal conviction and on conscious, systematic ethical achievement, they evolve from within a sociological fundamental theory which may be described as the uniting of individuals in a common spirit, which is not the sum but the product of the uniting individual will, which only exists in and through its active work. In one particular direction this spirit of the whole absorbs into itself the will of each individual, in order that that may again be affected by the spirit of the whole; in other directions, however, it is left free to work out other social ideas in its own way. It is no sterile individualism, nor is it an institutional spirit, which produces and supports the individual, but it is a vital process of interaction between the individuals who compose the society and the product of this union.

The idea of fellowship is not determined by inherited moods and feelings, by a fixed framework of life which maintains itself by its own miraculous power, in which currents of feeling sway to and fro between active strenuous effort and passive adherence, but by the Divine purpose of Life—clearly recognized and systematically realized, making demands on every single soul, yet transcending all—the Holy Community, the authentication of grace, preparation for the future life. This is a curious blend of the ecclesiastical and the sectarian spirit, in which the latter is the stronger. Actively and visibly exercised first and foremost within a religious fellowship, this spirit spreads outwards to the whole of life as a sociological fundamental theory which similarly defines the State, the communes, and the whole infinitely subdivided group-life. This produces a certain affinity with Democracy and Liberalism, but without the rationalist demand for equality, and also without the revolutionary spirit which is peculiar to the democracy of the Latin peoples. This kind of individualism, indeed, tends to be absolutely conservative, since it upholds with care the delicate balance between the individual and Society (as a constitution), and endeavours to secure it as far as possible from all disturbance. These are matters which force themselves upon the attention of every observer of American life; they also characterize English Dissent. These peculiarities are usually explained as Anglo-Saxon racial characteristics, whereas in reality these racial characteristics have themselves been produced by the discipline and education of Calvinism.[509]

Ascetic Protestantism

Thus the development of Calvinism into Puritanism and the Free Churches, combined with the development of the Baptist movement into a bourgeois body, and the development of the

[509] Cf. the study by *Max Weber*, which has already been quoted several times, on *Kirche und Sekte in Nordamerika*; there is a certain amount of material also in *Tocqueville* and *Bryce: The American Commonwealth*³, *1903*.

Pietistic sects on ecclesiastical lines, has produced that collective Protestant group which has already been described above as "ascetic Protestantism", in order to distinguish it from Lutheranism and Catholicism. At this point we again pick up the thread which we had to drop at the close of the last section.

It has already been made abundantly clear that Lutheranism taught that labour in a calling was both a service rendered to God and an outward expression of brotherly love. On the other hand, by its emphasis upon the purely inward aspect of religion, its lack of a clear standard of moral behaviour, and its acquiescence in the conditions of life which were created by Natural Law, but were often extremely unchristian, it was not able, on its own initiative, to bring about a coherent and systematic transformation of social life in general. Neither in theory nor in its attitude to life does it possess a systematic ethic. Again and again Lutheranism casts aside its asceticism (which it also possesses as the corollary of the doctrine of Original Sin), and gives itself up to repose in the blessedness of the Divine Mercy, and to the thankful enjoyment of Divine gifts in all that is good and beautiful, and whenever it becomes dubious about the world and about sin it withdraws into the refuge of its inner happiness of justification through faith.

Catholicism, on the other hand, likewise values the cosmos of the vocational system as the means of natural existence appointed by Natural Law. But this system of callings is applicable to the conditions of natural existence, and is thus merely the lower degree of that higher supernatural ethic, which inwardly is no longer connected with the claims of the active life, but which in the life of contemplation attains the highest degree of supernature or grace.

Ascetic Protestantism and the "Calling"

Ascetic Protestantism, however, regards the "calling" as a proof, and the ardent fulfilment of one's professional duty as the sign and token of the state of grace. Accordingly it gathers all the work of the "calling" into a coherent system of the utmost concentration of human faculties on the aim of the "calling", which is appointed to the individual through his providential position within the system. The principles and ideals of Ascetic Protestantism may therefore be summarized thus: the inner severance of feeling and enjoyment from all the objects of labour; the unceasing harnessing of labour to an aim which lies in the other world, and therefore must occupy us till death; the depreciation of possessions, of all things earthly, to the level of expediency; the habit of industry in order to suppress all distracting and idle impulses; and the willing use of profit for the religious community and for public welfare; these principles, which may vary in detail, are all in the main similar in character, and to a considerable extent also they have been and are being realized.[510]

Social Doctrines of Ascetic Protestantism

These principles also help us to understand the social doctrines of Ascetic Protestantism, which affect the sphere of life which lies outside religion. Under this head I include Neo-Calvinism, whose social teaching, for the same reason, has not been described in detail.[510a]

The Sex Ethic

The sex ethic is, of course, concerned with the preservation of the strict purity of family life. All sexual intercourse before marriage and outside the marriage state is strictly forbidden. This, of course, is the ordinary Christian point of view. Nevertheless, the ethic of the family itself is conceived in a very peculiar way. Asceticism, namely, demands the excision of all those erotic and emotional elements which Catholicism and Lutheranism had always believed they ought to tolerate as the sensuality resulting from Original Sin. The sex life of marriage was to them *medicina libidinis*. Here, however, it is firmly incorporated into the aim of the community to serve the glory of God. The life of sex is not to be used for enjoyment, but for the deliberate procreation of children. It is not an aim in itself, but it serves the continued growth of Society and the Church. Further, the production of children involves the duty of bringing up useful members of Society and believing members of the Church; this naturally implies the duty of providing a suitable education. It was Pietism and the sects which evolved the idea of a systematic, useful, and practical education, and which established schools for this purpose.

The relation between the sexes, conceived in a very individualistic way, softens the severity of Patriarchalism; woman especially, in the Baptist movement, gains her religious and therefore her social independence. From time to time the sects (like the mystics) have their feminine preachers and leaders of

[510] See p. 986. [510a] Cf. above, p. 691.

meetings. In the Calvinistic "Prophesyings" and conventicles of Voet, women were allowed to take a public part. In the community of Jean de la Badie, women, and especially the famous Anna von Schürmann, played a decided and independent part. Together with other reasons, the well-known position of woman in America is also connected with her religious position. It is only natural that in the whole effort to attain a more stable and more deliberate attitude towards life the attitude of children towards their parents should also become more independent. Schools and meetings for children, with the development of an independent *esprit de corps* and of independent responsibility, reveal the educational ideal of these groups. The Sunday School movement within the churches, the Young Men's Christian Association, and other similar movements all tend in this direction. The effect of this education, intensified by a democratic way of life, is one of the most striking phenomena which attract the attention of the European visitor to America.[511]

The Political Ethic

The political ethic, likewise, regards the State from a purely utilitarian standpoint. In this matter Calvinistic Natural Law prepared the way which was trodden later by the sects and the Free Churches. The only right the State has to exist is for the sake of order and of discipline, and thus to provide a basis for Society. The purely political conception of the State as an ethical end in itself, which was self-evident to the Ancient World, and which has reappeared within the modern world, does not come into the picture at all. This essentially utilitarian and essentially social, non-political conception of the State is indeed, as we have already seen in various ways, likewise a common Christian idea. It is the natural result of the transference of all true life-values into the religious sphere, which means that even in the most favourable light the rest of the life-values are only regarded as means to an end. Ascetic Protestantism, however, on the basis of rationalistic Natural Law, which, like the Puritan ethic, it instinctively takes over from Calvinism, goes much farther than Lutheranism and Catholicism.

In Catholicism the State belongs to the natural stage of existence, above which there rises the supernatural stage of Grace, which is completely indifferent to the State. In Catholicism, therefore, the State is sometimes utilized and glorified, sometimes

[511] See p. 987.

treated merely as the material for and presupposition of something else, sometimes shorn of all authority and trampled under foot by the world-organization of the Church.

In Lutheranism the State is also a part of the natural order, but as such it is a necessary form of the activity of Christian love and of the Christian spirit; but since it is still essentially a product of the natural evolution of reason which punishes and heals sin, and as such is guided by God, it gains (whether harmful or useful to the Christian aim of life) the supernatural dignity of a power which has been directly appointed by God, which, above all, must be endured and respected.

Early Calvinism, like Lutheranism, had an equally strong sense of authority, and only permitted a subsidiary ideal of utilitarian-rational interference in circumstances where the ruling powers of the State were unchristian in their behaviour. Those exceptional conditions, however, were not to be allowed to continue long, but as soon as possible they were to yield to an organized authority, and restore the social unity controlled by a State Church.

In Ascetic Protestantism, on the contrary, the organization of the State is likewise in principle deduced from the Natural Law of the fallen state, but it is always estimated according to its rational purpose, and subordinated to its responsibility not merely to God, but also to the people from whom it has received its mandate, whether legally or merely morally. The social unity controlled by a State Church has disappeared; the State no longer takes a direct part in the vital interests of the Christian churches and denominations; moreover, it has thus been forced down to the level of mere human expediency. The honours, offices, and dignities of the State are functions appointed by God and the people, but they do not proceed from inherent divine right within the government. No honours may be paid to a creature which would encroach upon the homage to be paid to God, and at bottom all are only functionaries of Providence in the natural cosmos of Society, which is designed to serve the glory of God by a way of life which is based on strict Christian principles. Within the State, therefore, there is a strong sense of the equality of all in the presence of God, a sense which is expressed particularly strongly only in the well-known customs of the Quakers, but which is in no sense an equalitarian view like that of the European democracy. This is prevented by the idea of Providence, which looks upon the social and political cosmos as divided by God, for the express purposes of Salvation, into different groups, faculties, and positions in life. This strong emphasis upon Providence is a relic of the doctrine of Predestination.

We may thus sum up the main features of the attitude of Ascetic Protestantism towards the State: it is inclined towards a liberal or democratic conception of the State, apart from equalitarian theories; it tends to regard the State simply as something which must be endured; it glorifies its own national inheritance more for its religious mission than for its political greatness; and it likes to regulate international relationships according to peace principles, which are also reasonable, and from the business point of view desirable. Ascetic Protestantism views imperialistic and nationalistic movements with a good deal of misgiving. Sometimes it rejects them on principle; sometimes it is able to justify them as an extension of Christian civilization whose sole genuine representative it feels itself to be; it has been entrusted with this destiny by God. It then regards itself in the light of the Old Testament as a "Chosen People", and absorbs Imperialism into the aim of Foreign Missions.[511a]

The Economic Ethic

The economic ethic, finally, teaches (likewise from the general Christian point of view) that labour is the result of the Fall, and is to be regarded as the penalty and the discipline of sin. But this idea is here developed into that of a rational, systematic discipline of labour, evolved, above all, in Puritanism, and thence taken over in a more or less logical manner; this ethic regards laziness and idleness as the source of all evil, and the result of a failure to impose discipline. With this systematic view of work (to which, incidentally, other than Puritan motives were sometimes added, as, for instance, among the Quakers the waiting and self-preparation for the Divine illumination), a strong and systematic impulse was given to production, while, on the other hand, with the same asceticism there is united a considerable limitation of consumption and a complete avoidance of all luxury (at least, of all that is obvious and that ministers to vanity and arrogance). It is only at this point that we see the full effect of that which has already been described as the favourable ethical disposition of Calvinism for bourgeois Capitalism. Thus this economic ethic became middle-class, one might almost say lower middle-class-capitalist, and it bore all the signs of the results of the capitalistic attitude towards life: systematic division of labour, emphasis upon specialization, the feeling for advantage and profit, the

[511a] See p. 988.

abstract duty of work, the obligation towards property as towards something great, which ought to be maintained and increased for its own sake. The owner of wealth or property is "the Lord's Steward", and administers a Divine gift which has been entrusted to him. An ethic of this kind placed at the disposal of the nascent modern bourgeois Capitalism both energetic and courageous *entrepreneurs*, and men who were willing to endure exploitation if only they could get work. This ethic differs from the Capitalism of antiquity and of the later Middle Ages by those very features which have just been described, and alongside of it the other existing kinds of Capitalism, of course, must not be overlooked.

This type of Capitalism, however, preserves its special Christian character by its taboo on pleasure-seeking and self-glorification, the sense of the duty of work for the service of God, strict honesty and reliability, the humane obligation to make provision for the workers and to give respect to employers, and the extensive use of wealth for philanthropic ends.

The system of fixed prices, the standardization and classification of goods according to their quality, the building up of business upon the strictest formal honesty, the principle "honesty is the best policy"—all arose at this point. It is the expression of a spiritual and moralistic opposition to the guild system and to unfair dealing in individual cases; it means that the life of business is constructed upon the calculation of the individual in relation to an abstract circle of purchasers, and upon the absolute necessity for correctness and honesty as regards estimates and deliveries. The inscription on the Bremen Exchange, which states that the merchant is the most honest man, should be interpreted from this point of view. The justification for the economic life lies in its value to the community, and in this sense it can be considered a blessing; in itself, however, the ideal attitude is that of the man whose spirit is inwardly entirely independent of possessions. It is even possible to go a step farther and to exalt poverty, which preserves from the dangers of wealth, just as, on the other hand, wealth, used in a Christian way, preserves the community from misery and want. Thus here also there is no idea of equality. This is prevented by the whole idea of Providence, and above all, where it was still a vital force, by the idea of Predestination. The conception is always that of a cosmos directed by God, in which the Christian Ethos only works itself out through reciprocal activities, division of labour, a variety of gifts and capacities. Thus, as Calvinism and the sects are of one mind on the question of the development of a voluntary Church, and on the question of separation between Church and State, so also their views coincide in the economic ethic of secular asceticism which determines the ethic of Ascetic Protestantism, renouncing its greater earlier freedom: Calvinism reaches this point of view under the urgent sense of need to prove in daily life the reality of its faith, and it therefore produces the systematic asceticism of labour; the passive, persecuted sect comes to this point by giving up its hostility towards the world, and by fusing its ascetic detachment from the world with the Protestant idea of the "calling". Further, both movements shared the following experience: on account of their Nonconformity and their freedom from the State, they were forcibly excluded from all official positions in the State and from its dignities; thus they were thrust out of the ruling classes and obliged to join the bourgeois middle class; this still further intensified the bourgeois capitalist element. Agriculture was not excluded, but it was only practised by the people of this class by farming, and by trading in property in land; but it has nothing to do with the feudal ownership of land.

Thus the difference between this ethic and that of the theoretical traditional economic ethic of Catholicism is clear. In this ethic, work and possessions belong to the natural sphere alone; the desire for gain does not directly concern the religious ethic at all; gain is regarded merely as a method of providing for one's needs according to one's rank in Society; whatever is earned beyond that should be used for charity; the most genuine charity, however, is actually exercised by those who possess nothing at all, by those who stand outside the ordinary work of the world altogether.

The difference between this economic ethic and that of Lutheranism is equally clear. Lutheranism, it is true, makes the task of earning a living part of the "calling" to brotherly love, but, in spite of this, it gives preference to the callings which belong to a settled order of Society consisting of agricultural labourers, manual workers, and officials; Capitalism and the calculating spirit which is continually striving to make more money is regarded by Lutheranism with detachment and extreme misgiving.

But even contrasted with primitive Calvinism, to which, with its State Church point of view, all methods of gaining a livelihood were of equal importance, which had not developed the asceticism of labour to this extent, and which had no trace of the lower middle-class spirit at all—this was something new. This was the result of that asceticism in which the Puritan, legalistic, organizing Calvinism came into contact with those sects which were comparatively ready to accept secular civilization; it was also the result of the social and political situation in which both Calvinism and the sects found themselves over against the official world.[512]

Ascetic Protestantism and its Relation to General Historical Development

Surveying all these developments as a whole, it is plain that the Christian social philosophy of Puritan Calvinism, of Pietism and the sects, and, to some extent, even that of the mystical groups, is a great unity, which, for historical significance can only be compared with the social philosophy of the Middle Ages. As in the Middle Ages, the main point for us is the theory, the intellectual orientation of a Christian work of civilization, and a Christian organization of Society. Here, as there, convinced supporters of the system, who are vitally concerned, will be in the minority. But they blaze a trail in the realm of thought, and they create ways of thinking which come to be accepted as obvious and natural, within which the general Christian consciousness and a unified attitude towards life can live and move; it does not then matter how much real seriousness there is behind each individual instance of this behaviour. The great problem of Christian supernaturalism—that of uniting and adapting itself to the practical life of Society—was solved in each instance on a great scale and in a popularly effective way: in Catholicism, by means of a universal Church, which regulates, supervises, and finally itself effects the ascent of Nature to Grace; in ascetic Protestantism, by a highly individualistic congregational system which was in harmony with modern individualism, and through the ascetic self-control of individuals who reduce the whole of secular and social life to the level of a mere method of glorifying God and proving the state of grace. Thus there are certain points of contact between the two systems, since both express the Christian hostility to the world in a systematic discipline and in asceticism.[513] They still differ fundamentally, however, since Catholicism places its ascetic ideal in opposition to the lower

[512] See p. 988.

[513] For analogies with Protestant asceticism in the monasteries so far as they introduce labour and in so doing develop systematic self-discipline, see *Max Weber: Archiv XXI, 28 ff.*; for occasional union of mysticism with the ethic of the "calling" as a means of discipline, see *XX, 50*, and *XXI, 22*.

stage of life in the world; therefore, the consequences of this lower degree break through everywhere, giving to the actual highest achievements of asceticism a directly legalistic, mortifying character. Protestant asceticism, on the contrary, gathers directly all the material of the natural life into the supernatural aim; thus it here loses its self-mortifying and dualistic character, and becomes a systematic work for the salvation of souls and for the Kingdom of God, within the setting of a secular "calling". Lutheranism certainly did not finally close the circle so firmly, and the idealistic mysticism which in some ways is so closely akin to it fell back very frequently into a purely dualistic asceticism with its emphasis upon mortification.

On the other hand, this inquiry closes with Puritan Calvinism and the "purified" communities of the sects. To what extent they will be able to dominate the modern civilized world permanently in a Christian manner is another question. This school of thought is still a power in worldhistory. But it is clear on all hands that to a great extent the State, Society, and economic life will no longer allow themselves to be dominated by it, and in their present position cannot possibly be dominated by it any longer.

Faced by all these considerations, we arrive at the last question of all—going beyond the immediate subject—the question of the connection between these views of general social conditions and their effect upon the whole of civilization. This question can only be answered with the utmost reserve, since, *1st*: until now the facts have only been known in part, and, *2nd*: the perpetually fluctuating power and range of influence makes it very difficult to give any certain interpretation of the facts.[514]

"Spiritual religion" or mysticism is not a product of particular social conditions. It proceeds from other causes: the experience of the incapacity of the churches to realize their ideal, weariness of the strife and conflict of religious parties, the pure inner dialectic of religious feeling returning to its ultimate source, the critical destruction of dogmas and cults, and weariness of the disappointments and confusions of the external life in general. Thus of itself it has no social influence upon life in general. Its inner circles do not penetrate into the masses, and its purely contemplative ideas do not grip the common life, but work purely personally, or hover in a literary manner over the whole. In modern times

[514] On the whole subject, which gathers up all his earlier ideas (in *Archiv XX* and *XXI*, and in the article in the *Chr. W.*) and carries them out further, see *Weber's Schlusswort, XXXI, pp. 584–598*. Cf. also, above, the exposition of asceticism, pp. 604–605.

certainly, its extension depends upon the existence of classes which live apart from the crude struggle for existence, and can seek spiritual refinement for their own sake, so far as it is not hidden in small evangelical sects, which also, however, have always a special sectarian trait. Beyond that it is connected with the modern scientific cultivation of the autonomous reason, in so far as this takes a religious turn. To this extent it reflects to-day the universal individualism of modern times, which indeed it still further strengthens. It accompanies social conditions, but does not arise out of them, nor does it influence them directly. Indirectly, however, the fact that it weakens the power and exclusiveness of the churches means that it has a very important social influence.

The ideal of the radical sects, on the contrary, was never developed out of the purely inward dialectic of Christian thought. In its primitive form, Christian thought left all such matters too much to a future which was to be brought about by God, even though it was expected that this would soon be realized, and it left all details in God's Hands, and not to the consideration and organization of man. After the Christian faith had adjusted itself to the present world and had become a Church, the expectation of a complete ethical world-renewal could only be introduced into Christianity from outside through the pressure of intolerable conditions; and, somehow or other, that inevitably implied human thought and human organization. Particularly threatening social and political conditions were then held to be the signs of world-renewals which were about to come, as a challenge to prepare the way of the Lord for the Kingdom of God; it was a mingled attitude of believing expectation of the Kingdom, and an actual effort to cause the new conditions. The sect-ideal, therefore, only rose to the heights of its power when the existing conditions required reform, when the history of the period seemed to point to some catastrophic event which God was about to bring to pass, which thus reawakened the expectation of the coming of the Kingdom of God.

Thus the ideal of the radical sect is always aroused only by the course of general social development. This is true also of modern Christian Socialism, which was only brought into existence first of all by the revelation of the results of the capitalist system, and, above all, by the great Socialist Movement; in its most advanced groups, in fact, the Socialist Movement is interpreted as a sign of a world-upheaval willed by God.

For that very reason, therefore, the influence of Christian

Socialism is always of a secondary nature, being exerted alongside those more general movements, which it merely interprets, appropriates, and rectifies. Christianity does not breed social revolution. It can only adjust itself, with a certain sense of strain, to the modern social revolution, which, although it is not violent, is still very radical in principle. The aim of Christian Socialism is to effect a change in the hearts and minds of men which is orientated towards God, and not towards the world. The modern realization of the fact that spiritual values are intimately connected with the material social basis of life must always be stressed very strongly, if it is to lead to a thorough social reform, or even to the revolution of Society. At present it is very difficult to estimate to what extent its efforts to educate the wealthier classes in their social responsibilities, and the working classes in a spirit of confidence and moderation, have actually influenced the class-war. The importance of Christian Socialism in England is well known. In other countries it is harder to estimate its significance. In any case, it exists. In these matters material circumstances speak louder than ideas; but they need to be filled with idealistic content. In this respect Christian Socialism certainly has a mission, although it will scarcely be able to build up the new social order.[514a]

Social Influence of Ascetic Protestantism

On the other hand, the social influence of Ascetic Protestantism upon the history of civilization has been penetrating and comprehensive.[515] Through its ecclesiastical ideal, which merges into the ideal of the Free Churches, the democratic constitution of its individual congregations, as well as of its general ecclesiastical structure, its autonomous individualism, based upon the Will of God and the fact of Redemption, and its systematic and positive industry, it has become one of the basic causes of the immense changes in modern Society; this spirit has only been brought into Catholic and Lutheran countries from outside; but it would never have been created solely by the new economic, political, and technical conditions of the modern world. This fact must be regarded as one result of this inquiry. At this point it is impossible to make a balanced estimate of the influence exerted by the forces which have moulded modern society; it is sufficient to point out that Ascetic Protestantism has made an important contribution to the whole. Of course, we might express the

[514a] Cf. *Sombart: Sozialismus und soziale Bewegung, pp. 19, 100, 252, 262.*

[515] See p. 989.

question differently—thus: Did this achievement only become possible to Ascetic Protestantism, or was it even forced upon it by its adjustment to the surrounding world of progressive Western Europe? In the course of this inquiry this point also has been discussed several times. The country round Geneva already contained impulses of that kind; undoubtedly France, Holland, and England contained still more. Also the fact that, in many countries, its members were forcibly excluded from the official world has helped to shape it. On the whole, however, in face of developments which agree with each other in so many entirely different forms of civilization, and sometimes in such unfavourable surroundings, it is surely permissible to emphasize here the primary significance of the religious and ethical idea, which, indeed, from the very outset bore within itself a great power of adaptation to practical and average needs.[515a] To-day, however, its spirit has very largely vanished from that which it essentially helped to create. Its creations have passed into other hands, and are being shaped by them according to their purposes. This is particularly true of the transformation of the results of the English Puritan Revolution by the French Revolution, and its intellectual and literary impulses. Against this "Enlightenment", however, created by the Latin and Catholic peoples, which sends out its rationalistic and abstract ideas in every direction, there contends to this day everywhere the conception of human society and its aims which has been formed in the school of Ascetic Protestantism. Pre-eminently its spirit is incarnate in the Anglo-Saxon world. So far as the social struggle of the present day is spiritual and concerned with questions of principle, it turns upon the question of this conflict between the Corporation-idea of Anglo-Saxon Calvinism and the Democracy of French Rationalism; Catholic and Lutheran Patriarchalism have retired into the background. This general opposition tends to modify group differences within Protestantism to an appreciable extent. Calvinism and the sect-movement have found each other. But Lutheranism also is being slowly drawn into the forward march of the Protestant social doctrines, and is being influenced by Ascetic Protestantism. This process of development will increase when, as we may expect with certainty, it is no longer supported by the State.

Protestant ecclesiasticism, which began as the Reform of Catholicism, and which had built up a new uniform and compulsory Christian civilization, was led to an ever greater extent

[515a] Cf. above, p. 631.

to sever its social doctrines from these early universal ecclesiastical developments. The first great structure which arose out of this process of separation was Ascetic Protestantism. It has founded and evolved the main body of Protestant civilization. But its power is weakening, and Protestantism is thus faced by new tasks, both in its own sociological development and in its corporate connection with civilization.

NOTES TO CHAPTER III

[197a] (p. 465.) On this point we must mention especially the well-known biography of Luther by *Denifle*, who emphasizes rightly that Luther was not influenced by Thomism, and indeed that he only had a limited acquaintance with this philosophy. When, however, this leads him to accuse Luther of ignorance of the whole great system of Catholic science, saying that in his ignorance he had stuck obstinately to a less valuable scientific form of Catholicism, and that therefore all his polemics are misdirected, we can only explain this by concluding that this is part of the modern Catholic apologetic. In reality, Occamism was the real reason for the break-up of the unity of Catholic civilization and theology, whose position had become untenable, and to that extent it constituted the natural foundation for a new interpretation and development of Christian thought. On this point cf. *W. Köhler: Ein Wort zu Denifles Luther, 1904*. The basis of Luther's thought upon Occamism is strongly and rightly emphasized in the extremely interesting book by *Hermelink: Die theologische Fakultät in Tübingen, 1477–1534, 1906*, in which for the first time there is clearly set forth the relation between Thomism and Occamism in this important transition period (on this point cf. my review in *G.G.A., 1909*). *Linsenmann: Gabriel Biel und der Nominalismus, Theol. Quartalschrift, 1865*, takes this same point of view which is so important for Lutheran thought. This Nominalism, however, still continues the main features of mediaeval Christian piety, in so far as it still regards the Universal Church and the Christian nature of the whole of Society as perfectly natural assumptions; the co-operation of the laity, of the secular authorities, of the councils is more strongly emphasized in this ideal, the rational metaphysical basis of theology is set aside, and its authoritative and revelational character is increased.

[198] (p. 467.) *Kautsky's* position is naturally that of a man who traces the origin of the Reformation to class movements (*Sozialismus in Einzeldarstellungen, I, 1, pp. 239–251*). To him Luther is an agitator who provides a religious sanction for the communistic-democratic opposition, and an unprincipled courtier who supplies a religious sanction for the rising absolutism; his great influence is supposed to be due to this dual position. The real hero of the Reformation is Thomas Münzer, who did not possess Luther's second detestable characteristic. Reasons for these statements are not given in this superficial sketch, which is entirely lacking in understanding. A similar view is expressed by *Kalthoff: Das Zeitalter der Reformation. hg. von Steudel, 1907*, from the point of view of the theory of the collectivist interpretation of history. The editor says: "In the economic and class struggles *K.* gives us an insight into the innermost driving forces in that whole mighty upheaval of civilization, and we thus are able to understand the personalities which emerge from the fight between declining and fresh groups of interests" (*VIII*). The author, however, makes no attempt to carry out this programme. *K.* contents himself with pointing out in a quite general way the bourgeois character of the Reformation, illustrated chiefly by Dürer and Hans Sachs. There is certainly something true in this, but it does certainly not mean that a class struggle was the chief cause of the Reformation —*Dilthey: Die Glaubenslehre der Reformatoren* (*Preuss. Jahrbb., 75, 1894*), and *Arnold Berger: Die Kulturaufgaben der Reformation, 1895*, and *Lutherbiographie, I², 1908*, emphasize strongly the indirect influence of the development of the towns, the increasing influence of the laity in the Church, and the solid virtues of the bourgeois way of life. Here, quite rightly, the Reformation

movement is placed within the absolutely necessary broad setting of the general history of civilization. But, as so easily happens in such a comprehensive view, the lines which converge in Luther become indistinct, and the definite concrete conception of Luther's own development also suffers. Luther is still essentially a monk who follows the great mediaeval way of the realization and concentration of the religious life, the way of monasticism, and he is also a theologian who first of all comes to his own position through inward experience, and the theological study of late Scholasticism, of mysticism, of St. Augustine, of St. Bernard, and of the New Testament, and only from this does he enter into relation with the tendencies of his time. In these books the authors also overlook the fact that Luther starts from the conception of the Church, and gives it a new connotation, but that he does not substitute for it a non-ecclesiastical form of mysticism and lay religion. This means that from the very beginning the aim is laid down which is implied in the ecclesiastical objectivity of the Word and the Sacrament, and the further consequence of the conception of the Church; further on this subject is treated in greater fullness. Therefore primarily Luther is an ecclesiastical theologian, and quite distinct from sectarian leaders, as well as from the representatives of a purely lay religion, whose outlook is wholly individualistic. Therefore all presentations of the subject err which do not conceive him as a Church reformer, but as a representative of the purely individualistic lay religion which many modern people of the present day prefer, and who, therefore, place Luther in an exaggerated historical succession of late mediaeval lay religion and bourgeois thought, instead of in the direct line of theological tradition. We have to be surer of the facts of the influence of the former element in his pre-monastic period; this can only be discovered through the medium of the study of late Scholasticism, mysticism, and Humanism, which in any case did contain new sociological points of view; this, however, in view of the nature of the subject, would be a very difficult task.—The relation between his doctrine, which had already been formulated in its main features, and the Lutheran propaganda, to the social tendencies of the time is now illuminated in the important work by *Barge: Andreas Bodenstein von Karlstadt, II, 1905*. According to this work Luther's own doctrine in its final form is everywhere on the side of government, and its interest in order, which desires the reform of the Church, the breaking of the power of the hierarchy, a policy of secularization, and a morally authoritative control of the excited masses of the population; Luther himself is only interested in social reform within these limits, after the first great ideal hopes of the Reformation had failed, which he had expressed in his treatise *To the Nobility of the German Nation*, and after the failure of the nobility to meet his hopes caused him to turn to the idea of small groups of genuine Christians with a Christian *Kastenordnung*; the cause of this failure was due to actual conditions. To Luther social reform was always only a secondary question; in fact it only interested him in so far as it provided a better basis for the religious life. The fact is that Luther's interests were purely religious, and that otherwise his was an entirely conservative nature. At the same time the social revolutionary endeavours of the peasants and of the proletariat of the great towns were taking place, whose religious elements were more Hussite or Taborite in character, and although they were drawn into the agitation caused by the Lutheran movement, they were neither spiritually nor theologically determined by it. Finally also there was a third group of reform movements which *Barge* especially mentions; it was composed mainly of small artisans with whom the clergy and schoolmasters were in sympathy; this group was strongly anti-clerical, and wished to see a free lay Christianity of the Congregational type which would entirely do away with Catholic ritual, theologically would get rid of the authority of the Church and an official ministry, and which wished to introduce all kinds of social and ethical reforms under the wing of the State and of the administration of justice, in the sense of a severer form of the Christian way of life and charitable activity, and also elementary Christian social reform in Society in general; all this, however, is not to take place through the territorial princes, but through the local authorities and the parish representatives; the latter groups accept radical anti-sacramental theology, and provide the soil for the Baptists, since everywhere the territorial lords or the stronger neighbouring powers suppress all communal independence of that kind. Here also there is an entire lack of any clear idea of a comprehensive and uniform reshaping of the Church, like that which was developed by Calvinism, at a later date, with similar ideas. These ideas are simply local and temporary in character, based on the expectation that in some way or another the order of the whole Church will come into being. As naturally this order did not arise, these aspirations provided a fertile soil for the development of Separatist communities or of the Baptists. Thus, from this side also we see that it is quite impossible to describe the Reformation doctrine as determined by the outlook of one particular class and its development. As *Barge* several times points out, a very great part was played, on the other hand, by the aversion to the Catholic Church and the independent spirit of the laity which had developed during the later mediaeval times; this latter movement was, of course, deeply rooted not merely in an opposition in ideals but in real social facts. We also ought not to underestimate the importance of Bible study by the masses in a time which was so penetrated with religious ideas. The enormous controversial literature, with its extremely detailed Biblical exposition which is quite unintelligible to us modern men, can only be understood from the standpoint of an independent religious interest in the attempt to square life and doctrine with the standard of the Bible. Further, we have to take into account the fact of a sediment of demagogy—the kind of thing which always forms part of universal agitations of this kind—which gives rise to the most varied and wild meaningless and chaotic extravagances.—I have just given an outline of the most important ideas in *Barge's* book, but at the same time I have made clear the points in which I disagree with him. "Lay Christian Puritanism", whose apostle, Karlstadt, he describes in a strongly partisan spirit (cf. *Karl Müller: Luther und Karlstadt, 1907*), is neither the logical result of Lutheran thought, nor is it a hopeful programme for German conditions; the reason for this will emerge in the analysis of Calvinism.

[200] (p. 469.) Well formulated in *Preuss: Die Entwickelung des Schriftprinzips bei Luther bis zur Leipziger Disputation, 1901, p. 34*; it was the Scholastic doctrine that "the sacraments of the New Covenant *opere operato* are channels of grace of a purely positive, as well as ethical and religious power. All that is required is that the recipient should place no barrier. This corresponded entirely to the whole mediaeval fundamental idea which conceived the relation between God and man as something, properly speaking, quite concrete, as an exchange of mutual activity, as a relationship of service and reward. This point of view (which Luther also shared at the beginning, but which was so little able to satisfy him that it almost drove him to despair) was for him, after that fundamental experience, in principle overcome; in place of the old relationship there now emerged a relationship which is interpreted as one based upon God's grace, as an entirely personal turning of God towards the sinner, and of the

faith of man, that is: his personal confidence in God, his purely personal relationship." The vital point is this: that Luther could find no peace in the Catholic sacraments, and that in his preparation for the Sacrament all he could feel was conviction of sin, the oppression of the law, and self-righteousness. This explains his different religious feeling, and it is from this standpoint that he appeals to the Pauline assurance of grace in Christ. *Böhmer* (*Luther im Licht der Neueren Forschung, 1906*), who accuses me of a misunderstanding by making the doctrine of the Sacrament the starting-point of Luther's theory when it should be regarded as an important result, says the same thing: "Grace is no longer conceived by him as a supernatural energy or medicine which is imparted to men through the sacraments, and which then ought to bring forth spiritual and moral results, but an attitude of God which is proclaimed in the Word of God and works through the means of the Word just as otherwise the manifestation of a spirit is manifested through a word" (*p. 17*). That is exactly my own meaning, and all that Böhmer says about me is due to a misunderstanding. Entirely in agreement with my own point of view is *Gottschick's* definition, *Die Lehre der Ref. v. d. Taufe, 1906, p. 13.*

[201] (p. 469.) On this point and that which follows, cf. my presentation of the subject in the *Kultur der Gegenwart, I, IV, 1: Protestantisches Christentum und Kirche.* In it also the literature upon which my views are based is given in full. In the second edition of 1909 I accepted the objections which had been raised. Essentially in the positive conception they made no difference; they were only concerned with my habit of contrasting the thought-world of the Reformation with the modern thought-world. That, however, is a point of view which Protestantism as a whole must adopt, because it is only so that we can understand the crisis through which it is passing at the present day. For the present work this point of view disappears. Here we are solely concerned with the special subject of the confessional Protestant social doctrines, compared with the Latin Catholic and the early Christian social teaching. Here, however, also it will become clear that fundamental assumptions have been maintained which only Latin Catholicism had gained; indeed, from the sociological and ethical side the continuity is much clearer than from the side of pure dogma, which is the aspect with which theologians are usually entirely concerned. Since, namely, the exclusive dominion of religious authority and the stable constitution of secular society in accordance with that as well as of the secular thought of the Middle Ages and of early Protestantism are common to both, and since the whole system in both cases is based upon this exclusiveness of authority and stability, and since, further, this exclusiveness and stability on the spiritual and secular side of an established Christian civilization and society both theoretically and actually is the work of the Middle Ages, this then forms the presupposition of Protestantism and this thought goes on working out in Protestantism. The deep differences are naturally not to be overlooked, but they move within a common framework. And it is precisely this common framework which the modern world had broken; indeed, that is the element which quite clearly is to be fixed in it alone as its character; cf. my discussion, *Das Wesen des Modernen Geistes, Preuss. Jahrbb., 1907.* With the breaking down of this framework, however, then only will the motives of Protestantism which are related to the modern world become free and find a development which leads far away from the meaning and spirit of the Reformers in whose minds that framework was most closely connected with the subject itself; see my article, *Luther und die Moderne Welt in das Christentum, Leipzig, 1907.*

[204] (p. 473.) This variation between direct Divine appointment and indirect

causation through Natural Law is characteristic of the strongly religious-positivist attitude of Lutheran thought. Both, however, are combined in the idea that in one way or another God alone is the Author of all these things, and that particular institutions are only direct manifestations of the otherwise indirect Law of Nature which mediates the Divine Will; see *Luthardt: Luthers Ethik, 1867, pp. 94 ff.*: "The natural ordinances and classes . . . belong only to this temporal and natural life. But although they are only secular classes, and are subordinate to reason, that does not imply that they are profane, but they are instituted, ordained, and willed by God, and God is present within them. For God uses His creatures like a 'mask' behind which He Himself is concealed and behind this 'veil' He does all things. . . . The view of the active presence of God in all His creatures and ordinances he has always maintained. If, however, these secular classes are the will and ordinance of God, and if He is present within them, then also there must be a relation between them and the Gospel. For they are both of God even though they are different—on the one hand, they are the ordinance of God the Creator and now of God the Redeemer." Here we must point out that it is at this point that the conservative conception of Natural Law and Natural Right arises within Lutheranism; cf. *Eugen Ehrhardt: La Notion du Droit Naturel chez Luther (Festschrift von Paris für Montauban, 1901, pp. 287–320)*.

[207] (p. 476.) The sects also had already discarded the idea of an ascent from Nature to Super-Nature as has been shown already. But also the late Scholasticism of the Occamists with its restored emphasis upon the absolute opposition between Grace and Nature had also discarded this conception together with the ideas of reconciliation and development which it involved; see *Hermelink: Die theologische Fakultät in Tübingen, 1906, pp. 111 and 122*. For the Primitive State this difference has already been set aside, since it is argued that there was no ascent from connatural perfection to supernatural perfection, but perfection in itself is conceived as a *debitum naturae*, and on account of the weakness of man only needs to be filled with supernatural grace; see *Linsenmann: a.a.O., pp. 648–651*. We may, however, say that Luther's discarding of those conceptions was so far original to the extent in which its motive was not the radicalism of the opposition but the idea of the essential connection between Grace and Nature within the Will of God. It is here that there arises the peculiar limitation in contrast with Catholicism that the Lutheran relationship between Grace and Nature makes possible on the one hand an inner combination, an immanence of Grace in Nature, but that on the other hand, since Nature is appointed merely by an act of will as the sphere for the exercise of Grace, all inner union and reconciliation between the two disappears and genuine Protestantism finds it much more difficult to have an inner relation with "Nature". The Catholic assertion that Protestantism has much less inward connection with Nature and with civilization is to that extent right, and is based upon this fact, a circumstance which is usually not noticed by Protestant controversialists.

[208] (p. 482.) *Rudolf Sohm* has illustrated his well-known thesis that Church and Law are absolutely inconsistent particularly by Luther, to whom he ascribes the complete removal of every element of law out of the conception of the Church: "Luther declared war on every kind of Church law, every kind of Divine Church law, and in principle likewise on all Church order which is merely human, historical, and therefore changeable, which gives itself out to be such of whatever kind it be" (*Kirchenrecht, I, 1892, p. 461*). I cannot consider this statement accurate in this form. Luther certainly spiritualized

to the utmost the conception of the Church and of religion, and he knew neither a quantitative doctrinal belief, but only a spirit which tended towards the Gospel as a whole, nor a compulsory orthodoxy, but only religious instruction alongside of the suppression of heretical expressions as a disturbing rebellion against the Christian order of Society. But since his spiritualized conception of the Church still has its outward tangibility through supernatural concrete signs in the pure Word which is to be kept pure, as also in the Sacrament which is to be rightly taught and administered, so, then, there arises out of this the necessity of creating an apparatus of legal protection and of legally regulated administration for them. Luther only does not attempt this as long as he leans wholly upon the idea of the miraculous power of the Word which will naturally effect everything by its own power, and as long as the old ecclesiastical order continues. Later, however, this super-idealism was disillusioned. In the period of fermentation and of varied local attempts at reform Luther allowed the congregations to try to create their own new order of administration and he gave this his sanction. When, however, nothing came of this and the Peasants' War brought in its train a dangerous abuse of these reforms, he desired a general new order for the sake of the country, and then in the new Territorial Church Luther had to tolerate a human apparatus of law for the assistance of the Word, and incidentally he even had to encourage it, for which the early beginnings lay in the purity of the doctrine and the sacraments and the necessity for an ordered ministry. Out of these relics of a visible and concrete Church there arose once more, as at one time out of the visibility of the episcopal office, necessarily a law. Here also this does not mean that Luther has denied his earlier position, but the reappearance of the consequence of the Church conception which at first had been severely checked; this Church conception implied a supernatural and therefore universal institution, which in certain definite aspects also needed to be outwardly tangible, with a permanent external constitution. If by a Church a supernatural institution is meant which is visible in revelation and in sacrament, this then produces also out of these supernatural elements a supernaturally established law, whether the basis of this law and its creation is left to the congregations themselves or handed over to the civil authority; inferences will always be drawn out of a basis of (supernatural) fellowship which demands the formation of law. Even though its carrying out may be entrusted to circumstances, regarded as purely human and liable to be changed at will, the law itself may change, but the demand for its formation remains. Only a conception of the Church, which has resolved itself into a purity of doctrine and sacraments which can dispense with the visible (which is a purely religious general spirit and a purely inner fellowship), can dispense with law. But then this would not be a conception of the Church at all, and it was not Luther's conception of the Church. That idea is purely the conception of religion as something vital which cannot be touched or defined, and its opposition to law is no longer the opposition between Church and law, but between religion and law, which certainly is a fundamental and real difference. This points, however, to a tension between religion and the Church itself which shows that in reality the two are not identical. Out of this tension there always arises the emancipation of religion from the objectivity of the institution and of the supernatural authority, and the turning towards an unlimited inwardness of mysticism and of spirituality, as, indeed, the mystics and Spiritual Reformers of the Reformation period have done, believing that they were developing to their logical conclusion the ideas of the Reformers. Cf. my discussion, *Religion und Kirche*,

Preuss. Jahrbb., 1895. The Church conception of *Sohm* fluctuated between that of a universal and supernatural institution and that of a purely spiritual and intellectual connection which consists solely in the wealth of its subjective personal effects. That, however, is a Church conception adapted to modern requirements. Here I must agree with Höfling's and Ritschl's conception, which *Sohm* borrows (*p. 467*). The passages from Luther on the contrary, which *Sohm* quotes, do not seem to me to prove his thesis, but only to show that Luther found it very difficult to combine the spirituality, voluntary nature, and inwardness of his idea of a religious community with the necessity of law which was required by the need of a pure message and an ordered ministry—that law remains to Luther always something human which only has to be tolerated, but that in its necessary issuing forth from the Word and the Sacrament in itself still is always, at least at the starting-point, a *jus divinum.* Thence also the development of the conception of the ministry in Lutheranism and of the constitution of elders in Calvinism. Here certainly there are inconsistencies, but they are involved in a conception of the Church which asserts at the same time that it is visible and invisible, voluntary and universal. These inconsistencies belong to the conception of the Church itself; they are not due to the combination of law with the conception of the Church. There will be more about this in the next section.

210 (p. 484.) For Luther's conception of the Church, which from the very outset was closely connected with the new idea of salvation, its independence of Huss, and its inner difference from the Hussite teaching, *v.* the excellent discussion by *Gottschick: Huss, Luthers und Zwinglis Lehre von der Kirche, Z. f. Kirchengeschichte, VIII, 1886.* In contrast with the Hussite idea of a fellowship of the elect, which works itself out through the institution of the Church, but which makes the divinity of the ecclesiastical institutions and of the priests dependent upon agreement with the ethical law of Christ and thus approaches the Donatist sectarian idea in spite of the assertion of the Catholic nature of the sacraments, with complete exclusion of all sectarian making the Church dependent upon the realization of the law of Christ, it is the institution of grace, or of the Word which by baptism includes all, but which only rules all by the word of grace. Therefore here also his emphasis on Scripture is different. *P. 377:* "Huss's Scriptural principle differs from that of the Reformers in this respect—for the Reformers the standard of ideas which forms the main content of the Scriptures, and which they, through the authority of the same, maintain against the authoritative demands of the Catholic ecclesiastical legal institution, is the Gospel of the free grace of God in Christ which grants forgiveness apart from all human merit; for Huss, however, it is the Gospel law."—The presupposition of all this is Infant Baptism and its general extension. Both Luther and the population in general which believed in the unity of the Christian Society regarded this as obvious; when in the Visitations Luther came across people who had not been baptized, baptism was administered immediately without anyone thinking that this was a compulsory religious observance. Cf. *Barge: Karlstadt, II, p. 142.* Luther never doubted the validity of Infant Baptism, and that means he never doubted the necessity for its universal administration, as *Karl Müller* rightly maintains against *Barge*; all he had to do was to make his idea of the nature of the baptismal process to agree with his general idea of the process of salvation, which he effected by his theory of a slumbering faith effected in the children. Cf. *Karl Müller: Luther und Karlstadt, 217–221.* Thus Luther's Church conception can never be understood merely out of his opposition to the Catholic Church, but also out of his opposition to

the sects, and here Infant Baptism and its universal character form the decisive element. Then there must be added alongside of this opposition to the Catholic conception of the Church the setting aside of the *jus divinum* of the hierarchy, the destruction of the concrete conception of the Sacrament and of Grace, the reduction of all the effect of the Church, and of redemption to a purely spiritual effect of the Word, that is: all the important features which are implied in the Catholic conception of the Church: its institutional character, its objectivity, its authority over the individual, universality and its dominion over the whole of Society, which is here, however, now conceived solely in a spiritual sense.—For the close connection of Luther's conception of the Church with the idea of Infant Baptism, in which the incorporation in the process of salvation of the institution of the Word which is based upon faith is completed and thus to everyone a basis is given which is independent of his own efforts; cf. *Gottschick: Die Lehre der Reformation von der Taufe, 1906*. Infant Baptism is commanded and I know of no place, even when the spiritual struggle was being most hotly waged, when the question of baptizing or not baptizing children was ever discussed. With that, however, the main thing has been decided: an institutional connection which manifests itself primarily in the general use of Infant Baptism.—That involves the idea of the *Corpus Christianum* which has been so strongly emphasized by *Rieker: Die Rechtliche Stellung der ev. Kirchen Deutschlands, 1903*, and by *J. N. Figgis: From Gerson to Grotius*, within which its secular and spiritual power are only different sides of one undivided whole. That, however, is the mediaeval idea of the unity of Christian civilization and Society. Out of this idea there result all the main features of Protestant social doctrine. *Böhmer* thinks that he is speaking against this thesis when he says: "Meanwhile in one theoretical point Luther also, it seems, remained in bondage to mediaeval thought, that is, in his view of the Church. To him, as to Catholicism, the Church was not a free association constituted by men, but an institution established by God whose work it is to proclaim the Word of God, to comfort men's hearts, and counsel their consciences. Thus have we here to do really only with a transformation of the mediaeval idea? Not at all; here we have only to do with a new formulation of the general Christian view of the Church in which once more the specifically Catholic element, namely, the opinion that a definite external legal order is essential to the Church, has been completely set aside. For faith in the Church as having been established by God through which and in which the Spirit of God is active in the world, is as old as Christianity" (*p. 120*). Certainly, but the decisive point is this, that alongside of the Church-type there is the sect-type, which is equally ancient, and it also has its roots in the New Testament; further, that the Church-type only effected an inner penetration of the Church and the world through Latin Catholicism in the *Corpus Christianum* or in the Christian Society which implied the duty of the Government to protect this unity by guaranteeing and protecting the institution, and that this idea is continued by Protestantism and therefore that the essentially Catholic element does not consist merely in uniting the Church to an external legal order. In its continually increasing opposition to the sect-type Protestantism conforms to the Church-type, and, indeed, to the mediaeval Church-type with its ideal of a uniform Christian Society; and therefore also its social doctrines in many respects are so closely related to those of Catholicism. Whether in that we see a limitation or an eternal truth is a matter of theological opinion. The fact remains that in the modern world the religious roots of the Church conception and therefore of it itself have become very weak, and that means that its social doctrines are also of a quite different type.—For the Lutheran conception of the Church in its intellectual form see *Kolde: Luthers Stellung zu Konzil und Kirche bis zum Wormser Reichstag, 1876; J. Köstlin: Luthers Lehre von der Kirche, 1853; R. Seeberg: Der Begriff der christlichen Kirche, I, 1885.*

[211] (p. 485.) The idea that, essentially, the Church ought as far as possible to control Society, and at the same time to assimilate civilization, has been very characteristically formulated by the late President of the Prussian Supreme Church Council, *H. von der Goltz,* in *Grundlagen der christlichen Sozialpolitik, 1908, p. 203:* "The Church (which to him is, naturally, the same as the 'religious community') appears in all three forms of social life (namely, the Family, the State, and Society), but it is not exhausted by any one of them, and cannot be supported solely by any one of these forms. As a Church (and, indeed, as a universal united Church, which has only been broken in historically by Catholic corruption) she asserts a right to an independent existence and activity, apart from all the social groups of natural and earthly life. This dominant position of the Church in the social world is based on the co-operation of four factors: (1) On the Christian conception of revelation, which recognizes in the historic Person of Christ not only the instrument, but also the content, of the revelation of the Invisible God, and the Church as the organ of the perfect final Word of God to men, as the supporter of the absolute religious-moral truth (that is, the objective and absolute conception of Truth); (2) the transference of the real goal of humanity into the future life, so that all that is earthly only appears as a school for eternity, and the Church is the mediator of the heavenly good (that is, the sole power of the Church to impart salvation); (3) the union of the separated groups and classes of the world of humanity into an international commonwealth, which ethically overcomes all social opposition (that is, the universality which is the result of the two previous factors); (4) the moral quickening, and the harmonious shaping, of the whole life of civilization, from the standpoint of religious principle, as the means of combining all moral tasks into a unity (that is, the acceptance of the life of the world which is the consequence of the claim to universality; the fact that this secular spirit is incompatible with the New Testament, *von der Goltz,* like all Churchmen, does not feel at all). Through the combination of these four factors the Church succeeded in forming for the spiritual life of religion its own historical body, which it made important as the highest and most complete form of social life. The Church has its most distinctive foundation in Revelation, its main aim is the education and union of mankind for eternity, it works through its international organization, and in the cultivation of human life in the realm of culture." This characterization is expressly applied to the Church as a whole, that is, both to Catholicism and to Protestantism (*pp. 24–30*). Only within this common framework do the differences appear between Catholicism and Protestantism. *P. 284:* "This conception of the position of the Church in the common life of humanity may, however, be interpreted in very different ways. The Catholic Church makes its organism an independent aim, and everywhere makes the external form as important as the spiritual content (?). Protestantism knows that all that is ecclesiastical only has value when it is aiming at an inwardly free, but also absolutely firm and certain, union, and (here lies the difficulty of the Protestant conception of the Church) of the core of the personality (!) with God." This logical and likewise unimaginative statement shows the complicated character of the Protestant conception of the Church. It does not become any clearer in the following attempt at a closer definition: "The Church may not treat her changeable

corporate form and doctrine, ritual and constitution as an aim, but as times change these things must be regarded as methods which are adjusted to these changes, in order to cultivate communion with God in the hearts of men, and to have a purifying and hallowing influence inwardly upon the world of civilization. And even if, in so doing, her rightful influence is threatened, she must not cling to external supports, but she must make her services desirable, and radiate the righteousness of God as a victorious power into the consciences of men. Only with such a high conception of her ethical tasks, based upon the right spirit, can the Church maintain her healthy (that is, not compulsorily formed, and therefore joyfully supported) relation to the tasks of civilization, and to the various groups of natural moral fellowship." In these expressions all the peculiarities of the Church conception, and all the particular difficulties of the Protestant Church conception, are found together; the latter consist in the combination of inner freedom and absolute stability, of universal dominion and spiritual propagation combined with the renunciation of all compulsory authority, of a future and eternal goal and a harmonious permeation of civilization, of an objective institution and a personal religion of sentiment. Also the relation of this Church to "natural" society, which *von der Goltz* constructs, is only a modern form of the Lutheran *Lex Naturae*, and of the social system which is evolved from it. Similarly, one of the most active ecclesiastical leaders of the Conservatives, *R. Seeberg*, describes a "healthy piety" as one which is both "Churchly" and friendly to civilization, that is, "pressing into the business of life and sanctifying it" (*Die Kirchlich-Soziale Idee und die Aufgaben der Theologie der Gegenwart, Zur syst. Theol., II, 1909, p. 327*). This is required "both by the nature of man and by the history of civilization and of religion" (*p. 328*). "All forms of the natural life in the State, and in politics, in trade and industry, in science and in art, also all the great doings of the mighty ones of the world, and all the work of everyday men and women, are to the Christian the workings of God, in which is prepared and realized the coming of his Kingdom. The distinction between the State and the Church, however important it may be in other directions, ought never to mean that God is only active in the Church, or that God's servants are free from the duty of serving Him in the family, in the national life, in society, and in the State" (*p. 334*). This means the dominion of the Church over civilization apart from the hierarchical methods of authority, and the dominating spirit of Catholicism. For *Seeberg* this is the natural meaning of Jesus, and of the New Testament: "The redeeming dominion of God (made effective through the Church and the ministry) is the creative and guiding principle of human history, and it so organizes this history along lines of development completed through mutual influence as to lead to the goal of the Kingdom of God. Both these primitive Christian (!) ideas determine the peculiar world-view of Christianity" (*p. 333*). Therefore, to *Seeberg*, as also to the Catholics *Mausbach, von Nostitz-Rieneck*, and others, the Church is the "principle of progress". Owing to the fact that it is based upon absolute Divine truths, the Church is naturally, in the main, absolutely conservative, but "the brake is also a method of progress, since without it the carriage would roll over the nearest precipice and be smashed to bits". All these ideas are in reality also the leading ideas of the Lutheran conception of the Church, only they have been translated into the flatness of modern academic terminology, without any understanding of the difficult problems which Luther felt these ideas contained.

212 (p. 487.) For the development of the authority and sole infallibility of the Bible, together with the establishment of this infallibility upon the practical

experience of salvation which is the sole experience of redemption in the Bible, see *Preuss: Entwickelung des Schriftprinzips bei Luther, 1901*. On *pp. 6, 14*, and *60*, the author rightly distinguishes it from the Humanist principle of Scripture which uses historical methods and studies the sources, thus leading it to an estimate of the original situation, but in no way leading to a basis of religious infallibility. He also treats very aptly the relation with mysticism which ignores the mediation of the Church and of the Bible in its immediate intercourse with God: Luther modifies the idea of the union of the soul with God to mean the union of the soul with the Word, and always relates the general principle of revelation and redemption of the Logos to Christ and the Word of Christ; he does this to such an extent that even the glory of the Creation through the Logos, the Christian view of Nature, is mediated through meditation on Christ and the Word. For the relation between Luther's free and critical treatment of Scripture and his view of the infallibility of the Scriptures which he held firmly at the same time, see *Scheel: Luthers Stellung zur h. Schrift, 1902*. Luther, and above all the Lutheran Church, found in the end that they could not unite both and they gave up the former in favour of the latter. That, however, was only the logical result of the need of ecclesiastical authority and organization. It could not be helped, there was simply nothing else to be done. The attempts of present-day theologians to return to Luther's earlier theory of Scripture, which combined criticism and authority and only used the Scriptures as the standard for practical religious life, presuppose first the stability of existing churches which could only have been gained by the orthodox theory of Scripture, and, secondly, will never be able to create unity, since nowhere at all can we draw an authoritative line. The principle of Scripture which is bound up with the conception of the Church and of absolute truth, and a unity in standard and doctrine, must inevitably develop into orthodox doctrine, just as the institution of the Papacy issues in the infallible monarchical seat of doctrinal authority, and modern orthodoxy which accepts higher criticism is in the same position as Catholic Modernism, which tries to turn the Papacy into a system of authority and supervision which is merely pedagogical in character.

[213] (p. 491.) *Rieker*, who has also triumphantly vindicated the significance of the mediaeval idea of the *Corpus Christianum* for Luther, has certainly found difficulties in this "Congregational" ideal. He has tried to solve them too easily by describing them as a mistaken bias towards the Baptist sect-type (he seems to base these remarks on some meagre suggestions by *Achelis* on this question); he seems to consider that this phase of Luther's life was a tribute which he paid to the tendencies of the time, with which he had little affinity (*Rieker, pp. 74–86; Achelis: System der Prakt. Theol., I, 35 ff.*). Against this interpretation *Walther Köhler* has reacted in a very instructive piece of research: *Die Entstehung der reformatio ecclesiarum Hassiae von 1526, Deutsche Z. f. Kirchenrecht, 1906, pp. 199–232*, and in an article, *Zu Luthers Kirchenbegriff, Christl. Welt, 1907, pp. 371–377*. His view is that the previous theory is a misunderstanding and an under-estimate of the Congregational ideal. That was followed by the penetrating research of *Drews*: *Entsprach das Staatskirchentum dem Ideal Luthers? 1908*, who answers this question in the negative, and who pleads that the Congregational ideal can very well be united with the fundamental idea of the Church, but that it was limited at that time because of the period of transition in which it was conceived; all that matters is the establishment of the Word, the method employed to do this is indifferent; since finally this could only be effected with the aid of the territorial lord, whose assistance Luther accepted as a service of

love but not as dominion. Still more decided in his views of the connection between the Congregational ideal and actual local conditions is *Karl Müller: Luther und Karlstadt, pp. 217–223, 123,* who emphasizes the necessity for this arrangement along with the ancient patronage system. Cf. also *Hermelink: Zu Luthers Gedanken ueber Idealgemeinden und von Weltlicher Obrigkeit, Z. f. Kirchengeschichte, 1908, pp. 267–322,* where it is shown that this Congregational ideal was connected with Apocalyptic expectations, and at the same time the anti-democratic attitude of the congregations was represented as far as possible by the local authority. For our subject the important point is that in all this in any case the idea of the Church itself is preserved, in spite of an apparent approximation to the sect-type; see also *Troeltsch: Trennung von Staat und Kirche, pp. 9–23.* For Luther it seemed absolutely obvious that in all this the religious form within a given territory and the territory itself should coincide (*Drews, p. 99*), and all the early renunciation of any attempt at overriding men's consciences still only meant a temporary attitude of *laissez-faire* based upon confidence in the Word; the civil authority further had to suppress all open blasphemy and sedition, that is, all disturbance of the unity of the Christian Society. Of this more anon. In these expressions about the Congregational ideal of 1522–1525, it is clear that there lies a peculiar problem which was not merely local nor temporary, and which is of extreme interest for the sociological significance of the Lutheran conception of the Church. It is an attempt within the general Christian Society, and the institutional Christianity composed of all who have been baptized, to found smaller groups in which radical Christian piety will be realized without any intention of allowing these smaller groups to remove the general ecclesiastical character from the Church. *Köhler* calls it "a parallelism of a Christian Society which is organized and controlled by the State and a system of smaller groups for worship and fellowship". "When Luther gave up the attempt to carry out this idea it was taken over by the Anabaptists, thence it was taken over by Bucer and finally from him by Calvin" (*Christl. Welt, p. 470*). The chief point, however, is this: that in so doing the Anabaptists cut themselves off from the wider circle of the Christian society which was being ruled: they used baptism only as adult baptism for mature Christians and they placed the fellowship composed of those who had been baptized in that way, in open opposition to the secularized morality of the so-called Christendom and the Church. Calvinism, on the contrary, transformed "the smaller groups" into the whole Church, and gave them the structure of a universal Church within which care is taken to develop the personal Christian piety of all the citizens and Church members. The Baptists discard the idea of the Church altogether; Calvinism transforms the ideal of these smaller groups into an institutional Church which agrees with the territory in which it is placed. In those expressions during the first half of the twenties (in the sixteenth century) Luther is obviously seeking a middle way. Since, however, from the outset the idea of the Church is absolutely predominant, it is not surprising that once a definite order had been established he developed the logical implications of the idea of the Church to their fullest extent, and gave up both the formation of smaller groups and also the idea of transferring the administration of Church-order only to the parishes. He was prevented from developing this idea in the Calvinistic sense both by circumstances and by his ecclesiastical idea of grace which was opposed to all legalism, while Calvinism in reality replaced the idea of the Church with a sectarian element of compulsion. This subject will be treated in greater detail in the section devoted to Calvinism.

[214] (p. 492.) The idea of a Society inspired by a uniform world-view is undoubtedly mediaeval, but it is still a vital problem which has not yet been solved. There cannot be a real social coherence at all without the unity of the world-view, and it is good for us to remember that in contrast to the modern anarchy in the view of the world which has such a disintegrating influence upon Society and religious thought, two so very different thinkers as the Romantic Novalis and the sober Empiricist Auguste Comte deliberately look back to the Middle Ages as the classic epoch of a social unity based upon unity of ideas. At the present day we have an example of the same thing in social democracy. Also the conservative parties and the Churchmen of to-day use the same principle, even though somewhat weakened; see *Loofs: Luthers Stellung zu M. A. und Neuzeit, 1907, p. 19:* "On the other hand, the gulf between Luther and the modern day has not been fixed so irrevocably as Troeltsch believes. Had we not ourselves until 1874 practically compulsory baptism? Is it not a fact that blasphemy is still an offence punishable by law? And have we not still to-day a civilization of authority of a Christian tinge which upon the whole has compulsory religious instruction? . . . Actually the idea of what constitutes blasphemy is interpreted very differently from the ideas of Luther, but from the formal point of view the difference is not so great." That is undoubtedly true, especially for Prussia, but it is still only a proof that the same motives are here at work as there were in the mediaeval social order, and that the Protestant compulsory civilization is to be interpreted in exactly the same sense as the mediaeval. Luther's retention of the unity of the religious idea has certainly not merely the significance of a mediaeval prejudice, but it is a result of a unified conception of Society and of an absolute revealed knowledge of truth which is entirely logical. When, however, this goal had been set up, methods were also desired in order to reach it, and the same process will be continually repeated.

[215] (p. 494.) Here also Luther's statements are contradictory according to the time when they were uttered, and the situation and the collection and interpretation of these statements vary greatly; it all depends upon the object which they are meant to serve; they may be used for apologetic or for controversy, for history or for doctrine. *Wappler* has published from the records of Zwickau a whole series of the records of religious trials, enactments of the Government, professional decisions of the Wittenberg theologians and jurists, which reveal the pressure on conscience exercised by the Visitation in a most terrible and petty manner; see *Wappler: Inquisition und Ketzerprozesse in Zwickau zur Reformationzeit, 1908.* He has combined with this a presentation of statements of Luther and Melancthon which emphasize very clearly the contrast between the earlier attitude of toleration and non-intervention on the part of the civil authority in the free spiritual struggle, with the later exhortation to punish all rioting and disturbance of the peace with banishment in order to preserve the external order of Society, and at the same time the Christian social order, until it was so far developed as to regard every heretical doctrine as the disturber of peace and unity to be punished with extreme severity, even to the point of death. When, however, he tests the Reformers by the modern idea of toleration which places ethics in the forefront and doctrine in a less important position, and then interprets their departure from this ideal because of their appeals to the Old Testament as the fruit of the sinister Old Testament spirit of revenge, he forgets in the first place that the Reformers, just like the mediaeval thinkers, had the same conception of absolute truth to whom the modern idea of toleration, with the possibility of various forms of truth (all having a

right to their individual existence alongside of one another), would have seemed like frivolous scepticism and blasphemy: he also overlooks the fact that the Old Testament is here called in in order to find a Scriptural basis for things which could not be justified from the New Testament, and which yet, because they were inevitable in practice, had to find a basis somewhere. Further examples in horrifying fullness are given by *Barge's Karlstadt* in spite of the modifications made by *Karl Müller*. From the Catholic standpoint *N. Paulus: Luther und die Gewissensfreiheit, 1905*, collects passages on the same subject. He explains the earlier demand for toleration as the toleration of a minority, that is, as a demand addressed to the Roman Catholic princes not to interfere with spiritual matters and not to hinder the Gospel, and he shows how at the same time Luther regarded the abolition of the Mass by the authority which was sympathetic towards the Reformation as a duty of a Christian Government. He also argues that freedom of discussion was only allowed to the Anabaptists and fanatics so long as he believed he could easily cope with them, but that so soon as real opposition developed this toleration ceased at once and was replaced by the severest suppression. In general this is certainly in both directions not far from the truth; but it leaves out of account the inner motive which caused Luther to act, not merely out of opportunism, but out of the necessity of his conception of the Church; this at first led him to lay stress on the purely inward spiritual building up of the communities, and a purely spiritual way of overcoming opposition in confidence in the invincibility of the pure Word. On *p. 27* there is an interesting quotation in which Luther replies thus to the argument that the Emperor was really in sympathy with his doctrine, and, therefore, that he would not take it amiss if he enforced it compulsorily: "We know that he is not certain of that matter, and that he cannot be certain because we know that he errs and strives against the Gospel: the Emperor is under the obligation to know God's Word and like us to further it with all his power." This is the real heart of the matter, as most of the other students realize by quoting this same passage, and it is intelligible that from such a fundamental conviction, amid so much obstinate opposition, Luther came to feel finally that force might be used, and, indeed, must be used in defence of the truth, both in the interest of the defenceless, the weak, and those who are easily led astray, as well as in the interest of the Christian unity of the Church and of Society. *Paulus* rightly censures the statement of the modern orthodox Lutheran apologist *W. Walther*: "Every impartial man must feel that Luther did the only right thing when he tried to arrange that in each country there should be only one Confession" (*p. 13*). There is no need to point to the Imperial law against heretics, to the social and political danger which was caused by the existence of the Anabaptists, to the pressure of the surrounding Catholic States (as the learned pastor, *Bossert*, with a great sense of superiority to *Wappler*, brings out) in order to excuse the Reformers who ought to be judged in a relative manner (*Theol. Litztg., 1908, p. 153*). The new law against heresy, the demand for censorship, and the unity of the Confessions, is ultimately due to the Reformers' conception of truth and of the Church, and the inconsistencies are inconsistencies which belong to the nature of this conception of the Church, which desires a universal Christian Church and social order, and yet at the same time to have an inward and spiritual influence. This proved impossible in practice: so force was tried, and these duties were entrusted to the civil authority as duties which belonged to the exercise of Christian love and were based upon Natural Law, which limited the purely spiritual character of ecclesiastical self-propagation to one of theological exhortation, which preceded the government condemnation-verdict, and to the toleration of a mistaken faith which is maintained in secret and makes no public expression of opinion. This is in reality the ancient Catholic law against heresy, as Paulus says, only "with this essential difference that Melancthon grants to the civil authority as the most important member of the Church the real decision in matters of faith, whereas on the Catholic side the decision of religious doctrine is kept in the hands of the infallible Church. Melancthon, indeed, also desired that in doubtful cases the princes would allow themselves to be guided by the council of the theologians; but in the last resort the civil authority always made the final decision" (*p. 43*). In that there is expressed the retention of the spiritual methods of working and the characterization of heresy as tumult and a disturbance of Christian Society; but also this implies the continuance of the Catholic idea of the unity of Christian Society, which for its part is a logical result of the conception of the universality of the Church. Within the common whole the emphasis has been shifted, and in this shifting of emphasis the spirituality of the new idea of the Church has been asserted. This has been very rightly emphasized as the vital point by *W. Köhler: Reformation und Ketzerprozess, 1901, pp. 21–26*, who also shows how difficult the Reformers found it to give up their original idea of the omnipotent character of thought or of the Word, and how finally the transference of the heresy legislation to the secular power as the protector of the Christian unity of Society still also required the preparation of a purely ecclesiastical heresy legislation, upon the basis of which the secular authority could then act. This handing over to the secular authority belongs to the establishment of the heresy law upon the Law of Nature which Melancthon argues (*p. 29*), which, gathered up in the Decalogue, prescribes the protection of the First Table, that is, especially of the office of the ministry, which is here sanctioned by the secular authority. The new element, however, is still there, that the suppression does not take place in the name of the Church and through the Church, but in the name of the Christian order of Society and through the State, whereas the only aim of the purely ecclesiastical heresy trial is the preservation of the purity of doctrine. The secular arm does not execute a sentence passed by the supreme authority in the Church, but the State protects Christian Society and itself in its own name. The effect, however, is the same.—It is incredible that *Hermelink: Der Toleranzgedanke im Ref.-Zeitalter, 1908*, faced with all that, can picture Luther as the herald of the modern liberty of conscience. Even in the mediaeval system it was not Christianity, but the neo-Platonic element mingled with it which was the father of intolerance!! Luther is supposed to have led the Church back to depend solely upon a spiritual and inward influence, and when the Reformers handed over the right of the punishment of heretics and the duty of establishing a unity of faith by compulsion, it only means that they held a conception of the State which had not yet been purified by their new knowledge—a conception of the State, that is, of the Renaissance, Machiavelli's Supreme Power of the State!! The Baptists, on the other hand, are said to have had nothing to do with toleration. "They were intolerant towards the State and non-Baptist Christendom in a dangerous manner", with which, in *Wappler*, one might compare the statements of the entirely passive Baptists!! Luther's conception of truth in which the "spiritual and invisible" is an established truth which God breathes into the hearts of believers, and in which "all that fights against this . . . is a bit of the devil's work", is said to be a relic left over from mediaeval Neo-Platonism, which only appears in isolated instances!! etc. Things could not be twisted in a more mad and stupid way, and this kind of apologetic it is which makes so many theological works insupportable to those who are not professional theologians.

[216] (p. 494.) On Luther's ethic the best book is still that by *Luthardt: Die Ethik Luthers in Ihren Grundzügen, 1867*. Here, however, all tensions and difficulties have been smoothed away, till the whole system looks as though it were completely uniform and logical. He has found this easier to do because he does not touch practically the whole of the social philosophy. The excellent work by *Eger: Die Anschauungen Luthers von Beruf, 1900*, is an historical work which emphasizes quite rightly the various tensions; he is, however, only wrong when he deduces the tension from the after-effect of monasticism instead of from primitive Christian Radicalism, or to the dialectic incapacity of Luther to gain a systematic deduction of civilization and the ethic of humanity conceptually and the inner difficulty of the whole matter. For the early period, *Braun: Concupiscenz*, is valuable. Excellent, and also of value for Luther himself, is *Hupfeld: Die Ethik Joh. Gerhards. Ein Beitrag zum Verständnis der Lutherischen Ethik, 1908;* here also it is precisely the subject of the social philosophy and the analysis of the tensions and inconsistencies which is ignored. On the contrary, these difficulties are treated with great energy, but without the knowledge of the main conceptions which illuminate the whole subject; *Lommatzsch: Luthers Lehre von Etisch-religiösen Standpunkt aus, mit besonderer Berücksichtigung seiner Theorie von Gesetz, 1879*. Excellent detailed researches are offered by *Gottschick: Ethik, 1908*. For my view as a whole I must refer to my work, *Grundprobleme der Ethik Z. f. Theol. und Kirche, XII, 1902*.

[217] (p. 495.) On this point *Kapp* is excellent: *Religion und Moral im Christentum Luthers, 1902; Herrmann: Verkehr des Christen mit Gott*[5], *1908; Thieme: Die Sittliche Triebkraft des Glaubens, 1895*. The essence of the ethic which is determined by religion is this, that here the religious relation itself is the absolute value and the absolute obligation, and that therefore all moral values—whether of self-cultivation or in the formation of a relation with one's fellow men—are placed at the service of this supreme aim. This is how Jesus understood the matter as has already been shown. And thus also is it interpreted by Luther; the repetition by Luther is a confirmation of an idea which has been developed by Luther; see above, *p. 37* (against this and agreeing with Harnack's objections meanwhile, *Thieme: Christl. Welt, 1909, pp. 771 ff.; Bedeutung der Nächstenliebe bei Jesus*). From this point of view the first duty is that of self-conquest and self-surrender to God, and the next duty is love to one's neighbour for the sake of God, with the intention of being united with one's neighbour in God. That both these ideas are the meaning of the Lutheran doctrine of the love of God and the love of man, see the apt proofs in *W. Walther: Die Christliche Sittlichkeit nach Luther, 1909, p. 35*, and in *Thieme: Triebkraft, pp. 17–53*. Let me quote a few passages from Luther according to Thieme: "Ingressus in Christum est fides, egressus autem est caritas, quae nos justitia Dei indutos distribuit in obsequia proximi et exercitium proprii corporis ad succurendum alienae paupertati, ut et ipsi per nos attracti nobiscum ingrediantur in Christum" (*p. 289*); or the well-known and important passage: "Out of all this we come to the conclusion that a Christian man lives not in himself, but in Christ and his neighbour: in Christ through faith, in his neighbour through love. Through faith he goes out of himself into God, from God he again descends through love and yet remains always in God and in the divine love" (*p. 284*); or: "When a Christian begins to know Christ as his Lord and Saviour through Whom he is redeemed from death and brought into His glory and honour, his heart becomes

so full of God that he would like to help everyone to enter into the same joy. For he has no higher joy than to rejoice that he knows Christ (that is, the real ethical fulfilment of personality). Therefore the Christian goes forth from himself, teaches and exhorts other men, exalts and confesses Christ before everyone, pleads and sighs that they might also come to such an experience of the grace of God. That is a kind of divine unrest in the midst of the highest repose, repose in God's grace and peace which will not allow a man to be idle, but urges him ever to aspire and wrestle with all his powers, to live only to exalt the honour and praise of God amongst men that others also may receive such a spirit of grace" (*p. 297*). That is the ethic of the Gospel expressed in somewhat different language as it has been expressed also by Augustine and Bernard in their language as love to God and love to creatures in God. *Thieme* asks the question, somewhat scholastically, whether in all this there is not a love of one's neighbour for his own sake, and answers it rightly by saying that it is precisely the highest welfare of the neighbour which is served when through showing him the love of God the love of God itself and that happiness is kindled within the neighbour himself. This idea lies virtually and unconsciously at the basis of the passages where all that is mentioned is help and assistance to one's neighbour. This is certainly right, and it explains why in the ethic of Luther as in that of Jesus the social conditions of ordinary life are of no ethical value in themselves, but they are only regarded as methods and opportunities to develop such values out of the religious temper.

218 (p. 496.) The following quotation illustrates the logical results of these ideas: "Now behold, these people do not need any sword or law of this world. And if all the world were true Christians, that is, true believers, then no prince, king, lord, sword, or law would be necessary" (*Lommatzsch, 207*). Renunciation of one's own honour (*Lommatzsch, 240*), at the same time with the admission that "only a few and very highly spiritual men" are capable of such praise. It would be a very good thing if some scholar would give us a study of Luther's relation to the Sermon on the Mount. The aloofness from the world which is expressed in the Gospel in eschatological terms, but which in Luther primarily has a mystical basis, finds its classic expression in the famous treatise on the *Freiheit eines Christenmenschen*. The chief passages of the German text (*Berliner Ausgabe, I*[1]): "Here then we will answer those who are angered by the aforesaid speeches, and who often say: 'Oh, then, if faith is everything and is enough to make us religious, why then are good works required? Let us make merry and do nothing.' No, my dear fellow, thou must not act thus, that were only possible if thou wert an entirely inward and spiritual man, but that will not happen till the Last Day. . . . Although man in his soul is sufficiently justified by faith, and has all that he ought to have, excepting that the same faith must increase into that life, yet he still remains in this bodily life upon earth, and must rule his own body, and mix with men. This is where works begin: here he must not be idle, the body must be exercised with fasting and prayer, with toil and labour, and with all moderate discipline, that it may become obedient, and conform to the inward man, and to faith, and not hinder and resist it as is its manner where it is not forced" (*p. 306*). "Thence, each man must learn how to chastise the body in all modesty; for he fasts, watches, labours, as long as he sees that the body needs to be kept down by the will . . ." (*p. 307*). "As Adam in Paradise, in order not to be idle, was told to labour, so a believing man also needs to labour,—not in order to make him a religious man, but that he be not idle, he is commanded to prepare and preserve his body to do such good works solely in order to please God". . .

(*p. 308*). This must be said of works in general and of those which a Christian man must exercise in order to subdue his own body. Now will we speak more of the works which he does to other men. For man does not live simply in his own body, but among other men upon earth. Therefore he cannot live apart from other men; he must speak with them, and have to do with them, although these same works are not necessary to salvation. Therefore in all his works his intention should be freely directed to serving, and being useful to other people, and to undertaking nothing save that which is of use to other people (*p. 312*). "However much the work of Christ was needed and has served to produce piety or salvation, so also are His other works, and the works of Christians, needed by them for salvation, since they are all services rendered freely for the good of others. . . . In like manner St. Paul, in Romans xiii and Titus iii, exhorts Christians that they should be subject to the authority of this world, not that this will make them religious, but in order that in so doing they may freely serve others, and the Government, by doing their will in love and freedom." Thus it is also possible for love's sake to submit to unchristian institutions and laws (*p. 314*). That the latter, from the point of view of such an ethic of love, has its difficulties, and requires actions which are inconsistent with this ideal, Luther was quite aware (*Lommatzsch, p. 287*); in any case, however, this motivation means a complete indifference to the actual political, legal, and economic values of the world.—It cannot be denied that these ideas can be traced to St. Augustine (see *Hunzinger: Lutherstudien, I, 1906*) and to German and Bernardine mysticism (*Braun: Bedeutung der Concupiszenz*). The most important thing, however, is to realize clearly that this is only the transformation of the radicalism of the Sermon on the Mount which became the prevalent point of view after the time of Augustine, the mystically based and interpreted exposition of the commands of absolute self-sanctification for God, and of absolute brotherly love, with the complete disappearance of the secular virtues of conflict and justice. The command to renounce rights and worldly honours, and completely to surrender the spirit to God has become the command of humility and of the love of self only in God, and the command of brotherly love as the manifestation of the love of God, has become the mystical love of the brethren in God, with the mortification of all selfishness. The *conversio ad Deum* means turning towards the only true Being, and the union of brethren in this one Reality; the substitution of the radical ethic of love for the merely relative virtues, gained in the struggle for existence, has become a turning away from the untrue and the unreal non-being of the world which leads to selfishness and multiplicity. In this interpretation, however, Luther follows throughout the primitive Christian Radicalism—indeed, he went into the cloister for that reason, for in the monastery alone, however much altered, the radical ethic had been maintained. Thence he only came through gradually to a new development of this Radicalism, which carried it into the everyday life of every individual, without externally removing it; in connection with this also the mystical interpretation went back more and more to the real meaning of the Sermon on the Mount.

[219] (p. 497.) It is undeniable that Luther's *Gemeindeideal*—that is, the regulation of the calling of pastors and the control of the behaviour of parishioners (which starts from the individual)—is connected with an interpretation of the Christian ethic in the sense of the communism of love and a strict observance of the Christian rules of life; the Leisnig Ordinance lays stress upon the latter element, and the little pamphlets entitled *Dass eine christl. Gemeinde Recht habe alle Lehre zu urteilen und Lehrer zu berufen*, and *Von der Ordnung des Gottesdienstes*

in der Gemeinde, emphasize the former; both, however, have the same aim. In the preface to the former Luther approves "that you have undertaken to make a new order of public worship and to hold goods in common according to the example of the Apostles (that is, of the Primitive Church)". *B.A., IV, 1, p. 111;* in the Ordinance itself it is said: "We have received a thorough knowledge that all the inner and outer possessions of Christian believers should serve and be used for the glory of God and for the love of one's neighbour, for one's fellow Christians according to the ordering of Divine truth and not according to human ideas" (*p. 117*); at the same time the congregation has provided for a strict Church discipline (*pp. 118 ff.*). This is undoubtedly an approximation to the sect-type; we must, however, remember that *W. Köhler* not only rightly points out that this is the source of the Baptist and Calvinist ideals, but also that other very important things were involved in both of these. Calvin especially is less concerned with the exercise of the priesthood of all believers than with the founding of a holy community ordered by God; cf. below. Luther is also clear that a community of those who "earnestly wish to be Christians and confess the Gospel with hand and mouth" (*p. 168*) cannot be a Church of the masses, at least not at first. Therefore, in the famous introduction to the *Messe deutsch*, there is the idea of a more select body of communicants within the external Church who attend the preaching service and undergo Christian instruction, thus distinguishing between "an ordered and certain gathering within which one could rule Christians according to the Gospel", and the great parish where is "only public stimulus to faith and to Christianity." "In this order one would be able to know, punish, improve, cast out, or excommunicate those who did not behave in a Christian manner according to the rule of Christ (Matthew xviii. 15). Here also it would be possible to ask the Christians all to give alms together; these would be given willingly and shared out among the poor according to the example of St. Paul, 2 Cor. ix. 1" (*pp. 167 ff.*). This is one of the chief passages upon which the Pietists later on based their idea of the *ecclesiola in ecclesia*; Luther, however, does not intend a withdrawal out of a secularized Church, but he wishes to create progressive kernel organizations of the converting Spirit within the Church. Luther, however, finds that he has not got the earnest Christians whom he requires, and, on the other hand, he is afraid that "this might lead to faction, so I am putting it out of my head", that is, he would not allow it to develop of itself (*p. 169*). Thus Luther renounces the idea of such "peculiar communities" (*p. 169*). *Eger, pp. 77–83*, has a right view of this subject.

220 (p. 498.) On this point, cf. especially the treatise: *Wider die himmlischen Propheten, 1524*. In this Luther follows Paulinism. But it is important to note that in so doing it is the ecclesiastical element of Paulinism which he follows. The socially conservative position which Paulinism adopted in its own day is not, it is true, like the Catholic ethic, an absorption of the secular institutions into the Christian ethic, but it is a waiting and a toleration and an enduring and a cautious use of the ordinances of a world which God still permits to exist. But even this very restricted acceptation of the world was only possible to Paul through his conception of grace, since this conception of grace fills the Christian community as a whole with the redeeming energies of Christ, and therefore takes away from them the responsibility of fixing a limit by a radical external separation and activity of the individual; see *Wernle: Der Christ und die Sünde bei Paulus, 1897, pp. 60–72*, in which, however, the connection between the Pauline "conception of the Church" and the idea of Grace is not sufficiently emphasized.

This predominance of the idea of grace gives to the whole of religious thought in general a bias to accept the existing order as a Divine decree which is not to be altered by force.

[221] (p. 498.) This idea of the impossibility of overcoming sin is a remarkable divergence from Paulinism, which in the certainty of a complete renewal and transformation of Christians considers it natural that sin should be overcome: in it also the defects of individual Church members were regarded as stains and shortcomings in the real ideal of the Church; these are to be got rid of by discipline, and will be burnt up in the Judgment and End of the World which is imminent. Cf. *Wernle: Der Christ und die Sünde*, and *Braun: Luthers Lehre von der Concupiszenz, pp. 107–112*. In that, however, there are also the sectarian elements of Paul as they are contained in that Enthusiasm which he proclaims alongside of the consummation of revelation in Christ. The sects until the present day for this reason continue to appeal to these ideas. In Paulinism both types are still together.

[222] (p. 499.) For the naturalness of the idea of the *Corpus Christianum* see the following passages in *Lommatzsch, 258, 275, 282, 527 ff.* That is plainly shown in the description of the three hierarchies of the civil authority, of the household, and of the clergy as estates of the Church. Cf. also *Rieker: Rechtliche Stellung, pp. 66–71*. Both recognize in this, and rightly, the continuation of the mediaeval idea whose origin in the ideas of the primitive Church cannot, however, be explained quite so easily and simply. In the second main section of this work it was my intention to make this clear. If that result is right, we may then draw the conclusion that in spite of all reactions to Paulinism and Augustinianism, the Reformation ethic, and the social philosophy which issued from it, continues the mingling of the Church and the world in an undifferentiated unity, and only rearranges the relation between the elements which compose this unity; so also *Ehrhardt: La notion du droit naturel, pp. 308 ff.*

[223] (p. 500.) Cf. *Luthard, pp. 76 ff.*: "Luther based his position on the distinction between the Kingdom of God and the kingdom of this world (as he calls it), or, in other words, upon the tenet of the inwardness of Christianity contrasted with the external life in the world, which is based upon the Creation (it would be more accurate to say, upon Reason). . . . After the doctrine of justification by faith there is perhaps scarcely any other doctrine which Luther mentions so often, and propagates so earnestly, as this doctrine of the spiritual and inward character of the Kingdom of Christ, and of the difference between it and the kingdom of this world, that is, the sphere of the natural created life. Primarily, the Gospel has nothing at all to do with the external life; it is wholly concerned with eternal life; it is not concerned with external ordinances and institutions which might come into conflict with the ordinances of the world, but with the hearts of men and their relation to God, with the grace of God, with the forgiveness of sins, etc., in short, with the heavenly life. The characteristic element of the Kingdom of Christ is the order of grace (and love), the characteristic of the kingdom and the life of this world is the system of law. Therefore they are quite different in quality, and do not belong to the same plane; indeed, they belong to different worlds. To the one I belong as a Christian, to the other as a man (this is the modern way of putting it, Luther would have said: 'I belong to the one through the Gospel, and to the other through the *Lex Naturae*'). For we live in two spheres of life, we are in heaven and upon earth at the same time. . . . 'Christ's Kingdom', says Luther, 'is, and ought to be, a Divine Kingdom, and yet the same spiritual Kingdom is interwoven with the kingdom of this world, and Christ and His disciples use the

world, but they do it all as pilgrims and strangers', just as Christ also has done. . . . Hence it is not the duty of Christ, or of the Gospel, to alter the ordinances of the secular life, and to set up new ones. All that part of life is under the control of its own laws, and of reason, and for that we do not need the Holy Spirit. . . . 'Therefore', says Luther, 'we must make a very clear distinction between the two spheres, between that in which sin is punished and that in which it is forgiven, between that in which rights are demanded and that in which rights are renounced. In the Kingdom of God, which He rules by the Gospel, there is no demanding of rights, and there is no question of law, everything is forgiveness and magnanimity and generosity, and there is no wrath, and no punishment, but purely brotherly service and good deeds. 'The creatures', says Luther, 'are all in existence before the Gospel comes, that is, all secular matters and ordinances which have been constituted by men according to reason, and by the Divinely implanted natural wisdom' (i.e. through the *Lex Naturae*). . . . 'Therefore also the servants of Christ ought not to have anything to do with these worldly matters, but simply to preach the grace of God. So far as those matters are concerned, jurists may advise and help and show people how to act.' . . . 'Thus everything will go on just as it is until the great change comes to all things; for until then the Kingdom of God has only an inward form, and Jesus rules simply in the hearts of men. . . . For it is not the outward which matters, but the inward; Christ was concerned simply with the inward. This alone is the meaning of the words of Christ—especially in the Sermon on the Mount—in which He gives His rules for a Christian life, that we ought not to swear, etc. He does not dream of laying down rules for the outer life; He is thinking only of inward and personal behaviour. His words do not apply to the external calling, and to the official conduct which that implies, but to the individual, and to his spirit, and the inward personal attitude of mind and heart. For otherwise, if we are to understand His Word as applying to external matters, Christ would overturn the whole order of the world. For it would give rise to an insoluble contradiction between the external behaviour in one's calling and office upon earth' (in this, indeed, he demands obedience to both systems of ethics, the 'personal' and the 'official', but, at the same time, he recognizes that inwardly they are essentially inconsistent with each other). . . 'For since Jesus only requires an inward attitude, and only asks for an external renunciation when faith and personal witness require it, He indirectly confirms all these external things, possessions and the rest, and also makes it plain that all renunciation which is not demanded by that duty is a dereliction of duty'. (Certainly a very indirect and arbitrary compromise with the teaching of Jesus.). . . The decisive point, which Luther always brought out in these questions, was that he had learnt to distinguish between the inward personal spirit of the Christian, and the outward attitude to the duty of his secular office and calling."—To that we must add this sentence of Luther's: "For thyself thou remainest within the Gospel, and thou abidest by the word of Christ, so that thou art willing to receive a blow upon the other cheek, and thou dost allow men to take thy cloak, if it only concerns thee and thine own affairs. Thus in this way all goeth well together, that thou dost satisfy both the Kingdom of God, and the kingdom of this world, outwardly and inwardly, if thou dost suffer at the same time evil and wrong, and yet dost punish evil and wrong, and if thou dost resist evil, and yet thou dost not resist it. . . ." Or the other saying: "So far as I am a Christian, I must not care about money, or gather it, but only trust in God with all my heart. But outwardly I may and ought to use temporal goods for my own body, and for other people, so far as my worldly person is concerned."—That is quite manifestly a dualistic morality, based on absolutely contradictory principles. The question is: How did Luther solve this evident problem? *Luthardt's* explanation is that Luther made a distinction between the order of Creation and the order of Redemption, between man as a human being and man as a Christian; from this point of view Redemption is the completion of the Creation, and the Christian is the true human being. This, however, is a theory which would only be possible to the modern reconciliation theology (i.e. the *Vermittelungstheologie* of the middle of the nineteenth century). For Luther the solution lay in the sphere of thought governed by the Patristic and mediaeval ideas of Natural Law; cf. *Ehrhardt: La Notion du droit natural,* who, however, has only an imperfect knowledge of the origin and significance of this point of view. While *Ehrhardt* first of all rightly confirms and illustrates the harsh contradiction between the secular ethic of law and the evangelical ethic of love and suffering (*p. 290*), pointing out that at the beginning Luther even went the length of rejecting the Decalogue as a document of merely legal morality, he also shows that Luther still retained the legal morality for the unconverted who need a discipline, a *frenum*, and a *remedium peccati*, and also for the real Christians who can only be protected by a system of law against the abuse and exploitation of their radical spirit of love and readiness to suffer, and, finally, because *de lege naturae* is necessary in order to secure peaceful relationships in the State, the family, and in economic life (*pp. 293 ff.*); for the latter see the passage in Luther's great *Commentary on the Galatians*: "saepe a me audistis, quod ordinationes politicae et oeconomicae sint divinae, quia Deus ipse ordinavit et apportavit eas, ut solem lunam et alias creaturas". "This way of thinking leads Luther to affirm that there exists a natural divine social order independent of the special revelation of God as such, which is in the Bible, an eternal order, and in its principles, at least, unchangeable" (*p. 295*). This is the well-known idea of the *Lex Naturae*, which is written in the hearts of men, and which has now been adjusted to the state of fallen humanity as a *frenum* and a *remedium peccati*, but which is also a necessary reasonable order of natural social things in harmony with the Natural Law. For the relative Natural Law, see the passage from the *Commentary on Genesis* quoted by *Lommatzsch, p. 286:* "Politia ante peccatum nulla fuit, neque enim ea opus fuit; est enim politia remedium necessarium naturae corruptae. Oportet enim cupiditatem restringi vinculis legum et poenis, ne libere vagetur. Ideo politiam recte dixeris regnum peccati. . . . Hoc enim unum et praecipuum agit politia, ut peccatum arceat. . . . Si enim homines non essent per peccatum mali facti, politia nihil fuisset opus." Thus he accepts also the relevant passages concerning the Natural Law both in Roman law and in the Canon Law, which otherwise he so sternly condemns. For him, however, the ultimate reason for the possibility of combining the natural legal ethic with the Christian love-ethic is finally the identification of the Decalogue with the Law of Nature on the one hand, and with the moral Law of Christ on the other; further, in contrast to his original rejection of the Decalogue he interprets it (in sharp distinction from the ceremonial and political law of Moses) as the total content of the moral demands of the Primitive State, of the Natural Law, and of the Christian Law, and makes great use of the Bible, as well as of illustrations from antiquity, in order to prove the source of the Law of Nature. In so doing, all the old Catholic ideas have again been completely accepted, as is shown by *Lommatzsch, pp. 60–90,* more clearly than by *Ehrhardt, p. 303*. Thus Luther says in his work, *Against the Heavenly Prophets*: "Moses' law and the Natural Law are one thing" ("ein Ding"). Cf. also *Lommatzsch, p. 63,* and the larger Catechism: "The Ten Commandments are likewise written in the hearts of all men, they are symbolical books" (*Müller, p. 460*). The Decalogue and the Christian law itself contain this dualistic ethic, which, therefore, represents the contradiction between legalism and the commandment of love which is the result of the adaptation of the Law of Nature to the conditions of the fallen State; thus this is the idea of the relative Natural Law, with which we are familiar. The difference between this conception and the Catholic development of the idea consists in this: that the dualistic ethic is not represented as a gradual process, or as an ascent from the ethic of the Natural Law to the peculiar achievements of the Christian ethic, in which the latter, in its entire radicalism, is only binding on a special class of people, but that every individual, equally, is laid under the obligation to obey both laws. We shall meet these inconsistencies at every turn in the exposition of the social doctrines of Lutheranism. *Ehrhardt* remarks somewhat naïvely: "But is not this distinction between the exterior and the interior man abstract and artificial? and what is the relation between justice according to Natural Law (a justice possible even to non-Christians) and the justice of God?" (*p. 318*). *Lommatzsch, p. 606:* recognizes the inconsistency, and the problem which it contains, more deeply and theoretically. In general, however, these writers do not know what to make of these statements; the reason for this is that either they have no knowledge, or only a very imperfect knowledge of the whole ancient Patristic scholastic set of ideas which deal with the Law of Nature, and its organic function which makes it possible for the ecclesiastical ethic to accept the world. They explain them sometimes as a reaction towards Catholicism, contrary to Luther's own principles, sometimes as personal peculiarities and uncertainties of Luther; a man like *Ehrhardt* can even deny that Luther identified the Law of Nature with the Decalogue (*p. 319*), and in all these statements he only sees an unconscious attempt on Luther's part to adjust the historical bias in favour of Natural Law, newly awakened by Humanism, to the Gospel! And *Lommatzsch* can say: "Scarcely ever, however, does Luther display more theoretical obscurity than in these definitions, this uncertainty affects nothing less than his view of the relation of the supernatural to the natural, or of the revelation of God in the wider sense, to such a revelation in the narrower sense" (*p. 71*). *G. Müller: Luthers Stellung zum Recht,* thinks (on *p. 26*) that the whole matter sounds very much like the ideas of St. Augustine, but he thinks that inwardly Luther had given them up!

224 (p. 503.) The clear recognition that the radical ethic would only influence small groups of men, and that therefore the Christian ethic for a mass community needed the complement of the secular ethic, comes out in the *Schrift von weltlicher Obrigkeit, B.A., IV, 1, p. 236*: A strict and really Christian fellowship would not be possible. "Thou must first fill the world with earnest Christians before thou canst govern them in a Christian and evangelical way. This, however, thou wilt never be able to do, for the world and the masses are, and remain, unchristian, even if all were baptized and called Christians. But as the saying is, Christians dwell far from one another. Therefore it is not possible that a Christian government (in the sense of the Sermon on the Mount) could be set up in common over all the world, or over one country or a great number of people. For the evil are always more numerous than the good; therefore to presume to try to rule a whole land or the world with the Gospel is like a herdsman who would put together in one stable wolves, lions, eagles, and sheep, and would allow them to mingle freely together. . . . Here, indeed, the sheep

would keep the peace and peaceably go to pasture and allow themselves to be ruled, but they would not live long, nor would one animal have more chance than another. Therefore we must deliberately separate the two kinds of rule and allow both to remain, the one which makes men good and the other which creates outward peace and prevents evil works; within this world neither is sufficient without the other." All this only makes sense on the assumption of the necessity for a comprehensive popular Church.—From another point of view Luther says the same thing in his famous introduction to the Psalter, in which he points out that the Psalter expresses all the heights and depths of religious and moral conditions, and is, therefore, better for the Christian community than the mere narratives of the heroic acts of the saints. "Finally, in the Psalter (through this presentation of various stages), there is certainty and a well preserved guidance, that in it, without danger, we can follow the example of all the saints (that is, of the religious souls who express their feelings in the Psalms). For other examples and legends from the 'dumb' saints (that is, solely the account of their deeds without an expression of the fluctuations of their inward life) produce many works which one cannot imitate: indeed, they bring before us works which are dangerous to copy, and which often cause sects and tumults and which lead and even tear men away from the Communion of Saints (that is, from the Church). But the Psalter keeps thee in the communion of saints and preserves thee from tumults; for it teaches thee in joy and fear, in hope and sorrow, to be and to speak as all the saints (that is, average religious men) have thought and have spoken" (*IV, 1, p. 8*).

[225] (p. 504.) The Decalogue, which in the Early Church and in the early Middle Ages was scarcely used at all in the teaching of the Church, was used a great deal in the later Middle Ages in connection with the confession (*Beichtspiegel*). (*Kawerau*, in the volume which has already been indicated, *p. 43*.) It was only regarded as a central Christian doctrine, by which the law and its opposite, grace, and also the doctrine of Substitution and the Christian ethic, are tested, in Protestantism, and indeed Calvinism, owing to its stricter ethical parish organization, used it still more than Lutheranism; the foundation, however, in both is the same. For the absolute position which it had here attained, see *Lommatzsch, pp. 60–90.* The more detailed development of the doctrine, with its underlying theory of the Two Tables (I cannot tell how far this idea was peculiar to Luther; in any case, in its detailed treatment and its opinions it is a mirror of the ideas of the Reformation), and with its identification of Natural Law, Christian law, and Decalogue (also it is thus the only connection which remains in this quite anti-philosophical theology between Reason and Revelation, Nature and Grace) is illustrated by *Eger, pp. 99–118*, and *Hupfeld, pp. 75–104*, and *Troeltsch: Vernunft und Offenbarung bei Joh. Gerh. und Melancthon, 1891, pp. 137–173;* while I was writing this work I was not then sufficiently acquainted with the significance of the whole group of ideas dealing with the Decalogue and the Natural Law in the whole body of traditional theology, nor did I realize its connection with Luther, and I attributed this doctrine too much to the mind of Melancthon. In this connection the great new element which Luther introduced was the distinction between the *justitia spiritualis* and the *justitia civilis*, between the *motus spirituales* and general natural ethical obligations; the latter are good in a Christian sense when, as the First Table requires, they are exercised "in faith". For this "exercising in faith" of the works which in themselves are required by the Natural Law, see the detailed presentation of the subject in *Thieme, pp. 19–102.* This sentence

throws a light on the whole: "In this work (that is, in faith in Christ) all works must be exercised, and from its goodness they receive an influence which is like a Divine gift" (*p. 76*). The difficulties, however, created by this gathering up in the Decalogue have not by any means disappeared. In the Primitive State the Decalogue and the Natural Law, "the Law of Nature and of Love", are certainly quite the same. At the Fall, however, through the secular order of law, the Natural Law was adapted to the fallen State, and now the question arises: how far can both of these once more be united in the state of sin? *Eger* (*pp. 92 ff.*) also formulates the problem thus, and in a very pertinent manner.—At this point there are the most important developments of Luther's ethic. The two poles of this development are shown by the works *Von Weltlicher Obrigkeit, wieweit man ihr Gehorsam schuldig sei 1523*, and the *Auslegung der Bergpredigt, 1532*. In the former work Luther says expressly the Catholics had thus combined the Sermon on the Mount and the obligations of practical life by relegating them to different classes of people, and by making the distinction between *consilia* and *praecepta*, whereas he regards the claim of the Sermon on the Mount and of Paul for the absolute ethic of love, which renounces law and force, as binding on all Christians without exception. The same Christians, however, are also taught to admit the claim of practical life, the recognition of law and authority; in the form, however, which it has displayed since the Fall, that is, in the legal order, which has been instituted as a *frenum* and *remedium peccati*; this legal order, namely, issues from reason; it has also been explicitly appointed by God (in the Old Testament), and, in the New Testament, it has also been expressly confirmed by Christ through His own obedience to it, His patience, and His endurance. The Christian now belongs to both these separate and contradictory orders of life; since the great majority are not true Christians in the sense of the Sermon on the Mount, and need the relative Natural Law, that is, the use of law and force for the good and order of their earthly life, and since also Christians need this order as a protection against the misuse of their willingness to suffer, he submits to this law out of love to the mass of the unconverted, and out of obedience to God's law. Both these orders are to be kept strictly separate; the civil authority in particular (which has been instituted solely for the repression of sin, and, therefore, is restricted to the external and secular sphere) may not interfere with the affairs of the spiritual and Christian sphere; least of all may the governments which have remained Papist and unbelieving do this, but otherwise their right to exist is not to be opposed. On the contrary, however, the spiritual ethic of love may not interfere with the State order of law, nor attempt to make its radical Christian piety of love into a law and a programme of social reform for the masses. For the latter need the law; the principles of the Sermon on the Mount applied to the non-Christian masses of the population would simply lead to all kinds of abominations. Christians, indeed, have a double position, and, like Paul, they must endure the non-Christian ordering of the world and let it continue to exist. It is clear that this treatise in which, in some strange way, people have tried to find the principles of freedom of conscience and of the modern State, still holds a very crudely dualistic standpoint; the Sermon on the Mount "certainly teaches that Christians should use no worldly sword or law amongst themselves; but it does not forbid that we should serve and be subject to those who wield the temporal sword and administer the law; but much rather because thou dost not need such things, nor ought thou to have them, nor ought thou to serve those who have not gone so far as thou, and who still need the same" (*B. A., IV, 1, p. 239*). This is the relative Natural Law which each Christian has to accept for the sake of the existing masses of non-Christians, even when, as an individual, he admits the claim of the principles of the Sermon on the Mount; indeed, no one ought to try to get rid of this obligation and constitute special groups of those who are perfect. The right meaning of the Sermon on the Mount is "that a Christian shall be so set himself to suffer evil and injustice without desiring to avenge himself, nor to protect himself by law, that he most certainly will not need worldly power and law for himself. But for others he may and should (as a judge, executioner, or soldier) seek revenge, law, protection, aid, and in that capacity do whatever he can. Thus authority will also help and protect him, whether of itself, or through the acts of others, but without any complaint or search of his own. When this does not take place he must let himself be accused and despised, and 'resist not evil', as Christ has taught us. And be thou certain that this Word of Christ is not a counsel for the perfect, as the Sophists do falsely say, but that it is a strict commandment binding on all Christians alike. . . . And do not go with the multitude, and the common customs, for there are few Christians upon earth. . . . And God's Word also is something other than a common custom" (*p. 245*). Here, again, the approximation to the sect-type is very evident; the difference, also, is plain, namely, the recognition of the relative *Lex Naturae* and of natural and existing conditions for the sake of the unity of the national Church (*Volkskirche*). This dualism, however, disappears almost entirely in the exposition of the Sermon on the Mount. Here the presupposition of action is the official position, and class, as it has been appointed by God, and a means of brotherly love as well as a Divine command which men ought to obey. The legal order is regarded as a system of classes, which, owing to the fact that they have been appointed by God, are holy. They are now simply "Divine callings" (*p. 292*). The exercise of one's calling, and the estimate of "the calling", and of the social system, as a system which has been brought about by, and maintained by Providence for the good of Christendom: this idea now becomes the main content of the Lutheran ethic. The love which exercises that which in itself is not necessary for a Christian, namely, submission to the legal order for the good of one's neighbour, leads to that idea of obedience, and of faith in Providence, which exalts the State, the social order, and the law as Divine ordinances, in which it is a simple duty of obedience to remain, and to serve one's neighbour. *Eger* has brought this out very well in his informative work, and at the same time he rightly points out that in spite of this the world-order is not yet considered to possess an ethical value of its own. Men serve God *in vocatione*, not *per vocationem*. In other directions, however, the whole view is altered. Since the State no longer feels that it has no right to attempt to influence matters of religion because it belongs to a lower order, but that now, as a Christian government, it is under the obligation to serve the Church and the Truth, so also Christians are no longer to maintain an attitude of merely passive endurance towards the law. This is what he now says about the legal system: "What does the righteousness of this world mean except that every man should do in his class what he ought? What does that same law of one's class mean? What does it mean to have rights as men and women, as children, and as domestic servants? or what does it mean to have civil rights? Surely all this means that they are to look after and rule other people, and thus exercise their office with care and faithfulness, and that also truly and willingly they are to render the same service and obedience to others" (*p. 300*). "All this has God commanded, so it cannot be unclean, indeed it is even the purity with which God is sought. Thus, if a judge exercise his office and condemn an evil-doer to death, in so doing this is not *his* office and action, but the office and act of God. Therefore it is a good, pure, and holy work (provided, of course, that he is a Christian), which he could not do if he had not already a pure heart" (*p. 306*). In explicit contrast to the renunciation of one's own rights which was required in the passage quoted above, people are now exhorted first of all to try to live in peace and to get on with people: "If, however, that cannot be and thou canst not endure it, thou hast the law and the government of the land whither thou mayest go to seek it in an orderly manner" (*p. 316*). These changes are just as decided as those which were described previously in relation to the connection between Church and State, freedom and compulsion, and both these alterations are related to each other. For the earlier demand for freedom and separation from the State was based upon a low estimate of the State and of the legal system. In its later form, however, Luther's ethic remained permanent, and the explanation of the Decalogue in the two catechisms has given it its permanent classic form down to the present day.

226 (p. 504.) Cf. *Eger: Anschauungen Luthers von Beruf, p. 124:* "It does not seem superfluous to point out how strongly the study of the Old Testament has affected the Lutheran view and caused this constantly increasing openness towards the world. The passages which have been just quoted about the value of earthly gifts and possessions have been almost entirely drawn from expositions of various writings of the Old Testament." "In the Old Testament there is indeed no trace of detachment from the world, of indifference to earthly things and earthly conditions; it is, therefore, under all circumstances a more sure method of gaining a wholesome understanding of that which the earth can offer than the New Testament which is exposed to so much misinterpretation (!) The sphere within which the Christian lives and works in trust in God is now in Luther's view God's world." Thus in reality Luther's economic ethic and his ethic of the family is drawn very largely from the Jewish Wisdom literature. Only this can scarcely be an unconscious effect of the Old Testament, but on the contrary an attempt to find in the Old Testament a justification for things which the New Testament would not tolerate. We shall see how Calvinism had to go much farther in this direction in order to maintain its Scriptural character.

227 (p. 508.) This depreciation of the values of the State and of Society, making them mere forms and presuppositions for the loving exercise of faith (since the love of one's neighbour is best exercised through using the institutions which serve the welfare of Society), still characterizes the ethic of modern Lutheranism. At the same time science is granted a certain standard of value as a means which is essential for the exercise of one's calling and for the "dominion over Nature" which is absolutely necessary to Society, and art as a "recreation" in order to preserve freshness in the work in one's calling. Cf. *Gottschick: Ethik, p. 127:* "The secular moral associations in their professional organization are the requisite means for maintaining the natural life of humanity which is the indispensable presupposition for the transformation of humanity into the Kingdom of God. Luther's objective theory of the *Lex Divina Naturalis* as the basis of Society is thus replaced by the witness of history, which shows that according to the Will of God the different classes of secular callings are intended to serve the purpose of the Kingdom of God. If this is true of the civil calling, in which one gains a livelihood, it is all the more true of the Christian calling, if to that are added all the moral and other tasks which result from the regular relations of the individual in the family, in Society, in the State, and in the Church." *Herrmann: Ethik*[3], *1904, p. 158:*

"We only then show ourselves as Christians in the world when it is natural to us to see the working of God in the inexhaustible formative power of Nature (that is, the *Lex Naturae* of Luther, without his application to definite and permanent institutions): hence we should value as the basis of our order of life and as forms of our activity which have been given to us by God, the naturally established human associations which we find in the world already." Just as Luther regarded the class guild, absolutist and agrarian form of life as a condition which was permanently demanded by Nature, and one which could be approximated to Christianity on the side of the external life, so here an unlimitedly mobile shaping of these things, including the modern militaristic, capitalistic, and scientific and aesthetic civilization, is regarded as the "form" of the natural life which is to be inspired by faith. Likewise, in *v. d. Goltz: Grundlagen der christlichen Sozialethik*, who in his "sociological" section develops the Lutheran doctrine of Natural Law by a modern doctrine of the "natural basic forms in the family, the State, and Society", and then places these "forms" under the influence of the Christian spirit; *p. 282:* "In Christianity religion takes over the guidance of human social life. . . . The dominion of the Spirit over nature is here led to a gradual completion, and all individual and social disharmonies are smoothed out, while the peculiar energies of the various social groups are also brought into harmony." Likewise also *Luthardt: Kompendium der Ethik, 1896*: "Since the spirit is only the truth of man and Christianity, the truth of the earthly life, so the truth of the morality of the natural life consists in this, that this morality shall be achieved with the sense and spirit and moral power which Christianity provides. . . . Gratia non tollit, sed sanat naturam." Everywhere any possibility of an inner opposition between the natural forms of the ethic of civilization and the radical spirit of love (whose eternal aims ought to fill them) has been entirely forgotten, and Luther's conflicts around this problem are simply regarded as "Catholic relics". The saying of *Luthardt* reminds us directly of the Catholic principle: "Gratia praesupponit ac perficit naturam", and shows at the same time the striking difference. In Catholicism Nature and Grace are different in degree, in Protestantism they finally come together as form and content.

229 (p. 509.) Cf. *Eger, pp. 124 ff.*: "That which has been said above about the alteration in the conception of faith and of obedience to the revealed word of God, and of the way in which obedience is ranged against the promises, and those again are set over against the commandments of God, finds its clearest expression in the passage out of the *Enarr. in Genesin*: 'Haec sunt verae laudes obedientiae, quae tantum est vel promissionum vel praeceptorum divinorum.' " A similar tendency emerges in the fact that the theory of 'faith and love" which was laid down in the *Liberty of a Christian Man* as the mark of the Christian life, is replaced by the principle of "faith and obedience towards God". "After we have placed our righteousness solely upon the promised Seed, promising also that we will be obedient to God, and that in this temporal life we will do and observe what He has commanded. . . . Therefore both must be together, faith and obedience to God." This makes the works of the Christian holy in contrast with those of the pagan because they are carried out in the spirit of faith in Christ and in obedience to God. The *Kirchenpostil e* has similar ideas: "God wills that after our sins have been forgiven we should live in obedience to His commands." "That which leads us to obedience is, more and more, not the revealed grace of God in Christ which wins our hearts, but the formal authority of the Divine word" (*p. 125*). The parallelism of the knowledge of faith and of the moral law is characteristic, both have taken the same course

of development, for the same reason, namely, for the sake of the conception of the Church. Curiously enough, theologians have complained a good deal of the first development, while they have praised the second, since it provides them with that humanitarian theory of Christianity which accepts the world, which they find so necessary at the present day. Therefore, in general, the limitations of the modern verdict on Luther, which praises his earlier individualism, which was like that of the sect-type, and complains of his prejudice in favour of a Catholic negation of the world, while it regards the dogmatism of Luther as an older man as a reaction towards Catholicism, and praises his attitude of acceptance of the world as modern progress. In reality, both the latter are inseparable from the Church-type, as the two former were inseparable from all tendencies towards the sect-type. This shows how fruitful the differentiation between the sect-type and the Church-type which was made in *II, 9* is for our subject as a whole. This will also be very evident in dealing with Calvinism and the Baptist movement.

230 (p. 510.) On this point cf. my treatment of the subject in the *Kultur der Gegenwart*. Characteristic passages in *Herrmann: Verkehr, p. 208*: "This does not mean leaving and fleeing from the world as they (the Papists) imagine; for thou mayest be in whatever kind of life or position that thou wilt—for thou must be something because thou art living upon earth—God has not told thee to depart from them, but to live among them; for each man has been created and born for the sake of other men. Wherever now thou art I say, and in whatever position thou dost find thyself there thou must flee from the world." "Thus I am separated from the world and yet am in the world." Thus also *Luthardt* says rightly: "Therefore in the sphere of outward activity we are not to mark off a special sphere of ascetic activity, but we are to bring the ascetic factor into all our activity" (*Ethik Luthers, p. 63*). *Braun: Concupiszenz:* "Thus there lies truth in the paradox: by the very fact that Luther drove the monastic ideal to its farthest limit he destroyed it in its very root" (*p. 57*). That is what Max Weber and I mean when we speak of an "asceticism within this world" of Protestantism, in opposition to the Catholic asceticism, which is above—or perhaps better—alongside of, this world.

230a (p. 513.) This statement of the midway position of Lutheranism between a system of moderate asceticism and ecclesiastical guidance of Society on the one hand, and a sectarian enthusiastic radicalism on the other hand, is specially adduced for the Christian social problem of the present day. According to the genuine Christian social idea it would be good to retain the free non-legal spirit of the ethic of love, and to leave social reform itself solely to political and social experts who should draw the spiritual energies they need for their task out of this spirit. Certainly *R. Sohm* expresses himself to me in a letter: "the Gospel is understood as containing a social programme. Through that the Gospel became a new law which was established now in a relative and now in a radical form. But, as I believe, the development consisted in the fact that this standpoint was superseded, and I consider that the first great step towards progress in this direction was taken in Luther's Reformation. The second step, which led to the present day, came through the Enlightenment. . . . The ethical consequence of brotherly love which is given through the love of God cannot be gathered up in some law or programme which will hold good for all time, and they are, therefore, no essential part of the Gospel, which for all time is a message of salvation which is ever valid, whose content is solely religious and which brings forth social energies but no social programme." In any case, however, that is not the meaning of Lutheran thought in its application to social things, for according to Luther's idea the latter are not free and mobile, but through the Law of Nature they are bound up with an entirely anti-capitalist tendency; the modern social development was rejected by Luther in the name of Nature as well as in the name of the Gospel as the next section will show. On the other hand, however, even the Gospel for Luther is not the personal spirit of love which offers power to Christianize social institutions which in themselves have become necessary in the course of history, but an individual ethic of unconditional love and readiness to suffer which does not penetrate and shape the official morality of law and property, but tolerates and suffers it as an opposition introduced by sin which cannot be overcome. Calvinism would come better under this heading, which in point of fact penetrates existing Society with the Christian spirit and knows no invincible opposition between official and individual morality (public and private morality). But all such spirit must in application become a programme and a law, and thus it became that also in Calvinism, whereby its law was indeed not unchangeable, but it adapted itself with great elasticity to the various conditions of life among the Calvinistic nations; this will become plain in the third section. The classic theory formulated by *Sohm* is rather a very modern theory, as he himself seems to suggest. Its assumption is the insight into the impossibility of stabilizing social institutions and the judgment of these things according to their immanent purely secular necessity, and with that precisely the withdrawal of religion to that which is purely spiritual and religious. It contains at the same time the equally modern demand that the Christian spirit should penetrate the social world, that is, the demand for a uniform ethic which, in contrast with Luther's dualism, should accept the ever-changing social world, and still at the same time penetrate and mould it with its own spirit. The question is, however, whether and how this is possible at all in face of modern social life, and whether it does not make it necessary to have a most inward transformation of the Christian ethic in order to draw in the secular life values even when a penetration of spirit of the existing necessities merely is demanded, and even when these are to be seriously conformed to the ideal. Here, however, we have reached the problems of the modern Christian ethic, which rather resemble those of Calvinism than those of Lutheranism; but it is no longer possible to solve them in the traditional Scriptural manner (i.e. O.T.) of Calvinism. Not from the Bible, but from the Christian spirit, that is, from the progressive Christian principle, these questions must be answered to-day, if it is really possible to answer them at all. This, however, is rather different from the old Lutheran position. This is a modern way of thinking along evolutionary historical lines, as indeed indirectly the words of *Sohm* seem to suggest. The new position is a result of a process of progress which arose out of the history of the Middle Ages, passed through Protestantism, and which leads from Protestantism to a modern form of Christianity which arose out of the latter, but is not identical with it. This fundamental content which can everywhere be recognized reveals itself also in the problem of the social doctrines of Christianity; cf. my work on Protestantism in *Kultur der Gegenwart, I, IV, 1, pp. 634–649.*

231 (p. 516.) On this point see *Möller-Kawerau: Lehrbuch der Kirchengeschichte, III³, 1907; Riecker: Die Rechtliche Stellung;* and, above all, *Sohm: Kirchenrecht, I.* The work of *Sohm* is not only extremely able, but it also has a very unprejudiced eye for the historical and actual which has not been dimmed by modern ideas of Church-order. Here the Lutheran doctrine is understood in its most inward and real sense. The paradox of *Sohm's* argument only arises in this,

that it treats the over-idealistic miraculous Lutheran conception of the Church which Lutheranism itself has completed by a very realistic secular Church law as something which also without this completion can and should exist; and the vulnerable historical point is the identification of that idealistic Lutheran conception of the Church with that of the Primitive Church, which had no legal tradition at all and which works not with conceptions which are detached from law, but with legal conceptions which have not been defined, and, above all, which places the ministry under the Enthusiastic conception of the charisma. Of that more anon; also see above, *pp. 481 ff.* The point at which I believe that I must diverge from *Sohm's* treatment of the facts will be treated later; cf. *Note 236.*

[232] (p. 518.) On this, above all, see *Sohm*: the starting-point, the productive, miraculous power of the Word and not of the congregation (*pp. 511–513*); the pastoral character of jurisdiction based upon a free spirit of love and submission (*pp. 522 and 529*); the charismatic character of the ministry which depends upon the willing affection and permission of the congregation, only otherwise to be appointed according to order (*pp. 500–505, 518*); judgment on doctrine a matter for the pastors, but only as professional organs for self-interpretation of the Scriptures or as the mouthpiece of Christ (*pp. 521, 492 ff.*); the order of love in the congregation in contrast with the order of law (*pp. 494–496*). For Lutheranism the decisive point is faith in the wonderful spontaneous power of the Word of God to form churches, see the passage in *Sohm, p. 492.* Similar passages, *p. 616*; it is the main idea also in the later orthodoxy, see *Schmidt: Die Dogmatik der ev.-luth. Kirche*[6], *1876, p. 432.* This supernatural and objective spirituality, combined with the idea that the legal State which aims at secular well-being is not sufficient for this sphere but may serve it, is the source of the characteristic expressions of Luther about the relation between the sacred and the secular even in the case of those which sound most modern.

[234] (p. 519.) Cf. *Sohm, 622 and 627*: "And if it were necessary that the secular government, on occasion, should take up the question of those who despise the ban of the Church" (at first purely spiritual, carried out by the pastor and the congregation), in the Wittenberg Concord of 1545, which was signed by Luther and which dealt with the future form of Church government. *Sohm* rightly describes this as the specifically Lutheran view, as contrasted with the view of Melancthon and of most of the others who wanted to give to the Church courts the immediate power "to judge according to the Holy Scriptures and also according to the usual laws which are in our country . . . *arctiora mandata* with the menace of serious punishments, like fines, imprisonments, etc." and who wished to compel the secular authorities "straight away, without delay, to carry into effect the verdict of the ecclesiastical authorities" (*p. 628*).

[235] (p. 519.) On the whole subject, see the illuminating remarks of *Sohm: pp. 542–633.* Here also the right explanation for this development out of the renunciation of the supernatural idealism, from *Sohm's* personal point of view an effect of lack of faith for which he makes Melancthon especially responsible, cf. *612.*—As *Sohm* shows, Luther always protested against this development; but the passages quoted by *Sohm* reveal rather a protest of a theological and Scriptural nature against decisions of a juridical and Canon law nature than a conflict between the voluntary order of love and a legal order of compulsion; for Luther is ready to hand over sinners in life and doctrine to the secular arm for further secular penalties. This means that the twofold order is differentiated more in theory than in anything else: actually in practice it all amounts to a legal and compulsory attitude even in matters

of Christian doctrine and discipline. The latter were found to be necessary and the formal decisions of Luther were practically ineffective. It could not be helped, *p. 619*: "The desire for a legal order was here stronger than faith in the rule of Christ and the power of the Word. Men desired a Church-order as an aid for the Word. Very well, it came, but it came in order to appoint the territorial prince as the lord also of the Church."—For the way in which it came, see *K. Müller: Anfänge der Konsistorialverfassung, Hist. Z., 302, pp. 1–30.*

236 (p. 521.) In this I have expressed my own attitude, as briefly as possible, to *Sohm's* famous thesis. It contains the important sociological viewpoint that every kind of Church-order is the law of the Church, and as that which is appointed to protect great supernatural things it is itself drawn into this supernatural order, and in so doing it receives qualities which make it quite incommensurable for the precise and actual jurists. Further, within this law there is the inconsistency that it binds and hampers the quite individual religious life by formal and purely objective standards. Only this is a contradiction which does not belong to the fact of a law in the Church, but to the conception of the Church as an institution which protects by strict rules an objective treasure of revelation. The ideal conception of the Church as of an institution which can be freely developed and ruled by the Word is a Utopia of faith. Historically the question is whether Luther purely and exclusively sanctioned this Utopia of faith as *Sohm* believes, and whether the introduction of a Divine Law in reality can only be laid to the account of Melancthon, the politicians and the consistories, or, in other words, whether Luther (who had retained so many mediaeval Catholic elements of the conception of the Church, especially that of the objective doctrine which can alone give salvation and of the united Christian Society) at this point really went so far as to exclude all Divine Law from the Church and every kind of Divinely based rule for securing pure doctrine and the ordering of morals. The answer depends on the interpretation of Luther's doctrine of the office of the ministry. *Sohm* interprets the Lutheran conception of the ministry (*p. 473*) quite simply from the point of view of the primitive Christian charismatic idea and overestimates Luther's own expressions about the charismatic character of the ministry, *p. 474*: "The heart of the doctrine of Luther . . . that the pastor exercises his office 'only on account of the congregation', only in the name of 'the Church'. His ministry, from the spiritual point of view, he can only have from God through the gift which God has given him, but the exercise of the ministry is only possible to him, not legally, but solely because he is permitted by the congregation (!)." Luther, however, alongside of this supernatural charismatic conception of the ministry also undoubtedly had the supernatural legal conception which represented the ministry of the pure Word as the truth of Scripture and formed the official expression of the community ordained by God, which is bound to the assumption of an orderly calling excluding all disorder and fanaticism. The latter, in the prevailing point of view, is rightly regarded as the central point of a spiritual law since existence and a proper calling *de jure* are required for it, and the exercise of the Scriptural understanding of the congregation is bound up with these official interpreters of the Word; it is only the manner of the calling which is left free to human custom. The above presentation of this subject is based upon this latter conception.

237 (p. 522.) For these *externa disciplina*, which the Government is bound to exercise as *custos utriusque tabulae* from the point of view of the State, and as *membrum praecipuum ecclesiae* from the point of view of the Church, see the words

of *Melancthon* quoted by *Sohm*: "Magistratus est custos primae et secundae tabulae legis, quod ad externam disciplinam attinet, hoc est prohibere externa scelera et punire sontes debet et proponere bona exempla. . . . Etsi enim magistratus non mutat corda nec habet ministerium spiritus, tamen habet suum officium externae disciplinae conservandae etiam in iis, quae ad primam tabulam pertinent (that is, in questions of worship and orthodoxy in doctrine). . . . Cum quaeras, quae sint officia magistratuum, tibi pingito magistratum cui de collo pendeant tabulae duae legis Moysi. Horum custos esse debet politicus gubernator, quoad externam disciplinam attinet. Nam haec sunt summae leges, ex quibus ceterae honestae leges omnes tamquam ex fontibus derivantur." For the way in which these *externa disciplina* for the maintenance of a Christian external order are to be used by the secular officials, see the *Visitations Instruction* of 1527, *Sohm, p. 607*: "Officials, jurymen, town councillors, noble judges, also ought to punish matters which are not to be borne among Christians . . . like the following: frivolous swearing and using the Name of God in vain, *item* gluttony, drunkenness, gaming, idleness, *item* treating matters of faith flippantly or contemptuously in wine- or beer- or drink-houses, or quarrelling about them (thus a system of denunciation, which, according to *Wappler's* reports of law proceedings actually became very dangerous to many Anabaptists), adultery and fornication, disobedience of children to their parents, and especially when these attack their parents with words, or with their hands, *item* if the children get engaged without their parents' will or knowledge." Absence from Church, disturbances in Church, and, of course, false doctrine, are all punishable offences. The punishments which are preferable are imprisonment rather than fines, which are considered "self-interested". Later on, the consistories exercise the same discipline in their own name (*p. 615*) with fines, imprisonments, and corporal punishment, also with the great ban which is the result of the civil boycott, "*suspensio ab officio* exclusion from the council, denial of the right to exercise his trade or his livelihood". People even thought of building a special consistorial prison. These things only show how everything was dominated by the idea of the uniform Christian Society. Luther also desires all these things, only not at the disposal of the spiritual authority, but of the secular authority as such, which he justifies by the fiction that all these crimes also have a civil aspect which the State ought to punish as a contravention of its own order! Calvinism, on the contrary, places all these matters under the control of the ecclesiastical court of discipline itself, which has the power to inflict very effective "purely spiritual" punishments, and thus, through the Church, by spiritual means, it establishes a social order which Lutheranism handed over to the civil government, and which, in the mixed consistories, came under the standpoint of the interests of the State entirely, and for that reason it did not develop a religious and ethical influence at all.

[238] (p. 522.) *Gerhard* in *Schmidt: Dogmatik, p. 452:* "Status sive ordines in ecclesia a Deo instituti numerantur tres, videlicet ecclesiasticus, politicus et oeconomicus, quos etiam hierarchias appellare consueverunt. Oeconomicus ordo inservit generis humani multiplicationi, politicus ejusdem defensioni, ecclesiasticus ad salutem aeternam promotioni. Oec. ordo oppositus est a Deo vagis libidinibus, polit. tyrannidi et latronciniis; eccles. haeresibus ac doctrinae corruptelis." These divisions are very ancient, see *XXVIII, p. 624*; also *Böhmer: Luther, p. 220*; in a Bishop Gerhard of Cambrai, 1036 (*Luthardt: Comp., p. 267*), and then again in Stephen of Prague and Nicholas of Clemanges, *Köhler: Staatslehre der Vorreformatoren* (*Jahrbb. f. deutsche Theologie, XX, p. 95*). Also in

Wimpfeling, 1501, see *Roscher: Nationalökonomik, p. 37*. In the last resort that really is the Platonic classification of classes in his *politeia*. The theory goes right through the whole ethic and dogmatics of Lutheranism, and has again been taken up by the ethic of modern confessional Lutheranism, whereby it is admitted that they owe to Pietism a broadening beyond the narrow conception of callings into the "general Christian humanity, for example, of home and foreign missions"; see *Luthardt: Compendium der Ethik, pp. 267–269*.

[239] (p. 523.) For this idea of the *Corpus Christianum*, see specially the excellent treatment of the subject by *Rieker*; similarly *Sohm, p. 540*: "We only gain the right standpoint for the complete understanding of the question with which we are concerned when we get rid of all our present-day ideas about Church and State and transport ourselves into the spirit of the Church politics of the sixteenth century, which were still very much determined by the Middle Ages. The conceptions of Church and State in the present sense are still unknown, the fundamental conception is that of Christendom. In Christendom God has appointed 'two swords': the spiritual and the secular. It is the duty of both to govern Christendom, but with different aims and therefore with a different authority, the one with spiritual authority and the other with secular authority. The nature of these 'two swords', and therefore of their mutual relationship in authority, had to be determined. This is what Luther did. His doctrine of the division between the two forms of government represents solely the reformed doctrine of the Middle Ages of the 'two swords'. Clearly it does not regard the question according to the relation between two organizations, but solely the question of the relation between two authorities . . . , which both belong to a great organism of Christendom." Because the whole civilization of Lutheranism is based upon this, I have described this in the *Kultur der Gegenwart, 4*, as a certainly very penetrating transformation of mediaeval civilization. *Böhmer, p. 121*, however, gives it as his opinion that this is "simply an assertion and, indeed, an assertion which excludes absolutely a clear insight into the nature of Protestantism as well as of Catholicism"!

[239a] (p. 523.) For the ethic of Lutheranism, cf. *Troeltsch: Joh. Gerhard und Melancthon; Hönnicke: Studien zur altprot. Ethik, 1902* (also my review, *G. G. A., 1902, pp. 577–583*); *Hupfeld: Ethik Joh. Gerhards, 1908* (also my review, *Th. L., 1909*); also the *Geschichten der christlichen Ethik*, by *Gass* and *Luthardt*; *Th. Ziegler* remains, here also, on the fringe of the subject. Instructive presentation of the modern Lutheran ethic, but quite steeped in the Lutheran spirit, *Gottschick: Ethik, 1907; Luthardt: Compendium der Ethik, 1896*, rich in quotations from the orthodox ethic; *Hofmann: Theolog. Ethik, 1878*, an excellent even though modernized description of the spirit of the Lutheran ethic. Both the latter are visibly full of the spirit of the triumph of this ethic in Church and State after the interim period of the Enlightenment, and they give some idea of the instinctive connection between the modern Conservative party and the spirit of the Lutheran ethic. A magnificent analysis of the Lutheran ethic in relation to the Calvinistic ethic is given by *Schneckenburger*, cf. *Darstellung des Lutherischen und Reformierten Lehrbegriffes, 1855*.—We must always remember in every presentation of the Protestant ethic the Lutheran special dogma of the exposition of the Sermon on the Mount, according to which this only rules the spirit of Christians towards Christians without legally binding them to their concrete examples, and, above all, assumes alongside of this exhortation to a spiritual outlook at the same time the civil and legal official and vocational ethic as a legal order instituted by God. That is a fundamental Scriptural dogma as important as the doctrine of justification by faith, and it stands over against

the Catholic dogma that the Sermon on the Mount contains the evangelical counsels of a one-sided perfection ethic alongside of the ethic of the world for the special class of the monks, as well as against the sect-dogma that the whole of Christian Society ought to obey these rules, and therefore as a religious group ought to withdraw from the State and from the world. This is a fundamental dogma of exegesis of Lutheranism contrasted with Catholics and Baptists. Hence also the characteristic historic construction of the Lutherans according to which the post-apostolic and primitive Church ethic under pagan influences again became uncertain about the right understanding of the Sermon on the Mount (*Hofmann, p. 294*). In reality, the Protestant dogma of the Sermon on the Mount was not yet present and could not be present. It only became possible through the mediaeval development over which the relative opposition must not lead us astray.

[240] (p. 524.) For further proofs, see *Buddeus: Isagoge historico-theologica ad theologiam universam, Lpz., 1720, II, 4*: "De theologia morali simulque de theologia mystica itemque jurisprudentia divina et prudentia tum christiana tum pastorali." Even this title shows the variety of the contents; the retrospective survey of the history of the Lutheran ethic (*pp. 652–672*) emphasizes it expressly and laments that there is no systematic treatment of the subject, although Luther and Melancthon were supposed to have renewed all the subject-matter of ethics. To that then comes in addition the "theologia conscientiaria", or casuistry (*p. 616*), about whose connection with the Lutheran practice of confession (which had to differentiate between the sins which led to loss of grace and those which did not lead to it) *Hupfeld* makes a very instructive contribution to the subject. Also on this side there is an analogy with the Catholic ethic: the ecclesiastical ethic can only hold together the heterogeneous elements which it contains by means of casuistry and the confessional in spite of its Protestant autonomy and emphasis upon inwardness. Something similar is revealed by the Calvinistic system of Church discipline. The difference lies merely in the absence of the legal binding nature of the verdict; see the statement by *Gass, II, 1, p. 157*, on *Balduin: Tractatus toti rei publicae utilis sive de casibus conscientiae, 1628*. I here give the outline of the material according to B. (1) The real philosophical ethic in the Aristotelian sense is occupied with questions of the virtues, temperaments, etc., all of which is absorbed into the Christian central virtue of love; see *Luthardt: Compendium, 122–165*. (2) The other part of ethics is the doctrine of Natural Law: "Altera philosophiae practicae pars seu jurisprudentia naturalis de officiis hominum legibusque divinis, quibus illa diriguntur, praecipit." For the second section the main authority is Cicero, while Aristotle, it is true, "ad vitae civilis usum unice accommodatus est", but "prudentiae potius quam obligationis legumque divinorum habuit rationem" (*p. 308*). The Church Fathers combine this Natural Law with revelation, the Schoolmen mingled Aristotle, the *jus civile* and the *jus canonicum* in a confused way. Melancthon, Benedict Winkler, and others then restored the right relationship. Finally, *Fal. Alberti*, in his *Compendium juris naturae orthodoxae theologiae conformatum*, whom the jurists Dav. Menius and Veit Lud. v. Seckendorf followed, deduced the Natural Law from the Primitive State, only in so doing they did not lay sufficient emphasis upon the special conditions and modifications produced by the Fall. In any case, it is "praestantissima philosophiae practicae pars, quae vel maxime vitae civilis negotiis inservire debet (*p. 344*)". (3) The third part of ethics is the real Politica, the doctrine of the effectuation of civil welfare in all classes and callings: "eo magis illa tractatio est necessaria, quo amplius ejus est usus,

siquidem non tantum prudentiae civilis et aulicae, sed et christianae et theologicae et ecclesiasticae principia et fundamenta ex ea petenda sunt" (*p. 317*). Here also there is a large literature which only in more recent times as "politica sive prudentia civilis" has become clearly defined in relation to the doctrine of the universal Law of Nature, which in earlier days was to a great extent mingled together with it. The primitive form of this "Prudentia civilis" is the Mosaic Law, "omnes enim istae leges aequitati naturali sunt consentaneae" (*p. 419*); then the Wisdom literature of the Old Testament which had "prudentiam non minus quam ad doctrinam moralem seu vitam recte instituendam spectant" (*p. 320*). The results have been put together by the well-known theologian *Dannhauer*, in a *Politica biblica*. Further, Aristotle has to be considered; it is, however, felt that he is not quite sufficient to meet the requirements of the present day; after that there follow notes on more recent literature on politics and State administration, among whom Bodin and Machiavelli, who exaggerates the rights of princes, must not be overlooked. To this belongs also political economy whose connection with the Christian class state and the Natural Law is shown by *Roscher: Geschichte der Nationalökonomik*. *Buddeus* names above all Seckendorff's Christian State: "de omnium ordinum emendatione secundum indolem disciplinae Christinae praecipit" (*p. 721*). (4) Above these three or four sections of practical theology there then rises the real *theologia moralis*, the doctrine of the *motus spirituales*, or the *theologia moralis mystica*, whereby this mysticism is only permissible if it is pure, that is, if it is based upon faith in the Atonement and faith in the Bible: "Per theologiam mysticam, puram scilicet, nihil aliud intelligi quam ipsam theologiam moralem stricte sic dictam quemlibet potest docere collatio. Mysticam namque theologiam ita nonnulli definire solent, quod sit divina et arcana de Deo rebusque divinis sapientia, qua mens hominis regeniti illuminetur, voluntas virtutibus divinis instructa ab inquinamentis peccatorum purgetur, ut illa cum Deo arctissime uniatur. Id vero est, quorsum et theologia moralis tendit" (*p. 672*). The books by *Alberti*, *Dannhauer*, and others I have unfortunately been unable to read.

242 (p.529.) Cf. on this point *K. Köhler: Luther und die Juristen, 1873; E. Brandenburg: M. L.s Anschauung vom Staate und der Gesellschaft, 1901* (*Schriften d. Vereins f. Ref.-Gesch., 70*); *G. Müller: Luthers Stellung zum Rechte* (*Schriften des evang. Bundes, 43–44*), *1906; E. Ehrhardt: La nature du droit naturel chez Luther, Festschrift der Pariser Fakultät für Montauban; Cardauns: Lehre vom Widerstandsrecht im Luthertum und Calvinismus, Bonner Diss., 1903.—Bluntschli: Gesch. d. allgemeinen Staatsrechtes und der Politik, 1864, pp. 46–60*, does not penetrate deeply enough into the subject; he makes certain criticisms which to some extent are in touch with modern liberal criticism. *Bergbohm: Jurisprudenz und Rechtsphilosophie, 1892*, a radical criticism of all Natural Law from a purely legal Positivistic standpoint has neither knowledge nor understanding of the ecclesiastical Natural Law, and speaks especially of the Natural Law of the Reformers (*p. 159*) with complete ignorance of the subject. *Hinrichs: Geschichte der Rechts und Staatsprinzipien seit der Ref. I, 1848*, gives little about Luther, more about Melanchton and orthodoxy.

243 (p. 529.) Here is the radical difference from Occam's Natural Law, *Ehrhardt, 304*. Cf., for example, the "exhortation to peace in reply to the Twelve Articles of the peasants": "So there is the Natural Law which governs the whole world, that no one may be his own judge nor revenge himself" (*B. A., IV, 1, p. 319*). "Can ye not think that if your demand were right each man would judge the other, and there would be no longer any authority or government, order or law in the world, but simply murder and the shedding of blood . . . ? Now it is said of the common Divine and Natural Law that

even the heathen, the Turks and the Jews, must keep it, if order and peace in the world is to remain" (*p. 321*). "You are going beyond God, and taking away from the government its authority and its rights, and indeed all that it has. For of what use is the government if it has lost its authority? . . . . In authority consists all its wealth and all its life" (*p. 320*). Still more clearly in the pamphlet *Ob Kriegsleute auch in seligem Stand sein können, 1526.* So also in the modern Lutheran ethic, cf. *von Hofmann*: "As a member of the State the Christian is obliged, by means of that which the legal order offers, to maintain his own rights against their abuse by the official ruler. When this is out of the question, then only one of two things is morally possible, either to endure compulsion or to exchange this State for another" (*p. 278,* see also *p. 273*).

246 (p. 532.) *Figgis: From Gerson to Grotius, pp. 62–107,* places Luther with Machiavelli. *Buddeus: Isagoge, 323,* sees in Lutheranism the right mean between followers of Machiavelli and the *Monarchomachi* (opponents of monarchy): "quorum illi imperantibus plus quam decet coneedunt, hi plus quam decet adimunt". He also finds in Bodin relative truths; the related elements in the view of Hobbes on the contrary seem to have been nowhere recognized; only Pufendorf, who in many respects had a Lutheran way of thinking (see *Bluntschli, p. 130 f.; Lezius: Toleranzbegriff Lockes und Pufendorfs, 1900, pp. 58 and 68*), has noticed this; see *Bluntschli, 121.*—These ideas of Lutheran Natural Law are those which lie entirely at the basis of the legal philosophy of F. J. Stahl, and in Stahl they experience their first comprehensive and otherwise very able philosophical basis; cf. the instructive analysis of *Stahl* in *E. Kaufmann: Studien zur Staatslehre des monarchischen Prinzips, Hallenser Diss., 1906.* The connection with Luther is carried out right into details: the Government and authority a power that has been absolutely given and set over individuals (*p. 79*); the social institutions, the family, property, the State, based in the Divine Will and not in immanental necessity, but appointed with the Creation and with Nature working themselves out along their own naturally reasonable laws (*p. 82*); law is ethical even in its transformation into an external compulsory authority which has been effected by the Fall (*p. 83*); the State and Society limited to the working out of the purposes of well-being and order within the world for which authority and order is necessary, in that, however, it is quite independent and not influenced by revelation (*p. 94*); the source of natural Reason is equally the source of the Divine power and appointment (*p. 94*). All those statements are purely Lutheran; it is the Natural Law "of irrationalism", as *Kaufmann* rightly sets it over against the Natural Law of Rationalism; only *Kaufmann* in a quite erroneous conception of Luther as a representative of modern autonomous individualism has not recognized this connection (*p. 99*). The special factor in time and in history for Stahl is solely the intensification of the "irrational Natural Law" exactly towards the legitimist monarchy for which Luther felt no necessity. Princes or magistrates were all the same to him.—It is from this point of view that we can understand right down to the present day the politics of Conservatives who combine a policy of dominion with all the consequences of the thought of power with a Christian piety which is restricted to the inward life of the spirit and temper, and who maintain an ethical connection between the two separate spheres only by means of the theory of the patriarchal relationship of authority and respect, which should subsist between those who rule and those who are ruled. Cf. the demand of Stahl quoted by *Kaufmann* (*p. 96*): "Thou ought not to break this connection without reason (with the authority that has come into existence historically), thou must have reverence for that which God has either ordained

or permitted to take place; thou shalt not merely obey the Government where such exists but thou shalt yield faithfulness and affection to the dynasty which is rooted in history." Otherwise the existence alongside of each other of a policy of force, which includes all kinds of harshness, of a system of power which has to be established legally, and of a love ethic which believes in Providence, the result of sin, in which then all that is left over is to protect as far as possible the positive law and authority and a compromise in which the love ethic keeps the abstract doctrinaire spirit in the background.—Also in Bismarck the striking phenomenon of his policy of force, and his Christian piety which existed alongside of each other, can only be understood if one understands the ideas of that Lutheran and Stahl principle of the "Natural Law of irrationalism" alongside of a Christian piety which was entirely untouched by it; in the Calvinistic and sectarian Cromwell, and also in Gladstone and Lincoln, a position of this kind would have been quite impossible. For this separation between an external policy of force and an inward piety of feeling Bismarck liked to appeal to Luther; see *Lenz: Bismarcks Religion* (*Ausgew. Vortrage und Aufsatze, deutsche Bücherei Nr. 18*), *Art. Bismarck* in *Religion in Geschichte und Gegenwart; Meinecke: B. s. Eintritt in den christlich-germanischen Kreis H. Z., 1902; O. Baumgarten, B. s. Stellung zu Religion und Kirche, 1900;* now, above all, *E. Marcks: Bismarck, I, 1910.* The impression of Bismarck's political thought upon German Christian piety has been extraordinary even down to the present day; but the glorification of force which has been rendered necessary by sin, with the withdrawal of the Christian ethic more to private relationships, is not only a peculiarity of the Prussian religion of the present day, even though it is only here that it has gained an enthusiastic acceptance as something quite natural which was alien to Luther's ideas and for other reasons also to those of Bismarck.

[247] (p. 532.) Cf. the expression of opinion in the *Kreuzzeitung* on the aristocratic selection-theories of the well-known evolutionist sociologist *Otto Ammon*: "The weakness of the doctrine of the Blue and Red democracies cannot be represented more strikingly than in this book"; they are results "against which even from a strictly conservative standpoint there is nothing to be said"; see *Stillich: Die politischen Parteien in Deutschland, I, Die Konservativen, p. 32;* appeal of the *Kreuzzeitung* to Machiavelli's theory of Power, *p. 58.* Or see the statement in the Conservative election programme of 1849: "The Conservative candidate must be a political man. He must know that force in the life of a State is an eternally effective factor, and that it (although in itself unreasonable) may always be used if it produces that which is reasonable, as is proved by its being a fundamental condition of the life of the State" (*Stillich, p. 218*).

[250] (p. 534.) Cf. the section in *Stillich: Die Rechtsauffassung der Konservativen, pp. 161–178.* The inequality of law according to differences of class and the justice which takes account of the conditions of the time in contrast to the abstract equality before the law (*p. 166*). A mad example of Kadi justice is the verdict of the Duke Charles of Burgundy in *von weltl. Obrigkeit, IV, 1, p. 272,* to which Luther appeals: "A knight who engages the affections of the wife of his enemy and promises her that he will spare the life of her husband, and then, in spite of that, kills his enemy, is condemned to take the woman to wife, and then after the bridal night he is unexpectedly beheaded, and all his goods are given to the lady. See how such a judgment is freely due to reason, and goes so far beyond the law of all books that everyone must acknowledge its justice and find in his own heart that it is right."

[251] (p. 535.) For the foundation of institutions in God and the meaning of this foundation, see *Ehrhardt, p. 303*. It is always meant indirectly. How this is understood is shown by the fact that Luther held that the Holy Roman Empire was appointed, that is, founded, by God, although Luther held that the *translatio imperii* by the Pope was a piece of trickery; *W. Köhler: Luthers Schrift an den Adel, 1895, p. 242.* "Starting from the idea of the absolute and unlimited arbitrariness of God . . . Luther recognizes in the Pope's action a Divine intention, he places the Pope's action under the guidance of God, seeing in the Pope the mechanical instrument of the Divine and Almighty Will." Thus *Professor Suchsland* explains the Conservative theories of authority in the State, in morality, in law, in marriage, absolutely from the strictly scientific standpoint, that is, on the presupposition of the principle of selection; the theory of a "Divine appointment" is then held to be merely the transcendent dogmatic element of faith which is only something additional (*Stillich, p. 33*).

[252] (p. 535.) On this point cf. *Corpus Reff., XXI u. XVI;* also *Köhler: Luther und die Juristen, pp. 100–105; Troeltsch: Gerhard und Melancthon; Ellinger: Melancthon, 1902, pp. 585–589;* here his tendency to the aristocracy of the towns, just as it was with Erasmus; very good rendering in *Hänel: Mel., der Jurist* (*Z. f. Rechtsgeschichte, hg. v. Rudorff, VIII, 1869*). The following passage is relevant: "His standpoint is that of Scholasticism, in spite of his aversion to it, and that which in all his writings distinguishes him from the Scholastic writers is neither a greater precision in the definition of ideas nor a more independent and free method, neither new and fruitful ideas, nor even merely a deeper utilization of Aristotle, but solely the popularization of the subject-matter, the attempt to bring the philosophic way of thinking nearer to life, and naturally, above all, the altered view of the relation between Church and State" (*p. 269*). Only the doctrine of non-resistance must still be emphasized, as *H.* himself says in another place: "Behind the political ideas there are independent and peculiar conceptions and principles, as, for instance, especially, that man is created for Society, and that in Society conditions of authority and submission obtain which must be recognized and logically developed. But they are conceptions and principles which are Divinely implanted. It is this which makes the State a Divine institution. . . . The existing State and the existing law are Divine even when they are oppressive and stifle freedom; even a Divinely appointed and unbelieving ruler must be respected in his rights as a scourge of God. Every self-willed and thoughtless alteration in the constitution and in the laws must be rejected; even departures from Reason must be tolerated, so long as they do not go wholly against Nature and then spoil it" (*p. 260*). Then, how under the influence of the problems which faced the Schmalkald League, Melancthon and Luther recognized the right of resistance, and incidentally adopted the Rationalistic individualistic conception of the Law of Nature, is shown by *Cardauns, pp. 14–19*; here, incidentally, are the preparatory stages of Calvin's doctrine. Unfortunately, *Cardauns* does not show how these doctrines disappeared from Lutheranism; their disappearance was probably connected with the general "Fundamentalist-Lutheran" reaction, and the reactionary propaganda which emanated from Saxony, through which, then, the forces which made for reform and progress were driven into Calvinism. In later Lutheranism the problem of resistance centres chiefly round the problem of the relation between the territorial lords and the Imperial power, in which a strictly Imperial and Conservative party stood in opposition to a Calvinistically influenced party, which was much freer and which centred in Jena; see *Stintzing: Geschichte der deutschen Rechtswissenschaft, II, 1884, pp. 40–54.*—The gradual

decline of the liberal conception of Natural Law in the School of Melancthon, see *v. Kaltenborn: Vorläufer des Hugo Grotius, 1848.*

[252a] (p. 537.) Cf. *Cardauns, p. 13*: at the beginning Melancthon follows the opinions of Luther; then, however, he shows "in opposition to Luther from the beginning, not only under the influence of external happenings", his preference for class control of the ruling power. *Cardauns* points out his preference for Ph. de Commynes (for the latter, *ibid., p. 30*, and *Baudrillart: Bodin, 1853, pp. 10–13*), also echoes of the Erasmian doctrine of the State, *Cardauns, pp. 31 ff.*—For the connection between his hatred of the non-Sacramentarians and his aversion to a republic, see *von Schubert: Bündnis und Bekenntnis, 1529–30, 1908, p. 9; M. s. Schule v. Hinrichs, I.*

[253] (p. 537.) Cf. *Stintzing: Geschichte der deutschen Rechtswissenschaft, I, 1880.* Very characteristic here is the deduction of the jurist Konrad Lagus (*pp. 302 ff.*): distinction between the *jus naturale primaevum* and the *jus naturale secundarium*, the latter "granted to man by the grace of God against his corrupt nature". "The law which flows from that the Romans call *jus gentium* because it is observed among all peoples. It is also called *jus divinum*. The Calvinists are wrong when they restrict this term to the standard laid down in the Gospel. For there are many *leges vere divinae* which are expressed neither in the Gospel nor in the Mosaic Law. The *jus divinum* is everything which corresponds to the Will of Christ and which purely human Reason requires for the protection of the existence of human society. This *jus naturale* has several degrees which are given in the Decalogue (by the distinction between the First and the Second Table). Its commandments—and, it is true, both those of the First and of the Second Table—can be inferred from human nature and Reason. Only, since the impulses of the sinful nature of man are so powerful that he often acts against the *judicium naturale*, it is not sufficient to leave obedience simply to his good-will. That is why it became necessary to invent other *legum carceres* in order to force men by public authority to obedience. These reflections lead to the positive law *jus civile*, "quod publica necessitate exigente civium suffragio (!) in aliqua re publica constituitur". In *Kling, I, 307*, we find the same conclusions and the same way of treating the conceptions *jus naturale primaevum* and *jus naturale secundarium* as technical conceptions. It means the same thing that I have distinguished all through this book as the difference between the "absolute" and "relative" Natural Law. It is just the same in the standard jurist, *Joh. Oldendorp, I, p. 371*: the *jus naturale secundarium* is said to be gathered up in the Decalogue as a means against sin; thence it was taken over into the Roman Twelve Tables which the Romans are supposed to have learned from the Greeks, and the Greeks from the Hebrews. It is only with the aid of these examples that we see clearly into the meaning of the thought of early Lutheranism.

[254] (p. 538.) For the details, see in *Stintzing, II*; the doctrines of the theologians of the seventeenth century, in *Schmidt: Ev.-Luth. Dogmatik, 459 ff.; Hollaz:* "Causa efficiens principalis magistratus est Deus triunus, qui certis personis officium magistratus committit vel immediate (Exod. iii. 10; Num. xxvii. 18; 1 Sam. ix. 15) vel mediate (John xix. 11) . . . Hodie ad officium magistratus personae habiles moderante Deo legitime perveniunt vel per electionem vel per successionem vel per justam occupationem." *J. Gerhard:* "Magistratum potestate aliqua instructum esse pater ex Rom. xiii. 1. . . . Potestas illa magistratus non est absoluta, illimitata et indeterminata, sed ad leges et normam superioris alicujus potestatis restricta. Cum enim potestatem suam a Deo magistratus acceperit, ideo Deum superiorem recognoscere et illius voluntati

ac legibus in usu hujus potestatis sese conformare tenetur. . . . Quando ergo politici absolutam potestatem [that is, Bodin's doctrine] summo magistratui tribuunt, id non est accipiendum simpliciter nec respectu superioris sc. Dei, sed dumtaxat respectu inferiorum magistratuum [this is in direct opposition to the main doctrine of Calvinism] . . . Propter peccatum protoplastorum non solum spiritualibus et aeternis futurae vitae bonis, sed etiam corporalibus et externis hujus vitae commodis genus humanum excidit. Sed Deus ex miranda et nunquam satis praedicanda benignitate propter filii intercessionem non illa solum sed etiam haec restituit ac reparavit ac media illis conservandis ordinavit. . . . Per magistratum politicum Deus conservat pacem et tranquillitatem externam, administrat justitiam civilem, defendit facultates, famam et corpora." All this takes place through the Natural Law of Reason, only the later doctrine emphasizes mainly the Divine appointment of the existing order; upon this a jurisprudence which works up the empirical law material then bases itself, without caring very much about the theoretically asserted deduction from the Natural Law and Reason.—The doctrine of the jurists is summarized by *Reinking*: "The fundamental idea of his political convictions is the (mediated) Divine appointment of all authorities. He who attacks it breaks faith and is disobedient, and must expect to be punished by God, even when in extreme cases the resistance can be excused, i.e. when it is exercised against a prince who by despising the fundamental laws and by legal violence has become a 'tyrant' (here, too, this is a relic of Natural Law Rationalist individualism!). To him the best of all forms of governments seems to be that of monarchy, because it is the most ancient and the most natural order, which most easily preserves peace, and which most nearly resembles the Divine government of the world" (*Stintzing, II, 197*). In matters affecting the law of the Empire, *R.* takes the Imperial standpoint; the Empire is the fourth world monarchy of the Book of Daniel, which will last for ever. Authorities are the Roman law, and the law of feudalism, and the mediaeval jurists. "*R.*'s work is interwoven with every fibre in the traditions of the Middle Ages so far as his decided Protestantism has not freed him" (*p. 199*). The opposing modern school of Arumäus and Limaeus, which was influenced by the Netherlands and by Calvinism, seems (according to *Stintzing's* illustrations) to have had modern ideas only in reference to the Imperial law. The analogous development in Catholic Absolutism (not, however, among the juridical philosophers), see *Kaufmann, pp. 16 ff.*, and in *Bossuet's Politique Tirée de l'Écriture, 1709;* in English Absolutism similar conclusions in *Filmer's Patriarcha, 1680.* The Law of Nature only became suspect to orthodox Lutherans after the Natural Law of Grotius had emancipated it from theology; see *Stintzing, II, 129;* over against that *Reinking* writes a *Biblische Polizei, d. i. gewisse aus heiliger göttlicher Schrift zusammengebrachte, auf die drei Hauptstände, als geistlichen, weltlichen, häuslichen, gerichtete Axiomata, Frankfurt, 1653;* the large number of editions proves that the book found deserved acceptance (*Stintzing, II, 207 ff.*). Similar in spirit is *Seckendorff's Deutscher Fürstenstaat, 1655,* and *Christenstaat, 1685.*—For the relation of *Grotius* and *Pufendorf* to these ecclesiastical schools of thought, see *Bluntschli und Hinrichs,* for *Masius,* see *Bluntschli, p. 184.*

255 (p. 539.) On this cf. *Roscher: Geschichte der Nationalökonomik in Deutschland, 1874.* In spite of the opinion that the Reformation really constituted a renewal of economic thought as well, *R.* recognizes its purely Scholastic character (in this respect) in his description of both the main representatives of the Lutheran doctrine of Society; *Melchior von Ossa* (died 1557) and *L. von Seckendorff* (died 1692): "Our friend Ossa stands likewise with one foot in the

theological period of political economy, and with the other in the juridical period. Besides the Bible, the Church Fathers, and Aristotle he quotes chiefly from the *Corpora Juris*", *p. 115*. That the latter is not in opposition to the Christian Natural Law has already been shown, and is also proved by the title of the main section of the work by *Ossa*: "*Von Gottseliger, weisslichen, vernünftigen und rechtmässigen Regierung und Institution*". Here the identification of the Bible, Reason, and law are distinctly expressed. The description of *von Seckendorff* is similar: "That theological, or at least religious, colour of the science of the State and political economy, which the Reformation had not only retained from the Scholastic period, but had also considerably warmed and deepened, was quickly disappearing among *S.'s* contemporaries" (*p. 240*). On the development from the first to the second, see *p. 252*: the Prince becomes from a patrimonial lord a new head of the State; in spite of all the piety of the time, political science and the system of political economy "became, to a great extent, emancipated from the whole admixture of theology and jurisprudence"; only then did political science and political economy go beyond aphorisms and become systematic sciences. For the way in which the Church was hampered, and for the use of Scriptural examples for doctrines of Reason, even among authors of a modern outlook, see the remarks on *Obrecht, p. 152*. The main interest was concerned with the preservation of the system of the division of classes, which was also served by the ordinances about dress, and to some extent by the laws about luxury (*pp. 119, 121, 127 ff., 247*); it has been instituted by God like the State itself, to whose conception it belongs. The second main interest is the increase of the power of the territorial lord, who, however, remains bound in the patriarchal manner to Natural and Divine Law, and may not rule in the Machiavellian fashion (*pp. 106, 129 ff., 204*).—For the theologians the whole is a concern of the authorities, who in so doing have to behave according to the Natural Law and the Divine Law, as the appointed organ for the working out of that which was suitable; thus *Hutter*: "Praecipua officia magistratus politici sunt: (1) curam gerere utriusque tabulae decalogi, quod ad externam disciplinam attinet, (2) ferre leges de negotiis civilibus et oeconomicis consentaneas juri divino et naturali; (3) sedulo providere, ut leges promulgatae veniant in executionem; (4) delinquentibus pro qualitate delicti poenas irrogare, obedientes fovere et praemiis afficere"; or *Hollaz*: "Magistratus civilis est ordinatus ad bonum publicum idque quadruplex: (1) ecclesiasticum, cum reges nutritii ecclesiae et episcopi extra templum; (2) civile, dum civium commoda tuetur et hostes externos finibus patriae propulsat; (3) morale, quatenus honestas praescribit leges, quibus subditi in officio continentur, ut vitam tranquillam agant in pietate et honestate (1 Tim. ii. 2); (4) naturale, quo imperantes prospiciant subditis de commeatu et aliis necessariis instar Pharaonis (Gen. xli. 34)". *Schmidt: Dogmatik, 460*. For the special nature of the content of the economic Natural Law, see further below. For the relation between the growing modern political economy and its individualistic rationalistic hedonistic character to that of the ecclesiastical Law of Nature, see *Oncken: Geschichte der Nationalökonomie, I, 1902*.

[256] (p. 542.) This fundamental theory finds its classic expression in Luther's Greater Catechism: it is the duty of the individual to submit to the existing institutions as in the "media per creaturas bona percipiendi". For "creaturae tantum manus sunt, canales, media et organa, quorum opera et adminiculo Deus omnia largitur hominibus. . . . Quam ob rem et haec edia [namely, parents, authorities, and the general relationships between one man and

another] . . . non sunt respuenda neque temeraria praesumtione aliae rationes et viae investigandae, quam Deus praecipit". Thus parents, governments, and Christian fellow-men have received their task from God in their post which has been given them by Nature, "ut omnis generis officia nobis ostendant et exhibeant adeo, ut haec non ab illis, sed per illos a Deo peculiariter accipiamus". (*Symb. Bd. ed. Müller, p. 390*). The most important commandment among those which relate to human relationships, that is, of the Second Table, is the fourth: "thou shalt honour thy father and thy mother" (*p. 405*). At first this position of the family is described in its immediate significance, but as the highest ideal of sociological relations: "Hunc parentum statum et ordinem Deus praecipue hoc ornavit elogio ante omnes, qui sub ipso sunt, status et ordines, ut non simpliciter praecipiat parentes esse amandos, sed honorandos. . . . Est enim honor res amore multis modis sublimior, utpote quae non tantum amorem in se complectatur, verum etiam singularem quandam modestiam, humilitatem et reverentiam, quae cuiquam quasi majestati hic occultae habenda sit" (*p. 406*). But this fundamental theory covers all kinds of authority, and since differences of authority, owing to the inequality among men, are everywhere present, it finally covers all relationships in general: "In hujus praecepti explanatione neque illud praetereundum est, quod ad multiplicem obedientiam superiorum attinet, nempe eorum, qui versantur in imperio et rei publicae procurationem sustinent. Si quidem e parentum potestate omnes aliae propagantur et manant." Thus there follow the relations to authorities, to which, of course, the local authorities and the lords of the manor belong; then teachers of all kinds, and the pastors, then the neighbours, and finally employers of labour and servants, "ita, ut omnes, quotquot domini appellatione censentur, vice parentum sint ab iisdemque potestatem ac vim regnandi accipiant. Unde quoque secundum Scripturam omnes dicuntur patres, utpote qui in sua gubernatione officium patris obire ergaque subditos patris animum inducere debeant. Quemadmodum et olim apud Romanos et alios plerosque populos heros herasque patres et matresfamilias nominabant. Ita quoque suos magistratus et principes dixerunt patres patriae, nobis Christianis in dedecus et ignominiam" (*p. 412f.*). This implies the duty of care for others on the part of parents and masters: "Neque enim Dei voluntas est, ut aut perditi nebulones aut enormes tyranni hujus officii procurationem obeant . . ., sed cogitent potius, quod et ipsi Deo obedientiam debeant, ut officium suae fidei delegatum ipsis curae sit ac sollicitudini utque liberos, familiam et subditos suos non tantum nutriant et corporalibus alimentis provideant, sed omnium maxime ad laudem et gloriam Dei propagandam educant" (*p. 417*). Certainly it is generally true: "erga fratres, sorores et proximum in genere nihil amplius (Deus) praecipit quam amore prosequendos esse" (*p. 106*); after that, however, follows the statement that it is a much higher thing to honour than to love, and in the general graded character of all conditions (coram Deo omnes quidem pares sumus, sed nos inter nos hoc dispari et ordinato discrimine non possumus non discrepare, *406*) love everywhere is mingled with elements of authority and subordination, and everywhere it is replaced by grateful humility or a paternal authority.—Just as classically formulated is this fundamental theory with its religious basis within the modern Lutheran ethic by *von Hofmann*: "Our assistance to the world is conservative. The humility of our love to the world excludes all arbitrary action" (*pp. 156ff.*); see also *Stillich, p. 89*: "The preparation for the social organization of Society desired by the Conservatives is that of the family. The latter", says the venerable leader of the Saxon Conservatives, *Freiherr v. Friesen*, "purposes the harmonious co-operation of all the individual members in a definite whole, whereas the bureaucratic (that is, the modern) State, in the principle of equality, destroys that which was originally equal, for its own special purpose, and the individual atoms which it thus gains it forces violently into its own scheme." Even down to the present day these are the fundamental sociological features of the world-outlook among the Conservatives, so far as their policy is a policy of a world-outlook at all. It is, however, also clear that this view is closely connected with an anti-individualistic immobilized general situation in politics and economics, and that an urban mobile individualistic and capitalistic civilization would need different ethical and religious convictions. That the difficulties of the Lutheran Catechism lie in ethics still more than in dogma every pastor knows who works in great cities and among working-class communities. It represents a fundamental theory of sociological questions which cannot be carried out in our modern city civilization. On this point cf. *Traub: Ethik und Kapitalismus*[2], *1907*.

[258] (p. 547.) On this point see *J. Köstlin: Luthers Theologie*[2], *1883, p. 482*: "Luther defines marriage as 'conjunctio unius maris et unius feminae insepara-bilis, non tantum juris naturae as the Canonists express it: sed etiam voluntatis et voluptatis, ut ita dicam, divinae'. Its purpose or its *causa finalis* he sees in the procreation of children, in the *procreatio sobolis*. Before the Fall it had already been instituted as a means of providing the Church and the State with useful members. 'Thus marriage and the household are not merely *fons et origo generis humani*, but at the same time they ought to serve as *paratio ecclesiae* and become *fons rei publicae*.' After the Fall it also serves the purpose as a remedy against lust and a check to its sinful outbreaks. Indeed, he now describes this as *primus finis*, whereas otherwise the original purpose remains *finis magis principalis*. Thus in his mind that desire still retains its sinful character, but 'approbatio et beneplacitum Dei tegit miseram turpitudinem libidinis et removet iram Dei imminentem illi concupiscentiae'."—The inner nature of marriage itself Luther explains very beautifully in the Greater Catechism, in the exposition of the Sixth Commandment, particularly at the end, where he is dealing with the subject of "chastity" within marriage: "Ubi enim volumus conjugali castitati locum esse, ibi necessum est ante omnia, ut vir et mulier in amore concordes conversentur, ut alter alterum ex animo mutua quandam benevolentia et fide complectatur. Quod si praesto fuerit, ipsa quoque castitas sua sponte sine mandato consequetur" (*Müller, 426*). In addition, cf. *Wald. Kawerau: Die Ref. und die Ehe, 1892* (*V. f. Ref.-Gesch., Nr. 39*); *Marianne Weber: Ehefrau und Mutter, pp. 282–285;* here it is rightly pointed out that "the new ideal of womanhood which lays the chief stress upon the moral qualities of the house-mother, on love and loyalty, on the fear of God and trusting God, on reliability and honesty" (*Kawerau, 71*), has been strongly influenced by the ideals of the *Book of Ecclesiasticus*; further, cf. *Rade: Stellung des Christentums zum Geschlechtsleben* (*Rel. Volksbb., V 7/8*), *1910;* a collection of the most important passages in *W. Walter: Für Luther wider Rom, 1906*. For the view of the matter as it affects economics and the theory of population, see *Roscher: Geschichte der Nationalökonomik, pp. 57–59*. For concupiscence, see *Braun: Luthers Lehre von der Konkupiszenz*. This, however, is not simply a relic of the Catholic and monastic system; the thought lies much more in the system, as we shall see in similar ideas on the State and work. In the dry definitions of the later Lutheran Schol-astic thinkers (*Schmidt, Dogmatik, 461–465*), this feature disappears, but only behind the positive character of the command. Luther's "relics of Catholicism" are connected with the early Christian opposition between the world and

salvation, and they concern essential problems of Christian thought, as indeed the problem of sex relations undoubtedly is.—For Luther's pessimism about actual conditions, see *G. Kat*: "Quoniam vero apud nos adeo foeda et nefanda omnium vitiorum et scortationum lerna cernitur, hoc praeceptum quoque adversus omnia impudicitiae genera et species constitutum est. . . . Tantum ergo hoc praeceptuma nobis exigit, ut quisque tum pro se vitam castam agat, tum proximo quoque in hoc obinenda et tuenda sit auxilio" (*Müller, 423*).—*Rade, p. 51*, says: "The transference of the chief emphasis to the inmost centre of personality and the proclamation of Christian freedom which sprang out of that was bound to have as a result a complete change of judgment about the external processes of the life of sex. And we can only regard it as a relic of Augustinian and Catholic tradition that still under the influence of Luther's example in the Protestant Church the universality of human sin was attributed to the sex origin of each individual." This deduction, which is certainly possible from the logical point of view, from the principle of Christian freedom, was, however, not made by Luther. The life of sex and erotic love are precisely not gifts of God with their own beauty to be freely used and shaped, but they are simply a tribute paid to Nature, which the Christian can and ought to make a means for the exercise of the love of one's neighbour. Naturally, the presuppositions which determine our point of view, namely, the biological conception of "lust" and the poetic glorification of eroticism, do not exist for Luther; with him, rather, the predominant idea is the doctrine of lust as a result of the Fall.

[259] (p. 548.) On this point cf. *Köstlin: Theologie Luthers, II, 485–490, 553–564; J. Köstlin: Staat, Recht und Kirche und die ev. Ethik, Stud. u. Kritt., 1877; Brandenburg: L.'s Anschauungen von Staat und Gesellschaft; Lenz: Luthers Lehre von der Obrigkeit (Preuss. Jahrbb., 75, 1894); Jäger: Politische Ideen L.'s und ihr Einfluss auf die innere Entwickelung Deutschlands (Preuss. Jahrbb., 1903); K. Köhler: Luther und die Juristen. Lenz* pays too little attention to the connection with the mediaeval world of thought, and connects the modern State too directly with Luther's ideas; *Brandenburg* rightly emphasizes the former, but undervalues the positive value of Reason and the Divine appointment of the State, which certainly only comes out in Luther later on. *Gottfried Arnold: Unparteyische Kirchen- und Ketzerhistorie, 1700, II, 11 and 12, 18–28*, represents Luther's politics with an emphasis on the features of detachment from the world; the newest is *Karl Müller: Kirche, Gemeinde, und weltliche Obrigkeit nach Luther, Christl. Welt, 1910;* the question of the State is, however, scarcely mentioned in this book.

[260] (p. 551.) Cf. the tractate *Ob Kriegsleute auch in seligem Stand sein können, 1526*, and *Vom Krieg wider die Türken, 1529*. Here again the Old Testament has to be drawn in so as to justify a not really Christian idea. Later, of course, Luther thought less harshly, and perhaps also less logically, about these things; see *Cardauns, pp. 1–17*. But upon the whole the particularism and the rejection of a policy of intervention is a main feature of genuine Lutheranism, as the works of *Schubert* which have been mentioned show. On problems of war and treaties, see above all *Hortleder: Handlungen und Ausschreiben von Rechtmässigkeit des deutschen Krieges, Gotha, 1617 und 1618*, where the material is collected, especially *II*; see here the discussion by *Ratzenberger*, who argues that Melancthon, Jonas, Bugenhagen, Menius, etc., had fallen away from Luther's pure doctrine of resistance (*p. 39*), also *Theolog. Jahresbericht, XXVIII, p. 460*, on *Schweizer: Der Donaufeldzug von 1546*.

[261] (p. 552.) *Lenz* gives it as his opinion: "In this double relationship of a Christian government in its negative function of preserving peace, maintaining

law, and furthering material interests, and in its positive duty to secure peace, I believe, lies the solution of the much discussed problem, and of the harmony which is lacking in the life and doctrine of the Reformer. . . . Two kingdoms, both founded by God, are spread throughout the world, the creature and the Gospel, indivisible in every Christian, and yet theoretically to be kept separate like soul and body, idea and appearance; but the faith remains in an ideal freed from all the burdens of earth in the Kingdom of God" (*pp. 435 ff.*). This is a distinctly modernized solution of the problem; in reality, Luther firmly maintains the old solution of Scholasticism, the solution with the aid of conceptions of Natural Law and the Gospel, only transplanted from the mediaeval idea of an ascent from Nature to Grace, to the new sphere in which both are within each other. Otherwise Luther himself appeals to Augustine: "Thus I have written about the secular authority as glorious and useful as no teacher has done since the time of the Apostles, excepting possibly St. Augustine" (*Krieg wider die Türken, B. A., IV, 1, p. 441*). In his writings about the Peasants' Revolt and the war he teaches the dualistic morality of the use of law, force, and authority on the one hand, and of the suffering and sacrificial ethic of love of the Sermon on the Mount on the other hand, in an often absolutely amazingly harsh distinction; see, for example, *pp. 322 ff.*: "What do you think that Christ would say to it that you bear His Name and call yourselves a Christian body when you are so far away from that, when, indeed, you do and teach so abominably against His law that you are not even worthy of being called Turks or heathen, but much worse, since you violently oppose both Divine and Natural Law which is observed among all the heathen (by rebellion and the encouragement of a Christian form of communism) . . . Further, we will now speak of the Christian and evangelical law, which does not bind the heathen like the former law, for as you boast and like to hear that you are called Christians and also wish to be regarded as such, so you must also endure that I hold up to you your law. Give ear now, beloved Christians, and listen to your Christian law. Thus speaks Christ (Matt. v. 39): 'Resist not evil, but he who impels thee to go with him one mile go with him two, and who takes thy cloke let him take thy coat also and he who strikes thee upon the one cheek, offer him also the other. . . .' Indeed, Christ says (Matt. v. 44) that we ought to wish good to those who do us evil, and pray for our persecutors and love our enemies and do good to those who injure us. These are our Christian rights, dear friends. . . . A child, indeed, would understand from these sayings that it is a Christian law not to resist evil, not to take to the sword, not to defend oneself, not to revenge oneself, but to deliver up one's body and one's possessions, and let anyone take it who will. We indeed have enough in our Lord Himself who will not leave us as He has promised. Suffering, suffering cross, cross is the Christian's law and there is no other." Or, *p. 365*: "There are two kingdoms: the one is the Kingdom of God, the other the kingdom of the world (in this instance he does not mean the realm of evil, but of the natural creation of Reason). . . . God's Kingdom is a kingdom of grace and mercy and not a kingdom of wrath or of punishment. For it means nothing but forgiveness and protection, loving and serving, doing good, having peace and joy, etc. But the kingdom of this world is a kingdom of wrath. In this kingdom there is nothing but punishment and resistance, judgment and condemnation in order to force the evil and to protect the good. Therefore also this kingdom possesses and wields the sword. . . . The texts which speak of mercy belong to the Kingdom of God and to Christians, they do not apply to the secular law. For a Christian must not only be merciful, but he must also suffer all manner of evil, etc. But the kingdom of this world, which is simply the servant of the Divine wrath over evil men and the precursor of hell and of eternal death, and it must not be merciful but severe, etc. . . .; it looks upon the evil men that it may punish them and hold them in check and in peace for the protection and the deliverance of the good." This, indeed, is something other than the relation between the idea and the appearance.

[262] (p. 553.) His pessimism is strongly emphasized by *Brandenburg*: "Thus at the beginning at least he had an ideal floating about in the air of a Christian society which should be governed by an authority informed with the Christian spirit. This authority, however, was not to be subordinate to the spiritual authority and directed by it; otherwise its actions would be forced and valueless; but while it possessed an equal right externally it was to be combined with the spiritual authority in the same Christian spirit. . . . This thought runs right through Luther's *Address to the Nobility of the German Nation*. But the dream soon faded, and when he awoke Luther found himself alone with a few like-minded souls among the heathen, and he gained the conviction that this was how it would remain. Henceforward he had no more interest in trying to picture how a Christian Society might be created and ought to be, for, he thought, it indeed will never come to pass; the few Christians scattered throughout the world will never be able to form a closely knit community. The world as it is cannot be governed with Christian love according to the Gospel (*p. 9*). . . . Therefore Luther says: 'If thou sufferest violence and injustice, thou must say that is the government of this world. If thou wilt live in the world, that is what thou must expect. Thou wilt never succeed in bringing about that it should happen otherwise. If thou wilt live among the wolves, then thou must howl with them. Here in this world we are serving in an inn where the Devil is master, and the world is the landlady, and all kinds of evil passions are the servants; and these all are the enemies and opposers of the Gospel. Thus if thy money is stolen or thou art injured in thy honour, that is just what thou hast to expect in this house.' Nowhere do I find the essential element in Luther's outlook on the world so clearly expressed as in this illustration. The monk wishes to forsake the service of the devilish landlord by flight, the struggling Church desires to tear the rule out of the hands of the innkeeper by external means of authority and gain control of the domestics; at first Luther hoped to be able to convert the inhabitants and fill them with the Christian spirit; now, however, he has given up this hope, but in spite of that he wants to stay in the terrible house. For he is not there of his own will, but because he has been placed there by his God. Therefore he desires to do his duty here, to let himself be beaten and ill-treated if it pleases the evil master and his servants to do this, but he will not stir from the spot till his Lord calls him away, and every good hour which he enjoys he will rejoice in as a special grace" (*pp. 5 ff.*). *Brandenburg*, in my opinion, lays too much stress upon these passages—at least alongside of them there are others in which the Christian order of life in public and private morality seems to be something possible and desirable, upon which, indeed, his ethical text-book, the Greater Catechism, is constructed. In my opinion the really characteristic element is rather his alternation between that despairing pessimism and the triumph that the genuinely evangelical order has at last become a reality. The principles, on the other hand, in which *Lenz* (*p. 440*) describes the continued influence of Lutheran ideas as the "vital mark of our people" ("in them is rooted the right of our sword, its might, and our obedience. With forceful power they fetter everyone to the public will, and in freedom millions serve them without

difference of creed. They are interwoven with every public office, with our customs of marriage and family life, with our ideals of war (!) and all our (!) work of peace. Upon this foundation our whole classical literature (!) has grown up, and these ideas still dominate large sections of our art (!); only through them has genuine tolerance and free research (!) become possible"), are only very partially of Lutheran origin. A continued influence of the Lutheran idea of the State and of Society in reality only takes place in the *Weltanschauung* of the Conservative party, and, above all, in its standard-bearer *Stahl*, who, however, found himself obliged to incorporate Calvinistic and Independent individualism into the newly formed Lutheran idea of the State; cf. *Stahl: Der christliche Staat.*

[263] (p. 554.) Cf. *L. von Seckendorff: Teutscher Fürstenstaat, 5, 1687* (at first *1656*), especially *c. 1, 5* and *8* of the third section. The author, however, confesses in the Foreword: "I have often been obliged to put the *Regula* instead of that which in reality I ought to find, but which I found nowhere, or very little."—Especially characteristic of the spirit of the whole is *pp. 194 ff.*: "The main aim of all this is the healthful preservation of the police, or of the whole Government, in its august power and greatness, and the ultimate aim is the glory of God." In Christian States, however, the task is not merely that of the maintenance of authority, the prevention of crime, and the preservation of peace, but also the moral furtherance of the subjects, "a constant approximation and exercise, which among the ancient pagan peoples of Greece and Rome was sought in many kinds of instruction from learned philosophers and poets. But in a Christian State the Government can and must go still further in this matter". It must cultivate right sentiments and dispositions, and since this cannot be brought about by compulsion and by the law, the discipline of the Church, the home, and the school must also be used for this purpose. "Notwithstanding this, however, there are certain matters in the administration of a country which concern every person in it; these are dealt with by the Government, since they also can bring harm and vexation to others in the same land if they are not wisely regulated. As, for instance, a seemly outward celebration of Sundays and festivals, the avoidance of shameful drunkenness, and where, after a certain time of day, one must stop tippling and treating. Further, a regular calling and activity and the avoidance of idleness . . ., for which purpose also an excellent method is the provision of a house of correction for those naughty persons, for the improvement of their life and for the relief of the minds of other people. The preservation of a seemly order and precedence between the various classes and subjects, according to their honour, their position, and their office, in all events and gatherings, both in clothing and in other outward things . . ., in order that confusion, misunderstanding, and vexation may be prevented." This conservatism, however, is only to serve the cause of peace and order, but it is not to exclude all idea of progress (*p. 215*). "The Government is bent on introducing into the country more and more what will be useful and will serve the way of peace and understanding, by all kinds of friendly methods, and granting of immunities, it desires to show that it desires to encourage progress and advancement in many ways."—*Joh. Gerhard*, in his *Loci* (*ed. Cotta, 1775*), *vols. XIII and XIV*, develops the Natural Law and Christian ideas of the State in great breadth and detail, with, however, the lack of vision, which considers it quite possible to realize the ideal of a Christian society with a Christian spirit of the government, pure Church doctrine and the humble obedience of the subjects: "Utraque potestas ad ecclesiae collectionem conservationem ac propagationem itemque ad Dei

gloriam ordinata est. Mutuas enim sibi tradunt operas. . . . Sine ecclesiastico ministerio commode quidem, at non pie; sine politica potestate pie quidem, sed non commode vivi potest. (*XIII, 225*) ! The "Magistratus sunt Dii terrestres" (*XIV, 305*) ! This lack of vision is also reflected in the ideal of the Primitive State, which in development without the Fall would have been, in spite of that, a "subjectio", but only a "subjectio filialis" instead of a "subjectio servilis" (*p. 240*). On treaties: "Foedera ipsa urgente rei publicae necessitate cum infidelibus et diversae religionis hominibus instituta non possunt absolute et simpliciter improbari; cavendum interim, ne adhaereat fiducia in humanum auxilium ac diffidentia erga Deum neve defensio ecclesiae, quae est solius dei opus, foederibus illis transscribatur" (*XIV, 14*). Support of oppressed co-religionists in foreign countries only allowed as diplomatic (*XIV, 72*). All that is said about the Sermon on the Mount is that it is parabolic in character and must not be taken quite literally, and of the law it says simply: "Observa etiam quod magistratus dicatur constitutus subditis *in bonum*, nimirum ut bonum publicum promoveat justitiam administrando, justos defendendo, sontes puniendo. Quare cum hoc bono et dono divinitus concesso utimur, hoc est cum officium magistratus imploramus, *recte omnino* facimus" (*XIV, 135*). As in the Church, the Church law has been introduced as the Divine law, and is in general no longer a problem, so also for the State and for Society, law and might have ceased to be a problem, they are a *bonum divinitus concessum* (*p. 137*). The comprehensive polemic against the Anabaptists is a thorough transformation of the Sermon on the Mount, in the light of other passages of Scripture, which is continually being renewed; the spirit of the whole is that of the most extreme Philistine theological politics.

[264] (p. 554.) On this point cf. *Roscher: Geschichte der Nationalökonomik* and *Aug. Oncken: Geschichte der Nationalökonomie, I, 1902;* and also the well-known treatises by *Schmoller: Zur Geschichte der Nationalökonomischen Ansichten in Deutschland während der Reformationsperiode, Z. f. d. gesamte Staatswissenschaft, 1860, pp. 461–716; Wiskemann: Darstellung der in Deutschland z. Z. der Reform. herrschenden Nationalök. Ansichten* (*Jablonowskische Preisschrift, 1861*); also *Uhlhorn: Geschichte der christlichen Liebestätigkeit, III, 1890; Uhlhorn: Katholizismus und Prot. gegenüber der sozialen Frage*[2]*, 1887;* see *Eck* in the detailed introduction to *Luther's Von Kaufhandlung und Wucher, Bd. IV, 1, pp. 494–513; K. Köhler: Luther und die Juristen, pp. 111–124; H. Böhmer: Luther im Licht der neueren Forschung, pp. 130–139; Brandenburg: Luthers Stellung zu Staat und Gesellschaft; Frank G. Ward,* presentation and estimate of Luther's views of the State and its economic tasks; *Conrad's Abhh., XXI, 1898;* finally, my own presentation of the subject in *Kultur der Gegenwart, pp. 544–552.*—For the general economic setting in which the position of the Reformers moved, see *Lamprecht: Deutsche Geschichte, V and VI; Schmoller: Das Merkantilsystem in seiner historischen Bedeutung* (*Umrisse und Untersuchungen, 1890, pp. 1–60*), the numerous researches of *G. von Below,* especially the *Untergang der mittelalterlichen Stadtwirtschaft* (*Jahrb. für Nationalök. und Statistik, 1901*) and *Territorium und Stadt, 1900*; examples of the economic situation in the towns in *Bothe: Frankfurter Patriziervermögen im 16. Jahrh., Archiv für Kulturgeschichte, Beiheft 2, 1908;* for rural and provincial conditions, see *Schauenburg, 100 Jahre Oldenburgischer Kirchengeschichte, V, 1908.* For the seventeenth century, see compilations in *Händtke: Deutsche Kultur im Zeitalter des 30 j. Kriegs, 1906,* see *Below: Die Frage des Rückgangs der wirtsch. Verhältnisse vor dem 30 j. Krieg* (*Vierteljahrsschrift für Soz.- und Wirtschaftsgeschichte, 1909, pp. 160–167*). At the present day we must take it for granted that the great economic and social upheavals of the sixteenth century arose independently

of the religious movement, and that in them Lutheranism at first adopted an essentially reactionary attitude, whereas the casuistical ethic of Catholicism was in a position to make compromises with them.

[269] (p. 555.) On the "traditionalist" character of the Lutheran doctrine of property, see *Max Weber: Geist des Kapitalismus, Archiv. XX, pp. 44–50*; on the ethical objection to competition which is evident, particularly in Luther's doctrine of prices, *Schmoller, 491 ff.* Luther himself says (*Kaufhandlung, BA, p. 527*): "We ought to be satisfied with a very moderate standard of living . . . not day and night try to reach something higher." Oncken calls this the "ascetic" conception of industry in contrast to the "hedonistic" conception which entered in with Adam Smith (*pp. 152, 149*). In the question of usury Melanchthon is more inclined to compromise than Luther, and the later orthodox Lutherans did not perpetuate Luther's severe attitude towards usury, *Neumann: Geschichte des Wuchers*; that, however, does not mean a new principle, but only the modification which we notice everywhere of Luther's ethical radicalism.

[272] (p. 557.) This non-feudal character is also a marked feature of the mediaeval economic ethic; on the relation of both elements in the mediaeval town and in the Canon Law, see *Oncken, I, 125*, who is excellent on this point; *Oncken* describes it as the system of the "gebundene Geldwirtschaft", which is opposed to the later "ungebundene" capitalistic economy of the towns. The Reformers only opposed the latter kind. Only so were they in a position to prefer the Roman law, which is quite opposed to the feudal constitution and favours both an economy based on money and the principate of the territorial lord. The modern tendency of the Reformers consists essentially in handing over economic matters to the territorial lords, who are obliged and entitled to increase possessions and industry for the good of the whole; cf. *Schauenburg: s. Theol. Jahresbericht, 496*. Thus with the blessing of Lutheranism and without ecclesiastical control they entered the path of mercantilism as well as that of an absolutist social policy. Otherwise already Scholasticism had empowered the territorial lords to gather treasure, and thus they were exempt from civic morality (*Oncken, I, p. 128*).

[273] (p. 558.) Cf. the highly characteristic passages in *Kaufhandlung, BA. IV, 1, pp. 523–527*, on the four ways in which we ought to behave in a Christian way in business: firstly, that we ought to allow ourselves willingly to be exploited if the Government does not prevent it; secondly, that we ought to give to those in need freely; thirdly, that we ought to lend without receiving it back again. Then only comes the fourth way, that we buy and sell goods for goods or goods for money as a measure of value and a method of preserving value; for the latter end, however, the fixing of the *pretium justum* by the Government is necessary. Yet still more plain is the much-quoted letter to the people of Dantzig in the year 1525, in which he says that the taking of interest is forbidden by the Gospel, but then continues: "But the Gospel is a spiritual law by which one cannot govern, but about which each man must decide for himself whether he will observe it or whether he will leave it alone. And one may and ought to force no one to it, any more than to faith; for here it is not the sword but the Spirit of God which must teach and govern. Therefore the spiritual rule of the Gospels must be separated from the external secular rule and the two must not be mixed with each other. . . . The Gospel teaches, indeed, that one is to have no care for possessions at all, but whoever forces me he takes from me that which is mine." Thus according to human law he would sanction at least a limited and officially fixed interest of 5 per cent.

(*Oncken, I, p. 144*). This, again, is the well-known dualistic ethic of Luther on account of which Luther's attitude on the question of interest has often been called hesitating and uncertain; that, however, is not so inwardly and in itself in the Christian demand it is not so; it only becomes so when the serious effort to realize it in practice is given up and when a secular use is recognized in addition.

[274] (p. 558.) Thus Luther is ready to tolerate the sins which inevitably belong to the desire for gain which characterizes the system of trade which is allowed: "Therefore thou shalt not burden thy conscience with that, but thou must bring it to God as another sin which cannot be overcome to which we are all prone; commend it thus to God with the paternoster and leave it to Him, for necessity and the kind of work drives thee into this failing, not knavery and envy, for I am speaking here of good-hearted and God-fearing people who do not wish to do wrong. Just as the duty of marriage is not carried out without sin, and still on account of necessity God winks at it because there is nothing else to be done" (*BA., IV, 1, pp. 519 ff.*). It is exactly the same with the toleration of the compulsory character of the State as the "kingdom of wrath".

[276] (p. 560.) On this contrast see *Schmoller, 569, 591, 692, and 719*; on a motive of Socialism present among the Reformers, and only restricted in favour of the situation conditioned by original sin, see *Schmoller, 708 ff.*; on the religious and ethical motives for the regulations in defence of the poor and the debtors (as in the Canon Law), see *Schmoller, 529 and 591*. The Socialistic element, which—on a religious basis, and with the presupposition of sin and inequality—the canonistic Lutheran doctrine contains, is also emphasized by *Oncken, p. 135*; there also note the connection between the physiocratic doctrine and this "natural economic ethic".

[281] (p. 561.) For the social organization in Luther's view which quite corresponds to the mediaeval idea, see *Brandenburg, p. 11; Schmoller, pp. 475, 485–487, 688*. How natural Luther found the guild organization is shown by the anecdote in his Table Talk, according to which Luther claimed that among the tailors there ought to be special groupings for making breeches, jerkins, or coats, in order that the work might be better (*Schmoller, p. 487*). There is a wealth of material for the social history of Lutheranism in *Drews:* "*Einfluss der Gesellschaftlichen Zustände auf das kirchliche Leben*" (*Z. f. Theol. und Kirche, 1906*), and "*Der ev. Geistliche in der deutschen Vergangenheit*", *1905*. To a great extent the theory continues the barren scholastic threefold division; the third estate is never constructed in its constituent parts, the urban and agrarian, and then further in their mutual organization; above all, the fourth estate of servants, day-labourers, serfs, and slaves never appears in a category by itself. As a rule the theologians deal with the *status economicus* as a domestic economy in which the servants are included and which as far as possible they regard as a self-contained household; cf. the meagre statements in *Schmidt: Ev.-Luth. Dogmatik, p. 462*; here the only distinctions that are made are the *societas paterna*, that is, the smaller family group, and the *societas herilis*, that is the *legitima dominorum et servorum conjunctio divinitus instituta ob mutuam utilitatem*, and for all further detail people are commended to the study of the Decalogue. The real social theory and policy is left in the hands of the authorities, of the princely police, and of the financiers; the theological ethic emphasizes only the general principle of patriarchalism.—A book which *Gottfried Arnold* often quotes and uses, called *Spiegel aller Stände*, by *J. Cuno*, I was unable to obtain.

[282] (p. 561.) On this point Luther exclaims against the demand of the peasants that serfdom ought to be abolished (*BA. IV, 1, pp. 334 ff.*): "There ought to be

no serfs because Christ has set us all free. What then is that? This means Christian freedom would be quite carnal—did not Abraham and other patriarchs and prophets also have bondmen? Read St. Paul and what he teaches about the servants who in his time were all slaves! Therefore, this article is clean against the Gospel and sheer robbery, for every man who considers his body thus his own has stolen it from his master. For a serf can, indeed, be a Christian and have Christian freedom, just as a prisoner or a sick man is a Christian and still is not free. This article wishes to make all men equal and make the spiritual Kingdom of Christ into a secular external kingdom which is impossible. For a secular kingdom cannot exist without personal inequality where some are free and some are bound, some are lords and others are subjects." In another passage he exhorts even the Christian prisoners of war who have been enslaved by the Turks to endure their state of slavery patiently: "Thou must think that thou hast lost thy freedom, without which thou thyself canst do nothing apart from the will and knowledge of thy master without sin and disobedience. For in so doing thou dost rob and steal thy body from thy master, which he has bought or otherwise gained that it henceforward is not thine but his possession like a cow or any of his other goods"!! *BA. IV, 1, p. 479.* Thus the fresh expansion of serfdom in the agricultural districts and estates on the eastern side of the Elbe from the time of the sixteenth century was entirely unhindered by Lutheranism (see *Gothein: Agrargeschichte in Religion in Geschichte und Gegenwart, I, p. 2807*). A legal stabilization of human rights did not take place at least in Germany until the time of the Enlightenment, and until the present day it is only from this point of view that this is possible.

[283] (p. 561.) *F. J. Stahl: Der christliche Staat, p. 8,* the patriarchal fundamental theory; *p. 17,* the opposition of the modern principle. The continuance, or, rather, the reawakening by the Restoration of these tendencies in modern Conservatism, is described in a most interesting manner with a large number of extracts from the Conservative Press by *Stillich: Die politischen Parteien in Deutschland, I.* Stillich, however, sees in this only an expression of the Conservative class struggle, and overlooks the connection between this class struggle and the reawakening of the pure ideological motives of Lutheranism, through which alone it can be carried on in the name and with the energies of a popular outlook on the world; see *p. 55* for the class, or as we say to-day in order to distinguish it from the mechanical individualistic principle, the organic conception of Society of the Conservatives; see likewise *pp. 87 and 219; p. 143* for the economic traditionalism which is bound up with that.

[285] (p. 562.) Cf. the presentation of this political economy by *Roscher* and especially by *Oncken, I, 226–236*: "Political economy as a specific form of the mercantilistic literature of Germany bears on the one hand a populationist character, and on the other a character of the science of State finance. In a 'productive' town and country population, and in a flourishing 'aerarium', the wealth of the land consists. One must also say in praise of the political economists that they have honestly and eagerly tried to cope with the tasks which have faced them: it cannot be denied, however, that when at that time the wealth of a sovereign prince was measured by the number of his subjects, this mostly happened in the sense in which in our own day a landowner is esteemed according to the number of his cattle." Noteworthy is the similarity of the Catholic and the Protestant branch of this political economy in its theological ethical presuppositions and its practical political results. Only the Protestant tendency is represented in more fullness and variety (*p. 232*). Oncken calls

attention rightly to the "semi-Socialist character" and the tendency to the "middle class" (*p. 229*), but he does not sufficiently emphasize the connection with the religious ethic. It is everywhere quite plain that the emphasis on peace, order, the exclusion of competition, the stabilizing or new regulation of the class-organization, proceed from the standpoint of the ethic of love, which is opposed to the free struggle for existence. The "free course of commerce" is "evil and foolishness" (*p. 251*). The whole exclusiveness and the lack of individual initiative are both due to religious motives as well as based on circumstances without its being possible to describe the religious theory as simply a reflection of the actual circumstances. It is a reaction behind the lay culture or civilization of the town of the later Middle Ages which is based on the one hand on the actual political and social development of conditions of power and economics, but on the other hand also on the reactionary religious theory of Luther about economic and social questions which is quite independent of the former. That the formation of greater States, with a unity of administration which follows with this from another point of view is progress, or the presupposition of progress, is a matter of course; only that kind of idea is not consciously intended by Lutheranism, whether of the theological or of the juridical political kind.

289 (p. 567.) Cf. *Uhlhorn, III, 315–414*. One of the chief defects in this otherwise excellent book is that it does not recognize and emphasize the return to the principle of charity as such, and therefore it does not discern the real reasons for this return. They lie in the failure of the early Lutheran patriarchalism, which believed that in the cosmos of "callings" all were cared for, and only provided the *Kasten* for exceptional cases. It is of the essence of the new period of Protestant philanthropy since Pietism arose that it no longer depends upon the organization of the State, nor upon the official activity of the Church, but that it organizes its charity freely from the laity and from the local congregations. Instead of that, in order to explain this new period *Uhlhorn* suggests that it is due to the influence of the philanthropy of the Enlightenment, which decidedly had very little part in it. Further, *Uhlhorn* rightly lays a great deal of emphasis upon the influence of Calvinism and of Catholicism; also the fact that the opposition of the official Lutheran Church is a sign that it regards these returns to Calvinistic and Catholic lay activity as something new and strange. That in reality the Catholic principle of charity was being approached in this activity is shown by the way in which Fliedner and Wichern appeal to the institutions of the Primitive Church, as well as by some involuntary expressions of *Uhlhorn*: "There is a danger of falling into a very widespread habit of almsgiving all the more because the various associations have little or no connection with each other, and the applicant has only a very external link with the association. . . . But the most serious result would be if those people were right who say that the number of charitable associations which at present exist is a symptom that the historic groups, the State and the Church, are breaking up as in the Roman Empire and towards the close of the Middle Ages" (*p. 412*). The similarity of these associations with the Catholic Religious Orders is often noted and carefully denied.

290 (p. 568.) Cf. *Uhlhorn, III, 347 ff.–364*, and especially *Wernle: J. H. Wichern, 1908*. In the Commission of the Central Committee for Home Missions, *Wernle* summarizes the content of Wichern's Memorial of 1849: "Within the sphere of the State the Home Mission ought to fight against the revolutionary spirit, and also care for the welfare of the prisoners and of discharged criminals. In the ecclesiastical sphere it is her main task to give to every baptized Christian

the full opportunity of hearing the pure Word of God; this means that Bible Societies, Bible Study Groups, special Missions, etc., must be instituted. In the general sphere of morals it must oppose prostitution, drunkenness, and bad literature, and finally in the social sphere it must do all that is possible to maintain and to save family life; it must care for the poor and the sick; it must organize Christian Workmen's Unions over against the Communist organizations; it must take special care of manual labourers who are in great need and of apprentices for whom colonies on the land should be created" (*p. 38*). For the reasons of failure he says rightly: "The methods of saving almost all proceed from a very marked lack of understanding of the true intellectual, political, and social distress of the modern day; they accept the old Christianity of authority and the old political and social order as apparently sanctioned by Divine authority, and, therefore, as something which is quite natural. . . . Above all, they are unable to place over against the modern emancipation movement any great positive aim in which the deeper longings of the recent time might be able to find itself" (*p. 39*). Further, however, ecclesiastical Lutheranism did not accept these proposals, which already seemed to it to be too revolutionary. "It is the tragic element in the life of Wichern that all his enthusiasm and his energy of love broke in vain on the rock of this rigid Lutheran tradition. In addition to Lutheran ecclesiasticism, the greatest hindrance . . . was the political reaction, and especially in the fact that it sanctioned the Home Mission" (*p. 48*). In vain Wichern tried to avoid this political disintegration (*p. 49*).

[291] (p. 568.) Cf. *Göhre: Evangelisch-soziale Bewegung, 1896*. It is interesting to note how in Rud. Todt and his central association, Lutheranism, completely overwhelmed by the knowledge of the new situation becomes quite bewildered, believes that it ought to evolve a new social theory to meet the new conditions, and composes this theory under the influences of Socialism and the Sermon on the Mount. Yet even Todt's State Socialism retained strongly patriarchal conservative features. Stöcker's work developed this latter dual tendency still farther, and finally sacrificed the social reform tendencies to middle-class patriarchal High Church ideas; *Göhre, 107*. The *Kirchlich-Soziale Konferenz*, which inherited Stöcker's ideas, went farther in this direction. The Protestant Workmen's Unions also display the same dualistic point of view; *Göhre, pp. 116 and 125*. The cause of that, however, is not merely political, but also the after-effect of the old tradition of Lutheran ethics.

[292] (p. 568.) So, for example, the earlier Hanoverian Church leader, *Uhlhorn: Kath. und Prot.* Appealing to the tradition of Lutheranism, and in decided opposition to the changes in the Lutheran spirit introduced by Stöcker, he wishes to see the Church solely occupied with the preaching of the Word and he lays down as the social service of the Church: (1) the re-emphasis on the dignity of labour in which the modern work in factories can be ennobled in a Christian manner, just as slavery was ennobled in the Early Church; (2) the proclamation to the masters of a patriarchalism which recognizes the infinite value of every Christian soul; (3) Sunday observance, the building of churches, the institution of new parishes; (4) the creation of smaller and more living congregations; (5) bringing under the control of the Church the very varied philanthropy which flourished in very different forms, sometimes Pietistic and sometimes almost Catholic, and the making of this charity into a definite task of parochial Poor Relief. Otherwise, however, the Church ought solely to place the Word of God upon the lampstand, so that "Christian" statesmen, jurists, political economists, members of parliament, manufacturers, bankers, and

workmen "then freely, according to their special insight, can effect social reform". To the Church itself, this is not commanded: "The Church is only concerned with that pertaining to spiritual possessions, righteousness, peace, and the Holy Ghost, and these possessions need to be gained whatever the external conditions of man may be" (*p. 44*). This, however, presupposes that those Christian statesmen, etc., will find also a social order which will correspond with the Christian ideal of Lutheranism, and that that which they discover will neither disturb nor alter Lutheran dogma and ethics!—Less unconcerned in this respect is *Nathusius: Die Mitarbeit der Kirche an der Lösung der Sozialen Frage*[3], *1904*; he therefore desires a High Church intensification of the independence and power of the Church, and he gives the "Christian" statesmen, etc., some hints upon what assumptions they ought to base their thought and their action.

[293] (p. 568.) Cf. *Wenck: Gesch. d. Nationalsozialen, 1905*. Naumann completed the process of development from charity to Christian social reform, and from this to a social formation based purely upon general political and economic causes which cannot be effected by religious ideas directly, and in so doing he gave the religious element back again to its more limited sphere. This again leads him to the tradition of Lutheranism, but with the important alteration that he requires a general social development which is strongly opposed to the main ethical idea of Lutheranism; this led naturally to a critical and disintegrating reflex effect upon Lutheran dogma and its ethic, as his *Briefe über Religion* shows. On the other hand, he emphasizes increasingly the indirect importance of the religious element for the freedom and value of personality in contrast to the oppressive influence to be expected from a bureaucratic capitalism.

[294] (p. 568.) Cf. the *Reports of the Ev.-soz. Kongress* since 1890, especially the address by *P. Drews* at the last Congress in 1909; otherwise, *Göhre, 135–162*. Since Stöcker left the Congress and the Conservatives became increasingly reluctant to identify themselves with this movement, the Congress has become more and more a place for the discussion of all the important leading questions of the Lutheran ethic, both practical and theoretical; this is also proved by the fact that it is now under the chairmanship of the leader of progressive Protestant theology, Adolf Harnack. The development of thought, which can be traced in the Reports, of a free Protestantism, gradually turning its attention to ethics rather than to dogma, is extremely instructive and attractive, but we are here concerned merely with the first beginnings of a new statement of the problems, behind which the scientific ethic of modern Protestantism only marches very reluctantly, and which with its earnestness actually affects very small groups. But at the present day, where do we find a really penetrating social ethic at all?

[295] (p. 569.) Cf. on this point *Elisabeth v. Richthofen: Ueber die historischen Wandlungen in der Stellung der autoritären Parteien zur Arbeiterschutzgesetzgebung und die Motive dieser Wandlungen, Heidelberger Diss., 1901, p. 72:* "The hostility between industry and agriculture, which at first (that is, among the adherents of the Christian Social party) seemed to lead to the support of the working classes against their 'capitalistic exploiters', has finally culminated, as the result of the need for labour, in an aversion to the introduction of measures for the improvement of the situation among industrial workers. . . . The Conservatives have renounced all initiative in social politics, and have withdrawn to the standpoint of a purely agrarian representation of interests. Traditional views and social relationships united them with men of that type who wish to maintain, as far as they possibly can, a patriarchal, dominating system of

labour which alone corresponds to the principle of authority for which they stand." Cf. also *Stillich*, especially the chapter *Die Gesellschaftsauffassung der Konservativen.* Always there is behind all this a certain sense of the value of the ethical principles of obedience and of authority, on the basis of the theoretical statement of the essential inequality of mankind which is not merely dictated by class interest, but which is connected with all the fundamental Christian and Lutheran tenets; see the passages in *Stillich, pp. 164–167.* Further, it is everywhere the peculiarity of the Lutheran Natural Law, to emphasize in Nature the inequalities and hindrances which oppose an ideal social order from which it derives ethical values of obedience and of care for others, instead of wishing to overcome and remove them in a direct and reforming way through ethical idealism; certainly a very serious ethical question from the consideration of which we ought not to allow ourselves to be diverted by class-war exploitations of the principle. The problem of equality forms in reality one of the most obscure and difficult points in the modern social doctrines of a liberal and Socialistic nature.

[297] (p. 570.) The Protestant idea of the "calling" is exalted in this way in the influential works of *Ritschl: Geschich. d. Pietismus,* and *Uhlhorn: Geschich. d. christlichen Liebestätigkeit,* and *Uhlhorn: Prot. und Kath.* The critical voices of the sixteenth and seventeenth centuries which summon Lutheranism back to opposition to the world are here represented as Catholic ascetic, and, what is identical in both, as sectarian reactions which then were completed in Pietism. This, however, is a misinterpretation of the dualistic elements in Luther's own doctrine.—That both regard the "permeation of civilization" essentially in the Conservative anti-modern sense is shown by *Uhlhorn: Prot. und Kath.*, where he gives the advice that the question of Labour should be handled as Paul handled the problem of slavery (*p. 46*), and *Ritschl*, who in his *Göttinger Jubiläumsrede* (*Drei akademische Reden, 1887*), taught that Liberalism, social democracy, and the Catholic doctrine of Society had arisen out of the same root of individualistic Rationalism, while he claimed for Lutheranism an historic anti-Rationalist basing of Society upon power and force, somewhat in the sense of Heinrich von Treitschke, and thus explained the filling of the relationships of life which have thus been created with trust in God and loyalty to one's "calling" for the anti-mediaeval modern civilization; this leads, then, to insight into "the Conservative task of the State understood in the light of history" (*p. 61*). The intention is similar when in the book by *Loofs: L.'s Stellung*, Luther is represented as the victor over the mediaeval world and the founder of the modern world; the "modern world" of Loofs is possibly Prussian free Conservative or National Liberal of the Right.

[299a] (p. 571.) *Ritschl's Jubiläumsrede* has a right feeling for this special character of the Lutheran Natural Law contrasted with that of Catholicism and Calvinism. Rightly there also the Catholic, Liberal, Socialist (and Calvinist) idea is connected with Greek Rationalism, even though otherwise the account of the history of the Christian social doctrines is far from clear. We must, however, note that Greek speculation had already foreshadowed that difference, and had taught alongside of the Rationalist-individualistic Natural Law also that anti-Rationalistic positivist Natural Law; cf. *Hirzel: Νόμος ἄγραφος Abhh. d. Sächs. Ak., 1900*; also *Karst: Entstehung der Vertragstheorie, Z. f. wiss. Politik, 1909, pp. 524–528.*

[300] (p. 571.) For its general influence on civilization, see *Arnold Berger: Die Kulturaufgaben der Reformation, und desselben Luther.* For the dual tendency of these effects, see the opinions of the good Protestant historian, *H. Baumgarten,*

in his famous self-criticism of Liberalism (*Preuss. Jahrbb., 1866*): "Luther's almost exclusive emphasis upon the inward side of religion caused this aspect to predominate in our character for centuries. . . . Our Lutheran princes, too, had a policy, and one which was quite new and had never been seen before . . . the policy of moral scruples, of paternal conscientiousness, of sterling excellence in small things and impotence in large questions, of great industry in a narrow circle, and stupid laziness when great matters were afoot. It was a policy of this kind which established and encouraged the solid bourgeoisie of our towns, the comfortable prosperity of our villages, the success of our schools and universities, the conscientious industry of our officials, the seriousness of our science, the purity of our family life; it has created, or at least developed, everything of which we may be proud, everything which makes for happiness and prosperity in our domestic, private, and economic life. It has, however, also created that *Kleinstaaterei* which honours a man only as the father of a family, but which has no use for him as a man and a citizen, that wretched Philistinism which keeps our nation in bonds, that terrible habit of cherishing the most daring fantasies and then of sinking to the ground in despair before the slightest difficulty. This spirit has sucked the energy and virility out of the life of the State, and has turned it, properly speaking, into a sort of Kindergarten, which has preserved us from all the dangers of this wicked world, but also from all its greatness" (*p. 456*). *Baumgarten* then goes on to say that this Lutheran "inwardness" also caused the cosmopolitanism and lack of national spirit present in our classical literature and philosophy. And it is a fact that all this is connected with the specifically Christian side of Luther, but the question has also another aspect. Bismarck, too, whom *Baumgarten* admired for his greatness, but to whom he was opposed in other ways, also appealed to Lutheranism. But the Lutheranism to which he appeals is certainly not the definite Christian element in Luther, but his irrational conception of the Natural Law of power and authority, which for two hundred years certainly only served to support the claims of the existing authority, but which with the rise of Prussia were brought out afresh by Stahl as arguments against Liberalism and the Revolution and developed in a brilliant way; since then, in its connection with the Christian idea of sin and of inequality (in the non-religious sphere), it has served the interests of a highly realistic policy of might and authority which allows the Christian, as an official member of the institutions determined by sin, to develop all the consequences of the naturalistic idea of power and authority. It is thus, namely, that *H. v. Treitschke* has represented Lutheranism. In so doing, however, as with Bismarck and other Conservatives of the modern day, the idea of power has frequently become an end in itself, the duty of the State to care for the Christian character of Society has been placed in the background, and the co-operation of the policy of power with the religious end of life has been left in a general way to Providence, who has made humanity what it is at any rate; cf. *Lenz: Bismarcks Religion.* German social legislation, therefore, is no longer the result of a conception of the State which is Christian in principle, but it is an incidental use of Christian ideas for political ends in which that which had been separated fortunately is once more united.

[303] (p. 573.) On this point, see *Haendtke: Deutsche Kultur im Zeitalter des 30 j. Krieges, p. 70*: "It is beyond doubt that at that time from the economic point of view Germany was still very much hampered by mediaeval views; for in what other land would it then have been possible (1684–5) to forbid, for example, the ribbon-loom which was so important, as took place at Nürnberg

at the request of the lace-makers, or as happened at Frankfort-on-the-Maine; in 1666 permission was refused to set up a weaving-loom such as had already been seen in 1665 at the Frankfort Fair. . . ." Also in other places it was unthinkable that the question of machinery was made "'une affaire de conscience' by the 'premier confesseur et prédicateur de L'Electeur de Saxe'." We ought to place alongside of that the often-quoted sentence of *Uhlhorn* that the machine is in itself Protestant!—*Laveleye: Prot. u. Kath. u. deren Beziehungen zur Freiheit und Wohlfahrt der Völker, deutsch 1875*, deals with Protestantism in general, it is true, but in point of fact it refers always only to Calvinism. The only points which apply to Lutheranism are the reference to the increased intellectualism of a doctrinal and book religion. In this realm of thought there is need for some much more exact research.

[307] (p. 575.) In reference to the great European "Restoration" (of the early part of the nineteenth century), its world of thought, and its social history, there is no really satisfactory work, which represents its difference from the modern world. Church histories in particular, which should have a good deal to say on this question, are totally inadequate. Either they glorify the reawakening of faith, which to them is something quite natural contrasted with the sin and evil of the modern world, or they complain of the destruction of the beginnings of reform which they regard as the result of reactionary politics and selfishness. A deeper understanding of the subject is found in the brilliant book by *Meinecke: Weltbürgertum und Nationalstaat, 1908,* which deals with a different subject. This writer does justice not only to the Liberal school of thought (which is usually the only one to which attention is paid), but he traces the connection from "Stein to Friedrich Wilhelm IV, that is, the Romantic-Conservative branch of the idea of a national state" (*p. 19*). Here also we come upon the reawakening of the irrational positivist Natural Law in *Burke, 126 ff.*, in *Adam Müller, 128, K. L. v. Haller, 212 f.*, and the religious interpretation of the Law of Nature as the natural reason guided by God in the process of development (*211*), the maintenance of this idea of development alongside of anti-revolutionary conditions which morally are required, and which belong to the Christian-patriarchal-aristocratic forms of life (*217*), contact with the ideas of Darwin without giving up the religious interpretation (*212*), the focusing of this Christian-realistic policy, in opposition to the revolutionary doctrinaire policy in a Christian universal policy, a new Catholicism (*221*), the entrance of these ideas into Pietist Lutheran circles and the reawakening of the old Lutheran sociology, combined with a compromise with the modern idea of a national State, and with increased emphasis upon monarchist Legitimist ideas (*226–232*), the complicated blend of these ideas (*245–291*), Bismarck's development out of these theories (*300–315*). All this, however, is regarded too much from the "Romantic" point of view, whereas in reality Romanticism merely formed a bridge to the old ecclesiastical-sociological ideas, and after that the Christian and ecclesiastical sociology plays its part alongside of the nationalistic and philosophical-cosmopolitan theories, and after the victory of Bismarck-Nationalism it is to-day again endeavouring, in quite an unromantic way, in connection with certain definite interests, to dominate the situation. The fact that this Romanticism looked first of all towards Catholicism was because it alone offered the two elements of authority and internationalism which seemed necessary in order to counteract the influence of the Enlightenment, whereas the Lutheran churches with their "advanced" theology, and their dependence on the State, were at first of no use for this purpose. Since in this respect they have gained their own organized

independence, they, and not Catholicism, which contains within it strongly Liberal elements, are the real home of Conservatism.

[308] (p. 577.) *Hundeshagen*, in his *Beiträgen zur Kirchenverfassungsgeschichte und Kirchenpolitik, 1864*, has shown for the first time that the essential difference in Calvinism is to be sought in this sphere; in this book the writer counsels his colleagues in Church history to make the basis of their research into the question of the conception of the Church "the visible empirical social group formed by the churches and their laws of life and growth which are still too little known" instead of dogmatic speculative research (*IX*); that is, he is summoning them to treat Church history from the sociological point of view. "Not merely in Geneva, but wherever Calvinism extended it found great social crises already in existence, and it intervened as a stimulating but also a purifying element which, while it caused ferment, also produced order out of chaos. For Calvinism the sphere of conflict is never merely religious or ecclesiastical in the purely religious sense; the Roman Catholic faith never opposes it simply as such, but everywhere definitely combined with dynastic interests and principles of government. Thus it was in the nature of the situation that Calvin and his co-workers like Zwingli had to take into account not merely individuals but smaller and greater nationalities. Thus for Calvin also the Gospel is not merely an energy which saves all the individuals who believe in it, it is not merely a comfort for individual burdened consciences, not merely the overcoming of errors which are dangerous to the soul, but it is at the same time the means of healing all public and universal ills, the element of purification and renewal for larger social groups and the foundation-stone upon which this work of renewal must be based" (*pp. 294 ff.*). This passage gives very apt expression to the difference between Calvinism and Lutheranism.—The recognition of the fact that in this special form Calvinism also contains an element of considerable approximation to the tendencies of the modern world (once again in contrast with Lutheranism) relates this book to more modern researches: *Gierke's Althusius; Jellinek: Die Erklärung der Menschen- und Bürgerrechte*², *1904;* and the treatise by *Max Weber* on the *Geist des Kapitalismus und die prot. Ethik, Archiv XX und XXI*. The following works also follow the same line: *Rieker: Grundsätze ref. Kirchenverfassung*, and *Figgis: From Gerson to Grotius, 1907; v. Schulze-Gävernitz: Britischer Imperialismus und englischer Freihandel, 1906*, and my presentation in *Kultur der Gegenwart, IV*², *Protestantisches Christentum und Kirche*. In this matter also, however, *Hundeshagen* has already been before us: "*Ueber den Einfluss des Calvinismus auf die Ideen von Staat und Staatsbürgerlicher Freiheit*", *1840*, also *Baudrillart: Bodin et son temps, 1853*.—The primary reason for the growth of Calvinism in France and the Netherlands (in addition to that of geographical proximity) seems to have been its independent ecclesiastical Church formation and its more decided opposition to Catholicism. Cf. *K. Müller: Preuss. Jahrb., 1903*, and *Rachfahl: Wilh. v. Oranien und der Niederländische Aufstand, I, 1906, p. 145*.

[309] (p. 577.) Cf. *A. Kuyper: Reformation wider Revolution* (German translation by *Jäger*, 1904). This book is not only Kuyper's government programme, but, consisting of lectures delivered at the University of Princeton, which is strictly Calvinistic, it constitutes a kind of collective creed of modern orthodox Calvinism. Otherwise in an absolutely unprecedented degree Neo-Calvinism is here read into the primitive Calvinism of Geneva. It is the book of a dogmatist and a politician, and as such it is extremely instructive; as an historical work, however, it is very misleading.

[311] (p. 578.) Cf. *von Bezold: Staat und Gesellschaft des Ref.-Zeitalters* (*Kultur der Gegenwart, II, V, 1*), *p. 81*: "In many respects Calvin's work is reactionary;

he is especially sharply opposed to the Humanist artistic and natural science tendencies of his day. When, however, in spite of that Calvinism is here regarded as an actual ferment which caused the rise of modern Europe, this applies very largely to its propaganda and development outside Geneva." The rest of this section will show how true this last observation is; I would only add that the basis for this development was already present in primitive Calvinism. The earlier part of this quotation is only true within certain very definite limits. Cf. *Arnold: Calvin, 1909.*

312 (p. 579.) Cf. in general *Kampschulte: J. C., seine Kirche und sein Staat, 1869–99; Cornelius: Historische Arbeiten, 1899; Doumergue: John Calvin* (7 vols.); *Marcks: Coligny, I, 1892; Rieker: Grundsätze Reformierter Kirchenverfassung, 1899;* and *Sohm: Kirchenrecht, I;* for Church history see in particular *Karl Müller.* The two works of *Choisy* are particularly important, *La Théocratie à Genève,* and *L'état chrétien à Genève aux temps de Bèze*; an analysis from the point of view of ethics and of the history of dogma in the masterpieces of *Schneckenburger* and *A. Ritschl,* to which we must add *Lobstein: Ethik Calvins, 1877*; also *Rachfahl: Oranien, I, 1, 1906; I, 2, 1907; II, 1908.* The results of the researches of the Jubilee year, 1909, are given by *W. Köhler* in *Th. J. B.* for 1910. The following works ought also to be noted: the *Calvinreden* of the *Siebeck Verlag,* the *Calvinstudien* of the *Elberfeld group,* published by *Bohatek,* and *Calvin and the Reformation,* four studies by *Doumergue, Lang, Bavinck,* and *Warfield*; finally, *C. F. Arnold: Calvinrede.*—In the research of the present day the relations between early Calvinism and Martin Bucer and Strassburg emerge very clearly; this aspect of the subject is treated by *Lang* in his *Evangelienkommentar, 1900,* and also by *W. Köhler: Gött. Gel. Anzeigen, 1902; Anrich: Die Strassburger Reformation, Ch. W. 1905; von Schubert: Calvinreden, p. 141.* Of Calvin's own writings the chief are the *Institutes* and his *Letters.*—For histories of dogma, see *Loofs* and *Seeberg.*—Above all, there is a great deal of useful material in *Göbel: Geschichte des christlichen Lebens in der rheinisch-westfälischen Kirche, I, 1849; II, 1852; III, 1860;* this book deals especially with the analogies between Calvinism and Pietism and the sect-type of which there were many illustrations in the development of Calvinism in the Netherlands and on the Lower Rhine. This valuable, although somewhat unctuous book, first shows the matter in a true light, whereas *Ritschl's Gesch. d. Pietismus* treats the Calvinism of Calvin simply as an imitation of Luther and a reaction towards Catholicism. Such a statement is only intelligible in the light of Ritschl's curious doctrine that the sect-type is Catholic, and therefore that any approach to the sect-type means Catholicism and "mediaeval reaction". This doctrine makes it impossible to understand the matter; rather, together with the Baptists, Calvinism ought to be described as radical Protestantism and "*Biblizismus*" (that is, a Church in which the Bible occupies a central position), whereas Lutheranism remains closer to Catholic conservatism and its institutional spirit. This has been shown in the previous section, and is of the highest importance for the understanding of the special nature of the social teaching of Calvinism compared with which Catholicism and Lutheranism are relatively closer to each other, and in spite of all differences they move within one common type. *Schneckenburger, I, 6,* remarks very truly: "First of all Lutheranism after Catholicism is the direct continuation of Latin Christianity, a spiritualized transformation of the same, and an actual reform which is connected with its historical development. In the Calvinistic church development the aim is not so much a mere reform and spiritual continuation of historic Latin Christianity as a phenomenon which in principle is a new formation of Christianity directly formulated from the Scriptures according

to its original standard form." This is confirmed by the undeniably greater dislike of Catholic and Old Catholic thinkers (among the latter *Kampschulte* and *Moritz Ritter*) for Calvinism than for Lutheranism. Quite similarly also *Ranke* expresses himself in one famous passage about the Augsburg Confession.—A survey of recent literature on Calvinism is given by *Knodt: Bedeutung Calvins und des Calvinismus für die prot. Welt im Lichte der neueren und neuesten Forschung, 1910.*

[313] (p. 581.) Cf. the beginning of *Book IV* in *Calvin's Institutes*. Here the Church is regarded as the treasury of grace independent of the individual: "Quia ruditas nostra et segnities externis subsidiis indigent, quibus fides in nobis et gignatur et augescat et suos faciat progressus usque ad metam, ea quoque (Deus) addidit, quo infirmitati nostra consuleret; atque ut augescat Evangelii praedicatio, thesaurum hunc ad ecclesiam deposuit. Pastores instituit ac doctores, quorum ore suos doceret Eph. iv. 11. Eos autoritate instruxit. Imprimis sacramenta instituit, quae nos experimento sentimus plus quam utilia esse adjumenta ad fovendam et confirmandam fidem. Nam quia ergastulo carnis nostrae inclusi ad gradum evangelicum nondum pervenimus, Deus se ad captum nostrum acomodans pro admirabili sua providentia modum praescripsit, quo procul disjuncti ad eum accederemus" (*Inst. IV, 1, 1*).—"Quia nunc de ecclesia visibili disserere propositum est, discamus vel uno matris elogio, quam utilis sit nobis ejus cognitio, immo necessaria: quando non alius est in vitam ingressus, nisi nos ipsa concipiat in utero, nisi pariat, nisi nos alat suis uberibus, denique sub custodia et gubernatione nos tueatur, donec excuti carne mortali similes erimus angelis. Neque enim patitur nostra infirmitas a schola nos dimitti, donec toto vitae cursu discipuli fuerimus. Adde, quod extra ejus gremium nulla est speranda peccatorum remissio nec ulla salus" (*IV, 1, 4*). An individual is born into this Church as you inherit an entail; cf. *Contre les Anabaptistes, Corpus Reformatorum, 35, p. 522*: "Ainsi l'homme qui n'a esté receu en l'alliance de Dieu des son enfance, est comme estranger à l'Eglise, iusques à ce que par la doctrine de salut il soit amené à foy et repentance. Mais alors sa semence est aussi quant et quant faict domestique de l'Eglise. Et pour ceste cause les petitz enfants des fidèles sont baptisés en vertu de cette alliance, qui est faicte avec leurs pères, en leur noms et à leurs profits." The spiritual nature of the sacraments which Calvinism teaches thus changes nothing in the conception of the Church. Infant Baptism should take place in the presence of the congregation, but it is always a witness to the child's birthright in the Church which it already possesses; cf. *Briefe, II, 34, 38, 245, 423*. In the Sacrament of the Lord's Supper, moreover, Calvin has retained the idea of objective wonderful spiritual food, even though solely spiritual, in the interest of the idea of the Church, and, therefore, he regarded himself as a Lutheran. Although he lays stress on the exercise of discipline and makes the demand for a worthy reception of the Sacrament the centre of his idea of a holy community, he expressly guards against all separatist and sectarian consequences. Where the Word and the Sacrament are, there for him is the Church, as for Luther, and since it is impossible to know the inner state of each individual, no separation between believers and unbelievers is allowed. *C.R., 35, p. 68:* "Car la majesté de la parolle de Dieu et de ses sacrements nous doit estre en telle réputation, que partout ou nous la voyons nous soyons certains que là il y a Eglise, nonobstant les macules et les vices qui pourront estre en la vie commune des hommes." The power of excluding individuals from communion, which is to be exercised by the Church, is good, but it is always only a method of punishment and education used by the Church, never a separation of the pure and holy from the Church of the pure doctrine and the pure Word, however much sin she

may contain: "Je laisse à dire qu'encore posé le cas que nous ne deussions avoir aucune considération que des hommes et de leur meurs (this is supposed to be a false assumption of the Baptists), nous pourrions estre souvent abusez en reiettant une compagnie et ne la daignant estimer Eglise à cause des imperfections qui y seraient. Car il se pourrait faire tout les coups, que nous ferons iniure à beaucoups de sainczt personnages, dont le nombre est caché entre les meschants comme le bon grain dessoubs la pouille." These are almost literally all the characteristics of the idea of the Church contrasted with that of the sect which I have previously noted (*II, 9*). Cf. also the completely Lutheran formulas for the Church conception, *Briefe, I, 6, 57, 76, 271; II, 158, 409*: "I know very well, thank God, that the true efficacy of the Sacrament does not depend upon the worthiness of him who dispenses it." Further, the strongest emphasis is laid upon the ministry called and established in an orderly manner, without which there can be no congregation and no Church; the ministry is regarded as the vessel which carries the wonderful power of the Church, which is independent of the personal worthiness of each individual minister; *Briefe, I, p. 266; II, 18, 47, 52;* cf. *272, 357*: Laymen can never be considered suitable for any office; also "the elders" are not purely lay, for they are ordained in the same way as a minister (*Choisy, 356*). From this there naturally results that so far as the influence of the State authority extends, only the true religion may predominate: *Briefe, I, pp. 9, 311, 344, 445f.; II, pp. 117, 200.* The circuitous route which Luther followed in order to reach this view was not necessary for Calvin, after events had spoken clearly. Toleration is granted only to the Truth, and this toleration must predominate. The most characteristic expression of this absolute assurance of possessing the sole Truth is Calvin's remark about the "false martyrs" (the Anabaptists), although Calvin himself at the same time describes martyrdom as the highest witness to the Truth; see *C. R., p. 35*: "Et mesme c'est ce qui discerne les martyrs de Dieu de ceux du Diable que de mourir pour iuste cause. Pourtant tout ainsi que c'est une constance louable que de souffrir la mort, si mestier est, pour le tesmoignage de la vérité: aussi c'est obstination enragée que de souffrir pour mauvaise querelle. Tellement que celuy qui en souffre le plus, est d'autant plus à vituperer." This is a spirit of self-assurance which entirely takes away the breath of the modern man, but it constitutes the heart of the Church conception and of the dominion of the Church, the heart of the greatness of those men. Cf. also Calvin's self-estimate, *Briefe, I, 451*: "So far as I am concerned, my masters, I am quite certain in my conscience that that which I have taught and written did not arise out of my own head, but that I have received it from God, and I must stand firmly by it if I am not to be a traitor to the Truth." He writes in the same vein to the Council (*I, 444 and II, 67*). At the same time the spiritual nature and inwardness of the Church is preserved, as by Luther, through the statement that the Church does not force men to believe, but that the State only compels people to lead an externally Christian life and to use the means of grace in the interest of society; faith is a miraculous gift of God and conquers only through the inner power of the Word.—The rest of this section will show that the Church, together with the State, must and will also accept and dominate civilization in general; further, Calvin expresses everywhere in his views on the Anabaptists that this previous statement is the logical result of the conception of the Church, *C. R., 35, p. 92*: "Touchant de la fin ou ilz pretendent, ie n'en diray que deux motz: qu'ilz (the Baptists) se monstrent en cela ennemis de Dieu et du genre humain. Car c'est faire la guerre à Dieu de vouloir mettre en vitupere ce qu'il honoré (that is, in the

Old Testament and through the actual course of history); de vouloir fouler aux piedz ce qu'il a exalté. Et on ne saurait mieux machiner la ruine du monde et introduire partout qu'en taschant d'abolir le gouvernement civil." The emphasis on this objective institutional character of the Church increases with the various editions of the Institutes, *Köstlin: Ueber Cs. Inst.* (*Stud. u. Krit.*, *1868*), *p. 481*; *Rieker* tends to emphasize the "fellowship" element in the Church conception more strongly than the "institutional" (*p. 71*); he considers that "the latter threatens to absorb the former in course of time". This, however, only took place in Independency which precisely on that account cannot claim pure descent from the thought of Calvinism; so long as *Rieker* abides by the Calvinistic idea pure and simple, he himself must also lay a great deal of emphasis on the institutional element and the agreement with Luther (*pp. 75, 81 ff., 87*). The "combination between predestination and a sectarian individualism" is nowhere completed by Calvin since predestination is always connected with the "vehicle" of its outworking in the Word and the Sacrament. In Calvin also, as in Luther, we find the doctrine that the Church is present wherever the Word and the Sacrament are present even within Catholicism (*Briefe, I, 352, 371, 437*). The individualism of the doctrine of predestination is important enough, but it has nothing to do with a "fellowship" conception of the Church.—Moreover, to speak of an element of Natural Law in the Calvinist conception of the Church, as does *Sohm, Kirchenrecht, p. 697*, seems to me a complete misunderstanding of the subject; this is always an interpretation of primitive Calvinism in terms of modern Calvinism. The historical problem lies precisely in this transformation, and in this section this subject will be dealt with very thoroughly.

[314] (p. 583.) That in this respect also Calvin at first simply follows Luther is shown perfectly plainly by the one fact of Luther's treatise against Erasmus, *De servo arbitrio* (for the meaning and importance of this work, see the careful book by *Zickendraht: Der Streit zwischen Erasmus und Luther, 1909*). For the independent development of the doctrine of predestination, see *Alex. Schweizer: Die Zentraldogmen der reform. Kirche, 1854–56*. For the importance and the effect of this doctrine upon Calvin's doctrinal system, and, above all, on his ethic about which there has been much controversy, see the various leading ideas in *Hundeshagen, pp. 301–306*. Yet there can be no doubt that for Calvin this doctrine was of central importance; see *Scheibe: Calvins Prädestinationslehre, 1897*. Ritschl's opinion that the doctrine of predestination was only an additional element in Calvin's system which arose out of his strict obedience to the Scriptures, is a strange and curious idea which can only be explained from the point of view of his endeavour to turn Calvin into a mere imitator and disciple of Luther; see his *Geschichtl. Studien zur christlichen Lehre von Gott., Jbb. f. deutsche Theol., 1865 and 1868;* from my own point of view the agreement with Scotism, which is here asserted, is only due to analogy and not to origin.

[315] (p. 583.) *Lobstein, 82–86*. Luther always looked upon suffering as essentially the result of sin and justified by it. The importance of distinguishing the *gratia universalis* from the grace of election which softens the doctrine of Original Sin, accepts the fact of Reason and culture, gives room to the *Lex Naturae*, and generally weakens the rigidly pessimistic and ascetic features; see *Bavinck* in *Calvin and the Reformation*, and also *Kuyper, pp. 110–118*. This side of the question, which is usually overlooked, is very important for the problem of asceticism and its relation to civilization.

[316] (p. 585.) Cf. *Hundeshagen, pp. 396, 401, 447, 448*. On the intellectual nature of Calvinism, see *Choisy: L'état chrétien, p. 523*, and *Kuyper, 103–331*;

the latter with an admixture of very powerful apologetic, highly characteristic of the aims of modern Calvinism. *Schneckenburger* has some excellent passages on the intellectual character, self-consciousness, and calm assurance of Calvinism; for the fact that this led to the acceptance of Western culture and of Humanism by Calvinism which, in spite of its predominant pessimism and asceticism, is much stronger than in Lutheranism, see *Arnold: Calvinrede.* The higher position of spiritual and intellectual culture in Calvinism is also very finely expressed in *C. F. Meyer's Novelle über die Bartholomäusnacht.*

[319] (p. 587.) On the great emphasis on the Bible in Lutheranism and Calvinism, see *Schneckenburger, I, pp. 16, 20, 27; Otto Ritschl: Dogmengeschichte des Prot., 1908, I, 53–192. Göbel, II, 114, 154, 347,* results for worship and song; *118,* the form of worship, which is very simple and founded on the Bible, resembles that of the Waldensians and the Moravians; *I, 326,* Laski's view of the Bible "stands midway between the Lutherans with their lack of constitution and the separatist Anabaptists"; *311,* the same tendency in Calvin, who in so doing "also really attained the re-entrance of the separated Anabaptists which since then in Geneva and in the whole Calvinistic Church scarcely happened again (?), and then soon also they were tolerated in a way which never happened in the Zwinglian (and Lutheran) churches". This analogy with the Scriptural principles of the Baptists is very clearly recognized by *A. Ritschl: Gesch. d. Pietismus, I, 72.*

[320] (p. 590.) For the special character of Calvinistic individualism, see *Schneckenburger* and especially *Max Weber: Archiv. XXI, pp. 5–14,* in which *Weber* rightly points out the very different meaning which the word "individualism" can be used to cover. It may mean the mediaeval freedom of movement and the variety of graduated relationships along with a relative equality in the spiritual content of life, or the modern consciousness and sense of difference with the greatest possible equality in the legal and social sphere, or Catholic mysticism and Catholic liberalism, or Lutheran happiness of justification, or the self-concentration and self-control of Calvinism. Calvinism is characterized not by an increased individualism, but by a particular kind of individualism; see *Weber, p. 12,* also cf. *Rieker, p. 72,* and *Seeberg: Begriff der Kirche, I, 1885, p. 123,* who, however, underestimate the connection between the effect of predestination and the ecclesiastical means of grace, because they think that the later Independents and the sects were derived directly from Calvinistic individualism. This, however, in view of its Church conception, which it borrowed from Luther directly, is impossible. For Calvin the Church and predestination are in no way rival forces, and the conception of the Church is placed within the setting of predestination. From the ethical point of view, however, this individualism always has more touch with that of the sects. But although the legalistic spirit, the emphasis on the will, the derivation of fellowship from the association of individuals, brings Calvinism very near to the sects and increases the spirit of individualism, this sense of individualism is again removed by the conception of grace which gives rise to the doctrine of predestination. *Schneckenburger* has brilliantly opened up this subject, and shown the interplay of both these tendencies. He was also the first to notice the resemblance to the sect, *I, 26*: "The external Church has almost only *necessitas praecepti* and it very nearly rejects them quite in the sectarian manner"; *50:* "The far greater significance of the institutional character of the Church for the Lutherans"; *157:* "The Church does not make the believers what they are, but the believers make the Church what she is; this is the principle expressed in a very outspoken way by Vinet, and is directly opposed to the Lutheran

conception of the Mother Church"; *167:* "It was and is always the practical way of sect-formation through which certain inconsistencies in doctrine, and more frequently merely ascetic or disciplinary discords, are resolved." Cf., however, also the reverse side of this question in the section on the *Unio cum Christo, I, 133–143,* where the removal of these consequences by the doctrine of Predestination and of Grace is described.

[323] (p. 593.) On this point his work, *Contre les Anabaptistes, C. R. 35,* is very important. In this work Calvin treats the conservative branch of the Baptist movement on the whole very leniently, only blaming them in a condescending manner for their foolishness and lack of culture. He admits especially that so far as the demand for a holy community and excommunication is concerned, there is a common standpoint which the Baptists also had gained from the Bible, and he only opposes their atomistic separatism, their tendency to regard solely the moral worth of the individual, and their subjectivism which overlooks the objectivity of grace and their hostility to culture. So far Calvin, in fact, accepts the early Lutheran group ideal (*W. Köhler: Christl. Welt, 1907, pp. 371–377*), and he corresponds to the tendencies of a lay Christian Puritanism as it has been called by *Barge.* Only it should be emphasized very strongly that Calvin did not try to reach that ideal of the holy community from the standpoint of lay Christianity and the priesthood of believers, but through setting up a supernatural Church-order based on the Scriptures, which is of Divine authority. He also removed the question of appointment to, and control of, the ministry from the congregation, handing it over to the general body of the pastors and to the Council, leaving to the congregation only the right of protest. The lay elders also were elected by the pastors and the Council, they were not chosen by the congregation, and they had a semi-clerical character; see *Choisy: L'état chrétien, p. 536.* Attempts at a more far-reaching congregational democracy were suppressed by the pastors (*Choisy, 79, 149, 153*). Certainly the fundamental idea of Calvinism was the purity of the body of communicants, based upon Pauline teaching, only this purity was maintained on ecclesiastical, authoritative lines, not on those of a sectarian lay religion. On that account, because all exclusion was effected by the State-clerical institution of discipline and had civil consequences, the celebration of Holy Communion was always an act both of the municipal community and of the Church at the same time (*Choisy, 358*). Only thus did Geneva become the "Holy City", the "New Jerusalem", as men liked to call it (*Choisy, 430, 436*). This, together with the different attitude towards culture, is the difference between primitive Calvinism and the New Jerusalem of the Baptists at Münster; in contrast with Luther it is the supernatural character of the Calvinistic Church-order which made possible the erection of a stable community and kept it in close touch with the Church-type, whereas Luther in the rejection of that "new law" in reality would have been at the mercy of congregational democracy and the sect-type, if he had followed his earlier plans out in detail, or if he could have done so. Only in France, when congregations were set up which were free from the State, did the congregations begin to elect the elders (*Briefe, II, 469*); for the Palatinate Calvin had outlined a mixed system of election (*413*). The election of pastors, however, lay always in the hands of the pastors (*II, 330*). Further, democratic tendencies towards lay Christianity, the election of pastors and elders by the congregation, discussions on the sermon into which the congregation was drawn, which indeed closely resembled the Baptist communities, which became so important for the Netherlands and the Lower Rhine (*Joh. a. Laski,* see in *Göbel, I, 318–351, 412*).

[324] (p. 594.) The illustrations of this question are in *Schneckenburger*, *Choisy*, and *Göbel*. The purity of the body of communicants as the main point, *Schneckenburger, I, 64ff.; Göbel, II, 73;* baptism as an obligation, *Göbel, I, 122, 175ff.; Schneckenburger, I, 254.* The connection between these ideas of excommunication, the purity of the body of communicants, and baptism, with the Baptist movement, and the tendency (which was also present in Calvinism) from this point of view to break down the ecclesiastical spirit altogether, is emphasized a good deal by *Göbel, I, 88–99*: "Since for other and more important reasons this separation did not take place, because it was considered desirable to maintain itself as a Church and not to become a sect, there remained, therefore, in all the congregations a great deal, and in some everything to be done in order to reach even to some extent the high aim of a true congregation consisting only of believers." *I, 111,* scruples against Infant Baptism and the oath; *113,* Labadism and Pietism only opposed because their effect is sectarian; *211,* central significance of the home rather than of the congregation, because the former is more capable of being really Christianized.

[325] (p. 595.) On this spirit of legalism, see *Schneckenburger, I, 109–131; Lobenstein, 51–57; Inst., II, 7, 6–9;* here the statement, *II, 7, 12*: "Tertius usus legis, qui est praecipuus et in proprium legis finem propius spectat, erga fideles locum habet, in quorum cordibus jam viget et regnat dei Spiritus." The law does not serve chiefly to make sin known as in Lutheranism, but it regulates the behaviour of the individual who has been born again; therefore, in the Calvinistic Catechisms law does not precede but follows faith. This has nothing to do with Catholicism, for obedience springs out of faith, but with the strictness of a holy community; it is combined with predestination through the idea of perseverance and the doctrine (which Calvin himself rejected) of the signs of the state of grace. On this point, in addition to *Schneckenburger*, see *Göbel, II, 137, 145, 206, 215.* The only analogy is the legalism of the Baptists, whose moralism, however, is set aside by Calvinism by tracing everything back to predestination.

[327] (p. 596.) On this point see the brilliant sections in *Schneckenburger* on the mystical indwelling (*I, 182–255*). Christ as Lord and Law-giver (*I, 126*); the Lord in Whom the Church is planted (*I, 136*). Of course, I do not mean that we are here confronted with an historical influence of the Baptists, but simply with the consequence of an idea which Calvinism held in common with the Baptists. The same consequences, the same effects. At the same time the difference which arises out of the rest of the assumptions on both sides is quite clear. It is, however, remarkable that so far as I know no one has pointed out this resemblance before. *Choisy*, certainly, points frequently to the Christocratic conception which distinguishes Calvinism from Lutheranism.

[328] (p. 597.) On the Covenant idea, see *Schneckenburger, I, 159; Göbel, I, 385,* already Olevian in *Heppe, 205–240.* That this is the root of Calvinist Free Church development is shown by *Göbel, 401*; *418,* the Church on the Lower Rhine; *423,* a voluntary Church based on personal confession of faith and personal obligations; *443,* the resemblance of this idea of the Church to that of the sect fully recognized. In consequence of this, the idea of the germ of the Church existing within the Church; *Göbel, II, 71,* closed and open communities; *II, 415,* two congregations in each parish. *Göbel* emphasizes in this the transition to Pietism just as Coccejus, with his Covenant theology, did more for Pietism than Voet with his organization of Conventicles in which Coccejus did not share. Coccejus has done more to break up the idea of the Church inwardly and spiritually through the idea of the Covenant than the

orthodox Voet, who only wished to help Church discipline through his Conventicles.

[330] (p. 598.) Cf. *Choisy: La Théocratie*. Here and in *Schneckenburger* genuine ecclesiastical Calvinism is described; in *Choisy* that of the Genevans and of Calvinism; in *Schneckenburger* that of orthodoxy. *Göbel*, however, whose sympathies were Calvinistic and Pietist, points out everywhere the connections with Pietism, which were in harmony with his own sympathies, for which reason also he often detects resemblances between primitive Calvinism and the sect-type. For this reason his book is very instructive, whereas otherwise, even in *Schneckenburger*, the legal and ascetic features of Calvinism are often attributed to Catholicism. It is, however, true that *Schneckenburger* likes to make his subject more intelligible by using illustrations from Methodism, Quakerism, Pietism, and Puritanism.—For the ecclesiastical nature of Calvinism which remained in spite of all this, see *Choisy, p. 262*: "Calvin does not admit that man is free; he excludes this idea from his theological, and from his social system. The Kingdom of God is not offered to man to be freely accepted; it is established by persuasion, no doubt, but also by the repression of all rebellion by constraint. Calvin does not admit that the glory of God consists in offering His Sovereign Will to the will of man, who accepts it freely or who denies it, who obeys or who resists it, who gives himself or refuses to do so. For him the glory of God is maintained when man bows down before His law in an attitude of submission whether free or forced. Sins against God and His Word are considered violations of the law." This applies equally to the elect and the reprobate. Here is the main difference between Calvinism proper and every form of Free Church and Pietistic modification or accentuation of Calvinism, and also of all forms of sectarianism.—The connection which still exists between both, in spite of all that, is also recognized by *Luthardt: Gesch. der christl. Ethik, II*: "However vigorously Calvin tries to disclaim any connection with the Anabaptists, the connection with that twofold way of thinking (spiritual mysticism and the legalistic holy community) cannot be denied. And although at the beginning perhaps it was unconscious, it was later quite consciously expressed and made to count." The matter is still more clearly recognized by *Ritschl: Geschichte des Pietismus, I, 61–98*, in which also the different attitude of Lutheranism towards excommunication and Church discipline is made very clear. Cf. *I, pp. 7 and 96*. Ritschl's argument that this resemblance to the sect-type is due to its French revolutionary, equalitarian popular character, is certainly more characteristic of the Prussian conservative Ritschl than it is of Calvin. The Lutheran Ritschl, who exalts so highly the Lutherans because they regard the Church in an objective sense, cannot even imagine that such things are simply Christian, that is, that they represent an indestructible element of primitive Christian thought. Further, in Calvin there is no question of "equality".

[331] (p. 601.) For Calvin's ideal of heroism and its conscious connection with Platonism (probably also and still more with Stoicism), see the section in the book mentioned below by *Beyerhaus, pp. 153–155*. Calvin's Humanism is certainly coloured by the ethic of Stoicism, much more deeply than Melancthon's merely Scholastic Humanism. He is the most Humanist of the Reformers; see *Arnold, pp. 11 ff.* Cf. also the analysis of the commentary on *Seneca's De Clementia* in *Beyerhaus, 1–25*. In his ethic it seems possible to discern the effect of Humanism and of juristic thought to the same extent in which one discerns in Luther's ethic the influence of monasticism.

[332] (p. 602.) In Calvin there is no distinction as there is in Luther between

personal and official morality. Calvin has, it is true, Luther's formulas; cf. *Contre les Anabaptistes, CR. 35, p. 77*: "Or il est vray qu'en particulier l'usage du glaive ne doit estre permis a nul pour faire resistence au mal. Car les armes des Chrestiens sont prieres et mansuetude, pour posseder leurs vies en patience et vaincre le mal en bien faisant selon la doctrine de l'Evangile Luc. 21, 19. Rom. 12, 21. L'office de chacun de nous est de souffrir patiemment si on nous fait quelque outrage plus tot qui d'user de force et violence. Mais de condamner le glaive publique, lequel Dieu a ordonne pour nostre protection, c'est un blasphème contre Dieu mesme." There is a similar passage in *Lobstein, p. 121*. But the opposition between the legal order and its spirit of punishment and authority, its connection with the struggle for existence against the purely voluntary order of love, has been quite lost. The legal order is solely a useful member appointed by God in the upbuilding of rational society as already in the Old Testament. This comes out most plainly and in an almost identical manner in the Calvinist exposition of the Sermon on the Mount, whose results are gathered up in the work *Contre les Anabaptistes, C.R., 35*, in the *Institutio, IV, 20, 17–22*, and in the exposition of the *Decalogue, II, 8*. The Sermon on the Mount is to be understood in the light of the Old Testament as an expression of the unchangeableness of God; Christ has added nothing to it and altered nothing, but since He has not opposed the social and legal order of the Old Testament He has confirmed it; all that He did oppose were the misinterpretations of the Pharisees. Therefore even the harsh laws against adultery belong to the law of Christ. *Inst., II, 8, 26:* "Christo non est institutum legem aut laxare aut restringere, sed ad veram ac germanicam intelligentiam reducere, quae falsis Scribarum et Pharisaeorum commentis valde depravata fuerant." Thus from this point of view the oath, law, tyranny, war, and possessions are regarded as permitted by the Sermon on the Mount. Also the practical interests of Society require an exposition of this kind; cf. Beza's opinion about the death penalty for double adultery (*Choisy, p. 185*): "Et ce d'autant que pour punir ce crime capitalement, il faut avoir esgard non seulement à l'impudicité, mais aussi et principalement à l'interest de la société humaine, laquelle ne peut subsister si la distinction des familles, héritages et successions n'est conservée, ce qui rend ce crime naturellement capital, comme expose tres bien Mr. Calvin sur l'histoire de Juda, Genes. 28, 24." The story of the woman taken in adultery is interpreted in a different sense. Thus Calvin sees in the Sermon on the Mount simply the use of civil ordinances and law without personal hatred and passion for the objective end of the securing of the law and of the protection of Society (*Inst. IV, 20, 18*, and *R. 35, p. 44*). Calvin knows that even that is difficult and rarely happens. This is all undoubtedly practical and sensible, but the whole feeling is quite different from that of Luther's ethic. The reason for the different conception lies in this that the ethic of Calvin does not have its central point in the free outpouring of love, but in purity of conscience and in heroism and self-denial for the setting up of the Christian community. Love in the meaning of Luther is not its fundamental conception; hence it feels no opposition between love and law and force, see *Choisy: La Théocratie, p. 258*. On this point Calvin himself speaks very plainly. The sum-total of ethics is to him (*Briefe, II, 100*), "that we are strong in hope and in endurance, that we are self-restrained and sober in the avoidance of worldly lusts, that we give great pains to control the passions of the flesh, that the endeavour after righteousness and piety live in us strongly, that we are earnest and eager in prayer, that the thought of eternal life should draw us upwards." Of Moses he says, characteristically (*II, 221*): "Whence he gained his strength, namely, because he became firm, through gazing upon God." The *Theologia Germanica*, which Luther prized so highly, Calvin rejects "as a prating of the devil, which has been made by his cunning in order to confound the simplicity of the Gospel" (*II, 258*).—In a very special way he expresses himself on the subject of love in writing to Renata of Ferrara (*II, 470 ff.*) in order to defend hatred of evil; Renata especially did not wish to see her brother-in-law, the murdered Duke of Guise, insulted, and Calvin writes as follows: "To my observation, that David teaches us by his example to hate our enemies (Ps. xxxi. 7, and clxi. 3), you say that that was at the time when under the rigid law it was still permitted to hate one's enemy. Now, madam, an exposition of that kind could overthrow the whole of Scripture, and therefore we must avoid it like deadly poison. For we see that David exceeded the very best men that we could find to-day. . . . If, however, he says that he cherishes a deadly hatred of the reprobate, so doubtless he is boasting of his right pure ardour, which is quite in order if the following three conditions are fulfilled: (1) that we do not draw ourselves and our own personal interest into the matter; (2) that we act with wisdom and foresight and do not judge lightly; (3) that we are restrained and do not go beyond that to which we are called. You can read more on this subject in several passages of my exposition of the Psalms. Precisely on that account even has the Holy Ghost given David to us as a kind of patron saint that we should follow his example. It is, indeed, actually told us that in his zeal he was a type or a foreshadowing of our Lord Jesus Christ; see Ps. lxix. 10, and John ii. 17. Do we then want to exceed Him who is the source of all sympathy and mercy in gentleness and kindness? If we do, woe to us! Let us make an end of all explanations: we then will be content that St. Paul applies particularly this exhortation to all believers that the zeal for the house of God shall eat them up (Ps. lxix. 10 and Rom. xv. 3). . . . The method (against a false conception of love) is this: to hate evil, but not to think simply of individuals, but to leave each to his own judge."—This is an example of the positive and impersonal character of the Calvinist ethic. To this also belongs the exposition of the renunciation of revenge in Hoornbeck, quoted by *Weber, XXI, p. 13*: "Denique doc magis ulciscimur, quo proximum, inultum nobis, tradimus ultori Deo. Quo quis plus se ulciscitur, eo minus id pro ipso agit Deus!" A similar example on *p. 32*. Here we are worlds apart from Lutheranism. Characteristic also is the passage which *Beyerhaus* quotes from *C.R., 57, 143*: "Car en cela monstrerez . . . vous que vous estes vrais zelateurs du service de Dieu, quand vous tuerez vos propres frères, et que rien ne sera espargné: que l'ordre de nature sera mis sous le pied, pour monstrer que Dieu domine par dessus tout, et qu'il a son degré souverain." For Luther the natural order of love (in its perfection in the Primitive State) was identical with the Divine Law of morality; Calvin, however, under some circumstances makes a distinction between the Natural Law of love and the positive Divine Law of the unconditional glorification of the sovereignty of God. This leads also this ethic back to the fundamental difference in the conception of God.—In any case this is a quite different spirit from that of the Lutheran ethic and also from that of the New Testament. Calvin finds Scriptural justification for it in the Old Testament, which, therefore, for this purpose he reads into the New Testament. His fundamental idea is the fulfilment of the eternal unchangeable law through the grace of election in the new Israel which is formed by Christ. *Choisy* emphasizes this fully everywhere. I would only add that without this Calvin's practical work would have been quite impossible, just as impossible as that of Luther actually became. From the point of view of the New Testament it is impossible to effect any direct change in the world. The whole of this previous inquiry has shown us this and Calvin's use of the Old Testament, for all that is practically important, is only a further proof of this statement. Even to-day we have the same interpretation in, for example, *Rauschenbusch: Christianity and the Social Crisis, 1904*; in which the writer argues that the teaching of Jesus was drawn from the Old Testament prophets and His Kingdom of God from the prophetic ideal of Society, and he describes the Church as apostate because she has fallen a prey to the mystical individualism of the Greek spirit! For all political and social matters Calvin appeals, in fact, to the Old Testament; see *Rieker, I, 234, 345, 393, 405*. Cf. *Choisy: L'état chrétien, 156 ff.*

[333] (p. 602.) This emphasis on Christian Socialism above all in *Choisy: La Théocratie, 244 and 278*. Only here does Christianity become consciously and systematically social after it had followed a very devious or fanatical course of development among the Anabaptists and the sects. Cf. above, *pp. 82 and 423*. Also at this point we see more clearly the resemblance between Calvinism and the sect-movement as well as its limits. Calvinism understands Christian Socialism as a life-unity of Church and State (*Choisy, 250–254*) and modifies the over-idealistic standards of the sect to practical common sense. That is why Calvinism and Calvinism alone has been successful in a far-reaching education of peoples. *Choisy, 205:* "The Protestant peoples are there in order to show that the ecclesiastical and social work of Calvin, his colossal effort to realize upon earth the social ideal of the Kingdom of God, have not been in vain." This primitive Calvinistic Christian Socialism differs from modern Christian Socialism by its predominantly ethical and ideological character, whereas the Christian Socialism of the present day is based upon the economic historical and technological foundation of modern social theory. At that time such things were scarcely thought of at all because circumstances did not make it necessary. Calvinism, however, even then was concerned with the question of the material economic substructure of the ethical life, and it knew the value of statistics. Of this more anon.—On this Christian social feature down to the present day there are admirable observations in *Karl Hartmann: Englische Frömmigkeit, eine Studie, 1910* (*Beilage zum Jahresbericht des prot. Gymnasiums zu Strassburg*). This work contains a great deal of illuminating material about Calvinism and the sects, and everywhere it confirms the point of view which is here presented.

[336] (p. 604.) A number of examples in *Kampschulte* and *Choisy*. Unfortunately *Schneckenburger* gives no analysis of this. Like so many other thinkers, in this legalism he only sees the rigorism of a spirit which approaches dependence on "works". He lays stress upon the fear of exaltation of creatures, on the rational and methodical systematic nature of Calvinist behaviour; and the relation to the future happiness with the constant tension of aiming at a goal in the future life which contrasts strongly with Lutheranism and its sense of security in the present life and its happy faith. Only he makes no attempt to understand these ideas in connection with Christian asceticism and its history. Also in *Luthardt: Geschichte der christlichen Ethik* this does not happen. The theologians in their treatment of ethics almost always discuss simply problems of form, that is, of the basis or sanction, and the source of energy or of religious power, but not the content or the aim of morality. This aim, however, in an ethic which over against the world which is lost and corrupt by Original Sin and wishes to secure the happiness of heaven, is ascetic. And at this point the Calvinistic ethic, contrasted with the Lutheran, is much more dualistic, more systematically directed towards the other life and the depreciation of this life, without,

however, taking away the value of this life altogether, but in order to use it. *Ritschl*, in his acute way, has described Calvinistic asceticism as "a clear approximation to the monastic withdrawal from the world" (*Geschichte des Pietismus, I, 76*); it is the attitude of "Franciscan Tertiaries". "So far as the Christian ideal of life of Calvinism is anti-Catholic, this is due to Luther's influence; so far as it departs from Luther's conception it goes back again into line with the Franciscan ideal of life." *P. 78*: "Ascetic holiness, namely, strict rejection of all worldly recreation and of all games." The derivation and description of the ideas of this Calvinist "asceticism" are, however, quite inadequate in this book; indeed, it is almost comic (*p. 76*). A penetrating conceptual analysis has only been given by *Max Weber*; see especially *Archiv. XXI, 73*. *Göbel* gives a mass of examples and analyses the subject less clearly: *I, 444–448*, resolutions of Synods; here (*p. 447*) the asceticism of the "calling"; "a Christian shall use the time which he still has to live in a serious manner (that means without pleasures), faithfully fulfil his 'calling', and otherwise in his leisure time he ought to fill the time with God-fearing conversations, taking great care to avoid books of fables and to read aloud from the Holy Scriptures and other hallowed treatises"; *II, 72*, self-description of the Calvinistic members of the Church as "Christians", while all the others are called "children of the world"; *II, 47*, further resolutions of the Synods against pleasures, even against those which the Government has instituted and expects to be used; *II, 105*: "the Calvinists are distinguished by an earnest piety and a strict morality, by a careful observance of the First Table of the Law, by great honesty and sobriety, especially in relation to public pleasures (dances, Church consecrations, shooting festivals, banquets, theatres), and through the frugality and order, industry and honesty which is connected with that way of living." The characteristic element is everywhere unlimited industry with solely spiritual recreation, the cutting down of the sense-life to the unavoidable minimum, but without bodily injury or mortification, the purely utilitarian treatment of all secular things as mere means and the exclusion of all that is earthly from this aim, the methodical and systematic discipline and direction towards a final end in the other life. In all these things Lutheranism is much more lax, spontaneous, instinctive, and, above all, less logical. The attitude of Lutheranism in these things is, above all, one of absence of theory and lack of logic, just as its whole ethic with its repetition of justification is not directed towards a logical end, but towards the enjoyment of the salvation offered us in Christ in each experience. *Schneckenburger* has developed this latter point in a very striking way; see also my review of *Hoennicke* in *GGA., 1902*. It is true that Lutheranism knew sufficient about denial of the world; cf. these words of Luther quoted by *Schneckenburger*: "Weeping goes before works, and suffering is a greater thing than all we do." The question is, "Sese passibilem Deo praestare," man must become clay in the hands of God who will mould him. Even where in the older books of doctrine good works are specified, he only knows "abnegatio sui, toleratio crucis" and "precatio" (*I, 140*); this passage shows at the same time the difference between Lutheranism and the active asceticism of Calvinism. The idea of "intramundane asceticism", which is here used, is already found in *Göbel, III, 334*: "The Roman Catholic external renunciation of the world and external system of sanctification contrasted with the Evangelical inward overcoming of the world and joy and peace in believing." This simply means the same thing expressed by *Weber* and myself as the opposition between an asceticism apart from or within the world, which, however, it is easier for a Pietist to understand and value than for a rigid

Churchman like *Ritschl* or even a Rationalist like *Rachfahl.*—Further, see the article entitled *Askese* (*geschichtlich*) by *Heussi* in *Schiele's Lexikon*, which follows my point of view. The article entiled *Askese* (*ethisch*), by *Scheel* at least instinctively distinguishes the two main tendencies which I discern of the metaphysical and the disciplinary kind of asceticism; otherwise he has not recognized sufficiently the special character of Christian asceticism; the asceticism of Buddhism, Neo-Platonism, of fanatical and ritual cults, is something quite different. Christianity, when it found that the world was going to last and that it must renounce the idea of the miraculous coming of the Kingdom of God, was obliged necessarily to transfer the spirit of tension directed towards the other world to another part of its world of feeling. Thus its asceticism arose, but it was a Christian asceticism, and it is always important to distinguish clearly between its own nature and the various influences from outside which have affected it (from Neo-Platonism, paganism, etc.). *Scheel*, from his modern immanental standpoint, questions whether Protestantism is justified in retaining the conception of asceticism at all; he says, however: "I have not been able to find a sure opinion about asceticism in general which would correspond with its fundamental religious and ethical convictions." Certainly, and for good reasons. "Intramundane asceticism" is, indeed, from both points of view, Lutheran and Calvinistic, not so easy to justify, and yet in both confessions its main ideas are present. Here the resolute dualism of Catholicism is easier to justify. The inner complication of Protestantism, its position between Immanence and Transcendence, between a pessimism which regards the whole world as lost in sin and the acceptance of the world, emerges clearly particularly in its idea of asceticism. That is why it is so difficult to conceive this idea clearly. Where, however, within Protestantism asceticism is clearly emphasized and required, there appears the dangerous element which this important factor contains by reason of its indefinite character. The tendency of asceticism within Protestantism is always towards breaking away from the Church, whether in the sectarian or the mystical and idealist sense, since asceticism in Protestantism is not placed under the control of the Church or of a religious order, but it is an entirely voluntary matter or the personal duty of the individual.—The latter anti-authoritative effect of asceticism (*Max Weber: Archiv. XXI, 65 ff., 93*) has been recognized pre-eminently by *Ritschl.* Thus actually in Calvinism it leads to Pietism, as *Ritschl* rightly discerns. *Ritschl's* own conception of Lutheranism as a glorification and moulding of the world in one's "calling", made possible through trust in God and the happiness of justification, is certainly a highly modernized Lutheranism which allows the dualistic ascetic and pessimistic elements in trust in God, that is, in truth under the influence of modern ideas of Immanence, to disappear. That which he regards as the heart of Lutheran, and therefore of genuine, Christianity, namely, trust in God, which is based upon the ecclesiastical objective means of grace, and which makes possible both different degrees of active holiness and adaptation to the world in popular Christianity, does not occupy in any sense a prominent place in the early sources, and also has only been brought to light by *Ritschl* as their unconscious presupposition, which was hidden behind doctrinaire ideas.

337 (p. 608.) *Rachfahl*, in his attack upon *Weber* and myself (*Calvinismus und Kapitalismus*, *Internationale Wochenschrift*, *1909*), has felt able, by appealing to some encyclopaedia articles, to treat the conception of "intramundane asceticism" in a very condescending manner. But he understands nothing at all of theological matters; I believe that what I have written is sufficient in

order to justify afresh the use of a conception which must have some kind of name and which modern Rationalists—theological and non-theological—do not understand at all. When *Rachfahl* appeals to *Loofs: Luthers Stellung, pp. 21 ff.*, *Loofs* is there only opposing the opinion that because such asceticism exists, Protestantism must be relegated to the Middle Ages, and is, therefore, of no further use for the modern man. This, however, is not my view in any sense, as *Loofs* himself knows, since he thinks that if I had had more opportunities I would have shown more understanding for asceticism. *Loofs* interprets what I have said about Luther's connection with the Middle Ages as value judgments, which they are not meant to be at all. That Luther "got stuck" in the Middle Ages was neither the expression I used nor is it my opinion. I emphasized only the difference compared with the modern world as it actually is; and there is no doubt that in its practice and its theory the modern world has very little room for asceticism. But in saying this I am not giving a value judgment upon asceticism in itself. The mediaeval world contained many elements which are still live issues at the present time, and the ascetic elements which the Reformers held in common with the mediaeval period contained permanent problems and vital interests which will certainly return once more, although in a completely different form. I would refer my readers to *Jakob Burkhardt's Weltgeschichtliche Betrachtungen*, one of the deepest and most thoughtful books of recent times. My difference with *Loofs* is related in reality to the question of the unity and extension of modern thought. I regard this as a much bigger question than *Loofs* does, and I consider that the situation of the Church is far more serious than he does; see my article, *Die Entstehung des modernen Geistes in Preuss. Jahrb., 1906.* In the question of simple facts about the nature of Protestant asceticism on the contrary, I believe that I am, upon the whole, in agreement with *Loofs.—Rachfahl*, in his second statement (*JW., 1910*) *Nochmals Calvinismus und Kapitalismus*, declares that he thinks it wise to withhold confidence in my statements about asceticism until they have been accepted by *Loofs*, *Kawerau*, *Kattenbusch*, *Scheel*, and *Lang*. To some extent these men are outstanding scholars, but at this particular point of the definition of Catholicism, Lutheranism, Calvinism, and the Baptist movement with the assistance of the conception of asceticism, they are all under the influence of the well-known ideas of *Ritschl*, which, closely connected with theological confessional value judgments, have, in my opinion, a quite wrong orientation. Further, those scholars themselves would certainly dissociate themselves from *Rachfahl's* banal observations about asceticism (*pp. 728 ff.*).

338 (p. 609.) Cf. *Inst., III, 7, 1–2; Lobstein, pp. 79 ff., 86*, and especially *108–112*: "If we are to live we must have the necessary means of life. Also we cannot avoid that which leads more to pleasure than is absolutely necessary. We ought to observe a spirit of true moderation which must be determined by the thought that life is a pilgrimage towards heaven." "Our principle ought to be to use goods for the purpose for which God has created them. But He did not create them merely for necessity, but also in order to give pleasure. He has thought of the desire of the senses since He has created flowers and has given to gold and silver, ivory and marble, a beauty and a brilliance which makes these metals and stones more costly and valuable than others." "Thus, then, the best and the safest path to pursue is to subordinate this present life to the eternal; we ought to enjoy life as though we did not enjoy it; we must learn to endure poverty patiently and wealth in moderation; we must guard ourselves against turning those things which are the means of this life into hindrances for the eternal life. Secondly, we must beware against

thinking too much of earthly goods; this tendency shows itself both in the flight from poverty and lowliness as in honour and desire for gain. Thirdly, we must always remember that we have to give an account of our use of earthly goods. Finally, God wishes us in all the deeds of our life to regard our 'calling' in order to judge our actions by this standard and to orientate our lives by it." I give the following extract from a sermon in which science and art are treated according to these principles: "Quand un homme sera le plus exquis en science qu'on sauroit imaginer, si faut-il que nous apprenions de nous humilier, et que toute hautesse soit mise bas, que le savoir humain que Dieu nous aura donné pour lui servir, soit assujetté à sa parole." It is the same with eloquence. "Vray est que tous les deux procedent de la pure bonté de Dieu. Mais si faut-il venir là, que celui qui sera parvenu à la vraye clarté celeste, die, Je suis tien, Seigneur; et tout ce que tu m'as donné, aussi vient de toy: que tu le reçoives dono sur tout: puisque tu m'as fait la grace de estre instruit par ta parole, fay que tout le reste rende l'honneur et l'hommage tel que il appartient à ceste science admirable, que j'ai apprinse en ton escole. . . . Dieu a ressuscite les sciences humaines qui sont propres et utiles à la conduite de nostre vie, et, en servant à nostre utilité, peuvent aussi servir à sa gloire. . . . Nulle bonne science n'est repugnante à la crainte de Dieu ni à la doctrine qu'il nous donne pour nous mener en la vie eternelle, moyennant que nous ne mettions point la charrue devant les beufs; c'est à dire que nous ayons ceste prudence de nous servir des artzs tout liberaux que mechaniques en passant par ce monde pour tendre tousiours au Royaume celeste." Cf. also *G. Lasch: Calvin und die Kunst, Christliches Kunstblatt, 1909*, in which the differences between Calvin and Luther in this sphere come out very clearly. This also reveals their attitude towards the Renaissance. Only when we recognize this use of earthly means with reference to a heavenly purpose is it right to describe the *meditatio futurae vitae* as the central point of Calvin's ethic; see *M. Schulze: Med. fut vitae im System Calvins, 1901.* Further, *Lobstein* points out that in his struggles at Geneva Calvin's practice was more austere than his theory.

[344] (p. 612.) *Weber's* treatise in reality does not aim merely at the derivation of the capitalist spirit from the Calvinistic idea of vocation, but at the explanation of the modern bourgeois way of life, within which the "capitalist spirit" is only one element. He is concerned in the main with the modern characteristics of the bourgeoisie, and not with the elements which modern capitalism has inherited from the ancient world and from the later Middle Ages. *Rachfahl* and *Kurdt* have not understood this in the least. For my part I would rate still higher the difference which *Weber* emphasizes between Calvin and Calvinism, which has played its part in the formation of the bourgeois way of life. I would like to emphasize as an explanation of the "bourgeois" spirit in this later Calvinism still more than *Weber* does the setting, the exclusion from the official world, from feudalism, and from the right to hold large estates. But there can be no doubt about the close connection between the "bourgeois spirit" and later and present-day Calvinism. This has been made possible particularly by the fact that Calvinism has reduced the Christian ethic from a spiritual and Utopian ethic of love to one of strict fear of God, industry, faithfulness in one's calling, and honesty. The difference between this bourgeois ideal and the feudal aristocratic world which was much happier with the authority religions of Catholicism, Lutheranism, and Anglicanism, and whose morality was inwardly entirely free from the democratic spirit of humanity (but also from the really spiritual morality of love), is obvious; incidentally this is expressed quite frankly now and again. Likewise, however, also the difference

from the morality of the ancients; before me there lies a *Jahrbuch für die geistige Bewegung, 1911*, published by disciples of *Stefan Georges*, with an article by *Friedrich Gundolf* on *Wesen und Beziehung*, in which the Protestant bourgeois ethic and its secularized inheritance appear as the curse from which only a free, autonomous development apart from any "calling", but out of the unity of body and spirit, can help the situation. Here the inconsistency is rightly felt even though to me the argument seems practically hopeless.—On the question of the Huguenots, see *Marcks*; on its gradual development in the bourgeois direction, see certain passages in *Elster* and *Laveleye*. Its peculiar character still needs to be specially investigated. *Max Weber* scarcely touches it, and *Schneckenburger* not at all. It is, however, certainly more nearly related to the genuine spirit of Calvinism than the bourgeois world of the Netherlands, the Lower Rhine, England, and America. I do not know what the position is in Scotland, where the nobility in particular took a great part in the Reformation movement; in any case, however, very characteristically the nobility finally went back into Anglicanism.

[345] (p. 612.) Cf. *Briefe, II, 267*: "More than two years ago, in a private conversation, John Knox asked me what was my view about the regiment of women. I answered frankly that it was a departure from the original true order of nature, and on that account that it must be regarded as one of the penalties of the Fall, as, for instance, slavery." Cf. also *II, 13*.—Further, with reference to marriage: in the pure state of nature marriage was without "libido", but "accensa post lapsum libidine . . . illam ipsam conjugalem societatem in necessitatis remedium esse ordinatam, ne in effrenem libidinem proruamus" (*Inst., II, 8, 41*).—The oath is a Divine appointment for the good of Society under the conditions of evil which have been brought in by sin (*Contre les Anabaptistes, CR., 35, p. 98*); likewise the power of the sword of princes and governments (*ibid., 78*).—Further statements about the relative Law of Nature, or, as it is here put (*p. 84*), about the "results of sin limited by the universality of grace", see in *Kuyper, pp. 73–76*, where Calvin shows himself entirely as a supporter of the general teaching of the Church: "Through its profound conception of sin Calvinism has merely laid the essential foundations of the life of the State, and at the same time two things are impressed upon us: (1) that we ought to accept the life of the State and the Government as means of deliverance which are now absolutely necessary; (2) but also that we, in virtue of our natural instinct, ought always to be on our guard against the danger to our personal freedom which lies in the supreme authority of the State" (*p. 74*). The new element lies in the second point, whose significance will immediately be explained. There is a great deal of material (on the relative Natural Law, however, only as suggestions, *pp. 131–133*) in the extremely careful and convincing work of *G. Beyerhaus, Studien zur Staatsanschauung Calvins* (*Neue Beiträge herausgegeben von Bonwetsch und Seeberg, VII*), *1910*. There are some passages also in the extremely superficial book by *A. Lang: Die Reformation und das Naturrecht* (*Beiträge zur Forderung christlicher Theologie*), *1909, pp. 20–22*. I cannot understand how in face of his own quotations Lang can say that Calvin found no place for Natural Law in his system. For Calvin this is simply a natural presupposition, and it permeates all his arguments wherever this idea was present. In the *Institutes* naturally this takes place least of all. *Beyerhaus, p. 66*, says very rightly: "If Lang had systematically studied Calvin's Commentaries, especially, for instance, the explanation of the Decalogue, *CR. 52, 261 ff.*, as well as *CR. 57, 554 ff.* (also *Beyerhaus, pp. 96 ff.*, and *p. 157, nr. 4 b*), he could scarcely have made the assertion that 'the Natural

Law plays no part in Calvin's judgment of legal and social conditions', and his whole verdict upon the meaning of the *Lex Naturae* for Calvin would have been essentially altered." The fact is that *Lang* has no insight into the inner structure of the Christian Natural Law and its function for the idea of a Christian civilization. Hence also the quite wrong assertions about Luther, who also is supposed to have seen nothing in Natural Law and the restriction of the understanding of Natural Law to Melancthon. So he comes to make the statement that the Natural Law is really contrary to the true view of Luther and of Calvin, only in haste "for lack of a conception of the State clearly formulated according to the fundamental ideas of Protestantism" (*p. 50*), it was taken over out of mediaeval Catholic theories which arose in Catholicism "and therefore in error", and were then adopted by Liberalism!

[346] (p. 613.) This point of view is expressed in countless passages. The doctrine of law and the Decalogue is introduced with the statement: "Porro haec ipsa, quae ex duabus tabulis discenda sunt, quodam modo nobis dictat lex illa interior, quam omnium cordibus inscriptam et quasi impressam superius dictum est. Proinde (quod tum hebetudini, tum contumaciae nostrae necessarium erat) Dominus Legem scriptam nobis posuit: quae et certius testificaretur, quod in lege naturali nimis obscurum erat, et mentem memoriamque nostram excusso torpore vividius feriret" (*Inst., II, 8, 1*). "Nihil est vulgatius, quam lege naturali hominem sufficienter ad rectam vitae normam institui. Nos autem expendamus, quorsum indita haec legis notitia hominibus fuerit; tum protinus apparebit, quousque illos ad rationis veriratisque scopum deducat" (*II, 2, 22*). Cf. also *Briefe, II, 140*. The same idea occurs also in Gratian. The law is unchangeable and eternal for the future; it was, however, also unchangeable before Moses (see the sermon of *Lobstein, pp. 59–62*), hence this unchangeableness of God means that there is no difference between the law of Moses and that of the Sermon on the Mount, which, therefore, likewise is a perfected form of the Natural Law (*Contre les Anabaptistes, CR. 35, p. 95*). In *Beza* the expression is "Loy divine, naturelle et universelle", or "Règle perpétuelle et infallible de toute justice", or "Loy de Dieu et de nature", absolutely the *Terminus technicus* for the Decalogue (*Choisy: L'état chrétien, pp. 180 ff., 294, 296*); the history of the Old Testament as an illustration of the Law of Nature in the interesting record of the *Vénérable Compagnie* in *Choisy, pp. 179 ff.* This is a further reason which justifies the use of the Old Testament.—Cf. also the section on *ordre de nature* and *jus naturae* in *Beyerhaus* (*pp. 66–76*), the Stoic extension of Natural Law into the animal world (*pp. 148–152*), and the analysis of the commentary on Seneca (*pp. 3 ff.*).

[347] (p. 613.) The main passage in *Inst., II, 8, 11*. Pervading spirituality as the nature of the First Table (*Inst., II, 8, 16*): "Praecedat oportet vera religio, qua in Deum viventem animi referantur, cujus cognitione imbuti . . . in omnibus vitae actionibus tamquam in unicum scopum aspirent." Otherwise the division into two parts belongs also to the Natural Law (*Inst., II, 2, 24*, and *Inst., IV, 20, 9*): "Officium magistratus extendi ad utramque legis tabulam, si non doceret scriptura, ex profanis scriptoribus discendum esset: nullus enim de magistratuum officio disseruit, qui non exordium faceret a religione et divino cultu."

[348] (p. 613.) *Inst., IV, 20, 8:* "Magna hujus dispensationis ratio posita est in circumstantiis." Here is the place of the "naturalis aequitas et officii ratio" (*Inst., IV, 20, 11*). "Libertas singulis gentibus relicta est condendi quas sibi conducere providerint leges: quae tamen ad perpetuam illam caritatis regulam (that is, the Law of God and of Nature) exigantur, ut forma quidem varient,

rationem habeant eandem. Nam barbaras et feras leges . . . pro legibus habendas minime censeo" (*Inst., IV, 20, 15*). Further material in paragraph *16*. It is from this point of view that we can explain the positive peculiarities of the Jewish and Roman law, which we would consider impossible to combine (*Choisy, pp. 184 and 514*). Thus the historical development of states and of law, in spite of all differences, is something which has been indirectly effected by God through the natural causal nexus; it is the ancient doctrine of God as the *causa remota* of states, of law, and of constitutions: "Perinde istud valet, non humana perversitate fieri, ut penes Reges et Praefectos alios sit in terris rerum omnium arbitrium, sed divina providentia et sancta ordinatione, cui sic visum est, res hominum moderari, quandoquidem illis adest ac etiam praeest in ferendis legibus et judiciorum aequitate exercenda" (*Inst., IV, 20, 4*). "Quodsi non in unam dumtaxat civitatem oculum defigas, sed universum simul orbem circumspicias ac contempleris vel aspectum in longiora saltem regionum spatia diffundas, comperies profecto divina providentia illud non abs re comparatum, ut diversis politiis regiones variae administrentur" (*Inst., IV, 20, 8*). The "institution of the government by God" is thus—apart from the supernatural history of Israel—as in Luther, always conceived as mediated by Providence and that means the natural causal nexus. It is the Stoic doctrine of Providence and of the cosmos of the political and social world (see *Beyerhaus, pp. 3, 71, 109, 62, 127*). Thus the apparent positive law goes back to Providence and the Law of Nature: "Solent plerique nimis scrupulose inquirere quo quisque jure adeptus sit imperium: atqui hoc solo contentos esse decet, quod videmus eos praesidere" (*CR., 83, 244*). In this the historical and Natural Law point of view is united.

349 (p. 613.) Passive obedience to the point of suffering: *Briefe, II, 14, 64*; also *Inst., IV, 20, 1, and 20, 25*, especially *20, 27*: "Nunquam in animum nobis seditiosae illae cogitationes venient, tractandum esse pro meritis regem", or "nihil refert, qua sit apud homines conditione, cujus gentis legibus vivas: quando in rebus istis minime situm est Christi regnum." Greatest respect for the Government (*Briefe, I, 213; II, 80, 198, 220, 267*), advantage of the Reformation that it supports the Government more than the Papists (*II, 124*). *Lobstein, 104*. Treatment of the masses in Luther's style; *Choisy, 350*: "le peuple, qui est une beste farouche et dangereuse", *p. 352:* "une beste à plusieurs testes". Frugality as an ideal of life (*Inst., II, 8, 46*). A main interest and favourite expression of Calvin is the *cogere in ordinem* (see *Beyerhaus, p. 63*); passive obedience and the exclusion of the mediaeval doctrine of popular sovereignty (*p. 97*); but also a gradual modification of this doctrine of passive obedience and increasing rationalism (*pp. 123–129*). In this there is reflected only the inner contradiction within his whole theology, which on the one hand recognizes to a great extent the rationalism of the *Lex Naturae*, and on the other hand asserts the irrational character of the Divine Will. Calvin can say on the one hand "ut voluntas ejus sit pro lege et pro ratione et pro summa justitiae regula" (*Beyerhaus, 65, CR., 68, 685*); on the other hand he is able to identify the law of revelation and the law of reason. Under the influence of the first idea all government seems to be simply appointed by God, and the whole duty of subjects seems to consist in the exercise of self-humiliation; under the influence of the second idea the authorities are bound by the Law of Nature, and they are to be controlled by those who have called them to their office, even to the extent of the complete removal of the idea of sovereignty from the Government. This discord goes right through Calvin's teaching; as time went on, however, the conception of the State became more rational (*Beyerhaus, p. 88*).

[350] (p. 613.) A harsh expression of opinion about the State in the Augustinian and Lutheran sense (cf. above, *pp. 566–568*) we seek in vain. Everywhere and directly it is regarded as a Divine institution. It is "sancta Dei ordinatio et donum ex eorum genere, quae mundis munda esse possunt" (*Inst., IV, 20, 19*). It belongs to the absolutely necessary means of human existence: "Sin ita est voluntas Dei, nos, dum ad veram pietatem adspiràmus, peregrinari super terram, ejus vero peregrinationis usus talibus subsidiis indiget; qui ipsa ab homine tollunt, suam illi eripiunt humanitatem" (*IV, 20, 2*). The State is only considered from the point of view of its positive rational service to the Church and Society. Here Calvin is speaking as a lawyer and a practical man, in contrast with Luther, who was a monk and an idealist.—With reference to property there are traces of certain specific Scholastic ideas. Cf. *Beyerhaus, 76*. They are, however, of little practical significance. The *Institutio* says, simply: "Sic enim cogitandum est, unicuique evenisse, quod possidet, non fortuita sorte, sed ex distributione summi rerum omnium Domini"; thus, property is regarded as a Divine institution, as well as the legal system which safeguards property (*CR., 35, p. 87*). In his discussions with the Anabaptists, where one might expect an explanation of primitive communism, he only says: "De ce qu'aucuns d'entre eux ont tenu touchant la communauté des biens, item qu'un homme peut avoir plusieurs femmes et mille autres absurdités: je me déporte d'en toucher. Car eux mesmes, estant confuz en leur follies, s'en sont retiré tout bellement pour la plupart" (*CR., 35, p. 103*). He considers the Baptists well-meaning fools who do not know the world, and are arrogant expounders of the Bible, who follow their popular fantasies. "Je demande à ces bons docteurs, que deviendra le monde!" (*CR., 35, pp. 87 and 92*); and if they think that among true Christians law and authority are unnecessary Calvin says simply: "c'est une resverie!" Practical life is impossible without the order of the State and of law, since there are so many unavoidable errors and obscurities in life, even when there is nothing wrong. For the way in which the State (without sin) is supposed to have developed as a patriarchal world empire, cf. *Kuyper, p. 73*. The fact that Calvin saw no practical significance in the communism of the Primitive State is connected with his whole change of the point of view of the ethic of love into an ethic of the glorification of God, and it is of great significance for his rationalism of the formation of the State and of Society, although it is little noted.

[351] (p. 614.) The meaning of the First Table, *Inst., II, 8, 16*: "Pura sit ergo conscientia vel ab occulissimis apostasiae cogitationibus, si religionem nostram Deo approbare libet. Siquidem integram et incorruptam divinitatis suae gloriam non externa modo confessione requirit, sed in oculis suis, qui abditissimas cordium latebras intuentur." The meaning of "spirituality", *II, 8, 6*: "Paulus affirmans legem esse spiritualem significat non modo animae, mentis, voluntatis obsequium exigere, sed requirere angelicam puritatem, quae omnibus carnis sordibus abstersa nihil quam spiritum sapiat." This is a quite different meaning for "spirituality" than that in vogue among the Lutherans, for whom the antithesis is spirit and law, love and rights (see above, *pp. 494, 497, 516*).

[353] (p. 615.) Examples of this State Rationalism, which proceeds not from popular sovereignty but from the idea of the purpose of the State, and therefore finally involves the ethical, philosophical, Christian, and also the legal obligation of the Government to the *salus publica* and, further, the advocacy of the Church will be found in *Beyerhaus, pp. 69, 95–97, 123–129*. The essence of authority is to measure all by this standard—"ad Dei cultum tuendum et

promovendum et populi totius commodum et utilitatem procurandam (*125*)"; all this is best guaranteed by a written constitution (*123*). This is something quite different from Luther's conception of authority (see above, *pp. 531–532*).

354 (p. 616.) There are examples of this subject in the very condensed twentieth chapter of *Book IV*; see especially the famous passage (*paragraph 31*) in which Calvin declares that a moderately aristocratic republic is the State form which approximates most closely to the ideal of Natural Law. Hence Providence has endowed most States with such organs in the course of the historical process: "quales olim erant, qui Lacedaemoniis erant oppositi regibus Ephori aut Romanis consulibus Tribuni plebis aut Atheniensium senatui demarchi, et qua etiam forte potestate, ut nunc res habent, funguntur in singulis regnis tres ordines, cum primarios conventus peragunt" (*e.g.* the German estates of the Empire and the States General in France). Of these *magistrats inférieurs* it is said: "illis ferocienti regium licentiae pro officio intercedere adeo non veto, ut, si regibus impotenter grassantibus et humili plebeculae insultantibus conniveant, eorum dissimulationem nefaria perfidia non carere affirmem, quia populi libertatem, cujus se Dei ordinatione tutores positos norunt, fraudulenter produnt." In this we see the compromise between Luther's authoritarian way of thinking, which Calvin fully shares, with his rational ideal of Society which secures the claims of the individual. For the constant criticism of State and of Society in its aim and purpose which this produced, see *Choisy, pp. 493 ff.; Beyerhaus, pp. 108–130.—Kuyper* also quotes some characteristic words of Calvin: "Haec maxime optabilis est libertas, non cogi ad parendum quibuslibet, qui per vim impositi fuerunt capitibus nostris, sed electiionem permitti, ut nemo dominetur, nisi qui probatus fuerit"; and *p. 77*: "Ye people to whom God has given liberty to elect your own rulers, see to it that ye do not use this favour unwisely by electing worthless persons and enemies of God to the highest posts of honour." That is a rational Natural Law which must lead finally to laying on the Government the obligation of observing the laws in as nearly an ideal way as possible, as, indeed, Calvin co-operated in this sense in the endeavour to observe the political laws of Geneva. It is a germ of constitutionalism, as *Kuyper, p. 89*, rightly points out and *Beyerhaus* confirms.

355 (p. 617.) The examples for this are given in great detail in both *Choisy's* books. It also permeates the whole tradition of the Calvinistic ethic in its varied and independent development. Even in the eighteenth century *Lampe* teaches in his ethic: "Finis, in quem ipse Deus mundum conservat, est ecclesiae conservatio et electorum salus. Si salus singulorum est rei publicae finis, tum liquet, quod quo perfectior est salus, ad quam leges societatis civilis tendunt, eo perfectior sit ipsa rei publicae forma. Salus temporalis et aeterna ita sibi invicem sunt innexae, ut illa absque hac inanis umbra sit." *Luthardt: Geschichte der Ethik, II, 219.* Here also we must observe the spirit of utilitarian individualism.

356 (p. 617.) The conception of a fundamental theory of this kind was expressly formulated by Calvin himself, since in his discussion of the Fifth Commandment he describes the sociological relation of the family with its authorities and the spiritualizing of authority as the fundamental common *ratio* which lies at the basis of all other social relationships: "Quoniam hoc de subjectione praeceptum cum humani ingenii pravitate valde pugnat (quod, ut est celsitudinis appetentia turgidum, aegre se subjici sustinet) ea, quae natura maxime amabilis atque minime invidiosa superioritas, in exemplar proposita est, quia facilius animos nostros emollire et inflectere ad submissionis

consuetudinem poterat. Ad omnem enim legitimam subjectionem ab ea, quae facillima est toleratu, nos paullatim, assuefacit Dominus: quando est omnium eadem ratio. Siquidem quibus attribuit eminentiam, quatenus ad eam tuendam necesse est, suum cum illis nomen communicat. In unum ipsum ita conveniunt Patris, Dei ac Domini tituli, ut, quoties unum aliquem ex iis audimus, majestatis illius sensu animum nostrum feriri oporteat. . . . Quapropter ambiguum esse non debet, quia hic universalem regulam statuat Dominus: nempe prout quemque novimus esse nobis ejus ordinatione praefectum, ut ipsum reverentia, oboedientia, gratitudine et quibus possumus officiis prosequamur. Nec interest, disquirere an indigni sint, quibus honor iste deferatur; nam qualescunque sint tandem, non sine Dei Providentia hunc locum assequuti sunt" (*Inst., II, VIII, 35*). This looks as though it were the same as the patriarchalism of Lutheranism developed from the ideal of the family. Only the continuation shows that this is meant somewhat differently: "Sed istud etiam obiter annotandum, quod illis obedire nonnisi in Domino jubemur: neque id obscurum est ex jacto prius fundamento: praesident enim eo loco, in quem erexit eos Dominus. . . . Quae ergo submissio illis exbibetur, ad suscipiendum summum illum Patrem gradus esse debet. Quare si in legis transgressionem nos instigant, merito tum non parentis loco nobis habendi sunt, sed extranei, qui nos a veri patris obedientia subducere conantur. Sic de principibus, dominis et universo superiorum genere habendum. Indignum enim et absonum est, ut ad deprimendam Dei celsitudinem eorum eminentia polleat, quae, ut ab illa pendet, ita in illam diducere nos debet" (*Inst., II, VIII, 38*). An all-round description of the nature of Society and of the relation of the individual members to each other, see *Inst., II, VIII, 46*: "Honest gain without desire for riches; the support of all in the enjoyment of their rightful possessions and, as far as possible, avoidance of strife with deceitful and faithless men, even at the cost of one's own loss; in cases of need the utmost readiness to help; correctness and strictness in keeping all legal obligations; obedience to legal authority; the obligation of all authorities to consider the welfare of those who are under their protection with a constant consciousness of their responsibility in the sight of God; duties of the clergy in dogmatic and ethical instruction and good example; trust and obedience of the people to the clergy; mild but authoritative education of children, respect of youth for age; friendly and understanding counsel to youth by age; willing and cheerful obedience of servants for the sake of God; brotherly and considerate attitude of masters towards their servants; each individual first occupied with the endeavour to fulfil his own duties; finally, constant looking up to and sense of responsibility of all towards the Divine law-giver."

[357] (p. 618.) This is the very important contribution of *Ritschl* to the understanding of Calvinism. From this point of view he has absolutely corrected the mystical individualism of Lutheranism and has tried to support Lutheranism by means of the Calvinistic idea of the Church; this also is an example of the increasing importance of Calvinism at the present day; cf. *Rechtfertigung und Versöhnung*[3], *I, pp. 203–216*: "In this Calvin has saved a principle which Luther in his original right feeling of the reciprocity of the idea of justification with life in the congregation of the faithful placed in contrast to the erroneous structure of the Roman Catholic Sacrament of Penance and its ecclesiastical system(?)" (*p. 216*). It would, however, be more true to refer this contrast to a certain mystical tendency of Luther which led him to treat the individual in isolation; in his early years this was one of Luther's predominating ideas; as time went on, however, it receded into the background and the idea of the

Church took its place, but the effects of the earlier ideas are still operative in Lutheranism as a whole.

[360] (p. 620.) The inequality continues in the other life, as Calvin argues from 1 Cor. xv. 41–42 (*Briefe, II, 66*). The higher position a man occupies the more is he bound to endure martyrdom (*II, p. 277*). Cf. also *Troeltsch: Praedestination, Ch. W., 1907*.—There are also characteristic passages in *Beyerhaus, 95*: "We ought to know 'que d'autant plus qu'un homme sera eslevé il est obligé aussi et à Dieu et à ceux sur lesquels il preside comme il n'y a nulle preeminence sans charge, voir sans servitude'. The sphere of these moral duties in which this 'servitude honorable' ought to exercise itself is placed in the comprehensive conception of the common weal which corresponds to the eudaemonistic State theories of the Ancient World." *P. 133:* "This dominion of individual *viri maximi*, which he regards as the original form, is described in the following words: 'mediocris status hominum, ut si qui aliis praessent, non tamen dominarentur, nec sibi regium imperium sumerent, sed dignitate aliqua contenti civilem in modum regerent alios et plus autoritatis haberent quam potentiae' " (*CR., 51, 159*). Example, Noah. This situation which Calvin describes as *vetustissimus mundi status* on that account enjoys God's special favour because it corresponds to the demands of a *moderata administratio*, that is, on the side of the Government it preserves the *aequalitas cum minoribus*, on the side of the subjects a willing spirit (*sponte magis eos reverabantur quam imperio coacti*). This aristocratic form of government "was first broken through by the ambition of Nimrod: he is the archetype of the tyrant, his name henceforward is a byword."—This blend of aristocracy and masterfulness with the free initiative of each responsible individual is a permanent characteristic of the peoples which have been educated or influenced by Calvinism; they are remote from the equalitarian Latin democracy of Rousseau's school; indeed, in this respect Rousseau was in no wise a disciple of Calvin, although people often tried to make him one. This is the reason why in England the Socialism of self-help co-operative societies and trade unions provided the first outlet for these ideas, and therefore genuine social democracy could only make headway with difficulty. In America also the slow progress of Socialism must also be due to this education in self-help. It is, however, true that even there this difference is being increasingly nullified by the effects of industrial capitalism of the present day, which are everywhere the same.—*Kuyper* considers this idea from all sides, and he sees in Calvinism the great modern principle of civilization. For the contrast between the American and the French Revolution, see this expression of Hamilton in *Kuyper, p. 80:* "The principles of the American and the French Revolution resemble each other about as much as the quiet Puritan house-mother resembles the adulterous wife in a scandalous French novel." In the same book (*p. 78*) the contrast between the French and the English Revolution is thus expressed by Burke: "Our Revolution and that of France are just the reverse of each other in almost every particular and in the whole spirit of the transaction."—Gladstone also says to Ruskin: "I am a firm believer in the aristocratic principle, the rule of the best. I am out and out inegalitarian. . . . How are you to get the rule of the best? Freedom is the answer" (*Morley, Gladstone's Life, II, 582*). For Gladstone the highest virtues are self-command, self-control, respect for order, patience under suffering, confidence in the law, regard for superiors (*II, 124*).—Carlyle also in support of his ideal appeals to Puritanism and Calvinism; see *Baumgarten: Carlyle und Goethe, 1906*: "The eternal right of the dignity of man, the aristocracy of the heroes and obedience, that is, submission to the better", this is his sociological ideal. The idea of equality is

at home in the radical section of the Baptist movement, in the Stoic Natural Law, and in the modern Natural Law, but not in Calvinism. From those sources it certainly has penetrated into Calvinistic peoples, but it has never radically triumphed. In the book which I am about to mention by *Hagermann: Erklärungen der Menschen- und Bürgerrechte*, on *p. 77* it is said of Milton: "We read in Milton that all men are by nature born free. However, this freedom is a Protestant freedom; he calls it 'a due liberty and proportioned equality, both human and Christian', as we have seen in the American constitution to some extent men have not advanced beyond this demand for equality . . ." In the same book (*p. 45*), see remarks about the origin of American equality from the literature of the Enlightenment. Especially instructive in this respect is *Held: Zwei Bücher zur sozialen Geschichte Englands, 1881*. Here the continuance of the Puritan conservative features within Liberalism is explicitly described, especially in Burke. Likewise everywhere here the connection is shown between the radical democratic theories and, in particular, the French equalitarian propositions (*pp. 340–342, 288–293*): "The spirit of Cromwell's God-fearing regiments was still alive and active in the social struggles of the nineteenth century, and it was due to this fact that in spite of all passion and confusion the working-classes remained true to the State and its laws." "Puritan views which restrained the spirit of democracy by a strong Christian sense of duty lived on effectively among the Dissenters; Hampden remained a more popular hero than Robespierre."—The history of the problem of equality would be one of the most important contributions which could be made to the understanding of the development of European Society. It is, however, still entirely unwritten; there are some suggestions in *Lorenz von Stein: Soz. und Komm., pp. 3–128*.

361 (p. 621.) Cf. the presentation of the fundamental theory in *Choisy: L'état chrétien, pp. 489 ff.*: "Calvinism is animated by a great spirit of equality, of justice, and of social solidarity. The person and the activity of man being . . . immediately dependent on God and His Word, it follows that all men are equally obliged to obey God and are equal before His law. No one is capable of doing good apart from a gift of God, a communication of His Spirit. Since things are so, no man of himself has the right to dominate over others. Authority belongs to God alone, and there is no respect of persons before God. This fundamental equality before God and His Law results in the authority of parents over their children, of magistrates over their subjects, and even of men of science and of talent over those who do not possess these gifts; this authority does not belong actually to those who exercise it: it belongs to God, who exercises it through them. In consequence it will be suspended as soon as they abuse it or use it contrary to the Will and the Counsel of God. Also at Geneva the Ordinance takes in hand the protection of the rights of children against unjust or negligent parents; and the ministers defend the cause of the people and its rights over against the magistrate, and the *Compagnie* and the *Consistoire* constitute themselves the champions of justice, of the equality of all before the law; they exact the punishment of highly placed culprits, of persons of quality, just as they do that of obscure and uninfluential culprits. However, if the Calvinist spirit is a spirit of justice and equality, that does not mean a spirit which abolishes all distinctions; it recognizes natural differences, Providential inequalities, special gifts, exceptional vocations, extraordinary talents. These inequalities, however, do not constitute from the Calvinistic point of view rights for those who enjoy them, but they constitute obligations of service. Calvinism has given to men of every kind the sense of their solidarity in their moral obligations and in their responsibility towards God." Further,

for the sense of individualism within this solidarity, see *Choisy: La Théocratie, p. 279*: "Also genuine Calvinists possessed to a high degree the sense of responsibility, the spirit of initiative, the need for veracity, and the moral energy of the will and full self-command." Descriptions of the fundamental theory, of the "relation between individuals", also in *Kuyper, pp. 19–24.* Here, however, there is an exaggerated emphasis upon the democratic results: "Their endeavour was to look first at God and then at their neighbour; this was their mood, their spiritual habit, which was created by Calvinism, and only from this devout reverence for God in which all were in the Presence of God did there develop a consecrated democratic sentiment. This means that all, whether man or woman, rich or poor, strong or weak, talented or ignorant, have no personal claims at all, all are God's creatures and lost sinners; this means, therefore, that both as an individual and as a people, both before God and in all human relationships, we are all on the same level, and no other difference between human beings ought to exist excepting in so far as God has given to one a higher position than another or more gifts than another, in order that he may give more service to others and that in others he may render more service to his God. For this reason Calvinism condemns not only every kind of slavery and caste system, but just as decidedly all concealed slavery of women and of the poor; it opposes all hierarchy among men and tolerates no other aristocracy than that which, whether in an individual or a race, obviously possesses a greater amount of moral or intellectual capacity through the grace of God, and thus shows that he does not wish to use this over-plus for himself in order to increase his own reputation, but that he wishes to use it for God in His world."

[362] (p. 623.) *Choisy*, in particular, brings out the character of a "Christian Socialism", the united care for external well-being, and the moral correctness of each individual exercised by the authority of Church and State, the common responsibility of the community for each member, the social reform and philanthropy which was carried out down to the smallest detail, and he illustrates this with numerous examples from the records. This Socialism is thoroughly anti-Communist, but everywhere it makes the community responsible for the individual members, and in certain instances it requires the greatest sacrifices of public and private means. In all this the clergy are the driving force; their methods are partly the penalties of the municipal court of justice and partly the hailing of offenders before the magistrate who dealt with minor offences. They demand the regulation of the price of corn, see *Choisy: L'état chrétien, pp. 117, 121, 244*; laws against luxury and sumptuary regulations for the sake of frugality as well as of the maintenance of class barriers and of decency (*pp. 118, 148, 231*); rate of interest corresponding to the business situation (*pp. 119, 190*); paying back of debts in the same value in which they were contracted (*p. 120*); the "Blue Monday" forbidden (*p. 153*); statistical inquiries according to districts about income, need of support, family circumstances, etc. (*pp. 166 and 257*); supervision of inn-keepers and cheap prices for wine (*p. 167*); impartiality and correctness in the administration of justice (*p. 196*); introduction of manufactures in order to give employment to the population, and a careful selection of those who are to be sent away from the overcrowded town (*p. 246*); strict morality and honesty of the troops in the occupied territories (*p. 290*); similar points of interest in *pp. 302 and 342.* All these matters came before the Council either in the form of a motion or a complaint. In other matters the court of discipline acted independently: it punished commercial deceit, dishonest coal-dealers, a velvet manufacturer

because one of his lengths was short by one inch, a tailor who gave preferential treatment to foreign customers, a surgeon who asked too high fees; it served as a peace-maker and a court of arbitration; it pointed out offences which had been overlooked by the civil authorities, protected the weak, and punished those who ill-treated children, etc. (*pp. 443 ff.*). "The Consistory intervenes in order to restore peace and unity in family life and to call individuals to do their duty; it takes in hand . . . reforms in favour of the helpless and the weak; it censures the lazy and the idle as well as fathers and creditors who were too harsh; it shows no mercy to usurers, monopolists, or tradesmen who defraud their customers. It strives against the coarse customs of the time, the brutality of the men and the careless negligence in the treatment of sick people" (*La Théocratie, p. 244*). It is, otherwise, clear that in this Church social policy the methods and ideas of the old policy of the guilds and the municipality are transferred to the whole commonwealth. *Doumergue* has proved many of these things in detail. The acceptance of these principles by the Church, which acted in common with the State and the systematic unified extension over the whole of Society, marks the difference between this policy and that of the mediaeval Church and of Lutheranism, which left most of these matters to the State and the guilds and otherwise undertook essentially caritative social policy.—In addition there were the taxes and loans in favour of the poor, both the poor of the district and the refugees, which were constantly increased until they reached the utmost limit; without considerable and constant financial assistance from outside the whole system would have been impossible to maintain in Geneva, whose very existence was always threatened. *L'état chrétien, pp. 428 ff.* In this financial solidarity the early Christian love communism was revived.—For the Christian social character as the main factor in Calvinism, see also *Rieker, p. 68,* and *Göbel, II, 123.*—For the development of this guild Christian Socialism into modern Christian Socialism, see *Held* and *von Schulze-Gävernitz: Zum sozialen Frieden.*

[368] (p. 628.) The congregational character of the Calvinistic Church is undeniable. For the congregation has a share in everything, even although it may be only through carefully selected lay representatives, as in the court of discipline or through the power to vote as in the election of pastors; cf. the sentence from *CR., XL, 9,* quoted by *Holl, p. 54*: "les pseudod-evesques ont ravy a l'assemble des fideles et tire a eux la cognaissance et puissance d'excommunier." But the official positions themselves are not the expression of the free choice of the congregation, but they are a Divine appointment, hence also they are not bound to come into existence through the activity of the congregation; see *Rieker: Grundsätze reformierter Kirchenverfassung, pp. 92, 126 ff., and 129 ff.* Thus even in Geneva the Church constitution was very aristocratic, the election of pastors was carried out by the pastors, the community was only asked to consent. The elders on the Board of Discipline were chosen partly by the Council and partly were nominated by the pastors. Proposals which went further, suggesting, for instance, that the congregations should carry out the elections themselves or even that the congregations should possess the right of discipline, were rejected and, indeed, by the pastors themselves; see *Choisy: L'état chrétien, p. 79,* likewise in the sphere of the constitution of the State (*p. 149*). Cf. the description which Calvin gave himself in the letter to Olevian, who was at Heidelberg, as a model for the organization in the Palatinate (*Briefe, II, 329–331*). The French Church constitution of the same character, see *Marcks' Coligny, I, 1, p. 331*; about Geneva, *pp. 297 ff.* The Synods also were not representative bodies, but governing bodies formed according to the Divine appoint-

ment (*Rieker, 158*). Everywhere, however, the tacit consent of the community is always presupposed, and the far-reaching right of protest was at least a democratic element.

[370] (p. 628.) This is the important section in *Institutio IV, 20, 8, Equidem-cogitatio*; cf. the synoptic impression of the edition *CR., XXIX, p. 1105*. It is in opposition to the earlier passage (*VIII, 20, 7*), where the monarchy which condemns all men to servitude appears to be authenticated by the Scriptures for the restraint of human evil. On that point in *Doumergue: Les origines historiques de la déclaration des droits de l'homme, 1905, pp. 10 ff.*, see the quoted passage from Calvin's lectures which plainly reflect the experiences of Geneva: on Micah v. 5: "The prophet here magnifies the singular kindness of God, that is to say, that the people will be restored to their liberty. And, in fact, it is a most desirable situation when the pastors (that means here the magistrates in general) are elected and created by the common voice of the people. For where empire and sovereignty is usurped by violence there is a tyranny which is too barbarous. There also, where the kings rule by right of succession and of inheritance, it does not seem very favourable to liberty" (*CR., XLIII, 374*).—On Deut. xvi. 11: "When we see these examples (that is, of bad kings) we know that it is an inestimable gift if God permits a people to have liberty to elect their leaders and magistrates . . . seeing then that it is an excellent gift, let us see that we conserve it and that we use it with a good conscience" (*CR., XXVII, p. 411*). This, then, became the official manner in which the Genevans spoke of their Republic as of a special gift of God which made it possible to Christianize the State, as *Choisy* shows in many places. Also in *Beyerhaus* there are similar passages (*pp. 116–129*).

[371] (p. 629.) Every biography of Calvin shows this fact about him, for example *Kampschulte, II, 355–357*. The negotiations with the magistrate about the *cri au peuple* and its effectiveness in *Choisy: L'état chrétien. P. 55:* Colladin preaches against usury and the Council treats that as mutiny. *P. 154:* Beza preaches on behalf of the ministers against the prices of corn, etc. *P. 190:* sermon against usury and the responsibility of the ministers: "They are bound to say freely when the magistrate does not do what he ought. Faults are being committed. Those who hear them mentioned inquire into the matter, and they reply sometimes in general, sometimes in particular. These matters are sometimes overwhelmingly manifest, and yet people do not want to see them. If we should be silent, what would the people say? That they are dumb dogs. . . . Do people think that they want to increase their power by ruining the magistrates, or that they are trying to foment sedition as if they did not know that they themselves would be the first to suffer? But they are afraid that instead of arousing others they will lose themselves. . ." *Pp. 251 ff.*: Six members of the Council (under Beza's influence) explained to the magistrate, with an appeal to religious duty, the necessity of declaring war on Savoy, and they summoned the Government "to put their hand to the matter immediately and without delay if we do not wish to make shipwreck of the precious liberty which it has pleased God to give and to conserve to us until now . . . and what would be still more to be deplored, expose the holy Name of God, our Sovereign Father and benefactor, to blasphemy and dishonour for which we would be gravely responsible before His judgment seat". The people are already murmuring against the Council. "Good magistrates must respect the voice of the people and the lamentations of men of good-will, especially in free states where without the people they are nothing." The right to undertake this war is "ratified by the desire and the consent of the whole of this faithful people,

which is instructed in the fear of God." The Council answers that it realizes the weight of this argument and hands it over to Beza to be considered. *P. 298:* the ministers decide against a resolution of the Council of the Two Hundred in appeal matters. To that is added a long struggle between the ministers and the Council, which regards this as rebellion. *P. 347:* the ministers protest against irregularities in an election and support this protest in sermons. When the Council protested on its part, the *Compagnie* testified to their "displeasure that these gentlemen do not unite themselves with the people". They declare "that being informed by the people of certain faults which are in the aristocracy, they are constrained to remonstrate with the magistrate". Further examples, *pp. 356, 375, 395, 396, 399, 610. P. 413:* the permanent significance of this *cri au peuple* in Geneva. *P. 467:* a striking comparison of the ministers with the present-day influence of the Press. *P. 469:* a good summary: "They were admirably well informed about the material, commercial, and moral circumstances of the population; this was due to the exercise of their functions as guardians of public morality. The part they played in supervising the doctrines and the customs of the citizens brought them into close touch with the details of the daily life of the Genevese. This rôle of popular defenders and tribunes, or, rather, of prophets of the law of God, contributed greatly to make them loved by the poorer classes; indeed, it made them persons who were admirably situated to serve as impartial mediators between the different social classes."—*Choisy* also rightly emphasizes the constitutional character of the whole commonwealth. *P. 498:* "The political edicts and the ecclesiastical ordinances enacted under the influence and with the participation of Calvin are an authority superior to the magistrate and limit his absolutist designs; it is the constitutional law which he is not allowed to abrogate, and which he may not touch without the consent of the people united in general council. . . . The power of the magistrate is limited to a right of control and of conservation." In case of conflict his only way of getting assistance is to call on the professional opinion of foreign churches. "Like the magistrate, the faithful ought to watch to see that all that is done in the Church is conformable to the ordinances of the Word of God; they may oppose the election of a minister whom they judge to be unworthy of his charge, and they can ask the competent authority to depose a minister who does not fulfil the duties of his office faithfully"—this alone is a decidedly democratic main idea, but characteristically the people is still only thought of in the person of its representatives who have been appointed by God. These representatives are in the highest sense the ministers, who therefore are particularly fond of comparing themselves with the Prophets of the Old Testament and their mission to the people (*pp. 72 and 123*). The people act directly only through the elections, but those who are elected are only nominated after a very careful process of selection.

[372] (p. 630.) This is the famous treatise *De Jure magistratuum*, which previously figured anonymously among the writings of the so-called *monarchomachi*, even in *Gierke: Althusius*[2], *p. 4*, which, however, *Cartier* (*Bulletin de la Soc. d'histoire et d'archéologie de Genève, Bd. II, 1898–1904, pp. 187–206*) has proved from the records of the Council to have been written by Beza. I have before me an edition of 1580 (from Basle) as a supplement to *Machiavelli's Principe*, together with the *Vindiciae contra tyrannos*. The Council refused to give their imprimatur to this work when they realized its content, for fear of the French Ambassador, and thus to a great extent the work appeared anonymously. *Cartier* indicates its content very aptly in the following sentences. *P. 188:* "The only will is that

of the only God, which is the perpetual and immutable rule of all justice (it is 'jus illud naturae, a quo uno pendet totius humanae societatis conservatio', *266*; conceived in its application to both Tables, *207*).—The peoples whom it has pleased to allow themselves to be governed either by a prince or by some chosen lords are more ancient than the magistrates, and in consequence the people is not created for the magistrate, but, on the contrary, the magistrate for the peoples.—All resistance of a subject to his superior is neither illicit nor seditious.—Rightful resistance by force of arms is not at all contrary to the patience and the prayers of Christians.—All ought to oppose those who wish to usurp power over their fellow-citizens or over others who are not subject to them.—The estates are above kings.—The estates or others who have been instituted to serve as a curb to sovereign rulers can and ought to restrain them in all the ways they can when they have become tyrants.—The public good and the rights of the nation are superior to those of the individual, even to those of the sovereign.—The unjust usurper of power can become a legitimate and inviolable magistrate provided that he gives his free and true consent to the terms by which legitimate magistrates are created.—If one is persecuted for religion it is right to make armed resistance with a good conscience."—All this sounds very modern and democratic, but we must not overlook the fact that the genuine Calvinistic restrictions in favour of historic right and its conception have been established indirectly by the Providence of God, and are, therefore, regarded as having been instituted by God Himself. I have noted them above in the text; they appear again and again in the whole book, with emphasis on the Christian spirit of obedience. Above all, this is important for the conception of the rise of the State and the social contract. The rise of the State is always in the Aristotelian manner conceived as organic; the social contract of a mutual obligation between subjects and rulers which binds the rulers to the observance of Natural and Divine Law is contained in this only silently and as a matter of course. Historic law is to be recognized everywhere; it is, however, only Divine when its content agrees with Natural and Divine Law, otherwise every robber would be obeying a Divine Law (*p. 287*). The mutual obligation is taken for granted with the existence of definite positive laws; if they are lacking it is based upon the tacitly assumed Law of Nature (*pp. 270 and 273*). There is no idea of a rational shaping of the State through a social contract; all that is aimed at is to assert that in the historic law the Divine and Natural germ does exist if this should be denied. And it is true only in legitimate ways through the subordinate authorities; private individuals can only act as those who have been commissioned by them, which, however, in the end means that the private individuals also are indirectly included (*p. 279*). When the tyrant has been corrected, then historic law must be restored, whether by himself or through someone else acting in his place; *p. 293:* "Si quidem cum non nisi certis conditionibus administratio illi (that is, the tyrant) sit commissa: minime censendum est, novas pactiones cum ipso iniri, quoties interpellatur ut vel priores conditiones ratas habeat easque deinceps observet, vel alteri locum cedat, qui de illorum observatione magis sit futurus sollicitur. . . . Ordines vero vel status regionis (that is, the subordinate authorities who are justified in resistance), quibus haec autoritas a legibus est collata, eatenus sese tyranno opponere atque adeo ipsi justas et promeritas poenas irrogare et possunt et debent, donec res in pristinum statum restitutae sint. Quodsi praestiterint, tantum abest, ut seditiosi aut perduelles habendi sint, ut contra officio suo et juramento probe defuncti tum demum censeri debeant" (*p. 266*).—The fact that Christ and the apostles did not resist the authority of the State, their whole emphasis on suffering, is explained by the fact that they were private individuals, and that there were no subordinate authorities in existence who could protect the law, and thus until the present day they are the norm for merely private individuals: "Dominus noster Jesus Christus, prophetae item ac apostoli, cum privati erant homines, sese intra metas suae vocationis continuerunt" (*p. 309*)! This means a most decided retention of historic law, and it is easy to understand that the Genevan Council approved of the content of the work. Even Luther, though only under the influence of the decision of the jurists of 1530, himself approached such views to the extent of accepting the idea of the right to execute a tyrant and the idea of the *mutua obligatio* between people and rulers, even Melancthon had already made the distinction between private individuals and *magistratus inferiores*; likewise Osiander (?); also the Erasmian and the Scholastic doctrine of the State is here in the background; see *Cardauns: Widerstandsrecht, pp. 8–15, 31 ff.*—Beza has clearly expressed the positive reasons for the justification of his theory. They are: (1) the Christian aim of the State and its aim according to Reason (*p. 216*); (2) the consequence of the lower court of justice (*p. 217*).—That theories of this kind could proceed drectly from Calvin's instruction is shown still more strikingly by *Knox's* theory, which was formulated in Geneva, and the treatise by *Goodman*, the second pastor of the English Church, which teaches the right of resistance almost without safeguards, *How superior powers ought to be obeyed of their subjects and wherein they may lawfully by God's Word be disobeyed and resisted, Geneva, 1558.* Calvin looked through this treatise, and the author reports that Calvin thought it harsh and needing to be used with caution, but that its main contention was right (*Doumergue, pp. 28 ff.*). The tractate by the English bishop, *Poynet: A short treatise of politic power, and of the true obedience which subjects own to the King and other civile governors, 1556,* written in Strassburg. *Cardauns, 37–40,* proceeds directly from the standpoint of *Calvin's Institutes.*

[374] (p. 632.) On this point cf. *Cartier, pp. 204–206; Figgis: From Gerson to Grotius; Baudrillart: Bodin et son temps, 1853; Cardauns: Widerstandsrecht, 1930; Treumann: Monarchomachen, 1895 (Staats- und völkerrechtlich Abhandlungen. hsg. v. Jellinek, Nr. 1); Elkan: Publizistik der Bartholomäusnacht,* and *Mornay's Vindicae, 1905 (Heidelberger Abhh. zur mittleren und neueren Geschichte, Nr. 9); Mèaly: Les publicistes de la réforme, 1903 (Thèse of the Paris Faculté de Théol. Prot.)*; for *Jurieu,* see *Doumergue, p. 22,* and *Luran: Les doctrines politiques de J., 1904.* In this respect it is unfortunate that the theological ethic of Calvinism has not been yet carefully examined, but in any case, from the time of Beza, its important representatives agree with the publicists and the jurists on this point. Thus the resemblance between the ideas of the *Monarchomachi* and the principles of Rousseau ought not to be overestimated. They are concerned with deductions drawn from the Scriptures, the Law of Nature, and theology; they are not concerned with the decided rationalism of an independent philosophy of the State. *Treumann,* who calls attention to the lack of a clear distinction between the social contract and the contract of sovereignty (*p. 50,* also *Elkan, 159*), as well as in reference to the "theocratic" limitations, has also recognized this, but he has not emphasized its importance sufficiently. The question is not one of the "retention of the ideas of contract without attacking the theocratic basis of the right of the ruler" (*p. 56*), but it is a question of the introduction of this idea also as an ingredient into all historic law; not one of setting aside an ideal of the State, which previously had been absolute, theocratic, and monarchical (*p. 77*)—there was never an ideal of this kind in Calvinism—but of the introduction of methods of control into the constitution which was itself

unaltered. The contract idea is, therefore, quite dissimilar from the conceptions of Hobbes, Grotius, and Rousseau, and it remains true to the standpoint of the historic and therefore Divine Law.—Thus their ideas lack also the necessary presupposition of the later philosophy of the State, of the social contract, and the contract of sovereignty, the original freedom and equality. It is true that *Elkan* (*p. 30*) says: "Ultimately the whole structure was based upon the idea of freedom for humanity, which was absolutely taken for granted. No one took the trouble to find an argument for this doctrine, scarcely anyone even dreamed of doubting it." Therewith he only proves the absence of this doctrine. In reality, the Calvinistic and non-modern character of this whole school of writers is based upon the absence of this doctrine. To them the social contract of equal and free men is superfluous because the Aristotelian organic doctrine is applied to the rise of Society; this, however, also implies inequality in rank, the distinction between private individuals and officials, the sovereignty of the objective law, not the subjective equal share in Reason. Further, the idea of equality is excluded by the spirit produced by the doctrine of predestination. The youthful work of *La Boétie* (who was certainly not a Calvinist): *Discours de la servitude volontaire*, which began at the standpoint of the original freedom and equality in the Stoic Humanistic sense, and declared that servitude arose out of willing submission, was rejected by the Calvinists (*Baudrillart, 68–73*), *Mēaly, 63*.—It should be noted that *Cardauns* derives the Calvinistic theory from the branches of Lutheran propaganda which were influenced by Hesse and Strassburg in the days of the League of Schmalkalden, and of the Magdeburg struggles, as, indeed, *Beza's* tractate in its first edition (1574) was introduced as being "*publié de ceux de Magdebourg l'an 1550*" (*Cartier, 187*). Also *Ritter: Anfänge des niederland. Aufstandes* (*Hist. Zeitschr. 58, 1887, p. 425*), quotes from a letter of 1556, in which a tractate is mentioned which deals with the problem of resistance and the justification of the *magistratus inferiores*, and he holds that this tractate refers either to the *Gutachten* of the ministers and lawyers of Wittenberg, or to the *Vermahnung der Pfarrherrn von Magdeburg, 1549*. Cf. also *Cardauns, p. 71*, Beza's appeal to the people of Magdeburg. In point of fact, all the ideas of the Calvinistic theory are also found, although in a confused way, in the works of many German writers. Only the Calvinistic doctrines have one main theoretical feature and principle derived from the fundamental religious idea of Calvinism—the idea of the glory of God, and of the equality of all in the presence of God, which clearly distinguishes them from those Lutheran theories, and, indeed, these theories themselves were an illogical and passing phenomenon, and at the best only a by-product of Lutheranism; this latter point is not sufficiently emphasized by *Cardauns*, see above, *pp. 530 and 532*.

[375] (p. 634.) Cf. *Martin: De la Genèse des doctrines religieuses de John Knox*, and *De la Genèse des doctrines politiques de J. K.*, in the *Bulletin de la société de l'histoire du prot. français, 1906, 193–211, and 1907, pp. 193–221*. Cf. also *Cardauns* and *Elkan*. Cf. also in the book by *Bastide* on *Locke*, to be mentioned shortly, the section entitled *Théories politiques en Angleterre au 16 et 17ème siècles, pp. 137–176*. The conservative legitimist Calvinistic character of the Presbyterian and Independent movement is here rightly emphasized in contrast to that of the "Levellers" and kindred groups. We shall see later on that the latter were nearer to the spirit of the Anabaptists than to that of the Calvinists. The forces which were at work in the so-called "Independency" were utterly different.—Pareus in Heidelberg also taught that kings might be deposed, see *Bastide, p. 144;* this idea was not peculiar to the English Revolution.

[376] (p. 635.) Cf. *Gierke's Althusius*[2], in which, with his admirable learning and industry, *Gierke* examines the origin of all these elements of thought. *Gierke* also rightly lays stress on the fact that the new theory stands out clearly from the previous religious theory, especially the presupposition of universal freedom and equality before the social contract (*pp. 29, 79, and 107*). Further valuable details dealing with this subject will be found especially on *pp. 28 and 30, 59 and 69, 76, 217, and 145*. The view that subordinate authorities are justified in resistance under certain circumstances is discussed on *pp. 34 and 35*. Indeed, a Lutheran, *Peter Gartz*, has described the doctrine of Althusius as a product of "Presbyterian error" (*p. 7*); it is, however, in reality a step beyond genuine Calvinism, and stands between it and the classic-Rationalistic Law of Nature.

[377] (p. 636.) The famous work of Grotius (which I have used in the translation in the *Kirchmannschen Philos. Bibliothek, 1869*) shows everywhere its purely humanist, philosophical, juridical character and its fundamental connection with Stoicism; the whole statement of the problem of war and of international law starts from the cosmopolitan Stoic idea of humanity; from this standpoint it is believed that confessional struggles and conflicts can be absolutely overcome. Therefore, in his opinion, the Law of Nature, the a priori rational foundation, is entirely independent of all theology and of all faith in God (*I, p. 31*). For the relation to the previous Protestant doctrine of the State the declaration regarding the Old Testament is characteristic: "Many would like to raise the Old Testament to the level of a Law of Nature, but they are wrong. For much that it contains proceeds from the decree of God, which is certainly not in conflict with true Nature" (*I, 60*). This means that the Law of Nature is no longer identified with the political ethic of the Old Testament. With reference to the New Testament he says: "I make use of the New Testament because that which is permitted to Christians I can learn from it alone. Unlike most other writers, however, I distinguish this content from the Law of Nature itself; for I am convinced that in this holiest of all laws a higher holiness is taught than the Law of Nature requires for itself alone. Yet I have always noted whether in certain instances some things are rather suggested than commanded. Since it is wrong and punishable to depart from the commandments (that is, also from that which is commanded by Natural Law), whereas it is the sign of a noble temper, which will not go unrewarded, if one always strives to follow the highest, that is, the commands of the Gospel, which exceed those of Nature (*p. 61*). This means that the Protestant habit of identifying the Natural Law and the Sermon on the Mount has been given up, and it also means the final emancipation of the Natural Law from the commands of the Sermon on the Mount, as is shown in the long argument which follows. Then there comes the vigorous establishment of the contract upon the presupposition of an original communism and an original freedom and equality (*I, pp. 70, 74, 76, 80, 90*); further, the rejection of anti-monarchist theories in the interest of a unified State authority which is far removed from religious conflict (*I, 195*). In accordance with this Grotius opposes the doctrine of predestination, and from the dogmatic point of view he takes the side of the Arminians and the Socinians.—The Natural Law of the period after Grotius departed still further from the Calvinistic basis. Of Rousseau, above all, *Gierke* says very pertinently that the idea of the contract of sovereignty is swallowed up in the social contract (*Alth., 91 ff.*); in so doing, however, he destroyed every historic right, and set up the ideal of small federated republics, in which the original freedom and equality should be preserved by basing all legislation upon the general will; this may correspond to the Swiss republics, but it has nothing to do with

the spirit of Calvinism; indeed, it is in complete opposition to it.—French Protestant apologists naturally approve of Rousseau's estimate of Calvinism; cf. the work by *Méaly* and also *Doumergue* (who is much more restrained) (*pp. 53, 55, and 63*). Nevertheless, it is wrong. To describe *Grotius* and *Pufendorf* as "representatives of Calvinist politics" (*p. 25*) is simply false; the Genevan lawyer, *Burlamaqui* (d. 1748), whom *Doumergue* quotes with special emphasis, represents a purely individualistic rationalism of freedom and equality, which is quite remote from Calvinistic thought. Also *Jurieu* (d. 1713) already shows this foreign influence (*pp. 22 ff.*).

[381] (p. 641.) Cf. *Kampschulte, I, 385–480,* especially *429 ff.; II, 342–387; Wiskemann: Nationalökonomische Ansichten zur Zeit der Reformation, pp. 80–87; Elster: Calvin als Staatsmann, Gesetzgeber und Nationalökonom. Jahrbb. f. Nationalökonomie und Statistik, XXXI* (based on *Kampschulte* and *Wiskemann*)*; Rachfahl: Calvinismus und Kapitalismus, Internationale Wochenschrift, 1909* (in which there are references to Calvin based upon *Kampschulte, Elster,* and *Lang*)*; Max Weber: Protestantische Ethik und der Geist des Kapitalismus, Archiv XX and XXI; Laveleye, Protestantismus und Katholizismus in ihren Beziehungen zur Wohlfahrt der Völker, deutsch, p. 127; Choisy: L'état chrétien; E. Knodt: Bedeutung Calvins und des Calvinismus für die Protestantische Welt* (*Vorträge der Giessener Konferenz*)*, 1910.*— *Weber's* treatise is to-day of fundamental importance. First of all he has handled the problem in its great setting of the history of civilization, and on its inward side he has linked the religious and ethical element with the social and economic element. For my own part I have adopted these views of his which I have found confirmed largely through a study of American life, and of that of the Lower Rhine, and have used them in my more general works on the nature of Protestantism and its significance for civilization, naturally not wholly without using my own judgment, but it is quite unnecessary to stress this point.— *Rachfahl* has attacked *Weber* and myself in the article which has just been mentioned; I do not, however, consider that in these matters he is a competent judge.

[382] (p. 641.) Passages in *Kampschulte, I, 430*; see also *Briefe, I, 433,* the recognition of the poverty which Jesus commanded contrasted with monastic poverty. Numerous examples of a similar anti-mammon spirit among his followers in *Choisy, 176 ff.*, to a proposal of the tradespeople to found a bank with the rate of interest of 10 per cent., they recognize the "belle apparence" of the project, but they fear "abus, désordres et dissolutions", point out the dangers of banking business in Paris, Venice, and Lyons, and they also point out the destruction of Jerusalem and of Rome through riches: "Si ce change est introduit, on dira, qu'à Genève chacun est banquier et qu'il n'a que des prêteurs. Si d'aventure Messieurs jugent néanmoins que ce charge sera commode, ils prient de bien considérer s'il sera tolérable de prêter à deux et demi par foire. . . . Ils pensaient que la cité serait plus forte en demeurant pauvre". *P. 346:* "The Venerable Compagnie announces that they will preach to the people on 'l'ordre, l'obéissance et la modestie'." *P. 229:* They demand "qu'on demeure en toute modestie et médiocrité". Calvin already was quite of this mind (*Elster, 191*): "Et en général, que chacun ait à se vestir honestement et simplement selon son estat et qualité et que tous, tant petits que grands, monstrent bon exemple de modestie chrétienne les uns aux autres."—The Church in the Netherlands still has too high a rate of interest, pawnbrokers' shops and deposit businesses are vigorously opposed as methods of exploiting the poor; see *Knappert: Geschiedenis der nederlandsche hervormde Kerk, 1911, pp. 178–182.*

[384] (p. 643.) This reaction of Geneva is emphasized by *Kampschulte, p. 429.* Before Calvin Geneva had already a State system of legislation on interest, which he simply took over. The fact that Calvin threw himself into the commercial atmosphere of the city, which is taken for granted, is illustrated over and over again by his correspondence. *Briefe, I, 33,* mercantile speculations in respect of Calvin's exile; *81 and 306,* recommendation of believers as apprentices; *209,* Calvin's own difficulty of raising a loan for himself; *283,* difficulties of placing a nephew of Viret in a shop or as a traveller or as a collector of debts; *294,* similar difficulties in raising securities for a colleague in the ministry. Advice to two citizens of Lausanne about financial transactions; *II, p. 109,* efforts on behalf of debtors in order to secure the credit of Geneva. Further illustrations of Calvin's interest in financial and business matters can be found in his correspondence; see the German edition of his *Letters,* especially the following pages in *II, 360, 140, 393, 442.* The same point of view is reflected in the extracts from reports quoted by *Choisy,* see especially *pp. 31 and 392; 34, 36, and 58; 47, 57, 140, 194, and 388.*

[387] (p. 644.) The details of this subject belong to the economic presentation of the subject; they are, however, not at all simple to represent statistically. To that we must add the fact that in the neighbourhood of Calvinism there were also other groups—Anglican, sectarian, and Lutheran—which also were to some extent influenced by Calvinism. The fact itself is well known and generally recognized. In addition to the literature which has already been mentioned I would call the attention of the reader to the good summary in *Arnold: Calvinreden, pp. 28–33*; here, *p. 31*: "Calvinism has produced this proverb, 'Faith removes mountains and works at the same time with axe and spade'. Lutheranism also gave dignity to labour, but since all this was referred to work in one's 'calling', the free initiative of the individual was less definitely released. . . . Calvin alone among the Reformers emphasized the fact that that which makes work productive is not merely the physical and the intellectual effort, but above all moral force. . . . The objective value of that which is achieved by labour, the economic result, consists, according to this view, not in temporary gain, but solely and only in the fact that honest work has been done. An idea capable of infinite expansion! This capacity for development is so easily overlooked because people look upon it as such a natural thing, as, indeed, it is." There then follows a sketch of the expansion and influence of Calvinistic industrialism and capitalism.—A characteristic example from the Netherlands is given by *Weber* from the work entitled *Political Arithmetic,* by the famous political economist *W. Petty: Antikritisches, p. 184*: "Dissenters of this kind (he means the supporters of the struggle for freedom in Holland, who were primarily Calvinists) are, for the most part, thinking, sober, and patient men, and such as believe that labour and industry is their duty towards God." This is not contradicted, but rather supported by the following passages from the same author, *ibid., p. 188:* "These people (namely, the Puritan Dissenters), believing the justice of God and seeing the most licentious persons to enjoy most of the world and its best things, will never venture to be of the same religion and profession with voluptuaries and men of extreme wealth and power who they think have their portion in this world."—The extension of bourgeois capitalism, in particular territories and the modifications which there obtain, is treated by *Weber: Antikritisches, pp. 186–188, 192*; conclusion, *pp. 571 and 594 ff.* Here we see how also within a setting, which in itself was unfavourable to Capitalism—as in East Friesland, New England, and Hungary—similar, or at least related, influences were also operative. This development

of Capitalism is not dependent merely upon a favourable environment.—*Göbel, II, 39,* gives numerous examples of Calvinism in the Netherlands and on the Lower Rhine: "Its members (of the Calvinistic community at Aachen) consisted almost entirely of wealthy and noble merchants, while all the Lutherans were only tolerated as assessors." *II, p. 47:* "The letters of credence of the delegates and elders to the synods had to be put in the form of mercantile letters of credit in order to avoid all danger of treachery or suspicion." *II, p. 106:* "And (after a description of their ascetic strictness of life) since both in Jülich and Berg they were excluded from all public offices, it was all the more natural that the whole trade of the Lower Rhine, and the whole of the industry of these parts which was here so important, especially fell into their hands, and that still to-day it is in their hands in particular. Hence the districts of Berg, Mark, and Jülich, which have developed a remarkable manufacturing activity and an extended trade, have become some of the richest and most remarkable parts of Germany, which at the same time have gained a name for great attachment to the Church and for personal piety." *II, p. 205*—the writer is here quoting from Labadie: "The elders and deacons fulfil their duties to the members of the Church and the poor in their own districts; the judges love righteousness and the tradespeople carry on their trade in the sight of heaven and the masters labour for eternity." For the economic significance of Labadism, see *II, pp. 238 and 259*; in this respect it is only a heightened form of Calvinism.—With reference to the economic ethic of English Puritanism, *Cunningham*, the well-known English economic historian, says in a small book entitled *The Moral Witness of the Church on the Investment of Money and the Use of Wealth, Cambridge, 1909, pp. 23ff.:* "As the defect of the present-day ethic of the Church (in England) is a one-sided tendency towards Socialism, so on the contrary the one-sided nature of Puritanism and its neglect of other factors was its peculiarity. Its fight against idleness and love of pleasure, and its recommendation of disciplined work, have made it absolutely capitalistic. Unemployment and idleness were the characteristic evils of the seventeenth century in England and Scotland; the great need for introducing a godly, sober, and righteous life into the community appeared to be that of getting the population to submit to the discipline of work. There were no half-measures in the Scottish treatment of vagrants, according to the Act of 1663. Capitalists who set up manufactories were empowered to impress any vagrants and 'employ them for their service as they see fit' for eleven years, without wages, except meat and clothing. Good subjects were recommended to take into their service poor and indigent children, who were to do any task assigned to them till they had attained the age of thirty, and to be 'subject to their masters' correction and chastisement in all manner of punishment (life and torture excepted)'. The seventeenth-century Puritans took a stern view of the discipline which was good for children, so that they might be kept from forming habits of idleness and drifting into evil of every kind. While there was a strong sense of the religious duty of insisting on hard and regular work for the welfare, temporal and eternal, of the people themselves, there was a complete indifference to the need of laying down or enforcing any restrictions as to the employment of money. Capital was much needed in England, and still more in Scotland, for developing the resources of the country and for starting new enterprises; freedom for the formation and investment of capital seemed to the thoughtful city men of the seventeenth century, who were mostly in sympathy with Puritanism, the best remedy for the existing social evils. They were eager to get rid of the restrictions imposed by the Pope's laws, which it was possible to bring up in ecclesiastical courts as well as to be free from the efforts of the King's Council to bring home to the employing and mercantile classes their duty to the community. The agitation against the interference of the bishops in civil affairs and the triumph of Puritanism swept away all traces of any restrictions or guidance in the employment of money. In so far as a stricter ecclesiastical discipline was aimed at or introduced, it had regard to recreation and to immorality of other kinds, but was at no pains to interfere to check the action of the capitalist or to protect the labourer. From the time when the rise of Puritanism paralysed the action of the Church (that is, the State Church), and prevented her from maintaining the influence she had habitually exerted, it has been plausible to say that Christian teaching appeared to be brought to bear on the side of the rich and against the poor. The Puritans were probably right as to the most serious evils of the day, and the economic means of overcoming them; they may well have felt that religious duty impelled them to the line they took." This book is otherwise also characteristic; it is an expression on the part of the clergy of their views on a Christian ethic of economics, and on its side it develops a modern adaptation of early Christian ideas to the modern capitalistic form of life which is to be accepted as the natural course of affairs. With reference to Bremen, which is overwhelmingly Calvinistic, a conversation between a leading tradesman of Bremen and a tradesman of Vienna about the difference in the way of living of the luxurious Viennese tradespeople and of the austere and frugal tradespeople of Bremen, which I found in the *Sonntagsblatt* of the *Bremer Nachrichten, Nr. 30 and 31 of 1910* ("*Von alter Bremer Art*"): " 'Do you know, Musje R. (the Viennese), why we don't act like that? . . . Because we are free citizens of the Empire.'—'But still', says the other, 'you are also important tradespeople!'—'And just on that account', the man from Bremen continues, 'we need a lot of money, and also we have to save. But in order that you may understand me, I must explain to you what a large tradesman in an free imperial city really means. He is a man who always works more in order to earn more, and who always earns more in order to work more, because in this way he does not use up his money, but gives it away in order to employ more hands and to be able to feed more hungry people. The Viennese merchant can buy estates and use up a good deal of his property. I don't think the worse of him for it. If there is distress in the land his Emperor puts his hand into his pocket. But here, if there is distress, the free State turns to its free citizens for help. The rich citizen is ready and willing to help and to give. Also the citizen who is in difficulties naturally flies for help to the citizen who is in better circumstances. If one of the citizens has earned a great deal he has many claims to satisfy, and he does this gladly both as a fellow-citizen and as a Christian. And now I would like to give you the prescription for the medicine with which I want to die! (The previous remarks were the prescription for life). It is in Matt. xxiv. 12, 13, "He who abides in righteousness and love unto the end will be saved".' " The man from Bremen says that the reason for his way of life is the republican character of the city of Bremen, but the religious turn of the conversation shows that what is here in question is the Calvinistic ethic, as, indeed, the whole article shows that the author is strictly religious.—In the passages which have here been quoted there emerges at many points the connection between this development and the position of the Calvinists as a minority and their exclusion from official life, as also is emphasized by *Weber: Antikritisches, p. 188.* In the light of other passages, however, this is not decisive.—An important point remains in the capitalistic development of Calvinism in the direction of the middle classes and the bourgeoisie. To this is due in England the contrast between the "squirearchy and the bourgeois middle classes, who in the Cobden movement were characteristically supported by Dissent" (conclusion, *p. 558*); bourgeois character, see conclusion *p. 573:* "It is now, however, one of the achievements of Ascetic Protestantism that it worked against these tendencies: the 'idolizing of the creature', the desire to secure the *splendor familiae* through the immobilization of property in order to bring in a large income, the aristocratic joy in 'high life', the voluptuous wallowing in aesthetic enjoyment and 'selfish indulgence' as well as the desire for insolent ostentation." This bourgeois development is, in my opinion, one of the main problems of our subject, and its causes are still most obscure; cf. the remark by *Weber: Antikritisches, p. 188:* "The interesting phenomenon which can be observed in the relation between the classes and the religious life—almost in all countries—is the gradual transformation of the originally (often even including the Baptist movement) vertical cleavage in the social system (that is, group-formation conditioned by religion) into a horizontal cleavage (that is, a situation in which religious characteristics belong to certain classes in Society); this is where the materialistic 'interpretation' of history steps in." This interpretation has, however, not yet been authenticated. In the course of the whole of this book I have continually been faced with this problem; I have, however, only been able to offer some meagre suggestions in explanation, especially on this point; sometimes it seems to me as though the minority position and exclusion from official life were the cause, sometimes as though it were due to the inward logic of the Calvinistic ethic, and often it seems as if both causes combined were the reason. In any case, at the beginning the social classification played a much smaller part, and humanistic secular culture and aristocratic customs predominated. There is a great contrast between the Calvinism described by *Marcks* in his *Coligny* and that which is described by *Dowden* and *Göbel*. Also it remains to be proved how far this shifting of emphasis was a general phenomenon.

[388] (p. 644.) No one has ever asserted that Capitalism is the direct product of Calvinism. We can, however, say that both possessed a certain affinity for each other, that Calvinistic ethic of the "calling" and of work, which declares that the earning of money with certain precautions is allowable, was able to give it an intellectual and ethical backbone, and that, therefore, thus organized and inwardly supported it vigorously developed, even though within the limits of anti-mammon. "There is no doubt that where an economic system and a 'spirit' with which it has a certain affinity meet, there ensues a development along uniform lines which is also inwardly unbroken (that is, where the spirit and the economic system agree, which is not always the case), of the kind which I had begun to analyse (that is, like the Calvinistic development)." The conjunction of these two elements itself is an historic accident, as I have said already in describing the similarly comparatively close affinity between the mediaeval system and the Catholic ethic. But out of such accidents (*Weber: Schlusswort, XXXI, p. 580*): "Humanity which through the meeting of religious and economic elements was created"; *p. 583:* "Protestant asceticism created for it (bourgeois capitalism) a positive ethic, a soul which needed that restless activity in order that 'spirit' and 'form' might be one"; *p. 588:* A current of 1) psychic elements which arose from a very specific moral and religious source, 2) combined with capitalistic possibilities of development from which the great historical developments proceed. The Christian ethic only attained a great actual importance for world-history when it was supported by an "accident" of this kind. In itself alone, when it did not receive this support, it simply remained

in the realm of theory. The combination of these elements then reacted, however, upon the religious and ethical spirit, as I prove in both instances. In the history of the Christian ethic there have only been two "accidents" of this kind, the mediaeval system and the Calvinistic system, whose expansion through the bourgeois sect will be demonstrated in the next section. There are other certainly often finer and deeper conceptions of the Christian Ethos to whom an historic influence of this kind was denied, because they were not favoured by such an "accident" or in their very nature were unable to find such support. If I speak here of "accident", this is naturally meant logically, i.e. that here there is no immanent development, not that these things have happened *sine Deo*.

389a (p. 645.) The rise and the nature of the "Capitalist system" is, as is well known, the main problem of economic and theoretical research at the present day. Analyses of the system are given by *Weber: Prot. Ethik, XX, pp. 11–35; Sombart: Die Juden und das Wirtschaftsleben, 1911, pp. 186–198;* and in his well-known earlier works, *Deutsches Wirtschaftsleben des 19. Jahrh.*, and, above all, *Der Kapitalismus;* see also the article *K.* by *Traub*, in *RGG*. An account of the "system" in England is given by *Held: Zur sozialen Geschichte Englands*, in which there are excellent observations on social history in general. *Held* lays more emphasis upon the external technical and other reasons for the growth of the system. He only deals with the spiritual and ethical foundations in the analysis of the theories of students of politics and political economy; but he does not follow the subject into the real popular ethos. *Weber*, however, has dealt with this question in studying the problem of the rise and nature of the "Spirit of Capitalism", *Sombart* in studying the problem as a question of the "economic spirit" (*Wirtschaftsgesinnung*), and both have explored the depths of the popular religious ethos. For the difference between the "Spirit of Capitalism" and "the Capitalistic system", which do not need to coincide, and often do not coincide, see *Weber: Antikritisches, pp. 201–202*. The domination of Capitalism over the minds of men does not take place until by "accident" both these elements meet. *Rachfahl* cannot understand this distinction, and he only makes fun of it. Further, I wish to emphasize that *Weber* and *Sombart* are mainly concerned with the attempt to lay bare the nature of Capitalism, and the religious and ethical elements are only of secondary importance. My aim, on the other hand, is to make clear the significance of Capitalism in the development of Calvinism. Thus behind our researches the points of view are very different.

390 (p. 645.) This is very clearly analysed by *Weber: Schlusswort, XXXI, 582 ff.:* "Of course at all periods praise and commendation for conscientious work have always been given to the laity (although only in a limited way in primitive Christianity, more among the Cynics).

"Luther's expressions of opinion in this direction are well known. Outside Protestantism, of course, there have been those who have taught the blessing that rests on secular work. But of what use is this if, as in Lutheranism, there are no rewards (in this case spiritual) for this way of life which will ensure that these theories will be put into practice? Or if, as in Catholicism, far greater rewards are offered for quite a different kind of behaviour, and further, when in the form of the confessional a means is given which over and over again makes it possible for the individual to unburden his mind of all kinds of errors which he has committed against the postulates of the Church? Whereas, on the other hand, Calvinism, in its development after the latter part of the sixteenth century, and similarly the Baptist movement in the idea of the necessity of ascetic proof, in life in general, and specially also in the life in one's 'calling', as the subjective guarantee of the *certitudo salutis*—as one of the most important signs of one's own certainty of election—created a very specific spiritual reward, which in its effectiveness within this sphere cannot easily be excelled for the ascetic way of life which it required."

[392] (p. 647.) This is one of the most important results of *Max Weber's* study. Only later on shall we be able to see its full significance, when, after the analysis of the Protestant sects, we come to the collective conception of Ascetic Protestantism. I maintain that these conclusions are right, although they have been criticized by *Rachfahl*; *Rachfahl*, indeed, admits the fact, but he allows much less significance to be attributed to its significance for the development of economic history, and he is determined not to grant that it arises definitely from the spirit of Calvinism. In the first place he has, indeed, alluded to the exceptions which *Weber* has made, which of course allow for the existence of a number of other motives which have contributed to the rise of modern Capitalism; *Weber*, indeed, names some quite different groups as supporters of this development, but *R.* has not taken them into account. In the second place, his knowledge of the doctrine of Calvin and of primitive conditions in Geneva is only indirect, and gained from the works of *Kampschulte*, *Elster*, and *Lang*, and, therefore, he misinterprets both in the political and in the economic sphere the consequences of the most distinctive religious thought of Geneva. He considers Calvin a traditionalist in the Lutheran sense; the only difference is that he thinks that Calvin has a broader view on the subject of interest, and that otherwise he emphasizes honesty and seriousness in work, that is, the various ethical elements in economic life. Otherwise, like *Kampschulte*, he regards Calvinism as an exaltation of religious feeling which is contrary to Nature, can only last a short time, and is unable to do anything great in the secular sphere. *Rachfahl* considers that modern progress is due to the Rationalists, and to Christians of the school of Erasmus who practise toleration, and also to the comparative emancipation of the Protestant State from religious considerations. The whole constitutes a defence of toleration in the wrong place. But toleration by itself does not mean anything in economic development; it all depends upon the economic nature of that which is allowed to be tolerated. This is very well illustrated by *Bastide, p. 214*, where he is dealing with toleration in England: "The example of Holland had struck the English; Sir William Temple . . . attributed the prosperity of this country to religious liberty and to the presence of numerous refugees. Finally, the arrival of the Huguenots (after the revocation of the Edict of Nantes), who were fleeing from persecution, and who made a great impression by their industrious habits and the quality of their work, confirmed the idea that the religious exile is a great help to public wealth. Sir W. Petty said that 'commerce is practised most vigorously in all states and under all governments by the heterodox section of the nation, and by those who profess opinions different from those which are officially received'. We can remember what importance Shaftesbury gave to the economic argument in his Memorandum on toleration. This argument often reappears. Charles Wolseley . . . in a little treatise upon liberty of conscience, mentions the departure for Holland of the dissenting weavers of Norwich. An anonymous author . . . without insisting . . . on the theological side of the question . . . replied to Dr. Dove 'that religious liberty was the school of noble and generous souls'. The artisans of Norwich who have emigrated are the best citizens: 'Are not the men who have religious principles sensible and serious men who do good to a nation? Are they not generally in all forms of trade and in other

callings the most industrious and the most prosperous?' " It is clear that here the allusion is not to toleration in itself, but to the acceptance or retention of a certain class of citizens; these citizens are precisely the Calvinists with their well-known commercial qualities. It is also clear, as these authors observe, that the experience of religious oppression and exclusion fosters the growth of those business qualities, and, finally, that these qualities are connected with moral and religious principles. We might produce similar arguments in favour of the Baptist and Pietist sects, who also, through similar experiences, develop similar qualities upon a similar foundation of religion and ethics. It is not Calvinism itself which is here being considered, but Calvinism as it has developed in the school of oppression and as a minority. This development, however, is still connected with the fundamental Calvinistic ethic in general, and with its economic ethic in particular. There have also been Catholic minorities in England, but we never hear anything of this kind about them. Cf. also *Weber* in *Antikritisches, Schlusswort, XXXI, pp. 565–569*, and *Antikritisches, XXX, 182–188.*—This toleration has also been to the advantage of the Jews. *Sombart* has made a study of their significance similar to that made by *Weber* on *Calvinism* and the sects. In my opinion, however, *Sombart* has overestimated and misinterpreted the rôle of the Jews. He is certainly wrong in his comparison between Puritanism and Judaism, based on the argument that the Calvinists lay so much emphasis upon the Old Testament. For the Calvinistic economic spirit is quite different from that of Judaism, and their connection with the Old Testament is very complicated; see above, *pp. 638–640*. Many resemblances, however, have been noted.

[393] (p. 650.) Calvin is an opponent of Baptist communism, against which he strives repeatedly, precisely for social reasons; for when all had sold their goods the rich would have to beg, and no one would have a house in which to dwell, or in which the poor could be sheltered (*R., XXXV, p. 488*). Otherwise his way of thinking is definitely social on a religious basis; see, for instance, the summary of Christian ethics (*Inst. III, pp. 7–10*), which forms a supplement to the explanation of the Decalogue (*II, 8*), and deepens it with the Christian point of view: "Nostri non sumus: Inde consequitur, ut ne quaeramus, quae nostra sunt, sed quae ex Domini sunt voluntate et faciunt ad gloriam ejus promovendam. . . . Quum enim nos privatam nostri rationem omittere jubet scriptura, non modo habendi cupiditatem, potentiae affectionem, hominum gratiam ex animis nostris eradit, sed ambitionem quoque et omnem gloriae humanae appetitum aliasque secretiores pestes eradicat" (*III, 7, 2*). "Perspicimus abnegationem nostri partim quidem in homines respicere partim in Deum" (*III, 7, 3*). Then follows the development of the first idea: "Jam in quaerenda proximi utilitate officium praestare, quantum habet difficultatis! . . . At Scriptura, ut eo nos manuducat, praemonet quidquid a Domino gratiarum obtinemus, esse nobis hac lege concreditum, ut in commune ecclesiae (that is, the whole Christian society) bonum conferatur ideoque legitimam gratiarum omnium usum esse liberalem ac benignam cum aliis communicationem." All possessions are "deposita Dei ea lege fidei nostrae commissa, ut in proximorum bonum dispensentur". There then follows the well-known Pauline parable of the organism: "Nullum membrum suam facultatem sibi habet nec in privatum usum applicat, sed ad socia membra transfundit. . . . Sic pius vir, quidquid potest, fratribus debet posse: sibi non aliter privatim consulendo, quam ut ad communem ecclesiae aedificationem intentus sit animus. Haec itaque . . . nobis sit methodus: quidquid in nos Deus contulit, quo proximum queamus adjuvare, ejus nos esse oeconomos, qui ad reddendam dispensationis rationem

adstringimur. Eam demum pòrro rectam esse dispensationem, quae ad dilectionis exigatur regulam. Ita fiet, ut non modo alieni commodi studium cum popriae utilitatis cura semper conjungamus, sed hanc illi subjiciamus" (*III, 7, 5*). At the same time we have to remember "non hominum malitiam reputandam esse, sed inspiciendam in illis Dei imaginem: quae inductis et obliteratis eorum delictis ad eos amandos, amplexandosque sua pulcritudine ac dignitate nos alliciat" (*III, 7, 6*). "Ita secum quisque cogitabit, se, quantus quantus est, proximis debitorem rei esse, nec alium exercendae ergo ipsos beneficentiae statuendum esse finem, nisi quum facultates deficiunt: quae quam late extenduntur, ad caritatis regulam limitari debet" (*III, 7, 7*). This is an absolute programme of Christian Socialism.—This point of view also determines Calvin's insistence on the restriction of interest, his fight against usury, the civil legislation about trade and consumption, and, above all, the establishment of the Church system of poor relief and social welfare. The *Compagnie*, under Beza, worked in the same direction, keeping their hand on the control of public life; *Choisy* gives many illustrations of this point. On the question of the care of the poor and the enormous sums which were spent on this, see *Uhlhorn: Liebestätigkeit, III, 141–169* and *Choisy* in general.—Where Church and State were not united the Christian social development was simply an intensive affair of the congregation itself, as in the refugee community in London organized by John à Lasko, and in the communities organized after the same pattern in the Netherlands and on the Lower Rhine; on this point see *Simons: Eine altkölnische Seelsorgegemeinde, 1894, Aelteste evangelische Gemeindearmenpflege vom Niederrhein, 1895, Niederrheinisches Synodal- und Gemeindeleben unter dem Kreuz, 1897;* here *p. 20:* "Thus the Synod, from the modern point of view, is not very far removed from Christian Socialism." For the Elizabethan social legislation, and its connection with Puritan ideas, see the work by *Cunningham*, which has already been mentioned, and *Held, 16–38.*—On these restrictions and the fact that the Calvinistic ethic also retained the *pretium justum*, see *Weber: Antikritisches, XXX, 188, 194, 201 ff.;* also *Laspeyres: Geschichte der Volkswirtschaftlichen Anschauungen der Niederländer, 1863, pp. 256–270:* theological views on Capitalism which, it is true, admit the taking of interest, but which would like to see it restricted, with consideration for the poor; on the other hand, attention is drawn also to the strongly theological elements in the economic theories even of non-theological thinkers (*p. 31*). Characteristically Calvinistic is the formula for the undertakings in Brazil (*p. 82*): "De hooghste Wet, rakende Brasil, behoovt te wesen de Eere Gods ende de Welstand der Participanten."

394 (p. 650.) There are some characteristic remarks in a letter of Calvin to Bullinger (*Briefe, I, 342*): "We must also take this city into account, and indeed we must give it a very prominent position in our thoughts. If I were thinking only of my own life or of my own circumstances, I could go somewhere else at once. But when I consider how important this corner of the world is for the extension of the Kingdom of Christ, I am sure I am right to do all I can to protect it." Calvin then goes on to advise a treaty with France, which he thinks is allowable, since Abraham made a covenant with the heathen Abimelech, and Isaac and David likewise made covenants with the heathen for the purpose of the Kingdom of God.

397 (p. 651.) Calvin's teaching on war, *Inst. IV, 20, 11, and 12;* the vigorous passage which defends war only appears in the later editions. The cause of Christ is only to be served through confession of faith, organization, breaking with the Catholic Church, suffering and endurance and trust in God. Human power is to be unconditionally renounced; if it is necessary, God will work a

miracle to save His Church. Numerous passages in the *Letters* take this point of view. Everywhere Calvin advised against taking up arms, and often on occasions which were either very favourable to the Calvinists, or times of great necessity.

[398] (p. 651.) This change of view comes out in several passages in Calvin's *Letters, I, 341*; in connection with the plan for a treaty with France, which might lead to France going to war with Charles V; in spite of all scruples he thinks that "we might ascribe it more to a blameworthy sense of security than to genuine trust in God, if we were to ignore means of assistance which, even though not desirable, are still permitted"! *II, 59:* Calvin blames the Germans, who in 1555, by their laziness, threw away their chances of being protected by God, and therefore had so little success in war. *II, 327:* writing to Bullinger: "Believe me, I can assure you certainly that there is no danger of disturbance on our side unless the King of Navarre is openly attacked. In his defence, certainly, I hope that many would rise and fight." *II, 345:* he deplores the rising of the Savoy Protestants against their lord. *III, 442:* he counsels the Calvinistic commandant of Lyons, in a very conditional way, to lay down his arms: "Further, if both wish to come to terms with you there would still have to be a legal basis for this, for without their help you cannot . . . carry the matter through. For something which has been begun without being called to it, and justified in it, can never work out well. I do not say that perhaps a good reason could not be found, but I do not know one, and on that account I would not venture to advise war to begin without being better informed." Here also Calvin's thought is not uniform, since if a legitimate reason can be produced both civil war and a war of religion are permitted. This also is the interpretation given by *Marcks* in his book on *Coligny, pp. 358, 361, 380,* especially *408;* finally, it comes to this, that a legal reason has to be found to justify a war; this is where sophistry begins.

[399] (p. 651.) *De jure magistratuum, 280.* If the Estates and the *magistratus inferiores* are not strong enough to control the tyrant, then it becomes permissible to call in help from outside: "Licebit etiam saniori parti oppressae auxilia aliunde conquirere, praesertim apud Regni confoederatos et amicos." He gives examples from the history of Israel, and of the Romans, and also recalls what was done by the Italian patricians through Charles the Great against the Lombards. In itself, however, the Kingdom of Christ has nothing to do with fighting: "Cum religio ad conscientias pertineat, quibus nullo modo vis inferri potest, non videtur illa ullis armis stabilienda et defendenda, quam ideo praedicatione verbi Dei, precibus ac patientia hactenus potius propagatam conspicimus. Extant praeterea loci permulti in scripturis, quibus ostenditur, quanta sit inter regna hujus mundi et regnum Christi spirituale differentia" (*p. 294*). To that are added the examples of the Prophets, of Christ, and of the Apostles. Only in those days there were no Christian lower magistrates. They confronted purely pagan governments, from whom they could not require any help for the cause of Christ, and to which they had to submit and suffer. Since now, however, there is a Christian State, with lower magistrates who have a duty laid upon them by God, the whole matter is quite different. "At ego contra praecipuum optimi piique Magistratus munus esse dico, ut quidquid mediorum autoritatis et potentiae illi a Deo concessum est, huc totum omnino conferat, ut inter sibi subditos Deus ipse vere agnoscatur agnitusque tanquam summus regum omnium rex colatur et adoretur." Thus the authorities must establish the true religion, even by force of arms if necessary among their own subjects first, then, however, also among others. Certainly all in a legitimate

way. The introduction of the true religion into a country can only take place with pure Divine means. "Hoc enim proprie Spiritus sancti opus est instrumentis spiritualibus utentis." Thus the knowledge of the true religion is to be spread through preaching, and only those who resist in an obstinate way are finally to be compelled to accept it! Where, however, the pure religion is already established by law, there the authorities are under the obligation under certain circumstances to assist the realization of this legal position, also by force of arms. Christ and the apostles were private individuals, and had to remain within the limits of their "calling", avoiding the use of arms. But the magistrates of a Christian State are, if there is no help for it, justified and obliged to resort to arms. They are also justified in calling on the aid of foreign nations; this statement is supported with many examples. This problem is treated similarly by the *Monarchomachi, Elkan, pp. 116 and 168 ff., Cardauns, pp. 5, 104,* where the passage from the *Vindiciae* is quoted: "'Universam (Ecclesiam) singulis, singulas ejus partes universis commisit Deus; itaque si unam ejus partem princeps religionis illius curet, alteram vero oppressam, si opera ferre possit deserat et negligat, Ecclesiam deseruisse censetur.' It is one of the established legal principles of the period that a prince of another nation may intervene to save a people oppressed by a tyrannical government."

400 (p. 652.) This pacificism is emphasized by *Hartmann: Engl. Frömmigkeit, p. 26. H. Oncken* is instructive, *Amerika und die grossen Mächte* (*Studien und Versuche zur neueren Geschichte,* dedicated to *Max Lenz, 1910*), *pp. 427 ff.:* "One of the peculiar results of the Colonial situation of this State was that from the very beginning it was comparatively independent of foreign politics and its dangers. And, at least among the Puritan and Baptist elements, it was taken for granted that war, the sorrowful privilege of monarchies and oligarchies, was to be renounced for religious and democratic reasons. . . . The predominance of religious feeling, which affected the development of this State behind the scenes in a great variety of ways, required insistently that the people of God should be sufficient unto themselves, and carry on their affairs without the use of arms; strict abstention from foreign policy also produced that fundamental rationalistic utilitarian element in the American nature which arose from sources affected by Natural Law." But, *p. 469:* "The first century of American history already shows that even a commonwealth which, from the days of the Pilgrim Fathers, was controlled by opposite influences, in the long run has to obey those laws, which, as inherent necessities, belong to the essence of the State and of dominion." More on this subject in *Oncken: Amerikanischer Imperialismus und europäischer Pacifismus, Preuss. Jahrbb., 1911.* Likewise, only with a different point of view and outlook for the future, *Masaryk* in a splendid article on *Roosevelt* from *März, 1910, Nos. 12 and 13.*

401 (p. 653.) Cf. *Gass* and *Luthardt; Alex. Schweizer: Die Entwickelung des Moralsystems in der reformierten Kirche, Theol. Studd. und Kritt., 1850.* In all these works the development of ethics from the point of view of its content is very largely ignored in favour of questions of the relation between philosophical and theological ethics, of freedom and the miracle of grace, of justification and of the moral law, statements of the problem which unfortunately usually almost exclusively dominate the theological treatment of ethics. There is more on the content of ethics in the *History of Ethics within Organized Christianity,* by *Thomas Hall, New York, 1910.*

402 (p. 654.) On this point see *Rieker: Reformierte Kirchenverfassung; Sohm: Kirchenrecht, pp. 642–657; von Hofmann: Kirchenverfassungrecht der niederländischen Reformierten; Choisy: La Théocratie* and *L'état chrétien;* also his inaugural lecture,

L'état chrétien calviniste au 16ème siècle, 1909. Here there is a pertinent emphasis upon the meaning of the Communion (*p. 11*): "The Communion is, in fact, in the Christian State, an act of obligation, a social and civic act. By participation in the Holy Communion the citizen and the inhabitant of Geneva professes his faith in the only true God and manifests his intention to submit to His Law. It is the homage rendered by the Christian to the Sovereign Legislator and Protector of the city, and to Jesus Christ His Son, the Redeemer, the Supreme Head of the Church. This is why one cannot admit to the Holy Table those who openly violate the Law of God and shamefully outrage His truth. This is why, on the other hand, no one can be permitted to abstain from Communion without having been officially or publicly excluded from participation in the Holy Communion. However, even although it is a civic act, and thus obligatory, the Communion ought to be an act of personal piety, etc." Sociologically, the Communion exercises the same function as the Sacrament of Penance in Catholicism, hence both attain a power of organization which does not characterize Lutheranism.

[403] (p. 655.) On this point I only venture to express my opinion with some reserve, since there are no works dealing with this theory of Society. The absence of the doctrine of the Three Estates is emphasized by *Rieker, p. 184*, organization according to possessions in the laws on luxury in *Elster, pp. 190–192*, the continuance of the categories of "callings" and guilds in *Choisy, p. 118, note 3*, and *Gierke: Althusius*², *24*. Here the "callings" are all treated as *consociationes collegarum, p. 22*, at the same time it is pointed out that they are "entirely free associations, which can be formed and severed at will". On equality in the sight of God, see *Choisy: L'état chrétien, pp. 484–490*. Here also belongs the careful avoidance by the ministers of all *Amtswürde* (dignity of the ministry), which does not allow the development of a conception similar to that of the Lutheran conception of the ministry. Concerning the peasantry, its neglect is deplored; see *Althusius, p. 25*. On the democratic consequence of religious equality, see *Rieker, p. 122*.

[404] (p. 655.) Cf. *Briefe, I, 256*, on the subject of the necessity for a mutual attraction to the knowledge of each other, as the presupposition of marriage, its relation to the aim of the holy community (*I, 351 and 369*); on the equal position of male and female in Christ, and the duties of women compared with those of the greatest heroes (*II, 193*) (to the imprisoned women in Paris); equality of husband and wife (*II, 268 and 451*); always, however, the husband is the head of the wife (*II, 391*); for the attitude of the State legislation and of the Board of Discipline in the control of the sex-life, see numerous examples in *Choisy: L'état chrétien*, especially *p. 401*; for the significance of marriage for Society (*p. 487*); on the whole subject, *Elster, pp. 194 ff.*, and the fine description by *von Schulze-Gävernitz: Britischer Imperialismus, pp. 47–49:* "Puritanism prepared the way for a view of sex-relationships which places the responsibility contained in procreation in the foreground, and makes possible an ethical construction of sex-relationships from the standpoint of the child."—A monograph on this subject would be of great assistance.

[405] (p. 659.) *Göbel* has rightly recognized this connection with the problem of numbers of the masses and of the Christian civilization of the people, and in both directions, i.e. the Free Church movement and Pietism, he has emphasized its significance; he has also seen clearly the resemblance to the Baptist movement. The problem began with the exiled communities in foreign lands, the Church under à Lasko in London, the Lutheran Calvinistic community in Frankfort, and the Dutch groups of exiles on the Lower Rhine (*Göbel, I, 326*).

Here the communities became thoroughly democratic (*I, 340 ff.*), they had to choose their own officials, and they had no connection with the civil authority. Of decisive importance was the community in London under John à Lasko. *Göbel* calls it "a wholesome reconciliation between the Lutherans and their lack of a constitution and the Separatist Baptists, and thus he made possible upon German soil the founding of a Reformed Church which holds a central position between both" (*p. 326*). "Under its freely elected preachers and elders it constituted itself independently of the bishop and the parish clergy, quite freely, according to its own principles; this, however, produced within it a clearly marked independent partially Separatist character, which distinguished it from the rest of the secular and civic life around; when, therefore, this community migrated, and in an expanded form settled in Emden, Wesel, Frankfort, and Strassburg, and when it spread still farther in the region round the Main, and especially in the Rhineland, it was, of course, natural that the Calvinistic Church which it established in those places naturally bore the same kind of ecclesiastical character, and that in its flourishing Christian life it bore the stamp of decision and bluntness, of world-renunciation and of hostility to the world" (*336*). The same is true of the older communities in the Netherlands before they regained the character of a State Church, which, moreover, was always only comparative, as *von Hoffmann* shows; it is also true of the English Puritans, as soon as they were forced into opposition after 1567 by the harsh Elizabethan legislation, see *Kattenbusch Art. Puritanismus in PRE³:* they formed "private associations which were usually called 'prophesyings'. The name was based upon 1 Cor. xiv. 13. They were societies for mutual edification and for the furtherance of a Christian life, and they originated in the community led by John à Lasko"; at the same time the tendency towards Presbyterianism was developed: "The secular authority has no power over the Church"; they desire "the complete autonomy of the Church", which for the time being was only possible in the form of separation.—Cf. further the description of the important resolution of the Synod of Emden, 1571, in *Göbel, I, 418:* "Thus in Emden there was established a Church-order which was set up not for a whole country, nor for a whole town, nor for a whole people, but only for those who joined it of their own free-will, and who submitted themselves to its order and Church discipline, and therefore also could leave it again at any moment." This applied first of all to the communities in the Netherlands. The connection between this new Church principle and the opposition of the State authorities on the one hand, and with the difficulties of a mass and popular Christianity on the other, is developed (*I, 423*). On the analogy of this Church-order and sect-type, see *I, 443:* "In general the whole (Lower Rhine) Church . . . would have gradually fallen into the danger of remaining a sect, or of becoming one again; if, on the one hand, they had not remained in connection with the at least outwardly strong and flourishing National Church of the Netherlands, and if they had not been preserved from such shrinkage by the development of their theology which took place in a splendid way at the Universities of Leyden (from 1575) and Franeker (from 1585), and, on the other hand, the union of synods, and, after 1609, their unexpected liberty and extraordinary expansion. All these things laid upon this Church the task of becoming, at least to some extent, a national or a territorial Church, and thus of leavening the whole country and the whole people with its own spirit. In spite of that, however, our Calvinistic Church could never entirely deny its Separatist origin, and there remained, therefore, within it the opposition between the world and Christianity, between the worldling and the Christian, between human statements and the Word of God, between the Papacy and the Gospel, so that as Church discipline slackened and the Church and Christian life became more secular, attempts were ever made anew, both from outside and from inside the Church, to restore the old severity and keenness, whether through the gathering together of individual awakened souls within the congregation, or through the separation of the latter from the great secularized Church, and the formation of special groups of their own." This explains even at the present time the character of Church life in the Wuppertal and the Pietism of Elberfeld and Barmen. This applies, however, also *mutatis mutandis* to all territories in which Calvinism is predominant, owing to the idea of the holy community and of ecclesiastical autonomy over against the State.

406 (p. 660.) For the development of the "subsidiary Calvinistic conception of the Church", cf. *Rieker, pp. 190–205; Kuyper, 52–60, 71–100,* sees in this the distinctive fundamental tendency of Calvinism which was not quite plain to its early leaders; the excellent book by *Rothenbücher: Die Trennung von Staat und Kirche, 1908,* describes the rise and the nature of the principle; the enthusiastic religious glorification of the principle as that of modern religion and the Church in general in *A. Vinet: Essai sur la manifestation des convictions religieuses, et sur la séparation de l'église de l'état, 1842* (translated into German by *Spengler, 1845*), and also *La liberté des Cultes*[2], *1852.* Cf. also *Troeltsch: Trennung von Staat und Kirche, der Staatliche Religionsunterricht und die theologischen Fakultäten, 1907;* to my joy *Rothenbücher* agrees essentially with the account I have given here of the Baptist movement and its origin. For the "Natural-Law" character of the Calvinistic Church conception, see *Sohm: Kirchenrecht, I, 655 ff., 697 ff.*

407 (p. 661.) It is extremely important to emphasize the fact that in early Calvinism the conception of Truth was such that it made it impossible for it to renounce dependence on the *brachium saeculare,* or to allow different forms of Church life to exist alongside of each other; cf. *Troeltsch: Trennung, etc.* When the Netherlanders wanted to organize their Church life upon lines which made room for the existence of various churches, the Genevese characterized this as a despicable principle of toleration like that advocated by *Castellio: Rachfahl, II, 727–731.* The churches of the Lower Rhine, which were practically Free Churches, still retained explicitly the idea of a State Church as the normal thing; see *Simons: Freikirche, Volkskirche, Landeskirche, 1895, p. 12.* When Calvinists found themselves under Catholic rule, and were forced to organize on Free Church lines, they always did it as a temporary arrangement, expecting the victory of the Truth, and maintaining that it is the duty of a ruler to submit to the Truth (*Rachfahl, II, p. 881; Rothenbücher, p. 20*). Where the hope of victory had been given up, and the Calvinistic Church life had to be organized alongside of other confessions, this still did not mean a general spirit of ecclesiastical liberty, it simply meant that toleration was restricted to Catholicism, Lutheranism, and Calvinism; it is the toleration of minorities when there is no help for it, but it is not the principle of liberty of worship and of conscience; see *Rachfahl, II, p. 728,* and *Frank Puaux: Les précurseurs français de la tolérance au 17ième siècle, Paris, 1881; Rothenbücher, p. 63.* The Pilgrim Fathers returned to a strict theocracy, in which the Baptists were punished with death because they represented the idea of toleration (*Rothenbücher, 120–123*).—Nor is it possible to say that Calvinism was organized on voluntaryist lines. *Rieker* has asserted this against *Sohm,* who claims that there is a relationship between Calvinism and the Law of Nature, and he might have emphasized it still more strongly (see *p. 133*). Independency is expressly rejected (see *p. 82*), and *Simons: Niederrheinisches Synodal- und Gemeindeleben, 1897, p. 15.* The idea of a contract, held so

strongly by Calvinism, applies to the State and the relation to the State, but not to the rise of the Church itself, as *Rieker* himself makes plain (*p. 73*). In the refugee churches of John à Lasko, which lived under a government with a different religious outlook, and then in the Netherlands, *H. von Hoffmann* (*Das Kirchenverfassungsrecht der niederländischen Reformierten, 1902*) makes it plain that the Church membership, both of those who had previously belonged to other forms of religion and of those who were already baptized, was only gained "through a covenant (contract)"; thus for the first time the Church here appears as a corporation, in the sense in which the word is used in modern law (*p. 86*). Only the expression is expanded in modern legal language, and in this case it is not quite applicable since the correlated idea of a "right to leave the Church (*Austrittsrecht*)" does not exist (*p. 83*). All that it comes to really is this, that it provides a way by which individuals could take a personal share in an institution which existed by Divine appointment; the Church Council, however, was always regarded as the primary method for exercising the royal sovereignty of Christ; thus, wherever there is such a centre, it is the duty of individuals to join this institution, which is the one and only body in which Truth and Redemption reside (see *pp. 87, 88, 75, and 96*)! Freedom to form churches on a voluntary basis is not a Calvinistic idea, but it comes from the Congregationalists and the Baptists; see *Rothenbücher, p. 30*. Calvinism, therefore, has always used it only for the outward constitutional form, it has never formed part of its nature; see *Rieker, 130–174*.—The "Natural-Law" conception of the Church is, moreover, an intellectual method, which has grown out of the juridical way of thinking; it has been used by all kinds of churches, and can easily be used in support of the idea of an institutional Church. In my opinion it has nothing whatever to do with the Calvinistic idea of the Church; see *Rothenbücher, 68–72*.—On the Scottish Covenants (with to some extent the text of the same), see *Champlin Burrage: The Church Covenant Idea, Its Origin and Development, Philadelphia, 1904*.—That in the Free Church movement there is at bottom a new conception of Truth which differs from that of early Calvinism is shown characteristically by *Vinet: Darlegungen, p. 276:* "If the National Church system were to make an end of all sects, or were to make it impossible for them to arise, this would not be a cause for triumph, but for reproach. . . . There is no life where there are no sects; uniformity is a sign of death." Cf. also *p. 278* and *p. 206*. "It has been said that seeking for the Truth is more important than the Truth itself; this might also be applied to religion in general, if, as we believe, it is right to say the first of all truths is that we ought to wish and seek for the Truth. The Truth is only half-realized if it is not sought. Here seeking is as important as possession. . . . This, we admit, is the heart of our theory" (*p. 293*). The real State Church system only arose, according to *Vinet*, out of the Reformation, and he considers that it is something which ought never to have been born (*p. 273*). Historically *Vinet* appeals chiefly to America (*p. 356*); this also illustrates the connection between the Free Church principle and democracy (*p. 366*). This democracy, however, only means the right of the people to self-determination; it does not mean a democratic Church constitution, and there is no equalitarian removal of that patriarchalism in Society or in the sociological fundamental theory (*p. 377*). *Vinet* considers this genuine Calvinism, but in reality it is spiritual idealism with its subjective tendencies.

408 (p. 662.) On the whole subject, see the excellent article in *PRE*[3] by *Loofs* entitled *Kongregationalismus*. The great work by *Dexter: Congregationalism of the Last Three Hundred Years, New York, 1880*, is out of print, and I was unable

to obtain it. Further, see the highly interesting book by *Burrage: The Church Covenant Idea*, which gives numerous examples of these Covenants in full, follows their development, and treats in detail their resemblance to and connection with the Baptist movement; see *p. 46:* "In the same year, 1580, it is now generally admitted, Browne very likely came into contact with foreign Anabaptists, and doubtless learned their simple ideas of forming their brotherhood churches or societies by a *Bund*, or a covenant with God. Their idea was that a Church may be composed only of believers. Browne accepted this view, but, following the opinion of his time in general, added, 'and their seed'. . . . It may be added that neither Browne nor any of his earlier followers seem to have been influenced to any great extent by the Scottish Covenants." Further, the Covenant of the Brownists, and of all other Covenants, was not merely a Covenant with God, but also with their fellow Church members; see the passage in *Browne's* own *Book which showeth the life and manners of all true Christians, p. 37:* "How must the Church be first planted and gathered under one kind of government? First by a Covenant and condition made in God's behalfe. Secondly, by a Covenant and condition made on our behalfe. Thirdly, by using the sacrament of Baptisme to seale those conditions and Covenants." Cf. further *Burrage: The true story of Robert Browne (1550?–1633), Oxford, 1906.* Here are the most important "spiritual" passages, *p. 56:* "There (speaking against the external Churchmanship of the Anglicans) is no duty, law, deed, cause, question, or plea, etc., which ought not to be spiritual, or is not determined by the Divine and spiritual right, law and Word of God." *P. 20:* Confronting Anglicans and Presbyterians he gives the motto: "The Kingdom of God should be within you." *P. 21*, against the use of Latin: "They spake the languages, saith the Scripture, as the Spirit gave them utterance." This connection with "spiritual" religion is still more important than that with the Baptist movement; on the difference between both see below. To *Burrage* we owe the discovery of several of Browne's writings, upon which his new book is based: *The Retractation of R. B., 1907*, and *A New Year's Gift, 1904*; for the use of these two books I am indebted to the kindness of the publisher.

[409] (p. 663.) On this point, see *Powicke: Henry Barrow, Separatist (1550?–1593), London, 1900*, a very instructive book and most illuminating for the Church-history of the period. Here (*pp. 215 ff.*)*:* "On the whole it may be said that Barrow was far nearer to the Anabaptists than he knew. . . . Indeed, apart from a number of comparatively superficial differences, due partly to circumstances, and partly to a more scrupulous fidelity to their common principle of reverence for Scripture—there was nothing in the sphere of Church practice which need have held Barrow and the Baptists apart, except the doctrine of Baptism. . . . But this refers only to his ecclesiastical position. As to theological differences, the case is not the same. Here what meets us is diametrical opposition rather than development. Barrow was a Calvinist, and accepted all the implications of this creed with full consent." *Powicke* regards the retention of Infant Baptism as due merely to his fear of being called an Anabaptist; I believe, however, that the deeper reasons which have already been mentioned were the cause of this. He rejects both the Baptist doctrine of free will and also the restriction of the body of the redeemed to those who have become members of a voluntary Church; this means the connection with still another Church conception (*p. 123*); against equality (*p. 94*), asceticism (*p. 149*); we must note anticipations of Quakerism (*p. 118*)*:* "B. anticipated George Fox in some points, e.g. in his refusal to take an oath on the Bible; in his objection to naming the days of the week, Sunday, Monday, etc., and in his dislike of

titles." The Separatist-Baptist result of Puritanism (*pp. 153 ff.*); it is one of Whitgift's main arguments, and individual Puritans seem rather embarrassed by Barrow. For the "spiritual" features, see especially the account on *pp. 92–93*, where Barrow is being examined; Barrow appeals to the exposition of Scripture through the Spirit which is the fruit of the Word: "Andrews: 'This savoureth of a private spirit.'—Barrow: 'This is the spirit of Christ and of His apostles, and most publicly they submitted their doctrines to the trial of all men. So do I.'—A.: 'What, are you an apostle?' B.: 'No, but I have the spirit of the apostles.' A.: 'What, the spirit of the apostles?' B.: 'Yes, the spirit of the apostles.' A.: 'What, in that measure?' B.: 'In that measure that God has imparted unto me, though not in that measure that the apostles had by any comparison. Yet the same spirit. There is but one spirit.' " This seems to me still more important than the resemblance to the Baptist movement, which is also strongly emphasized by *Loofs*. Could it possibly be that Schwenkfeld's influence is behind this?

410 (p. 665.) On this point see in particular *Burrage: The Church Covenant Idea;* the possibility of developing in the direction of the Baptists, the Independents, and a new conception of a Church of the people, *pp. 167–169*. "Yet certainly they would not turn for rescue to the Baptists, whose baptism on profession of faith they had spurned, and thus lay open their full indebtedness to Anabaptist principles." *Powicke* sees this question from the same point of view, showing very clearly how the Puritans swayed between the idea of a Calvinistic National Church and a Separatist voluntary Church; the opposition of Whitgift is characteristic; he held that without a settled authority in Church and State, and without the agreement of both, the principle of the unity of Society was threatened.—The transition from the State Church to Separatism was made possible to the Puritans through the purchase of livings, when they then were able to choose their own clergyman and remain loyal to him as a congregation; there were such cases even before Robert Browne, see *Burrage: New Facts Concerning Robinson, 1910, pp. 31, 24 ff.* Also frequently Puritan clergy, whose preaching licence had been taken away from them preached in private houses or in the open air, and gathered congregations round them on a personal basis; see *Dexter: The England and Holland of the Pilgrims, Boston, 1906, p. 125*.

411 (p. 666.) Cf. *Loofs: Kongregationalismus*; in particular also *Dexter's* book, which has already been mentioned, which is full of detail on social and cultural history, also the section in *Powicke* on the Amsterdam Church, and also that in *Burrage: Church Covenant, or the "Half-way Covenant", pp. 169–174*. There also the adoption of the Covenant principle by the Baptists. The ecclesiastical democracy of the Barrowists was not really democratic in spirit, but it was regarded as the agreement produced by the Spirit of Christ, and therefore supernatural in character, for which reason it was always laid down that all resolutions should proceed from prayer and meditation. Cf. *Powicke* (*p. 271*), where Ainsworth declares: "Christ's ruling power, which the Papists say is in the Pope, we say not (as this man calumniateth us) that it is in the body of the congregation, nor that it is in the prelates . . . nor (as the Puritans) that it is in the presbytery . . . but that it is in Christ Himself. . . . The Word of God is given to all and every member of the Church to read and exercise privately; but publicly—in the Church—there is a double use of it in prophecy and in office." *Dexter* sums this up thus: "The mainspring of power for people and officers alike is in the living Presence of Christ." This is undoubtedly the point of view of 'spiritual' religion; these statements exactly resemble those of *Schwenkfeld*, see *Sippel: Schwenkfeld Ch.W, 1911, p. 869:* The organization is, according to the

apostolic example, not the work of the believers, but that of the Holy Ghost. The practical control of the community is not the business of certain elected representatives, but of the living and ruling Christ. He alone represents the government of the Church. Jesus rules in spirit through those who are endowed with the gifts of the Spirit, both the individual congregation and the Church as a whole. In the community of the faithful the charismatic offices and gifts, according to 1 Cor. xii, manifest themselves for the common good. The famous farewell discourse of Robinson (*Weingarten, 33; Dexter, 587*), with his exhortation to the group not to cling to his (Robinson's) authority, but to expect and wait for new illumination, is likewise conceived from the point of view of "spiritual" religion; but it is not, on that account, to be overestimated, since a spirituality of this kind proceeds always from the Calvinistic interpretation of the Bible, and is only rejected by a rigid ecclesiastical orthodoxy like that of Lutheranism and Geneva. It is from this point of view that we must also understand Robinson's later concessions in the direction of spiritual fellowship with the members of other churches, and even his readiness in the settlement in Virginia to acknowledge an external civil authority of the bishops (*Dexter, 568 ff.!*); the practice of lay-preaching and of the lay-criticism of the pastors is also to be understood from this point of view. This does not exclude the idea that in ideal conditions there ought to be only Congregationalist churches, and this is what happened in New England. *Dexter, 567* thus describes the aim of their emigration: "Nor could they bring themselves to abandon the missionary purpose which they had cherished from the first, that they might demonstrate somewhere the value to mankind of a pure and democratic Church."—For their history and development in New England, see the important work by *Doyle: The English in America, London, 1887*, and *H. K. Caroll: The Religious Forces of the United States, New York, 1893*. A good deal of light is thrown on this subject by *Roger Williams* in his *Bloudy Tenent*, which will be discussed later; the Congregationalist churches will not allow the existence of any other churches, but they do not force all the colonists to become full members; in the first case they preserve the Calvinist idea of unity; in the second, the subjective liberty of conscience; of all they require outward conformity to the Law of Nature and to the Christian moral law; thus there is one section of the population without any Church at all, but these people must at least hear the Word of God; see *Bl. Ten., 250!*

412 (p. 669.) On this point see *Carlyle: Cromwell's Letters and Speeches*[2], *1846; Gooch: History of English Democratic Ideas, Cambridge, 1898; Shaw: History of the English Church, 1640–1660, London, 1900; Glass: The Barebones Parliament, 1653, London, 1889; Firth: Cromwell's Army, London, 1902; Gardiner: Cromwell, 1899*: all these works are very important, and to a great extent they supersede *Weingarten's* classic work *Die Revolutionskirchen Englands, 1868. Weingarten* has made too little distinction between the groups within Independency, and he has altogether misunderstood the distinction between the Baptist movement and ecclesiastical Protestantism.—*Weingarten's* excellent account of Cromwell, however, agrees entirely with the article by *Kolde* on *Cromwell* in *PR*[3]. The story of the religious development of Cromwell, of his relation to Harrison, of his adoption of "spiritual" ideas, still needs to be cleared up. "Spiritual" religion is represented in its extremist form by his two chaplains, Dell and Saltmarsh, as will be shown later. This also is a point which *Weingarten* has not noticed, and which distinguishes Cromwell from the actual Baptist movement. Here are some "spiritual" expressions: "The true succession is through the Spirit, given in its measure" (*Kolde, IV, 341*); the formulation of the only sign of a

real Christianity as of those "who believe in the remission of sins through the blood of Christ, and in free justification through the blood of Christ, who live upon the grace of God", is Pietistic in its outlook (*Kolde, 342*); "spiritual" also are the signs of a true minister required by the Examination Board: "They must not admit a man unless they were able to discerne something of the grace of God in him; grace of God which has to be so inquired for, as not foolishly or senselessly, but so far as man could judge according to the rules of charity" (*Glass, 133*); "spiritual" and not Baptist is his whole Church principle of "comprehension", which allowed different groups to exist freely within a Church which merely carried on an external administration: "A system of State aid and regulation of parishes leaving to individual churches a free hand for variety of doctrine and freedom in forms of worship."—*Glass, 131;* Cromwell's speech, 1657: "I think if there be freedom of judgment it is here. Here are three sorts of godly men whom you are to take care for, for whom you have provided in your settlement. And how could you put the selection upon the Presbyterians without by possibility excluding all those Anabaptists, all those Independents? As you have put it in this way, that, though a man be any of those three judgments, if he have the root of the matter in him he may be admitted" (*Glass, 133*). Francis Rous, likewise, the untiring Convener and worker in all the Ecclesiastical Commissions of the Long Parliament and of Cromwell, was also full of similar "spiritual" ideas; this is his declaration quoted by *Glass, 48:* "From Christ's time place is approved by truth and not truth by place. He that freed true worship from being tied to Jerusalem, and tied it to the service in spirit which may be in all places, gave true religion a large scope, even as large as the world itself." Further, Rous, as is well known, is a mystic whom *Ritschl: Gesch. d. Prot., I, 128–130,* considers influenced by "mediaeval example". "As in the English Church Calvinism of the Independent type came very near to the Anabaptists, so this work (by Rous) proves that in that direction they had also drawn upon the indispensable example of mysticism!" Also in the whole view of "Church comprehension" there are "spiritual" arguments and motives; cf. *Shaw, II, 75,* where this declaration is made to the Scots with reference to Ireton's report: "For the toleration of all religions and forms of worship that their letter objects, we know not whom they intend in that charge; as for the truth and power of religion, it being a thing intrinsical between God and the soul, and the matters of faith and the Gospel being such as no natural light doth reach unto, we conceive there is no human power of coercion thereunto, nor to restrain man from believing what God suffers their judgment to be persuaded of." There are suggestions of a connection with Schwenkfeld in *Sippell: Ch.W, 1911, p. 966,* and *William Dell's Programm, p. 81,* where the reference to Osiander would have been better if applied to Schwenkfeld. To the extent, as we shall see later, that Schwenkfeld's teaching was already a combination of "spiritual" and Baptist ideas, it naturally contains indirect Baptist influences.—For the relation of Cromwell to Harrison, see *Glass, 61 and 64; Firth, 318, 341 ff., 370.*—On the Independent army chaplains, Dell, Saltmarsh, Sedgwick, Hugh Peters, see *Firth, 320 ff.*, in Lilburn's regiment, John Canne; in Cromwell's John Owen, Thomas Patient, Robert Stapylton, see *Firth, 324 and 325–327.* On John Owen, the friend and confidant of Cromwell, as a Pietist who was above all sectional interests and respected by all, see *Heppe: Gesch. des Pietismus, 1879, pp. 43 ff.*; Dell and Saltmarsh are "spiritual" idealists; Hugh Peters, originally a Puritan, developed into a democratic Radical (*Gooch, 134–136 and 175*); Canne, who was first a Baptist preacher, became likewise radically

Anabaptist (*Gooch, 174ff.*); John Goodwin was originally an Anglican clergyman, but later he developed in the direction of "spiritual" religion (*Gooch, 132ff.*).—Cromwell himself had a strongly Calvinistically conservative strain. His conception of the Law of Nature was distinctly a class conception: "A nobleman, a gentleman, a yeoman, the distinction between these is rightly of great interest to the nation. Was not the natural constitution of the nation not almost trod underfoot with scorn and contempt by people with levelling principles?" (*Bernstein, 630*). As from the point of view of doctrine he was a Calvinist who held predestinarian views, his conception of revolution and of civil war was first of all that of the Calvinists and Huguenots. But the more, in the social chaos, things became confused, the more he explained events and inward resolutions as revelations and guidance from God for the course of events willed by God. This is fanaticism. He also tended to cherish the expectation of the speedy return of Christ, and in connection with that he cherished an indefinite hope of a universal reordering of conditions in the spirit of the Christian idea. But the maintenance of civic and State order, the rejection of all pure democracy and Communism, the appeal to the army as "a lawful power called by God", the appeal to the *salus populi* as the rational legal basis of the State—all these, on the other hand, are Calvinistic characteristics, in absolute contrast to the Chiliastic idea of reform, a view which he held for a time, owing to the difficulty of knowing the Will of God, but which he finally regarded as a point of view which led to the wanton destruction of all order. After the dissolution of the Parliament of the Saints he returned with increasing decision to the old Calvinistic theory of authority, since he regarded himself as the legal authority, called to this position by the people in the absence of all other legal authority. Of Independency he retained nothing beyond liberty of conscience. Otherwise his policy was such as could only be conceived on the basis of the Calvinistic relative Natural Law; he was always sure that "the cause of Christ and the cause of the people agree well together". Cf. my article *Moralisten, Englische* in *PRE*[3], *XIII, 443–448.*

[413] (p. 670.) On Locke, see *Bastide* and *Lezius*, especially *Rothenbücher*, where the further development of the philosophy of law and of the State is described (*pp. 46–112*). At the same time it is characteristic how everywhere the distinction is made between the theorists who have been more or less determined by Independent American ideas, and those who defend and exalt the modern Enlightenment against the Church. *R.* considers that the latter appear predominantly in Catholic countries where people are accustomed to a uniform religion, and where the Catholic unity is only replaced by the Enlightenment. The latter type is that to which the Deist religion of the State of Rousseau belongs, alongside of which freedom is given for particular private convictions. Also from this side Rousseau is anything but an inheritor of Calvinistic or even neo-Calvinistic ideas; see also *Jellinek: Erklärung der Menschen- und Bürgerrechte*[2], *1904;* also my *Trennung von Staat und Kirche, 1905.*—On the practical American form, see also the works named on *p. 928*, and also *Rothenbücher, 116–170.* When *Hägermann* points to the Law of Nature and to Locke, he does not realize the idea of the Christian Natural Law which is concealed within this theory, nor the way in which Locke is affected by Independency. Natural Law and Christian arguments are not in opposition as he thinks they are (*p. 151*). Hence Methodism in America has found such a response, and from the social point of view there is there still to-day a very massive orthodoxy and strict morality. Usually the European of the Enlightenment never quite understands this phenomenon.

[414] (p. 670.) For the fact that the Calvinism of the present day has in some directions very largely accepted the Free Church principle, see *Vinet* and *Kuyper*, and the great survey of *Rothenbücher* of the Free Churches in existence at the present time.—For the connection between this Church principle and political democracy, see *Rothenbücher, 472.*—The Pilgrim Fathers, even while they were still on the *Mayflower*, made a political covenant on the pattern of the Church Covenant; see *Burrage: Church Covenant, pp. 86 and 93.* "By 1639 the Covenant idea had become so popular in the minds of the Massachusetts and New Haven colonists that even towns were organized by covenant." Cf. also *Jellinek: Erklärung, pp. 36–39.* The connection between Calvinism and democracy is almost taken for granted in modern Calvinist literature, whether in the form in which Christianity and the Bible are completely identified with democracy, or in the theory that Calvinism is the final form of development of Christianity in which democracy and religion have finally become one, and which, therefore, is destined to triumph over the world. We find these ideas in *Vinet*, *Kuyper*, and *Rauschenbusch*. The French emphasize the agreement between Christianity and democracy; see the work which has already been mentioned of *Méalys*; further, *P. Sabatier: A propos de la séparation*², *1900*, and *R. Allier: Une révolution, 1806. Choisy*, who is such an excellent Calvin scholar, closes his inaugural lecture at Geneva entitled *L'état chrétien calviniste, 1909*, with the words: "To sum up; the theocratic régime, which was carried out by the Christian State of Geneva, was a rude but salutary training in justice, morality, and virile piety for that epoch. It prepared the way for liberty of conscience in the future and for the development of the spirit of fraternity and solidarity in the Christian democracy" (*p. 32*). On Dissent in England, see *von der Goltz: Staat und Kirche in Grossbritannien, Preuss. Jahrbb., 84, 1896.* Originally this union of Calvinism and democracy was only achieved to a limited extent in England, where the Independents of the Calvinistic turn of mind, especially Ireton and Cromwell, as far as possible remained even politically Conservative and legitimists, and it was only groups like the "Levellers", which had been influenced by Baptist ideas, which represented pure democracy; see *Rothschild: Der Gedanke einer geschriebenen Verfassung in der englischen Revolution, 1903*, also *Gooch: English Democratic Ideas.* Cromwell, indeed, declared in 1654 (*Carlyle, III, 29*): "liberty of conscience and liberty of the subject—two as glorious things to be contended for as any God has given us", but he immediately adds: "yet both these abused for the patronizing of villainies". In this, from his relative conservative standpoint, he rejects radical democracy. His own views on the connection between the Free Church movement and democracy were peculiarly confused.—This union of ideas was only clearly perceived, free from all the elements of early Calvinism, in America; on this subject, see the great work of *Tocqueville: La démocratie en Amérique*³, *1850.* In England it is only the work of the nineteenth century, where Dissent after the reforms of 1832 became the support of Liberalism and of democracy, and at the same time permeated these ideas with religious enthusiasm; see *Ostrogorski: La démocratie et l'organisation des partis politiques, I, 1903, pp. 21–26*; also *Held, p. 48.*

[414a] (p. 671.) On the sense of superiority in Calvinism in this respect, see *Kuyper, p. 15:* "Lutheranism remained ecclesiastical and theological; it is only Calvinism which both inside and outside the Church has left its mark upon all forms of human life. No one speaks of Lutheranism as the creation of a distinctive way of living; even the name is scarcely mentioned, whereas all who know history agree more and more in calling Calvinism the creator of a distinctive world of human life." *P. 26:* "It is as clear as day that the main force in the

development of the human race after Babylon, Egypt, Greece, and the Roman Empire, and after the Papal supremacy, has finally come into the hands of the Calvinistic peoples of Western Europe"; *p. 37:* "Calvinism means the completed evolution of Protestantism which in the sixteenth century led the development of our race into a new and higher phase . . . Therefore everyone who refuses to start from the standpoint of atheism or anti-theism must go back to Calvinism in order to learn to think and to live according to the Calvinistic principle, naturally in our day in a form which corresponds to the life of our time." Or cf. *Dexter, pp. 594 ff.:* "In the Plymouth Colony, and later in that of Massachusetts, the Free Church system flourished. It had a large part in shaping the thought and life of the colonists. It tinctured their political idea and aided powerfully in preparing the way for American Independence, and ever since their day it has continued a potent factor for good in our national life. In the Mother Country also, although hampered by many hostile conditions and not wholly free even yet to do its best work, it has become conspicuous and effective, and during the nineteenth century it has accomplished much of what it could not bring to pass in the seventeenth. . . . It would be a mistake to regard the Pilgrim Colony in America . . . as merely ecclesiastical in origin and development . . . it was one of the earliest manifestations of that resistless impulse of expansion and conquest . . . which changed the whole face of the globe. It opened a fresh and vitally important era in human history. It was practically the beginning of the civilized permanent settlement of an almost unknown Continent. It prepared the way for the birth of a new and mighty nation. The world's debt to the Pilgrims is not limited by any denominational lines. It is universal. The adherence of the Free Church systems may fairly claim to possess special justification for pride in the Pilgrim history, but nobody can monopolize it. All lovers of intelligence and civil as well as religious liberty have the right to share it." This is Americanism in its relative connection with Calvinism and sectarianism.—From the opposite point of view *Shaw* complains in his *English Church, I, 316:* "The earliest Reformation had never proclaimed such a separation of the civil from the ecclesiastical government. It was the fatal and malignant heritage of the genius and life of Calvin, and how adversely it has affected the later history of European progress can hardly yet be estimated."—There are numerous excellent observations in *Tocqueville's* book on the special character of Puritan Anglo-Saxon democracy contrasted with nationalist French democracy. In *I, 51* he gives rightly as the guiding principle of the whole the words out of the old *Matthew Magnalia Americana:* "Let us not delude ourselves about that which we call our independence. In reality, there is a kind of corrupted freedom which is common to men and animals and which consists in doing whatever one pleases. This kind of freedom is the enemy of all authority, it endures rules and regulations unwillingly; in giving way to this we descend below our own level; it is the enemy of truth and of peace, and God Himself has found it necessary to speak out openly against it. But there is a civil and moral freedom whose strength is in unity, and to protect which is, indeed, the nature of all power; this is the freedom to do fearlessly all that is right and good. This holy freedom in all fateful hours we will defend, and for this, if necessary, we will sacrifice our lives." Cf. also the observations in the preceding pages on the fundamental sociological theory of Calvinism; also *Ostrogorski, I, 93:* "From the moment when the individual soul awakened to affirm himself before God and Society 'man' had entered into the social and political life of England, never to leave it. In England he entered by the door of ethics, as he penetrated into France by that of logic." Cf. also in a similar vein, *Morley: Life of Gladstone, I, 163.*

[415] (p. 673.) On the history of toleration and the liberty of worship, which goes far beyond mere tolerance, see the article entitled *Toleranz*, by *Friedberg*, in *PRE*[3]; *Rothenbücher, 74ff., 116–131; Jellinek: Die Erklärung der Menschen- und Bürgerrechte*[2], *1904;* especially *Ruffini: La libertà religiosa, I, Storia della idea, 1900.* For the very limited tolerance of the Brownists, Barrowists, and Pilgrim Fathers, see the works which have already been mentioned by *Burrage, Powicke,* and *Dexter*; in New England, see *Jellinek, pp. 39–45*; toleration and the Long Parliament, *Shaw, II, 33–97*; among the Independents, *Jellinek, 36; Shaw, II, 46–52*; Goodwin and a memorial by the Brownists shows that they went a good way in this direction, cf. *Glass, p. 21 f.* (here with the "spiritual" argument, "Let every spirit praise the Lord"); on Cromwell and religious toleration, see *Glass* and *Kolde*; *Speech III* (*Carlyle, III, 68*) deals with the question of the fundamental laws which every system of legislation must regard as natural rights. "Again, is not Liberty of conscience a fundamental? . . . Liberty of conscience is a natural right; and he that would have it ought to give it. . . . Liberty of conscience, truly that is a thing which ought to be very reciprocal! . . . This, I say, is a fundamental. It is for us and the generations to come." Otherwise this toleration was very limited, as *Glass* proves with detailed illustrations. Milton travelled farthest along this line; in addition to the usual Puritan-Independent and "spiritual" motives he added the broader element of rationalism, which, however, remained confined to the idea of the Christian State. Locke took up the subject at this point.—Complete independence and freedom were demanded only by the Baptists and the spiritual idealists of the time. For the former see *Tracts on Liberty of Conscience and Persecution, 1614–1661* (a publication of the Hanserd Knollys Society, 1846). Roger Williams, whose name is held in high honour in America at the present day, was one of the most important representatives of this spirit; see *The Bloudy Tenent of Persecution for Cause of Conscience* of 1664, published with a biographical introduction by the same Society, 1848. R. W. was a Puritan of a very devout kind, who laid great stress on "holiness of life", and as such he was strongly opposed to any union of Church and State, a combination which had already taken place in the Congregationalism of New England; closely connected with that he was rigidly democratic and keen on an ethical system of politics, which led him (like Penn at a later date) to desire to deal with the Indians on a basis of justice and kindness, and he established missions amongst them; from this point of view he opposed the Colonial Charters, which made grants of land belonging to the Indians without any regard for their rights. This fact, together with protests against the mingling of affairs of Church and State, led to his being banished from the colony. In Providence he founded a purely democratic State with entire religious liberty (for the fortunes of this enterprise, see *Doyle*), and went over to the Baptists in 1639 (the biography remarks: "Infant Baptism and persecution, as in other churches, in sisterly embrace together", *XXVI*, and mentions, *p. XXXIII*, a Baptist asserting as one of the results of Infant Baptism that "hence also collaterally have been brought the power of the civil magistrate into the church", which shows a right sense of the fact that Infant Baptism implies the Church of the people or the National Church, and that this means finally the domination of the State in the Church). Roger Williams did not remain a Baptist for very long, however; he then gave up belonging to any denomination at all, believing (like Schwenkfeld, Coornheert, and Franck, as well as the Collegiants) that the true constitution of the Early

Church had long ago disappeared, since the days of the Apostles, in fact, and that now there was no longer in existence any Church at all which had been instituted by God. Thus he then adopted a position which was entirely individualistic and non-denominational (*XXVII*). His *Bloudy Tenent*, 1644, was linked on to a Baptist treatise in favour of liberty of conscience, which is defended (*XXX*). Only in the same year did the Independent, *John Goodwin*, come forward. R. W. went too far for the Independents: "They are willing to grant liberty only to those sound in fundamentals, the identical views of their brother Congregationalists of America" (*XXXV*). The feeling of the *Bloudy Tenent* is radically individualistic, although the argument as a whole is the Baptist argument, and only combines with this the specific Puritan sentiment of superiority to the world and of possessing a victorious mission to spread the Truth. "Spiritual" elements are not emphasized particularly, although it seems probable that the writer was acquainted with and influenced by spiritual and mystical literature. The following quotation seems to bear this out: "Whatever worship, ministry, ministration, the best and purest, are practised without faith and true persuasion that they are the true institution of God, they are sin, sinful worship, ministers, etc. . . . Without search and trial no man attains this faith and right persuasion. . . . Having tried we must hold fast upon the loss of a crown" (*p. 8*). His "inwardness" often reminds us of Luther's earlier period (*p. 118*): "I hence observe, that here being in this Scripture (2 Cor. x. 4) held forth a twofold state, a civil state and a spiritual, civil officers and spiritual, civil weapons and spiritual weapons, civil vengeance and punishment and a spiritual vengeance and punishment. . . . These states being of different natures and considerations, as far differing as spirit from flesh, I first observe that civil weapons are most improper and unfitting in matters of the spiritual state and kingdom, though in the civil state most proper and suitable." His exegesis is often explicitly mystical and idealistic in the extreme. See his appeal to the "famous Waldensian witnesses" (*p. 159*), to Luther (*p. 171*), against Calvin, appeal to Gal. i. 8 (*p. 181*). It is worthy of note that the Baptist treatise upon which this work is based itself appeals in detail to Luther's carlier "spiritual" conception of the Church (*pp. 15 ff.*). Roger Williams himself bases his individualism upon the doctrine of predestination (*p. 82*): "The Church or spiritual state, city or kingdom, has laws, orders, and armories . . . to defend itself against the very gates of earth or hell. . . . The Lord Himself knows who are His and His foundation remaineth sure; His elect or chosen cannot perish or be finally deceived." We shall come upon similar references to the earlier period of Luther and his "spiritual" ideas among the English mystics of the Cromwell period. A monograph on Roger Williams would be very interesting; in many respects he is very original.—*Kuyper*—although in a somewhat sophistical way—illustrates the adoption of liberty of conscience as one of the principles of Neo-Calvinism. He asserts (quite against the spirit of Calvin) that the "government of the Church on earth is democratic to the very marrow" (*p. 56*), and, moreover, he describes liberty of worship and religious toleration as an "essential" feature of Calvinism (*p. 92*). In so doing, however, Kuyper approaches very closely to that idea which is inevitably connected with the whole idea of toleration, namely, that all religious knowledge is merely relative, and with this he is renouncing an original principle of Calvinism. "By its strong emphasis upon religious freedom Calvinism abandoned the idea of the unity of the visible Church" (*p. 94*). "Since the very fact of the destruction of the unity of the Church naturally meant that the relative nature of all creeds must come into prominence, Calvinism, by making possible the formation of various churches of different kinds, also brought to light the limited nature of our belief in the Truth!" In ecclesiastical matters the State has no right to interfere, "not from a false idea of neutrality, nor from any idea of indifference to the truth, but because as the ruling authority it lacks the presuppositions which would enable it to give a true judgment, and the attempt to do this would too easily override the sovereignty of the Church" (*p. 97*). Hence the State must not attempt to hinder a Church from setting up a system of the strictest orthodoxy within itself, but every Church must also tolerate the existence of other churches alongside of itself, and must not call upon the State to put an end to their existence. "Nothing can destroy the fundamental rule, that the civil government ought to honour the whole body of Christian churches as the many-sided revelation of the Church of Christ upon earth" (*p. 98*). "The State ought to recognize that every citizen ought to be granted full liberty of conscience as an original human right, belonging to him by nature" (*p. 99*). This is precisely the spirit of the constitution of New Hampshire, quoted by *Jellinek, p. 21*. Certainly the only element in it which is Calvinistic is the assertion of the sovereignty of the Church over against the State. The relative element in these statements is due to the influence of the Baptists, of mysticism and of rationalism; Kuyper himself is unable to deny that "frequently (!) it was the Baptists and the Remonstrants who even three hundred years ago defended the system of the Free Church against Calvinism" (*p. 92*). Real toleration is found only among mystics and spiritual idealists and reformers, but among them this very easily merges into rationalism. The Baptist movement, with its absolute conception of Truth, is ultimately only tolerant to the extent of desiring to be independent of the State, and only from that standpoint does it advance to the inevitable conclusion that liberty of worship is also desirable. All these influences are fused in Neo-Calvinism. For the secular reasons for toleration which also existed, see *Max Weber: Archiv XXI, 42 f.*—The view upheld by *Jellinek* of the significance of this formulation and of the practical carrying out of liberty of conscience for the legal formulation of a still more comprehensive list of natural human rights, and therewith of the introduction of the conception into the constitution of the modern state in general, has been very largely questioned or depreciated. The second edition of his book takes some of these objections into consideration. The Catholic *Paulus* (*Kölnische Volkszeitung, Literarische Beilage, 1906, Nr. 39*) argues that the rights of humanity are exclusively derived from the Natural Law theory of the State and the philosophy of the Enlightenment; *Wahl: Zur Geschichte der Menschenrechte* (*H. Z., 103, pp. 79–85*), emphasizes, alongside of the religious influences, the general political situation of the states which were united together with their entirely different church organizations, and the influence of the ideas of the Enlightenment. That is probably right. *Hägermann: Die Erklärungen der Menschen- und Bürgerrechte, 1910* (*Eberings Hist. Studd., 78*), likewise lays stress on the literary influences of the Enlightenment and reduces the religious influences to a minimum, but his ideas about the latter are very confused. He has misunderstood Roger Williams and his opinions altogether, he does not know that a conception of Christian Natural Law exists, and the influence of Milton and Locke, which he rightly emphasizes, is not interpreted in connection with its religious basis. Much in the book is, however, instructive and interesting; he is right in pointing out that equality is a purely rationalistic growth, and his emphasis upon economic, political, and personal influences is thoroughly justifiable. *Jellinek* never argued that the American revolution was due to Puritanism, but it was only the rights of humanity and the argument for these which sprang out of Puritanism. In my opinion this is still true, even though he treats the Enlightenment too summarily. For all students of the religious development the explanations (text in *Jellinek*) contain the specifically religious sense of the invulnerability of conscientious convictions and of the religious element which ought not to be touched by the State at all; this shows the Calvinistic-Baptist origin of this development of the idea.—For a more recent work see *Klövecorn: Die Entstehung der Erklärung der Menschen- und Bürgerrechte, 1911.*

[416] (p. 674.) That the classic Law of Nature is the emancipation of the Stoic elements from their connection with the ecclesiastical dogma and ethics, and from the ecclesiastical myth of primeval history, appears in all the mass of average literature dealing with the Law of Nature, as described by *Glafey: Gesch. des Rechts der Vernunft, 1739* (see especially *p. 54; III, 193f.*), and *Hinrichs: Gesch. der Rechts- und Staatsprinzipien, 1848–52* (especially *I, 227; II, 13*). Aristotle, whose organic theory of the formation of the State was coupled together in the very mixed ecclesiastical theory of the Law of Nature with the contract theory and with the doctrine of the Divine origin of government, is entirely set aside; increased individualism now works solely with the Stoic doctrines of an original freedom—(whether actual or only virtually present)—equality, and goodness of men in the Golden Age, out of which there arose, through the egoism of men and their non-social qualities, the necessity for the development of Society in the form of the State, in order to protect the original goods granted by Nature. In so doing, however, the ideas of Stoicism are not only released, but they also lose their Christian aspect, since (*a*) the Law of Nature is derived purely out of the nature of humanity, that is, out of the social and reasonable character of mankind, without any admixture of the Law of Nature with the desire to imitate the justice of God, and without any sense of need for the direct connection with the conception of God at all; (*b*) since in the definition of the Law of Nature the difference between the Primitive State and the fallen State increasingly disappears, and the Law of Nature is interpreted as originating in humanity as it is in itself; (*c*) since the rise of the State and of Law does not appear as a merely relative Natural Law of the fallen state, but as progress in civilization for the preservation of the natural disposition against passions which would endanger its existence. Henceforward the views of men become independent of primaeval history and its desirable social organization, and develop into purely rational sciences, which allow scope for the Church and for revelation alongside of themselves, but which are really independent in principle. Cf. my article *Das stoisch-christliche Naturrecht und das moderne profane Naturrecht, H.Z., 1911,* also *Verhandlungen des I. deutschen Soziologentages, 1911.* When *Gothein* and *Kantorowicz* here point out the importance of Roman Law in this process of transition, I would like to observe that already in the confessional philosophy of law Roman Law was the *ratio scripta* and the historical-positive development of the Law of Nature, identical with the Decalogue in its spirit and its meaning. This process is quite evident in the development of Hugo Grotius, who belongs from the very outset to a circle which was inwardly not Calvinistic; he was also very much under the influence of Stoicism, and in his view there is a curious blend of utilitarian and idealistic elements; Grotius evolved his ethical theory, his theory of the philosophy of history, and his theory of law quite independently of all confessions; cf. the Heidelberg Dissertation by *W. Geibel* on *Ethik und Theologie des H.G.* For further details on this subject see *Gierke: Althusius*², and *Figgis: From Gerson to Grotius*; on the whole subject, see *Bluntschli:*

Gesch. des allgemeinen Staatsrechtes und der Politik, 1864, and *Bergbohm: Jurisprudenz und Rechtsphilosophie, 1892*; it is, indeed, hard to say how, once the ecclesiastical doctrine of Society had been destroyed, the modern doctrine of Society could or should have been established in any other way.

416a (p. 675.) In the *Bloudy Tenent* of Roger Williams there is one of the most important ideas for the possibility of the building up of Society and of the State according to the Law of Nature and the Second Table (of the Decalogue), without the interference of the State with the sovereign rights of the purely spiritual Church, but also without the need to create a Christian support for bourgeois morality and expediency. Even Heathen, Jews, and Turks are capable of a far-reaching politico-civil ethic, which in actual fact will always fit in to the Christian ethic, since indeed the Law of Nature is only the Second Table of the Decalogue. Roger Williams also combines with this idea a purely external utilitarian conception of the State; for the same reasons this is also the case in *Locke* (see the book about him which has already been mentioned by *Bastide*). When the religious duties and ideals are taken away from the ecclesiastical conception of the State it then falls a prey altogether to utilitarianism. On *Bayle*, see *Jodl: Gesch. d. Ethik, I², 420*; on Milton, *Stern: Milton und seine Zeit, 1877–99*. The unbroken process of development from the ecclesiastical-Calvinist Natural Law into a purely rational conception of Natural Law is seen in the New Englanders described by *Hägermann*, especially in *Otis*, whom he describes as the real father of the American system (*pp. 44–58*). Those who are familiar with the Calvinist doctrine of the State will here be able to note everywhere both the Calvinistic root, and the development in the direction of a rationalistic Natural Law. *Hägermann* quotes on *p. 52:* "He who desires to realize the doctrine of unlimited passive obedience, which allows no resistance to man at all, is not only a Nero or a rogue, but he is also a rebel against the sanity of human intelligence as well as against the laws of God, of Nature, and of his country." With that he couples freedom of conscience and the rejection of the priestly and the military caste, as, with an appeal to Saul, Roger Williams had also taught (*p. 53*). In Boston, therefore, he was compared with Isaiah and Ezekiel (*p. 47*). This is still clearly the atmosphere of Calvinism. *Hägermann* gives several other examples of this process of development.

417 (p. 675.) Cf. on this question the often-quoted article by *Max Weber: Kirchen und Sekten in Nordamerika*, and *Antikritisches, p. 202; Tocqueville: Démocratie en Amérique; von Schulze-Gävernitz: Deutscher Imperialismus und englischer Freihandel, pp. 42–64; Hartmann: Englische Frömmigkeit.* It is very interesting to note (*Rothenbücher, 149–165*) how American law, from the point of view of the idea of associations, tries to do justice, by means of suitable fictions, to the idea of the Church as an institution. Here two different worlds of sociological thought come into collision. This contact is well illustrated by a passage in the account of Locke's argument against patriarchalism and against the institutional idea in *Bluntschli, p. 173:* "The (opposing) argument is this: the children are bound by their fathers, and this argument is false. The father has no right to give away the freedom of his son. When the son reaches man's estate he is no less free than his father was. Since the states are in existence, and children are born into them and educated as dependent members of the families which make up the State, since the land and the possessions of the citizens are permanently controlled, since in these conditions it is only one at a time, and one after another that individuals attain their majority and become free, and not a whole number at once, the act of freedom which the man who has come of age has consummated

when he unites his life to that of the State is overlooked. He is free, if he will, to choose to belong to another State." In reality, this is the pivot of the whole question, and it is evident that there is here a very close resemblance to the ideal of the sect, which essentially claims that no human being is born into an institution, but that it is his duty to enter into a voluntary congregation on reaching maturity and of his own free will; this implies that Adult Baptism and not Infant Baptism should be the rule.—At the same time we must remember, on the other hand, that *Gierke*, in his *Genossenschaftsrecht*, derives the mediaeval conception of the corporation, of the institution, of the unity of the State, from the analogy of the ecclesiastical *Corpus mysticum*.

[418] (p. 676.) Here the *Life of Gladstone*, by *Morley*, is very instructive (*1903*). Gladstone developed from Anglican Conservatism into a combination of Calvinism and Liberalism which had a great influence upon the inner life of the English nation, and which has found its chief support among English Nonconformists. His Conservative successor, Lord Salisbury, called Gladstone "the great Christian", and the biographer adds: "nothing could be more true, or better worth saying. He not only accepted the doctrines of that faith as he believed them to be held by his own communion; he sedulously strove to apply the noblest moralities of it to the affairs both of his own nation and of the commonwealth of nations" (*I, 4*). For that very reason, at least to some extent, he even envisaged the possibility of Disestablishment. He separated the spheres of Natural Law and the churches, reserving the former to the State and the latter to Revelation and its various interpretations; cf. a characteristic statement of Gladstone's on "the highest ground of natural justice"; it is "that justice which binds man to man; which is older than Christianity, because it was in the world before Christianity was born; which is broader than Christianity, because it extends to the world beyond Christianity; and which underlies Christianity, for Christianity itself appeals to it" (*I, 563*); this is to him, for example, the rule for the war with China. *Erich Marcks* certainly remarks on this point, that this Christian-ethical policy was only possible because Gladstone's predecessors had already established the supremacy of England both on sea and land so that it could not be questioned, thus giving Gladstone the luxury of carrying on a moral policy, while at the same time he was fortunate in having Disraeli as the representative of the opposite policy; cf. *Marcks: Die Einheitlichkeit der englischen Auslandspolitik, 1910*. To-day we are again experiencing the same ethical Liberal tendency in the internal politics of England. The visits of English clergy to Germany in the interests of Peace are part of this movement. The following incident, which I read in a Church paper, is characteristic: a German "General Superintendent" writes with great astonishment to tell how his very devout host entertained him with true Christian hospitality, and then told him, perfectly naturally, that in the same guest-room which his friend was occupying, the radical Liberal Theodor Barth had also stayed. This certainly is not possible within Lutheranism, and this impossibility is one of the most difficult problems in the religious situation in Germany.—Further, we must not overlook the fact that English Liberalism has also a decided anti-religious, purely utilitarian tendency of the school of Bentham and Mill.—*Kuyper* here is typical, speaking of Gladstone as a "Christian statesman who was a Calvinist to the very marrow" (*p. 195*). He speaks of "a sacred spirit of democracy" (*p. 21*). "In Calvinism we first see the people itself come to the fore, and out of its own spontaneous impulse attain a higher form of social life" (*p. 31*). Here there rules the "universal grace", the "order of creation", or the *Lex Naturae*. "In the world we have to honour the effect of the

universal grace of God, and for this reason we must free the world from ecclesiastical bonds . . ." (*p. 24*). "All that proceeds directly from the Creation possesses all the presuppositions for an independent (i.e. free from the Church) development in Nature as such. . . . It is altogether the life of creation according to the ordinances of creation, and, indeed, in organic development" (*p. 84*). "Thus the Church retired to a position, where she was nothing more and nothing other than the community of the faithful, and thus the life of the world was set free, not from God, but from the Church. . . . Thus family life once again became independent. Trade and industry were now free to act on their own initiative; art and science were released from their ecclesiastical bonds and their own inspiration was given back to them, and the subordination of the whole of Nature to man, corresponding to the order of creation given by God in Paradise, was seen to be the true order" (*p. 23*). "Fundamental legal rights" (*p. 90*). "In the Declaration of Independence John Hancock expresses this in other words when he says that America, in virtue of 'the Law of Nature and of Nature's God' had come into being, that this nation acted as 'endowed by the Creator with certain inalienable rights' . . . that this Declaration was made with 'a firm reliance upon the protection of Divine Providence' " (*p. 79*). This conception of Natural Law is purely utilitarian: "The well-being of man must be the visible sign of His Divine Wisdom" (*p. 74*). This, however, is an American form of Neo-Calvinism: "Calvinism was transferred to America that it might develop there in a higher freedom" (*p. 30*). Here is the summary of this Neo-Calvinism (*p. 33*). "Remember how first the song of freedom arose through Calvinism, that consciences which had been oppressed now burst forth into praise, that our constitutional civil rights were only won and secured by means of Calvinism, and that at the same time that mighty movement went forth from Western Europe which permitted art and science to flourish, opened new roads for trade and industry, renewed family and social life in a brilliant manner, elevated the status of citizenship, placed the workman on a level with his master, brought with it a rich development of philanthropy, and, beyond all this, through its Puritan earnestness, it has exalted, purified, and ennobled the moral life of mankind" (*p. 33*). For *Kuyper* the State is still an institution of the Natural Law of the fallen State, a "mechanical" system of authority, placed over the world of Natural Law for the repression of evil, but for that very reason to be kept carefully within certain limits, in order that it may not interfere with human rights (*p. 86*). In spite of all these democratic-liberal, Free Church toleration, utilitarian-Natural-Law principles, *Kuyper* is still the leader of orthodoxy, and of the forces of reaction which are combined with the Catholic Party, just as American and English Calvinists as a rule are very orthodox and keep the churches within strict limits. Opposition to the French conception of the equality of Natural Law (*pp. 173 ff.*).—All this agrees with the statements in the American Declaration of Independence (*Jellinek, p. 9*): "We hold the following truths as self-evident, namely, that all men are born equal, that they have been endowed by their Creator with certain inalienable rights, that to these rights belong life, freedom, and the endeavour to attain happiness, that, in order to secure these rights, systems of government have been set up amongst men, which derive the just authority from the consent of the governed; that whenever a form of government works against these aims, it is the right of the people to alter it or to do away with it, to appoint a new government, and to establish it upon these principles, and to order its powers as may be best for its happiness and usefulness in the world."—How utterly different is the conception of the State in Germany (under the influence of

Lutheranism), and how this conception of a *Kulturstaat* still means for many people the absorption of the religious aims of life into the tasks of the State, appears especially in the attempts to interpret the separation of Church and State in a German way in *Otto Mayer: Staat und Kirche in PRE*³, and *E. Förster: Entwurf eines Gesetzes betr. die Religionsfreiheit, 1911*, especially *pp. 39 and 47*, with references to Freiherrn, v. Stein and Hegel; here it is argued that it is in the interest of the State to use the means it has at its disposal of the external care of the churches to support the unity and continuance of the chief great religions, because its nature is not regarded as purely rational and utilitarian. The same point of view in *Max Lenz: Nationalität und Religion. Preuss. Jahrbb., 1907*, here also upon a foundation of Lutheran sentiment.

[419] (p. 676.) See, for example, *Kuyper, p. 184:* "Calvinism is the high-watermark of progress; 'Modernism' does not mean progress since it has no new ideas of its own.—The material progress of this century (nineteenth) has nothing to do with progress in the sphere of principle." Thus Pietism also has been able to combine technical knowledge and the study of natural science in a quite neutral way with dogmatic orthodoxy. It is thus expressed by *Kuyper:* "Our Calvinistic denomination speaks of two ways through which we come to the knowledge of God, Nature and the Scriptures, and it is far more noteworthy that Calvin, instead of treating Nature with neglect, said that the Scriptures were like a pair of spectacles which gave us the power of reading the Divine Scripture in Creation which had been faint and defective before" (*p. 113*). "Thus the Calvinist was still a pilgrim, but a pilgrim who on the way to the eternal fatherland had a vast task to fulfil. Above, below, and around there stretched the world with all the wealth of Nature. This whole vast field must be cultivated. The earth, with all that is in it, was to be made subordinate to man. Thus there flourished in my present fatherland as never before industry and agriculture, trade and seafaring. The new life of the community awakened new needs. In order to be able to control the earth it was necessary to know the nature of the earth, of the seas, of the qualities and laws which govern Nature" (*p. 122*). It is along this line that we must interpret the orthodoxy of so many great English natural scientists. Also the entirely different attitude to missions among these peoples must also be explained from this point of view; it is not merely due to its desire for colonies and its gift for colonial expansion, although naturally these interests probably played some part. Everywhere it is the possibility of "making the best of both worlds" (*Dowden, p. 275*).

[420] (p. 677.) See *Powicke*, where much emphasis is laid on the presence of the "spiritual" element in early Congregationalism (*p. 218*): "A result of his two first principles working in combination: his faith in the Inner Light and his reverence for the written Word. For faith in the Inner Light, at least, in the case of the more deeply thoughtful and devout of its disciples, really meant faith in the highest intentions of spiritual reason; and this, when brought to a study of the written Word, could not fail to operate selectively, fastening on what was agreeable to the most worthy conception of God and man and tacitly ignoring all else." Thus also one section else branched off into Unitarianism.

[422] (p. 678.) On this point see *Göbel: Christl. Leben, I, 318–351*. Here already we meet the democratic tendency in congregational organization, and the strict separation from the world, also the "prophesyings". *Heppe* (*p. 20*) thus describes the Puritan "prophesyings": "The ruling idea was this—that Christianity was of necessity life, and, indeed, that it ought to be a serious life,

entirely regulated by the Word of God, in which the Christian must not be idle, but in which he must unceasingly exercise himself, proving himself by the Word of God, and striving for an ever more complete sanctification through prolonged prayer, through meditation and fasting, and, above all, through systematic asceticism." Note the element of asceticism.

423 (p. 678.) For the name and its history, see *Douglas Campbell: The Puritan in Holland, England, and America*[4], *1902, I, p. XXVII; Kattenbusch*, article *Puritaner* in *PRE*[3], who here absolutely identifies Puritanism with Pietism; *Heppe: Gesch. des Piet., p. 6.* The names *praxis pietatis* and others are also frequently found in the English literature of the subject (*Heppe, pp. 23, 30*). The terms "Precisians", "Puritans", or even "Martinists" were used even by Barrow; the latter term comes from the *Marprelate Tracts*; see *Powicke, p. 149.* Another term which occurs again and again is that of "godliness" or "saintliness", the "godly men" or the "saints". *Weingarten*, unfortunately, did not perceive or describe this tendency, as *Heppe, p. 14*, rightly points out: this is why he has not made clear its relation to Presbyterianism, Congregationalism, and the Baptist movement; yet only when these distinctions have been drawn is it possible to understand the collective expression "Independency".—Their opponents still liked to call them "Libertines", following the ancient custom of Geneva.

424 (p. 681.) The most important sources, *Works of the English Puritan Divines, London, 1845–48, 10 vols.*, used very largely by *Heppe* and *Max Weber.* Also *Heppe: Gesch. d. Pietismus*, in which, however, the position from the standpoint of the history of dogma of early Calvinism and of Lutheran Pietism is not made clear in any way, and there is no reference to the general history of civilization in which this movement was set. *Ritschl: Gesch. des Pietismus*, entirely ignores this Pietist movement; the accidental fact that *Ritschl* did not know English gave to his views and to those of his followers a very considerable and a very unfortunate twist. *Douglas Campbell* has a great deal of information, but the book needs to be used with caution; in his mind Puritanism is mainly Calvinism of the individualistic rigoristic type, and he regards this type of Puritanism as the origin, to a very large extent, of almost the whole of the present Anglo-Saxon world; thus his view of the basis of modern civilization is similar to that of *Kuyper*, only without his orthodox colouring; he also includes the sects within Puritanism. This work, which is in two volumes, reached a fourth edition, a clear sign of the response which there is to such views. For Pietistic Puritanism as a special group, distinct from Presbyterianism and Congregationalism, see also *Shaw: English Church, I, 6f., 51–53*; for a description of the Puritanism of the later years of the reign of Elizabeth and of the Stuart period, contrasted with the Puritanism of earlier days, which was supported rather by theologians and affected very largely by the anti-Catholicism of Geneva, see *Glass, 4–13*; this later Puritanism he calls "revivalism", and says it may be compared with the Methodism of a later period. See also *Dexter: The England and Holland of the Pilgrims, pp. 122ff.*; it is a "reformation within the Reformation", an "evangelical purpose". *Max Weber* also describes this form of Puritanism in its fusion with the sects, and also rightly distinguishes it from the primitive Calvinism of Geneva.—The question of the reasons for the rise of this Pietist movement, which was behind the Great Rebellion and was one of the formative elements in more recent English history, is raised by *Douglas Campbell, I, X*; he attributes it to the influence of the Calvinistic exiles from the Netherlands, who came over in great numbers (75,000 fathers of families), and who were welcomed by Elizabeth on account of their

usefulness in trade and industries. "These Netherlanders helped to make England Protestant, and this laid a lasting basis for her wealth; but, at the same time, they did an even greater work than this; for in helping to make her Protestant they also helped to make her free". . . . "It was Protestant England that ultimately controlled the ocean and the markets of the world, colonized America, and girded the earth with an empire" (*p. 429*).—For the aspect of the movement which affects the history of civilization, see *Taine: Hist. de la littérature anglaise, II, 1863, pp. 275–435*, and, above all, *Dowden: Puritan and Anglican, London, 1900*. Both these writers describe the Puritan hostility to the world and their systematic asceticism, which, however, does not mean withdrawal from the world but the active domination of the life of the world; in *Dowden* there is a very fine description of the secularization of the Puritan spirit in the comparison between Bunyan and Defoe (*274–278*); here he says of the secularized Puritan: "To make the best of both worlds was the part of prudence, and of the two worlds, that on which our feet are planted is, at least, nearer and the more submissive to our control. Divine Providence is doubtless to be acknowledged, but it is highly desirable to supplement Divine Providence by self-help. . . . Adventurer, trader, colonist, missionary, we hail him as one of our makers of empire." For the ethical hostility and the opposition to the Elizabethan literature, see *Douglas Campbell, II, 114–136*. There was good reason for the hostility and the literary class was very meagre. Here also is the explanation of the austerity of the Puritans, so different from the attitude of Calvin; it was due namely to their hostility to the worldliness, immorality, and brutality of the rest of the nation (*pp. 152–163*), here, however, the Calvinistic element is greatly underestimated; social and political reform efforts (*pp. 171–176*); see also *Glass* for an estimate of the value of the legislation of the Barebones Parliament, in which the minority consisted of Pietists of this kind; here Pietists opposed Baptist fanatics.

[425] (p. 682.) For the class relationships see suggestions in *Glass, pp. 6 and 23 f., Dowden, p. 255 f.;* especially *Glass, p. 32:* "Puritanism was a movement of the people, with not a few leaders among the aristocracy. For a time its temper was high and courageous, hopeful and even audacious in new experiments. Its religious spirit tended to abolish or modify social distinctions: all mortal men were alike sinners before God, and peer or peasant, if true members of the congregation, were equally saints. Its favoured ecclesiastical schemes and platforms were of a democratic kind. Its political ideal was not a loose and incoherent democracy; it aimed at vigour in government, and was willing to confer immense powers upon chosen individuals; but its political culmination was a Republic." *P. 4:* "The mundane spirit of the Renaissance (?) in its lower form of commercial interests by degrees allied itself with Puritanism." Later (*p. 275*): "The middle classes advanced in wealth, power, and in influence. After the jagged precipices and forlorn valleys—scenes of spiritual exaltation or despair—a tableland was reached—safe, if unheroic—where man might plough and build." *Douglas Campbell* has investigated the problem with vigour, but he solves it too externally with his favourite theory of the influence of the Dutch immigrants; he describes the facts of the situation, however, in the following terms: this movement was the rise of the middle classes through the religious movement to a position of importance which they had never held before, which had permanent results in its effect upon the rise of England and America to a power over the rest of the world, after Elizabethan England had been behind the rest of Europe, owing to its defective adoption of the culture of the Renaissance; *pp. 483 f., 490–492:* "No people on earth have a higher

order of virtue than the English middle classes. They bear a courage which never falters, an earnestness of purpose which brooks no obstacles, a love of justice and fair play, a devotion to home and country, and an instinctive morality and real belief in a Higher Power which are not so common among the Latin races. . . . Their daily life was a sermon on the Christian virtues of industry, temperance, and charity"; *496:* "The opposition to the arbitrary power of the Crown grew with the development of the industrial classes. The tiller of the soil, as Irish history has shown, can exist even when denied almost every human right. But manufactures and commerce require the air of freedom. . . . The wealth came, but with it the ideas and spirit that in the next century (under Cromwell) bred a revolution." The Dissenting middle classes were shut out from official positions, and, therefore—like the Jews—they turned to business, to a capitalistic form of agriculture, to manufacturing, and to trade, this tendency being further strengthened by the Huguenots (*II, 401*), their importance for the Liberalism of the nineteenth century (*II, 404*)*:* "They forced the passage of the Reform Bill, widening the suffrage. Then they began to look round for social, legal, and other political reforms." They now began to follow Puritan America: "Rejuvenated England has followed America in her system of popular education, freedom of religion, freedom of the Press, the secret ballot, prison reform, and the entire reformation of her legal system." The origin of the secret ballot from the Dutch system of election within the Church, see *II, 437*. In spite of his insistence on the fact that all these things were due to the influence of Puritanism, *Campbell* does not throw much light upon the inner psychological connection. The ascription of these effects to "Puritanism" in Holland renders it particularly necessary to explain the latter; *C.*, however, takes this for granted. Further, the influence of Puritanism in England and in the Netherlands was a mutual one. There are similar descriptions of the English middle classes in *Held, p. 48*. *Weber*, in the articles which have often been mentioned, deals with the psychological analysis of this whole subject in a very fine and illuminating manner; he takes points which have merely been touched upon or suggested by these other authors and expands them along this line. For the transmission of this spirit to New England and through the Dutch to New York, see *Campbell, II*, and *Doyle: The English in America*.

[426] (p. 685.) Cf. *Göbel, I; Heppe; Ritschl, I; Knappert: Geschiedenis der nederlandsche hervormde Kerk gedurende de 16e en 17e Euw, Amsterdam, 1911;* for the constitution see *von Hoffmann: Das Kirchenverfassungsrecht der niederländ. Kirche bis 1618.* For present conditions, see *Rothenbücher, 425–429*. *Heppe* and *Ritschl* take almost no notice at all of the aspect of the question which concerns the history of civilization. The connection with England is brought out by *Heppe, 107–110, 140–144, 148, 156, 164, 185*. *Ritschl* scarcely touches this point, but, on the other hand, he analyses the contrast with primitive Calvinism, the connection with the fundamental impulse of Calvinism, the development of this Pietism out of a mere effort to provide more adequate means of grace and more pastoral care in order to build up believers in the life of sanctification, into a legalistic individualism, into a mysticism of the St. Bernard type, into evangelical emotionalism. He regards this as the destruction of ecclesiastical Calvinism by the spirit of the Anabaptists and of Catholic mysticism. He does not see, however, that in reality this represents the exaggerated endeavour of a whole people striving after holiness, and the natural result of the failure of rigorism in this task—thus a result of the Calvinistic principle itself—because his idea of the normal Christian life is summed up in the certainty of salvation, trust

in God, and loyalty to the duties of one's calling; this produces an ecclesiastical popular morality, from which, he says, Calvinism, through Pietism, has departed.—His endeavours to trace resemblances to Liberalism within Pietism are interesting (*p. 267*): "The student of history may assert, that . . . the expectation of inner and outer changes in the Church and in the world has hindered the Protestant Church no less than the well-meaning hopes of the political Enlightenment and of doctrinaire Liberalism endangered the health of the moral life of the people. Religion of the Pietist type is, at this point, assigned a close relationship with political Liberalism, whereas this school of thought considers itself to be exactly opposed to it. This, however, is due to the fact that originally Pietism did not trouble at all about the State as such, but that its endeavours which resemble Liberalism were all undertaken within the sphere of the Church. The adherents of the Enlightenment and of political Liberalism, however, know that Pietism prepared the way for their movements." Their ascetic and revivalist character is emphasized by *Knappert, p. 273*.—For their connection with the history of civilization in general see *Laspeyres; Douglas Campbell, II, 287–356; Busken-Huet: Het Land van Rembrandt*[2], *1886*. We must not overlook the fact that the Arminians, like the Anglicans, are defenders of the State Church or "Erastians", and that also for this very reason the theology of the Stuart period was Arminian, or at least it was called so. See also *Campbell, 304*, for the views of Oldenbarneveld on certain Calvinists whom he called "Puritans and double Puritans". Here the difficulty is not merely opposition to the doctrine of predestination. It is plain from the complaints of the Pietist section that their opposition was directed further against the worldliness of a politically, economically, and scientifically progressive nation which disapproves of asceticism. Above all, they strove against the exemption of certain practical callings from religious rules, and against the restriction of the latter merely to private and personal life. Often they almost hover on the brink of formulating the idea of an "intramundane asceticism". Cf. *Ritschl, I, 123*: "Voet accepts as the definition of mysticism the phrase of Gerson: *Vita contemplativa est status hominum extra mundum*. . . . Voet (who himself to a great extent accepted the mystical and ascetic literature of Catholicism (*Heppe, 151*)) discerned in this tendency the foundation of monasticism . . . and replies: *unde ipsos videre est separare invicem primae tabulae praecepta a praeceptis secundae tabulae*." *P. 274*: "It is, however, appropriate that if contemplation whose home is the cloister is to be carried out, the rule of the canonical hours must be rediscovered (i.e. the Puritan form of discipline and ordering of time, even to the extent of determining the length of time which may be spent in sleep). But this can only be permitted within civic activity, which is just as legitimate in the Calvinistic Church as it is customary among the Dutch people." *P. 278*: "Here we meet the ideas of self-examination and penitence, of self-denial and scrupulous behaviour, of the spiritual permeation of secular business and of the desire for perfection, and finally of public and private worship." *Busken-Huet, II, 84* (alluding to a book on the theologian Bogermann) gives an account of the ascetic requirements, and then adds: "Hunne levensbeschouwing was somber en stemmig als hun kleed. Zy geleken monniken, die hunne cel verlaten hadden, en het boze menschdom wilden overreden om, boete doende, de wereld voor zich tot een kloster te maken." This was everywhere the same as that word of Sebastian Franck, which I quoted earlier in this book (*Kultur d. G., N.S., 445*): "Detachment from the world and self-denial is the duty of all Christians; it is no use trying to throw the responsibility on to monasticism." *Rachfahl* calls all this only "common Christian morality". Unfortunately, *Knodt, p. 26,* also takes the same point of view.

[427] (p. 686.) A tendency to appeal to the lower classes among the people is asserted by *Heppe, p. 51*; *Knappert (172)* speaks of democratic tendencies in the Puritan preachers, which are in accord with their middle-class origin; the same is emphasized in the *Dissertation* by *Geibel,* which has already been mentioned, where it is asserted that wholesale business was (on the whole) carried on by the "Libertines" and trade by the Puritans or "Precisians"; see also *Laspeyres, Busken-Huet,* and *Douglas Campbell.*—An interesting illustration is given by Campbell of the supposed superiority of the Hollanders in the words of a London merchant named Lamb, who told Cromwell (*II, 327*): "In Holland, when a merchant dies, his property is equally divided among his children, and the business is continued and expanded, with all its traditions and inherited experience. In England, on the contrary, the property goes to the eldest son, who often sets up for a country gentleman, squanders his patrimony, and neglects the business by which his father has become enriched. . . . The honesty of the Hollanders in their manufacturing and commercial dealings. When goods are made or put up in Holland, they sell everywhere without question; for the purchaser knows that they are exactly as represented in quality, weight, and measure." *Laspeyres* says that the high position of Holland was due to religious toleration, and to the fact that persons who were engaged in trade were attracted into the country; also he speaks of the "moral advantages", such as frugality and honesty, which also helped to raise the whole tone of social life, and as a further factor he states that the question of religious denomination did not enter into business dealings (*pp. 122–124*). None of the other writers has mentioned this point, although both *Douglas Campbell* and *Busken-Huet* connect the flourishing state of the republic with its Puritan Calvinism. In general, too, the researches of *Weber* are very illuminating on this whole question; cf. *Weber: Antikritisches, u.s.w., pp. 186–188,* and his *Schlusswort, pp. 570–571.* He describes the Puritanism of the Netherlands as one which continually "broke down at important points, even though not at all points". Their missionary efforts in the colonies, for example, were suppressed; indeed, in the colonies as a whole the religious life was made to conform to the interests of trade, and in spite of certain scruples slavery was justified (*Laspeyres, 106, 111*).

[430] (p. 687.) Cf. *Münsterberg: Die Amerikaner, 1904,* and *W. von Polenz: Das Land der Zukunft, 1903*; both these books, however, throw very little light on this question at this point; even in *Tocqueville* there are only hints and suggestions; *W. Müller: Das religiöse Leben in Amerika, 1911,* does not give very much; there is more in the works of *Rauschenbusch. Max Weber* gives a good many individual examples, which are drawn from his study of the resemblance between the Pietism of the Lower Rhine and of Westphalia and the Puritan groups of England and America. Just because these groups are so different these resemblances are all the more valuable evidence for the existence of a definite social-ethical tendency and result of Calvinism (these two do not always coincide). *Weber* lays stress on the fact that these results happened in very unfavourable surroundings, like East Friesland and the young English colonies. It is, of course, understood that in each case other influences beside that of Calvinism have also contributed to bring about these results.

[431] (p. 688.) For the conception of Christian Socialism connected with Neo-Calvinism, see *Rauschenbusch und Holl: Calvinreden, p. 35.*—For the relation to Lutheranism, see the characteristic observations of *Kuyper, p. 15:* "In all

Lutheran countries the Reformation started rather with the princes than among the people, and thus it came to be under the power of the Government . . . and in consequence it has not transformed either social or political life by the power of its own vital principles. Lutheranism has remained churchly and theological; Calvinism alone has set its seal upon all the expressions of human life, both within and without the Church. No one speaks of Lutheranism as of the creation of a distinctive form of life, even the name is seldom mentioned; whereas all students of history agree in ever-increasing measure to salute Calvinism as the creator of a distinctive world of human life." Thus Calvinism feels itself to be the one great Christian social system alongside of Catholicism (*p. 10*): "Of Romanism alone can we say that it has incorporated its own thought about life in a distinctive world of sentiment and practical expression. But alongside of, and over against, this Romanism, Calvinism arose, not simply as a system of Church reform, but in order to create a quite different form of human life, to give to human society another form of existence, and to fill the human heart with other and different ideals and conceptions." "This unity of the conception of life we do not find in the narrow idea of Protestantism . . . but alone in the mighty historical process, which, in the form of Calvinism, drove its way through circumstances, and hollowed out a channel, through which the powerful current of its life could flow. It is, thanks to this consciousness of unity within Calvinism that you here in America, and we in Europe, can again take up our position alongside of Romanism, and over against modern Pantheism."—So far as Catholicism is concerned, here is the contrasting picture, mentioned by *Prezzolini: Wesen, Geschichte und Ziele des Modernismus, pp. 58–60:* "The Catholic ideal is a well-fed people, who think little, and are led and controlled by a theocracy. But this kind of social activity is utterly different from that which grew up during the nineteenth century, and, indeed, at two points: (*a*) in the predominance of the priesthood, and (*b*) in the exercise of charity. . . . The predominance of the theocracy is replaced by a strong emphasis upon the laity, and the idea of charity is replaced by that of the necessity for a fundamental social reform. . . . The attitude of Latin Catholics towards social democracy is divided. The Old Catholics represent the standpoint of love to one's neighbour and of good-will, and they are perpetually criticising economic Liberalism. . . . They believe that it would suffice if guilds on the mediaeval pattern and all kinds of co-operative societies were established, and more scope were given to the laity within the parishes. . . . Their highest ideal is that of a mediaeval society established upon a theocratic basis, with trade unions among the workpeople. The young Catholics are gradually becoming bolder; they desire more modern and quicker methods, and they do not shrink from imitating the methods of Social Democracy, and, in contrast to the Old Catholics, they refuse to combine with the reactionary bourgeois parties in politics." Hence, as is well known, in Italy they have been censured by the Pope.

[433] (p. 692.) Cf. *Hegler: Geist und Schrift bei Sebastian Franck, 1892, p. 168 n.* The significance of the Sermon on the Mount ought to be emphasized still more strongly, as this has been done in the writings of L. Keller, which will be mentioned shortly. For the significance of the Sermon on the Mount as an ideal of life among the Baptists, see *Gottfried Arnold: Unparteiische Kirchen- und Ketzerhistorie, 1700, II, pp. 529 ff.* We find the same thing in *Sebastian Franck: Chronica, Zeitbuch und Geschichtsbibel, 1536,* in the *Ketzerchronik, p. 146:* "Therefore there belong to these (to those who falsely reverence the Scriptures) all those who thus break up the Scriptures and who do not observe one word of God

as strictly as another, and who do not preach so willingly and so frequently from the fifth to the seventh chapter of Matthew and the sixth chapter of Luke as they do from the Epistles to the Romans and Galatians." Cf. also *Dilthey* in his important essay, *Auffassung und Analyse des Menschen im 15. und 16. Jahrhundert, Archiv. f. Gesch. d. Philos., V, 1892*; his words on *p. 378* are very striking: "In the Protestant community the principle of the inner Word was in conflict with that of the Scriptures—the Gospels with Paul—the Apostolic life with mankind as it is—the Christian ideal with statecraft—above all, however, the Word of the Bible with the progressive form of religious life produced by the Reformation."

[434] (p. 693.) Illuminating, though decidedly grim in its irony, is the treatise of Luther, in this connection, entitled *Wider die himmlischen Propheten von den Bildern und Sakrament*, of 1525 (*B. A. Ergänzungsband, I*). So far as both Luther and his opponents regarded the whole Bible, and Paul in particular, as an inspired authority, Luther's attack is certainly right, and it represents the logical consequence of his fundamental ideas. This situation is excellently described by *Erbkam: Gesch. d. prot. Sekten, 1848, pp. 167–171, 483–488.* The development out of mysticism is very well described in the book by *Braun*, which has already been mentioned, *Bedeutung der Konkupiszenz in Luthers Leben und Lehre, 1908.* The most recent study, based on newly discovered early works of Luther by *Scheel: Entwickelung L.s bis zum Abschluss der Vorlesung über den Römerbrief* (*Schriften des Vereins für Ref. Gesch., 1910*) underestimates the significance of the mystical element in an amazing way; see in particular *pp. 192 f.* and *201 f.* For Luther's connection with mysticism see also the excellent work of *H. Hering: Die Mystik Luthers, 1879.* See also above, *pp. 494 ff.*

[438] (p. 694.) Cf. *Karl Müller: Kirche, Gemeinde und Obrigkeit nach Luther, 1910,* especially *pp. 32–40, 84.* I consider *Müller's* argument entirely valid; it also agrees with my own conception, see above, *pp. 487–494.* Even in these smaller communities Luther has retained the general Church conception of an organ of salvation produced by the Word. His idea was simply that these groups were to be smaller and more closely knit circles within the Church itself, and that gradually from these groups the influence of the Word should be carried out into the popular and national churches. All that they possess is due only to the effect of the Word, but it is the real, strong, and visible effect of the Word which is concentrated here and which finally should be spread outwards over the whole. Thus the general idea of the Church is maintained, but within it there still takes place a certain approximation to the ideas of the sect. In all this the idea of the Church certainly predominates, and in consequence, upon the whole, Luther's development is essentially straightforward, as I have described it above. He did not suddenly incline towards the sect and then return to the Church; he only made the attempt to make room for the sect-idea within the Church. That, however, is a very difficult matter, and that is why in this question Luther did not get beyond the stage of drawing up plans. The decisive element is the idea of the Church, which determines all the rest. This has already been understood quite rightly by *Erbkam, pp. 9–13.*—I therefore do not agree with *Rieker* and *Achelis* that this approach to the sect simply meant that for a time and against his own principles Luther was influenced by the Baptists; in my opinion this approximation towards the idea of the sect was due to an inner conflict within his own thought which arose from his study of the Bible.

[439] (p. 694.) Appeals to the younger Luther, who is supposed to have betrayed his earlier ideals, are general among the Dissenters. *Hochhuth* gives examples in

his great series of articles from the published records of the *Hess. Archiven, Z. f. hist. Theol., XXVIII–XXXII;* especially *XXVIII, pp. 542, 631; XXIX, p. 179.* Here is the letter of an Anabaptist: "Even their own prophet, Martinus Luther, has also written about these things (in a little book which is called *Eine Weise christlichi Mass zu halten*) that people should come together behind closed doors and set things in order. Once again he said: 'I am not yet bold enough to begin such a thing lest it should be thought to be some kind of fanatical sect.'" Everywhere here the complaints are given as the reason for the Anabaptist movement that the new Church achieves nothing in the moral sphere, and that Luther did not venture to continue his first attempt for lack of genuine Christians to carry out his ideas.—The interpretation which *W. Köhler*, in the *reformatio Hassiaca*, has given as a working out of the same Lutheran ideas, is also connected with this subject. (*Entstehung der ref. eccles. Hassiae of 1526, Deutsche Z. f. Kirchenrecht, 1906, pp. 199–232*). Even when in the case of Lambert these ideas were attributed at an earlier period to Franciscan ideals, the instinct was still right because they are sect-ideals; but at the time the fact was overlooked that Luther himself in his earlier period had tried to unite these ideas with his later conception of the Church; cf. *W. Köhler: Zu Luthers Kirchenbegriff, Chr. W., 1907.*—Among the Independents, William Dell, who has already been mentioned, and who will be treated more fully in a later section of this book, referred expressly to Luther in his original combination of mystical, Congregationalist, and State Church ideas; see *Sippell: William Dells Programm einer "lutherischen" Gemeinschaftsbewegung, 1911.* So far as Schwenkfeld is concerned, *Ecke*, in his *Schwenkfeld, Luther und der Gedanke einer apostolischen Reformation, 1911*, and also *Sippell*, in his article, *Caspar Schwenkfeld, Chr. W., 1911, Nr. 37–41*, have shown the connection with Luther's ideas.—*Franck*, in the splendidly objective article, *Martin Luther*, in his *Ketzerchronik*, emphasizes the idea of the more exclusive Christian community with its own sacramental celebrations (*II, 173b*). *Hegler* points out everywhere that Franck and the Anabaptists have a close connection with the original ideas of the Reformation. —But *Gottfried Arnold* also is quite clear upon this point. Thus *Arnold* appeals to Luther's original rejection of war, in which he agreed with the Anabaptists; cf. also *Franck's Kriegbüchlein.* "After which Luther altered his opinion which had been previously formed in harmony with the Will of Christ, because he felt that the Gospel does not do away with Natural Law" (*Arnold, II, 11 and 12*). In his opinion, Luther's ideas were "stifled by the jurists" (*II, 20*). The urgent impulse towards real sanctification which characterized the earlier stages of Luther's career, in which Luther's monastic ideals were still active (*II, 46*), which, however, unfortunately he gave up later on (*II, 93*). The idea of particular smaller communities as a useful adjunct is emphasized in *II, 132*; practice of electing pastors by the congregation unfortunately given up (*II, 161*); likewise prohibition of usury unfortunately given up (*II, 162*).—*Spener's Pia desideria* appeals, it is true, in reference to the *Collegia Biblica* not to Luther's ideal of groups of genuine Christians, but to his ideal of the priesthood of all believers (see Edition of 1706, *p. 109*). Further, to Luther's recommendations of Tauler, Thomas à Kempis, and the *Theologia Germanica, p. 140*; he also emphasizes the Christian Utopian characteristics of the Lutheran ethic: avoiding of lawsuits (*p. 41*); communal holding of possessions in a different but analogous sense like that of the Early Church in Jerusalem (*p. 43*); everywhere in general recourse to the Apostolic Church and the assurance that that was no *respublica Platonica.* For the relation of the Pietist *Collegia Biblica* to Luther's "more exclusive groups", see *K. Müller: Kirche, Gemeinde, u.s.w., pp. 83 ff.*

[440] (p. 695.) The most important presentation of the subject is given by *Gottfried Arnold* in his *Kirchen u. Ketzergeschichte*, a Church history which is not yet out of date and which can still be used along with modern Church histories. It uses an unbelievable wealth of source-material, and brings one into the atmosphere of the Protestantism outside the Churches as no other book does. Further, there is also *Sebastian Franck's* famous *Geschichtsbibel*, in which the *Ketzerchronik* is incorporated; here the Anabaptists are described with special emphasis, and obviously out of a wide personal experience and exhaustive research. *Bullinger: Der Wiedertäufer Ursprung, Fürgang, Sekten, Wesen, Zürich, 1560.* This writer takes one into the hostile atmosphere of a national Church and into the relative right of defence; a national Church could not come to terms with these people.—Modern presentations of the subject suffer, above all, from this defect, that they do not distinguish between this Anabaptist, sectarian movement, and mysticism; while in actual fact the two were often united they are, nevertheless, distinct in the inner structure of thought. The custom of early heresy-hunters to call all heretics "*Schwenkfeldiani, Anibaptistae et alii id genus*" and then to include them all under one head, and Luther's habit of calling them all fanatics and saying that they perpetuate the Catholic heresy of good works, legalism, and monasticism, has greatly obscured our understanding of this subject. *Hegler*, who is the most expert and understanding student of this subject, has rightly warned us that we ought to distinguish between the two, and in so doing, above all, he has already pointed out the sociological differences between the two; *Anzeige von Harnacks Dogmengeschichte Theol. Litztg., 1908, pp. 253–258.—Ritschl* (*Gesch. d. Pietismus, I*) also follows Luther's and Bullinger's track; "as a Lutheran theologian" and Churchman he feels obliged "to adhere to the opinion of the Reformers" (*p. 7*), hence he argues that the Anabaptist movement and mysticism have developed out of Catholicism—mainly, it is true, out of the popular expansions of the Franciscan movement, whose origins, therefore, were not well known. At the same time he recognized the difference between the sect and mysticism as something which "in itself is quite a matter of indifference" (*pp. 28, 35*); but he thinks that the coupling of both together arose already out of monasticism, which, on the one hand, desires to renew the Apostolic life of detachment from the world, and, on the other hand, owing to the fact that it had no profession or occupation within the world, very naturally gave way to mysticism of an emotional kind!—*Ludwig Keller* has also maintained that the Anabaptists were non-Protestant in character (*Reformat. d. älteren Reformparteien, 1885, Staupitz und Anfänge d. Reform., 1888, Anfänge d. Reform. u. Ketzerschulen, 1897*), but for his part he does not attribute this to Catholicism, but to the voluntary Church, purely primitively Christian, which had a separate existence from the time of Constantine—the so-called early Evangelical communities who had a high standard of social morality and religious toleration—which, with Peter Waldo and the Anabaptists, only underwent a certain transformation, and which in his opinion represent the genuine Christian tradition as compared with Catholicism and Protestantism. Even though this idea of "early Protestant communities" at least in this form may be a fantasy picture, still the researches of *Keller* are certainly very instructive and stimulating. His chief defect is that he does not analyse clearly enough the essence of the sect in contradistinction to that of the Church, and that he includes under his conception of the sect all forms of opposition to the Established Church, mysticism, humanism, etc. In particular, the failure to distinguish between mysticism and the sect in the case of the Friends of God, Tauler, etc., makes it very difficult to get any clear picture of the real situation. He always makes

mysticism and the sect explain one another; "the theology of the latter must be used as the complement of German mysticism at every point in which the latter is in the habit of evading a definite pronouncement!" *Staupitz, 143:* Mysticism is said to be only "half the system of the earlier Protestants" (*ebd., 224*). If now the Anabaptist movement does not quite correspond to this mingled ideal, consisting of mysticism and a tolerant voluntary Church, this then must be ascribed to the fact that the Anabaptists in earlier times had transferred to the whole Church an ascetic doctrine and a rejection of the world which was only meant for Apostles (*ebd., 321*)—a statement which is nowhere proved. All this points to the fact that these component parts which *Keller* combines ought to be separated, and that the problem of the origin of each from the Middle Ages and of its relation to the Reformation principle must be stated. Then, however, the phantom of the early Protestant communities disappears altogether, and the relation between the Anabaptists and the earlier sects proved by *Keller* loses the striking significance which *Keller* gives it as the apologist of the "early Protestant communities"; he even argues that the Reformation was due to them through Staupitz.—*Thudichum: Die deutsche Reformat., 1517–37, 1907–1909,* follows *Keller's* line; he obliterates the difference between the sect and mysticism with the words (*II, 114*): "The expression 'mystics', which the newer Protestant theologians are so fond of using, which really means esoterists (*Geheimtuer*), is very unsuitable, and it is high time that we avoided this foreign word."—The whole question appears under a different aspect among those who hold that the Anabaptists and "spiritual reformers" are the logical result of the principle of Church fellowship and of liberty of conscience of the Reformation, like *Weingarten: Revolutionskirchen Englands, 1868, p. 442;* and *A. Dorner: Grundriss der Dogmengeschichte, 1899, pp. 253 ff.* Thinkers of this school usually overlook the fact that the Dissenters are also in the direct line of the mediaeval development, only they belong to a tendency which is different from that which the Reformers are carrying forward. The emphasis on a manifold relationship with the ideas of the Reformation, which had not yet become ecclesiastically settled, is quite right.—The able book by *Erbkam* still deserves attention at the present day; it contains much suggestive matter, but he is quite wrong in his conclusions. In his opinion the Anabaptists represent ethical mysticism, while the "spiritual reformers" represent intellectual mysticism. Together they are thus supposed to be a continuous supplement, brought down from the Middle Ages, of the objective and institutional character of the Church, which ought to have formed the complementary movement in Protestantism. These movements, however, broke away from Protestantism in an unhealthy manner, and some of them merged into pantheism; he concludes by pointing out the peril of separation from the Church as the organ of salvation.—A wealth of source-material, and an illumination of the whole movement from local points of view, can be found in *Hochhuth: Protestant. Sektengeschichte in Hessen, Z. f. hist. Theologie, XXVIII–XXXII.* Here also everything starts from the Reformation and the criticism of its defective moral achievement.—There is an excellent description of the German Anabaptist movement in *Cornelius: Gesch. d. Münsterschen Aufruhrs, 1855–60*; a socialistically coloured collective description in *E. Belfort Bax: Rise and Fall of the Anabaptists, London, 1903* (the closing chapter is particularly important with its indications of continuations in the English Revolution); from the Baptist standpoint, *A. H. Newman: History of Antipedabaptism, Philadelphia, 1897,* the most detailed account of the whole movement, unfortunately only until 1609; finally, the article "*Täufer*", by *Kramer: PRE*³.—

There is also a good deal of important material in *Göbel: Gesch. des christl. Lebens*. For the connection of this movement (including the Pietist Separatist groups) with the weaving and cloth-making industries, which appeared especially among the Waldensians, see *I, 37–39*; for the connection with the numerous Waldensians of the Rhineland, *I, 40–42*. Göbel connects with this also the victory of Calvinism over Lutheranism in these lands, since Calvinism was more closely related to the Waldensian ascetic Christians. A very good description of the Baptist movement as a sect-type (*I, pp. 143–149*). Here also his view is fair: "a quite definite tendency of Christian life which, in its fanatical form, could indeed be fought against and also violently stamped out, but in its truth and necessity could never be completely suppressed and overcome", "it also should be definitely recognized as a Christian movement" (*I, 135*). In Pietism he sees only the reappearance of this tendency; *I, 157*, and in other places. In all this, however, he has not distinguished clearly enough between the ideas of the sect-type and of mysticism.

[441] (p. 696.) Cf. the description in *G. Arnold, II, 264ff., and 524ff.*, who, however, separates himself clearly from them: "Although there was much human foolishness, blindness, and weakness among them, there was also to be seen in many a great simplicity and fidelity of obedience, because they tried to follow the letter of Scripture with so great exactitude, that also in so doing they fell into other untimely opinions (this means that they became exclusive and intolerant) and they themselves came into disrepute and fell on evil days." *Arnold* himself sides with the mystics. In *Arnold, II, 266*, we have Luther's opinion: "This monster can be controlled neither by sword nor by fire. They leave wife, child, house, and farm, all that they have." Also the opinion of Melanchthon: "No one should be distressed when they see the Anabaptists going to death so confidently and suffering so many things, because Satan has hardened their hearts." The Calvinist controversialist, Hornbeck, is somewhat milder: "It was not so much that the Anabaptists withstood the orthodox Protestants with their doctrine by adding another or a new doctrine, as that they did not quite understand the doctrine of orthodox Protestantism." In *Arnold, II, 524*, we have a later orthodox opinion: "If I regard the Anabaptists and the Mennonites they seem to lead forsooth a hypocritical kind of life, they avoid fine clothes, swearing, lying, gluttony, drinking, adultery, villainy, quarrels, and contentions like the devil, so that whoever comes into their community or their society stands almost amazed, thinking that he has not come among men, but among angels in the form of men, or, at least, that he is among living saints and elect, genuine Christians."—Of fundamental importance also is the description given by *Sebastian Franck* (*Ketzerchronik, 193–201*), whom *Keller* very wrongly calls a "genuine Baptist" (*Ref., p. 462*), and who in any case knows nothing about Keller's early Protestant communities. Franck says simply about their origin: "In the year 1526, both during and after the Peasants' Revolt, there arose a new sect and a separate Church founded upon the letter of Scripture which some call Anabaptists and others Baptists, who began to separate themselves from others with a particular baptism and to despise all other communities as unchristian; also they believed that no one could be saved or be their brother who did not belong to their sect or their party. They began to baptize all those who joined them for the second time, or, rather, as they gave out, to baptize according to the command of Christ. . . . Their overseer and bishop was first Balthasar Hübner, then Melchior Rink, followed by Joh. Hut, Joh. Denck, Ludwig Hetzer. . . . They appeared to teach nothing but love, faith, and the Cross, in much suffering they showed them-

selves patient and humble; they broke bread with one another as a sign of unity and love; they helped each other faithfully with lending, borrowing, giving away, and they taught that all things should be in common; they called each other brethren. If, however, anyone did not belong to their sect they scarcely greeted him, they would not stretch out the hand to him, they kept together, and increased so greatly from year to year that the world was afraid that they would cause an uproar." The terrible persecution and the number of martyrdoms convinced the masses that these were true Christians, and thus they again gathered large numbers of adherents. Then it seems that many Baptists went beyond the good which was undoubtedly in them. "They became in spirit somewhat uppish, they began to judge everyone, and in many places they became disunited amongst themselves and they had as many doctrines as they had leaders. . . . Although I entirely believe that it is true that many pious, simple people were and still are in this sect, and that many of their leaders also have been ardent for God, but to my thinking not with knowledge. However, one ought not thus to tyrannize over them when they are obstinate and will not allow themselves to be taught, but we must commend them to God, who alone can give faith, root out heresy, and give good counsel in the whole matter." These are the characteristic features of the sect-type until the present day. "In their communities there is so much excommunication that every community excommunicates the other, and there is as much freedom to believe what they will as there is among the Anabaptists. Whoever in their communities does not say Yes in all these matters, they say that God has stopped his ears, and they begin to pray for him with sighs and tears. If he does not soon change his mind they cast him out" (*193*[a]). Thence also a great confusion: "Although all sects are split amongst themselves, yet the Baptists are so specially disunited and broken up amongst themselves that I do not know how to describe anything certain and complete about them" (*193*[b]). If we tabulate the different shades of opinion which Franck describes, we find that there are two main groups: those who have joined settled organizations and are bound by the law of the Scriptures, and those who favour rather enthusiasm and mysticism, and therefore become individualists without fellowship, but who still find their adherence essentially in Baptist circles. Later on we shall hear more about this difference. The "free Baptists", which were so called from the time of Bullinger, were not Baptists, but spiritual idealists.—Schwenkfeld and Franck agree. Cf. *Ecke, 89, 204–212.*

[442] (p. 697.) Cf. the well-known collections of passages in which Lutheranism testifies against itself in *Döllinger* and *Janssen*. Still more striking is the treatment of the subject by the honest *Gottfried Arnold*, and this point of view also prevails in *Franck's Geschichtsbibel*. Quite rightly *Hegler* has attempted to understand Franck entirely from this point of view, just as *Ecke* has tried to do with Schwenkfeld. Also in the splendid book by *Paul Drews: Der evang. Geistliche i. d. deutsch. Vergangenheit, 1905*, the description of the moral condition both of the clergy and of the laity gives a very dark picture. It is not sufficient to explain this meagre success as the after-result of earlier Catholic education, or to recall the later chaos caused by war. The very limited moral success of the Reformation is certainly due to something in its own nature; see *Ecke, 88.* The ideals were too high and the means of education were limited. It was impossible to realize these ideals until Pietism undertook the care of souls, and later the more humane morality of the Enlightenment, and popular education were also of great use. How very limited this morality was, however, is revealed, for example, by the well-known autobiography of the notorious Magister Lauck-

hardt. The raising of the average morality of the masses has, indeed, in general only been achieved by elementary education and the modern State, in which then, however, the ideals were not primarily drawn from a highly idealistic Lutheranism.

[445] (p. 699.) Thus it appears as though Münzer left the circle influenced by Luther and went over into the conventicles of Zwickau (*Thudichum, I, 215*); *Keller* also has made it seem probable that Grebel was connected with the Waldensians (*Reformation, 381–388*); also it is obvious that many of the Baptist preachers had already been leaders of conventicles even before Adult Baptism had been introduced (*Ketzerschulen, 52*). In the protocols of the trials of the Anabaptists which are mentioned in *Wappler: Inquisition und Ketzerprozess in Zwickau, 1908*, there are several references to a Waldensian origin (*pp. 121, 123 ff.*). On the other hand, the heretical "godless painters of Nürnberg", with whom Denck was in touch, seem to have been of a very different character.

[447] (p. 702.) An opponent of Joh. Arndt says very strikingly, even though with the characteristic disapproval of Arnold: "Those people would be wrong who would apply to all the teachings contained in Arndt's or Tauler's books since ordinary life requires quite other manners" (*G. Arnold, II, 458*). This is also the central point of Bullinger's criticism of the Anabaptists; they are against the Christian love which embraces the whole of humanity and endurance of circumstances "willed" by God; cf. *Sebastian Franck: Ketzerchronik, p. 153.* On the other hand, Schwenkfeld directs his criticism precisely against the national Church and recognizes its connection with popular "sacramentalism" (*Ecke, 103*).

[450] (p. 706.) Cf. the sketch in *Barclay: The Inner Life, pp. 79–89.* The acceptance of the Calvinistic ethic of "the calling", in which the old Baptist asceticism is only carried on in the avoidance of all outward luxury and all external honours, is rightly emphasized by *Max Weber: Archiv f. Soz., XXI, p. 69.* The criticism of the Radicals from the standpoint of "spiritualist" asceticism frequently in *Hylkema: Reformateurs*; further, see *Kramer: PRE*[3], the article on *Menno und Mennoniten;* also *Göbel, II, 690–697.* Here is an extract from a letter by William III of Orange: "I have always been assured of the submissive and peaceful spirit of the Mennonites, who behave themselves with resignation and perfect obedience towards their superiors, leading a peaceful and laborious life and contributing willingly to the upkeep of the State and of the country in which they live, to which they render themselves useful by their industry and their work." Here also there is information about their industrial capitalistic character.

[453] (p. 707.) The Particular (that is, Predestinarian) Baptists are not to be connected with this. The latter are pure Calvinists who deduced Adult Baptism from the theory of the Free Churches, just as, on the other hand, the Free Churches in their day arose out of the ideal of believers' Baptism. That becomes plain when we remember the formal connection between the Free Church and the sect-ideal which was explained when we were dealing with Calvinism; *Newman, p. 393; Barclay, p. 318*: "They consisted of little companies of respectable, godly people, gathered from Presbyterian worship, into what they deemed a more Scriptural form of Church discipline, and gradually became convinced of the importance and Scriptural sanction of immersion."

[454] (p. 709.) Cf. *Glass: The Barebones Parliament. Weingarten* makes too little distinction between the Anabaptists and Independents; his statement on *p. 158:* "In Cromwell the Anabaptist movement reaches its high-water mark, but it was also his doing that Anabaptism ceased to be a power", is only

accurate to a very limited extent. Further, *Gooch: The History of English Democratic Ideas in the Seventeenth Century, Cambridge, 1898*, a very solid and instructive book, which *Weingarten* expands and carries further. For the economic and social historical side of the matter, cf. the important work by *E. Bernstein: Kommunistische und sozialistische Strömungen während der englischen Revolution des 18. Jahrh.*, in "*Geschichte des Sozialismus in Einzeldarstellungen*", *I, 1895, pp. 507–718*; here, of course, according to socialistic historical dogma all that is religious is only a transparent veil for economic social endeavours which are here present in their pre-Marxian, that is, their ideological, and, indeed, Christian Anabaptist, stage; further, *Belfort Bax: Rise and Fall of the Anabaptists, London, 1903*, in which the whole is indirectly ascribed to the Baptist movement.—All the accounts recognized the essentially Baptist character of the later radical movement, which removes the Presbyterian and Calvinistic-Independent character; both the accounts of the question and the sources make constant reference to strong remnants of radical Baptists; cf. *Weingarten, pp. 103–105*, the witness of Baillies, *Weingarten, pp. 127, 179, Anm. 2, 265*. Further, *Gooch, 73–75, 128–129, 174 ff., 267–270; Bernstein, 509, 522; Vorspiel im Jahre 1549, 525–527; Lollharden und Täufer*. For the relation to Luther see a pamphlet in *Weingarten, p. 114:* "The time of Jerome of Prague or of Luther was but a little better than the darkest time of Popery." That is the language of Baptists and of "spiritual reformers". There are many references to the radical Baptists who are distinguished from the peaceful General Baptists in *Barclay: The Inner Life*, and in the important book by *Firth: Cromwell's Army, 1902*, which, unfortunately, does not pursue this subject in further detail. Dispute of the Army Chaplains about Infant Baptism (*p. 325*); in favour of lay preaching, by Lieut. Chillandon in the tract, *Preaching Without Ordination*; the lieutenant became an Anabaptist preacher. *P. 336:* Lay preaching, especially that of the officers, came into being because the Presbyterian pastors were withdrawn from the army. *Firth, 334 ff.*, likewise *Bernstein, 546*. It was connected with Chiliasm, since at the coming of the Kingdom the settled ministry will disappear. This lay preaching of the officers and their religious discussions, easily led to religious-political theories (*Firth, p. 337*). Yet the right of free preaching was never unrestricted and uncontrolled; it ended with the cleansing of the army from all "Anabaptist" elements, whereby, however, Cromwell expressly desired to retain the more peaceful "Anabaptist" in the army. A pamphlet of 1655 (*Firth, 342 ff.*) thus addresses Cromwell: "And so were you at Dunbar in Scotland, or at least you seemed so by your words and your actions; for you spake as pure Independency as any of us all then, and made this an argument why we should fight stoutly because we had the prayers of the Independents and Baptist Churches. So highly did you seem to love the Anabaptists then, that you did not only invite them into the army, but entertained them in your family." The ethical religious argument for the war against the previous authority was at first that of the Huguenots, the Scots, and the Calvinists, the soldier's catechism in *Firth, 330*, and the tract by *Bridge* about the right of armed resistance in *Hanbury: Historical Memorials Relating to the Independents, II, 189 ff.* With the incursion of Chiliasm the argument becomes different: the task is now to prepare for the Kingdom of Christ. A tract by *Archer* entitled *The Personal Reign of Christ upon Earth, 1642*, which Herr *Sippell* has most kindly lent me, is particularly instructive upon this point. With that the conception of the right of war becomes very similar to that of the Baptists or is directly dependent upon it.—Otherwise the influencing of the army through politics is the result of the break with Parliament and signifies the rise of a definite political and social class in the army (*Firth, 318, 351–354*).

Originally consisting of men who had been impressed, it had no interest of its own. Since 1651 the army consists only of volunteers because its one aim is to fight for one's people and one's religion. The real headquarters of these volunteers was from the beginning in Cromwell's cavalry.—For the absolute Natural Law of the sect which arose with that at the same time in contrast to the relative Natural Law of the Church, and the Natural Law of the social contract of the Huguenot and Scottish type which was still conceived on class lines, see *Gooch, pp. 108ff.*, also *pp. 117 and 133–162* (*Ireton*); the transition to radicalism, *pp. 176* (Godwin) *and 180* (Milton); the radical Natural Law of the Primitive State, of Reason, and of Christ, without compromise with sin, *pp. 184ff., 119, 328.* Particularly in the treatise of *Berens* about the Diggers, which will be mentioned directly: "First we demand yea or no, whether the earth with her fruits was made to be bought and sold from one to another? And whether one part of mankind was made to be a lord of the land and another part a servant by the law of Creation before the Fall?" For Bunyan, see *Belfort Bax, pp. 379–381.*

[455] (p. 711.) For the "Levellers" the best account in *Gooch, pp. 139–157, 195–206, 256–259.* Here the conception of *Weingarten* seems the most singular; he sees in them disguised Rationalists and even the beginnings of Deism, because he does not recognize the absolute Natural Law in its identity with Reason and the law of Christ as the early sect-idea. The absolute Law of Nature appears to him to be modern Rationalism, which it is not. *Bernstein* goes still further: he thinks that the religious element was merely superficial and was only used as a cover for something else. The treatise by *Overton: Man's Mortality*, to which he appeals, *pp. 579ff.*, still only denies the so-called intermediate State and teaches a full physical resurrection. The Epicurean expressions of Walwyn (*pp. 581ff.*) show a good deal more, although they are reported by opponents. In Lilburn himself and the whole movement there can be no doubt at all about the essentially spiritual and religious basis. The rejection of dogma and of the plan of salvation, also its allegorizing tendency, reveals a spirituality of the type of Sebastian Franck, but not a concealed surrender of its religious basis. The treatise, entitled *The Craftsman's Craft, 1649*, quoted by *Weingarten: p. 307*, as well as the treatise written in defence of Walwyn, *The Charity of Churchmen* (both probably by the same writer), has been made known to me by the kindness of Herr *Sippell.* Of the religious element it contains more than the mere confession of the existence of God quoted by *W.* It defends Overton's expression of opinion about the mortality of the body (which was touched upon above), expressly asserting the resurrection of the spirit and its reincarnation; it protects itself, further, with a characteristic limitation, against the reproach of Anabaptism of the Münster pattern: "Where proofs are wanting there are resemblances insinuated in their stead; and comparisons made either in such things as are true of neither, or else the Party that is to be made odious is likened to such as are already *in some particulars not material; and yet thereby is suggested a similitude in all the rest.*" This, however, amounts to a confession of the Baptist ideal, apart from some particulars not material. Above all, there is the argument of the demand of the "Levellers" as a movement: "We answer, that we cannot suppose, nor do we think any rational man to believe, the thing unlawful in itself; *for then the primitive Christians did what was unlawful.*" The principle in itself is Christian and reasonable; only it must not be forced upon people with violence: "To make it lawful there must be an unanimous and individual consent of every man thereunto." This also shows in what consisted the *particulars*, which the "Levellers" disapproved in the Münster Anabaptists:

in the spirit of violence which was against the Christian spirit. The statement quoted by *Weingarten, p. 304*, shows, however, only the spirituality of the people, whose non-rationalistic spirit we shall learn more about later on.

[456] (p. 712.) Cf. *Gooch, pp. 214–225; Bernstein, pp. 583–608;* above all, the book by *Berens: The Digger Movement in the Days of the Commonwealth, London, 1906*, which provides the most important account of the subject. The fact that *W.* describes God as Reason, or Creative Reason, has led many people to think that these ideas are essentially rationalistic. *W.*, however, begins with the Familists and ends with the Quakers. The Creative Reason is the Logos identical with the indwelling Christ: "This spirit of Reason is not without a man, but within every man; hence he need not to run after others to tell him or to teach him; for this Spirit is his Maker, He dwells in him, and if the flesh were subject thereunto he would daily find teaching therefrom, though he dwelt alone and saw the face of no other man" (*p. 45*). "Even so, Christ, which is the spreading Power, is now beginning to fill every man and woman with Himself. He will dwell and rule in everyone: and the Law of Reason and equity shall be Christ in them. . . . This is the Church, the great congregation which, when the mystery is completed, shall be the mystical Body of Christ all set at liberty from inward and outward straits and bondage, and this is called the holy breathing, that made all new by Himself and for Himself" (*p. 67*). "The Golden Rule, do to another as thou wouldst have another do to thee, which God, Christ, and Scripture have enacted for a law" (*p. 171*). "The law of creation and equity of the Scriptures" (*p. 158*). "That their intent is to restore the Creation to its former condition" (*p. 37*). In this sense the idea is always also that of the *birthright* or of the inborn right, or of the rights of humanity. Here already we meet this significant idea, and, indeed, as one which is based upon religion. The birthright is, at the same time, the pre-Norman English right of the people, as once in the Wycliffe movement; before the Conquest the Law of Nature prevailed. Such passages are innumerable; this is the Christian Natural Law in the form of the sect which is well known to us, and, further, it is united with mystical spirituality. For *W.'s* relation to the Baptists, see *p. 65* (they are too external for him).—For Plockboy, see *Bernstein, pp. 685–694*, and *Laspeyres, pp. 105 ff.*—For Bellers, see *Bernstein, pp. 694–728.*

[458] (p. 714.) For this cf. my treatment of the subject which deals with Independency and the significance of the Cromwellian period in *Kultur d. G., IV, 12, pp. 588–600*. The material which is there united is here broken up into its various component parts, and each one is dealt with in connection with its position in the course of development. "Independency" is, indeed, something very great and complicated in which the most varied elements are united. My treatment of the influence of the Baptist element, which there was dealt with in a very general manner, and which, further, was too much at that time under the influence of *Weingarten*, is now more exactly defined. With that are removed the partially justified misgivings which were aroused by *Loofs* in his *Luther und Mittelalter: p. 15.*

[459] (p. 719.) Cf. the excellent article by *Mirbt: Pietismus*, in *PRE*³, *XV*, further *Ritschl; Heppe; Grünberg: Spener, 1893, 1905, 1906; Göbel: Geschichte d. christlichen Lebens in der rheinisch-westphälischen ev. Kirche, 1849, 1852, 1860. Stephan: Pietismus als Träger des Fortschritts, 1908; W. Köhler: Anfänge des Pietismus in Giessen, 1689–1695*, in the *Giessener Festschrift of 1907*. For the social connections, see *Gustav Freytag* in his *Bildern aus der deutschen Vergangenheit; Bertholdt: Die Erweckten im prot. Deutschland (Raumers historisches Taschenbuch, 1852 and 1853)*, here the Calvinistic, non-Spener character of the phenomena, which have been

described, is not taken into account; *Drews: Einfluss der Kirche auf die gesellschaftlichen Zustände, Z. f. Th. u. K., 1905; Uhlhorn: Liebestätigkeit, III, 236–261;* especially *Ritschl, II, 500–505; Max Weber: Archiv XXI, pp. 39–56. Weingarten* in general does not sufficiently distinguish the various currents of thought, and unfortunately he has paid no attention to the Pietist current in its difference from Congregationalism and the Baptist movement in England, even though incidentally he actually describes it excellently.—*Ritschl's* work—in its own way magnificent—is based upon the clear recognition of the sectarian character of Pietism, and for this reason, from the standpoint of a complete bourgeois and Churchman, is a polemic which on account of its absolutely inquisitorial penetration is of the highest importance. It is most interesting and instructive that in *Ritschl* this hostile attitude towards Pietism is caused by the fact that he saw clearly that only a Territorial Church system, based upon the doctrine of the remission of sins, and only a Church which is guided by an objective ministry, can support the moral relativism necessary for a popular Christianity of the masses and the relatively moderate Rationalism of a scientific theology. "Christianity, in the shape of a people's Church, in order to maintain its own existence, is obliged to take the middle path in matters of public custom, and also to allow for many varieties and degrees of individual religious experience" (*I, 178*). "The root cause of all Separatism lies in the fact that the relative character of ecclesiastical relations is not admitted" (*I, 450*). "Originally Pietism concentrated its attention upon the moral security of the salvation of each individual in opposition to the world, and on the rejection of all considerations which the Church usually practises towards the world" (*I, 450*). "Lutheranism, which gave all its attention to purity of doctrine, remained out of direct contact with the ethical and aesthetic needs which ought to be met within the sphere of the religious education of a people." Thus so far Pietism in his opinion was already prepared for by the Church itself (*II, 88*). "He who in his place does his duty as a Christian must thus judge in the faith that where the Gospel is purely and sincerely preached there God has His Church." (*II, 151*). "A life which starts from conviction of sin and a genuine conversion may still bring about very many more testing experiences of Christian perfection. It has, however, moved away from the sphere of the exclusive Church connection, and if it finds a corresponding sphere of fellowship in sect or clique or Enlightenment, this has not been foreseen in that principle" (*II, 194*). These statements illuminate excellently the spirit of the Church-type. There is, however, no need to emphasize, on the other hand, the fact that the sect and mysticism are nearer to primitive Christianity than the Church, and that the appeal to the Early Church in Jerusalem is relatively justified.—The latter point has been seen much more clearly and truly by *Göbel*: "All these orgies and dangerous excesses (of Pietism) are so closely connected with the (Scripturally) thoroughly justified ways of the Christian life that they still always ought to be regarded as Christian phenomena; indeed, frequently the right method only develops itself out of the excess which was originally combined with sinful one-sidedness and error; for instance, it was only through mysticism and Separatism that genuine mysticism and asceticism came to their right position both in individual believers and in special groups, as well as by a reflex action in the dominant Church itself" (*I, 3*). A splendid collective characterization, which completely agrees with my own conception (*II, 617–621*). *Mirbt* explains Pietistic asceticism as "occupation with Holy Scripture to whose ascetic elements the Pietistically inclined Bible-reader of that day, who was already under the influence of eschatological tendencies, brought understanding" (*XV, 804*).—The opinion of *Uhlhorn, p. 260:* "Pietism has not yet found the right attitude towards secular things, particularly to the State, to science, and to art. It regards them from its subjective standpoint (that is, from a non-ecclesiastical standpoint which is only interested in conversion and the maturity of the individual Christian), as justified so far as they are of use to it; unlike Lutheranism, it judges by itself that their substance is justified." (This is erroneously and obscurely formulated; it means that over against the peculiar mixture of world denial and world acceptance in Lutheranism the Pietistic ethic completes the ascetic consequence by linking up with the Calvinistic ethic (see *Max Weber: Archiv XXI, pp. 46–50*), which takes away from the secular all value of its own, but moulds it in a quite utilitarian way, rationally and methodically, as a means to an end; hence also the ideals of Pietism with regard to education are exactly the same as those of Puritanism.) Piety is for it not the principle of life which penetrates everything, but the sole content of life. For that reason Pietism has no interest in social questions. From its point of view such things are just part of "the world", which it regards in a cool and detached manner. In spite of the tendency to intervene everywhere in all these spheres of life, it still remains unfruitful. Pietism has helped to weaken the importance of the Church in these spheres of life, and it is also due to it that works of charity, especially the care of the poor, have been brought into the hands of the State."—It is important to notice that *Ritschl* has entirely ignored English Puritanism, which everywhere merges into Pietism. Ritschl knew no English, and this circumstance led to very one-sided results in the studies of those who followed him in this subject.—Here *Heppe* and Barclay must complete the picture.—For the social and economic effects, *Weber, pp. 55ff.:* "Quite obviously thus in German Lutheran Pietism the preparation of the religious need for a present inward, emotional sentiment thus contained a minimum of stimulus for the rationalizing of activity within this world, contrasted with the need of the preservation of Calvinistic "saints" which was directed only towards the future life, whereas they, for their part, over against the traditionalist piety of the orthodox Lutheran, which centred in the Word and the Sacrament, were always adapted to develop a maximum of methodical religious penetration of life." The increasing development of a merely emotional tendency is also connected with the social divergence of the movement towards the clergy and the nobility. "If here we should characterize one practical consequence of the difference . . . the virtues which Pietism brought forth may be described rather as those which, on the one hand, the loyal official, workman, and home-worker, and, on the other hand, the patriarchally minded employer would display in a condescension which is well-pleasing to God. Calvinism seems in comparison with that to have a greater affinity with the hard legal and active spirit of bourgeois capitalistic entrepreneurs."—The peculiarities of Württemberg Pietism, which in Germany is the only kind which has been really popular, are connected with the insignificance of the nobility in that part, with the disposition of a free peasantry towards religious individualism and with the early connection in that region of Pietism with the Church, against which, however, there react until the present day Separatist peasant movements; see *Mirbt* and *Ritschl*; also *Kalbe: Kirchen und Sekten der Gegenwart*[2], *1910.*—For the fact that Pietism within the Church belonged to the aristocracy, the clergy and the official world, and that of the radical Pietists to the lower classes as a result of the social upheavals of the wars of religion, see *Becker: Zinzendorf, pp. 240–243*; at any rate, that is the view of the Count.—For the genuine inner connection of Calvinism with Pietism, according to which the conventicles do not disturb the Church idea at all, and its inner opposition to and disturbing effect upon Lutheranism, see the views of *Zinzendorf: ebd., pp. 246–250.*—For the darker side of the Pietistic sectarian movement, see *Harnack: Alte Bekannte, Aus Wissenschaft und Leben, II, 277–288.*—Quite lately I have seen *Göters: Vorbereit. d. Piet. in den Niederlanden, 1911,* obviously a linking-up of the German development with the Netherlands.

[460] (p. 721.) Cf. *Ritschl: Gesch. d. Piet., III,* in which, however, the pedantic treatment of the subject, the derivation of all the "dangerous errors" of the "theological dilettante", Zinzendorf, from a "careless" interpretation of the Lutheran conception of the Church, is intolerable. In addition to *Ritschl,* the following book is indispensable, *Jos. Th. Müller: Z. als Erneuerer der alten Brüderkirche, 1900.* With regard to the main point, the recognition of the tension between the mystical supra-ecclesiastical ideal and the sectarian ideal of the Moravians, *Ritschl* had, however, quite a right understanding of the case, and he also rightly recognized the danger for the Church. Cf. also *Müller, p. 40:* "Where an approximate historical realization of this conception (of an 'evident community of Christ') is attempted, there the structure which arises out of it—whether it be an 'evident community of Christ' or whatever one may call it—will always be more capable of realizing the Christian ideal than the popular and State churches, in the midst of whom it lives. . . . At the same time, however, it follows necessarily out of the conception of an 'evident community of Christ' that, in a community which has arisen out of an historical situation, this character cannot remain attached to it as an inalienable possession, nor can it become a birthright, because every time it depends upon the personal Christian piety of the members." It is precisely upon the understanding of this difference between Church and sect that everything depends.—It is from this point of view also that we must answer the question which *Loofs* once put to me in a letter: Could Lutheranism—under quite other external circumstances—have produced an ethic exactly similar to that of the Moravian Church? The question is very instructive, since here the theoretical ethical basis is undoubtedly Lutheran both in its spirit and in the letter. We must, however, remember that the ethic of a sect and of a State Church is still always entirely different. The sect is very little confused by being drawn into official positions in the State, politics, law, or war, and therefore it does not need, like Luther, to deduce all these things from the Christian Law of Nature and to take them into the Christian ethic as matters of fundamental importance. The difference between official and personal morality, which is so important in Lutheranism, here entirely disappears, and all that remains is personal morality. This personal morality, however, on account of mutual control, the effects of the smallness and narrowness of the circle, and the habit of measuring everything by the standard of the Bible, resulted in a strict morality which fostered a spirit of clear detachment from the world. Scruples about the oath, official service and war, similar to those of the Anabaptists, are mentioned by *Müller, 27, 92; Ritschl, III, 244; Approaches to Communism, III, 296; Renunciation of State Law and Arbitration within the Community, III, 346–348;* it is the spirit of the Sermon on the Mount, which *Ritschl,* however, recognizes to such a limited extent that in all this he sees nothing but "freaks". But the ethic of proof and active holiness here play a much greater part (*Ritschl, III, 398, 439, 247*) than in ecclesiastical Lutheranism, as *Ritschl* and *Müller* both rightly admit. It is certainly quite possible to argue that the agrarian character of Luther's economic ethic, and the overwhelming industrial character of the Moravian ethic, is due solely to external circum-

stances (see *Ritschl, III, 347; Müller, 79 and 84*). This also, however, is connected with the difference between the free and mobile Church association (*Müller, pp. 24–27, 36, 40*) and the State Church. The former is adapted to the mobile industrial population which at that time was in request by mercantilism, whereas the State Church had to consider the peasantry which was bound to the soil and the landed nobility. Also the business enterprise of the community belongs to the nature of the sect, which must maintain itself, and does not live on benefices and subsidies from the State. The difference, therefore, is an essential one, based upon something inward, which, just because of the equality of the theoretical ethical foundations and because of the brokenness of the sect-character in the Moravian Church, is most characteristic for the sociological effect of the sect-type, which is so different from anything that the Church-type can produce. In addition, cf. *Max Weber: Archiv XXI, pp. 50–57.*—It has not yet been clearly established how far Calvinistic business morality may have also influenced the Moravian ethic in detail; this question still needs to be studied. It is, however, significant that the Count likes to take his parables from the world of business; speaking of the inwardness with which the treasure of grace of the Church becomes one's own possession of the heart, he says: "I will have fellowship, therefore I must have a treasure, a share in the society, to which I wish to belong. . . . And where can one find that better than in His immediate presence?" (*Becker: Zinzendorf, p. 20*); about the justification of the conventicle in the Lutheran Church: "What reasonable man would say that if twelve citizens introduced a merchant company for the furtherance of trade they ought *eo ipso* to be separated from all the other citizens and from their country?" (*p. 134*). It is also significant that in these words there is a connection with the non-Lutheran Natural Law of Grotius and Pufendorf (further, in detail, see *Becker, p. 117*); Spener also had already shown a preference for the Natural Law of Calvinism. This is connected instinctively with the sect-idea or with mere religious sociability. The Count also had much sympathy with a man called Bayle.

[461] (p. 724.) Cf. the brilliant presentation of the subject by *W. C. H. Lecky: History of England in the Eighteenth Century, II, 521–642*, which is very fair and impartial; here also the opposition to culture is emphasized in which, however, as is always the case in such groups, the purely practical sciences are made an exception. Otherwise there still exists belief in devils, demons, and witches, in direct illuminations and miracles, healings, and Divine inspirations, a special Providence which continually breaks through Nature in favour of believers. For asceticism, see *pp. 589 ff.* After Wesley had visited the British Museum he wrote: "What account will a man give to the Judge of quick and dead for a life spent in collecting all these?" For the constitution, see the excellent article by *Loofs: "Meth.", PRE³, XII*, and *Nuelsen: "Meth. in Amerika", PRE³, XIII*; for the ethic, see the fine section in *Schneckenburger: Lehrbegriffe der kleineren prot. Kirchenparteien, 1863, pp. 103–151*, and *Max Weber: Archiv XXI, pp. 57–61.*—With reference to Baptism, see *Loofs, XII, p. 779*; in Wesley's abbreviation of the Thirty-Nine Articles, baptismal regeneration is set aside; he does not deal with "de peccatis post baptismum", but with "of sin after justification"; in Article 15 the statement "Nos reliqui (alongside of Christ), etiam baptisati et in Christo regenerati, in multis tamen offendimus et, si dixerimus, quia peccatum non habemus, nos ipos seducimus" is set aside, as *Loofs* thinks, in favour of Perfectionism, but also, that which is closely connected with it to the disadvantage of Infant Baptism. *Nuelsen* quotes from the Catechism by *Nast:* The new birth "does not take place through Baptism, but it is effected by God

at the same time with the justification which is attained by faith" (*XIII, 14*). Baptism, therefore, is replaced by revival work in classes of children and the intensive work in the school. Candidates are received first of all for a period of probation if they reveal an honest desire for salvation, and final admission into the community is preceded by this first question: "Do ye renew in the presence of God and of this congregation the solemn vow which is contained in the Covenant of Baptism?" (*XIII, 18*). Here, however Baptism is always eliminated in practice. *Schneckenburger, p. 148:* "Both sacraments, therefore, fall more under the conception of commands of Christ to which one must submit. Therefore, quite logically, one section of the Methodists have developed Baptist ideas. Amongst American Methodists Infant Baptism has almost entirely disappeared (?)."—Everywhere the development from the Church-type into the sect-type is apparent. The Methodists of South America have done away with the probationary period altogether. *XIII, 18:* "Baptized children of Church members are placed on a level with members on probation, and when they have reached a suitable age to be able to understand the binding character of religion, and when they can give proof of genuine piety and upon the recommendation of a leader in whose class they must have been under instruction for at least six months, they can be received into the Church as full members, while they publicly accept the baptismal covenant in the sight of the congregation and answer in the affirmative the questions about doctrine and Church-order. The practice of confirmation is not known in Methodism, yet the pastors are obliged to divide the baptized children as soon as they are ten years old into special classes and to instruct them in those truths which are necessary to make them wise unto salvation" (*XIII, p. 19*). "In many congregations since the time of a pastor's ministry (at one station) has been lengthened, the Class system has been introduced, and instead of individual classes every Sunday there is a general Class Meeting (testimony meeting) or the weekly prayer and experience meeting. The testimony meeting of the youth association has been brought in" (*ebd., 17*). *Loofs* gives the following summary (*XII, p. 810*)*:* "At one time people were only received as members who had been at least two months on probation in a Class. Now the membership in the junior Society Classes counts as a probationary period, which means that the children of Methodists grow up into the Society just as they do in State Churches. Human nature being what it is, there must be several amongst these members who have thus grown up within the Society, who do not fit spiritually into the Methodist Church. A Methodist National Church is an impossibility. Methodism will never wholly overcome the difficulties which are caused by the tension between its growing expansion and its Society character (which cannot be quite removed from it), unless it ceases to be what it is."—Further, it is *Loofs* in particular who, in his presentation, allows the sectarian features to remain in the background in a remarkable way; these features are much more clearly expressed by the Methodist *Nuelsen.* He desires a similar awakening for Germany, where, in his opinion, everything is ripe for another Wesley, and where the movement ought not to be separated from the Church. Only against such an awakening we must place the fact that the functions which were at that time exercised by Methodism have among us been taken over long ago by social democracy, upon whom a message of the type of Wesley's would make no impression at all. *Loofs* also underestimates the difference in the inner structure when he thinks that it would be possible to combine a Territorial Church and Methodism. If the *Gemeinschaftsbewegung* (*Fellowship Movement*) among us were to grow to a similar size, then we also would find it impossible to unite the two types. Such things depend on numbers.—For the class limitation of Methodism, see *Lecky, 600–602.*

[464] (p. 728.) For Christian Socialism, in addition to the works which have already been indicated, see those of *Theod. Mayer, Ratzinger, Uhlhorn, Naumann, Göhre, Wenk, von Schulze-Gävernitz, Rauschenbusch, Wernle, Traub, Ragaz,* and *Kutter*, also the Biography of the Bishop *von Ketteler Pfülf, 1899,* and the articles "*Christlich-Sozial*", "*Evangelisch-Sozial*", "*Katholisch-Sozial*", in *Schiele's Lexikon,* also the essay by *Ragaz:* "*Zur gegenwärtigen Umgestaltung des Christentums*" (*Neue Wege, Basel, 1909*), and by *Liechtenhahn: Die religiös-soziale Bewegung in der Schweiz* (*Christl. Welt, 1911*), and also the collected addresses of the *Berlin World Congress for Free Christianity, Religion, and Socialism,* published by *Schneemelcher, 1911.*—For the fanatical early stages of Marxian Socialism, see *Sombart: Sozialismus und soziale Bewegung*[5], *1905*; he rightly emphasizes the strongly rationalistic and equalitarian element which the religion of the Enlightenment has brought into this kind of Chiliasm.—The religious social movement in Switzerland gives the clearest interpretation of the problem of Christian Socialism, and in it there are revealed most plainly the essentially Christian motives of this whole group of thinkers. The *Evangelisch-soziale Kongress* occupies an intermediate position. The "*Kirchlich-Sozialen*" of the Catholic and Lutheran kind are not Socialists at all.—In a practical judgment of matters we must not overlook the fact that the real social development approaches rather analogous mediaeval attempts to solve the problem of the struggle for existence. This is being illustrated in many ways at the present time.

In any case, it is clear that everywhere individualism is being restricted, and that soon there will no longer be too much individualism, but too little. As political tendencies are becoming increasingly Democratic, religion may once again provide a refuge for individualism. On this point see the excellent book by *Joh. Plenge: Marx und Hegel, 1911.* The book is conceived entirely from the point of view upon which my own work is based. For the future possibilities of our social development, see above all, *pp. 178–182.*

[465] (p. 729.) An infinite amount has been written about Tolstoi, but very little that is good. The article by *Johannes Müller: Chr. Welt, 1911, pp. 218–224,* is excellent: "The new life which Jesus represented and aroused was alien to his thought. This life which welled up out of invisible depths, filling, restoring, creating, the stable and free superiority to all things upon that point outside the world which lies within us, the divine 'Yea' to all that exists, the goodness which at bottom lies in all this, the truth which struggles for life, which sees the glory shining through and therefore sets God's seal upon it; the love, the outpoured life and the surrender of the soul without choice and without limits, the reverence and kindness, the wrestling for the immediate experience in the inmost soul, he knew not." That is a good word for the Christian ethic, but, however, the formation of this life in the concrete conditions of existence remains difficult enough. *Müller*, for his part, thinks also of a transformation of the world, and he regards Tolstoi at least as a signpost pointing to the forgotten radicalism of Christianity: "He opened my eyes to the fact that Christianity had become conformed to the spirit of this world, while the statement of theologians that it must be secularized in order to become a world-religion only had the effect of increasing the mistrust which had been aroused. *If only it had remained the way to life which is called a sect.*"

[466] (p. 730.) Appeals to Luther's teaching on the Spirit: in *Sebastian Franck: Ketzerchronik, II, 199*[b]; *Hegler: Geist und Schrift, p. 269; Gottfried Arnold, II, 229:* "It is well known from Luther's writings that in his earlier works he often

wrote very freely about this grace (the inspiration of the Spirit), indeed, often his language gave more offence than that of many people who were called Enthusiasts, and he also referred everything to the Spirit"; among the Quakers, *Arnold, II, 661, 671, and 673.—Otto: Anschauung vom hl. Geiste bei Luther, 1898,* also shows the beginnings, only with this exception that seeking opposition to the "fanatics" in the wrong place he explains Luther himself too much in the sense of a "Spiritualist".—For the measure of "Spirituality" in Luther, Zwingli, Calvin, Capito, Oecolampadius, and Bucer, see the interesting accounts in *Richard Grützmacher: Wort und Geist, 1902.* Luther and Zwingli also regard the doctrine of predestination in this sense as an expression of the immediacy of the experience. Capito even goes back to the old mystical idea that the inner illumination is only kindled in the elect through the Divine Spark which indwells man. Oecolampadius even published writings of Schwenkfeld. Bucer is absolutely a preacher of the immediacy of the Spirit in connection with predestination. To the extent in which Luther did not merely co-ordinate the working of the Spirit with that of the Scriptures, but made this (the Scriptures) the sole means, the doctrine of predestination retired into the background and the idea of the Church and the objectivity of salvation came into the foreground. Calvin avoided all this by the idea which he established at the outset that predestination worked out in the Scriptures, the ministry, and the Church. —It is plain how much Spirituality of this kind there was among the Reformers. Therefore these ideas appeared afresh again and again out of the influence of their writings. *Sippell* gives a particularly interesting example in *W. Dells Programm.* The sermons which I have been able to get at in an edition of Dell's works of 1817(!) reveal everywhere a distinct and conscious affinity with the "spiritual" elements in Luther. The same is true of the Lutheran Antinomians, who were the horror of the Puritan Precisians and the men of the *jus divinum* in the Church; see *Sippell, pp. 2–4.*

470 (p. 733.) For primitive Christian "Enthusiasm", see *Gunkel: Wirkungen des hl. Geistes nach der populären Anschauung der apostol. Zeit und nach der Lehre des Apostels Paulus*[3], *1909; Weinel: Geist und Geister im nachapostol. Zeitalter, 1899; Taufe und Abendmahl bei Paulus, 1903;* for the mysticism of Paul there is very instructive material in *Reitzenstein: Die hellenistischen Mystereinreligionen, 1910.* From this point of view we can also understand the idea of an opposition between Paul and the Christ according to the flesh, which becomes to so great an extent a starting-point for fantastical conclusions. All mystics after Paul have also thought like that about dogma. *Reitzenstein* emphasizes rightly that there is in Paul also "conflict between the autonomy of religious feeling and the rigidity of tradition" (*p. 58*); the "mystical ideas freed themselves imperceptibly at the outset from the tradition which had begun to form within the Church upon Jewish soil, and the struggle which soon followed brought him the consciousness of freedom which for him now is everywhere where the Spirit of the Lord is" (*p. 60*).—Also *Deissmann: Paulus, 1911,* brings this out without, however, in this respect sufficiently recognizing the conflict between the primitive community and the starting-point for all "spiritual" mysticism. The emphasis on the combination of historical and "spiritual" elements is very apt. *P. 154:* The first leads to the sect, the second to *spiritualismus.*

471 (p. 740.) For this cf. above all *Preger: Gesch. d. deutschen Mystik,* one of the great classics of Church-history. In different places also there is a great deal of material in *Ritschl* and *Harnack. Denifle* identifies this kind of mysticism with Scholasticism, and says that he sees no difference between them; this seems to me very much the point of view of an apologist and does not touch the psycho-

logical depth of the problem. The reason that *Ritschl* and his disciples accepted this statement so eagerly was that in that way they wished to complete the equation of Catholicism with mysticism, like that of Catholicism, the Anabaptist movement, the sect, and monasticism. In that way, then, from the standpoint of the Lutheran Church, mysticism is dismissed.—Further, particularly in *Ritschl's Geschichte des Pietismus*, there are a number of most acute conclusions based upon detailed study, in which his Churchly instinct displays the essential anti-ecclesiasticism of mysticism, even in its expressions, which still seem to be quite in harmony with the Church and with dogma. But even so there can be no question of any identification with Catholicism. The well-known statement by *Harnack* that anyone who is a mystic without becoming a Catholic is a dilettante, I cannot feel is in any sense right. On the other hand, however, the equation of mysticism and *spiritualismus* with the essential idea of Protestantism, which is the tendency of *Weingarten*, *A. Dorner*, *Barge*, and also *Dilthey*, is certainly not right, even though we ought not to depreciate the strongly "spiritual" element in Luther. It is that element in Luther which the modern man understands best of all. The Luther monument at Worms bears not in vain solely "spiritual" sayings.—Very valuable also is the great work by *F. von Hügel*, one of the leaders of so-called Modernism: *The Mystical Element of Religion as Studied in St. Catherine of Genoa and Her Friends, London, 1908*; this book gives one such an insight into the wealth of the component parts which constitute the Christian world of thought as is given in few other works; in the course of time Christianity has become an entirely complex religion.

[472] (p. 740.) For the whole, see above all *Gottfried Arnold*, and also *Ludwig Keller: Erbkam; Geschichte d. Pietismus bei Göbel*, *Heppe*, and *Ritschl*. There is a good deal in *Hegler: Geist und Schrift bei Sebastian Franck*, who, on *p. 277*, tries a grouping; further, *Maronier: Het inwendig word, Amsterdam, 1890; Rich. Grützmacher: Wort und Geist, 1902*, also the fine treatment of the subject by *Dilthey* in *Archiv f. Gesch. d. Philos.* Of ecclesiastical theologians the nearest to this tendency were *Capito* and *Oecolampadius*; *Bucer's* relationship to it still needs to be examined. Cf. also *Hegler: Beiträge zur Gesch. d. Mystik in der Reformationszeit*, issued by W. Köhler, 1906; this consists of extracts from writings by members of the group influenced by Sebastian Franck. In *Sippell: Ueber den Ursprung des Quäkertums*, there are some valuable remarks; a very apt observation about the difference between Enthusiasm and mysticism, *Chr. W., 1910, p. 460*.—A splendid collective characterization also of this tendency in *Göbel, II, 680–690*, who also sees very clearly the difference between the sectarian Separatist groups (Labadie and Spener) and the mystical Separatist groups (above all, Gottfried Arnold).

[474] (p. 746.) Cf. the statement of *Ernst Ludwig Gruber*, which is quoted in *Göbel, II, p. 681*: "The true Separatists do not begin any new sect, neither do they try to build up that which was broken down, but they retire into the inward sanctuary, into their heart, wherein they seek to serve God in Christ Jesus through His mercy, in spirit and in truth, for whose gracious revelation and appearance in them and without them they then wait with joyful and believing hope, and, for the rest, they lead a quiet and exemplary life; also, so far as they have means and opportunity, they try to show all the love they owe to their own members and to their fellow-men. There is not much to say about their outward service of God because they have no formed and distinct rules, habits, and times, but they arrange such in accordance with the daily, hourly, and momentary impulse of God and the opportunity which is offered to them with prayer, singing, reading, and the handling of the Divine Word to the

edification of themselves and of others." On this point see further the description of the mystical Separatists in *II* and *III*; there the sociological characteristic of the "Philadelphian period" (*III, 71–86*), also the "Philadelphian invitation" (*III, 99*). *Göbel*, however, only treats the movements of Calvinistic and Lutheran mystical Separatism in West Germany. The subject is wider than that. Already in *Preger* there are all kinds of material of a quite similar kind for mediaeval mysticism, further material in *Hegler's Schrift und Geist*. *Göbel* and *Ritschl* describe only the comparatively small Pietistic conventicles in which, owing to the fact that they were excluded from participation in public affairs, was diverted into the channels of religious brooding; these religious *Grübelei* groups were sometimes emotional, sometimes very dull, and sometimes overexcited. Among such people there is no trace of the great ideas of mysticism of the kind represented by Sebastian Franck, Castellio, and Coornheert. Only the latter, however, can be compared with the Church way of thought in greatness and theoretical acuteness.

[476] (p. 748.) *Ritschl*, who is the harshest and most acute opponent of mysticism, is very instructive upon this point. As he develops his institutional Church interest in close connection with popular Christianity, he is obliged to teach that the forgiveness of sins is an attribute of the congregation or of the Church, in which the individual as a member of the Church shares through Baptism. Corresponding to this he opposes in mysticism nothing so much as its neglect of both the correlates: objective assurance of the remission of sins and the Christian community as an institutional Church. No one has recognized these connections as clearly as he has. Therefore from this point of view he has based his own ecclesiastical dogma upon the correlation of Christ, the assurance of the forgiveness of sins and the Church. His teaching, however, is particularly interesting because he questions the atonement as the basis of the forgiveness of sins. He is, therefore, obliged to construct this doctrine as the endowment of the Church, with a certainty based upon the supernatural authority of Christ, in God's readiness to forgive sin, and in so doing he comes very close to the Socinians, amongst whom, however, he misses the correlation with the Church. Thus it is extremely interesting to read his detailed explanation of the "Spiritualist" *Dippel* and *Zinzendorf* (*Geschichte des Pietismus, III, 429–435*), of whom the former denies the atonement and the latter maintains it, and both destroy, or at least weaken, the idea of the Church. Through emphasis on the Church and her objective assurance of remission of sins, for which it is not the atonement which is needed but Christ's guarantee, he resolves the conflict between the two in a "higher third".

[477] (p. 748.) For this simplification, see *Otto: Anschauung Luthers vom hl. Geiste;* also *Kant-Friesische Religionsphilosophie, pp. 18–23*; only it is wrong to refer the corresponding endeavours after simplification of the theology of the Enlightenment to Luther; it is Pietism and *Spiritualismus* which this theology here follows. Luther's development of the "verbum consummatum ac breve", out of the objective means of salvation, of the Word into doctrine, is the unavoidable result of ecclesiastical theology, which has an absolute external authority and must have it in the orthodox sense of the conception of the Church, and which then, naturally, must also develop this authority out to the circumference in order to leave no obscurities in which fanaticism could establish itself.

[478] (p. 751.) Cf. my *Trennung von Staat und Kirche, pp. 21 ff.* The deduction of a uniform Church system and of intolerance, also of the opposite attitude from the manner of the conception of truth, seems to me a very important point to recognize. Yet at that time I did not recognize sufficiently the difference

between the Baptist movement and *Spiritualismus*, in ascribing the opposite position simply to the Anabaptist movement. As the Church is connected with a definite conception of truth, so also the sect and *Spiritualismus* are connected with a definite conception of truth. The sect renounces compulsion and conformity, but not the absolute character of the conception of truth; *Spiritualismus* makes it relative in various forms of expression of a truth which is only to be attained spiritually and inwardly, and which, therefore, can never be finally and adequately formulated at all.

[479] (p. 752.) The relationship between *Spiritualismus* and the moralist sectarianism and the Enlightenment, which for orthodox minds like that of *R. Grützmacher* is a natural thing, is also a leading idea of *Ritschl*, who absolutely derives the Enlightenment from this disintegration of a sound Church system. Thus he forms at this point the astonishing equation of Catholicism, monasticism, sectarianism, mysticism, and Enlightenment, in which every member at the same time represents the unhealthiness of the other one, and over against which there only remains *Ritschl's* moderately rationalist but still essentially positively supernatural Lutheran ecclesiasticism, which is adapted to a modern popular ethic. Thus, at that time also, following *Ritschl*, *W. Bender* in *Dippel: Der Freigeist aus dem Pietismus, 1882*, has described the self-transformation of mysticism into Enlightenment. These statements, however, in *Ritschl* are obviously nothing more than an apologetic for his ecclesiastical Lutheranism, and *Bender's* statement is positively false. The change of opinion into Rationalism which takes place just as much in orthodoxy as it does in Pietism and in mysticism, must have its reason in something which equally lies beyond them all; this is proved by the fact that this same phenomenon occurs after quite different presuppositions. In orthodoxy the transition takes place by means of its intellectual, scholastic element, in holiness-Pietism by means of its moralist element, and in secular and scientific matters by means of its purely utilitarian, empirical element, in mysticism by means of its idea of a timeless religious element which is contained in Reason or the soul as such. In every case, however, the Enlightenment does not arise out of religious interests, but out of the political and social upheaval, and out of the emancipation of interests from the leading religious ideas of the past; this is accompanied by a completely new, that is, causal natural-science orientated philosophy, and by a development of new technical possibilities which is connected therewith. The Enlightenment was the stronger movement, and in all groups it sought the element which was akin to it at that time; naturally this is different every time. The change into Enlightenment on that account never took place naturally anywhere. In England the change was achieved by the Whig revolution and prepared for by the Cromwell revolution. The Enlightenment only penetrated into European life on the Continent as the result of this struggle and of this victory, and in other countries it never made its way completely without a struggle. The fight was carried through, above all, by absolute royalty. The fact that then the new movement everywhere drew out of the old that which was akin to it is indeed clear. In this sense many Christian ideas—altered—also live on in the Enlightenment, above all the idea of Natural Law and Natural Right, which I have studied in its development; see my essay, *Das stoisch-christliche Naturrecht und das moderne profane Naturrecht, H.Z., 1911, Vol. 106.* All the individualism of the Enlightenment is connected with the Christian subjective tendency which existed apart from the churches, as *Plenge: a.a.O.*, brings out very aptly in many places. Its ultimate reason, however, the social upheaval and the definite rise of the bourgeoisie, is likewise connected with the

previous Protestant development, but with only the ethical social effect, which was quite unintended, of increasing the commercial bourgeoisie; on this point, see *Max Weber*.—The connection between Deism and the radical parties and "Spiritual Reformers" of the English Revolution has not yet been made thoroughly clear. In Locke's principle of toleration it is clear. But Locke's theology and also that of Toland suggest the presence of Arminian and Socinian influences. Among the average Deists the opposition of the Dissenters to the whole Catholic element is clear, but there is no trace of a merging of mystical or Pietistical ideas in Rationalism. In Germany, Edelmann and Lorenz Schmidt, influenced by Spinoza, do not represent a phase of Christian mysticism.—*Dilthey* also seems to me to overestimate the "rational element" in the "Universal Theism" of Franck and Coornheert.—The difference between "spiritual religion" and the rationalistic theology of the Socinians, Arminians, and the Deists is also quite interesting on its sociological side. These Rationalists liked to remain within the churches, confining their efforts to introducing liberal ideas, or else at least they were content if they were tolerated; the reason for this was that they realized that in their scientific arguments they possessed a driving force which was much weaker psychologically, and that they were only able to reach the intellectual classes; their own power of forming churches did not suffice. When they were forced to separate from the churches they revealed an energy in propaganda and instruction, a scientific instinct for truth which is quite alien to mysticism and "Spiritual" religion in general. It would be very attractive to study the sociological aspect of the rationalist group-formations through the centuries down to the free religious group-formations of the present day. They do not in any way resemble the free mystical groups, neither have they any similarity with Holiness groups, nor with the Church. *Ritschl*, with his extraordinarily acute power of detecting any divergence from the Church-type, compares this tendency with the school (*Rechtf. und Vers.*[2], *I, pp. 320–323*), and he deduces from this characteristic its approximation to the sect-type, its intellectual propaganda, its lack of emphasis upon worship, and the frequency of division about opinions on doctrine. The uniting element is only intellectual agreement combined with all the needs of expansion and instruction, but also with all the dangers of division and the lack of that comprehensive spiritual substance which belongs to the common possession of the permanent witness of the churches.

480 (p. 753.) *Ritschl's Geschichte des Pietismus* gives a good deal of information upon this point also. Otherwise it is not possible to generalize on this question. This is precisely the difference between the "spiritual" ethic and every kind of ecclesiastical and sectarian ethic. Above all, it is important to recognize that asceticism has here more of a metaphysical and directly religious meaning than one of discipline, and just on that account it can also easily develop into libertinism. In connection with these groups, therefore *Weber's*, description of asceticism does not apply at all, unless perhaps owing to its Calvinistic origin they understood asceticism from the beginning in the Calvinistic sense; an example of this is Tersteegen, who thought that Zinzendorf was frivolous.—Information on ethics also in *Hegler: Geist und Schrift, pp. 148–150, 166, 170–184*. In Franck the social doctrines are essentially the same as those of Luther, only the spirit of resignation is still more evident.—Reference to the absolute Law of Nature, which is here naturally equated with the Divine Seed and the Divine Spark, with the higher Divine Nature which humanity contains, but which also agrees with the natural moral consciousness and is identical with the Decalogue—in *Hegler, pp. 209, 243, 116*; the Ten Commandments con-

tained in the "inner Word" (*pp. 92 ff.*). The "Natural Law of love" in the mystic Sperber (*Ritschl, I, 304*); likewise *Dippel, I, 337*; conscience and Natural Law, the eternal Word and the supernatural Light (*I, 354*), which *Ritschl* naturally immediately regards as Illuminism. In *Barclay, p. 225*, some elders declare that the Holy Ghost is imparted not only through the Word, but also through "His handywork in the whole creation, the Law of Nature written in the hearts of mankind, the light of conscience".—*Saltmarsh*, whose *Sparkles of Glory, 1647*, in a Jubilee edition of 1847, has been sent to me by Herr Sippell, is most interesting. There breaks forth from the degree of Nature, or the Law of Nature, impelled by its conscious sense of its incapacity to attain an ultimate value, the law of the Spirit as a higher stage: "The Christian is one who should live in an higher region than flesh or nature; and when God sayth 'Come up hither' he shall live there even in the Spirit with Him; so as though grace destroys not nature, yet it perfects and glorifies nature, and leads it out into higher and more excellent attainements, than it can find in itself. Nature lives by this law: preserve thyself, thy life, thy lands, thy rights, and privileges, avenge thyself, an eye for an eye and a tooth for a tooth and love only thy neighbour. Grace lives by this law: deny thyself, forsake lands, life, houses, take up the cross, if he take thy cloak let him have thy coat also, love thy enemies, bless them that curse thee." That reminds us of the Catholic application of the idea of development, but it is conceived rather differently. Nature, which finally asserts itself in the competitive struggle and the desire for self-preservation, becomes an ethic of love directed by God, "disengaged from the love of power, dominion, riches, earthly glory". The morality of the New Testament is only a literal preparatory stage and preparation for this third stage of the ethic of love, which is to be exercised in the freedom of the Spirit. These are conceptions of Natural Law and of grace which I have never met anywhere else, and which contain an element of profound truth.

[482] (p. 756.) Cf. the great work by *Barge*, who, however, takes up a very one-sided position in favour of Karlstadt for the sake of the political-social position, which also for Karlstadt lay quite on the circumference. The mysticism of Karlstadt would certainly have been both unable and unwilling to create anything permanent in this direction. But Luther's ruthless attitude towards the opponents of his idea of the Church is here, however, rightly and instructively brought out quite clearly. In the official picture of Luther these traits are usually very much toned down. Also *Scheel: Individualismus und Gemeinschaftsleben Z. Th. R., 1907; R. Grützmacher, 156–158; Gottfried Arnold, II, 231–239.*

[483] (p. 758.) Cf. *Grützmacher, Art. Schw. PRE*³, *Wort und Geist, pp. 158–173; Gottfried Arnold, II, 246–261*, who goes into great detail here and does not disguise his sympathy. *Grützmacher* as well as *Preger* refer to possible influences of the Bohemian-Moravian Baptists and their theory of the *Verbum substantiale* and *Verbum grammaticale*. In any case, from the point of view of religious psychology his theory is very subtle, see *Grützmacher: Wort und Geist, p. 165*: "The Scriptures are only an image and a parable of that which was worked in the hearts of the Prophets through inspiration." "Whereas one can neither write nor express with the lips spirit and life, but can only express it in parable, so must one know how to distinguish as is meet between the Scripture and the living Word of God (that is, the inward Word), and not give symbols of that which is *rei et veritatis*." "For although God has spoken through His Spirit with the holy men by whom the Scriptures were written, and gave to them what they ought to write, this does not mean that He spoke to them through writing syllables and letters as we would do, but through spirit,

power, and life (which according to their nature cannot be written down in a book, but only according to a parable or a picture), to which, then, a spiritual judgment will belong through which the written Word is distinguished from the living Word of God and the image from the truth." "The holy men of God who were moved to write and to speak by the Holy Ghost were not able to express and to give to others in tablets of stone and in the Scriptures the wealth which they had received as they felt it livingly within their hearts. Scarcely were they able to give any picture of it at all, and with sound voice or Scripture to witness in the Holy Spirit. The pen was unable to express the heart entirely on paper, neither could the lips give utterance to that which it had tasted of the living fountain, but therefore they have given us their message, as much as is necessary to us, in parable, and through that means they have pointed to the one and only Saviour, Fountain, and Light (that is, to the Christ who reveals Himself within our hearts)". Several times Schwenkfeld tried to get into friendly contact with Luther, but always in vain. At the last attempt Luther gave the messenger a note with the words: "The silly fool who is possessed by the Devil doesn't understand anything or know anything of what he is talking about. . . . And this is my last word: the Lord curse thee, thou Satan, and thy spirit, and all thy ways and all that belongs to thee" (*Arnold, II, 251*). Other orthodox theologians were more just in their opinions: "He wanted to be neutral, a sceptic, an unusual man." "He agreed neither with the Papists nor with the Lutherans, nor with the *Sakramentierer* [i.e. Zwinglians and others.—Tr.] nor Anabaptists, but in every sect he only approves of something, and he goes off on a new and peculiar form of religion of his own" (*Arnold, II, 242*). He himself expresses his views in a similar manner: "That I now belong to no party or sect as men call them, neither to the Papists nor to the Lutherans, neither to the Zwinglians, nor to the Baptists on account of my conscience, has many reasons and this brings to me not a little persecution. . . . I do not try to hide the fact of this separation, and I hold it as certain that the Christian should go with his heart out of this wicked world in order that he may again and again direct his heart into the heavenly sphere where his treasure is, even Jesus Christ" (*ibid.*). On *p. 242* he emphasizes very clearly the opposition to the popular and National Church, which was becoming increasingly rigid in its objectivity. In Pennsylvania there are to-day still four congregations of Schwenkfelders, with 306 members (*Newman, p. 156*).—The newest and the fullest account of the subject is the book by *Karl Ecke: Schwenkfeld, Luther und der Gedanke einer apostolischen Reformation, 1911*, a very valuable book. It is written from the standpoint of the Pietistic Fellowship Movement, and in Schwenkfeld it celebrates the founder of his movement, who, in agreement with Luther's original ideal of the *ecclesiolae*, was, however, on the other hand unable to go with Luther in his tendency towards popular Christianity and the sacramentalism which was bound up with it (especially *p. 103*); in the writer's opinion Schwenkfeld developed Luther's original idea from the Bible into a pneumatic charismatic form of fellowship Christianity, and in so doing he reached the true idea of Christian fellowship. In spite of the most cautious treatment of Luther, Luther here comes out in a similar light to that in which he is treated in *Barge's Karlstadt. Ecke* defends his hero against the charge of "heretical mysticism" like that of Franck, for example, who "has never scaled the heights of the Reformation experience of salvation" (*p. 96*), as against mysticism and Anabaptism in general in order to explain him purely from the point of view of primitive Christianity. This, however, is only true in so far as the Bible itself actually contains elements of sectarianism and of mysticism.

Otherwise, *Sippell: K. S. Chr. W., 1911,* rightly inserts him once again in the mystical and sectarian succession as a combination of both. Schwenkfeld's judgment about Luther's treatise *Himmlische Propheten, Ecke, p. 80* is worthy of note: "Would to God that people would look carefully into this little book with their eyes wide open, looking at Christ our Lord therein and at His divine truth, and would that they might compare this with the previous writings of Dr. Martin, and that they might know whither and how far he has now come, and that they might understand how much misery, instability, and error are therein and in the future will still be born out of this."—Very interesting opinions of Schwenkfeld about the Baptists in *Ecke, 204–212, 89.* So far as ethics are concerned it is characteristic that Schwenkfeld complains that the Lutheran merchants did not observe Luther's ethic at all, but only the forgiveness of sins and predestination (*p. 163*).—The influential ideas of the disappearance of the primitive Church, of the ecclesiastical formalism which has prevailed since then, of the immanence of an apostolic reformer with Divine credentials, of the future outpouring of the Spirit and of the End which will then follow; see *Ecke, pp. 227, 323–334.* The Chiliasm of the Anabaptists was of a different kind, although its basis was the same; from this point of view also a light falls upon the question of the emergence of eschatological ideas in Independency and Pietism. Every attempt to take the question of a Holy Community seriously for the masses leads to Chiliasm.

483a (p. 759.) For Weigel, see *Grützmacher: Wort und Geist, pp. 185–195*; here Weigel appeals to the younger Luther: "In the books of Luther ye had better seek; there ye will find even such words as ye have heard from me at this present in especial in his earlier writings." His radical subjective theory of knowledge ("All knowledge comes from the knower"), and the identification of the psychological religious movement of thought with the thought of the Logos or of the Divine Nature of Christ in us, has also procured him a place in histories of philosophy; see *J. E. Erdmann: Grundriss, II*[3], *1878, pp. 483–488,* and *Windelband: Geschichte der neueren Philosophie*[3], *I, 483–488.* It is genuine Neo-Platonic mysticism in which its Christian character is only preserved by the assumption of a positive agreement with the Logos and Christianity.

484 (p. 762.) Cf. the excellent book by *Hegler*; *Gottfried Arnold,* who adopted Franck's idea of the *Ketzergeschichte,* and continued it, and in general is very close to his position (*II, 281–283*); *Dilthey: Archiv V, 389–400. Dilthey* does not emphasize, in my opinion, the connection with mediaeval mysticism strongly enough, and he modernizes too much. The relation between his ideas and the modern philosophy of religion after Lessing, Kant, Schleiermacher, and Hegel, is indeed evident. In Franck, however, there is no question of the historic movement of truth; his conception of truth is completely non-historical, absolute, entirely spiritualized; he champions a dualism which is hostile to the world, which excludes a progressive and victorious religious movement, and is absolutely opposed to modern ethics; finally, he treats the Scriptures more along the lines of allegory and occultism than as the history of religion, or psychologically. His individualism, which dispensed with external forms of worship, and his mystical idea of immanence, meet with the approval of modern people, as is shown by the new edition of his *Paradoxa, 1910,* published by the Diederich Verlag. Luther took no notice of Franck, who, owing to his individualism, condemned himself to be ineffective; only after Franck's death did Luther thus express himself: "He had not wished to write anything against such an evil man because he despised him too much; he was a blasphemer, the Devil's own and favourite mouthpiece. . . . So far as I can understand and

judge he is either an Enthusiast or a 'Geisterer', who is content with nothing except 'Spirit', 'Spirit', 'Spirit' ('Geist', 'Geist', 'Geist'), who has no use for the Word, the Sacrament or the ministry. . . . He has wandered through all kinds of filth, and has at last got stifled in it" (*Arnold, II, 282*). This was Luther's verdict on one of the noblest and freest souls of that period. In Germany he was soon forgotten, but his influence was felt for some time in the Netherlands. *Arnold* could only get hold of his writings with difficulty! Cf. in addition, also, *Hegler's Programm*; "*Sebastian Franck's Lateinische Paraphrase der deutschen Theologie, und seine holländisch erhaltenen Traktate*", *1901*; also *H. Ziegler: Z. f. wiss. Theol., 1907*; also *Hegler's Beiträge zur Geschichte der Mystik*. Herr Sippell will report about Franck's writings in England, which he has found in some of the archives there. It seems to me that a man like Saltmarsh is unintelligible without Franck; their ideas are everywhere akin to each other, and at the same time they are most winning, human, and gracious.

[485] (p. 764.) Cf. the excellent book by *Buisson: Sébastien Castellion, sa Vie et son Œuvre, Paris, 1892*. For Castellio's mysticism and spirituality, see *I, 310–314; II, pp. 38, 99, 194–197, 201–213, 259*. The essence of this toleration with its "spiritual" basis, which still counts so strongly with the general Christian atmosphere that from the point of view of toleration it only envisages differences between Christians, but otherwise takes it as a matter of course that the "Spiritual Christian truth" will propagate itself, see *I, pp. 366, 373; II, 38, 290, 295*. Castellio compares particular dogmas to the small coin which varies in every country, while he compares the truth of the Spirit with the gold which is accepted everywhere. Thus we can understand how it came to be later on that in England and America toleration was only exercised within Christianity and did not include atheism. This is not illogical, but it is the result of the "spiritual" argument for toleration. The only difference between this idea of toleration, with its confidence in the victory of the Spirit, and Luther's earlier position is this, that for Castellio the "Spirit", with its looser and often allegorical relation to the letter of Scripture, is a simpler and less defined principle than Luther's idea of the Spirit, which is always combined with the "Word". A greater freedom of movement thus arises. But it would be erroneous to consider this freedom as one which is without restrictions. This enlarged conception of toleration, however, is based upon a different conception of truth from that of the Reformers. The truth lies in the power of the Spirit which is sealed subjectively in the conscience, whereas all that is external, literal, ceremonial, and institutional is merely relatively valuable, a veil for the truth which can only be lifted by the Spirit. Absolute truth is limited to the spirit; it is, however, here also clear and inescapable. All that is literal, both Bible and dogma, on the contrary, belong to the sphere of relative truth. At the same time this truth is entirely subjective, only to be tested by the individual in his own experience. It is thus neither the conception of truth of modern science nor that of the ecclesiastical organ of salvation, but it is that of "spiritual" religion and of mysticism.—We can well understand why his opponents were so horrified; in these ideas they beheld the essence of Satanic dangers, "academic scepticism", "arrogant fantasy", the removal of all possibility of a true Church and a stable authority (*II, 25–39, 122, 249, 255, 258*). Very characteristic is Beza's objection to the idea of trust in the spiritual self-propagation of the truth: "What then is the Church to do? She must cry to the Lord, you will say, and He will hear her. . . . Yea indeed, she will cry to the Lord. . . . But he who is hungry also cries to the Lord, but at the same time he does not wait for an angel to bring him something to eat, but the food which another gives

him or that he himself will have acquired by honest and right means, he will take as from the hand of God" (*II, p. 27*). Here in reality is the real point at issue. In this idea of mystical trust in the victory of the Spirit and the relativism which tolerated various kinds of literalisms, the ideal of the united Church and self-affirmation in the feverish mass struggles of the time could not possibly be carried through. Castellio's weak point, therefore, lies in the lack of clearness of his conception of the Church. He never thinks at all about the formation of sects or conventicles, but always about the triumph of the Spirit in a spiritual way for the whole (*II, 37, 230*): "Be content with agreement with the principal points of religion which are clear and evident in the Holy Scriptures, then they are at every point in agreement with you." True Christians, however, are rare (*II, 232*): "Those who thus care about numbers (like Calvin), and for that reason treat people with compulsion, resemble a fool who, broaching a big barrel and only finding a little wine therein, fills it up with water in order to have more, and in so doing he does not increase his wine, and he even spoils that which was good. For which reason we must not be surprised if to-day the wine of the Christians is so little and weak since it is mixed with such a lot of water!" In order to keep the Church pure he considers that it would be sufficient to exclude people from fellowship without any civil punishment (*II, 235*): "These are the right methods of resisting heretics: by words if they use words, by force if they use force." All this is still much further removed from modern ideas of toleration than Buisson thinks.

[487] (p. 766.) For the relationship between Castellio and Coornheert, see *Buisson, II, 324 ff.*; for C.'s mystical doctrine, see *Heppe: Geschichte des Pietismus und der Mystik in der reform. Kirche namentl. d. Niederlande, 1879, pp. 80–86.* "These saints are and live in Christ, who is the Light of the world and therefore they alone can know God. Taught by God Himself, by means of His living Word, namely, the Logos, and by the Spirit of truth, and led into all truth, and illuminated by the unction of the Spirit, they need not henceforth that any man should teach them" (*p. 84*). "Christ has become Man . . . and has risen gloriously in order that we through His active obedience in us should in Him become Divine" (*p. 88*). An acquaintance also with Franck and Schwenkfeld is highly probable. *Dilthey: Archiv V, 486–493*, brings him too near to Erasmus, even though he says also that "he went far beyond that which Erasmus considered it politic to say in his writings" (*p. 492*). *Rachfahl*, who in general takes his cue from Erasmus, with his Dutch liberal ideas, as the supporter of the Netherlands national spirit, makes him a true disciple of Erasmus (*Oranien, I, 451*). This, however, is not true. He is only a Humanist in his acceptance of the "Natural Law" and in his Stoic character, in which, indeed, he is also at one with the Reformers, Castellio and Franck. He certainly emphasizes this underlying element and its identity with the Logos much more strongly. In the main, however, he is an idealist and a mystic who makes the ladder of sanctification from detachment to freedom from sin the centre of his teaching, ascribing everything to the inward working of God; see also *Busken-Huet, II, 47–56.* His ideas upon the Church I take from extracts which Herr Sippell has collected and allowed me to see, but the publication of which he has retained for himself.

[487a] (p. 767.) For the Collegiants in detail see *Hylkema: Reformateurs*, and *Sippell: Ueber den Ursprung des Quakertums, Chr. W., 1910, pp. 483–487.* I likewise thank Herr Sippell for making known to me the "*19 Articles*" and their "explanation", which is often mentioned by *Hylkema*, the publication of which he has likewise retained for himself. For the connection of the Rynsburger with the Anabaptists, see *Newman: Antipedobaptism, pp. 321 ff.*; for their "inward"

character quite in the manner of Coornheert, see *Barclay: The Inner Life, p. 90.* For Coornheert and his followers, as representatives of the Inward Word and companions of *Sebastian Franck* and *Schwenkfeld*, see also *Maronier, pp. 307–309;* for the beginnings of the Collegiants, see *Barclay, pp. 89–92,* and for their later development from 1650 onwards, see *Hylkema.* A biography of *Coornheert,* or, at least, an account of his theology, would be very valuable, and would illuminate his connection with the past and with the future. The prevailing one-sidedly denominational conception of the history of the Reformation could thus once again at an important point be restricted.

[488] (p. 769.) For this cf. in general *Hegler: Geist und Schrift,* and *Keller: Staupitz. Keller* calls these idealistic Baptists the "better Baptists"; *Maronier* does the same (*p. 327*); others call them "free Baptists", which is a *contradictio in adjecto.* For *Bünderlin,* see *Hegler, p. 51; Entfelder Hegler, 273;* and *Keller, 360.* For *Thamer,* see *Neander: Th. als Repräsentant moderner Geistesrichtung, 1842,* and *Hochhut: Z. f. hist. Theol., 1861.* Like Sebastian Franck, Coornheert, and the Collegiants, Denk finally denies all spiritual ministry, even that with which he was entrusted by the Baptists; without a supernatural call like that of the Apostles there is no ministry. This again is Schwenkfeld's idea, or can it be that in this respect Schwenkfeld himself is going back to an earlier mystical theory? This is equivalent to the removal of all churches and sects in general, see *Keller: Denk, 1882, p. 226*; in this book his writings are analysed. His so-called "*Widerruf*" is only the reaction from the Baptists to mysticism.

[489] (p. 770.) For the whole subject, cf. *Hegler* and *Gottfried Arnold.* For the "spiritual religion" of *Servetus,* see *Tollin: Servet und d. Bibel, Z. für wiss. Theol., 1875.* For *Paracelsus* see the fine essay by *Eucken* in the *Beiträgen zur Einführung d. Geschichte der Philosophie.* For *Böhme* see in this connection merely *Ritschl: Geschichte des Pietismus, II, 301–305,* and *R. Grützmacher, 195–204.* The religious philosophy and metaphysics of these thinkers do not concern us at this point; on this question see the *Grundriss der Geschichte der Philosophie*[3], by *J. E. Erdmann,* which still to-day is an incomparable book (*I, 462–502*), also *Gottfried Arnold.* Here they appear solely in their "spiritual" and mystical effect, which makes their connection with the historic facts of salvation, upon which churches are based, superfluous, or makes them mere aids for producing the real, decisive, quite individual personal process. *Ritschl* has rightly seen that with the clear vision of hate; for *Kepler* see likewise *Eucken, pp. 38–53*; here the characteristic confession of Kepler to an orthodox opponent: "Tibi Deus in naturam venit; mihi natura ad divinitatem aspirat" (*p. 43*). His attitude towards the Scriptures in *Deissmann: Kepler und die Bibel, 1894*; there also the analogy with *Sebastian Franck* is emphasized (*pp. 28 ff.*).—For *Amos Comenius,* see the article by *Schiele* in his *Lexikon* and the publications of the *Comeniusgesellschaft,* which quite logically has also taken the other "spiritual" Reformers under its wing, often, unfortunately, in the uncritical manner of their leader, *Ludwig Keller,* even though in so doing he was following a right instinct. For the connection between asceticism, *Spiritualismus,* and Pietism, with an empirical pedagogy and philosophy, see the very illuminating remarks by *Max Weber: Archiv XXI, pp. 53 and 97.*

[490] (p. 771.) On this point see *Gottfried Arnold,* to whom he is a favourite saint, but who was regarded by the orthodox with great hatred as an arch-heretic and blasphemer—a sign of the inclination of several branches of Pietism towards him; in addition, the exemplary research which works up the whole subject by *Nippold: Z. f. Hist., 1863 and 1864.* Here the discussion between Joris and Menno Simons (*B. 33, pp. 141–149,* and *B. 34, pp. 533–557*), which

illuminates in an excellent manner the difference between the sect and mysticism: the spirit versus the letter, liberty versus law. The three types (*B. 34, p. 554*), where Blesdyk explains: "Some (the sects) have a false confidence in external virtues and they sacrifice everything for a literal faith . . ., others (the churches) have a false confidence in a self-chosen form of worship . . . or in the illusion which they call faith that Christ has died for them and has become their righteousness and their sanctification. . . . And this false confidence they support and maintain, some with many external works, the others with talking about and reading the Holy Scriptures, which they declare to the people according to learned commentaries (but they call it God's Word), and with the use of the Lord's Supper, which they regard as the seal of redemption and justification." Over against that Joris, as a newly raised-up prophet, proclaims the Religion of the Spirit (*p. 554*). The discussion with *Coornheert, 34, pp. 627–641*, especially *p. 635*: "Hereby the defender (of David) reproaches Coornheert, saying that he does not understand what David means (in so far as C. adheres to his belief in the incorporation of the Spirit in the Bible instead of in the new prophet), because he confuses it with the views of Franck and Schwenkfeld with which he himself (C.) agrees. For David does not teach like these that in the last days no one will teach the other either by word of mouth or in writing, but he calls the 'letter' or the external doctrine that which is taught by the wise of this world without the spirit. Over against this he describes that which is spoken by the true ambassador of Christ (that is, by David himself) through the Holy Ghost in the times of the Holy Ghost or of perfection, as Spirit and life." This is borne out by the content. No class distinctions in this sect (*34, p. 575*). New editions at the end of the sixteenth century (*B. 34, pp. 566, 627, 667*). Reproaches of the Jorist movement against Knutzen, 1674 (*34, p. 672*). Arnold's vindication also testifies to the impression upon radical Pietism.—For the sect of the Nazarenes, see *Kalbe, 275–285*. One of my relations, who belonged to this group, had in his possession all the mystical literature which was usual, including Gottfried Arnold and the "Berleburger Bibel".

491 (p. 773.) Cf. *Gottfried Arnold and Nippold: Z. f. hist. Theol., 1862*. Here, however, the English development of the group is only treated in a very meagre way. For the latter see *Belfort Bax, 338–380*; he connects the Ranters and the Quakers with them; see also *Barclay: The Inner Life of the Religious Societies of the Commonwealth, 1876, pp. 25–35*. No class movement (*Nippold, 370*), recognition of the existing order of Society and external adjustment to existing conditions, including ecclesiastical (*377*); hostility of Coornheert (*388 and 356*); the ideal ethic in the sense of a libertine mysticism (*516*), the origin of principle of the Holy Community and the system of penitential discipline in the Baptist movement (*539–542*); the hierarchical secret organization for worship, but without apostolic succession or institutional form, merely the inner calling of the Spirit and the recognition of this calling by an act of consecration (*549–563*). It is a peculiar mixture of spiritual mysticism, visionary Enthusiasm, Catholic hierarchy, and the Baptist Congregational ideal, with, at the same time, a very strong emphasis upon the perfection and union with God of the Primitive State which is to be restored in the Third Dispensation. For this reason *Berens* connects Winstanley closely with the Familists (*pp. 15–18*).—For the Irvingites, see *Kalbe, pp. 439–455*.—Further prophetic communities are the Ubbonites (*Heppe, p. 68*), others in the two treatises of *Nippold*.

492 (p. 773.) Cf. *Heppe, pp. 240–374; Ritschl, I, 194–246*. The dualism of the idea: "Mysticism and the idea that the converted can have no fellowship with

the unconverted" (*p. 316*). The opposition of the pure mystic, *Gichtel*, is characteristic "who could not feel at home within an exclusive sect, because he himself had no desire to form a sect at all" (*ibid., 317*).—Continuance of the influence of the Labadists upon the Church in the Netherlands (*Heppe, 394–464*): "The Conventicles were the sphere in which usually Pietists, Labadists and Hattemists met in fellowship" (*p. 399*); in the German Reformed Church (*Heppe, 482 and 489*). Thereby the communistic and monastic experiments came to nothing, but the tendency remained to Separatism, to non-historical mysticism, to Enthusiasm, to Chiliasm, to Perfectionism, and now and again also to the uncontrolled sexual tendencies of a Perfectionism of that kind. For offshoots of this movement in the Philadelphian societies, which include the so-called "Buttlarsche Rotte" (Separatist movement, led by Eva v. Buttlar (1670–1717)), see *Hochhut: Geschichte und Entwickelung der philadelphischen Sozietäten, Z. f. hist. Theol., 1865*.—For resemblances to and connections with the Waldensians and the Baptists see *Maronier, p. 136*; on the journey from Geneva to Middelburg, Labadie actually took refuge among some Waldensians in the Palatinate.

[494] (p. 774.) For the intercourse of Spinoza with Collegiants and Mennonites, see *Kuno Fischer: Geschichte d. n. Ph., I, 165, 137 ff.*; for his relationship with mysticism, *ibid., pp. 153–155*, in his correspondence: "For salvation I do not hold it necessary to know Christ according to the flesh; quite otherwise, on the other hand, do I think of that eternal Son of God, namely, of the eternal Wisdom of God which has revealed itself in all things at its highest in the human spirit and amongst all men at its highest in Jesus Christ; for without this Wisdom, which alone teaches how we can differentiate between truth and error, good and evil, no one can be saved." That is the doctrine of the "Spiritual Reformers". *Windelband* also points out connections of this kind in his *Geschichte d. n. Ph., I, 213. Hegler, p. 288*, rightly puts the question whether perhaps, especially in Holland, Spinoza had come into touch with Sebastian Franck. Also *Hylkema: Reformateurs, Haarlem, 1900 and 1902*, places Spinoza in this connection (*II, 367, 473–477*). It is not until we realize this, so it seems to me, that we understand the religious and ethical side of Spinoza's thought. Geulincx belongs undoubtedly also on the religious and ethical side to the same general group of ideas, as *Heppe* rightly emphasizes.

[495] (p. 776.) For this new wave of mystical life, see the deeply interesting book by *Hylkema*. It is a perfect mine of the characteristic peculiarities of this kind of "spiritual religion", and it exhibits in an amazing manner parallels with the English movement. The name, however, is rather unfortunate, also the connection between the history of dogma and the earlier mysticism, and the relationship with the Baptists, is not brought out sufficiently clearly; the political and social doctrines, as well as the theological ideas of this Spiritual Reformer, are interpreted too much in the sense of modern rationalistic and politico-social phenomena.—No class restrictions (*I, p. 80; II, 205–208*); a common opposition to the Church and the Baptists (*I, 138, 169, 185; II, 7*); radical non-ecclesiasticism (*I, 100 ff.*), opposition also to the ascetic Pietism within the churches (*II, 86 ff., 472*); equation of the true ethical content of the "spirit" with conscience and reason (*I, 161, 167, 176*); ethics in relation to the State (*I, 147–178*), the inward aspect, see also *II, 1–111*. The theoretical independence and remoteness of this religious idea, in relation to all morality in general, is brought out very well in *II, 83–111*; among the Collegiants the Calvinist and Puritan characteristics take the lead, in the other movements the chief features are communistic, sectarian, and democratic. Among the former

it is very interesting to note how it agrees with the economic features of Ascetic Protestantism, as they have been described by *Max Weber*; *van Hoek* cries aloud to his Collegiant brethren: "Vergenoegt u met een seedig gelat en gemoed, met deftighijd in handel en wandel!" (*II, 14*). Here also the systematic-rational element in Calvinistic asceticism, so strongly emphasized by Max Weber, finds its classic expression (*II, 49*). "Liever dan er ook maar de minste ruimte aan te geven (i.e. to the flesh) wil hij het stelselmatig tyraniseeren. Juist omdat het vleesch op gemak gestelld is, zal hij sich zetten tot strengen arbeid, etc."—Among the real Spiritual Reformers and pure mystics, on the other hand, this system gives way in order to make place for the liberty of the Spirit. There is a great difference between the mysticism which recognizes the Calvinistic ethic of the "calling" and uses it as a means of discipline, and Quietistic contemplative mysticism. Also fanatical world-reformers have little to do with the Protestant ethic of the "calling"; here the prevailing spirit is that of the radical sect, with its visions of world-renewal.

[496] (p. 780.) For the whole subject see *Hylkema*, who throws a good deal of light upon the connection between Dutch and English spirituality; in particular he shows the significance of the influence of the Collegiants on the Seekers and the Quakers; further, and above all, *Barclay*, who presents an extraordinary mass of material in a confused and most obscure manner; his treatment of the subject, however, carries one completely into the atmosphere of the time, and reveals on all hands the differences between Independents, Baptists, and pure mystics, as well as the various developments of these groups, and the way in which they agreed and disagreed with each other. He rightly sees that the decisive factor in this situation is the problem of war and non-resistance, in addition to the need to discern the genuine mystics.—The most instructive work of *Sippell* is based upon the material in both these books, and develops the suggestions which they give; see *Ueber den Ursprung des Quäkertums, Chr. W., 1910*, and *Dells Programm*. Above all, he has thrown a good deal of light upon the mystical treatises and their connection with the Collegiants, and thus indirectly with Coornheert, and he has also followed up the question of the references to Luther's earlier "spiritual" congregational ideal. I owe a good deal to verbal information from Herr *Sippell*, who has also most kindly placed at my disposal several rare treatises of that period which were in his possession. Thus I have learnt to know *Dell's Sermons* and *Dell's Select Works, London, 1773*, and the wonderful little mystical treatise by *Saltmarsh*, entitled *Sparkles of Glory, London, 1847*, as well as *Eaton's Honey-Combe*. It is only through these treatises that one can understand the period. For *Dell*, see the interesting work by *Sippell*; Sippell appears, however, to me at any rate, to undervalue the relation with Congregationalism, which itself contained mystical elements and to estimate too highly the connection with Luther. Dell's doctrine, however, is in reality Congregationalism transformed into "spiritual" mysticism, which further accepts the purely technical support of the ecclesiastical system by the State, as was obvious under Cromwell; in this connection we can also think of *Schwenkfeld*, as *Sippell* himself has remarked recently (*Chr. W., 1911, p. 966*). We may also state as a fact that there took place among the essentially Calvinistic Puritan Independents a development from originally pure dogmatic Calvinism to the Enthusiastic Independents under the influence of Baptists and Spiritual Reformers; above all, under the influence of the excitement and agitation of the period (*Barclay, pp. 150–159*). This, however, is not pure mysticism; cf. the passage which Barclay quotes from *C. H. Spurgeon*: "It happened that the Puritans were getting into the sere and yellow leafe; and

the Independents and Baptists and others sects who were at times thoroughly and even remarkably spiritual, were growing worldly, political and vain-glorious. They had the opportunity of grasping the carnal sword, and they embraced this opportunity; and from that very moment very many of them lost the spirituality for which they had been eminent. The danger was lest the Evangelical sects should quietly settle down into one State Church . . . and preach each one after his fashion. . . . At that very moment God sent into the world George Fox. . . . He stood up in the face of the Christian world, and said to it, 'No, thou shalt not do this. Thou shalt not conform thyself to the world. Thou shalt not go into an unholy alliance with the State; there shall be in the midst of thee a spiritual people who shall bear their protest that Christ's Kingdom is not of this world, and that religion standeth not in forms and ceremonies, but is a matter connected with the inner man, and is the work of God's Spirit in the heart." This shows the whole difference between "spiritual religion" and the spirit which has just been described above of the Baptists, Hussites, Huguenots, and Calvinists, who approved of war for the establishment of the establishment of the Kingdom of Christ. The same difference is seen in the observation of *Barclay* on *p. 625*: "The Christianity of Cromwell's soldiers at the commencement of our civil wars cannot be doubted, but it is more than doubtful whether it improved in quality by the conflict. They had, however, seen enough of war to be apt disciples of Fox, and many of them became preachers of the Gospel of peace and goodwill to men."—For the English followers of Boehme, see *Barclay, p. 214*; for the Seekers and their connection with the Collegiants, *pp. 73* and *410–413*; for the Ranters, *pp. 414–428*; *Barclay* thinks that they owe their origin to the "Libertins" of Calvin's time, and to the mediaeval "Brethren of the Free Spirit", whereas to me this seems a mere resemblance which can be explained by the fact that they have a common basis.—The spiritual course of many souls is reflected in this report about Salmon's treatise (*p. 428, I*): "First he became a Presbyterian; they appeared to him to hover gently and soar sweetly in a more sublime region than the Episcopal people. Then came Independency on the stage, a people far exceeding others in the strictness of their form. Then the doctrine of Believers' Baptisme. He became a Baptist preacher, braved persecution, and built a tabernacle. Then came that voice from the throne of the Almighty: 'Arise and depart, for this is not your rest.' "—See also the account in *Firth: Cromwell's Army*. Here "spiritual" religion penetrated through lay-preaching, and through the substitution of "spiritual" chaplains like Dell, Saltmarsh, Sedgwick, and Hugh Peters for the Presbyterian chaplains, who withdrew (*p. 320*). The gradual elimination from the Army (*p. 340*): "a sober Congregationalisme became the dominant form of religion." Cromwell interprets the coming Kingdom of God in a spiritual sense, in contrast to the Fifth Monarchy men, and therefore he desires to allow existing outward institutions to continue (*p. 341*). Monk complains that these "spiritual" men are very little use in the Army (*pp. 344 ff.*); "spiritually minded" officers cashiered (*346 ff.*). Here is a description of a Captain Jackson: "In the language of the time he was one of those who had passed through all forms, and was above all forms and above all ordinances, whose religion was not made up of laws and duties, but all exaltation and inward bliss. For such, he said, all external forms of duties and performances are turned into praises and thanksgivings. Now there is nothing but mirth in them, there is a continual singing of birds in them, chirping sweetly, in a sweet harmony of soul-ravishing delightful music." He was under the thumb of a Presbyterian colonel, but he was very useful as a military man, for which cause Fairfax did not wish to sacrifice him. That even in this Cromwell would not let things go too far, and punished those who held Socinian or Antinomian theories, as "derogation to the honour of God" is shown in the case of a Captain Covell (*347 ff.*).—In this whole connection *Sippell* ascribes a very restricted influence to the Familists (*p. 2*); he thinks that the "enthusiasm" and mysticism come from the eschatological tendency of Puritanism (*pp. 5–10*). However, in Everard, Dell, and Saltmarsh the whole mystical, "spiritual", literary tradition is undeniably in the background (*Sippell, pp. 80–88*).

[497] (p. 784.) On this subject see especially *Barclay*, who gives information on the most important particulars; obviously, however, he wishes to give the impression that Quakerism is a voluntary Church of a Pietist and Scriptural kind. See also *Weingarten*, who traces its descent from the Anabaptists, and *Sippell*, who ascribes its origin to the mystics, and also the *Journal of George Fox* (German translation, 1910), with the beautiful introduction by *Wernle*, who emphasizes chiefly the fact that the Quakers take the Sermon on the Mount as an ideal which is meant to be actually realized in life. In my opinion the whole question of the character of Quakerism is only intelligible when we take the following points into account: (*a*) that primitive Quakerism, with its emphasis upon inwardness and its "enthusiasm" was entirely unorganized and lacking in support; (*b*) that it only achieved organization when it began to follow the example of the community organization of the Baptists; (*c*) that this organization, once it had been completed, led the Society inevitably into a closer compromise with the world, until (*d*) the Society attained the Puritan morality of the "calling" and an almost ecclesiastical form of Church-order and tradition. Quakerism is a synthesis of mysticism and the Baptist movement (which was finally urged into close contact with the Puritan outlook), which from the beginning it had rejected so resolutely.—This is the main result of Barclay's study in accordance with which he tones down its mystical and enthusiastic origin. The connection with the constitution of the Mennonites (*p. 247*): "Does not this clearly show the way in which the doctrine of the Light, associated with the doctrines and practices of the Mennonites, passed into England and found a powerful and active exponent in George Fox?" The abiding difference (*p. 249*): "In Friesland he, a Quaker missionary, says, that they (the Baptists) hung exceedingly on their outward visible things, so that I am confident it was as easy for the Apostle taking the sect of the Pharisees off from circumcision, offerings, temple, and the traditions of the elders, as it is for us to bring these people away from their external celebration of the ordinances called Baptism and the Lord's Supper." The connection with the Mennonites and Collegiants especially (*pp. 352–358*).—Tension between both elements was, therefore, not lacking (*pp. 431 ff.*). The difficult problem of the establishment of the membership on the basis of the assumptions of mysticism (*pp. 359–366*), likewise the appointment of the minister and the teaching elders as the recognition of a spiritual endowment by the community (*p. 445*). The solution of the problem of "infallibility", that is, of the decisive authority which determines questions of membership and position, is the Spirit in whom one must trust (*p. 446*): "None ought nor can be accounted to the Church of Christ but such as are in a measure sanctified or sanctifying by the grace of God and led by His Spirit; nor get any made officers in the Church but by the grace of God and inward revelation of this Spirit." It was in the impossibility of solving this problem that Luther's idea of small groups of pure Christians proved impracticable. Among the Quakers, however, this interpretation of the leading of the

Spirit was interpreted along two lines: (*a*) it led to the idea of birthright-membership, that is, to the supposition that the children of Quakers will become filled with the Spirit, and that, therefore, they must be educated as far as possible on very intensive religious lines; (*b*) so far as officials were concerned, the guidance of the Spirit came through the vote of the majority, who chose and controlled their own officers. This constitutes the process of secularization, which *Barclay* laments from time to time (*pp. 527 and 362*).—The acceptance of the Puritan ethic of the "calling", supervision of the community by the laity, who interfere in every detail of business and family life (*pp. 490–501*); here we find the supervision of labour and wages conditions, strict avoidance of all kinds of luxury, exclusion of mendicancy, and the impossibility of finding a poor man in the community. The only standard for activity is usefulness; in one group the members are forbidden to plant flowers; that is a luxury, instead of flowers they are to plant potatoes and turnips. Here also the economic results are described in which he agrees with *Weber: Archiv XXI, pp. 61–72*, and especially *Bernstein, pp. 680–685*.—For the Quaker State in Pennsylvania, see the extremely interesting book by *Sharpless: A Quaker Experiment in Government, Philadelphia, 1902*.—*Barclay* complains of the numerical decline within the Society, and attributes it to lack of propaganda and laxity in excluding unworthy members, and to marriage with non-Quakers. The reason for that decline, however, is inherent in the sociological principle of the Society, which can only expand widely in times of religious awakening. A gain in numbers from a natural increase in population is only experienced within the churches, who, through Infant Baptism, increase along with the population, and who are able to combine their standards with a religion for the masses. I met with similar complaints among Unitarians and Congregationalists when I was in America. With such principles this is inevitable, and it can only be avoided by an approximation to Church principles, which, indeed, the birthright membership of the Quakers really is (see *Barclay, p. 362*).—For the policy of the Quakers in questions of poor relief, provision of employment, etc., and for the effect of the removal of poverty within a small circle, but aloofness from the working classes and the tendency of the Society to become bourgeois, see *Barclay, pp. 157–521*, and *Bernstein, 683*.—On Bellers, see the highly interesting information given by *Bernstein, pp. 694–718*. It is the radical Christian Baptist element in Quakerism, which is here expressed, combined with a Puritan emphasis upon work. The book bears the characteristic motto: "Industry brings plenty. The sluggard shall be cloathed with rags. He that will not work shall not eat."

[499] (p. 788.) For the *Unio mystica*, see the pertinent remarks in *Hupfeld: Ethik Gerhards, pp. 204–232*; for *Arnd*, see *Lasch: Arnds Wahres Christentum, Monatsschrift f. Pastoraltheologie, 1909*; a good deal in *Göbel*, who loves to trace mysticism so long as it remained within the Church; for further books, consult the literature mentioned in connection with Pietism. *Ritschl* understood very well the difference between "indifferentism" and the "sect" and the peculiarity of their way of forming fellowship. With his usual charity he calls this kind of thing a "clique" (*II, pp. 359–362; I, 475, 483*); he sees in the spiritual leaders of the Friends of God an imitation of the Catholic director, in mysticism the ultimate cause of the martial Jesuit order, or a luxury which is due to the fact that there are "enough people who think like that (like Tersteegen) some of them weavers whose imaginative powers and devoutness were no help to their mechanical work, partly rich people who did not need to work, partly women, especially unmarried women, who always have the time and the capacity for mystical contemplation" (*I, 478*)! According to his idea, such people ought to

be in a convent, and the whole doctrine simply comes from the cloister. In contrast with this, however, he can endure the ascetic sects: "For Separatism betrays a secret attachment to a confessional Church the more ardently it fights against the impurity of the same, at least to the extent that it assumes the necessity for a particular Church formation at all" (*I, 483*). This is a complete misunderstanding!—For the attitude to the State and to Society, see *Gottfried Arnold* and *Dippel, II, 315* and *327*, also *Göbel, II, 698–735*, and *III, 166–193*. *Dippel's* treatment of the subject has some Quietistic features, but in reality its whole spirit is not monastic as *Ritschl* seems to think, nor is it due to Thomas Aquinas, but it is genuinely Lutheran. He recommends agriculture and farming, considers work a kind of asceticism and a means of self-support, as well as the love of one's neighbour, treats private property as the result of the Fall, etc. He has, however, an aversion to official work under the State, a tendency which we see in Luther so far as individuals were concerned, but not with reference to official position, and he objects to a professional ministry, which, of course, for Luther would have been quite impossible. *Gottfried Arnold* accepts the existing situation in the genuine Lutheran sense, just as *Sebastian Franck* accepted it in his day. In *II, p. 365*, he says, very truly: "The practice of the early Anabaptists and of the English Baptists differed from that of the Separatists in Germany to the extent in which their piety was not bound up with any political claims or any tendency to social reform. Their complete detachment from the world, and their quite individual tendency towards self-denial, which often led to Quietism, made them feel that the thing to be most desired was the isolation of each individual." This description, however, only fits the mystics; among ascetic Pietists and Church reformers the reasons for such a passivity were different, and *Ritschl* has not gone into them further. Those reasons were the impossibility of any social reform from the point of view of German Lutheran Absolutism, and the acceptance of the ethic of the "calling" from the Calvinists, which from the very outset was bourgeois and conservative.—For *Christian Thomasius*, see *Ritschl, II, 552*, and *R. Kayser: Christian Thomasius und der Pietismus, 1900*.—If we speak of radical Pietism we must then distinguish between the ascetic sectarian wing and the mystical indifferentist wing; in Lutheranism the latter has been decidedly more important and influential than the former, whereas, on the other hand, within Calvinism the former has been most important down to the present day, and from this source receives ever fresh reserves of energy and fresh impulses for progressive movement. For mysticism in the Calvinistic Church, see above, *pp. 774–789*; also *Heppe, p. 70; Ritschl, I, 122–130; Max Weber: Archiv XXI, p. 44*. In the study of Dutch and English mysticism outside the churches we have already shown its connection with the mystical elements in the Baptist movement and the early spirituality of the period of the Reformation.—For the reappearance of mediaeval mystical literature there are numerous instances in *Ritschl*, also *Keller: Reformation, pp. 470 ff.* Very interesting also is *Hegler: Sebastian Francks lateinische Paraphrase der deutschen Theologie, 1901, p. 16:* "In the orthodox period the estimate of the *Theologia Germanica* was keener among the Calvinists than among the Lutherans."—The different attitude of mystics and "spiritual" men towards practical ethics, that is, the lack of contact with Calvinistic rational asceticism and the ethic of the "calling" in favour of a more passive suffering and non-theoretical attitude towards the world, has often been suggested by *Ritschl* and *Max Weber* (*Archiv XXI, 41*), but it has not been traced to its real reason, which lies in the fact that the fundamental doctrines and sociological quality of mysticism are different. Here, then, there is no systematic utilitarianism, and the main impression is one of spontaneity in response to moods, feelings, and passing impressions. But just because of that fact they again come nearer to Lutheranism, from which they only differ in ethics by a stronger theoretical rejection of the flesh. But here, indeed, Luther's followers for their part were also very uncertain.

[500] (p. 790.) Cf. *Plitt: Zinzendorfs Theologie, 1869 f.; Becker: Zinzendorf und sein Christentum im Verhältnis zum kirchl. und religiösen Leben seiner Zeit, 1900. Ritschl* is also very acute in his analysis; he considers that the Count was originally attracted to the spirit of Philadelphianism and "indifferentism" in the sense in which *Arnold* uses it, and that he only approached sectarian ideas through the influence of the Moravians. This expression of opinion has been questioned by *Becker* (*Studd. u. Kritt., 1891*), since he points out that Zinzendorf always remained a Lutheran. *Ritschl*, however, is right in the main because the Lutheranism in question was supra-ecclesiastical and interconfessional in character, that is, it is Lutheran Christ-mysticism and an ethic of feeling, and the difference between that and Lutheranism in the ecclesiastical sense was only not realized by the Count. In this matter he was amazingly naïve and non-reflective. Mystical features in *Ritschl, III, 407, 384*, above all in *Becker, 76–82, 249–262.* His misgivings about the Moravians refer to their sectarian character, "their tendency to separatism, to form themselves into harmful sects if they had only something external to show for it"; "that was an Italian Waldensian false spirit" (words of Zinzendorf in *Müller, 100 ff.*). He himself explains clearly why from his personal mysticism he came to see the need for membership in a community: "The Moravian constitution had to take place; otherwise we would have had to invent some other form. For at bottom it is a fanatical idea to say, What have we to do with sects? With human organizations? We want to be a Church of Jesus Christ. But what kind of a Church then? The invisible Church? Then you would have to become hermits once again. The visible Church? Then know that there is no visible Church without a definite religious form" (*Müller, 99*). These words are highly illuminating as showing the difference between the sect-type and mysticism and idealism. This fact also explains his opposition to the Church discipline which the Moravians wished to introduce, and to the development of their religious body into a state within the State; see *Becker, 225–232.*—For the aesthetic individualism, which was due to this outlook and very little to the voluntary character of the movement, see the interesting sketch by *Sam. Eck: Ueber die Herkunft des Individualitätsgedankens bei Schleiermacher, Giessen, 1908.* For the transformation of Spener's conventicles into free religious "sociability", as something which is due to the social nature of man and therefore also justified in religion, as well as on the other hand the development of conventicles into free associations, which are intended to fertilize the territorial churches by concentrating an inward and spiritual Christianity round their chosen leaders, see *Becker, 163–178; 153:* "The Zinzendorf Brotherhood has nothing to do with that which is usually described as Church development, but it is solely a religious movement within the popular churches which organizes itself into free groups and associations." Zinzendorf himself seems to have held this point of view: "In the opinion of Zinzendorf the future belongs to the free religious association which is founded solely upon Christ crucified, and whose only aim is to exalt Him, and therefore desires to serve the popular churches from this point of view which is its sole standard."

[502] (p. 792.) It is impossible to illustrate this question in detail. A certain amount can be found in *Keller: Reformation, 483–488*; the monthly review of the

Comenius Society studies this question unceasingly from Keller's point of view; see also *Troeltsch: Das Historische in Kants Religionsphilosophie, 1904.* Similarly *Kronenberg: Geschichte des deutschen Idealismus, I, 1909,* makes the statement that German Idealism signifies the breaking through of Christian mysticism "into the universal human". His treatment of Hamann and Jacobi is very fine. The fact that he practically identifies Christianity, mysticism, Protestantism, Romanticism, Platonism, and that he argues that the spiritual conflict is due to the original opposition of this tendency to Enlightenment, Rationalism, Scholasticism, Ecclesiasticism, is very little help in making clear what is right in his assertion of mystical and spiritual influences upon German Idealism.—The criticism of *J. Plenge* is very instructive because he entirely neglects the sociological point of view; see his *Realistische Glossen zu einer Gesch. d. deutschen Idealismus, Archiv für Sozialwissenschaft, XXXII, 1–35*: "Critical subjectivism experiences a brief period of critical brilliance, supported by the social optimism of a bourgeoisie which has attained its freedom. . . . It seems to have been an anticipation (that is, in face of the task of a renewal of Society in connection with the religious idea) which was only possible through the specific development of the problem of Reason which had grown up within the sphere of Christian subjectivism" (*p. 34*).—For the very interesting and influential *Lavater,* see the excellent studies by *von Schulthess-Rechberg* and *Heinrich Maier* in *J. C. Lavater, 1902,* as well as my *Anzeige HZ., 93.*—On the whole subject see *Sell: Die Religion unserer Klassiker, 1904.* Even to-day the best treatment of the subject is that of *Gelzer: Die deutsche poetische Literatur seit Klopstock und Lessing, 1846. Sell, p. 175,* expresses it excellently when he says that the common element in the classic writers consists in this: "It is the conviction of the complete relativity of all that is offered as revelation, with a complete recognition of that whence all revelations come and of that which it receives: of God and the soul." Goethe is, upon the whole, not unchristian, but absolutely outside the churches. "This Pietism (of Lavater and others) could and must interest Goethe because it was a form of personal religion invented by oneself, not a religion based upon authority or mere custom or because of submission to any kind of authority" (*p. 176*). "According to that, Goethe (apart from the central period of his life, when his whole attention was directed to antiquity) was a man who was self-taught and followed the Bible in his own way, a believer who only obeyed the witness of his own conscience" (*p. 189*). Goethe's expression is instructive: "There is the standpoint of a kind of religion, that of pure Nature and Reason, which is of Divine origin. This will eternally remain the same, it will endure and be of value so long as Divinely endowed beings exist. It is, however, only for chosen souls, for it is much too exalted ever to become general" (*p. 206*); that is not meant in the rationalistic sense; Goethe's intention was something spiritual, with the inclusion of Nature in the revelation of the spirit of the All. The well-known word about Christ: "If I am asked whether it is in my nature to yield to Him in reverent worship I answer, Certainly. I prostrate myself before Him as the divine revelation of the highest principle of morality" is likewise quite in the meaning of mystical idealism, excepting that God at the same time similarly reveals Himself powerfully in other realities, as, for example, in the Son as the most favoured revelation of the generative principle; "the worship of Christ is only a conditional recognition of something which he has experienced of Him" (*p. 190*). Very significant is the religious education in the pedagogical period of the years of travel, because it outlines a peculiar form of worship which corresponds to these ideas; further, it is quite different from that of the churches and reveals the sense of need to give to the new conception of Christianity also a form of worship and a community for instruction and education; it is the idea of an educational system and a form of worship which is to be freely entrusted to various groups.—To this connection belong Björnson and Ibsen, who both started from the Pietism of their family. Ibsen's idea of the Third Era is the same as the *Evangelium aeternum* of Lessing, the three stages of the mystics, or the threefold Gospel, and it can be traced right back to Joachim of Fiori; see also *Weinel: Ibsen, Björnson, Nietzsche, 1908.*—The whole subject deserves to be made a subject of independent research.

[504] (p. 795.) On this point see the works of *Dilthey* and *Haym.* The anti-ecclesiastical element in *Schleiermacher's Reden* can only be held to be an esoteric expression if we misunderstand the sermons preached at the same time; *Ritschl* has rightly felt this; see *Schl.'s Reden und ihre Nachwirkungen auf die evangel. Kirche in Deutschland, 1874*; see also *Troeltsch: Schl. und die Kirche* (*Schl., der Philosoph des Glaubens, 1910*).—No one has seen better than Kierkegaard the aesthetic and immanential character of Romantic religion as well as its radical individualism; Kierkegaard rejects the aestheticism and the theories of immanence, whereas he lays great stress upon radical individualism.—The completion of this individualism by a Romantic tendency, which copies the Catholic Church, as for instance in Novalis, is shown by Paul de Lagarde in his German writings, which, in spite of many fads, belong to the most important studies that have ever been written about the modern religious situation; he thinks that the whole situation means the break-up of the previous churches and the preparation for a new religion through a Gospel renewed from before the time of Paul and an ethically deepened spirituality.—*A. Bonus: Die Kirche* (*Aus die Gesellschaft, hsg. v. Buber, XXVI*) is very characteristic in its complete loss of the idea of the Church, and it is distinctive for countless people who are thinking along those lines.—Influential groups like that of *Johannes Müller* at Schloss Mainburg reveal the character of an ethical mysticism: awakening of the Divine Seed in man through Christ to a free personal development from the Spirit which is one with Christ, but which goes far beyond the letter; the incarnation of man by obedience to natural laws of the personal life, revealed and made known by Christ, is nothing other than the spiritual doctrine of the awakening of the Divine Spark in contact with Christ—all, however, removed into the sphere of activity. This group is also typical in its opposition to the Church and the sociological character of its spirituality; see *Müller's Bergpredigt* (turned into contemporary German, 1906).—The conception of Christianity, which *Eucken* describes as the necessary development of the same, is "spiritual"; see *Können wir noch Christen sein, 1911, p. 190*: "We are then in line with the movement of world history if we demand a further changing of the visible into the invisible, and if we desire to see a still clearer distinction drawn between genuine reality and that which can be touched by the senses. Therefore, we are not departing from our contact with Christianity, the religion of the Spirit, if we regard the happenings of the spiritual life as the only thing that matters and which ought to be treated accordingly." *P. 200:* "Religious fellowship must take its stand upon the truths . . . which belong immediately to the life process, which do not come first of all out of metaphysical speculation or out of historical tradition, truths, that is, which represent and are related to the facts of the appearance of a new world in man and the further formation of this world through struggle and conflict, the facts of a fundamental fighting and victorious spirituality."—A very original form of mysticism which is indifferent to Christianity has been developed by *Maeterlinck*, whose influence upon the present day can likewise

be interpreted from this homogeneity; see *The Treasure of the Humble.* Mysticism develops in a deliberately anti-Christian sense under pessimistic influences in *Schopenhauer* and *Ed. v. Hartmann,* and is still more hostile in character in their disciples *Arthur Drews* and *von Schnehen.* Here, by the extinction of the whole theistic and personalistic element, all desire to form a community and every form of worship falls away completely, and the central point of the Christian cultus, Jesus Christ, is set aside altogether; all the same these religious philosophers believe that they are able to revive a declining religion by this kind of religion of the immanence of the individual spirit within the All, apart from all fellowship, practice of worship, and basis in history.—Highly characteristic also is *Simmel: Das Problem der religiösen Lage* (in the collection *Weltanschauung, Philosophie und Religion, 1911*), who conceives religion as something entirely neutral without any definite content or stimulus, and therefore he excludes all connection with worship or with history.—Modern mystical lyrics, like those of *R. M. Rilke,* also belong to this tendency, and similarly the religious tendency of the *Diederich Verlag* and the whole modern claim to be not irreligious but apart from the churches, as well as many other things of the same kind.

[504a] (p. 797.) It is not uninteresting to classify contemporary Protestant theology from this point of view. Present-day orthodoxy has a strongly Pietistic element mingled with a strong emphasis upon the inward life; but since in the inward experience of the spirit it always considers, above all, that the Bible, the Sacrament, and the Church constitute the supernatural agent of the immediate experience, it retains a sufficient amount of objectivity, authority, an external standard and miracle in order to be able to think and work as a Church; from this point of view the Virgin Birth and the Resurrection are interpreted from the standpoint of inward experience; it is ecclesiastically "*potent*".—Schleiermacher and his disciples are essentially "spiritual" in their outlook; but he reacted from this "spirituality" to a modernized form of Christ-mysticism, and in so doing he retains a Christian form of worship and a canon of doctrine which are to some extent conceivable, the recognition of redemption through the supernatural impression of the personality of Christ as united to God; in accordance with this he would maintain the Church and a community for worship, while he would give up the very individual arrangements of the Christian life-substance which is clothed in the form of the popular Church; from this point of view a stable ecclesiasticism in the old sense will never be attained.—The followers of Hegel went in the same direction, in so far as they wished to remove religion from pure intellectualism and a mere party and scholastic connection; or they made the "principle" of the Spirit entirely independent, in contrast with the "Person" of Christ, and in so doing they only retained for the Church the spiritual fellowship which was entirely anonymous.—Ritschl and his genuine followers reduced the body of doctrine in a peculiar way, but they demanded for it a strictly authoritative ecclesiastical value, and for that very reason they laid great emphasis upon the Church, and drove mystical spirituality out of every hole and corner; Ritschl was triumphant when he could prove to his orthodox opponents their Pietistic modifications of the conception of the Church, showing them that he was more ecclesiastical than they. His doctrine, therefore, is completely planned to fit the possibility of a popular and Territorial Church.—Herrmann maintains a Christ-mysticism similar to that of Zinzendorf and Schleiermacher, which asserts a kernel of certainty given from without, which guarantees confidence, and is thus a redeeming revelation, but otherwise everything is left to personal conscientious conviction; therefore, from the side of the Church he believes

in Luther's confidence in the supernatural proclamation of Christ which itself effects conversion, which needs no other artificial aids, and is able to carry itself out by its own power; the consequences of this position for Church-order have been deduced by Rudolph Sohm and Erich Förster; this would lead in practice to Congregationalism, within which all that matters is faith and trust in God; in this case there would be nothing to fear from any anti-ecclesiastical influence. The so-called Religious Historical School goes back entirely to "spiritual" religion, and is, therefore, ecclesiastically "impotent". My own theology is certainly "spiritual", but for that very reason it seeks to make room for the historical element, and for the ritual and sociological factor which is bound up with it. Naturally I am aware of the difficulties of such an undertaking.—*Harnack* (see especially his remarks about the *World Congress for Free Christianity, Aus Wissenschaft und Leben, 1911, I, 146–152*) considers that a theoretical solution of the problem is altogether impracticable, and he only wishes to see an intelligent tolerant form of Church government, which would leave the pastors freedom of movement; this really means the destruction of the Church as a system, and it would be preserved solely by the exclusion of very "advanced" pastors; the limits within which their "advanced" views might be tolerated could only be determined by the verdict of some committee, acting according to the best of its knowledge, taking the general personality into account; this, then, might form a bridge to happier forms of organization later on: a conception which thoroughly corresponds with the mingling of spirituality and historicity in his theology (see *ibid., Christus als Erlöser, pp. 81–94*). From that point of view also we must interpret a work like that of General-superintendent *Kaftan: Wo stehen wir? Eine kirchliche Zeitbetrachtung, 1911*. He exalts the ecclesiastical "potency" of the orthodox, and casts up at the Liberals their ecclesiastical "impotence" which he says is due to the features which lay most stress upon "spirituality". In order to save the Church he would banish the "subjective" members from it. The characterization is not false. Still we must draw attention to the fact that qualities are essentially bound up with "ecclesiastical potency", which ethically are very hard to bear, and that the qualities which go with "spiritual impotence" are qualities which correspond to gentleness, goodness, and inwardness of Christianity. This presents, in fact, the sociological antimony between the claims of organization and those of the development of a free personality. *Mutatis mutandis* the political parties are in a similar position, with the exception that they do not theoretically serve the formation of the personality. If, however, the matter really were so, another way than that of *Kaftan* would be desirable, for if his way were followed the Church would be saved at a very great cost, and it would alienate spiritually minded men everywhere.—There are some fine remarks upon the whole subject in *Sell's* article *Die zweifache Theologie, Ch. W., 1911*; see also my memorial speech, *Richard Rothe, 1899. Rothe* only preserved himself from the ultimate consequences of pure "spirituality" through his Christology, but even in this he comes very close to theosophy; here he reminds us of Schwenkfeld, Paracelsus, Böhme, Oetinger, and Arnd.—For the whole see also the book which has already been mentioned by *Bruhn*.

505 (p. 798.) Pertinent remarks upon this tendency in Novalis and in the French Romanticism in *Windelband: Die Philosophie im deutschen Geistesleben des 19. Jahrhunderts, 1909, pp. 32–36*; for St. Simon see *Lorenz Stein: Sozialismus und Kommunismus*. Herder, in his time at Buckeburg, had tendencies of that kind. To what a limited extent, however, such tendencies arise out of the real spirit of Romanticism is proved by present-day Neo-Romanticism, which renews

the old aesthetic, differentiating spirit, and which has again entirely cast off the positive historical tendency, possibly only in order to experience a similar transformation.

[508] (p. 802.) For further details, see *Ritschl* and *Göbel*. The *Geschichte der Ethik*, by *Luthardt*, *II*, *248–340*, and *Gass*, *II*, *1*, *pp. 283–325*, and *359–368*, shed practically no light upon this subject. *Dippel* has written a work on social ethics entitled: *Christenstadt auf Erden ohne gewöhnlichen Lehr-, Wehr-, und Nährstand oder kurze doch eigentliche Abbildung der aus dem Reiche der Natur entstandenen und im Zorn Gottes bestätigten Ordnungen unter den Menschenkindern.* Extracts in *Walch: Religionsstreitigkeiten*, *pp. 729f. and 753f.* The existing social order of Natural Law belongs only to the economy of the Law or of the Father.—*Saltmarsh*, in his *Sparkles of Glory*, expresses similar ideas. A completely new order of humanity is to arise which will be entirely free from legalism moving only in the spirit of love and idealism, but in itself becoming a real organism through love. Until that time comes Christians are to live apart from the world in quietness and humility.—Sebastian Franck tolerates the existing situation in the sense of the Lutheran Natural Law with a great deal of emphasis on resignation and a pessimistic view of humanity (*Hegler*, *pp. 260–263*, *243*, *116*, *179–184*); Schmoller and Wiskemann are also in sympathy with Franck to a certain extent.—Gottfried Arnold also is conservative in his attitude towards the present day, but idealistic and revolutionary with regard to the future, so far as this problem is concerned (*Ritschl*, *II*, *311*, *315*). Winstanley and Lilburn, on the other hand, expect the renewal of Society in the democratic and communistic sense through the Spirit, and they work consciously though without violence towards this goal.—The sex ethic and the permission of woman to preach should be noted, for this in itself constitutes the removal of ecclesiastical and especially of Lutheran patriarchalism. Otherwise, the finer conception of sex ethics does not appear until we come to the modern spiritual idealists, who combine the religious idea of personality with an aesthetic-immanent conception of Nature. On this point *Schleiermacher's Letters* on *Schlegel's Lucinde* are characteristic; see *Rade: Stellung des Christentums zum Geschlechtsleben*, *pp. 61–89*, in which, however, the whole question is connected too closely with Luther instead of with the tendency in mysticism and spiritual idealism to emphasize the subjective side of personality. Schleiermacher's ideas are entirely non-Lutheran.—The fine works on sex ethics by *Lhotzky: Das Buch der Ehe*, *1911*, and *Johannes Müller: Beruf und Stellung der Frau*, *1911*, also belong to this school of thought. It represents entirely non-ecclesiastical sex ethics. Johannes Müller is particularly characteristic of the modern spiritual, idealist ethic; his attitude is not quietistic but energetic and resolute, aiming at the new creation of humanity through the awakening of the "original being" or Divine Spark, latent in every soul, which is wakened by the impression of Jesus and which creates a spirit leading to free personal development. It is a spiritualized Chiliasm. This teaching naturally exerts its highest influence on purely personal relationships and therefore affects sex relationships. *Müller's Bergpredigt*, translated into ordinary German in 1906, contains, however, some very vague and impossible idealistic ideas of reform in the State, economics, and Society, which do not even remotely do justice to the complicated condition of the actual life of Society.

[510] (p. 809.) At this point my presentation of the subject converges with the well-known researches of *Max Weber* on *Der Geist des Kapitalismus*, *etc.* (*The Protestant Ethic and the Spirit of Capitalism*, translated by Talcott Parsons, George Allen & Unwin, 1930, 10s. 6d. net). *Weber's* researches start from

the endeavour to discover the constitution of modern capitalism, with its emphasis upon trade and its bourgeois character as distinguished from the capitalism of the ancient world and of the later period of the Middle Ages. On the basis of practical observation in Westphalia and the Lower Rhine, in Scotland, England, and America, he represents one of the constituent factors as Ascetic Protestantism, whose nature *Weber* analyses with a view to understanding its significance in economic history, or better still in the history of civilization. My study has a different aim. It only intends to give a clear presentation of the Protestant social ethic for its own sake. I therefore set aside Weber's further references. On this point I was able to follow his presentation of Ascetic Protestantism precisely because every time I studied this subject afresh I felt that his argument had proved itself to be a brilliantly acute piece of observation and analysis.—For the rest, however—as I would like to take this opportunity to remark—my researches do not start from those of Weber. Externally they were caused by the task with which I was entrusted, of reviewing (for the *Archiv*) the book by *Nathusius: Die Mitarbeit der Kirche an der Lösung der sozialen Frage* (*The Co-operation of the Church in the Solution of the Social Question*). When I was engaged in this task I found that there were no books in existence which could serve as a basis for the study of such a question, and I then began to try to lay the foundation for such a study myself. This book was the result of my endeavour. When I began this work, however, I found that all the interests of my research contributed to it: the sociological phenomena connected with the conception and nature of the Church, which were based on the familiar doctrine of *Rothe* (see *Religion und Kirche*, *Preuss. Jahrbb., 1895*), interests which concern the history of the Christian ethic (see *Grundprobleme der christlichen Ethik*, *Z. f. Th. u. K., 1902*), and, above all, my researches into the meaning of the *Lex Naturae* (they run through a whole number of treatises from my *Melancthon und Gerhard* onwards). Finally the book embodied the programme which in 1901 I outlined in my review of *Seeberg's Lehrbuch der Dogmengeschichte*, *Gött. Gel. Anzz., 1902, pp. 21–30*. Weber's work, however, did not appear until 1903. Without Weber certainly, I should have been unable to gain a clearer conception of Ascetic Protestantism than that which had already been prepared by Schneckenburger and Ritschl. Indeed, we only need to study the works of both these eminent, acute, and extremely learned men in order to arrive at this conception. Weber's own important discovery is the setting of this conception within the whole framework of universal, economic history and history of civilization; at the same time also we must not overlook the psychological penetration of his dogmatic-ethical analyses. They are based upon penetrating studies of Baxter, Spener, Bailey, Sedgwick, Hoornbeck, and the works of the Puritan divines, London, 1845–1848.

511 (p. 810.) Cf. *Weber: Archiv XXI, p. 79 f.* "A sober procreation of children" is the aim, according to Baxter; Spener has similar ideas, with concessions to the coarse Lutheran view. . . . According to an idea prevalent in many Pietistic circles, the highest form of Christian marriage is that which preserves virginity; the next best is that in which sexual intercourse serves the purpose exclusively of the procreation of children, and so on, down to those which are entered upon for purely erotic reasons, or for external convenience, which from the ethical point of view may be regarded as concubinage. In all this, the marriages which are contracted at a lower level, and those which are contracted for external reasons, are preferred to those which are based on eroticism (because the former are based on rational considerations). The theory and practice of the Moravians may here be left out of account." Thus Whitfield

expresses himself in an offer of marriage: "I bless God, if I know anything of my own heart, I am free from that foolish passion which the world calls love. . . . I trust I love you only for God, and desire to be joined to you only by His commands and for His sake" (*Lecky, II, p. 589*). Further, *Weber, p. 79 f.*: "As in that rational interpretation of sex relationships among nations which have been influenced by Puritanism, there grew up, finally, that refinement of spirit and ethical penetration of marriage relationships and the delicate blossoms of married chivalry—in contrast to that boorish patriarchal spirit which among us is often present, even in the circles of the *Geistesaristokratie*—this does not need to be developed further here; the protection of the freedom of conscience of woman and the extension of the idea of the priesthood of all believers to include her were also, by including this question, the first breaches in the patriarchal ideas. In the *Th. JB., 1911*, *W. Köhler* calls attention to a paper by *Ellen A. MacArthur* in the *Ecclesiastical History Review, 24, pp. 698–709*, on the subject "Women's Petition to the Long Parliament"; on this he remarks: "Why did women come to the fore just then when the Puritan rule and Quakerism were about to emerge? From what circles do they come? What are their motives? The Calvinistic influence is quite clear." Parliament certainly answers: "Good women, we entreat you to repaire to your houses and turne your petitions into prayers at home for us." For the reasons of the position of woman in America see *Bryce, II, 742*: "The cause is the usage of the Congregationalist, Presbyterian, and Baptist Churches, by which a woman who is a member of the congregation has the same rights in choosing a deacon, elder, or pastor as a man has."—For the often emphasized tendency of Ascetic Protestantism towards an extended system of popular education without philosophy and academic theology, but combined with Scriptural instruction and realistic technical education, see also *Dell's Education Programme* in *Sippell, 63–71*, whose similarity with that of the Quakers and Pietists Sippell also emphasizes. He desires a strict discipline of youth, general elementary education, as many high schools as possible, but no scholastic, theological, philosophical, and privileged universities: "Especially the mathematical sciences must be highly honoured at the universities such as arithmetic, geometry, geography, and the like which do not have evil results, and are also very useful for human society and the various needs of this present life."

[511a] (p. 812.) The illustrations of this point are scattered through the whole of this book; of special importance also is the study by *Tocqueville* and *Kuyper*. There is also a certain amount of material in *Bryce, II, 617–854*; characteristically he is fond of comparing American piety with that of Scotland and the English Nonconformists. On the State in *II, p. 701* he says: "The State is not to them as to Germans or Frenchmen and even to some English thinkers an ideal moral power, charged with the duty of forming the characters and guiding the lives of its subjects. It is more like a commercial company, or perhaps a huge municipality, created for the management of certain business in which all who reside within its bounds are interested. That an organization of this kind should trouble itself, otherwise than as a matter of police, with the opinions or conduct of its members, would be as unnatural as for a railway company to enquire how many of the shareholders were total abstainers."—Cf. also *Veit: Englische und deutsche Frömmigkeit, Ch. W., 1906*.

[512] (p. 815.) I am here giving again an outline of *Weber's* ideas on the capitalist relations of Calvin and the sects, although I have already indicated it above. Here alone have we reached the point at which it can be fully introduced, because in this respect the matter of importance is not so much Calvinism

as Puritan, Pietistic, ascetic Calvinism, and its agreement with the sects. *Rachfahl* has not noticed this, although *Weber* has emphasized it clearly enough, and his study includes a large number of sects.—One example of the question, purely from the latter point of view, is the description of Quakerism in *Weingarten, 397–405*. The characteristic expression of *Rentmeister Gottes* (The Lord's Stewards) is used in *Heppe, 188,* and also in *Lodensteyn's Meditation on "Die Darbringung der zeitlichen Güter eines Christen an ihren Eigentümer"*. In the form of a conversation with God, in this Meditation he makes the Christian hand over quite formally all his possessions to God, whose steward he desires to be.—For further study of this subject, see *Weber* and also the anticipatory statements above (*pp. 709–723*). I believe, however, that through my presentation of the sects, and especially in the clear distinction between mysticism and the sect-type, I have in some particulars made *Weber's* idea clearer, and also that through the manifestation of the sectarian elements in primitive Calvinism I have made the fusion of Calvinism with the sect-type more intelligible.—In my opinion *Sombart's* brilliant book, *Die Juden und das Wirtschaftsleben,* does not weaken the force of Weber's argument at all. Above all, it justifies the whole formulation of the problem as the search for the origin of the "capitalist spirit", which supports the "capitalist system", which is the absolutely necessary presupposition for its modern mass-form, and is anything but easy to understand. Further, it shows one of the component parts of the modern capitalistic spirit, which is always recognized and emphasized by *Weber,* but which in that connection was not to be further analysed. Above all, however, through *Sombart's* researches that tendency of the capitalistic spirit, with which Weber was most concerned, is not touched upon—a tendency which is still more important for the understanding of modern civilization, the tendency, that is, which is directed towards bourgeois mass capitalism, with its modern idea of professions and specialists. The bourgeois spirit of modern civilization had to be explained in relation to the treatment of Capitalism, which had always been working from the time of antiquity, and was not specifically bourgeois and in relation to the technical, political, and colonial stimuli. Further, see above, *p. 720*. For the rest, I repeat, that in all this I have no intention of making a contribution to the history of Capitalism; this I must leave to the experts in this very difficult sphere. All that I have to do here is to interpret the social teaching of Protestantism, alongside of which everything which belongs otherwise to the history of Capitalism can here remain untouched.

[515] (p. 818.) On this point cf. the various statements in *Max Weber,* whose interests are concerned precisely with this problem. He has formulated thus the programme of research (*p. 109*): "The task is . . ., to show the significance of ascetic rationalism (that is, of Ascetic Protestantism with its utilitarian character which systematizes labour), for the content of the social-economic ethic, that is, for the kind of organization showing the development and function of social groups through their varying forms from the conventicle up to the State. Also, its connection with Humanistic Rationalism and its life-ideals and cultural influences, with the further development of philosophical scientific empiricism, with the technical development and the spiritual values of civilization, must be analysed. Then, finally, its historical growth must be followed through the different stages—from the early mediaeval beginnings of an asceticism within the world to its disintegration in pure utilitarianism, and through the particular spheres in which ascetic religiosity has been widespread. Only when this has been done will the significance for civilization of Ascetic Protestantism, in relation to other plastic elements of modern civilization,

emerge." The programme is very difficult to carry out as long as the history of Humanism, of humanistic culture, and of the classes which it affected, as well as the history of modern philosophy in its social aspects, has not been made perfectly clear. Both in the works of specialists, as well as in those of Church historians until the present time, this subject has never been fully cleared up. The history of technical developments, which in no way coincides with that of the natural sciences, would also need to be clearly presented. Weber's programme is thus, in my opinion, not yet possible to realize, but the idea is very stimulating, like other suggestions of *Plenge: a.a.O.* Such a programme of the history of civilization is particularly instructive as contrasted with Lamprecht, who, with quite other methods, is aiming at a similar scientific goal of knowledge. Lamprecht's methods are based upon "psychological" laws, which enable him from the outset to prescribe the order of facts in definite series, whereas my own method is essentially directed towards the analysis of the concrete particular situation with reference to its content and its special causal relations, which are only connected with this concrete situation. To this extent also in this work I would like to show the contrast between my method and that of Lamprecht, who tries to reach an extremely valuable goal of knowledge by impossible methods.—I am in entire agreement with the methodical reflections about the connection between the history of Christianity, and the history of civilization which *Harnack* has developed in his lecture *Ueber das Verhältnis der Kirchengeschichte zur Universalgeschichte, Aus Wissenschaft und Leben, II, 41–62.* Only I believe that in this work I have shown that the religious development reveals a firmer and more independent attitude, especially in relation to political constitutional developments, than Harnack thinks.

CONCLUSION

Developments in Christian Social Doctrine since the Eighteenth Century

Our inquiry is over. It was only possible to treat it exhaustively as far as the eighteenth century. The developments which have taken place from that period down to the present day could merely be suggested. With the nineteenth century Church History entered upon a new phase of existence. As a result of the dissolution of the unity of civilization controlled by a State Church, combined with the development of the independence of modern thought, it has since then no longer possessed a fixed and objective ideal of unity. The result has been that the social philosophy of the Christian community has also suffered an undeniable disintegration, through its dependence upon continually changing conditions. These groups are living in a new world, the world of modern bourgeois capitalist society and of bureaucratic militaristic states. The relation between Church and State has been weakened, and in some cases entirely severed. Social theory has developed out of a naïve preoccupation with antiquity, the Bible, and theology into an independent science, which examines entirely afresh the relation between the land and the population, the connection between the economic substructure and the spiritual superstructure, and the sociological laws and conditions which govern the growth of fellowship; this social theory has far outdistanced the social philosophy of the Church.

Above all, the modern bourgeoisie, the Law of Nature, the emancipation of the fourth estate, and, finally, scientific rationalism have created a new sociological fundamental theory of rationalistic individualism, which is connected, it is true, with the older ideas of Christian individualism, but which in its optimistic and equalitarian spirit is sharply opposed to it. The repercussions caused by this atomistic and essentially individualistic democratic spirit (which is plain even within Communism and Socialism) were only partly determined by the social philosophy of the Church; they are due also to the biological spirit of natural science or to the organic spirit of Platonism; both are in sharp opposition to the leading ideas of Christian social philosophy. Further, the actual practical restrictions of modern individualism, the neutralization of the competitive struggle, which had been unleashed for two hundred years by bourgeois individualism, and allowed to spread throughout the world, is likely to become an effect of purely economic and political conditions of power, in which the division of the product spheres and the influence of the producers bring assured quotas; and, when these spheres are fixed, both the mobility of the population and the production of offspring will be compressed within fixed limits. Radical individualism will probably soon be an interlude between an old and a new civilization of constraint. This individualism may be compared with the process of taking the materials of a house which has been pulled down, sorting them out into the actual individual stones, out of which a new house will be built. What the new house will look like, and what possibilities it will provide for the development of Christian ethics and of Christian social philosophy, no one can at present tell. Christian social philosophy will bring to the task both its common sense and its metaphysical individualism; but it will have to share the labour with other builders, and like them it will be restricted by the peculiarities of the ground and of the material.

Under these circumstances it is impossible to give a description of the present situation, and to deduce from it principles for the future. Even if the undertaking were restricted to a mere description of the different Christian endeavours, schemes, and associations of the present day, the whole situation is so complicated that the subject would have to be treated in a separate work. In order to conclude this survey, therefore, it is not necessary to deal further with the present situation; all that is required is to collect and formulate the results of this inquiry in some brief general statements.

Our inquiry began with the social and ethical tasks and possibilities of Christianity at the present day. It then reverted to the point at which the form in which the social development of the religious idea was expressed, severed its connection with the secular social formations. It discovered that these connections take very different forms, according to the special conception of the Christian idea, and of the organization which corresponds to this conception. Our inquiry then traced the course of development of the different church and group formations, and of the social ethic which corresponded in each case to this development. It was finally confronted with the fact that all these social developments were determined by the general conditions of civilization, and in every instance the question had to be asked: At any given time, what was the relationship between the two forms of influence, and how did they mutually react upon one another? Thus we find that the results of this inquiry are connected with the whole conception of the nature and history of Christianity in general. In the following paragraphs these results are briefly summarized.

RESULTS OF THIS SURVEY

Three Types of Christian Thought

(1) It has become clear how little the Gospel and the Primitive Church shaped the religious community itself from a uniform point of view. The Gospel of Jesus was a free personal piety, with a strong impulse towards profound intimacy and spiritual fellowship and communion, but without any tendency towards the organization of a cult, or towards the creation of a religious community. Only when faith in Jesus, the Risen and Exalted Lord, became the central point of worship in a new religious community did the necessity for organization arise. From the very beginning there appeared the three main types of the sociological development of Christian thought: the Church, the sect, and mysticism.

The Church is an institution which has been endowed with grace and salvation as the result of the work of Redemption; it is able to receive the masses, and to adjust itself to the world, because, to a certain extent, it can afford to ignore the need for subjective holiness for the sake of the objective treasures of grace and of redemption.

The sect is a voluntary society, composed of strict and definite Christian believers bound to each other by the fact that all have experienced "the new birth". These "believers" live apart from the world, are limited to small groups, emphasize the law instead of grace, and in varying degrees within their own circle set up the Christian order, based on love; all this is done in preparation for and expectation of the coming Kingdom of God.

Mysticism means that the world of ideas which had hardened into formal worship and doctrine is transformed into a purely personal and inward experience; this leads to the formation of groups on a purely personal basis, with no permanent form, which also tend to weaken the significance of forms of worship, doctrine, and the historical element.

From the beginning these three forms were foreshadowed, and all down the centuries to the present day, wherever religion is dominant, they still appear alongside of one another, while among themselves they are strangely and variously interwoven and interconnected. The churches alone have the power to stir the masses in any real and lasting way. When mass movements take place the sects draw closer to the churches. Mysticism has an affinity with the autonomy of science, and it forms a refuge for the religious life of the cultured classes; in sections of the population which are untouched by science it leads to extravagant and emotional forms of piety, but in spite of that it forms a welcome complement to the Church and the Sects.

Christian Thought dependent on Sociological Factors

(2) The results of this survey throw light upon the dependence of the whole Christian world of thought and dogma on the fundamental sociological conditions, on the idea of fellowship which was dominant at any given time. The only peculiarly primitive Christian dogma, the dogma of the Divinity of Christ, first arose out of the worship of Christ, and this again developed out of the fact that the new spiritual community felt the necessity for meeting together. The worship of Christ constitutes the centre of the Christian organization, and it creates Christian dogma. Since the God whom the Christians worship is not to be regarded as another god of the Mysteries in the polytheistic sense, but represents the redeeming revelation of the monotheistic God of the Prophets, the dogma of Christ develops into the doctrine of the Trinity. All the ideas which have been borrowed from philosophy and mythology are only used as a means of expressing ideas which have grown up out of the inner necessity of this Christian community for worship. Within the spheres of the Church, the Sects and Mysticism, however, this doctrine of Christ is interpreted very differently.

The Christ of the Church is the Redeemer, who in His work of salvation has achieved Redemption, once for all; working marvellously through the ministry, the Word, and the sacraments in the Church, He imparts to individuals the benefits of His Saving Work.

The Christ of the sect is the Lord, the example and lawgiver of Divine authority and dignity, who allows His elect to pass through contempt and misery on their earthly pilgrimage, but who will complete the real work of Redemption at His Return, when He will establish the Kingdom of God.

The Christ of mysticism is an inward spiritual principle, felt in every stirring of religious feeling, present in every influence of the Divine "Seed" and the Divine "Spark"; this mystical

Christ was Divinely incarnate in the Christ of History, but He can only be recognized and affirmed in inward spiritual experience; this principle therefore agrees in general with the "hidden ground" of the Divine life in man.

The same course of development can be traced in other doctrines. As the Christ-dogma absorbed into itself Jesus's original message of the Kingdom of God, so also the various transformations of the Christ-dogma determined the fate of this second fundamental Christian doctrine. The Church is the Kingdom of Christ, and is therefore identical with the Kingdom of God in the world, or at any rate it is the method by which it is continually produced afresh. In the sect Jesus is still the Herald of the Kingdom of God which He ushers in Himself; the sect is inclined to Chiliasm. In mysticism the dominion of Christ means the dominion of the Divine Spirit, from this point of view therefore the Kingdom of God is only within us.

The doctrine of Redemption undergoes an analogous process of development. From the viewpoint of the Church the work of Redemption was finished by the Atoning Death of Christ; this "finished work" endows the Church with the power to transmit remission of sins and sanctification. The sect believes that real redemption lies in the Advent of Christ and the establishment of the Kingdom; the whole previous process of history was a mere preparation for this consummation. In mysticism redemption is conceived as a process which is continually being repeated; it culminates in the union of the soul with God; in this experience Christ only serves as a quickening impulse or a symbol. In actual life, of course, these different types mingle and combine with each other, just as the different types of the Christian fellowship also mingle and combine. But this abstract analysis makes the history of dogma much clearer and simpler. This system of doctrine is neither a development of the Christian idea of God along the lines of Immanence, nor an amalgamation of the mythology of the ancient "mysteries" with speculative philosophy, nor an accumulation of ecclesiastical doctrinal definitions, nor an immediate expression of the Christian attitude towards life at any particular time. The religious doctrine was the expression of the religious vitality and development of thought which was focused first of all in the cultus, and then radiated forth from it again, so far as for this purpose ideas were necessary at all. Philosophical and purely dogmatic considerations were quite secondary. No one had ever felt the need for a dialectical interpretation of the instinctive conception of the idea of God itself which lay behind the cultus, and behind the idea of fellowship, which prevailed at any particular time. Individual ideas were simply linked together and classified. The real religious fundamental idea itself lay in the unconscious, and it was also embedded in the instinctive idea of fellowship and cultus which belonged to that conception. It was, of course, only natural that individual thinkers should ponder deeply upon these questions, and that, from the viewpoint both of theology and of the philosophy of religion, that they should attempt to search into the depths of her Christian knowledge of God; but so long as they remained attached to any kind of fellowship, even they found that the sociological character of the ideal of fellowship, which was vaguely defined in their minds, affected and limited their ideas on dogma.

On the other hand, an essentially dogmatic criticism also involves a shifting of emphasis in the fundamental sociological sense. This, however, throws a great deal of light upon the nature and the destiny of theology, on the scientific elaboration of Christian thought.

The theology of Catholicism—which represents the essentially ritual and sacramental development of Christian thought—is the formulated fixation and insertion of the *depositum fidei* of the institution of Redemption into the framework of the idealistic development of the metaphysic of late antiquity.

The theology of Protestantism—with its principle of the Church which spiritualizes public worship and the Sacrament—made the purified doctrine into an intellectual system, which, however, retains its connection with the sermon in public worship, and with the authoritative basis of grace and doctrine; in consequence it oscillates between a system of ideas which are valid in themselves, and a group of dogmas based on history and supported by miracles, an uncertainty which has only been increased by the influence of modern science.

The sect, which belongs essentially to the lower classes, and which therefore does not need to come to terms with thought in general, goes back to the pre-Church and pre-scientific standpoint, and has no theology at all; it possesses only a strict ethic, a living Mythos, and a passionate hope for the future.

"Spiritual Religion" alone conceives Christian piety as a living creative movement of the present day, and as a factor in the universal movement of religious consciousness in general. Hence it alone has produced a truly scientific theology, a real religious philosophy, based upon universals, and with a hope of real development before it. Hence of all Christian systems of thought it alone has been taken over and developed by the great thinkers of modern Idealism. Since, however, it arose out of the failure of the real ecclesiastical spirit, it finds it difficult to establish satisfactory relations with the churches, and with the conditions of a stable and permanent organization. This accounts for the difficult problem of the relation between Christianity and the modern cultured classes of the present day.

Conception of Truth, and the Idea of Toleration

(3) The diversity of ideas which the Christian conception of truth contains is evident in these three different types of religion, and this explains the complicated and inconsistent relation of Christianity to the authority of the State and to the idea of toleration.

The aim of the Church is to be the Church of the people and of the masses; it therefore transfers all divine and sacred character from individuals to the objective organ of redemption, with its divine endowment of grace and truth. The Church possesses a redeeming energy which is directly miraculous, and in contrast to all other kinds of human power. Thus it possesses an absolute directly divine truth and doctrinal authority over against all human subjectivity. In its very nature such truths must be uniform and universally authoritative. Thus in the Church itself this unchangeable truth is justified, and indeed bound to maintain its supremacy over pastors and teachers, and also over the laity. Every idealistic attempt to ascribe this development of the truth to the inward miraculous power of the Church itself, without compulsion, breaks down in the practical impossibility of carrying it through, and simply results in a return to compulsion. This attitude of compulsion must, however, finally express itself externally, because errors and customs which dishonour God ought not to be tolerated, and because it is not right that people who have been born into the membership of the Church should be allowed to fall a prey to temptation. Finally, the Church must see to it that the whole nation shall hear the message of salvation, and that everyone shall have at least contact with divine salvation. Mercy requires it, and the absolute divine origin of the truth of salvation justifies this procedure. Here it is permissible to force people for their own good. This, however, demands the co-operation of the material power of the State, without which neither the inner uniformity of the Church, nor the building up of popular and territorial churches, would ever have come into existence. In all this the Church is only fulfilling its duty towards Divine Truth. This line of argument explains the rise of the complicated question of the relation between Church and State.

The point of view of the sects, however, is quite different. They do not wish to be popular churches, but Christian denominations composed of "saints". The sects are small groups which exist alongside of the State and Society. They also maintain that they possess the absolute truth of the Gospel, but they claim that this truth is far beyond the spiritual grasp of the masses and of the State, and therefore they desire to be free from the State. Further, since it is precisely this absolute Gospel which forbids them to use force, authority, or law, they also must renounce forcing their opinions upon anyone, either within or without their community. Hence they demand external toleration, the religious neutrality of the State. Within their own borders, however, they practise a spiritual discipline of doctrine and of morals. They possess the tolerance of an idealism which believes in its own cause, and they forbid their followers to deduce from the absolute character of Truth the right to use violence in order to enforce it upon others. They do not expect to see the Truth permeating the masses before the Last Day. Where various sectarian groups exist alongside of each other, they permit the exercise of purely spiritual controversy and merely ethical rivalry without losing faith in the absolute character of the truth they possess. This truth is not meant for the masses, or for humanity in general; and it will only attain its final consummation at the Last Day. Their conception of toleration and freedom of conscience is of a toleration extended to groups like their own by the churches and the ruling powers; within their own borders, however, they had very little idea of toleration, since here Scriptural law prevails. Since, however, in order to uphold this unity they renounce State aid, and at the most can exercise the method of social boycott, endless divisions arise among them. It is a fact that real conformity can only be secured with the aid of the State and the exercise of compulsion.

Finally, the point of view of spiritual idealism and mysticism differs entirely from that of the churches or the sects. From its standpoint the truth of salvation is inward and relative, a personal possession which is unutterable, and lies unspoken beneath all literal forms. The merely relative significance of the Biblical, dogmatic, or ritual form in which Truth is expressed makes mysticism independent of all historic forms, and the inner Unity of the Spirit quite naturally unites all souls in the common truth which is purely spiritual, and impossible to formulate. From this point of view, and from it alone, are toleration and freedom of conscience also possible within the religious community, since the organization becomes merely a method of ecclesiastical administration, while the religious life itself can move freely under various forms of expression which are relatively justified. This, however, led to difficulties, for from this point of view it was very difficult to decide by what authority it was possible to determine the standard of what constituted Christianity in general. The usual answer, "the Spirit recognizes the Spirit", was found to be useless in practice. Hence this standpoint easily led to the giving up of all and every kind of organized fellowship, or to a withdrawal into private groups of a purely personal character composed of kindred souls. As well as conformity mysticism threatens to sacrifice fellowship altogether, and it easily falls into a comparative individualism. The problem of Christian toleration and liberty of conscience in relation to the conditions of the formation of religious fellowship belongs to this group of ideas. There is no escape from it. There are only varying practical suggestions of approximate utility which emerge out of this tragic interplay of forces.

History of the Christian Ethos

(4) Another result of this inquiry is the light which it throws upon the history of the Christian Ethos, a subject which, as is well known, presents extraordinary difficulties. The Ethos of the Gospel is a combination of infinite sublimity and childlike intimacy. On the one hand, it demands the sanctification of the self for God by the practice of detachment from everything which disturbs inward communion with God, and by the exercise of everything which inwardly binds the soul with God's Will. On the other hand, it demands that brotherly love, which overcomes in God all the tension and harshness of the struggle for existence, of law, and of the merely external order, while it unites souls in a deep spirit of mutual understanding, as well as in the most self-sacrificing love, which, even in its simplest expressions, gives a true hint of the nature of God Himself. This is an ideal which requires a new world if it is to be fully realized; it was this new world-order that Jesus proclaimed in His Message of the Kingdom of God. But it is an ideal which cannot be realized within this world apart from compromise. Therefore the history of the Christian Ethos becomes the story of a constantly renewed search for this compromise, and of fresh opposition to this spirit of com-

promise. The Church in particular, however, as a popular institution, is forced to compromise; this she effects by transferring to the institution the sanctity and the grace of forgiveness proper to it as an institution; the Church completed this compromise by making a covenant with the Stoic idea of the relative Law of Nature, which has prevailed since the Fall, which permits for the term of the earthly life the existence of law, might, tyranny, war, private property, and the desire to acquire possessions; it regards these things as the results of sin as well as means for the healing of sin.

When this compromise had been effected, however, within the Church, the average morality of the world and the strict morality of holiness then separated and went their different ways. The ethic of holiness became fused with the dualistic asceticism of late antiquity, and organized the monastic system, whence it once more influenced the world by permeating secular life with its higher ideals. Thus there arose a dualistic ethic which the classical Catholic theory worked into an ingenious system of evolution: the ascent from Nature to Grace.

Ecclesiastical Protestantism destroyed this dualism, and wove both its elements into the ethic of the "calling": Lutheranism carried this out with a careless acceptance of existing conditions, which are due to the presence of sin in the world, Calvinism and Ascetic Protestantism in an attempt to restore in a rational manner the holy community within the life of the world.

Alongside of these ecclesiastical compromises, however, there stood from the beginning the sect, which desired to realize the ideal of the Sermon on the Mount in all its purity; this view forced it into sharp opposition to the world. In the form of the passive and persecuted sect it realized the ideal with the fewest concessions in small and quiet groups, and comforted itself with the thought of the coming Kingdom of God, until, through its connection with Ascetic Protestantism, it also found a way of becoming incorporated with the life of this present world. In the form of the aggressive sect, when the End of the World seemed imminent, it felt justified in using force, and tried to establish the Christian order of life by violent methods; naturally, the experiment was never permanently successful; also such outbreaks always damaged the real Christianity of the sect, for then the Apocalypse and the Old Testament took the place of the Gospel.

Finally, untroubled by any of these questions of compromise, mysticism and "spiritual religion" went its own way, proclaiming the freedom of the Spirit and liberty of conscience, antinomian in the good, and also incidentally in the bad, sense; even where it was severely ascetic it maintained its spirit of freedom. This is the piety which acts or refrains from action as it is "moved by the Spirit", to use the language of the Quakers; that is, its action is controlled by its sense of inward communion with the living and holy God, and it expresses itself in a purely inward personal communion of individuals. This point of view certainly prevents its influencing the masses, or effecting any kind of organization of life on a large scale. But from the very outset this type of Christianity does not expect to influence the life of the world on a large scale; or if it does cherish such hopes it bases them purely on confidence in the interior "power of the Spirit". In the general way, it leaves to chance the question of the extension of its spirit into the general life of the world, and of a consequent inner transformation. In all these ethical movements, however, the impelling power is that of Christian hostility to the world. To-day this fundamental Christian tendency has been sensibly weakened by the tendencies of modern life: with its Utilitarianism and its optimism, with its ideas of Immanence, its Naturalism, and its aesthetic glorification of Nature, often to the extent of being unable to interpret its own meaning. But it breaks forth anew from the fundamental ideas of religion and out of the self-destruction of every kind of purely secular optimism. In the midst of all the pleasures of civilization and of all mere sceptical pessimism, once again it summons the Christian ethic to face its task.

To-day, therefore, the main problem of the Christian Ethos is still the problem of supernaturalism, and of its unavoidable result, asceticism, in the metaphysical-dualistic or in the disciplinary rigorist sense, an asceticism which is never merely a simple denial of the world and of self. On the other hand, its second main problem is how to supplement this religious onesidedness with an ethic of civilization which can be combined with it. The Church effected this supplement by drawing on the philosophy of late antiquity, and incorporating into its own ethic the idea of the moral Law of Nature. When the sect gave up this idea of a supplement of this kind altogether, it became uncultured and insignificant, while mysticism became complete and solitary resignation. Whenever both these movements rose to importance, they likewise introduced, each in its own way, a supplement. To-day, however, in an entirely new state of civilization these earlier supplementary movements have become impossible. A new supplementary process, therefore, is necessary. In a permanent world the Christian Ethos cannot live and be entirely self-sufficing. The question is simply this: How can this supplement be shaped to-day? The answer to this question constitutes an imperative demand for a new Christian ethic.

Significance of the Marxist Method for the Study of Christian History

(5) The last important point which is illuminated by our historical survey is that of the right to apply a method of social history to Christianity, and the limits within which this may be exercised. The "Marxist" method, especially those elements within it which seem clearly justified, is gradually transforming all our historical conceptions, and naturally it also transforms all our ideas about the present and the future. Scholars of the "class-war" school have undertaken to represent the whole of Christianity as an ideological reflection of economic development, and in so doing they have not only impressed the comrades within their own Party. In a finer and more instructive way quite recently Maurenbrecher applied this conception to the origin of Christianity. In opposition to the exclusive and doctrinaire application of this method, however, the whole of this survey has shown that all that is specifically religious, and, above all, the great central points of religious development, are an independent expression of the religious life. Jesus, Paul, Origen, Augustine, Thomas Aquinas, Francis of Assisi, Bonaventura, Luther, Calvin: as we study their thought and their feeling we realize that it is impossible to regard them as the product of class struggles and of economic factors.

On the other hand, however, it is clear that in the causal connection out of which their peculiar form of religious thought gains concrete stimulus, force, movement, and aim, social and even, finally, economic influences are at work, though this is not always apparent, and their significance varies considerably. As in all other spheres of life, so also in that of the history of religion, the conception of the causal connection is considerably widened and altered by giving fresh attention to this co-operating element. As previously we have been in the habit of placing scientific-historical, philosophical, race-theory biological causalities in the context out of which and in which the concrete movements of religious history arise, so also this newly discovered causality must be accepted in its full significance. In theory this means nothing new, once we have become accustomed to the idea of seeing religious revelations developing out of a causal connection;

we will not deal further with their supposed "necessity", or with "supposed laws of history". Causality knows no hierarchy; no degree of greater or lesser importance, and so it is no depreciation of previous theories (as many people suppose) if this newly discovered causality is granted just as much right to exist as those which were previously in a position of honour. In practice, however, this does mean a considerable shifting of emphasis. It then becomes clear that Christianity and the idealistic ethical and religious aspirations and endeavours of late antiquity (which were so closely akin to Christianity) were certainly connected with the final result of the social history of the Ancient World, and therefore they also met and united to form the new world; we have seen how the Middle Ages maintained its existence with the support of the Church and of the Christian Ethos within a relatively simple and undeveloped social setting, and that only thus did a Christian civilization become possible; we have seen that the individualism of the Reformation presupposed the collapse of mediaeval society, and that the triumphant realization of the Reformation can only be explained from the standpoint of political and social conditions; we have seen that the difference between the two great divisions of Protestantism is very largely caused and conditioned by its political and social setting; we have seen how modern Protestantism is bound up with modern bourgeois society and with their ideals of civilization, and, finally, we have seen that Capitalism, the modern Nationalist and Imperialist State, and the vast increase in the population of the world, constitute a crisis for the previous Christian ethic. The social position and relations of the sects reveal the hidden reasons for sudden changes of religious thought, which could not have been explained from their merely intellectual dialectic.

All this means that the history of religion is being drawn far more deeply into the stream of events, and into the varying conditions within the fundamental elements in life. Thus it becomes still less possible to find an unchangeable and absolute point in the Christian ethic, since this also only means the mastery of an existing situation, which is determined pre-eminently by social conditions and the establishment of an ideal which corresponds to this situation. The history of religion, however, has long been moving towards such a conception, ever since it learned to place the religious life within the general current of historical evolution. Thus it becomes clearer than ever that each factor is relatively conditioned as a synthesis which cannot be repeated, and as a spiritual-ethical mastery of this particular situation, which often sees truth much more clearly in the instinctive side of life than in the theory which overlooks and condones so much. Thus, finally, it becomes impossible to regard whole periods and groups solely as preparatory phases for an Absolute which can never be found in history. We then perceive the force of that pregnant phrase of Ranke (to which reference has often been made) that each epoch—not in its crude actuality, but with the aims and ideals which it has instinctively formed—exists directly for God. This truth also applies to the mastery of the tasks which arise out of the natural basis of life, from the economic social situation, out of the political conditions of power, by thought, in which thought can never be independent of the material which it has mastered, and by which it is frequently set in motion. On the other hand, however, all attempts to make Christianity into a changeful reflection of economic and social history are either a foolish fashion, or under cover of the most recent science they conceal a hidden attack on the religious value of Christianity.

Nature of the Christian Ethos

(6) All these results are of an historical nature. The question, however, naturally arises: Does an extended inquiry of this kind about the Christian world of life and thought really yield nothing more than historical light on the past and on its influence upon the present? Does it not also teach something lasting and eternal about the content of the Christian social Ethos, which might serve as a guiding star for the present and for the future, something which would aid us not merely to understand but also to transform the situation? It certainly is in the position of being able to teach us something of this kind. But perceptions of eternal ethical values are not scientific perceptions, and cannot be proved along scientific lines. These perceptions have been selected from life in history, which the living conviction and the active will fully apprehend in the certainty that here we perceive absolute Reason in the revelation which is addressed to us and formed in the present connection. Only in this sense is the attempt now made to emphasize the permanent ethical values which are contained within the varied history of the Christian social doctrines.

Firstly: The Christian Ethos alone possesses, in virtue of its personalistic Theism, a conviction of personality and individuality, based on metaphysics, which no Naturalism and no Pessimism can disturb. That personality which, rising above the natural order of life, is only achieved through a union of will and the depths of being with God, alone transcends the finite, and alone can defy it. Without this support, however, every kind of individualism evaporates into thin air.

Secondly: The Christian Ethos alone, through its conception of a Divine Love which embraces all souls and unites them all, possesses a Socialism which cannot be shaken. It is only within the medium of the Divine that the separation and reserve, the strife and exclusiveness which belong to man as a natural product, and which shape his natural existence, disappear. Only here do the associations formed by compulsion, sympathy and need of help, sex instinct and attraction, work and organization attain a connection which transcends them all, a connection which is indestructible because it is metaphysical.

Thirdly: Only the Christian Ethos solves the problem of equality and inequality, since it neither glorifies force and accident in the sense of a Nietzschian cult of breed, nor outrages the patent facts of life by a doctrinaire equalitarianism. It recognizes differences in social position, power, and capacity, as a condition which has been established by the inscrutable Will of God; and then transforms this condition by the inner upbuilding of the personality, and the development of the mutual sense of obligation, into an ethical cosmos. The ethical values of voluntary incorporation and subordination on the one hand, and of care and responsibility for others on the other hand, place each human being in circumstances where natural differences can and should be transmuted into the ethical values of mutual recognition, confidence, and care for others.

Fourthly: Through its emphasis upon the Christian value of personality, and on love, the Christian Ethos creates something which no social order—however just and rational—can dispense with entirely, because everywhere there will always remain suffering, distress, and sickness for which we cannot account—in a word, it produces charity. Charity, or active helpfulness, is the fruit of the Christian Spirit, which alone keeps it alive. Whatever pettiness and desire to convert may be bound up with it must simply be regarded as human limitations within something which is great and noble.

In conclusion: The Christian Ethos gives to all social life and aspiration a goal which lies far beyond all the relativities of this earthly life, compared with which, indeed, everything else represents merely approximate values. The idea of the future Kingdom of God, which is nothing less than faith in the final realization of the Absolute (in whatever way we may conceive this realization), does not, as short-sighted opponents imagine, render this world and life in this world meaningless and empty; on the contrary, it stimulates human energies, making the soul strong through its various stages of experience in the certainty of an ultimate, absolute meaning and aim for human labour. Thus it raises the soul above the world without denying the world. This idea, which is the deepest meaning of all Christian asceticism, is the only means by which strength and heroism may be maintained in a general spiritual situation, in which the emotional life is infinitely deepened and refined, and in which the natural motives for heroism are either altogether lost, or else the attempt is made to try to reawaken them on the side of brutal instinct. This idea creates a perennial source of strength for strenuous activity, and a certainty of aim, both of which make for simple health and soundness of mind. All social Utopias, then, become superfluous; over and over again experience teaches that the ideal cannot be fully realized; but this does not mean that the seeker for Truth and justice need lose heart and fall back into scepticism, a temptation to which serious and truth-loving souls are prone, and the effects of which are very manifest among the finer spirits of the present day. The life beyond this world is, in very deed, the inspiration of the life that now is.

What is the best Form of Organization for Christian Religious Life?

(7) These social and ethical ideas and energies spring out of the Christian religion. To enable them to do this it is necessary to maintain the vitality and to extend the scope of these religious energies; again, in order to achieve both these ends, an organization is needed which will lead them forward and continually produce them afresh.

This leads us to the question: What does our present inquiry teach us about this problem, which is a question of vital importance, about the formation of the religious community itself and its incorporation into the other great movements? Can we not learn something from a large work of this kind to help us to overcome our miserable ecclesiastical situation, which is daily becoming worse?

Here also the yield is a rich one, although it is more a matter of free insight into what is expedient than a scientific proof. The first thing we learn is, that the religious life—on the plane of spiritual religion—needs an independent organization, in order to distinguish it from other organizations of a natural kind. It strives after this from the moment it conceives of an independent existence, and this always remains one of its most important problems. Public worship forms the centre of such an organization; the derivation of comprehensive energies from it, or the organic attachment of them to it, is the great problem. Unless it is organized into a community with a settled form of worship, Christianity cannot be either expansive or creative. Every kind of reaction to a mere "freedom of the Spirit" in the hope that it will grow and thrive without organization, is a Utopian ideal which is out of touch with the actual conditions of life, and its only effect is to weaken the whole.

Secondly, so far as the form of this organization is concerned, it has become evident that the Church-type is obviously superior to the sect-type and to mysticism. The Church-type preserves inviolate the religious elements of grace and redemption; it makes it possible to differentiate between Divine grace and human effort; it is able to include the most varied degrees of Christian attainment and maturity, and therefore it alone is capable of fostering a popular religion which inevitably involves a great variety in its membership. In this respect the Church-type is superior to the sect-type and also to mysticism. This is why the main current of historical Christianity becomes the "History of the Church", and this is why the first result of the missionary work of the Early Church was "the universal Christian Church". At the same time, however, it cannot be denied that this does mean a modification of Christian thought in order to bring it down to the average level, to the level of practical possibility; and it is a principle of far-reaching adjustment and compromise.

In the third place: the Church-type itself, just because of this element of tension between pure Christianity and adjustment to the world which exists within it, has had a very changeful history, and is to-day becoming entirely transformed. Roman Catholicism is the pure and logical form of the Church-type; to an ever-increasing degree it has sacrificed the inwardness, individuality, and plasticity of religion to the fixed determination to make religion objective in doctrine, Sacrament, hierarchy, the Papacy and Papal Infallibility; the only outlet it gives to the sect-type and to mysticism is through the Religious Orders and the devotions of the Church. Since the crisis in the fifteenth century, when men's confidence in its right to dominate was shaken, it has therefore set itself to become more and more objective and centralized. Protestantism, on the other hand, has developed in the opposite direction, seeking to make the idea of the Church more subjective and inward, by placing the objective organizing element in the Holy Scriptures and in the spiritual power which dwells within them, and also in the ministry which expounds the Word. Luther based his hopes on the all-converting power of the Spirit and of the Word, a hope which was speedily disappointed, while Calvin sought the support of a stable ecclesiastical constitution with authority to control the faithful.

All the ecclesiastical institutions soon found that they were unable to maintain and carry on their existence by moral force alone, and they were obliged to appeal to the civil power for aid. Without its help no ecclesiastical system can be permanent, uniform, and undivided. This situation cannot be conceived without compulsion, and compulsory religion cannot be conceived without the help of the State. In periods when a naïve type of faith is widespread, this kind of compulsion is not harmful, nor does it militate against religion. If one is quite sure of the truth, and if the general instincts of the nations are united on this point, then the preservation from folly, error, and the danger of being led astray is only sensible and healthy; it is the assumption upon which the spiritual unity of Society in general is maintained, which it is not right to sacrifice to the doctrinaire and super-idealistic ideal of free self-legislation on the part of the individual.

In the fourth place: precisely because the Church-type is thus connected with the unbroken unity of an instinctive world-outlook of great masses of people the uniform Church-type is inwardly suitable for such periods alone. We have seen, in the course of this inquiry, that since these assumptions have disappeared the Church-type has been going through a process of decay and even of destruction. The days of the pure Church-type within our present civilization are numbered. Ideas which the modern world accepts as natural and obvious do not agree with the views of the Church. Compulsion is no longer a defence of the whole against individual disturbance; it only means the forcible restraint of currents of real vitality. Either completely or partially the civil power has retired into the background, and soon it will cease to have any influence at all.

In countries where the religious situation contains many different elements, the various ecclesiastical systems constitute a large body of opinion, in which each particular communion claims to possess the sole Truth, thus neutralizing the religious influence of all. The churches are losing their hold on the spiritual life of the nations, and many of their functions are now being exercised by educationists, writers, administrators, and by voluntary religious associations. Under these circumstances the Catholic

Church-type has been forced to exercise an increasingly powerful and external dominion over the consciences of men. The Protestant churches, on the other hand, have not exercised the same influence. This is due to two causes: (1) because they are not sufficiently vigorous to be able to do this; and (2) because their subjective interpretation of the idea of the Church contains strong tendencies which are directly opposed to a development of this kind. Thus they have not been able to withstand the influence of the sect-type and mysticism, both of which are tendencies which have a close affinity with the modern world. The Protestant Church-type, therefore, has persisted with the aid of sectarian ideas and the relativism of idealism and mysticism. Protestantism no longer represents the pure Church-type, although the ecclesiastical spirit of conformity has raised indignant enough protests against this irresistible development, and either secretly or openly casts longing glances at Catholic ideals. Protestantism is developing at present along the following lines: separation between Church and State; suspension of the endeavour to form new churches; the independence of the individual congregation; the transformation of State churches into popular churches in which there is a united system of administration, while the individual congregations are left a free hand to manage their own affairs; by this very fact, however, these churches contain a certain amount of high explosive which is a continual menace to their existence. Even beneath the veil of an apparently stable united confessional Church, the lack of denominational principle on the part of most of the members has produced this situation. More and more the central life of the Church-type is being permeated with the vital energies of the sect and of mysticism; the whole history of Protestantism reveals this very clearly. While Catholicism does all it can to hinder the development of these tendencies, they are both becoming stronger and stronger within the Protestant churches. In the mutual interpenetration of the three chief sociological categories, which must be united with a structure which will reconcile them all, lie its future tasks, tasks of a sociological and organizing kind, which are more pressing than all doctrinal questions. Along this path all efforts to achieve a reconciling unity have failed. An "Ecclesiastical Protestant system of dogma" no longer exists. Thus it is evident that union and cohesion must be sought in some other sphere than in that of dogma. This will only be possible on the assumption that the churches which have been created by compulsion, on a basis of authority and rigid conformity, may become homes within which

Christians of very varying outlook can live and work together in peace.

The ecclesiastical organizations maintain themselves by their own historic weight, and, once they have been created, they can serve other ends than those for which they were originally constructed. The pain and travail which the State Church system has cost in its day may be regarded as a sacrifice which the effort of building it has cost; but it does not need to be continually repeated. The home which was constructed by compulsion and relentless insistence upon rigid conformity to a uniform type of doctrine and organization can thus be inhabited by finer spirits and especially by souls of very varied types; they will then, it is true, have to guard the spirit of mutual toleration within certain wide limits. While a mere system of Free Church organization, or a system based on the separation between Church and State, only ensures liberty of conscience alongside of and outside of the churches while within them it fosters a very real spirit of intolerance, a system of that kind would be able to maintain a national (or popular) Church, and yet preserve at the same time liberty of conscience (so ardently desired) within the Church itself, so far as that is at all possible. The spirit of the Church-type would thus be maintained in its great conviction of an historical substance of life which is common to all, a substance which, in the various smaller religious groups and declarations, would be expressed, partly in one group and partly in another, which would preserve the whole from stagnation. We thus retain the sense of a common faith and the consciousness of a great inheritance as a "Minimum of the Church" as Richard Rothe used to say.

Christianity and the Modern Social Problem

(8) What has become of the question, however, from which we originally started?—the question of the significance of Christianity for the solution of the social problem of the present day? This social problem is vast and complicated. It includes the problem of the capitalist economic period and of the industrial proletariat created by it; and of the growth of militaristic and bureaucratic giant states; of the enormous increase in population, which affects colonial and world policy, of the mechanical technique, which produces enormous masses of material and links up and mobilizes the whole world for purposes of trade, but which also treats men and labour like machines.

Bearing in mind the whole trend of this book, we only need to formulate this question thus in order to recognize as its most important reply that this problem is entirely new, a problem with which Christian-Social work has never been confronted until now.

In face of the vast and serious nature of this problem the radical ideals of social reformers of the Chiliastic sects seem like child's play and childish fantasies; admirable and noble, no doubt, but Utopian even in their modern form of a Christian Socialism which dreams of a radical social transformation of the world. From the very outset mysticism declined to make any attempt to find a solution of the problem; in all this confusion it only discerns how impossible it is for the world to give the peace which passes all understanding.

All the Christian churches—the Lutheran Church least of all, however—are evolving schemes for the alleviation of all this distress which weighs on our hearts and minds like a perpetual menace, and each church does its part eagerly and unselfishly. But in all this the churches are only returning in essentials to the old and great main types of their social philosophy, which they are trying to mobilize afresh for the titanic struggles of the present day. Now, as we have seen, there are only two great main types of social philosophy which have attained comprehensive historical significance and influence. The first is the social philosophy of mediaeval Catholicism which is based on the family, guild, and class, which was able to combine a relative dependence on the struggle for existence, the establishment of all fellowship upon personal relations of authority and reverence, the relatively simple economic forms and needs of the pre-capitalistic period, the remains of old solidarities in conditions which involved being bound to the soil or involved in the fortunes of some ancient family, with the Christian Ethos of the personal value of the individual and of the universal fellowship of love within the ecclesiastical organization of life. The second is the social philosophy of Ascetic Protestantism, which developed out of that kind of Calvinism which was tinged with a Free Church, Pietistic outlook, and also out of those ascetic sects which had almost broken with the churches altogether, which is inwardly related to modern Utilitarianism and Rationalism, with diligence in one's calling and the glorification of work for its own sake, with political democracy and Liberalism, with the freedom of the individual and the all-dominating idea of the social group, which, however, knows how to neutralize the ethically dangerous consequences of modern life by the religious ideas of the responsibility of the individual, and of the duty of love, both of the individual and of the community, through the taboo on luxury, mammon, and love of pleasure, and finally through heroism in serving the cause of Christ all over the world.

Other Christian-Social ideals which developed alongside of these two main types were unable to make any impression on the hard mass of social realities; against this rock they fling themselves in vain to-day.

Both these powerful types of social philosophy, however, in spite of their great and enduring achievements, have now spent their force. So far as Catholicism of the patriarchal guild type is concerned, its failure is due to the fact that it is almost a sheer impossibility to realize its aims at the present day; a further cause of failure is the fact that these ideals cannot be carried out in practice, owing to the weakened religious forces of Catholicism; this also produces other results which are almost intolerable. Ascetic Protestantism, however, which had attempted to establish the rule of Christ over Society by a rational method, controlled by the ruling idea of religion, finds to its dismay that the results of its theory have long ago slipped away from its control, and that they have cast aside as useless all the original restrictions and landmarks, whether religious, intellectual, or metaphysical. On the other hand, by its cool austerity, its restraint and its concrete outlook, its proselytizing zeal, and its inartistic and Puritan characteristics, it is opposed to all the instincts of modern civilization; from the purely religious standpoint also its tendency to legalism and Pharisaism, to feverish activity and a mechanical outlook, is very far from being in complete agreement with the deepest Christian ideas.

Under these circumstances our inquiry leads to the conclusion that all Christian-Social work is in a problematic condition. It is problematic in general because the power of thought to overcome brutal reality is always an obscure and difficult question; it is problematic in particular because the main historic forms of the Christian doctrine of society and of social development are to-day, for various reasons, impotent in face of the tasks by which they are confronted.

If the present social situation is to be controlled by Christian principles, thoughts will be necessary which have not yet been thought, and which will correspond to this new situation as the older forms met the need of the social situation in earlier ages. These ideas will have to be evolved out of the inner impulse of Christian thought, and out of its vital expression at the present time, and not exclusively out of the New Testament, in precisely the same way as both those great main types of Christian-Social philosophy were evolved out of the Christian thought of their own day, and not solely from the New Testament. And when they have been created and expressed, they will meet the fate which always awaits every fresh creation of religious and ethical thought: they will render indispensable services and they will develop profound energies, but they will never fully realize their actual ideal intention within the sphere of our earthly struggle and conflict.

As little as any other power in this world will they create the Kingdom of God upon earth as a completed social ethical organism. One of the most serious and important truths which emerge as a result of this inquiry is this: every idea is still faced by brutal facts, and all upward movement is checked and hindered by interior and exterior difficulties. Nowhere does there exist an absolute Christian ethic, which only awaits discovery; all that we can do is to learn to control the world-situation in its successive phases just as the earlier Christian ethic did in its own way. There is also no absolute ethical transformation of material nature or of human nature; all that does exist is a constant wrestling with the problems which they raise. Thus the Christian ethic of the present day and of the future will also only be an adjustment to the world-situation, and it will only desire to achieve that which is practically possible. This is the cause of that ceaseless tension which drives man onward yet gives him the sense that he can never realize his ethical ideal. Only doctrinaire idealists or religious fanatics can fail to recognize these facts. Faith is the source of energy in the struggle of life, but life still remains a battle which is continually renewed upon ever new fronts. For every threatening abyss which is closed, another yawning gulf appears. The truth is—and this is the conclusion of the whole matter—the Kingdom of God is within us. But we must let our light shine before men in confident and untiring labour that they may see our good works and praise our Father in Heaven. The final ends of all humanity are hidden within His Hands.

INDEX OF NAMES[1]

[1] Volume II. begins at p. 455.